# The Book of

# History's
# Greatest
# Mysteries

Publications International, Ltd.

**Let's get social!**

⊙ @Publications_International

❢ @PublicationsInternational

**www.pilbooks.com**

# Contents

✳ ✳ ✳ ✳

Benin Bronzes ✦ Masks of Mali ✦ Millions of Years in the Making ✦ Heads of the Gods ✦ The Question of Pedra Furada ✦ The Bay of Jars ✦ Rock of the Andes ✦ All That Glitters ✦ The Ancient Wise Men ✦ The Paracas of Peru ✦ Lost Treasure

# Chapter 1

# Vanished Explorers and Lost Expeditions

## Arctic Doom: Sir John Franklin's Last Voyage

*An 1845 British expedition to find the Northwest Passage disappears in the harsh Arctic waters of northern Canada.*

✳ ✳ ✳ ✳

CENTURIES AGO, THE Northwest Passage was the elusive goal of maritime exploration among the major seagoing powers of the time. If such a passage existed, it would unlock a new sea route between the Atlantic and Pacific Oceans. European countries had sent multiple expeditions, beginning with John Cabot's 1497 voyage, in an attempt to find a route. Many of the world's most famous explorers, including Jacques Cartier, Sir Francis Drake, Sir Martin Frobisher, and Captain James Cook, felt the allure of this challenge. But centuries later, they were still looking. It would not be until 1905 that Norwegian explorer Roald Amundsen charted the treacherous middle passage section and found his way to the Beaufort Sea.

### The Franklin Expedition Sets Out

The HMS *Erebus* and HMS *Terror* sailed from England in May of 1845. They carried a total of 134 men and represented the best-equipped ships to ever go in search of the Northwest

Passage. The ship hulls were reinforced to deal with Arctic ice, and the rudder could be pulled into a ship's cavity if it appeared it would be damaged by ice. These were robust, cold-weather vessels that had already been tested in harsh and frigid conditions. They had steam engines and an internal steam heating system to keep the crew warm in polar conditions. The ships were loaded with three years' worth of provisions and even carried libraries of more than 1,000 books.

The ships stopped briefly in the Orkney Islands and then proceeded to Greenland. In Greenland, more provisions were brought onboard, and the crew sent their final letters home. They then sailed to Baffin Bay where they were sighted by two whaling ships. This would prove to be the last time the crew was seen alive.

What happened next has been pieced together gradually over the ensuing 170 years.

## Traces Remain

A series of search and rescue expeditions (32 in all) set out between 1849 and 1859. Traces of the expedition appeared here and there in the form of cairns, abandoned camps, artifacts, and graves. The ships themselves had vanished. The British government called off its own searches in 1854.

Thanks to the 1859 discovery of the Victory Point Note (a letter found tucked into a stone cairn on King William Island), we know something of how events unfolded. The letter was written by two crew members and highlighted their travails. According to the letter, the expedition spent the winter of 1845–46 on Beechey Island. That summer, they traveled down Peel Sound. Somewhere off King William Island the two ships became trapped in the ice. The crew was forced to spend the next two winters on the island. In June of 1847, Franklin died. The note went on to say that the crew had by then abandoned their ships and were heading for the Canadian mainland, which lay 248 miles away. It's fairly certain that about 40 crew members died near the mouth of the Back River. But what happened to the rest of the crew remained a mystery.

Over the ensuing decades, more traces of the expedition were discovered. Grave sites, relics, and the oral testimonies of the local Inuit population all pointed to a grim end involving slow starvation, sickness, and possibly cannibalism. Finally, the mystery of what happened to the two ships was solved in the twenty-first century. In 2014, the remains of the *Erebus* were discovered in 36 feet of water in Wilmot and Crampton Bay on the eastern side of Queen Maud Gulf. In 2016, the other ship was found south of King William Island in Terror Bay.

Many details of the ill-fated voyage will never be known, but the general picture is clear. Officers and crew battled the elements, malnutrition, disease, and even lead poisoning until they finally succumbed to the odds.

# What Happened to George Mallory?

*The famed British mountaineer George Herbert Leigh Mallory attempted to climb the highest mountain in the world three times between 1921 and 1924, with the goal of being the first person to attain the summit. His team's first two attempts to scale Mount Everest failed. On a third attempt, Mallory and a partner came very close but ultimately paid for the attempt with their lives. What happened? And did they reach the top before they died?*

✳ ✳ ✳ ✳

IN THE EARLY afternoon of June 8, 1924, British mountaineer Noel Odell watched two black specks traverse a snowy ridge high above him. The two climbers were very close to the final pyramid of the summit. But then a veil of clouds obscured Odell's view and he permanently lost sight of them. It was the last time George Mallory and Sandy Irvine were seen alive.

Mallory was a famed climber with a long history of daring, albeit reckless, ascents in Europe. He was exposed to mountain climbing as a schoolboy and continued to gain experience in college. After finishing his education, he became a teacher and was even known to take his pupils climbing with him. His career was interrupted by the First World War, where he served as a lieutenant. Then opportunity came calling; in 1920 he was invited to join the first English Everest reconnaissance expedition under Colonel Charles Howard-Bury (expedition leader) along with a group of highly respected climbers.

On this visit, the team produced some of the earliest maps of the Everest region. The mission was at least partially successful, as they managed to reach a height of 23,000 feet. From that point they determined that a later expedition could take a viable summit route via the northeast ridge. But many members of the expedition became sick from exhaustion and altitude sickness, resulting in their turning back. Mallory's second visit met with even more setbacks, including an avalanche that killed several members.

## 1924

Mallory returned to the mountain a final time in the summer of 1924. On reaching base camp, he wrote to his wife, "I feel strong for the battle but I know every ounce of strength will be wanted." He was right. Even though this expedition included supplemental oxygen tanks for the highest altitudes and better gear, attempting the summit would involve extreme conditions that could quickly kill even the most seasoned mountaineer.

On June 8, Mallory and Irvine set out for the summit, with Odell remaining at the final camp to provide logistical support. In his own words, Odell wrote, "At 12:50 . . . My eyes became fixed on one tiny black spot silhouetted on a small snow-crest beneath a rock-step in the ridge; the black spot moved. Another black spot became apparent and moved up the snow to join the other on the crest. The first then approached the great rock-step and shortly emerged at the top; the second did likewise. Then the whole fascinating vision vanished, enveloped in cloud once more."

## What Might Have Happened

Details about the attempted summit are scant. Most climbing authorities believe the pair never made it to the top. Their clothing wasn't protective enough, their skills (especially Irvine's) were inadequate, and the changing weather that day probably brought with it additional hazards like blizzard conditions and fluctuating temperatures.

In addition, they were carrying bulky oxygen containers that would have hampered movements. It isn't clear what quantity of oxygen they carried either. In a letter to his wife, Mallory wrote, "My plan will be to carry as little as possible, go fast and rush the summit. Finch and Bruce tried carrying too many cylinders." Later he said "we'll probably go on two cylinders— but it's a bloody load for climbing." If they ran out of oxygen at some point during the attempt—and it seems he must have— then simple tasks like walking uphill would have become major challenges. A barometric drop from storm conditions would have meant even less oxygen in the air too.

The difficulties of the final stage of the mountain are much better understood now, and because of this, it seems unlikely that the summit was attained. The two would have been working at the limits of human endurance.

## A Body in the Snow

The story of this famous first attempt reverberated down the decades in mountaineering circles. It wasn't until 1953 that Everest was finally conquered by Sir Edmund Hillary and Tenzing Norgay. When they reached the top, they had fifteen minutes to search for evidence of Mallory before they had to descend, but they found nothing. More ascents followed, but the bodies of Mallory and Irvine weren't found.

In May of 1999, a team of explorers headed up Everest to search for evidence of what happened to Mallory and Irvine, and of how close to the summit they may have come. On setting up camp in the determined search area, the team spread out to search the zone they suspected would yield clues and possibly Irvine's body. The assumption was that Irvine might be discovered in that vicinity because his ice axe had been found nearby in 1933.

While the others headed out and upslope, team member Conrad Anker descended onto a snow terrace, and, after some zigzagging, discovered a body. To everyone's surprise, it was Mallory's. The team examined and photographed the body, searched it for artifacts, and then partially covered it. They specifically looked for the camera he had supposedly been carrying, but it was not found. If it had been recovered, it might have yielded evidence of whether the pair had reached the summit.

They also looked for another important item: Mallory had been carrying a photo of his wife. If he reached the summit, the plan was to leave the photo there. The photo was nowhere to be found, even though his wallet and other papers were still in his pockets. This tantalizing absence keeps many hoping that someday proof of their successful summit will emerge. But for now, no one truly knows if they made it.

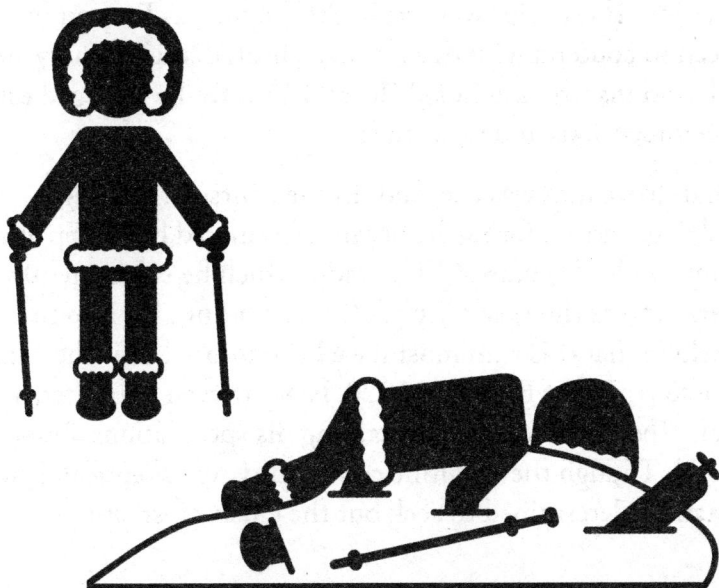

# Percy Fawcett and the Lost City of Z

*In 1925, the decorated British war hero Percy Fawcett was a well-known figure, having established credentials as a geographer, as well as being known as a meticulous archeologist and cartographer. He was well acquainted with the rigors of jungle and wilderness exploration in South America, having ventured into remote regions of the Amazon previously. Yet even though he was an excellent field explorer with years of experience, he promptly disappeared somewhere in the dense rainforest during his final expedition, never to be seen again.*

✳   ✳   ✳   ✳

LIEUTENANT-COLONEL PERCY HARRISON Fawcett was born in 1867. He joined the military at the age of 19, became a spy, and travelled widely during his army years. His travels sparked an interest in archeology, and this in turn led to work for the Royal Geographical Society. Between 1906 and 1924, Fawcett made no fewer than seven exploratory trips to South America. These trips were truly challenging, as Fawcett was forced to contend with dense jungle, heat, disease, deadly animals and insects, and hostile local tribes. Yet he emerged each time impervious and unscathed.

What drove him was a legend: In the course of reading, studying, and exploring, he became fascinated by old Spanish conquistador legends of El Dorado, which he subsequently referred to as the Lost City of Z. His readings led him to conclude that this ruin must have been located near the Matto Grosso region of Brazil. In 1920, Fawcett even published a book, *The Lost City of Z*, containing his speculations about the legend. Though the scientific community was skeptical, Fawcett remained determined to seek out the elusive lost city.

## The Final Journey

In April of 1925, at the age of 58, Fawcett returned to Brazil for another expedition. On this trip, his son Jack and Jack's friend Raleigh Rimell accompanied him. At the end of May, Fawcett sent his last known communication to his wife, Nina. This letter was sent from Dead Horse Camp, in the Matto Grosso region. In this letter, he mentioned being low on supplies while remaining optimistic about the expedition. Then the party vanished.

The last eyewitness accounts of the expedition are conflicting. Some accounts seem to suggest the party was killed by either tribal peoples who were in the area at the time or possibly by bandits. Others have noted that at least one of the party seemed to have an unknown illness soon after the beginning of the expedition. Lack of food and exhaustion have both also been suggested.

Since 1925, dozens of expeditions have tried and failed to discover remains or artifacts of the expedition. In 1951, the reputed bones of Fawcett were received by Orlando Villas-Boas, a local activist for indigenous peoples. A preliminary analysis of the bones suggested that they were Fawcett's but a subsequent analysis confirmed that they were not. Other pieces of "evidence" have surfaced over the years, but none have been helpful or conclusive.

The mystery has never been solved, but along the way, a minor industry in the form of various books, documentaries, and fictionalized account has sprung up. We may never know what happened to Percy Fawcett, but the enigma of his disappearance continues to fascinate us.

# An Open Secret

*Was Amelia Earhart the victim of an accident or some kind of conspiracy? Her choice not to keep up with technological know-how is most likely to blame for her disappearance.*

✳  ✳  ✳  ✳

PIONEERING AVIATOR AMELIA Earhart set records and made headlines because of her talent, courage, tireless work ethic, and willingness to craft her own image. But no one is perfect, of course. Earhart failed to keep up with the technologies that helped other pilots to call for help and made flying a much less dangerous job.

## Opening the Books

After Orville and Wilbur Wright made the first powered airplane flight in 1903, an ugly patent war began among inventors in the U.S. A huge number of researchers from all kinds of backgrounds—the Wrights themselves were bicycle mechanics, publishers, and journalists—had made incremental improvements on one another's work, brainstormed similar ideas, and generally squabbled over who was making the best progress. Think of it as a grade-school classroom where all the students are grownups, and they've propped up folders and textbooks to hide their tests from their classmates.

These aviation pioneers would have out-pettied today's worst startup companies in Silicon Valley. They went to court over minute details of one aircraft versus another, citing their own notes and evidence that had largely been kept secret. But after a decade of brutal lawsuits and public fighting over who was first, who invented what, and where the credit was due, the United States entered World War I. Aviation companies were de facto forced to pour their proprietary research and patents into a large pool shared by all of America's aircraft industry.

Making their technology "open source" was part of the war effort, but as with software and other inventions today, the open industry led to better and more rapid developments. After World War I ended, pilots began to set records left and right using ingenious inventions like the artificial horizon—something pilots still use in cockpits today, in a modernized form, of course. And some pilots made their livings in traveling air shows as airplanes became more and more familiar, but no less mesmerizing, to the American people. Amelia Earhart was one of these pilots, traveling to build buzz for her own career.

## The Morse the Merrier

Earhart was a gifted and remarkable pilot, the first woman to ride in a plane (as a passenger) across the Atlantic and then to fly across it as the pilot. She started a professional organization for women pilots and took a faculty position at Purdue University. She and fellow groundbreaking pilot Charles Lindbergh were like movie stars by the 1930s, and Earhart was witty and engaging when she spoke with the press or members of the public. Her career was at a perfect point for her to make an outsize gesture in the form of a trip around the world. She wasn't the first, but she was definitely the most famous.

Technology leapt ahead during her career, and Morse code was in wide use by the time Earhart began her trip around the world. The world's leading navigation instructor offered to teach Earhart radio operation, Morse code, and cutting-edge navigation, but she didn't have time before her trip, which had already been delayed by a failed first attempt.

The navigator she chose also did not know Morse code. When they grew disoriented in poor weather over the Pacific Ocean, they could not call for help in Morse code, and their radio reception was too poor to send or receive verbal messages to or from the Navy ships assigned to support the open water sections of their flight.

The "what ifs" of Earhart's failed final journey continue to stoke pop culture across the decades, and who can say what could have happened if she and her navigator were able to get help? Without specific coordinates or landmarks, which Earhart likely could have relayed to her support team, even modern rescuers can't cover large swaths of open ocean with success. Morse code might have made the critical difference.

# Henry Hudson's Unknown End

*Surprisingly little is known about the life of one of history's most iconic sea explorers, including his final end, after being set adrift on the bay that was named for him.*

✳   ✳   ✳   ✳

H ENRY HUDSON WAS probably born in the 1570s. Historians conjecture that he may have been born in London, may have been highly educated, and may have come from a comfortably wealthy background. In other words, we know very little about his early life. What we do know is that when he entered the historical record in 1607, he had by then become an experienced mariner.

Hudson apparently had an intense drive for sea exploration. In 1607, the Muscovy Company of England hired Hudson to go look for a northerly route to Asia via Canada—the legendary Northwest Passage. Though he failed in this endeavor, his travels yielded plenty of information about the islands and coasts of the far north. In 1608, he tried again, this time trying for a northerly circumvention of the Russian coast. The following year he actually tried to find routes both to the east and west.

## The Good Ship *Discovery*

The expedition of 1610–11 was to be Hudson's last. Funded by the Virginia Company and the British East India Company, Hudson set out once again at the helm of his new ship, the *Discovery*, to find the elusive northwest route to Asia. Following the Labrador coast, the expedition entered the Hudson Strait, and followed the coast south into Hudson Bay (both being geographical features subsequently named for the same explorer).

When ice made further exploration impossible, the crew wintered in James Bay. The following spring, Hudson began making plans to explore further west. At this point, the crew had been through hardships that included extreme cold and meager rations. By June, the crew had mutinied.

The mutineers took over the ship and expelled Hudson, his son, and seven crewmen to a small boat with just a few supplies (including guns, powder, some tools, and a cooking pot), setting them adrift in the bay. Then they set sail for England. Hudson and his crew were never seen again.

Beginning in 1612, a number of searches were launched. One explorer, Nicolas de Vignau, claimed he saw the wreckage of an English ship on the southern shores of James Bay and believed it to be connected with Hudson's last voyage. And in the 1950s, a stone was discovered in Ontario with "H.H.," "1612," and "captive" carved into it. The carving date of the stone has never been verified though. Could he have carved it?

While tales of Hudson's explorations and discoveries have faded somewhat into historical obscurity, it should be noted that his journeys were instrumental in opening up further explorations and opportunities for succeeding generations. Both the fur trading and whaling industries benefitted, for example, as did budding New World cartography. Though his story has unfortunately lost some historical prominence in recent years, his name is likely to at least endure in the place names of towns, rivers, bays, bridges, and even retail stores.

# The Disappearance of Ludwig Leichhardt

*German explorer and naturalist Ludwig Leichhardt migrated to Australia in 1842 with the intention of exploring the country's mysterious interior. He had already mounted two significant overland journeys when he set out with an expedition party in 1848 to travel east-to-west through the forbidding terrain of the Australian outback. He was never heard from again.*

✳ ✳ ✳ ✳

LUDWIG LEICHHARDT WAS born in 1813, in Prussia (now part of Germany). He developed a keen interest in natural sciences and exploration from a young age, and focused on philosophy, geology, and physiology, picking up six languages along the way. Academic interests aside, his true passion was exploration. He was an excellent field scholar, notable for creating accurate maps, writing close and detailed accounts of the places he visited, and collecting valuable botanical samples. His medical skills also came in handy when in remote places—he may have saved the lives of several of his companions when they were injured on an earlier trip.

After returning from a groundbreaking yearlong expedition that stretched from Brisbane to Port Essington, he received accolades from The Royal Geographical Society in London and other institutions. His success led him to immediately begin planning another expedition, an east-west jaunt across the continent from the Darling Downs in Queensland to a settlement far to the west on the Swan River.

## The Final Journey

The goal was daunting, but Leichhardt was both meticulous and confident. His assembled party began their trek in February, 1848. They included seven volunteers. Their starting point was Cogoon Station, the westernmost property on the

Darling Downs. The last confirmed sighting of the party was in April 1848, when they reached McPherson's Station. After that point, no reliable information about their whereabouts was ever obtained. The group disappeared without a trace.

Many search parties have headed into the outback over the years, hoping to find clues about what happened to Leichhardt. None have been successful. The mystery has led to a swath of theories about what happened, each more speculative than the last. Did the party simply die in a harsh environment from natural causes such as dehydration, disease, or exhaustion? Or was there an unknown conflict with aboriginal peoples?

Evidence on the ground has been scanty—especially considering how much equipment (including many metal components) they left with. In 1900, Leichhardt's brass gun plate was discovered on the border between Western Australia and the Northern Territory. This suggests that the expedition made it this far, but nothing can be proven. Since then, the trail has run cold, but the mystery continues to fascinate.

# A Balloon Flight to the North Pole

*In 1897, Swedish engineer S. A. Andree and two crew members set out for the North Pole in a hydrogen balloon. They left from the Spitsbergen archipelago and expected to sail directly over the Pole in a matter of days. What actually happened was a very different story.*

✳   ✳   ✳   ✳

S. A. ANDREE grew up in the small town of Granna, Sweden. He was drawn to the exciting scientific discoveries of his day and became fascinated with aeronautics as a young adult. His chosen obsession: ballooning. He bought his own balloon in 1893 and took it on nine expeditions, travelling across Sweden, the Baltic Sea, and Finland. In all, this first balloon traveled about 900 miles.

After learning the fundamentals of balloon flight and experimenting with drag ropes—a technique he believed would allow him to "steer" the balloon in the direction of his choosing—Andree began publicly touting the idea of a Pole-crossing balloon flight. Many seasoned balloonists scoffed at his idea, but many politicians and scientists, eager to see Sweden catch up with Norway in the realm of Arctic exploration, were swayed by Andree's enthusiasm and assurances that the flight would be successful.

## The *Eagle*

Andree was successful in securing funding for the expedition and commissioned the famous balloon builder Henri Lachambre to create his balloon. The final three-layer silk balloon was 67 feet in diameter. Andree christened it *Ornen*, Swedish for "eagle."

Unfavorable conditions scrapped the original departure date from Spitsbergen in the summer of 1896, but the following summer, the three-man crew launched on a clear sunny day with a favorable wind from the southwest. But almost immediately they ran into trouble.

Upon takeoff, over a half ton of drag rope became tangled and detached from their holds, making the balloon impossible to steer. The balloon was also too heavy to gain significant lift, and so nearly 500 pounds of sand ballast were also dumped. The shore crew watched the balloon disappear over the horizon, trailing its remaining drag ropes. The crew was not seen again for more than 30 years.

Lightened, the balloon began rising—and rising. It eventually gained 2,300 feet. The pressure from this elevation caused the balloon to lose even more hydrogen than was expected. In all, the balloon was aloft just over two days. When it ran aground on pack ice, it was nowhere near the North Pole, nor was it near anything else.

The *Eagle* had been packed with plenty of provisions, including snowshoes, skis, and sleds. After sorting and condensing, the men left the crash site with heavily-laden sleds. Months later, they managed to arrive on the island of Kvitoya.

### A Mystery

For the next 33 years, the fate of the *Eagle* was unknown. In 1930, a Norwegian sealing vessel came to Kvitoya and discovered the bodies of the crew, along with journals, a tin box containing Strindberg's photographic film, and other artifacts. Thanks to these discoveries, we know that the explorers pulled their sleds to the island, shooting and eating seals and polar bears along the way, enduring the incredible hardships of freezing winds, arctic temperatures, damp clothes, and constantly facing the possibility of polar bear attacks.

The ultimate cause of their deaths is unknown. It may have been from trichinosis via undercooked polar bear meat. It may have simply been the harsh Arctic conditions (which were steadily worsening as winter closed in) that eventually did them in. What's ultimately remarkable is that they survived as long as they did.

# Roald Amundsen's Arctic End

*Norwegian explorer Roald Amundsen was one of the great world explorers in the early decades of the twentieth century. His legendary expeditions to both the northern and southern polar regions are still considered heroic today. But his final venture into the arctic resulted in his disappearance.*

✳ ✳ ✳ ✳

BORN INTO A ship-owning family in Norway in 1872, Roald Amundsen was fascinated with exploration from an early age. Due to his mother's wishes, however, he pursued a career in medicine. When he was 21, she died, and he promptly abandoned medicine for a life at sea.

Amundsen joined his first polar expedition at the age of 25. Only six years later, he was leading his own expeditions. In 1903, he led the first successful traverse of Canada's Northwest Passage. In 1911, he successfully led an expedition to the South Pole. Next, he took on the Northeast Passage above Siberia. Suffering incredible hardships along the way (including frostbite, broken bones, and polar bear attacks), Amundsen acquired the stature of an invincible explorer whose exploits always seemed a little more harrowing and heroic than those of his peers. But ultimately his luck ran out.

In 1926, Amundsen and two other well-known explorers, Italian aeronautical engineer Umberto Nobile and American explorer Lincoln Ellsworth, travelled on a dirigible over the North Pole. The flight was successful, but Amundsen and Nobile descended into an acrimonious public dispute over who should have been credited as the leader of the expedition. The two broke off whatever friendship they had, but in 1928, a twist of fate nearly brought them back together again.

## The Airship *Italia*

Nobile had later planned for another expedition into remote parts of the arctic in their airship *Italia*. In 1928, they embarked on a flight that ended with a crash landing northeast of Spitsbergen. When news of the crash spread, international efforts to rescue the explorers began. Amundsen, perhaps motivated by the idea of rescuing—and one-upping—his recent adversary, promptly joined the efforts. He left his house on June 16, taking a night train to Bergen, where he met up with the crew of the French naval seaplane. Two days later, the Latham 47.02 departed in the late afternoon from Tromso, Norway, and headed north. It was never seen again. A few hours after their departure, a radio station at Masoy on the Finnmark coast received a request for an ice report from the Latham. An hour later, a telegraph operator at the Geophysical Institute in Tromso heard part of a message from the airplane, and this was to be the last anyone heard from the crew.

No one knows what happened next. It is reasonable to think that the plane crashed in the Barents Sea soon after. Whether this was due to fog, ice, or mechanical failure remains conjectural. Two months later a fishing boat spotted one of the plane's landing floats in the open ocean. Additional debris was discovered in the coming months, but the bodies of Amundsen and the crew have never been found.

# The Lost Corte-Real Brothers

*When a person goes missing, it is not uncommon for family members to retrace their last steps in an effort to locate them. This is exactly what Miguel Corte-Real did when his younger brother, Gaspar, disappeared while on an exploratory voyage in 1501. Neither brother was ever seen again.*

❋ ❋ ❋ ❋

THE CORTE-REAL FAMILY had a habit of impressing kings. The family of nobles originated in the fourteenth century with Vasco Anes da Costa, a Portuguese knight whose services were so appreciated that King Edward I granted him the name *Corte-Real*, meaning "Royal Court," to be used by his family. The knight's oldest son, João Vaz Corte-Real, also gained the favor of Portuguese royalty by undertaking many voyages to the west, reaching Newfoundland in northern Canada. Two of his three sons, Gaspar and Miguel, often joined him in his exploration, and for their efforts, the family was given the Azorean islands of Terceira and São Jorge to govern.

Miguel, born in 1448, was the older of the two exploring sons, and Gaspar, born in 1450, was the bigger risk taker. After their father died in 1496, the brothers continued the family tradition of exploration. In 1499, they received word that King Manuel I had expressed a hope that a northwest passage to India existed and was providing a grant to any Portuguese sailor willing to take on the risk of finding it. Gaspar jumped at the chance, and in 1500, he set sail in a fleet of three ships.

## Land Found, Brothers Lost

Landing in what he believed to be India (but was actually Greenland), Gaspar and his crew spent months exploring the shoreline and interacting with the native peoples. The frozen winter waters forced him to sail back to Portugal that winter, but he and Miguel both returned to the area in May of 1501. However, Greenland, known for its harsh Arctic environment, proved too icy to land boats, even in early summer. Instead, the brothers headed south, until they reached the pine trees and rivers of Labrador. Together, the brothers explored the coastline, charting about 600 miles of it, before deciding someone should head home to report their findings. So, Miguel took two ships and returned to Portugal, while Gaspar turned his ship south to continue his exploration. That was the last time anyone saw him.

When Gaspar failed to return to Portugal by May of 1502, Miguel took three ships and sailed back toward Labrador, intending to search for him. The ships made it to Newfoundland, where Miguel suggested the trio split up and meet again at a future time. Two of the ships later returned to the rendezvous location, but Miguel's ship, like his ill-fated brother's, was never seen again.

## No Answers

The last Corte-Real brother, Vasco Añes, organized another search party to find his brothers, but the king, perhaps wisely, forbade him from sailing along with it. The ships returned without locating any trace of Gaspar or Miguel, nor has any evidence of the brothers or their ships ever been found. Did both brothers succumb to storms in the cold Atlantic Ocean? Were they attacked by unfriendly inhabitants of the lands they explored? Or did they simply get lost?

Portuguese exploration of the North Atlantic ended soon after the disappearance of the Corte-Real brothers, and some historians debate whether the pair truly contributed significantly to our knowledge of North America, or whether their feats have been magnified by their mysterious disappearance. Still, Gaspar is remembered with a statue in the famous Monument of the Discoveries in Lisbon, a tribute to Portugal's historic, and sometimes dangerous, Age of Discovery.

# The Demise of the Ninth

*The Ninth Roman Legion consisted of approximately 5,400 men who fought in the Roman Empire's wars and quelled rebellions. Much was written about their exploits, until AD 108, when records of their existence came to a sudden halt. So how did thousands of men simply disappear from history?*

✳ ✳ ✳ ✳

IT IS SAID that when Julius Caesar became governor of Cisalpine Gaul, a region in what is now northern Italy, in 58 BC, at least four legions of soldiers came along with his title. Most historians believe that the Ninth Legion was one of the groups he acquired, and over the next few decades, the group of fighters gained a reputation for being Caesar's preferred soldiers, seeing action in the Gallic wars and battles in Dyrrachium and Pharsalus.

After Caesar was assassinated in 44 BC, the legion continued in its service to Rome and was stationed in Hispania, the Roman name for what is now Spain and Portugal. It was here that they earned the nickname "Legio IX Hispana," a nickname that stuck with them for the rest of their existence. The legion then went on to fight against the Germanic tribes along the Rhine River and spent many decades in Britain. During this time they experienced more notable triumphs—including putting down the rebellion of King Venutius in northern Britain—but also crushing defeats—like the disastrous Battle of Camulodunum, in which 2,000 legionnaires were massacred in one night.

Yet despite some serious setbacks, the legion regrouped, restored their determination, and went on to win decisive victories against the Caledonians in what is now Scotland.

## The Last Word

In AD 108, the Ninth Legion rebuilt a fortress at York, inscribing a stone gate with a tribute to Emperor Trajan and signing it "the Ninth Legion Hispana." This was the last known written record of the legion's existence. After this time, the stories of their battles, whether victories or losses, simply end, and aside from a smattering of tile stamps dated no later than AD 120, no other artifacts have ever been found that feature the name "Ninth Legion."

The reasons for the legion's disappearance have long been debated. One theory, first popularized by German historian Theodor Mommsen in the 1800s, suggests that the Ninth Legion was wiped out by Celtic tribes. Mommsen believed that one tribe, known as the Brigantes, inhabitants of what is now northern England, may have revolted, attacking the fortress at York and managing to kill the entire legion. However, little evidence of such an occurrence has ever been found, aside from a letter written by the Roman historian Marcus Cornelius Fronto to the emperor Marcus Aurelius in which he vaguely mentions a "great numbers of soldiers" killed during the reign of Emperor Hadrian.

## Relocated?

Other historians believe the Ninth Legion may have simply moved to a new location, trading their fortress in England for a new home in the Netherlands. It was not uncommon for legions to transfer to different locations, and indeed, an excavation in the city of Nijmegen in 1959 uncovered tiles inscribed with the words "Ninth Legion." Or, according to some archeologists, the legion may have transferred to London, with some believing that skulls uncovered near the city belonged to members of the Ninth.

The most commonly held theory is that the Ninth Legion met its demise during battle, either against Celtic tribes or possibly in Elegeia (a region in what is now Turkey) or Judea. Some even believe the defeat of the great Ninth Legion is what prompted the construction of Hadrian's Wall, a defensive wall built across the entire expanse of England, dividing the southern Roman Britain from the unconquered northern Caledonia. But, like all of the theories concerning the Ninth Legion, this idea is purely speculative. Like the legion itself, the true fate of this band of soldiers may be lost forever.

# Roman Legionnaires in China

*It seems like a tall tale: Roman survivors of the battle of Carrhae in 53 BC somehow manage to make their way to China. Is there any truth to the story?*

✳ ✳ ✳ ✳

WEALTHY STATESMAN MARCUS Licinius Crassus rose to power and prominence in the last days of the Roman Republic. Along with Julius Caesar and Pompey, he was a member of the First Triumvirate, the famous political alliance which pushed the Republic to its breaking point.

Though Crassus was incredibly wealthy (and frequently called "the richest man in Rome") he was avaricious and jealous of the military successes of others, particularly Caesar's. When he was awarded the governorship of Syria, he saw his chance for fabulous wealth and military glory.

## Marching to the East

Crassus wasted no time assembling a great army and bringing it to Syria. From there, he headed east towards the Parthian Empire. By doing so, he unilaterally broke the peace treaty between the two empires. His forces were hardly equipped to endure the harsh desert environment they were entering, but Crassus was confident he would crush the Parthians.

When the Romans came into contact with the Parthians, Crassus became even more arrogant, believing his forces vastly outnumbered the Parthians. He was completely right. But that would make no difference, as the Parthian forces consisted of light cavalry that could dance around the slow-moving Roman units with ease. Their hit-and-run techniques mowed down line after line of stationary Roman infantry with a withering barrage of arrows.

After a full day's engagement which saw his forces decimated, Crassus was compelled to meet with the Parthians for negotiations. But before negotiations could even begin, Crassus and his generals were killed. It is believed that, of the remnants of the Roman forces, 10,000 were captured.

## Subsequent Rumors

It seems likely that the 10,000 Roman prisoners of war were transported to a far corner of the Parthian Empire, probably to the northeast. This kind of resettlement of a former enemy to a remote location was a typical tactic in the ancient world. By doing this, the Parthians would have prevented the prisoners from realistically escaping. These trained soldiers would also have been immensely valuable as a military presence on a volatile frontier. But the northeastern frontier of the Parthian Empire was nowhere near China.

What actually happened to the soldiers in the years immediately following is unclear. But then, nearly two decades later, during a conflict recorded by Chinese historians at the battle of Zhizhi, the Romans seem to show up again. A Chinese army attacked a Parthian border town near a place now known as Taraz, in modern day Kazakhstan.

The historians wrote that certain defenders held their shields defensively in a "fish scale" pattern. The Chinese army was impressed by these warriors and, after winning the battle, brought them along as mercenaries. The Romans were then settled in a newly founded city where they guarded against raiders. There were 100 to 1,000 of these foreign soldiers. They were noted for some unusual practices such as using tree trunk counterweight construction devices—practices well-known to Mediterranean peoples of the time.

It is *possible* that these Romans actually did somehow end up settling in the area. But is it probable? We still aren't sure. A 2005 DNA study revealed that some villagers of the modern day village of Liqian do have Caucasian ancestry. However, the analysis did not link this ancestry to southern Europe. In fact, it seemed more similar to that of the Uyghurs of the Xinjiang Province in the west of China. Another study done two years later did not draw the same conclusions and cast serious doubt on the purported Roman connection.

In 1993, local excavations revealed fortifications using a type of trunk fixed with stakes. The dig was tentatively dated back to the time when the legionnaires would have arrived. And the trunk system used was typically Roman—not Chinese. It is now on display at the Lanzhou Museum.

Roman coins and pottery have also been unearthed at local digs. One tantalizing find was a helmet engraved with Chinese characters reading "one of the prisoners." But since the area was near the Silk Road, it is entirely possible that these archeological finds simply reflect the fact that items from all over the world traveled this famous trade route, ending up in locations far from their origins. Similar items have been found as far away as Vietnam and the Korean peninsula.

Tantalizing clues do not add up to solid history however, and for now, all we have is a tenuous theory. While it makes for a fascinating story, in all probability those soldiers had dispersed well before the supposed settlement in western China.

# Sir Ernest Shackleton and the End of an Era

*Antarctica, with its permanent ice and snow, is our planet's most desolate continent. Devoid of any indigenous human population, the frozen expanse is home only to those hardy enough to withstand its weather extremes for the sake of science. Not surprisingly, it has also been the setting of many mishaps, disappearances, and deaths.*

✳   ✳   ✳   ✳

BETWEEN 1819 AND 1821, Russian explorers Fabian Gottlieb von Bellingshausen and Mikhail Lazarev circumnavigated the Southern Ocean, becoming the first known explorers to discover the continent of Antarctica. Over the next few decades, interest in the southern continent was limited, however, as most considered the region too icy and remote to be worthy of exploration. At the time, this was correct, but in the late 1800s, a new curiosity was sparked when an Antarctic expedition from Dundee, Scotland, returned from the continent with artist renderings of the landscape and animals that thrived in the cold climate.

Much like the trends that are driven by pictures and videos posted on today's social media, the artistic drawings published from the Dundee Antarctic Expedition kicked off what has come to be known as the Heroic Age of Antarctic Exploration. The era began with a Belgian expedition which counted amongst its members Roald Amundsen, who would later lead the team that first reached the South Pole. But despite its optimistic beginnings, the Heroic Age ended much less successfully, with the ill-fated Shackleton-Rowett Expedition.

## A Rocky Start

Anglo-Irish explorer Sir Ernest Shackleton had already led two journeys to the Antarctic. During his first expedition, he made it to within 97 miles of the South Pole, a feat for which he was knighted on his return. His second expedition ended in disaster when his ship, *Endurance*, became trapped in ice and sank off Antarctica. The crew was forced to travel 720 nautical miles by lifeboats until they reached South Georgia Island.

Shackleton's last journey to Antarctica would truly be his final voyage. The expedition was financed by his friend John Q. Rowett, and Shackleton's goals were to circumnavigate the continent, map the coastline, and to search for any unknown islands in the area. Along with a crew of 19 men, Shackleton sailed from London on September 17, 1921, on the expedition vessel *Quest*. The ship was small and uncomfortable, rolling and bobbing with every swell on the sea. Even the most experienced sailors grappled with frequent bouts of seasickness, and several men disembarked the ship early in the voyage, unable to handle the constant queasiness. The *Quest* was also plagued by damage and breakdowns, requiring repairs at every port of call and slowing the expedition considerably. On November 22, *Quest* docked in Rio de Janeiro, Brazil, where Shackleton hoped a complete engine overhaul would improve the ship's poor performance.

## Final Resting Place

*Quest* was anchored in Rio de Janeiro for four weeks. On December 17, the evening before the ship was finally ready to depart, Shackleton fell ill. Some theorize he may have even suffered a heart attack, but the stubborn expedition leader refused medical attention or any delay. The next day, the voyage continued on a path toward South Georgia Island, but the crew noticed their leader was acting strangely listless and subdued. *Quest* anchored at Grytviken in South Georgia on January 4, 1922, and Shackleton disembarked to explore the island, writing in his diary that evening that it had been a "wonderful" day. But just after two o'clock in the morning of January 5, the ship's doctor was called to Shackleton's cabin, where he was complaining of severe back pains.

Not long after the doctor arrived, Shackleton suffered a seizure and died. The official cause of death was "atheroma of the coronary arteries and heart failure," or a blood clot in a vessel of the heart.

The crew of *Quest* attempted to return Shackleton's body to England, but his wife, Emily, requested that he be buried on South Georgia Island. Frank Wild, the second in command on the ship, made the decision to continue on with the expedition, determined to fulfill his friend's mission. But progress was slowed and stymied by pack ice, which threatened to trap the ship, much like *Endurance*. After a rather uneventful and melancholy voyage, the crew returned to Grytviken, where they constructed a memorial cairn in honor of Shackleton. *Quest* returned to Plymouth, England, on September 16, 1922, almost exactly one year after its original departure.

With its constant setbacks, and the untimely death of its leader, the Shackelton-Rowett Expedition was seen as a failure amongst many scientific experts of the time. Shackleton's death was also the death of the Heroic Age of Antarctic Exploration, though new technologies and advancements would soon usher in a whole new era of discovery. Today, Shackleton's grave can be found in the Grytviken cemetery, and the ashes of Wild, who died in 1939, were buried to his right, where they are marked with a granite block inscribed with the words, "Shackleton's right-hand man."

# Sailing into the Unknown

*It might be assumed that Christopher Columbus was the first European to set sail in search of a route to India. That assumption isn't exactly true, however. The first known expedition with a route to eastern Asia in mind occurred two hundred years earlier. But unlike the many stories we have of Columbus and his voyage, that first voyage remains shrouded in mystery.*

✻  ✻  ✻  ✻

BROTHERS VANDINO AND Ugolino Vivaldi were born in Genoa, Italy, where they earned reputations as merchants and explorers. Intending to combine their two interests, they sought to discover a passage to India by ocean, hoping to find new spices and curiosities to trade back home. In May of 1291, they set sail in two galleys, piloted by sailors from Majorca and accompanied by two Franciscan monks. Some historians theorize that the monks may have been familiar with the *Opus Majus*, a work by fellow monk Roger Bacon. In it, Bacon suggests that the distance between Europe and India is not terribly great, perhaps bolstering the monks' optimism that the brothers would quickly find the subcontinent. Still, the Vivaldi brothers gave themselves a generous ten-year schedule in which to complete their exploration.

The two ships sailed through the Straits of Gibraltar and turned south, following the coast of Morocco until they reached Cape Chaunar on the Atlantic coast. In the fifteenth century, this area would be nicknamed *Cabo do Não*, or "Cape No," by Portuguese sailors. The sailors believed that any mariner who attempted to sail beyond the cape would find navigating impossible. According to Venetian explorer Alvise Cadamosto, who wrote of his expeditions in the 1507 book *Navigazioni*, sailors who ventured beyond Cabo do Não were at the mercy of the sea, doomed, perhaps, to never escape her watery grasp.

And yet, hundreds of years before the cape earned its pessimistic moniker, the Vivaldi brothers sailed past it. They were never seen again.

## What Happened to the Vivaldis?

In 1312, Italian navigator Lancelotto Malocello set sail from Genoa, intending to retrace the Vivaldi brothers' steps in an attempt to find them. Malocello wound up in the Canary Islands, an archipelago located 62 miles west of Morocco and Western Sahara.

While he never located the brothers, Malocello stayed in the Canary Islands for more than 20 years, where the island of Lanzarote was named after him. Many historians believe the brothers did, in fact, make it to the Canary Islands, perhaps landing on the island of Alegranza, which, interestingly, nearly matches the name of one of the brothers' ships, *Alegranzia*.

But some theorize that the brothers made it much farther. A Genoese sailor named Antoniotto Usodimare claimed, in 1455, to have met a descendant of the last surviving member of the Vivaldi expedition near the mouth of the Gambia River. According to Usodimare, the brothers had made it as far south as the Gulf of Guinea before they had become stranded and were later seized and held captive.

Over time, the brothers became the focus of legends in which they were said to have successfully circumnavigated Africa, sailing all the way to Ethiopia before succumbing to ill fortune or shipwreck. But the truth of what really happened to Vandino and Ugolino Vivaldi may never be known. Despite their mysterious disappearance, brave and adventurous explorers who came after them continued their curious wanderings into the unknown seas.

# Lost in the South Pacific

*Just before Louis XVI was executed on the morning of January 21, 1793, during the French Revolution, he is said to have asked a very off-topic question: "Any news of Lapérouse?" Although an answer would come decades later, it would raise even more questions about the fate of the French explorer.*

✳ ✳ ✳ ✳

JEAN-FRANÇOIS DE GALAUP, Count of Lapérouse, was born in France in 1741 and enlisted in the navy at the age of 15. Navy life seemed to suit the young man. Often known simply as Lapérouse, he proved his worth during the Seven Years' War and the Anglo-French War when he was given command of a ship, the *Amazone*. He was made captain of the ship in 1780, and then transferred to the *Astrée*, where he continued to engage in battles throughout the American Revolutionary War, in which France fought alongside the American colonies against the British.

The navy captain's efforts during the Revolutionary War caught the attention of King Louis XVI, who, in 1785, chose Lapérouse to lead an exploratory and scientific expedition around the world. The king was fascinated by geography and the idea of discovering new lands, and saw the expedition as a way for France to strengthen its political standing in the world. So, on August 1, 1785, Lapérouse and a crew of 220 men set sail in two frigates, *La Boussole* and *L'Astrolabe*, from the port of Brest in western France. Ten scientists were aboard the two vessels, which were each equipped with the latest scientific instruments of the time.

## A Promising Start

The expedition was expected to take three years, and the ships were well-stocked with hundreds of barrels of food and a thousand tons of items to trade at each port of call. After sailing south across the Atlantic, the ships visited the Sandwich

Islands and then rounded Cape Horn and headed north, stopping at Easter Island and the Hawaiian Islands, where Lapérouse became the first European to set foot on Maui. By June 1786, the expedition made it to Alaska, then sailed south along the coast, exploring British Columbia and California.

La Boussole and L'Astrolabe next sailed west across the Pacific, and by the end of 1787, Lapérouse and his crew had visited the Philippines, Korea, Japan, and Russia, before heading south toward Australia. The ships reached Botany Bay on January 24, 1788, where they were welcomed by Captain Arthur Phillip, the first governor of the Colony of New South Wales, and Lapérouse and his crew spent six weeks resting in the area before restocking the ships and planning the next leg of their journey. Before setting sail, Lapérouse sent a letter back to France in which he estimated the expedition would be completed by June of 1789. But after La Boussole and L'Astrolabe left Botany Bay on March 10, 1788, Lapérouse and his crew were never seen again.

## Answers and Questions

Although Louis XVI sent a rescue party to search for Lapérouse in 1791, its efforts were fruitless. The king was executed soon after supposedly posing his question about Lapérouse's whereabouts, never receiving any answers about what happened to him. Then, in 1826, Irish sea captain Peter Dillon discovered the wrecks of two ships on the island of Vanikoro, in what is now the Solomon Islands. He speculated that they were La Boussole and L'Astrolabe, but it wasn't until 1964 that the wrecks were officially identified as those belonging to Lapérouse. While no one knows for certain what misfortune befell the captain and his crew, historians theorize that a storm pushed both ships into the rocky reefs of Vanikoro, where many of the men were massacred by local islanders. According to some of the locals, a few of the surviving sailors built a raft from the remains of L'Astrolabe, but where they sailed and what happened to them is a mystery.

In 2008, a French expedition, consisting of 52 crew members and 30 scientists, retraced the route Lapérouse most likely took from New Caledonia to Vanikoro. But even today, the fate of Lapérouse remains unknown. Artifacts recovered from *La Boussole* and *L'Astrolabe* can be seen at the Lapérouse Museum in Albi, France, and the Maritime Museum of New Caledonia, and places named in honor of the explorer include everywhere from Mount La Perouse in Alaska, to La Perouse Bay in Maui, to the La Pérouse crater on the Moon.

# The Disappearance of George Bass

*Surgeon and explorer George Bass married Elizabeth Waterhouse in England on October 8, 1800, but their honeymoon was short-lived. In January of 1801, Bass left his new wife in England while he traveled to Australia to seek his fortune. They would never see each other again.*

❋   ❋   ❋   ❋

GEORGE BASS WAS born in England in 1771, where, as a teenager, he studied medicine at a hospital in Boston, Lincolnshire. He went on to attend the Company of Surgeons in London, and in 1794 he joined the Royal Navy as a surgeon. His new career took him to Sydney, Australia, where he arrived in September of 1795.

But Bass wasn't content to simply perform his duties as a surgeon; he wanted to explore his new surroundings. Sailing in small boats he nicknamed *Tom Thumb* and *Tom Thumb II*, Bass made several short trips down the coast of Sydney, inspecting ports and navigating rivers that had not been charted before. In 1797, he procured a larger boat and sailed south to Port Phillip, located in what is now Melbourne. While on this trip, Bass hypothesized that Tasmania, then known as Van Diemen's Land, was probably separated from the mainland by a strait.

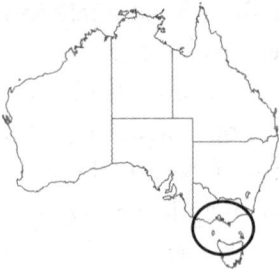

To prove his theory, Bass, along with his friend and ship captain Matthew Flinders, circumnavigated the island in the sloop *Norfolk*. Flinders was impressed with his friend's tenacity and determination to confirm his belief. He recommended to John Hunter, the governor of New South Wales, that the waterway between the two landmasses be named Bass Strait.

## Marriage and Mystery

In late 1800, after returning to England and marrying Elizabeth Waterhouse, the sister of his former shipmate Henry Waterhouse, Bass acquired a merchant ship called *Venus* and filled it with goods he hoped to sell in Port Jackson. He left Elizabeth behind and sailed back to Australia in January 1801. But he was unable to get a good price for his merchandise, so he turned to other plans.

On February 5, 1803, he set sail on the *Venus*, intending to head for Tahiti and then Chile. Some suggest that Bass was planning to engage in illegal trade with the Spanish colonies on the coast of Chile. But his true intentions were never revealed, as Bass and the crew of the *Venus* were never seen again.

Most historians believe that the *Venus* was lost at sea, but some speculate that Bass and his crew made it to South America, where they were arrested for smuggling goods. The crew would have been forced to work in silver mines as punishment. But by 1808, all British prisoners held by the Spanish in Chile were freed and returned to Europe. Bass and his crew were not amongst the freed prisoners, and their fate remains unknown.

Today, the Bass Strait, separating the island of Tasmania from the Australian mainland, stands as a reminder of the explorer's resolve to chart new discoveries.

# The Race for the Pole

*In 1909, Norwegian polar explorer Roald Amundsen was planning an expedition to the North Pole, intending to be the first person to reach it. But then he received the news that Robert Peary had already accomplished the feat. Instead of being discouraged, Amundsen simply aimed for the opposite pole. But he wasn't the only explorer heading south.*

✳ ✳ ✳ ✳

I N 1901, ROBERT Falcon Scott, a captain in the British Royal Navy, led an expedition to the Antarctic on the ship *Discovery.* The three-year expedition resulted in some important scientific findings, and Scott, along with a team including Ernest Shackleton and Edward Wilson, journeyed to within 530 miles of the South Pole. Shackleton would return to Antarctica in the 1907–1909 *Nimrod* expedition, when he set what was then the Farthest South record by reaching a point only 97 miles from the South Pole. This, along with Amundsen's announced plans to reach the pole, prompted Scott to launch a new expedition on the whaler *Terra Nova.*

*Terra Nova* set sail from Australia in October 1910, and faced challenges almost immediately. The ship faced fierce storms, and was trapped in sea ice for 20 days, hampering its arrival to the southern continent. But it reached the Ross Ice Shelf in January 1911, and Scott and his crew made camp on Ross Island, quickly assembling a prefabricated 50-by-25-foot wooden hut for shelter. While most of the crew settled in, first officer Victor Cambell sailed the *Terra Nova* east to explore more of the continent. On his way back, he was surprised to find Amundsen and his crew camping in the Bay of Whales. He rushed back to inform Scott, and the race to the South Pole was on.

## Disappointment

In October of 1911—spring in the Southern Hemisphere—Scott and a group of 16 men began a march south. Carrying plenty of supplies, members of the group turned back and returned to camp at specified latitudes, until only five men remained: Scott, Edward Wilson, Lawrence Oates, Henry Bowers, and Edgar Evans. On January 16, 1912, as they trudged through the frigid cold and what seemed a never-ending expanse of white, a dark fluttering object caught their attention. It was a black flag attached to a sled, sitting at the South Pole. Amundsen had won the race, reaching the pole a month earlier.

Although Scott did reach the South Pole, he and his men were despondent by their failure to be first. And what happened next has been debated for decades. Whether a result of their heartbreak, poor planning, or unpredictable weather, Scott and his team faltered on their way back to camp. Thanks to blizzards, frostbite, and gangrene, progress was painfully slow. Evans was the first to succumb, dying from severe frostbite and other injuries on February 17. One month later, Oates, who had been suffering from gangrene in his feet and hands, stepped out of the group's tent and never returned.

## Icy Tomb

On March 29, Scott recorded his final diary entry while a blizzard raged outside the tent, writing, "We shall stick it out to the end, but we are getting weaker, of course, and the end cannot be far." Members of the *Terra Nova* expedition sent out several search parties, but to no avail. It wasn't until November that members of the crew finally discovered the bodies of Scott, Wilson, and Bowers, lying in their tent. The crew entombed the bodies in a cairn of snow and rocks, and carpenters on the *Terra Nova* built a wooden cross, which now stands on Observation Hill near McMurdo Station.

Despite the deaths of Scott and his men, and their failure to be the first to reach the South Pole, the *Terra Nova* expedition ultimately resulted in valuable scientific contributions. The crew returned from Antarctica with more than two thousand plants, animals, and fossils, many of which had never before been studied.

Today, Scott's Hut, the prefabricated shelter erected by Scott and his crew, still stands, well-preserved in the dry, cold, Antarctic air. The cabin is a reminder of the ambitious, but ill-fated, *Terra Nova* expedition, which should be remembered for more than its tragedies.

# Desert Disappearance

*In 1979, Peng Jiamu, a biochemist at the Chinese Academy of Sciences, was promoted to vice president of the research organization. One year later, he disappeared in the Lop Nur Desert, leaving behind questions that continue to perplex explorers today.*

✳   ✳   ✳   ✳

A s a boy, Peng Jiamu was fascinated with nature and its secrets. He studied biology at the Central University of China, graduating in 1947, and became a biochemist at the Shanghai Institute of Biochemistry and Cell Biology. In 1956, the Chinese Academy of Sciences organized a research expedition to the remote province of Xinjiang, where Peng and his fellow scientists spent years exploring the endemic species in the region and measuring the potassium levels in the Lop Nur Desert salt lake.

Peng relished the chance to study this area, as he always desired to get out and explore the wildest areas of his vast country. The region around Lop Nur was especially interesting, as the area is full of archeological treasures. Sometimes called the Wandering Lake, because of its unusual propensity to shift its location,

Lop Nur is surrounded by ancient tombs, Bronze Age artifacts, and mummified remains. So, it was here, in 1980, that Peng decided to organize his own expedition, to continue his study of the remote desert.

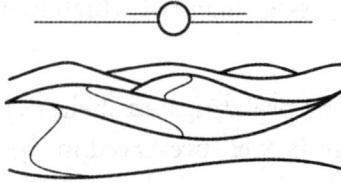

## Scientific Martyr

Unfortunately, Peng launched his research at a time when the weather was harshest, and soft riverbeds and moving sand dunes proved difficult for his team's vehicles to navigate. What's more, the expedition brought a limited amount of food, water, and fuel, and within just five days, the team was already in trouble. Leaving a note saying he was going out to search for water, Peng left the safety of the group and ventured out into the desert alone, never to be seen again.

The Chinese government launched an expansive search for Peng with the help of the miliary and police, but no trace of the scientist was ever found. Over the years, conspiracy theories have formed to explain Peng's disappearance, with some saying that he defected or was kidnapped by Americans, and others saying he was terminally ill with cancer and wandered off to commit suicide. Most believe he simply fell, perhaps dehydrated and disoriented, on the unstable rocks and soil of the desert, where his body was eventually hidden by drifting sands.

The Chinese government declared Peng a "revolutionary martyr" for exploration, and he is considered a symbol of scientific progress in the country. Peng himself believed what he was doing was a worthy undertaking, always searching for an opportunity to explore the overlooked corners of his nation. "Science," he once declared, "is to walk a road not traveled by other people."

# Chapter 2

# Criminals Who Got Away

## Whitey Bulger

*Though he served time in Alcatraz, Leavenworth, and Lewisburg federal penitentiaries, notorious Irish mob boss James "Whitey" Bulger Jr. spent much of his adult life in street clothes. His longtime freedom came largely thanks to a South Boston schoolmate who helped turn Bulger into a longtime FBI informant who put rival mobsters behind bars.*

✴ ✴ ✴ ✴

A "SOUTHIE" (PRODUCT OF South Boston), James Bulger Jr. descended from poor Irish immigrants and wasted no time showing a penchant for trouble. He joined a gang called the Shamrocks as a youth and was known for street fighting and thievery. While one of his brothers, William, would serve more than two decades in the Massachusetts Senate and for seven years as president of the University of Massachusetts, Whitey served in vastly different places. One was a reform school as a young teenager, followed later by federal prison.

When he was 18, Bulger joined the United States Air Force. There, he earned his high school diploma and trained as a mechanic. Making a positive impact, however, proved to be an elusive chore for Bulger. Several assaults placed him in military prison. Then, in 1950, he was arrested for going absent without leave. He received an honorable discharge two years later, only to find even more trouble with the non-military police.

Armed robbery and hijacking a truck landed Bulger in federal prison for the first time in 1956, when he was still a young man. While there, he volunteered for a series of controversial, CIA-sponsored experiments with controlled substances, including LSD. Bulger later claimed that the effects of the drugs brought him to the brink of insanity, saying he and other inmates were recruited deceptively into the program. Participation did bring abbreviated sentences, however, and Bulger was paroled back to the streets in 1965 after spending nine years in Atlanta, Alcatraz, Leavenworth, and Lewisburg federal penitentiaries.

Bookmaking and loan sharking were just the start of Bulger's post-prison pursuits back in Boston. He hooked up with brothers Donnie, Eddie, and Kenny Killeen, among others, in a gang that had ruled the streets for decades. Their home base, a small café, later became known as Whitey's Triple O's. When a rival gang began causing trouble in the late 1960s and early 1970s, Bulger soon earned a reputation as a man who wouldn't let matters take care of themselves.

## Sometimes, It's Who You Know

"Whitey"—a nickname bestowed upon him by local law enforcement but one that he hated—became implicated in the deaths of at least three people during those years. At least one was shot execution-style between the eyes. Bulger later took over operations of the renowned Winter Hill gang after its leader, Howie Winter, was arrested in 1979 for fixing horse races. Bulger was involved, too, but *somehow* managed to stay out of trouble.

As it turns out, that freedom from trouble was largely thanks to a former "Southie" schoolmate, FBI agent John Connolly, who had hired his old friend years earlier as an informant. Bulger had been providing Connolly and the FBI information for years that had helped take down several top leaders of the Italian mob throughout New England. Connolly intervened to protect his informant in the 1979 arrests, and was instrumental in Bulger's surprising, 46-year run of freedom.

That's right—46 years! During that time, Bulger was responsible for heinous murders, shakedowns of drug dealers that allowed him to route funds to the Irish Republican Army, and crimes of all shapes and sizes. He also did a considerable amount of traveling with his girlfriend and sidekick, Catherine Greig, and even pocketed a share of a legal, $14 million winning lottery ticket that was sold at a Boston store he controlled in 1991.

For a stretch, Bulger was the FBI's second most-wanted criminal, behind only Osama Bin Laden. After four-plus decades of freedom, and a dozen years after his old friend Connolly was indicted for routing confidential information, lying in FBI reports, and taking bribes, Bulger was arrested in Santa Monica, California, in 2011. He faced 48 federal charges, including 19 murder counts, and was convicted on 31 of them in 2013. Bulger began serving his life (plus five years) sentence in several federal prisons. Shortly after arriving at Hazelton in West Virginia in 2018, the wheelchair-bound 89-year-old was beaten to death by fellow inmates.

# Matteo Messina Denaro: Capo dei Capi

*Follow one of the most wanted and powerful criminals in the world through his life of destruction and carnage. Having commanded a criminal empire while being a fugitive for over three decades, Denaro was truly the "boss of all bosses."*

✳ ✳ ✳ ✳

MATTEO MESSINA DENARO was born with Mafia blood running through his veins. His father, Francesco Messina Denaro, aka Don Ciccio, was *capomandamento* (head of a territory) of Castelvetrano, a town in Sicily, Italy. In addition to his father, his brother, sister, and cousin were also involved in the "family business," with the goal of continuing its success into the latter half of the twentieth century.

Known as *Diabolik* (after a comic book character), Denaro learned how to use a gun at the young age of 14, and bragged on several occasions how he had "filled a cemetery all by myself." As he grew into adulthood, he was known as a playboy, having a flashy style and a penchant for fast cars and designer clothes and jewelry. He enjoyed playing computer games, and he had an extramarital daughter, which was uncommon within the conservative Mafia.

In a continuation of his violent streak, it is said that he killed a Sicilian hotel owner who had accused him of inappropriate contact with young girls. And in 1992, he allegedly took part in the murder of rival Mafia leader, Vincenzo Milazzo, and his pregnant girlfriend, Antonella Bonomo. Overall, it is estimated that Denaro was responsible for over 70 murders.

## Claims to Infamy

In May and July of 1992, Denaro played an important role in the Sicilian Mafia (Cosa Nostra) terrorist attacks—the Capaci bombing and Via D'Amelio bombing. These attacks would result in the deaths of magistrate Giovanni Falcone and his wife (Francesca Morvillo), as well as anti-Mafia Italian magistrate Paolo Borsellino. Eight police escort agents were also killed. It was a devastating tragedy to the public, but the Mafia considered it an incredible success.

But they would not rest on their laurels: Cosa Nostra launched four additional terrorist attacks in the following year in Via dei Georgofili in Florence, in Via Palestro in Milan, in the Piazza San Giovanni in Laterano, and Via San Teodoro in Rome. These attacks resulted in deaths and injuries, as well as serious damage to centers of cultural heritage. As with the 1992 bombings, Denaro would be heavily involved in the planning and execution of these attacks, as well as tracking and tailing victims and potential victims in preparation for the bombings. After these bombings, Denaro went into hiding.

During the trial of the Capaci bombing, Denaro and associates kidnapped 12-year-old Giuseppe Di Matteo in an effort to force his mafioso father, Santino Di Matteo, to retract his damning testimony of who and how the attack was pulled off. Unfortunately, after being held captive for over two years, Giuseppe was strangled and his body dissolved in acid on the orders of mobster Giovanni Brusca. A court sentenced Denaro and five others to life imprisonment for this heinous crime.

## A Mafioso Reborn

After his father passed away in 1998, Denaro took over as capomandamento of Castelvetrano and nearby cities. At his height, it's said that he had over 900 men in his employ, and he consolidated the 20 Mafia families of Trapani into one mandomento.

He earned the bulk of his wealth by extorting businesses for "protection money," being active in the international drug trade, and skimming money off the top of various public construction projects; he was able to take advantage of the latter due to his family's ownership of various sand quarries. He did operate a few legal ventures, such as a supermarket chain and olive groves, but he operated his olive oil production at a maximum profit margin due to taking advantage of cheap labor.

"Wait," one might ask, "If he was on the run from the police, how did he manage to still be this successful in legitimate business as well as the criminal underworld?" He was able to achieve this level of success through the sacrifice of other members of Cosa Nostra and his loyal family. Over the subsequent decades, it seems as though everyone took the fall for him: his lover and her brother, Maria and Francesco Mesi; his brother-in-law, Filippo Guttadauro; Giuseppe Grigoli, Rosario Cascio, and Vito Nicastri, who laundered money through their supermarkets, construction companies, and wind and solar energy investments, respectively; and Denaro's brother and sister, Salvatore and Patrizia.

In 2020, the walls of his empire finally began to crumble. After capturing most of his remaining allies and seizing most of his assets, the Italian police closed in around him. In January 2023, Messino was finally taken into custody at La Maddalena clinic in Palermo, an upscale cancer treatment center where he had been seeking treatment over the past year. He had been using a fake identity, but the police were still able to track and find him due to his failing health.

Even before his capture, he had been found guilty *in absentia* for his role in the bombings of 1992 and 1993; while facing life imprisonment, he died in 2023.

# Kicking the Folsom Prison Blues

*Of the many attempted escapes from California's Folsom Prison—the facility made famous in song by Johnny Cash—that of Glen Stewart Godwin in 1987 was the most famous and successful. As of 2024, Godwin was still considered to be at large.*

✳   ✳   ✳   ✳

GLEN STEWART GODWIN, born in Miami in 1958, might be a footnote in crime history but for two notorious prison escapes. He was convicted of the 1980 murder of drug trafficker and pilot Kim Levalley in Palm Springs, California. He had beaten Levalley, stabbed him 26 times, and tried to cover his tracks by blowing up the body in a truck using homemade explosives. After trying to break out of California's Deuel Vocational Institute in 1987, he was transferred to maximum-security Folsom State Prison, where he pulled off a nearly impossible escape.

His wife, Shelly Rose Godwin, and former Deuel cellmate Lorenz Karlic are thought to have smuggled in a hacksaw that Glen used to cut his way to freedom on June 5, 1987. He dropped into a manhole and crawled through a storm drain that emptied into the American River, cutting through bars at the river's entrance and navigating the river on a waiting raft. It was one of precious few escapes from Folsom prison. Most of the previous ones resulted in death or recapture.

Godwin fled to Mexico, where he earned a seven-and-a-half-year sentence in 1991 for drug trafficking. He was accused of murdering a Mexican cartel member behind bars while awaiting extradition to the United States, but managed to escape from Puente Grande—the same prison that once held El Chapo—in September 1991. A $20,000 reward for information leading to his capture has been offered by the FBI, but as of 2024 Godwin was still on the loose.

# Jason Derek Brown: Fugitive Extraordinaire

*How does an unassuming Californian man become one of the FBI's most wanted men in America? From children's toy seller to wanted killer, follow the mysterious trail of this phantom thief.*

✳  ✳  ✳  ✳

FOR ONE OF the most wanted people in the world, Jason Derek Brown had a fairly normal childhood. Born on July 1, 1969, in Los Angeles, California, he went to school in affluent Laguna Beach. In the late 1980s, he served a mission for the Church of Jesus Christ of Latter-day Saints in Paris before earning a master's degree in international business. At some point after graduation, he moved to Salt Lake City, Utah, and owned two businesses: Toys Unlimited and On the Doorstep Advertising. Brown portrayed himself as a wealthy man, enjoying cars, motorbikes, and boats. However, his two businesses weren't enough to support his expensive tastes; Brown defaulted on at least one large loan and was tens of thousands of dollars in debt by 2004. It is alleged that Brown would occasionally go into car dealerships and attempt to purchase a car with a fake social security number and address. His inability to support his lavish hobbies and his track record for scamming businesses all serve as probable motives for the awful crime he would soon commit.

## The Point of No Return

On November 29, 2004, Brown allegedly shot five rounds into the head of Robert Keith Palomares, an armored car guard, outside of an AMC movie theater in Phoenix, Arizona. Brown then stole $56,000 in cash and fled the scene on a bicycle. Palomares was pronounced dead at the hospital, and nearby witnesses described the shooter as being mid-twenties and of Hispanic descent. Authorities did recover the bicycle and were able to lift fingerprints that matched Brown, resulting in him becoming a prime suspect.

In the meantime, it's believed that Brown immediately fled Arizona for Henderson, Nevada, before swapping out his BMW for a Cadillac Escalade. He left the BMW in a storage facility in Las Vegas, and then drove down to California. Police tracked him to a relatives' house in Orange County, California, but he had already fled to San Diego. But rather than fleeing across the border into Mexico, he strangely drove north, all the way up to Portland, Oregon. Unfortunately for police and the FBI, after that he became a proverbial "ghost."

In the years since, the FBI has received more leads on Brown than any other person on their Most Wanted list; unfortunately, none of them have ever led to anything substantial. The only confirmed sighting of Brown came from an acquaintance of his who had been part of his mission trip in France. Upon recognizing each other at a stop light in Salt Lake City, Utah in 2008, Brown immediately sped through the light and was never seen again. The witness stated that he had a deeper tan and longer hair compared to 2004. The FBI is unsure whether he is in the country, living within the Mormon community in Utah under an assumed identity, or if he fled for Québec, France, or Thailand. Jason Derek Brown has been covered quite a bit in the media, including on *Dateline*, *American Greed*, and several others, and his story was dramatized in the 2022 true crime film, *American Murderer*.

# Audacious Outlaw (The Jacques Mesrine Story)

*What happens when you take a witty man with a penchant for crime and outlaw behavior, and add in Looney Tunes-like situations with the law and prison? You get Jacques Mesrine, who successfully escaped from prison multiple times and became internationally known as the "French Robin Hood."*

✳  ✳  ✳  ✳

JACQUES RENÉ MESRINE was born in Clichy, a suburb outside of Paris, France, on December 28, 1936. He was a delinquent from an early age, having been expelled from a prestigious Catholic school after attacking the principal. He was drafted into the French army in the 1950s where he served as a paratrooper. While despising how rigid and orderly the military was, he enjoyed and excelled in his counterinsurgency operations; this was the seeming catalyst event that would explain his continued patterns of violence throughout life. In 1961, he married Maria de la Soledad, and they had three children together before separating in 1965. That same year, he joined the far-right terrorist organization, *Organisation armée secrète*, and he was sentenced to 18 months in prison for robbery. After finishing his sentence, he attempted to walk the straight-and-narrow by first working at an architectural design company, and then at a restaurant. However, the allure of the criminal world proved too tempting for Mesrine, and he returned to it in 1965.

# Man on the Run

Mesrine had a reputation for being a man that you didn't cross lightly. He also had a love of women and living a "high octane lifestyle," and he was rarely seen without a female accomplice at his side. The first known criminal mistress was Jeannie Schneider, whom he was with when he robbed a jewelry store in Geneva, a hotel in Chamonix, and a fashion store in Paris before they fled together to Québec after robbing a gambling den. There, they got jobs working for Georges Deslauriers, a grocery and textile millionaire; however, they lost them a few months later when Schneider got into an argument with Deslauriers's longtime gardener.

A year later, in 1969, Mesrine and Schneider fled to the United States after attempting to kidnap Deslauriers. Thankfully for Deslauriers, the sedative they used didn't affect him, but this would kick off a penchant for kidnapping that Mesrine would never quench.

While attempting to stay hidden from U.S. police, who were aware of the couple's crimes in Québec, they did the exact opposite of "laying low" by strangling an older woman, Evelyne Le Bouthillier, who had given them refuge. Their whirlwind tour of the States ended a few weeks later when the police caught up to them in Texarkana, Arkansas, and extradited them to Québec. Mesrine and Schneider were acquitted of the murder of Le Bouthillier, but Mesrine was sentenced to ten years in prison for the attempted kidnapping of Deslauriers. He did successfully escape from prison, but was rearrested the next day. Together with fellow prisoner, Jean-Paul Mercier, and five others, Mesrine successfully escaped from Saint-Vincent-de-Paul prison in 1972; they succeeded by cutting through fencing with wire cutters. Mercier, a known murderer and Quebecois terrorist, was the perfect partner with whom Mesrine could execute the next part of his grand plan: attack the prison he had just escaped from in an effort to free the remaining 53 maximum-security prisoners.

This may seem rather silly at first. However, Mesrine had a known hatred for maximum-security prisons, despising in particular how he and others were treated in them. In between his usual bank robberies, he and Mercier went back to the prison and, upon seeing that it had greatly increased security, got into a shoot-out with guards that resulted in the injury of Mercier and two guards. The "boldness" of the escaped convicts caused the Canadian government to pursue them with renewed vigor.

## "The Man of a Thousand Faces"

One might wonder how he was able to commit so many crimes while being one of the most wanted men in Canada. This was through his mastery of disguise. He would often change his hair cut and style, donning various outfits and other disguises so that he could move around rather freely. He was also known for wearing flashy, high-fashion clothing most of the time, and his fair manners with civilians contrasted heavily with the brutality of his run-ins with the law. The fact that he was kind to average people, coupled with his penchant for donating to homeless people, earned him the other nickname, "The French Robin Hood." While he did seem to enjoy the high-stakes life of crime, he also seemingly used it to rebel against what he perceived as major problems; one example of this was his aforementioned hatred of maximum-security wings in prisons. He had previously held extremist right-wing views, but these had shifted over to more left-wing opinions as his contempt for police and prisons grew.

Despite his skill with disguises, Mesrine did not find Canada the easiest country to move around in. This prompted him to briefly move to Caracas, Venezuela, before returning to France in late 1972. In France, he resumed his bank robberies until 1973 when he brandished a gun at a coffee shop cashier during an argument. When a police officer tried to intervene, Mesrine seriously injured him; Mesrine was arrested and sentenced to twenty years in La Santé maximum security prison. Escape from La Santé was thought to be impossible, so Mesrine went about escaping through different means. Feigning illness, he was able to go into the courthouse bathroom where a revolver had been hidden by an accomplice. Using the revolver, he took a judge hostage as a "human shield" and was able to escape. He was free for around four months before an accomplice informed on him, and he was returned to La Santé. While in prison, he authored and smuggled out his autobiography, *L'Instinct de Mort* ("Death Instinct"). In it, Mesrine claimed to have committed over 40 murders—a figure considered a gross exaggeration by most. His book is what spurred France to pass the "Son of Sam law," which prevents criminals from profiting off of the publication of their own crimes.

La Santé managed to hold Mesrine longer than any other prison—but this was not meant to last. In 1978, he acquired a gun, keys, and—with famed escapee François Besse and an unknown man—they broke out of the cellblock and into a fenced-off yard walkway. Grappling iron in hand, Mesrine forced some workmen with an extendable ladder to follow them with said ladder. Reaching an isolated part of the exterior wall, they hooked the grappling iron to the top of the ladder and slid down a rope over the wall. The unknown man was shot dead by police when he attempted to get over the wall, but Mesrine and Besse successfully hijacked a car and avoided the police cordons. With this daring escape, they became the first men to ever successfully escape from La Santé.

## End of the Line

After their daring escape, the pair didn't rest on their laurels. Over the next year, they would proceed to rob several businesses and even a casino. Some of these robberies would result in exciting and dangerous gun fights breaking out with the police. They made quite a pretty penny from these robberies, stealing 130,000 francs from the casino, and 450,000 francs in ransom after kidnapping a banker. In between these crimes, Mesrine would take various interviews, such as the August 4, 1978, issue of *Paris Match* (a weekly news magazine) where he threatened the Minister of Justice. Feeling immense pressure from their inability to capture him and his very public gloating, French law enforcement agencies made him "l'ennemi public numéro un" (public enemy number one). Despite this, his mastery of disguises and avoidance of the criminal underground made him difficult to pin down. He also traveled a lot for pleasure and "work": Sicily, Algeria, London, Brussels, and back to France in November 1978.

That same month, Mesrine kidnapped another judge who had previously sentenced him as a form of protesting against maximum security prisons. While his accomplice was captured, Mesrine managed to run past a bunch of police officers before handcuffing one young policeman to a pipe. The following June, he kidnapped Henri Lelièvre, a millionaire in the real estate industry, for a ransom of six million francs.

He was finally tracked down with the help of former Directorate of Territorial Security policeman, Jacques Tillier. Tillier had been a vocal adversary of Mesrine; he lured Tillier to a secret meeting place, under the guise of an interview, where he shot Tillier through his face, arm, and leg. Tillier survived, and he was able to pass along a relevant license plate number to police.

The license plate belonged to Mesrine's latest mistress, Sylvia Jeanjacquot. By checking past parking tickets she had accumulated, law enforcement was able to figure out the areas the couple frequented. The couple were spotted and followed to their apartment, and were surveilled 24/7. When the couple left for a weekend trip a few days later, police set a trap for them that resulted in law enforcement firing into their vehicle, striking Mesrine 15 times. Jeanjacquot was shot in her eye and arm, but ultimately survived. Mesrine was given a "coup de grâce," which fueled accusations of unlawful execution by law enforcement.

# A Webb of Lies

*Donald Eugene Webb holds the record for the second-longest stint on the FBI's Most Wanted list. How did a career criminal with a remarkable knack for assumed identities stay out of the hands of the law for nearly forty years?*

❊   ❊   ❊   ❊

ONALD EUGENE WEBB was born Donald Eugene Perkins in Oklahoma City, Oklahoma, in 1931. The details of his childhood are unknown, except that he was raised by his paternal grandfather. In 1959, he legally changed his name to Webb; the reasons for this change are unknown. Throughout his adulthood, Webb worked several different jobs, such as a butcher, salesman, restaurant manager, and vending machine repairman. Despite holding down gainful employment, he had a taste for the criminal, having been convicted for burglary, breaking and entering, armed bank robbery, several possession charges, grand larceny, and car theft. The only known prison time he served was a two-year sentence in the mid-1970s.

It was believed by the FBI that Webb was an associate of the Patriarca crime family, based out of New England, and involved in an organized crime group in the Miami area. It was through these two crime syndicates that Webb was able to fence his stolen goods and likely received support for his many robberies.

The FBI considered Webb a "master of disguise," having a plethora of them in his arsenal. An example of this in 1979 saw Webb and two accomplices posing as sewer and water inspectors in order to burgle homes in Albany, New York. They were discovered and charged, but they posted bail and didn't return for their court date.

## Murder for One

In December of 1980, police chief of Saxonburg, Pennsylvania, Gregory Adams, pulled over a man who is believed to be Donald Eugene Webb. Adams asked for identification and the suspect gave him fake documents. The suspect exited his vehicle and proceeded to fight with Adams—in the process, he disarmed Adams, pistol-whipped him, and beat him to the point of being nearly unrecognizable.

Nearby witnesses recall hearing four "pop" noises and a large "boom" sound; it is believed that the first noises were from Webb's semiautomatic .25-caliber Colt pistol, while the final "boom" was from Adams's revolver. A medical examiner later determined that Adams was shot twice in the chest—one shot collapsing a lung, and the other ripping through his heart—and once in his arm. The suspect took Adams's gun and keys, and disabled Adams's police car microphone before fleeing in his own car. A nearby resident did find the dying Adams and was able to confirm that he did not know his attacker. Unfortunately, Adams lost consciousness on the way to the hospital, and ultimately died of his injuries.

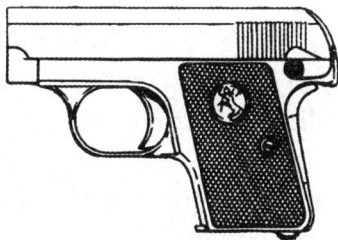

The aforementioned Colt pistol, blood matching Webb's blood type, and a New Jersey driver's license under the name Stanley John Portas were all found at the scene. The name on the license belonged to Webb's wife's late husband, who had passed away in 1948, and was a known alias of Webb. Later that night, Adams's revolver was located approximately seven miles away; two weeks later, the suspected getaway car was found abandoned at a motel in Warwick, Rhode Island. More blood matching Webb's blood type was found on the steering wheel, which seems to suggest that Webb was injured in the confrontation with Adams.

Webb was officially named the main suspect in the killing; he was charged in absentia with murder, attempted burglary, and unlawful flight to avoid prosecution. The manhunt for Webb officially began on December 31, 1980, and he was added to the FBI's Most Wanted list in May of the following year. In the subsequent years, there were confirmed sightings around Fall River, New Bedford, and Boston, Massachusetts, and unconfirmed ones in other parts of Massachusetts, Washington, Canada, and Costa Rica.

## Closure at Last

Webb would remain in hiding for nearly forty years, and the public wouldn't receive any closure until 2017 when his widow, Lillian Webb, finally revealed that she had been harboring him for nearly twenty years. Under immunity from the prosecution, she confessed to sheltering him since 1980. She added that he had suffered a compound fracture in his leg from a gun wound during the killing of Adams, and he was treated at Tobey Hospital in Wareham, Massachusetts, under a false identity. Regarding his inevitable end, she said that he suffered strokes later in life until he finally died in 1999. She led investigators to his remains buried on their property, which were tested and confirmed to belong to Webb.

Two weeks prior to Lillian Webb's confession, Mary Ann Adams Jones, Gregory Adams's widow, filed a lawsuit for civil damages against Donald, Lillian, and his stepson, Stanley Webb. Additionally, FBI investigators had discovered a hidden room behind a closet in the basement of Lillian Webb's home in North Dartmouth, Massachusetts, that had not existed when she originally purchased the house. This evidence was how the FBI was able to apply enough pressure to Lillian to get the closure they and Mary Ann needed.

# Whatever Happened to Bradford Bishop?

*On a seemingly innocuous March day in 1976, Yale graduate and foreign diplomat Bradford Bishop returned home from work and murdered his entire family. What led up to the heinous murders, and how has he evaded an international manhunt ever since?*

✳ ✳ ✳ ✳

WILLIAM BRADFORD BISHOP Jr. was born in Pasadena, California, on August 1, 1936. He enrolled in higher education, earning a bachelor's degree from Yale and a master's degree from Middlebury College. Additionally, he earned a master's degree in African Studies from UCLA. Post-graduation from Yale, Bishop married Annette Weis, his high school sweetheart. They had to move around quite a bit due to Bishop's service in the United States Army, which he said he enjoyed; Annette, not so much.

He spoke five languages fluently: English, Italian, French, Spanish, and Serbo-Croatian. It was due to this knowledge that he spent four years working in counterintelligence. After his time in the Army, he worked for the State Department and served as a diplomat in several overseas postings; this included places such as Verona, Milan, Florence, Ethiopia, Gaborone, and Botswana. His last posting before his crimes was in Washington D.C. Bishop, Annette, their three sons, and his mother, Lobelia, all lived in Bethesda, Maryland, at this time.

## "A Glitch in the Storybook Tale"

For a number of years, Bishop had been pursuing a promotion in the Division of Special Activities and Commercial Treaties. On March 1, 1976, when he did not acquire his sought-after promotion, he left early from work. It was then believed that he withdrew several hundred dollars from his bank before going to Montgomery Bank and purchasing a metal mallet and gas can. He filled the gas can and his car's tank before driving to a hardware store to purchase a shovel and pitchfork.

Upon returning to his home in the evening, he allegedly used the metal mallet to bludgeon his family to death: first his wife, then his three sons—who were asleep upstairs—and finally, his mother, who had just returned from walking the family dog. After committing the horrific and brutal murders, he allegedly drove the bodies 275 miles to a dense swamp five miles south of Columbia, North Carolina. Digging a shallow hole, he dropped the bodies in and lit them on fire. Their bodies were discovered soon after by a park ranger who had spotted the fire.

Ten days after the murders, a neighbor called police to report the family's disappearance. Upon investigating their home, the officers discovered blood on the front porch, and on the floor and walls of the front hall and bedrooms. Police connected the grisly crime scene to the burnt bodies discovered in North Carolina; they used dental records to confirm the connection.

Police were able to track Bishop's car to a secluded campground in Elkmont, Tennessee, about 400 miles from the Bishop family's graves. Within his car, police found dog biscuits, a bloody blanket, a shotgun, an ax, a shaving kit with Bishop's medication inside, and blood within the spare-tire well. The next day, a grand jury indicted Bishop in absentia on five counts of first-degree murder and other charges.

## Dust in the Wind

Neither Bishop, nor his dog have ever been seen since. The most credible sightings occurred in July 1978, January 1979, and September 1994. The first was where a Swedish woman, who had worked with him in the past, apparently spotted him twice at a park in Stockholm. The second spotting was by Roy Harrell—his State Department colleague and the last acquaintance to see him before the murders—in Sorrento, Italy. According to Harrell, he had made eye contact with Bishop and asked, "Hey, you're Brad Bishop, aren't you?" The man responded, "Oh no" before fleeing and never being seen in Italy again. The final spotting of Bishop was on a Swiss train platform by a neighbor who had known the Bishop family. The neighbor stated that he saw Bishop getting into a car, and added that he appeared "well-groomed." There have been various other sightings of Bishop in places such as Belgium, England, Finland, the Netherlands, Germany, Greece, and Spain, but these sightings are not considered credible. It is presumed that he is still out there somewhere, likely hiding in plain sight by simply lying low and avoiding arrest.

# Story of a Sociopath

*"La Pistolera" is responsible for three cold-blooded murders and breaking out of a Mexico City prison. Over half a century after her daring escape, Sharon Kinne's whereabouts and fate are still unknown.*

✳  ✳  ✳  ✳

SHARON KINNE WAS born Sharon Elizabeth Hall on November 30, 1939 in Independence, Missouri. When she was 16 years old, she met college student James Kinne at a church event. This would begin a several-months-long romance that lasted until he returned to college in the fall. Sharon soon informed him that she was pregnant with his child; this prompted him to return to Independence and the two married on October 18, 1956. After James finished college at Brigham Young University, they set down roots in Independence where James got a job as an electrical engineer and Sharon gave birth to a baby girl, Danna, and later a baby boy, Troy.

Unfortunately, their married life wasn't all sunshine and daisies: James was finding it difficult to support Sharon's lavish spending habits, and he correctly suspected that she was having an extramarital affair. They were both contemplating divorce when their worries were cut short by the ring of a gunshot. According to Sharon, on the evening of March 19, 1960, she heard a gunshot from their bedroom where James was currently sleeping. Upon investigating the sound, she claimed to see their two-and-a-half-year-old daughter holding one of James's pistols next to his body on the bed. James had suffered a gunshot wound to the back of his head, and he passed away on the way to the hospital.

## The Bodies Are Piling Up

Despite not having enough evidence to initially charge Kinne with her husband's murder, the prosecution eventually did charge her on May 31st, 1961. This was the same day she was charged for the murder of Patricia Jones. She had been having an affair with Patricia's husband, Walter T. Jones Jr., whom she had met in April of 1961 at a car dealership. Kinne apparently viewed him as a potential prospect for a second husband, but he had no desire to end his marriage. Realizing that convincing him was futile, Kinne allegedly met with Patricia, shot her four times with a .22-caliber pistol—the same type of gun that killed James—and stashed her body in the woods.

Kinne was found guilty on January 11, 1962, and sentenced to life in prison. Her defense moved that the conviction be vacated on the grounds that the jury had made its verdict based on "surmise and speculation" instead of "substantial evidence." This motion was originally denied by the judge, but it was brought all the way up to the Missouri Supreme Court, where they reversed it and ordered a new trial.

The second trial began in March, but a mistrial occurred after it was discovered that a law partner of one of the prosecutors had once been employed by one of the jurors. A third trial began in June, but the jury deadlocked seven-to-five in favor of acquittal; this resulted in yet another mistrial. At around the same time this trial began, the trial for the death of Patricia Jones began. Kinne won this one, being acquitted by a jury on all charges due to "too many loopholes" in the prosecution's defense.

## A Murder in Mexico

While out on $20,000 bond, Sharon Kinne left town on a trip to Mexico City in September 1964 with her alleged lover, Francis Samuel Pugliese. The couple posed as husband and wife while registering a room at Hotel Gin. Claiming that she felt unsafe, she purchased a gun, which they added to their existing collection of guns. On the evening of September 18, she ventured out alone from their hotel room and met Mexican-born American citizen, Francisco Paredes Ordoñez, at a nearby bar. According to Kinne, she left the bar with him and went to his room at Hotel La Vada to look at his photography collection.

While in his room alone with him, he allegedly made sexual advances towards her, resulting in her taking out her gun. She claims she had the intention of only scaring him, but she ended up shooting him in the chest. Hotel employee, Enrique Martinez Rueda, heard the shots and ran in, but was shot in the shoulder. He locked her inside the room, fled, and called the police. Police theorized that she had gone out with the intention of robbing someone, and that Ordoñez was an intended victim.

Kinne was arrested and charged with homicide and assault with a deadly weapon. Pugliese was originally arrested and held without charge, but authorities later charged him with entering the country illegally and carrying an unlicensed gun. Pugliese was ultimately cleared and deported back to the United States,

but Kinne didn't get off so easily. On October 18, 1964, she was convicted of the homicide of Ordoñez and sentenced to a ten-year prison term.

She attempted to appeal the verdict, but it only lengthened her term because, while a judge overturned her attempted robbery charges, he upheld her murder charge; this increased her sentence from ten to thirteen years. She was returned to a women's prison in Iztapalapa, Mexico City, to serve her sentence. The inmates nicknamed her "La Pistolera" (the gunfighter), a moniker which the press then adopted.

Interestingly, at Kinne's trial, investigators found evidence that one of the guns the couple carried was the same one that killed Patricia Jones. However, because Kinne had already been acquitted, she could not be retried.

On December 7, 1969, Kinne was missing from an evening roll call. It is suspected that she bribed guards to "look the other way," or that she may have caused a blackout to occur that night, facilitating her escape. A country-wide manhunt was underway and even the FBI got involved because of the Mexican authorities' belief that she might try to sneak back into the United States. However, the manhunt and investigation was short-lived, as authorities believe that she ultimately fled into neighboring Guatemala.

# Chapter 3

# Missing Treasures and Artifacts

## This Cup Runneth Over with History

*For centuries, men have pondered the existence of the Holy Grail, the cup Jesus is said to have shared with his disciples at the Last Supper and that might have been filled with his blood after his death on a cross. Actual or mythical, the Grail has a very real place in medieval literature—and modern speculation.*

✳ ✳ ✳ ✳

THE CHRISTIAN BIBLE tells us that Jesus held up a wine-filled chalice and offered it to his disciples at the Last Supper, telling them that the wine they were about to drink represented his blood—signifying a covenant with God that would give them eternal life. It's no surprise, then, that the chalice has been sought after for centuries by Christians and others. It's been dubbed the Holy Grail, from medieval literature all the way up to a 1989 Indiana Jones movie, and comes with countless stories about its past and potential whereabouts.

While the chalice might date to Jesus and the Last Supper more than 2,000 years ago, the first appearance of a mysterious grail in literature does not go back quite half that far. The first such reference is in an unfinished romance, *Perceval, the Story of the Grail*, by French poet Chrétien de Troyes in the twelfth century. It began showing up more frequently in subsequent literature. A Robert de Boron poem, *Joseph d'Arimathie*, around 1200 noted the significance of the Grail in Christ's final days and at his crucifixion, where Joseph of Arimathea is said to have used it to collect the blood of Jesus.

Perceval was the first knightly pursuer of the Grail in literature of that era, but slightly later works had Sir Galahad of King Arthur's court famously finding the chalice, or at least searching for it or admiring it with Arthur's other knights in a Grail castle. Some tales describe it as a bowl, dish, or platter—perhaps once serving up a severed head to a rival—in addition to its traditional portrayal as the wine vessel of the Last Supper.

## But Where Can It Be?

If the Grail does exist, where can it be? The answer is apparently not where Indiana Jones outmaneuvered the Nazis in his search for the treasure in *Indiana Jones and the Last Crusade*. Some literary accounts have Joseph of Arimathea relocating the Holy Grail to Glastonbury, in England, after the death of Jesus, burying it, and marveling at how the ground covering it started to produce flowing red water, presumably from running through Christ's blood.

Many of the legendary stories about the Grail involve the Knights Templar, a mysterious organization of medieval times that fought to defend the Holy Land during the Crusades. One well-known story has this group stealing the Holy Grail from the Temple Mount and storing it along with other religious relics, among them the Ark of the Covenant and parts of the cross from the crucifixion of Christ. It has been the subject of conspiracy theories for centuries, and places like Midlothian, Scotland, and Glastonbury have earned acclaim as possible locations where this ancient treasure could have been hidden and, someday, might resurface.

Whether or not the Holy Grail exists, once existed, or was simply a mythical representation, there's no denying its impact through centuries of art, literature, music, and film—even making an appearance in an episode of *The Office* (American version) and the *Assassin's Creed* video game franchise. Poems, paintings, and prose have immortalized the Grail as one of the most mysterious and elusive relics in history.

# History's Most Famous Sword

*Ask someone to name a sword—any sword—and it's likely one name will roll off the tongue. Excalibur, the magical and mysterious sword of King Arthur, was the steely legend of medieval times and has countless stories to tell and retell.*

✳   ✳   ✳   ✳

**T**HERE ARE CONFLICTING versions of how King Arthur came upon his mighty sword, Excalibur. One tale tells us that he attained the British throne by pulling it out of an anvil, or a stone, or an anvil atop a stone. Robert de Boron's poem "Merlin" recounted that only the true king would be able to pull the sword from the anvil on Christmas Eve, a feat that Arthur accomplishes twice—the first time accidentally, and then again publicly after returning the sword to its place.

Another version has the Lady of the Lake, also known as Nimue, presenting the sword to King Arthur in exchange for a favor that would be requested years later. Excalibur protects the king and his knights in battle over the years, and eventually gets returned to the lake on Arthur's death. At that time, a mystical boat surfaces to take him to the island of Avalon, where he presumably will be healed to eventually lead Britain when the country needs him most.

The latter is the most prevalent version of how Arthur and Excalibur were joined, though the sword-from-the-stone story has come to follow Excalibur through history. Welsh legend includes an ancient sword called Caledfwlch and an old Irish tale tells of Caladbolg, swords thought to be near the root of the name Excalibur.

## A Powerful Sword Indeed

Excalibur could cut solid steel, some said. Among its other powers, it shone brightly enough to light up the night—the equivalent to the illumination of 30 flashlights. It provided protection for Arthur and his knights from all wounds. And, most notably, every time King Arthur pulled it out he was able to win battles, no matter the odds. With it against the Saxons, Arthur was able to single-handedly slay hundreds.

Excalibur's scabbard, or sheath, also possessed magical powers. His sister once stole the scabbard, leaving Arthur and the sword vulnerable for a stretch. The king and his knights had other weapons, but Excalibur was the most powerful and most valuable. When he returned it to the lake in his dying days, a hand—presumably that of the Lady of the Lake—soared from beneath the water's surface to secure it.

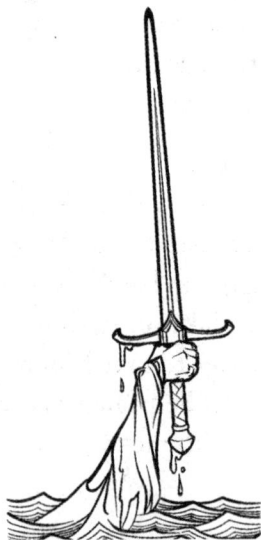

There are those who have searched for Excalibur over the years, and some who have even purported to have found it. In 2017, a young girl found a four-foot sword in a Cornwall pool where some say Excalibur was once thrown. It's a big claim, given that Arthur's own existence has been debated every which way for centuries. The stuff of legend, some might say.

# The Face of Controversy?

*The Mask of Agamemnon is stunning to look at—one of the most talked-about golden artifacts from the ancient Greek Bronze Age. Despite its captivating qualities, the legend behind the identity of the mask is even more gripping.*

✳   ✳   ✳   ✳

"I HAVE GAZED UPON the face of Agamemnon." These were the famous words of archeology pioneer Heinrich Schliemann after laying eyes on a golden mask still attached to its corpse in 1876. The Mask of Agamemnon was discovered, along with other artifacts, by Schliemann at the Bronze Age site of Mycenae in southern Greece. It remains displayed today in the National Archeological Museum of Athens, and has been referred to as the "Mona Lisa of prehistory."

The gold funeral mask depicts a man with a long face, long nose, thin lips, and eyes that could be seen as open or closed depending on one's perspective. It is one of seven masks found at the Mycenae site that day, this one discovered in a shaft tomb labeled Grave V. It's thought to have been made by placing a thick sheet of gold over a wooden replica of Agamemnon's face and then hammering out the details. Additional detail was etched in later. But exactly when is a question that remains the subject of debate.

Agamemnon was the Mycenaean king of Greek mythology, appearing in Homer's *Iliad* among other works. His story is one of sacrifice, anger, sadness, and revenge. In leading the Greeks in the Trojan War, Agamemnon is said to have sacrificed one of his daughters, Iphigenia, to the goddess Artemis in order to produce wind that would allow Greek ships to sail to Troy. Not surprisingly, this did not sit well with his wife, Clytemnestra, upon his return to Mycenae following the war. Struck with grief and anger, his wife killed him.

Schliemann contended the mask served as proof that Agamemnon actually lived. It's not surprising that this was greatly fact-checked by the scientific community. *Archaeology* magazine ran a series of articles debating the authenticity of Schliemann's discovery. Some suspected the mask was fraudulent. Others contended it was real—the common consensus, it seems—but that it was created some 300–400 years before the Trojan War, thought to have taken place sometime between the eleventh and thirteenth centuries BC.

Schliemann seemed to come around to the idea, in the days leading up to his death in 1890, that the mask did not actually depict Agamemnon. He also seemed to have developed a sense of humor around the subject. "So this is not Agamemnon," he reportedly said. "These are not his ornaments? All right, let's call him Schulze."

# Alaric's Lost Treasure

*Somewhere at the bottom of a river in Italy lies one of the biggest treasure hoards the world has ever seen. Gold, silver, precious jewelry, ancient coins, and other relics all await some lucky treasure hunter's eventual discovery. But is any of this true?*

✳ ✳ ✳ ✳

ALARIC WAS A king of the Germanic peoples historians called the Visigoths. Considered barbarians by the Romans of the fourth century AD, this group of Goths had had close contact with the Roman Empire for decades, sometimes working for them and sometimes warring with them. Alaric himself was typical of times: he had been both a soldier in the service of Rome and an adversary of the Empire.

After years of experiencing Rome's broken promises and double-dealing, mixed with the occasional ransom payment, Alaric decided to lead his forces into Italy. In 410, he successfully sacked the city of Rome. It was the first time the city had fallen to an enemy in almost 800 years. Months later, Alaric died in southern Italy. It's only natural that rumors, legends, and outright falsehoods would accrue around such an epochal event. One such story involves the massive treasure Alaric took from Rome.

## Jordanes the Legend Maker?

Nearly 150 years after the legendary sacking, a historian named Jordanes wrote an account of those times. But Jordanes was not the most reliable source. Critics believe his very pro-Goth writings were stitched together from sources both reliable and otherwise. He claimed that the Visigoths diverted the flow of "the river Busentus near the city of Cosentia" in southern Italy, and had a band of captives dig Alaric's grave in the river's bed. They buried him with a great treasure and then allowed the river to resume its course. Jordanes concludes "and that none might ever know the place, they put to death all the diggers."

Among many others, the eighteenth-century English historian Edward Gibbon took up the story, writing, "the secret spot where the remains of Alaric had been deposited was for ever concealed by the inhuman massacre of the prisoners who had been employed to execute the work." The treasure itself supposedly represented the vast wealth of Rome at that time, amounting to (depending on the source) up to 150 or so tons of silver, up to 25 tons or so of gold, assorted wagonloads of loot, and even the Menorah from the Second Temple (looted by the Romans in AD 70 from Jerusalem). Other sources give different amounts and types of treasure, including silk robes and valuable spices.

## Does It Even Exist?

Explorers, archeologists, and even the Italian government continue to search for the location of Alaric's treasure hoard. Many places have been suggested but none of them have turned up even a single coin. It should be noted that rivers shift their courses and earthquakes occur repeatedly in southern Italy, so even if sources can be trusted, the treasure may have settled more deeply into the ground, lie in a location no longer covered by water, or even be widely dispersed thanks to river currents. But the question will continue to haunt historians and treasure seekers: Was a vast amount of valuable treasure buried with the Visigoth king? Or was what we know of it more story than history? The mystery remains.

# Hope for the Second Temple Menorah

*The menorah, one of the definitive symbols of Judaism, is also one of the most important ritual elements of the faith. One made of solid gold from the Second Temple in Jerusalem has been missing for perhaps 1,600 years. Theories of its past vary widely, and rumors that it remains hidden somewhere today still fuel hope among some in the Jewish community.*

✳   ✳   ✳   ✳

SOLOMON'S TEMPLE, WHICH stood in Jerusalem between the sixth and tenth centuries BC, is said to have housed 10 menorahs—the seven-branched candelabra that symbolizes the Jewish faith. A menorah made of pure gold was the centerpiece of the Second Temple, a reconstructed place of worship built around 500 BC. This golden menorah of the Second Temple was a beloved symbol of Judaism both before and after it was carted off to Rome in AD 71, upon Roman destruction of the temple.

There's one place you can still see that menorah—at least a picture of it. It appears on the frieze of the Arch of Titus, located on the Via Sacra in Rome. There, it's shown resting on a large base with other artifacts being taken away by Roman soldiers during the fall of the Second Temple. The menorah is thought to have resided in Rome from AD 71 until the Roman Empire fell to the army of Germanic leader Odoacer.

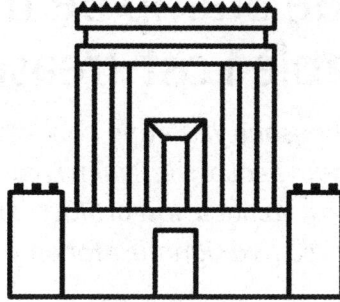

There are numerous theories as to what became of the Second Temple menorah following Rome's conquering. Some believe the Vatican ended up with it, stashed it in its archives, and is hiding the menorah to this day. The Vatican has repeatedly denied ever having possession of Second Temple artifacts. Some believe the original menorah was buried and replacements made to throw Roman soldiers, and other later searchers, off the "scent."

Some think the Second Temple menorah was simply destroyed at some point, while others claim it was melted down for the gold. There's another theory that it was thrown in the Tiber River during the conquest of Rome, and from there it either became buried in a river bed or was swept away—never to be found. Finally, there's a version of the story that had the menorah whisked to Carthage by vandals, and then falling into the hands of the Byzantine Empire upon the conquering of Africa's largest city around the sixth century AD. Byzantine Emperor Justinian, believing the menorah was cursed, returned it to Jerusalem, and it went missing in the seventh century when the Persians took Jerusalem.

With no documented sightings of the menorah for nearly 2,000 years now, it's unlikely the artifact will ever surface. The Temple Institute in Jerusalem crafted what they deemed to be a life-sized, exact replica of the original for display in the Jewish Quarter (and for a future Third Temple). The institute used an estimated $3 million in 24-karat gold for the replica.

# Could a Jade Stamp Be the Most Valuable Lost Treasure?

*Used for close to a thousand years and now lost for even longer than that, the Heirloom Seal of the Realm is considered by some to be our planet's most valuable lost artifact. It was a stamp made of jade that once served as a signature for only the most powerful rulers of China.*

✳ ✳ ✳ ✳

THE HEIRLOOM SEAL of the Realm, also known as the Imperial Seal of China, was carved in 221 BC from a sacred piece of jade for new emperor Qin Shi Huang, founder of the Qin Dynasty. The pure jade, known as Heshibi and once owned by the Zhao state Qin Shi Huang had just defeated, was to be made into a seal at the emperor's direction.

Jade is filled with symbolism in China. Some common themes include inner beauty, purity, and grace. Some also believed that jade represented immortality and thought that if they drank it in liquid form, it would grant eternal life. Seals were common in China and were considered to be more authentic than signatures. They were typically made from cheap stones, but the more powerful could have theirs created with valuable ones.

Though the seal was used to authenticate documents, Quin Shi Huang said his represented a mandate from heaven. He had it inscribed with the phrase, "Having received the mandate from heaven, may the emperor lead a long and prosperous life." For Quin Shi Huang, that life lasted under 50 years. It is uncertain whether his death came from an illness or a poisoning.

## The Seal Lived On

The Heirloom Seal of the Realm was passed down through subsequent reigns, including the Wei Dynasty, the Jin Dynasty, the Sixteen Kingdoms period, the Sui Dynasty, and the Tang Dynasty. It is documented that, sometime during the period of the Five Dynasties and the Ten Kingdoms (AD 907–960), the seal went missing. Along with its disappearance came many theories as to what happened to it.

One theory is that the seal was melted when one of the emperors burned himself and his family alive. This theory was debunked by experts who noted that jade would not have melted in the fire. They also noted that if the seal *was* in the fire, it may have burned, cracked, or changed color, but it would not have disintegrated.

Other theories suggest that the seal went missing under the rule of certain emperors such as Emperor Taizong of Liao, or perhaps one of the Yuan Emperors. None of these theories have been proven true, leaving historians and others to draw their own conclusions. Some consider the Heirloom Seal of the Realm to be the most valuable lost treasure in the world. Several over the years have claimed to have found the Heirloom Seal of the Realm, but each time experts have deemed these "discoveries" imitations.

# Inca Gold: True Treasure or Tall Tale?

*Is the story of lost Inca gold a mere fairy tale about long-lost treasure, or are there priceless artifacts actually hidden somewhere in the mountains of Ecuador? It's a question that historians and treasure hunters have been trying to answer for hundreds of years.*

✳   ✳   ✳   ✳

THE INCA EMPIRE was divided back in the sixteenth century because its ruler, Atahualpa, and his half-brother Huascar were at war over who would control the civilization. Because the empire was divided against itself, a leader of the Spanish conquistadors, Francisco Pizarro, decided it was the perfect opportunity to seize control. He did this by kidnapping

Atahualpa and threatening to kill him. To get him back, the Incans offered the conquistadors a large amount of gold.

Pizzaro agreed to the deal at first, and gold quickly came piling in. Unfortunately, the conquistadors decided to kill Atahualpa, dissolving the deal with the Incan civilians. It left the Incans with 750 tons of gold—worth about $30 billion in today's dollars. Legend has it that the gold was either buried in a cave or thrown into a lake, both of which would be located in the mountains of what is today Ecuador. This sparked the beginning of one of the most famous treasure hunts of all time.

Fifty years after the treasure had been hidden, an indigenous man is said to have found it and showed his Spanish son-in-law the location. This brought great wealth to the Spanish man and his family, who never spoke of the gold until he was on his deathbed. It is said that one of his final actions was revealing the location of the lost Inca gold, along with providing a map with written directions, dubbed the *Derrotero de Valverde*.

## No Easy Money to Be Had

The journey to find the treasure is not to be taken by the novice treasure hunter. For starters, the exact whereabouts of the gold are unknown. Many have tried to decipher and follow the map left by the Spaniard, but to no avail. One must also account for the uninhabited forests and shifting landscapes due to earthquakes over the years. And not everyone who ventures into the mountains in search of the gold has returned.

In the mid-1800s, a treasure hunter named Barth Blake claimed to have found it. "I could not remove it alone," he said, "nor could thousands of men." Blake tried to return home what gold he could carry in his hands, but legend holds that he disappeared at sea. Some speculate he was pushed overboard in a failed theft attempt.

Another treasure hunter who survived the journey was Mark Honigsbaum. He wrote *Valverde's Gold*, a book in which he claims that the Incans threw the gold into a man-made lake. Though he never found the lake, he maintains his claim and believes that if there ever was gold to be found, it would be long gone by now. On the off chance the gold still rests at the bottom of a lake, he likens discovering it to "finding a needle in a haystack."

# Great Bell of Dhammazedi Tolls for No One

*Handheld bells and those located at the tops of towers certainly enjoy better fates than that of the Great Bell of Dhammazedi. The largest bell ever cast at some 20 feet tall and 13 feet wide, it sits at the bottom of a river—a sunken remnant of the fifteenth-century reign of King Dhammazedi.*

✳  ✳  ✳  ✳

THE AFFAIRS OF modern-day Myanmar and Burma were in good hands under the rule of King Dhammazedi in the late 1400s. During his two-plus decades as ruler of the Hanthawaddy Kingdom, Myanmar went through a "Golden Age" in which residents prospered and art flourished. One of the grandest things to come out of the period was the Great Bell of Dhammazedi.

Although some advised against the creation of a giant bell, fearing it would be too large to be rung, King Dhammazedi was determined to see his plan through. He decided the bell would be built at and presented to the most sacred Buddhist temple, the Shwedagon Pagoda. It was cast from various metals, including gold, silver, copper, and tin. Once completed, it was a sight to behold. Thought to be the largest such bell ever cast, it weighed 294 tons and stood 20 feet tall and 13 feet wide. Skeptics were proven wrong when it rang, though the noise was claimed to be unpleasant.

All over the Great Bell of Dhammazedi were words that were described as "indecipherable" by a gem merchant who traveled from Venice to see it. As surprising as it was that the bell could make a sound, surely moving it would border on impossible. Against all odds, however, the bell was stolen in 1608.

## Taking the Plunge

By this time, the Golden Age of Myanmar was a thing of the past. The region was gathering attention from explorers, settlers, merchants, and eventually conquerors. Among the latter was Filipe de Brito y Nicote, a warlord and adventurer from Portugal. He arrived in the 1590s and led sacks in the capital of Lower Myanmar. Soon after, de Brito became the governor of Syriam and used his authority to hunt for treasures. This quest eventually led him to the Shwedagon Pagoda, where he decided to steal the Great Bell of Dhammazedi.

De Brito's plan was to have his men roll the giant bell down a hill, where it was to be placed on a waiting raft on the Pazundaung Creek. From there, elephants would drag it along the Bago River until they reached de Brito's ship. The ship would then bring the bell back to Syriam, where it would be melted down and turned into cannon. It turns out the plan had its challenges.

Although de Brito and his men were able to get the bell onto the ship, they miscalculated how heavy it was. The weight of the bell broke the galleon of the ship, and the bell fell into the Bago River. That was the last sighting of the Great Bell of Dhammazedi more than 400 years ago, though it certainly hasn't gone unseen due to lack of effort.

Many have tried to recover it. In recent years, there have been efforts by a professional deep-sea diver James Blunt, who has made more than 100 dives to its last known location. Although that location is generally agreed upon, retrieving the bell has proven daunting. Experts believe it is buried beneath some 25 feet of mud and nestled between two shipwrecks. With almost zero visibility, retrieving it would require advanced technology and some serious funding.

The BBC announced in 2000 it was planning a project toward recovering the bell, but the idea was eventually scrapped. With a treasure such as the Great Bell of Dhammazedi just waiting to be uncovered, its rescue would seem to be only a matter of time.

# Treasure in a Tropical U.S. Territory?

*Could Palmyra Island, the only incorporated, unorganized territory of the United States, hold a pirate treasure from more than 200 years ago? Some think the answer is yes, while others believe that treasure is at the bottom of the Pacific Ocean.*

✳   ✳   ✳   ✳

ALMOST DUE SOUTH of the Hawaiian Islands, in the geographical center of the Pacific Ocean, sits a sun-soaked island called Palmyra Atoll. No one lives permanently on its 4.5 square miles, but up to two dozen scientists or nature conservatory workers might be there at a given time. It's run as an incorporated, unorganized territory belonging to the United States—the only such American territory of its kind.

What Palmyra Atoll is most famous for, however, is not its political status, but a pirate legend involving an early nine-teenth-century Spanish ship called the *Esperanza*. This ship might have deposited a windfall of treasure on the island or in nearby waters. On New Year's Day 1816, the *Esperanza* left Peru, planning to stop in the Spanish West Indies for goods its crew could trade back in Europe. It carried with it a fortune in gold and silver that had been looted from Incan temples.

The *Esperanza* likely never made it to the West Indies. Strong storms cracked her mast, causing one set of problems. The ship then came under vicious attack from an independent cruiser, and the *Esperanza* crew was captured. There are differing stories as to what happened from here. One account has the *Esperanza* sinking in the Pacific, while crew was held captive on the other ship. Another account has the attackers taking possession of the *Esperanza* and leaving their own ship to perish, making off with the riches aboard the ship they had conquered.

## Search for the Treasure

Whichever version of the story one believes, the search for the Incan treasure remains central. Heavy winds are said to have thrown the sailors into an uncharted atoll—what we now know as the Palmyra Atoll—stranding all aboard on what they described as "hillocks of land." They took the loot from the ruined ship and buried it in the island sand, according to some. Still others believe some of the riches were lost at sea, either in the initial battle or near the atoll.

In time, a group of the sailors rebuilt the broken ship into a smaller boat they sailed out to sea. Each of the 80 or so who set sail brought a portion of the gold and silver with them. Their ship was never seen again. Some of the men who remained on the island built another small ship and made an attempt to reach the mainland, but only one is known to have made it— James Hines, who managed to reach a hospital in what is now San Francisco.

Hines lived for about a month there, writing briefly about his journey and telling the story to a young attendant. He told of the treasure, describing it as 1.5 million Spanish gold pesos and an equal amount in silver. Several voyages were made to the atoll in subsequent years and other expeditions were made to search for the *Esperanza*, but the treasure has never been found.

# Some Diamonds, and Their Mysteries, Are Forever

*The Florentine Diamond is that rare gem that has mystery and intrigue shrouding both its origin story and its current whereabouts, making it one of the most talked-about diamonds in the world. One thing is certain: its 137-carat weight and unusual form made it spectacular.*

✳  ✳  ✳  ✳

THE GREAT YELLOW diamond of the Medici family was actually a light-yellow color with subtle green overtones. The Florentine Diamond—with aliases including the Grand Duke of Tuscany, the Dufner Diamond, and the Austrian Diamond—hailed from India and had an unconventional shape. That much is known. The rest of this 137-carat masterpiece's genesis, however, is up for debate. The same can be said of its current whereabouts.

Some say Lodewyk van Bercken, a Flemish diamond polisher who invented the pear cut diamond, cut the Florentine Diamond for Charles the Bold, Duke of Burgundy, in the late 1400s. The duke is purported to have been wearing it when he was defeated in battle. The story goes on to say a peasant happened upon the duke's body, took the stone, and thinking it was made of glass sold it for a pittance. It then changed hands several times, with some of its owners believed to be Ludovico Sforza, Duke of Milan, and Pope Julius II.

Another story has Ludovico Castro, a Portuguese governor, winning the stone by defeating Indian King Vijayanagar in the sixteenth century and leaving it in the hands of Roman Jesuits before it was purchased by Grand Duke Ferdinand I—Ferdinando I de' Medici—of Tuscany. Most agree that it was Ferdinand's son, Cosimo II, who took the stone to a diamond cutter in Florence in 1615, when the finished gem was unveiled.

From there, its history and appearance are better documented. The Medici family, a great contributor to Italian art and architecture in the fifteenth, sixteenth, and seventeenth centuries, held the stone until their line came to an end. It was valued at $750,000 U.S. at the time it was transferred to the Austrian Crown Jewels in Vienna. That's likely comparable to $50 million today. The gem was, for a time, worn as part of an *aigrette*—a decorative piece of a hat—while in Austria.

World War I was responsible for the mystery of where the Florentine Diamond might shine today. As the Austrian empire fell, its imperial family is thought to have taken it into hiding in Switzerland. It was then reported stolen, along with other crown jewels, and possibly whisked off to South America.

Some say it reemerged briefly as part of a hat exhibit in Vienna, while others contend it was recut to a smaller size and sold in the United States. A Jean-Baptiste Tavernier drawing of the stone from the 1600s and a few black-and-white photos are all the evidence in existence of the stone's actual appearance, making it unlikely the Florentine Diamond will be identified—at any cut or weight—any time soon.

# World's Most Expensive Egg Hunt Is Ongoing

*Jeweled eggs worth tens of millions of dollars may seem like a strange concept. The 52 Imperial Fabergé Eggs, however, are some of the most coveted pieces of art in the world. Or in some cases, they were. Six of the eggs remain lost or missing.*

✳  ✳  ✳  ✳

As an easter gift in 1885, Russian Tsar Alexander III gave his wife a unique jeweled egg. Inside sat a golden hen on a pile of golden straw, and inside the hen were a mini-imperial crown made of diamonds and a ruby pendant. The egg was made by the House of Fabergé in St. Petersburg. Alexander's wife fell in love with the gift, prompting Alexander to appoint Fabergé as "goldsmith by special appointment to the Imperial Crown." What started as a generous gift marked the beginning of a renowned tradition: Fabergé's Imperial Easter Eggs.

Each year, Fabergé would create the most intricate, elaborate, and creative themed eggs to be gifted among the royal family. The eggs would open up to reveal a surprise, delighting onlookers each time. While there is a recorded history of 52 such eggs, only 46 have a known location today. Each of the six missing eggs holds its own story, capturing the attention of treasure-hunters and historians alike.

The first missing egg, "Hen with the Sapphire Pendant," was created the very next year. There are no photos or drawings of this second egg, but it was described as a hen covered in gold and rose diamonds, removing a sapphire egg from a diamond-covered nest or basket. Its last known location was the Kremlin in 1922. Some suspect the egg was sold to raise money for the government, while others believe it may have been lost during the Russian Revolution.

## Rounding Out the Half Dozen

The other five lost eggs span unveiling dates from 1888 to 1909. The first of those, the golden "Cherub with Chariot," was decorated with sapphires and diamonds. Opening it revealed a small clock inside. Its whereabouts are unknown, though some think it may have been purchased by industrialist Armand Hammer. "Nécessaire," was given to Alexander III's wife the very next year, in 1889. It was covered in rubies, emeralds, and sapphires. It was taken to the Kremlin in 1917, and in November of 1949 the egg was seen on display in London's Fabergé exhibition. Three years later, it was sold to an anonymous buyer who never shared its location.

"Mauve," named for its color, was given to the royal family in 1897. The simplest of the lost eggs was described as an "enamel egg with miniatures of the Tsar, his wife, Tsarina Alexandra, and their oldest child, Grand Duchess Olga" inside. The miniatures are located in St. Petersburg but the egg itself has disappeared, leading some to believe it had been hidden before the revolution.

The other two lost eggs date to the first decade of the twentieth century. The "Royal Danish" egg was given to Dowager Empress Maria Feodorovna in 1903. One of the larger Fabergé masterpieces, it featured the symbol of Denmark's Order of the Elephant on top along with portraits of the Feodorovna's parents, King Christian IX of Denmark and Queen Louise, inside. Its last known location was the Gatchina Palace in 1917. The "Alexander III Commemorative Egg," made in 1909, was also given to Feodorovna. There are no known photos of this egg, though it is said to have had a "miniature gold bust of Alexander III, the Tsar's father, and the Dowager Empress' former husband." Information is scarce as to where it might be. Some believe it may have been destroyed, while others think it was purchased by a private buyer.

With some of the existing Fabergé eggs having been valued at upwards of $30 million U.S., there's no telling what value might be placed on the six missing ones. Nor might we ever know, given the relative silence and lack of information about them. If there's one thing we know, however, it's that Easter season brings out the best in egg hunters.

# Famed Raphael Portrait a WWII Casualty

*Many valuable pieces of art went missing during World War II. One significant item was Raphael's* Portrait of a Young Man. *The 500-year-old painting was stolen by the Nazis from a museum in Poland in 1939 and hasn't been seen since 1945.*

✳  ✳  ✳  ✳

AN OIL PAINTING that would be worth more than $100 million today, *Portrait of a Young Man* was created by the Renaissance master painter Raffaello Sanzio da Urbino, better known as Raphael, in the early 1500s. Showing a seated young man posing, slightly turned but looking directly out from the canvas, it is considered by some to be Raphael's self-portrait. The man has fair skin and shoulder-length brown hair, wears a black beret with fur draped over his left shoulder, and positions his left hand near his heart. The latter is said to symbolize self-identity, contributing to the self-portrait theory and the great value that the art community places on the work. But it is not known whether Raphael ever identified the painting's subject matter.

*Portrait of a Young Man* became cherished by Poland's elite class. Together with Leonardo da Vinci's *Lady with an Ermine*, it was purchased in 1789 by Prince Adam Jerzy Czartoryski of Poland and made its home at the Czartoryski Museum in Krakow. It could be admired there until 1939, when—at the beginning of the German invasion of Poland—Prince Augustyn Czartoryski decided to hide several valued paintings, including *Portrait*, *Lady with an Ermine*, and Rembrandt's *Landscape with the Good Samaritan*, and hide them in the town of Sieniawa. The Nazis, however, found the stash two weeks later and whisked the works back to Germany. *Portrait of a Young Man* was last seen in 1945.

Hans Frank, Germany's General Governor, is thought to have brought the painting to his villa for his personal collection. Americans arrested Frank on May 3, 1945, and managed to recover the likes of *Lady with an Ermine* and *Landscape with the Good Samaritan*, returning them to the Czartoryski Museum. *Portrait of a Young Man* was never recovered.

The Czartoryski family went to great lengths to try to find the missing painting. They had no luck while hampered by Poland's position behind the Iron Curtain, and fared no better upon resuming their search in 1991. Some believe the painting lives on, secretly, in a private collection somewhere. Others believe it was likely destroyed in the war. Optimism remains, however: its original frame hangs in the National Museum of Krakow, awaiting the painting's return.

# Replica *Circumcision* Stands in Place of Original

*The Circumcision, a Rembrandt depicting the circumcision of Christ, was lost sometime between its painting in the 1660s and the early 1700s. The remainder of a small collection that initially included this work remains otherwise intact, but what's thought to be an accurate replica substitutes for this original.*

✳ ✳ ✳ ✳

THE CIRCUMCISION OF Christ was a familiar subject for Rembrandt. He first sketched such a scene in the 1620s, shortly after completing his apprenticeship. He did it using a needle on yielding film, finishing the "small plate" with incredible speed. Two decades later, well into his career as one of the greatest artists of his—or any—day, he sketched *Circumcision in the Stable*, a scene not necessarily about Christ but showing a group of light-bathed people gathered around a woman and her child.

His *Circumcision of Christ*, thought to hail from the 1660s, was considered the ultimate depiction of the scene described in the Gospel of Luke. It was recorded in 1719 as one of the seven paintings of Rembrandt's Passion Series in Karsch's electoral gallery catalogue in Düsseldorf, Germany. However, by 1756, only the other six works were mentioned in a letter from a court painter and curator. Curiously, *The Circumcision* was not among them. Something had happened to the masterpiece along the way.

No one knows how, where, or exactly when the original went missing. What became known as the Braunschweig *Circumcision* has been vetted for its accuracy in approximating the original oil painting, and in this regard it appears to score high marks. Its dimensions and rounded top match those of the six original paintings of the Passion Series, and the subject matter—including all 19 figures in the scene—correlate to the 1719 cataloguing of the original.

# Most Valuable Unrecovered Painting Plays Silently

The Concert *by Vermeer not only ranks as the most valuable work of art stolen in the famed 1990 Isabella Stewart Gardner Museum heist, but is considered—at north of $250 million U.S. in today's dollars—the most valuable unrecovered painting in the world.*

✳   ✳   ✳   ✳

ISABELLA STEWART GARDNER acquired *The Concert* for a mere $5,000 at an 1892 auction in Paris. Thought to be a mid-career (1660s) masterpiece of Dutch painter Johannes Vermeer, the painting shows three musicians in a quiet, intimate setting. One, a woman in yellow, is seated while playing the harpsichord. A long-haired man with his back to the viewer plays the lute, while another woman facing the viewer seems about to break into song.

The two paintings in the background of the scene form an interesting dichotomy. One is a serene woodlands scene; the other is Dirck van Baburen's *The Procuress*, which is set in a raucous bordello.

The painting has been revered for its complex angles and geometry, its rarity in that only three other works by Vermeer featured three subjects, and its unique serenity. Though music is being made by the subjects, the painting conjures a calm, quiet feeling. It's almost as if the viewer is intruding on a special moment, without being able to hear a single note.

In all probability, *The Concert* is the single most valuable unrecovered painting in the world. It was one of 13 works famously stolen from the Isabella Stewart Gardner Museum in Boston in 1990 in the largest and most lucrative art heist in history. Masterpieces by Manet and Rembrandt were among the paintings stolen in the early-morning hours of March 12 when thieves, posing as police officers, tied up museum guards and spent about an hour looting the place. Valued today at an estimated $250 million U.S. dollars, *The Concert* makes up about half of the total value of the missing works. The painting could be the most valuable stolen item in the world.

## A Rarity Indeed

In addition to the artistic quality of the work, *The Concert* holds magnificent value for its rare place among surviving Vermeer pieces. There are fewer than 40 Vermeers in existence. The most agreed-upon number seems to be 37, but some doubt the authenticity of a few of them, so the number might be as small as 34.

If the painting does still exist after more than two decades missing, searchers should know they're looking for a rather small masterpiece. *The Concert* was only slightly larger than two feet square. It was displayed on a small tabletop in the museum's Dutch Room, back-to-back with Govaert Flinck's *Landscape with Obelisk*, which was also stolen.

Details of the heist indicate that the robbers returned to the room where they bound the museum guards and asked them if they were okay before making off with the stolen goods. No arrests have been made, and none of the stolen pieces has ever been recovered.

# A Painting So Nice It Was Stolen Twice

*One of the last of the many masterpieces painted by Vincent van Gogh,* Poppy Flowers *remains missing after it was stolen not once but twice—a little more than a decade apart. A second reemergence of the work does not seem likely.*

✳ ✳ ✳ ✳

A FEW YEARS BEFORE his death in 1890, Vincent van Gogh produced a painting that became known by many names. *Still Life, Vase with Daisies and Poppies, Vase with Flowers,* and *Poppy Flowers* were among its most common monikers. As one might glean from those titles, it was a small painting of a vase abundant with flowers, most of them bright yellow poppies, and along the bottom of the floral arrangement are three red poppies, seemingly wilting.

The vase rests on a brown floor against a dark background, making the vase the main focus of the painting. On the floor are yellow petals that have presumably fallen from the poppies. Van Gogh used the "impasto" technique, applying paint in thick, textured layers to create a three-dimensional look. The technique was considered perhaps the most notable aspect of the work. That is, until it became more famous for its popularity among thieves.

*Poppy Flowers* made its way from Paris to Cairo sometime after the artist's death. It was on display in the Mohamed Khalil Museum in the late 1970s when thieves made off with it. Three Egyptians were thought to be responsible for this first theft, though the government of that country has not revealed the details. What's known is that it was, years later, recovered in Kuwait and returned to the museum.

Then, in August 2010, the painting was stolen again, this time in broad daylight. No one has been accused of the theft, but culture ministry employees were charged with "negligence and professional delinquency." The suspects were said to have pushed a couch up to the spot where the painting was being displayed and cut it out of its frame, all while going undetected by the museum staff. What's more, just seven of the museum's 43 security cameras were operational, and none was active at the time. Valued at $55 million, the painting has yet to be recovered. Rewards have been offered for any information regarding its whereabouts.

## *Chez Tortoni* Lost in Gardner Museum Heist

*Thirteen works were stolen from Boston's Gardner Museum in 1990. One was* Chez Tortoni, *Edouard Manet's late-nineteenth-century oil-on-canvas depiction of a gentleman in a Paris café.*

✳  ✳  ✳  ✳

ART AFICIONADOS AND historians alike know quite well the story of the Isabella Stewart Gardner Museum heist. Two men dressed as police officers slipped into the Boston museum in the early hours of March 18, 1990, and got away with 13 works of art that have never been seen again. Among them were works by Rembrandt and Vermeer, and a small oil painting of a young gentleman writing or sketching while wearing a top hat in the Café Tortoni in Paris.

*Chez Tortoni* was painted by Manet between 1879 and 1880. Manet was in his late forties at the time—only a few years from his death at 51. The painter produced a series of works depicting "café society," in this case putting his subject in a well-known

Paris eatery that was a popular favorite among the artist community. The man in the painting sits near a sunlit window, accompanied by a half-full beverage, perhaps wine or beer.

Even more than the subject, the painting is best known for its brush strokes. Broad and tactile, they stand out, as if the paint itself was where Manet truly wanted the eye to focus. Admirers of the work could once see it in the museum's Blue Room. In fact, it was the only painting stolen from the museum's first floor, and the only one whose frame was not left in the room by the thieves. During their time in the building, they managed to leave *Chez Tortoni's* frame in the office chair of the museum's security director.

Though a $10 million reward was offered, no information leading to the return of any of the stolen works has surfaced. Though it hasn't been seen since 1990, *Chez Tortoni* has made a few appearances in popular culture in recent years. It was seen in the background of an episode of *The Vampire Diaries*, and on two episodes of the French Netflix series *Lupin*.

# "Lost" *Medusa* Painting Shrouded in Snakes, Mystery

*It's thought that da Vinci painted a representation of the Greek mythological protectress Medusa early in his career. No one knows for sure, however, and speculation on the subject will likely never be resolved, leaving historians to believe what they will.*

✳   ✳   ✳   ✳

THOSE WHO GAZED into the eyes of Medusa, a woman with living snakes for hair, would turn instantly to stone in Greek mythology. There are several different interpretations of what the protectress looked like before she was beheaded by Perseus, who then used her head as a weapon. One of the most interesting representations of Medusa is thought to have been produced by the great painter Leonardo da Vinci.

His *Medusa*, which remains lost—assuming it really was one of his early works—was described by Giorgio Vasari in his 1568 biography *Vita di Leonardo*. He said da Vinci went to his room, where only he and various "strange animals" entered, and "formed a great ugly creature, most horrible and terrifying, which emitted a poisonous breath and turned the air to flame; and he made it coming out of a dark and jagged rock, belching forth venom from its open throat, fire from its eyes, and smoke from its nostrils, in so strange a fashion that it appeared altogether a monstrous and horrible thing; and so long did he labor over making it, that the stench of the dead animals in that room was past bearing, but Leonardo did not notice it, so great was the love that he bore towards art."

How Vasari might have seen the *Medusa* is not known. Some have speculated that Caravaggio might have based his own variation of Medusa on having witnessed the da Vinci painting, but no one knows for sure.

More than 200 years after the Vasari book, historian Luigi Lanzi in 1782 wrote about a painting of Medusa in Florence's Uffizi Gallery, referencing da Vinci and his realistic portrayal of the head and serpents. However, the *Medusa's Head* painting he was documenting was likely a copy of da Vinci's work, rather than the same one Vasari wrote about, or even another version of Medusa da Vinci is thought to have painted on a wooden shield. In fact, several painters over the years—inspired either by the da Vinci stories or Greek mythology—have used the unique head of Medusa as inspiration for pieces of art.

# "Lost Leonardo" Has an Identity Crisis

*Was* The Battle of Anghiari *lost during its painting? Or did it ever exist to begin with? Also known as "The Lost Leonardo," the presumed da Vinci painting has sparked controversy over its whereabouts and whether or not it ever came to fruition.*

✳ ✳ ✳ ✳

EONARDO DA VINCI was commissioned by Florentine statesman Piero Soderini to create a wall painting in Palazzo Vecchio's Salone dei Cinquecento—the Hall of 500—in 1504. The work was intended to be his most significant and sizable, so he started by producing a cartoon, or test drawing, in the Basilica of Santa Maria Novella. It was described as "a violent clash of horses and a furious battle of men fighting for the flag in the Battle of Anghiari."

Supposedly, things quickly took a turn for the worse when da Vinci began painting the real thing. He decided to use a thick undercoat for the base of the painting, which was presumably mixed with wax. Unlike his prior painting, *The Last Supper*, he wanted to use oil paints for *The Battle of Anghiari*. Some believe that it was the oil in the paint that caused problems, leading to the new painting dripping profusely. Others blame the rain and frequent humidity.

Only the lower portion of the painting was salvaged from oblivion. The upper part of the painting's colors mixed with the middle part, ultimately ruining it. Da Vinci then decided to abandon the project.

The Hall underwent reconstruction from 1555–72, and what was left of *The Battle of Anghiari* was lost. In the early 2000s, a self-proclaimed Italian art expert, Maurizio Seracini, hypothesized that *The Battle* still lived in the Hall—hidden on an older wall behind Vasari's *Battle of Marciano in Val di Chiana* (1572).

Sensors were used to determine a 1- to 3-centimeter gap between the old and new wall, which just might be big enough for *The Battle of Anghiari* to have been preserved.

In 2007, Florence's city council and the Italian Minister of Culture investigated. With Seracini heading the investigation, there were some controversial moves. He decided it was best to drill small holes in Vasari's painting to reach the old wall and take samples. The samples revealed paint remnants on the old wall that were similar to paints da Vinci had been known to use—proof, as far as Seracini was concerned. Further plans to investigate were halted.

Some art historians have come forward with a bold claim: *The Battle of Anghiari* can't be found because it was never painted in the first place. They believe the technique of using layers of gesso (a primer) and oil was used to prep the wall for the painting instead, rather than for the painting itself. They claim the technique could not be used to paint anything because the paint would not have held. These historians claim the many replicas of *The Battle* came from the cartoon version, and that the paint samples came from the wall, rather than from art.

# Bronze Gone! *Hercules'* Whereabouts Remain a Mystery

*Michelangelo's hands gave the world many a well-known masterpiece that has stood the test of time. He also created a more fleeting statue of a hero that has been missing for more than 300 years. Made of pure marble, the eight-foot Hercules captivated onlookers until its disappearance in 1713.*

✳   ✳   ✳   ✳

S TANDING EIGHT FEET tall, Michelangelo's *Hercules* was a sight to see. The Italian sculptor and painter carved the statue—massive yet intricate in detail—after his mentor and father figure, Lorenze de Medici the Magnificent, died in 1492.

There are two schools of thought as to why he created the statue. The first is that, overwhelmed with grief over the loss, Michelangelo wanted to dedicate a work of art to de Medici. He chose a subject who, in Greek mythology, represents power and bravery.

The second theory is that it was Medici's son, Piero, who requisitioned the work. Their family was then among the most powerful in Florence, and such a piece would have been a symbol to the world that Florence, like Hercules, would let no obstacle stand in their way.

On his own, Michelangelo would not have been able to purchase the marble needed for *Hercules*, making this theory a plausible one. Unfortunately for Piero and his family, the Medicis were exiled. Apparently, a statue was not enough to keep them in favor among the Florentine people.

In 1495, with the Medici family gone, Michelangelo had the statue back in his possession. He gifted it to the Strozzi family, another powerful group in Florence. The Strozzis used the *Hercules* as a statement that associated their family with strength in politics. The well-known statue remained in the Strozzi Palace for many years.

The *Hercules* was passed on again in 1529 to the king of France, Francis I. It is said that Michelangelo was not particularly fond of its relocation from Florence. He felt as if it would not resonate with the French the way it did for the people of Florence. He was right. It was placed in a garden in the Palace of Fontainebleau. The garden was destroyed in 1713, and the Hercules has not been seen since.

# *Isabella in Red* Stands Tall Among Copies

*One of the most painted women of her era, Isabella d'Este may be most famously remembered dressed in black in a Titian original. However, Isabella in Red—a copy that Rubens made of another Titian more than 400 years later—remains a popular attraction at Austria's Kunsthistorisches Museum.*

✳   ✳   ✳   ✳

NOT UNLIKE A Jaqueline Kennedy Onassis of her day, Isabella d'Este inspired women of the fifteenth and sixteenth centuries with her fashion sense, love for the arts, and political influence. She was the marchioness of Mantua, also serving as regent when her husband, Francesco II Gonzaga, was absent. Her innovative style and political stature combined to make her not only one of the most revered women of the Italian Renaissance, but also one of the most painted.

The most famous portrait of Isabella, known as both *Portrait of Isabella d'Este* and *Isabella in Black*, was produced by Titian in the 1530s. It hangs in the Kunsthistorisches Museum in Vienna, Austria, alongside two other color portraits of Isabella—*Ambras Miniature* and *Isabella in Red*. The black and red versions show their subject wearing a *balzo*, a type of headdress made famous among Italian noblewomen at the time, largely because of Isabella.

It is thought that the original *Isabella in Red*, painted by Titian perhaps before the version in black, became lost sometime during the sixteenth century. The *Isabella in Red* in the Kunsthistorisches came from the hand of Sir Peter Paul Rubens, a Flemish artist and nobleman who served as court painter in Mantua at the beginning of the seventeenth century, when the piece is thought to have been created.

Isabella sits in a red velvet dress before an aqua background. Her curls in this painting are reddish-brown, unlike the blonde ones of *Isabella in Black,* and art connoisseurs rave—as they do for the Titian painting—about the luminous skin appearance captured by the artists.

# Lost *Vision* Filled with Mysteries to Ponder

*Blake's* Vision of the Last Judgment *went missing sometime in the early 1800s. Earlier versions of the painting, and of Blake's portrayal of the Final Judgment described in the Bible, have given us imagery that scholars and religious minds have dissected at great length over the years.*

✳  ✳  ✳  ✳

**M**ANY OF WILLIAM Blake's contemporaries considered him a sort of madman. The English poet and painter, born in 1757, did not gain great acclaim for his work during his lifetime, which was spent almost entirely in London. It was only after his death, in 1827, that he began to be recognized as one of the greatest British artists in history. In particular, the mystical and philosophical aspects of his work were seen by some as pure genius.

Blake, a Christian, said he regularly experienced visions as part of his life. Clearly, they influenced his paintings. Perhaps the best-known example was *Vision of the Last Judgment,* a tempera and gold painting he created for an 1810 exhibition, at which he planned to present his notes in describing the work. The exhibition was cancelled, however, and somehow the 5- by 7-foot masterpiece became lost to the ages.

Fortunately, there were several more versions of Blake's rendering of the biblical Final Judgment, and even an 1808 watercolor of the actual *Vision of the Last Judgment* that Blake had painted for Elizabeth, wife of George Wyndham, the

Third Earl of Egremont. The watercolor is part of the Petworth House and Park collection, and gives art lovers the best chance to discuss what Blake was trying to share with the world. There is much to interpret, and each interpretation—by design—is bound to be different, even personal.

## A Very Personal Last Judgment

As suggested by its title, the painting is not Blake's rendering of the Last Judgment or even speculation about the Last Judgment. It's a "vision," something the artist spent much of his life experiencing. Another clue about the imagery being very personal to its audience comes in its shape. The myriad things happening in the painting seem to be taking place within the confines of the human skull. The shape says a lot about how the contents of the painting were to be perceived and absorbed. The events of this "judgment" are in the mind of each viewer.

On the surface, a great deal of the imagery, presented with a unique, swirling energy, corresponds to stories from the Christian Bible. Christ is in heaven, on the throne of judgment, surrounded by angels, elders, and apostles. A tabernacle with a cross sits above him. Baptism and the Last Supper—representing beginning and end—are represented among the swirling imagery. The human figures in the painting are heading in one of two directions. Those on Christ's right are being raised into heaven. Those on his left are heading in the opposite direction, being cast downward.

English writer and critic William Michael Rossetti came upon the notes Blake was planning to share at the cancelled exhibition, providing further evidence that the artist saw this judgment as a very personal experience. "Whenever any individual rejects error and embraces truth," Blake wrote, "a Last Judgment passes upon that individual." The painter went on to explain, "If the spectator could enter into these images in his imagination, approaching them on the fiery chariot of his contemplative thought...then would he arise from the grave."

While it's highly unlikely the original *Vision of the Last Judgment* will ever arise from its grave, wherever that might be, the art community is fortunate to have versions of Blake's work—indeed, his vision—out there to ponder.

# Francis Bacon: His Own Worst Critic

*Study After Velazquez III, the third in a famous series of paintings by Francis Bacon, became one of the more notorious lost works of art not only for its disappearance but for the condition it was brought to when it fell off the map.*

✳ ✳ ✳ ✳

**N**OT TO BE confused with the English philosopher and statesman bearing the same name, the artist Francis Bacon was born in Ireland in 1909 and became known for his striking, unsettling paintings, many of which portrayed crucifixion. Among his other favorite subjects were self-portraits and popes, the latter of which brings us to a lost painting made famous by the circumstances of its disappearance.

During the 1950s and 1960s, Bacon painted a series of works based on Spanish painter Diego Velazquez's 1650 work, *Portrait of Pope Innocent X*. The Bacon versions were raw, even hallucinatory, and the series is considered one of the masterworks of twentieth-century art. It earned Bacon a great deal of acclaim and was considered a highlight of his career.

However, *Study After Velazquez III* has also earned a place in history for the nature and circumstances surrounding its downfall. "I think I tend to destroy the better paintings . . . I try and take them further, and they lose all their qualities," Bacon once said about his penchant for tearing apart his own works.

*Study After Velazquez III*, unfortunately, appears to have been a victim of Bacon's destructive bent. It's unclear whether it was an alcohol-fueled rage—not unusual for Bacon—that wiped out the third painting in the famed Velazquez series, which some say contained perhaps 50 canvases. When two other Bacon paintings that were thought to be lost turned up in 1999, some wondered whether *Study After Velazquez III*, with its hazy vertical lines and mystery, would someday turn up as well. Most believe Bacon obliterated the canvas altogether.

# A Different Kind of Gold Rush in the Catskills

*A buried treasure worth more than $100 million could still be up for grabs in upstate New York, according to the deathbed ramblings of American mobster Dutch Schultz almost a century ago. Those ramblings, along with tales, maps, and legends, have captured the attention of fortune seekers since 1935.*

✳ ✳ ✳ ✳

ARTHUR SIMON FLEGENHEIMER, better known as Dutch Schultz, loved throwing people off the trail in his days as a well-pursued mobster and bootlegger. His greatest instance of such deception might have come after he was shot in 1935, as he clung to life in a hospital for 24 or so hours before taking his last breath. Or, perhaps Dutch was telling the truth!

Schultz was born in the Bronx in 1901 and seemed destined to be a troublemaker. He started committing crimes like theft and petty burglary from a very young age. He was just 17 when he went to prison for the first time for burglary. Before becoming a famous mobster, he changed his name, saying his birth name was "too long for newspaper headlines."

Schultz began making his fortune at the start of the Prohibition in the 1920s, when he took a job as a speakeasy bouncer in the Bronx. The place was owned by a gangster named Joey Noe, and together they began to build a territory. The Noe-Schultz gang opened many more speakeasies in the Bronx and even expanded their businesses to the Upper West Side. Noe died soon after, leaving Schultz as the leader. He managed to find ways to smuggle about $2 million worth of alcohol into his speakeasies each year, turning a huge profit.

As the Great Depression hit in the 1930s, Schultz was at the height of his crimes. He was participating in illegal gambling and taking over restaurants with force. Violent fights and killings with rival gangs became commonplace. The federal government had been following Schultz and was finally able to charge him with tax evasion in 1933. Schultz beat the charges and eluded jail time, but attorney Thomas E. Dewey wanted to take him down for his gambling. This angered Schultz to the extent he wanted Dewey killed.

## A Treasure, and Backfired Plans

The National Crime Syndicate, a group of several crime organizations, was made aware of Schultz's desire to murder Dewey. Fearing that such an assassination could lead to a huge police crackdown and investigation, they unanimously agreed to have Schultz killed instead. They were unaware that Schultz, along with his bodyguard Bernard "Lulu" Rosenkrantz, had decided to take his fortune in cash, bonds, jewels, and gold and stash it somewhere in Upstate New York, presumably in the Catskill Mountains.

Hitmen successfully shot both Schultz and "Lulu" in Newark subsequently. Schultz, who had been shot four times, died shortly after his bodyguard on October 24, 1935. Before he did, though, Schultz went on—at times barely coherently—about the treasure in the mountains. There was said to be a map exchanged at some point. And when the police questioned Schultz in the hospital, he made a cryptic reference to Satan, which led some to believe the loot was stashed near the town of Phoenicia, which has rock structures called Devil's Tombstone and Devil's Face.

Many have tried to uncover what is believed to be a bundle of riches worth more than $100 million in today's money. Rival gangs, locals, random vacationers, and treasure-seekers from all walks of life have attempted to locate it. Movies, books, and documentaries have fueled the curiosity around the treasure's location. Some speculate that it never existed, while others assume it was found a long time ago but never claimed publicly. Whether the story of Schultz's treasure is true or yet another of his curveballs, it remains compelling almost a century after its first telling.

# A Royal Casket Case

*Polish Princess Izabela Czartoryska housed her collection of Polish antiquities in Poland's first museum, the Temple of the Sibyl at Pulawy. When World War II broke out, Nazi soldiers plundered the collection and distributed its contents among themselves.*

✳ ✳ ✳ ✳

## Do Enlighten Me

A MEMBER OF ONE of Poland's most prominent aristo-cratic families, Princess Izabela Czartoryska was a writer, patron of the arts, and an important figure of the Polish Enlightenment. Unlike its neighbors in Western Europe, Poland's Age of Enlightenment was not focused on eliminating oppressive monarchies. In fact, Polish kings were elected and held little power. Instead, reforms centered around preventing abuses of the Sejm (parliament), which mandated unanimous voting. It was easy for other countries to bribe members of the Sejm and halt important decisions. As a result, most reformers of the time came from nobility.

In 1795, when Poland was annexed by Russia, Prussia, and Austria, Izabela Czartoryska was deeply saddened by her country's loss of independence. Together with her husband, she worked to completely transform her family home into an intellectual and political meeting place—a place for Polish culture to survive and thrive even when their country could not exist. She commissioned Chrystian Piotr Aigner, a Neoclassical architect, to create a park on the property with various structures, including the Temple of the Sibyl where she housed her collection of Polish antiquities. As a museum, it was opened to the public in 1801.

## Troves of Treasures

Czartoryska collected several items of national significance, many of which were the gifts of numerous other donors also dedicated to her mission. Of these precious relics, 73 from her personal collection were placed together inside a Royal Casket. The box itself was made of wood with ebony facing, equipped with gold fittings and handles in the shape of lions. The inscription on it read: "Polish mementos assembled in 1800 by Izabela Czartoryska."

Inside the box were several removable drawers and compartments lined in sapphire-colored velvet. The artifacts included Sigismund the Old's sixteenth-century pectoral cross made of red jasper, Stephen Báthory's silver penknife, the gold watch belonging to King Stanislaw Leszczyński, and Queen Marie Leszczyńska's silver rosary. Various other rings, brooches, and medallions were kept in it as well.

## A Royal Betrayal

After the fall of the November Uprising in 1831, Czartoryska's collection was moved again and again to prevent vandalism and theft. It was transported to Paris to the residence of Adam Jerzy Czartoryski, Izabela's son. Subsequently, it was brought to Kraków to be part of the Princes Czartoryski Museum collections, which opened to the public in 1876. At the start of World War II, the Royal Casket and the rest of the collection was moved once again, this time to the Czartoryski family estate in the town of Sieniawa. The relics were hidden in the basement of the palace's outbuilding.

Unfortunately, the relics' location did not stay secret for long. A German worker for the Czartoryski family betrayed its hiding place to *Wehrmacht* soldiers, who proceeded to break into the basement and loot the collection in its entirety. They took the items to an unknown location and distributed them among themselves. The Royal Casket, along with the other priceless artifacts of the collection, is still waiting to be found to this day.

# A Peking Man in a Parking Lot

*Priceless fossil relics illustrating the process of human evolution went missing during the chaos of World War II. Now, they might be buried beneath a warehouse parking lot.*

✳   ✳   ✳   ✳

## Zhoukoudian, 1929

WHILE WORKING IN the caves of Zhoukoudian, about 30 miles southwest of Beijing (formerly Peking), Wenzhong Pei and a team of archeologists happened upon the bones of early hominids—the first ancient humans ever discovered in mainland Asia. This discovery completely shook the foundations of anthropology and was invaluable in the reconstruction of early human history. Peking man, as these fossils are called, is characterized by a large cranial capacity and limb bones nearly indistinguishable from modern man's. Next to the fragments of teeth and bone, scientists uncovered sophisticated stone tools like axes, chisels, and hammers.

## Smuggled for Safekeeping

Sadly for the archeologists working the Zhoukoudian site, the outbreak of the Second Sino-Japanese War in 1937 interrupted excavations. Imperial powers have always been known to steal treasures from the people they conquered, and Japan was no different. In an effort to protect their discovery, Chinese scientists begged their American colleagues to smuggle a set of nearly 200 fossils into the United States for safekeeping. The Americans agreed to help, wrapping the bones in cotton and packing them into boxes that were supposed to be transported to Camp Holcomb, a U.S. base in Qinhuangdao, and then shipped on board the SS *President Harrison*.

But *President Harrison* never reached China. Having heard that the U.S. Navy planned to evacuate a group of Marines from Qinhuangdao following the Pearl Harbor attack, the Japanese launched an attack on the ship, taking 167 servicemen prisoner. In the chaos that followed, Camp Holcomb's boxes of fossils vanished, never to be seen again.

## A Break in the Case

In April 2010, paleontologist Lee Berger of the University of the Witwatersrand in South Africa received an email from Paul Bowen, the son of former U.S. Marine Richard Bowen. Bowen claimed that his father was stationed at Camp Holcomb in 1947 during the height of the Chinese Civil War. When fortifying their camp from attackers, the Marines dug foxholes and trenches to make room for their machine guns. Halfway through digging a new hole, Richard Bowen's shovel struck something solid: an old footlocker. He opened it to find an eerie sight: a bunch of skulls, staring back at him. It was night-time, and the idea of being near the bones spooked him, so Bowen hurriedly reburied the box and moved elsewhere to dig.

Berger contacted Wu Liu and Xiujie Wu of China's Institute for Vertebrate Paleontology and Paleoanthropology to investigate the story further. Could this account from over 60 years ago be true? Together, the three managed to locate the site of the former U.S. Marine base where Bowen was stationed . . . only to find that it was now an industrial hub of warehouses and parking lots. Although they could not excavate the area, Berger and his colleagues are hopeful that the bones are still buried there. Local officials have even agreed to monitor the excavations whenever the area is scheduled for redevelopment. The Peking Man fossils, wherever they are, deserve their rightful place out of the ground and into the spotlight.

# Off-the-Rails Hunt for Nazi Gold

*Treasure hunters in southwestern Poland have long scoured the Owl Mountains in search of a hidden Nazi train loaded with tons of gold and other stolen valuables. But with no evidence of such a train existing, was it ever real?*

✳ ✳ ✳ ✳

## Silesia: A Treasure Hunter's Paradise

THE REGION OF Silesia has changed hands multiple times in its history. Beginning as a Polish province, it was possessed by the Bohemian crown in 1335, and then passed to the Austrian Habsburgs in 1526. Later, in 1742, it was taken by Prussia. After World War II, Silesia was finally returned to its home country as compensation for eastern land incorporated into the Soviet Union. The Red Army forcibly expelled millions of Silesian Germans to the west, leaving behind empty homes vacant of everything except the furniture they couldn't carry with them.

In an attempt to house those displaced by the Soviet annexation in the east, the Polish government relocated them into the newly-deserted Silesian towns across the country. The settlers moved in slowly, feeling strange about essentially taking over the homes and gardens of families they never knew. Their hesitation was quickly eased, however, upon the discovery of gold, jewels, and antiques hidden in and around their new homes: In their haste to leave, many Germans buried their valuables, intending to return and retrieve them later. New Silesians sold their findings for small fortunes.

## Getting Klose-r

Nearly every Silesian was on the lookout for buried treasure, and soon other Poles from outside the region joined them. But rumors began to swirl about an even more impressive treasure, one bigger than anything that could be discovered in the jars and chests buried beneath farmer's fields. Because the Nazis considered Silesia to be safe from Allied forces, many of their assets were allegedly moved into the region, including factories, weapons, precious works of art, jewels, and gold. Supposedly, during the last few months of the war, an armored train filled with these treasures left Wrocław, arrived at Świebodzice station, but never reached its next stop in Wałbrzych.

Like with most rumors, it's difficult to find a definitive source of these claims. One story came from Herbert Klose, a German military officer who worked as a high-level police official in Wrocław. When he was caught and interrogated by the Polish secret police, Klose revealed that he helped local police collect valuables for safekeeping, storing them in unmarked iron chests for transport outside the city. Klose couldn't take part in hiding the chests himself due to an injury, but the other officers completed the task without him. Another story involved American soldiers investigating the location of the missing Reichsbank reserve, leading them to discover seven thousand bags of gold hidden in a vault inside the Merkers salt mine. As more and more of these tales came to light, it seemed like the discovery of a gold-filled train could be a possibility.

## Project Riese: A Giant Undertaking

But where could such a train be hiding? The answer may be found in a series of abandoned tunnels under Książ Castle. Seized by the Nazi regime in 1944, the castle became part of Project Riese, a system of seven structures connected via enormous underground tunnels. Construction work was carried out by forced laborers from the nearby Gross-Rosen concentration camp. Although the purpose of the project remains uncertain, sources suggest that it was planned as a network of factories. The castle itself would have served as the official residence of the Führer.

It stood to reason that such an extensive network of incomplete train tunnels would be the perfect place to hide looted Nazi treasure. For years, treasure hunters surveyed the tunnels, noting any shafts, adits, and crosscuts that could provide access into them. Every new passageway discovered renewed their hope in finding a golden treasure trove.

## Kilometer 65

In 2015, two treasure hunters—Piotr Koper and Andreas Richter of mine exploration company XYZ—claimed to have found the legendary Nazi train. The men opened secret negotiations with the Polish government for 10 percent of the train's value in exchange for its location. Images taken with ground-penetrating radar seemed to indicate that a 100-meter train had been found next to the Wrocław-Wałbrzych railway line at kilometer 65. Not everyone was convinced, however. Janusz Madej, a mining specialist leading the scientific team, reported that the anomalies found were too close to the surface to be the mythical train. Indeed, after seven days of searching, no trains, tracks, or tunnels were found. The radar images were revealed to have been the result of natural ice formations.

## Urban Legend, After All?

Nearly a century has passed since the Nazis evacuated the tunnels of Project Riese, and no hidden treasure has ever been discovered. There is a very good chance that the tunnels contain none of the gold promised within it, but this unlikelihood has not deterred the most adamant of treasure hunters. Nowadays, the rumors have swelled to include riches of less-conventional origin, including futuristic weapons, supercomputer prototypes—even evidence of aliens. As long as there's still hope of discovery, the train and its contents will continue to be on the minds of treasure hunters everywhere.

# The Hunt for the Honjō Masamune

*Swordsmith Goro Nyudo Masamune was perhaps the finest maker of swords in all of Japan. His most famous sword, the Honjō Masamune, was declared a Japanese National Treasure in 1939. Then, it went missing.*

✳   ✳   ✳   ✳

## Master Masamune

IN A COUNTRY already known for its quality sword craftsmanship, Goro Nyudo Masamune was unmatched in his profession. Although medieval steel production was still an imperfect art, Masamune could create exceptionally clean materials in his forge, producing swords and daggers of superior beauty and high quality.

Most of Masamune's swords were created during the late Kamakura period, from about 1288 to 1328. Signed works of Masamune are rare. His works are characterized by certain striking features, mainly *chikei*, running dark lines following the steel's grain pattern; *nie*, large crystals of martensite; and *kinsuji*, white, lightning-shaped lines of nie. Masamune is believed to have trained a great number of swordsmiths. Today, the Masamune Prize is awarded at the Japanese Sword Making Competition, presented to a swordsmith of exceptional talent.

## A Sword of Legend

The most famous of Masamune's creations is called the Honjō Masamune. Almost perfect in design, the sword was a result of Masamune's careful forging technique: A blend of both hard and soft steel were forged together at extremely high temperatures, then cut and folded again and again to produce a layered blade. Honjō Masamune's cutting edge was reported to have been no thicker than a single atom. Considered a national treasure of Japan, the sword was venerated as a powerful heirloom by the ruling shoguns. In particular, it represented the Tokugawa shogunate for a majority of the Edo period.

Several legends are associated with his magnum opus. One of the most popular involved a competition between Masamune and Sengo Muramasa, his rival, to see who could make a finer sword. Like Masamune, Muramasa was known for crafting swift, balanced blades. Unlike Masamune, however, Muramasa's swords were considered violent and bloodthirsty. The blade he crafted did not discriminate between whom or what it would cut, handing the victory to the superior Honjō Masamune.

Another legend involves Honjō Masamune's namesake, General Honjō Shigenaga. Shigenaga was attacked and bested in combat by Umanosuke, who used the sword to cleave his helmet into two halves. Retaliating, Shigenaga returned blow for blow, surviving the attack and taking the sword as his prize.

## Surrendered and Stolen

In the aftermath of Japan's surrender at the end of World War II, all weapons were required to be surrendered to Allied forces. The order included family heirlooms and antique samurai swords. The owner of the Honjō Masamune at the time, Tokugawa Ietsuna, honorably relinquished the sword, along with many other heirloom swords, to the Mejiro police station. A month later, the collection of 14 swords were surrendered to a United States representative of the Foreign Liquidations Commission of the Army Forces, Western Pacific, or AFWESPAC for short. The man's name was recorded as Sergeant Coldy Bimore.

Despite the sergeant's recorded name, researchers have come no closer to locating the whereabouts of the Honjō Masamune. According to the Foreign Liquidations Commission's records, no one by the name of Coldy Bimore has ever worked for the AFWESPAC. It is possible that the man in question gave Mejiro police officers a fake name. Equally as likely, his name could have been misspelled when phonetically translated from English to Japanese. As it stands, the trail for the missing sword ends there.

Not all is lost, however. In 2013, another Masamune sword was recovered and brought to the Kyoto National Museum. Although not as renowned as the Honjō Masamune, it was still historically significant. Goro Nyudo Masamune crafted the Shimazu Masamune as a gift to the Tokugawa family in celebration of Princess Kazunomiya's marriage. The Honjō Masamune's whereabouts may be unknown, but there is still hope that the national treasure of Japan will turn up someday in the near future.

# Up to the Neck in Jewels

*In 1928, the Maharaja of Patiala, a princely state in British India, commissioned an elaborate Cartier necklace made from his vast collection of jewels. Despite its great cost, the jewelry was not destined to remain in the family line for long.*

✳  ✳  ✳  ✳

## The Maharaja of Patiala

AT ONLY NINE years old, Maharaja Bhupinder Singh succeeded his father as the Maharaja, or ruler, of Patiala state. When he was invested with full power after his eighteenth birthday, Bhupinder Singh became very active in the public realm, serving as an honorary lieutenant-colonel during the First World War and representing India at the League of Nations in 1925. He became chancellor of the Indian Chamber of Princes shortly thereafter, and was later made a representative at the Round Table Conference held in London.

Bhupinder Singh was also known as a sportsman, particularly for being a cricketer. In addition to playing several first-class cricket matches, he also captained the Indian cricket team on their England tour in 1911. Because of his less-than-ordinary lifestyle, the Maharaja was drawn to extravagance. He became the first person in India to own an airplane, and had an airstrip specifically built to accommodate his purchase. Then, he turned his attention toward his jewels.

## Cartier Commission

In 1925, Maharaja Bhupinder Singh arrived at Place Vendôme in Paris accompanied by a retinue of servants wearing pink turbans, dancers, and, most importantly, six trunks filled with thousands of rubies, sapphires, emeralds, pearls, and diamonds. Among the latter was the famed De Beers Diamond, a 234.65-carat stone that Bhupinder had inherited from his father, Maharaja Rajinder Singh. Rajinder purchased the yellow, golf ball-sized diamond after seeing it exhibited in Paris in the 1880s. At the time, it was the seventh-largest faceted diamond in the world.

It took three years for Cartier, the French luxury conglomerate, to turn the Maharaja's impressive collection into numerous anklets, armlets, and *haath phools*, or hand flowers. The most extravagant piece of all, however, was the iconic *Collier de Patiala*, or Patiala Necklace. To this day, it remains the single largest commission ever executed by the company. The Patiala Necklace consisted of a neck collar and five rows of platinum chains. These were encrusted with 2,930 diamonds weighing around 1,000 carats, as well as several Burmese rubies. The yellow De Beers Diamond was the design's centerpiece. Cartier was so proud of its craftsmanship that the company sought Bhupinder Singh's permission to display the necklace before sending it off to India. The Maharaja agreed.

## Disappearance and Reappearance

The opulent necklace was worn regularly by Maharaja Bhupinder Singh, and then passed on to his son and heir Maharaja Yadavindra Singh. But the jewelry did not remain in the family's possession for long. In 1948, the Patiala Necklace vanished from the Royal Treasury.

Slowly, traces of the necklace began turning up, some in extremely damaged condition. In 1982, the De Beers diamond reappeared at the Sotheby's Patiala Royal Family auction in Geneva. In 1998, Eric Nussbaum, a Cartier associate, stumbled upon several platinum chains in a second-hand jewelry store in London. The large diamonds and rubies were missing.

Still, because of the jewelry's history and importance to the company, Cartier decided it would do its best to bring the necklace back to its former glory. After purchasing the chains, the jewelers replaced the lost diamonds with synthetic variants and cubic zirconia. It took four years to complete the restoration. Today, Cartier regularly exhibits the necklace, just as it did following its original creation. Though missing several of its original gemstones, the Patiala Necklace continues to exude the wealth and extravagance of its Maharaja.

# Maritime Museum Mystery

*Sir Horatio Nelson's diamond chelengk, presented to him by Sultan Selim III of Turkey, was stolen from Greenwich's National Maritime Museum in 1951. Years later, a master goldsmith reproduced the jewel for display in London.*

✳  ✳  ✳  ✳

## The Battle of the Nile

AS PART OF Napoleon Bonaparte's plan to invade Egypt in a campaign against British India, Commander François-Paul Brueys anchored the French fleet in Aboukir Bay. With the line's port sides facing the shore, Brueys was certain he had established a formidable defensive position against the incoming British fleet. Following convention, the British were expected to attack from only the starboard side.

Unfortunately for Brueys, the British fleet had other plans. Upon arrival, Sir Horatio Nelson ordered an immediate attack, advancing on the French line while splitting into two divisions. While one group cut across the head of the French line toward the shore, the other remained to engage the seaward side. The *Orient*, among other French ships, was trapped between British fire coming from both sides. The destruction of the French fleet was a major blow to Napoleon's ambitions in the east, and Nelson's achievement at the Battle of the Nile would be considered by many historians to be the most significant in his career.

## Presentation of the Chelengk

For his victory at the Battle of the Nile, Nelson was awarded a diamond chelengk by Sultan Selim III of Turkey. Historically, a chelengk referred to a bird's feather that was attached to a turban as a sign of bravery. By the end of the eighteenth century, however, the award changed in appearance. Instead of a feather, it became a jewel consisting of a central flower and seven upward-facing rays.

Nelson's chelengk was accompanied by 13 diamond springs—not seven—representing the collection of French ships conquered by the British during the famous battle. Hidden clockwork mechanisms allowed for the central diamond star on the jewel to rotate. The chelengk was reputed to have been taken from the Sultan's own turban. This gesture of honor was hugely significant, as the chelengk was the highest military decoration of the Ottoman Empire. Moreover, Nelson's chelengk was the first of its kind to have been presented to a non-Muslim.

Sir Horatio Nelson was so proud of his award that he wore the jewel on his bicorn hat for the rest of his life. He even added its image to his coat of arms. The chelengk became so intimately connected with Nelson's image that it was included on his memorial column in Trafalgar Square, commemorating the victory at the Battle of Trafalgar that cost him his life.

## Realistic Reproduction

Nelson's chelengk changed hands several times after his death. First, it was inherited by his brother and passed down the family for generations. Then, in 1929, heiress Lady Barclay purchased the chelengk and displayed it alongside other historical memorabilia in Greenwich's Painted Hall. After World War II, the chelengk was moved to the National Maritime Museum. It was exhibited for the public there until 1951, when it was stolen during the early hours of the morning and never seen again.

Such a fate was unbecoming of one of Sir Nelson's favorite possessions, and so, over 60 years after the original chelengk was taken, the artifact was recreated. London jeweler Philip Denyer used ancient stones cut around the same time Nelson's chelengk was made. He also referenced the original designs when reconstructing the jewel's tiny hidden clockwork. Although only a faithful recreation, Denyer's jewel captures the same spirit as the original. It is considered one of the most instantly recognizable jewels associated with British history.

# Bermuda Break-in

*Within the ruins of the* San Pedro *on Bermuda's reef, diver Teddy Tucker discovered a gold and emerald cross—the most valuable single object ever recovered from a shipwreck. Just days before Queen Elizabeth II's visit to the island, the one-of-a-kind cross was stolen and replaced with a cheap, plastic replica.*

✳  ✳  ✳  ✳

## The Tale of Teddy Tucker

ALTHOUGH NOT WELL-KNOWN outside of Bermuda, Edward "Teddy" Tucker became something of a local legend to those from his island home. He was born in 1925 to a prominent Virginian architect. As a young child, Tucker developed a heavy interest in ocean exploration—an interest that was only fueled by his proximity to the water. He spent his early days working on fishing boats, visiting the local aquarium, and scuba diving.

During World War II, Tucker served in the Royal Navy as an underwater demolitions expert. Afterwards, he and his wife, Edna, returned to Bermuda to settle down. Tucker was able to turn his passion for the ocean into a new, lucrative business for the family and began retrieving and selling scrap metal from the many shipwrecks surrounding the island. His new career made a critical contribution to the economy of Bermuda, creating millions of dollars for the island and helping to pay off the government's war debts.

## Searching the *San Pedro*

In 1951, while busy with work, Tucker was approached by a local fisherman. The man described a pair of large marble columns he had seen embedded in the coral among the other reefs: another place to dive. Because of Bermuda's treacherous waters and poor visibility (the island did not have a lighthouse until 1846), shipwrecks were not uncommon. On the website subsequently managed by his daughter, Wendy Tucker, Teddy described his search of the fisherman's site: While crossing a small sand pocket in the coral, he "saw what appeared to be the muzzle of a small cannon sticking out of the sand." After stopping the boat and putting on a face mask and flippers, he dove to take a closer look. Sure enough, it was a ship cannon, just as he had predicted. Tucker had just discovered the wreckage of the sixteenth-century Spanish treasure galleon, the *San Pedro*.

The next visit to the site would not take place for another four years, in 1955. On his subsequent dives, Tucker spent hours excavating wood, porcelain, and then—finally—gold. He found golden bars, disks, cubes, and hundreds of coins. On the seventh day of his diving marathon, Tucker lifted a large hull plank to reveal a cross face down beneath it. It was bright gold—22 carats—and barely bigger than his palm. He turned it around to face him. There, glistening green in the sunlit water, were seven large emeralds, each the size of a musket ball.

# A Cross Examination

The cross would soon be considered a historically-important find, one of the "most valuable pieces of sunken treasure ever found." Tucker's findings received worldwide media coverage. Multiple publications, including *Life*, printed stories about the discovery.

The media weren't the only ones interested in the cross. One American ambassador to Italy, Clare Boothe Luce, offered Tucker $100,000 for the cross. When he wouldn't accept her offer, she doubled it. Still, Tucker declined. He wished for the treasure to stay in Bermuda. Although Bermudian authorities originally announced that Tucker's items automatically belonged to them and they did not need to purchase the cross, they were eventually convinced to negotiate. Tucker sold the cross to the government for a fraction of its true value. It was then put on display at the Bermuda Aquarium.

In 1975, the emerald cross, accompanied by other treasures of the *San Pedro*, was temporarily relocated to the Bermuda Maritime Museum in anticipation of a special visitor: Queen Elizabeth II. Teddy was invited to host the viewing. Just when the Queen was about to arrive, Tucker approached the table. Something was off about the cross. Tucker's daughter, Wendy, described how the color drained from his face. Reaching out, he touched the cross and felt a veneer of gold paint—fresh, still wet to the touch. Sometime during its move from the Aquarium to the Maritime Museum, the cross had been stolen and replaced with a cheap, plastic replica. Still in a state of shock, Tucker presented what remained of the treasure haul.

The emerald cross, what Tucker called his "most treasured discovery," remains missing to this day. Not all is lost, however. Tucker continued his passion for diving, visiting over one hundred shipwrecks off the coast of Bermuda. To house the trove of artifacts he accumulated, he founded the Bermuda Underwater Exploration Institute—open to all visitors interested in sharing his thrill of discovery. Tucker even found his way into Hollywood: Writer Peter Benchley used him as an inspiration for Robert Shaw's sea dog character, Quint, in *Jaws*. Tucker's contributions to his home island won't be forgotten anytime soon. According to Benchley, Tucker helped give his home island the recognition it deserved, bringing "Bermuda to the world and the world to Bermuda."

# What Came First: the Great Mogul Diamond or the Orlov Diamond?

*What happened to a diamond with a history both rivaling and entangled with the Koh-I-Noor and one of the most iconic pieces of the Russian crown jewel collection?*

❋　❋　❋　❋

BELIEVED TO HAVE been discovered in the mid-seventeenth century, the Great Mogul diamond was unearthed at the Kollur Mine in southern India. The 787-carat rough stone was gifted to Shah Jahan in a gesture of diplomacy shortly after. The Mughal emperor assigned a Venetian, Ortensio Borgio, to cut the stone. Borgio refused to cut the diamond into multiple pieces, despite the general consensus that it would eliminate the inclusions in the stone, instead opting to grind away at the stone until all perceivable flaws were removed. This method proved to be an utter failure, removing a large portion of the massive diamond's weight. The Mughal emperor deigned to spare the Venetian's head, but fined him for everything he had, a total of 10,000 rupees.

The Great Mogul was seen and documented again around 1665, when Aurangzeb—the Shah's son—showed the stone to Jean Baptiste Tavernier. Tavernier noted in his writings that the stone was round with a slight crack on one of the lower edges and a flaw within. At this time, the stone was noted to resemble an egg cut in half. In this form, the diamond weighed approximately 280 carats. Tavernier's writings are the only surviving contemporary record of the stone in the possession of the Mughal empire.

## Disappearance

The stone remained with the imperial family until Mughal India was invaded and sacked by the Persian ruler Nadir Shah. Nadir Shah took the rose cut stone back to his home as part of his spoils of war, where it remained until he was assassinated in 1747, at which time the stone disappeared.

Following Nadir Shah's assassination, there is no further historical record of the Great Mogul Diamond. The only surviving record of the stone's existence is Tavernier's writings and drawings, and modern conjecture on the stone's path through political and military turmoil on the Indian subcontinent during the seventeenth and eighteenth centuries.

In the 1960s, the Iranian Treasury opened for examination, at which point, the experts found that none of the stones in the treasury resembled the Great Mogul. Theorists have long posited that the Koh-I-Noor (a large cut diamond that is part of the British crown jewels) is actually the diamond in question.

Tavernier's drawings lend credence to one specific theory of the diamond's ultimate fate. Lining up the centuries-old, primitive drawings of the diamond's facets with computer models of another famous diamond suggests a possible relationship between the missing Great Mogul and the Orlov Diamond of the Russian crown jewels.

## The Orlov Diamond

The origin of the Orlov diamond has accrued a proliferation of fanciful legends too. However, there is no well-documented history of the stone before a rich Iranian, Shaffrass, placed the diamond for sale in Amsterdam where it was ultimately bought by Grigory Grigorievich Orlov.

Depending on the story, Orlov bought the diamond for or on the behalf of Catherine the Great, with whom he had long been romantically involved. The diamond can be read either as a gift between lovers or a desperate token to regain the favor of the empress. Regardless of the diamond's purpose, Catherine named the diamond after Count Orlov and requested her jeweler create a scepter with the diamond at the center, now known as the Imperial scepter.

The scepter, and the Orlov Diamond, remain at the center of the Kremlin's Diamond Fund, acting as one of the most prominent reminders of Catherine the Great's reign and her cultural significance to Russia.

While there is some evidence to suggest that the Kremlin is the current resting place of the Great Mogul diamond, albeit in a smaller 190 carat form, the debate surrounding both the provenance of the Great Mogul and the origin of the Orlov continues—with no end in sight.

# The Gem of Sorrow: A Tale of Curses, Pen Names, and Ghosts

*A story that begins with misidentification ends with a legend that has persisted for almost two hundred years.*

✳   ✳   ✳   ✳

THE LONG AND treacherous story of the Delhi Purple Sapphire began with a case of misidentification. The distinctive purple amethyst was deemed a sapphire, and named as such, after being looted from the Temple of Indra and taken to England during a period of upheaval against British colonial rule on the Indian subcontinent during the nineteenth century.

Cavalryman Colonel W. Ferris took the stone back to England with him. He then suffered a series of financial blows and health issues. Every member of his family subsequently suffered through a series of strange illnesses. The stone passed to Ferris's son upon his death, and a second generation was also subjected to further calamities. So the story goes.

In 1890, Edward Heron-Allen became the stone's owner. The noted scholar became another victim of the stone and claimed that the amethyst was tainted. Heron-Allen set the stone in a ring featuring a snake, astrological symbolism, and two amethyst scarabs. Heron-Allen then claimed that the curse had abated (though he also claimed the ghost of a Hindu Yogi attempted to hunt both him and the gemstone).

Thinking the stone had lost its previous threat, Heron-Allen lent the stone out to a singer who then lost her voice after wearing the stone. After this incident and another related to his infant daughter, Heron-Allen attempted to rid himself of the stone by any means necessary, including an incident where the scientist tossed the stone into Regent's Canal only for it to be returned to him three months later by a jeweler who recognized the purple gem after it was dredged from the water. Ultimately, Heron-Allen stored the amethyst away in seven boxes stacked with good luck charms and locked it away in a bank, with a letter warning people not to open the box until 33 years after his death.

## The Natural History Museum

Less than a year after Heron-Allen's death, his daughter left the locked box and letter in the safekeeping of the Natural History Museum in London, where it stayed untouched and locked up tight until 1972, when a new curator discovered the box and Heron-Allen's letter, warning future owners of the gem of the misfortune that typically followed it around.

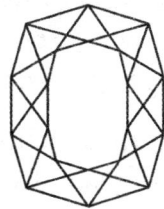

Since that young curator opened the box, the Delhi Purple Sapphire has resided at the Natural History Museum in London, splitting time between the museum vault and public display. The Museum believes Heron-Allen overinflated and manufactured much of the story, which he would go on to publish under a pen name.

Regardless of the logical answer here (a clever scientist engineers a hoax and publishes a fictional book about it), rumors still abound surrounding the supposed curse of the Delhi Purple Sapphire. In three separate incidents, a curator at the museum—John Whittaker—was asked to transport the amethyst to events. In the first, Whittaker was caught up in a storm and barely escaped without injury. In the second, he became exceptionally ill. In the third, Whittaker collapsed, passing a kidney stone hours later. Regardless of popular belief in the Delhi Purple Sapphire's curse, its chaotic history is well-known.

# A Tale of Two Kings, a Cardinal, and Too Many Merchants

*Is one of the gemstones in the British Imperial State Crown actually a fraud?*

✳ ✳ ✳ ✳

WEIGHING IN AT a remarkable 104 carats, the Stuart Sapphire is one of the 2,901 reasons that the British Imperial State Crown weighs 2.3 pounds. The sapphire is an oval measuring over an inch wide, nearly flawless, and a prime example of a sapphire's natural color. Exactly the kind of stone you'd expect a royal family to own.

The Stuart Sapphire, as the name suggests, has a long history with the Stuart Dynasty. Charles II, famous for his executed father and the decade-long period without a monarch that preceded his accession to the throne, is thought to be the first owner of the enormous blue sapphire. After his father's death, the crown jewels collection had been decimated, leaving the new king to rebuild the old grandeur of the monarchy. The Stuart Sapphire was likely one of Charles's new purchases during this time. Charles didn't reign for long, however, and his brother's trouble on the throne kick-started the stones' grand tour of Europe for the next few decades.

James II, the last Catholic monarch of Great Britain, got himself into trouble with the protestant kingdom he ruled. The country of Henry VIII would not accept a Catholic dynasty ruling the country. The moment James II produced a male heir, it was all over for him. James took the massive sapphire with him to France, where he passed it to his son, yet another James Stuart. James Jr., best known as the "Old Pretender," kept the stone his entire life, ultimately leaving it for his son Henry, who would become a Cardinal and wear the royal gem in his mitre.

## Back to England

At the end of his life, the Cardinal was the last surviving descendant of James II and, as he was a man of God, his worldly possessions were sold off, including the Stuart sapphire and a number of other relics of the deposed royal dynasty. At this point, Angelo Cesarini, the executor of the Cardinal's will, sent off a number of jewels to George IV of England—but not the Stuart sapphire.

George IV knew he hadn't received all the remaining Stuart jewels, and he wasn't happy about it. Then the Prince Regent for his father, mad King George III, the younger George enlisted Angioli Bonelli to head to Rome and track down any Stuart artifacts that hadn't made their way back to England.

Bonelli headed straight to Rome. He found a merchant who claimed to possess the Stuart Sapphire. Bonelli brought the enormous sapphire back to England, where George placed the stone in the crown jewel collection and Queen Victoria added it to her state crown, in a place of honor below the Black Prince's Ruby.

To this day, the Stuart Sapphire retains its place on the crown of British monarchs, though it's now relegated to the center back of the Imperial State Crown, with the Cullinan II diamond in its former center front position. No one knows for sure if the stone Bonelli acquired in Rome is truly the Stuart Sapphire that absconded with a disgraced King, but the enormous stone currently situated within one of the most iconic crowns within the British Crown Jewel collection isn't going anywhere soon.

# Brussels: Truly a Gem of a Heist

*In a matter of three minutes and with no shots fired, more than $50 million in diamonds were swiped from the Brussels Airport in 2013. To make matters even more unbelievable, at least 22 acquittals and just one conviction were the result of one of the most well-conceived and well-executed heists of all time.*

✳   ✳   ✳   ✳

F EBRUARY 18, 2013 WAS like any other day at Belgium's Brussels Airport. Planes were taking off and landing, with no indication of what would occur that night. Undetected by airport security, eight masked men sat parked on a construction site. They disguised themselves as police officers, wearing fake uniforms and even dressing up their cars with the look. Their goal: Snag millions of dollars' worth of diamonds that had been driven from Antwerp in an armored van. The gems were due to be transferred to a Helvetic Airways flight bound for Zurich.

At around 7:40 that evening, the men drove through a weak link they had created in a fence and quickly arrived at the scene. They calmly intercepted the transfer of the diamonds from the van to the aircraft. Brandishing Kalashnikov-type assault rifles, they ordered ground workers and the pilot to step aside while they piled up the loot. They took 130 bags of diamonds—not even all of it—and sped away without a single shot fired. It took three minutes to drive off with gems worth $50 million.

When the real police arrived, they found no one had sustained any injuries. In fact, the 29 passengers on the aircraft were not aware that a heist had occurred. All they knew was that they had to deplane due to the flight being cancelled.

One commentator described the event as "a very precise, almost military-organized and well-executed robbery." Some experts speculate that the heist was an inside job, due to the success the robbers had in evading security and getting away without a hiccup. How the thieves knew so much about the transfer remains unknown.

Soon after the heist, the escape vehicle was found burned and left behind, with none of the diamonds in sight. Though only eight men were said to have been involved in the actual heist, no fewer than 31 have been accused of having some level of involvement in it. And, as of 2024, only one—a man who helped with the planning but not the robbery itself—has been convicted, with 22 acquittals. Only a small portion of the loot has ever been recovered.

# From Golconda to the Guillotine: the Regent Diamond

*With a long and storied history, the Regent Diamond's name does little to account for the amazing story that began in a seventeenth-century mine.*

✳   ✳   ✳   ✳

WEIGHING IN AT a whopping 140.64 carats and worth £48,000,000 as of a 2015 estimate, the Regent diamond has been a fixture in high society since its discovery in 1698. Unlike many of the diamonds on display today, the Regent's provenance is mostly traceable. That is, except for its origin.

Most sources agree that the diamond was unearthed by a slave in the mines of Golconda, India. This region was already famous for the purity and size of its diamonds. The legend goes that the slave smuggled the diamond out of the mine concealed in a leg wound before attempting to use part of the proceeds from a future sale to buy his way onto a ship. The ship captain then killed him, taking the diamond for himself and ultimately selling it to Jamchand, a famed diamond merchant in India at the time.

From here on, there's little question of who had the diamond. Thomas Pitt, a British governor on the subcontinent, bought the diamond and almost immediately sent it to London, hidden within his son's shoe heel to throw off thieves. It spent the next two years being cut into its current shape. Pitt returned to England and thereupon began trying to sell the diamond in an effort to solve some of his money problems. Due to the size and quality of the diamond, few could afford to buy it and Pitt kept the diamond in his possession until 1717, when he sold it to Philippe II, the French Regent.

After the sale, the diamond remained at least somewhat connected to the French monarchy, adorning the coronation crowns of both Louis XV and Louis XVI before being added to a hat worn by the infamous Marie Antoinette. After the ouster of the French royal family, the diamond fell into Napoleon Bonaparte's hands, decorating his ceremonial sword throughout his reign.

Today, the diamond remains mounted in a Greek diadem designed for Empress Eugenie and is stored at the Louvre, within the French Royal treasury.

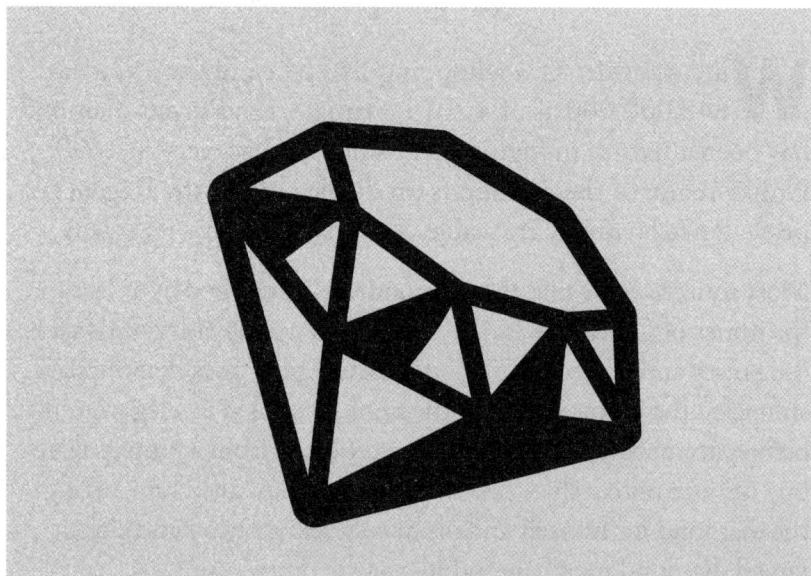

# Chapter 4

# Books We'll Never Read

## The Library of the Muses

*By far the most famous library in history, the Library of Alexandria held an untold number of ancient works. Its fiery destruction meant the irrecoverable loss of a substantial part of the world's intellectual history.*

✳  ✳  ✳  ✳

### The Library's Beginnings

THE CITIES OF ancient Mesopotamia (e.g., Uruk, Nineveh, Babylon) and Egypt (e.g., Thebes, Memphis) had cultivated archives and libraries since the Bronze Age, but the idea for a library as grand as Alexandria did not occur in Greek culture until the Hellenistic Age, when Alexander the Great's conquests brought both Greece and these former civilizations under Macedonian rule. Previous Greek libraries were owned by individuals; the largest belonged to Aristotle (384–322 BC), whose work and school (the Lyceum) in Athens were supported by Alexander.

When Alexander died suddenly in 323 BC, his generals carved his empire into regional dynasties. The Hellenistic dynasties competed with each other for three centuries (until each was in turn conquered by either Rome or Parthia). Each dynasty desired cultural dominance, so they invited famous artists, authors, and intellectuals to live and work in their capital cities. Alexander's general Ptolemy, who controlled Egypt, decided to develop a collection of the world's learning (the Library) and a research center, (the Museum, or "Temple of the Muses"), where scholars on subsidy could study and add their research to the collection. This idea may well have come from Demetrius of Phaleron (350–280 BC), Ptolemy's advisor and the former governor of Athens, who had been a pupil at the Lyceum, but the grand project became one of the hallmark projects of the Ptolemaic dynasty. Under the first three Ptolemies, the Museum, a royal library, and a smaller "daughter" library at the Temple of Serapis (the Serapeum) were built and grew as Alexandria became the intellectual, as well as commercial, capital of the Hellenistic world.

Egypt and Alexandria offered the Ptolemies distinct advantages for accomplishing their goals. Egypt was not only immensely rich, which gave it the wealth to purchase materials and to bring scholars to Alexandria, but it was the major producer of papyrus, a marsh reed that was beaten into a flat surface and made into scrolls for writing and copying. Alexandria was also the commercial hub of the Mediterranean, and goods and information from all over the world passed through its port.

## Bibliomania: So Many Scrolls, So Little Time

Acquiring materials for the libraries and Museum became somewhat of an obsession for the Ptolemies. Although primarily focused on Greek and Egyptian works, their interests included translating other traditions into Greek. Among the most important of these efforts was the production of the Septuagint, a Greek version of the Jewish scriptures. Besides employing agents to scour major book markets and to search out copies of works not yet in the library, boats coming into Alexandria were required to declare any scrolls on board. If they were of interest, the scrolls were confiscated and copied, and the owners were given the copies and some compensation. Ptolemy III (285–222 BC) may have acquired Athens' official state collection of the plays of Aeschylus, Sophocles, and Euripides in a similar way—putting up 15 talents of silver as a guarantee while he had the plays copied, then foregoing the treasure in favor of keeping the originals. Whether or not this is true, it speaks to the value he placed on getting important works and the resources he had at his disposal to do so.

Alexandria's efforts were fueled by a fierce competition with the Hellenistic kingdom of Pergamum (modern Bergamo, Turkey), which created its own library. Each library sought to claim new finds and to produce new editions, leading at times to the acquisition of forgeries and occasional embarrassment. Alexandria finally tried to undercut its rival by cutting off papyrus exports, but Pergamum perfected a method for making writing material out of animal skins (now called "parchment" from the Latin *pergamina*) and continued to build its holdings. Eventually, however, Alexandria got the upper hand when the Roman general Marcus Antonius (Mark Antony) conquered Pergamum and made a present of its library to his lover, the Ptolemaic Queen Cleopatra.

Estimates as to the number of volumes in the Alexandrian library ranged wildly even in antiquity, generally between 200,000 and 700,000. Estimates are complicated by the fact that it isn't clear whether the numbers originate from works or scrolls: Some scrolls contained one work, some multiple works, and long works like the *Iliad* took multiple scrolls. Over time, a complex cataloguing system evolved, which culminated in a bibliographic survey of the library's holdings called the *Pinakes*. The survey was put together by the great Hellenistic scholar and poet Callimachus of Cyrene (305–240 BC). Unfortunately, this important work only exists in fragments today.

## Burning Down the House

The Royal Library and its holdings were accidentally set aflame in 48 BC when Caesar (who had taken Cleopatra's side in her claim to the throne against her brother) tried to burn his way out of being trapped in the port by opposing forces. Further losses probably occurred in AD 271 when Emperor Aurelian destroyed part of the Museum while recapturing Alexandria from Queen Zenobia's forces. The "daughter" library of the Serapeum was finally destroyed by Christians under Emperor Theodosius near the end of the fourth century. But by then, much of the contents (like the contents of other great civic libraries of antiquity) had decayed or found their way into other hands, leaving the classical heritage scattered and fragmented for centuries. Much later, Christians dramatically blamed the burning of the library holdings on Muslim conquerors. Although this made for a good story, the legendary contents of the library were already long gone.

# Hesiod's Lost Epic Poetry

*An elusive and fragmentary epic poem with an intriguing theme appears in various works of antiquity, but a whole copy has never been found. What did the world lose?*

✳    ✳    ✳    ✳

**H**ESIOD WAS A Greek poet who lived sometime between 750 and 650 BC. His works are considered to be some of the earliest written European poems that have made it to the present day. During his lifetime, he won acclaim by participating in contests and recitals. Two of his epic poems have survived intact: *Theogony* and *Works and Days*. Hesiod's literary reputation is based on these works as well as the esteem many contemporary and subsequent Greek poets held for him. On this basis, we can theorize that his lost works were probably equally excellent.

One work in particular has fascinated scholars for centuries: *Catalogue of Women*. The surviving fragments of this work have been attributed to Hesiod but many scholars believe that it may not be his work, or at any rate was not entirely written by him. Regardless, the fragments of this epic poem are considered to be part of a larger work. The *Catalogue* itself may have been anywhere between 4,000 and 5,000 lines long.

Modern readers may be befuddled by the poem's title. In this case the word "catalogue" is used in the genealogical sense and reflects the subject of the work: collections of stories of various women, whether real or mythical, outlining their lineages and highlighting notable events in their lives. Some of the women mentioned are unknown to us, while others are famous heroines like Helen, whose story is central to the Trojan War. What especially sets apart *Catalogue of Women* is its strict focus on the female perspective, which is present in few other ancient Greek works. The poem likely served to elucidate the importance of women in the mythic past and their role in shaping the destinies of both the mortal and divine realms.

The structure of the epic probably followed a genealogical format, tracing the lives of women through many generations. This format is one of the reasons that Hesiod is connected to the poem: Genealogy seemed to be a central subject in his works and his *Theogony* similarly focused on outlining the ancestry of the gods. The work appears to have been divided into five books, structured around genealogical groups: the descendants of Aeolus, Inachus, Pelasgus, Atlas, and Pelops.

## The Five Books

The first book dealt with the genealogies of divine or semi-divine women. These women were often associated with mythological stories and had notable roles in the shaping of mythic history in Greece's earliest times. Whether they were based on real historical women is something we will never know, unless more text is recovered. The second book probably focused on real historical women, highlighting their notable deeds. The third book probably concentrated on genealogies related to the Trojan War. The fourth book may have explored the genealogies of women associated with Thebes, a city noted for its rich mythological traditions. It may have mentioned heroines like Antigone, Jocasta, and other women associated with the Theban cycle of myths. The final book may have been broader, considering women from different regions and cities.

Many fragments of this work can be found embedded as quotes in other works of antiquity. So, for example, we read in the one papyrus fragment, "And from Crete the mighty Idomeneus sought her to wife, Deucalion's son, offspring of renowned Minos. He sent no one to woo her in his place, but came himself in his black ship of many thwarts over the Ogylian sea across the dark wave to the home of wise Tyndareus, to see Argive Helen and that no one else should bring back for him the girl whose renown spread all over the holy earth." These fragments, when it is possible to set them in historical context, provide us with concrete details that are intimate, if not gossipy. What's fascinating—and tantalizing—about these bits of information is how they seem to tie various well known ancient Greek stories together, displaying the relationships between characters and behind-the-scenes details and backstories that, if only the poem were still extant, might make some of the better-known tales more vivid. Given the poem's focus, it would also shed light on the roles women played in Greece, as well as what they thought and how they interacted with men, each other, and society at large during this time.

# The Lost Plays of Aeschylus

*The "father of tragedy" supposedly wrote as many as 90 plays in his lifetime. No more than seven (plus fragments) have come down to us. Do we have any idea what all of those other plays were about?*

✳   ✳   ✳   ✳

ESCHYLUS LIVED ROUGHLY between 525 and 456 BC. He was one of the great writers of Greek tragedy—though details are sketchy. He fought in the Persian wars, participating in two battles at Marathon and Salamis. These wars were defining events; he lost a brother in one of the wars and his epitaph supposedly said nothing of his success as a playwright and instead mentioned that he had fought at Marathon.

History remembers Aeschylus for different reasons. Not only was he prolific, he was also extremely popular with his contemporaries. Though Greek drama already existed, his plays are seen as a beginning point. Part of the reason for this is due to the impact on Greek drama's subsequent development. He was an innovator who developed and expanded the traditional forms he inherited, making his plays more entertaining and dramatic. He incorporated wheeled platforms to change scenery and employed a kind of crane to lift actors. His costume designs were extravagant, and contemporaries also noted that his productions had some of the best stage imagery ever seen. Aristotle wrote that Aeschylus added second actors for minor parts and specifically improved dramatic dialogue.

## What We Know

His complete surviving plays include *The Persians, Seven Against Thebes, Suppliants, Oresteia* (a trilogy comprising *Agamemnon, The Libation Bearers,* and *The Furies*), and *Prometheus Bound.* These plays take as their subjects historical Greek events, interactions between gods and humans, plenty of deeds of vengeance, hubris, and of course, conflict with the Persians. In *Seven Against Thebes,* for example, the two sons of Oedipus agree to share rulership of the city, with each taking an alternating year. But after his first year of rule, Eteocles decides not to step down. His brother Polynices goes to war with him, the ultimate result being that they kill each other in single combat. Hubris, conflict, death, and a little moral superciliousness, then, as now, were a popular draw. Aeschylus was also a master of language and gave his audiences compelling dialogues and choral lyrics that had great emotional intensity.

There are fragments of lost plays too, and these seem to play out similar themes. In *Myrmidons* and *Nereids,* Aeschylus tapped one of Greek literature's greatest treasures, the *Iliad,* dramatizing key events that happened in that epic work. Of the rest, we have little more than the titles of the plays. These titles are overwhelmingly names, telling us little: *Athamas,*

The Cabeiroi, Callisto, Circe, Ixion, Orethyia, Penelope, Proteus, Telephus, The Thracian Women, and Xantriae, for example, are typical play titles.

## Tantalizing Discoveries?

While it's highly unlikely that we will ever discover the full scripts of any of Aeschylus's lost plays, sometimes fragments of his work show up in surprising places. Towards the end of the twentieth century, mummies stuffed with sections of papyrus were uncovered by archeologists, and the writings on these ancient remnants turned out to be excerpts of *Achilles*, a trilogy Aeschylus wrote about the Trojan War. While multiple ancient sources mention the play's existence, this was the first time in millennia that anyone had actually read the text. This tantalizing taste of ancient Greek drama makes us wonder—could more such discoveries lie waiting in forgotten tombs and under desert sands?

# The "Lost" Book of Enoch

*An ancient work alluded to by early Christians seems to disappear into the mists of history. Did it ever really exist?*

✳ ✳ ✳ ✳

THE BOOK OF Enoch did and does in fact exist. But for centuries, European Christians only knew of it by name, as it was mentioned in the writings of early Church Fathers and medieval ecclesiastics. But the text itself could not be found in any archive or library. The consensus was that the Book of Enoch had been lost.

## What Exactly Is in This Book?

The Book of Enoch is a compilation of separate works, most of which were written roughly between 300 and 200 BC. It was once in circulation among some early Christian communities and Jewish groups but is not now considered part of the Christian Bible.

Enoch is divided into five sections. The first section is on the subject of angels, Jerusalem, the Tree of Life, and the universe itself. The second considers the Messiah, the flood, Noah, judgment times, and paradise. The third focuses on matters of astronomy and Enoch's mission. The fourth looks at the flood, the future of Israel, and the messianic kingdom. The final section considers the challenges of the righteous and the wicked, ending with a discussion of sin after the flood and the eventual coming of the Messiah.

The Bible itself mentions two Enochs. The first appears in Genesis, as the son of Cain. The second also appears in Genesis. This Enoch is the son of Jared, son of Mahalaleel, and great, great, great, great-grandson of Adam. The book itself claims to be written by the latter Enoch, but the actual author or authors is unknown.

## How Did It Become Lost?

In the early days of Christianity, the Book of Enoch was valued enough to be quoted widely. Over time, however, attitudes changed. One of the book's central concerns—the nature and deeds of certain fallen angels—apparently ran afoul of prevailing conceptions. At least one Church Father, Filastrius, openly condemned the book as heretical. Given this disfavor, the text seems to have quietly disappeared from shelves, conveniently forgotten. Although it fell by the wayside, there remained a few erudite scholars and theologians who continued to make references to it. For example, the Byzantine chronicler George Synkellos of St. Tarasios referenced the book extensively in his eighth century work, *Chronography*. But though it may have been mostly forgotten in European Christendom, it was never truly "lost." In fact, the text is part of the Ethiopian Orthodox Church's biblical canon, and the Ethiopic translation is the only complete extant version.

From our perspective in the West, two events brought this early religious work out of obscurity. First, in 1773, Scottish traveler James Bruce obtained three copies during his travels in eastern Africa. A subsequent English translation was published in 1821, bringing it to the attention of many biblical scholars for the first time. Second, the early 1950s saw the publication of the Aramaic fragments of Enoch that were found among the Dead Sea Scrolls. The Book of Enoch, while still outside of the Christian canon (except within the Ethiopian Orthodox Church), is now viewed as an important source of ideas that probably influenced early Christian writers and the New Testament itself.

# A Tragedy of Loss: The Plays of Sophocles

*Sophocles is said to have written well over one hundred plays. Only a few of his works survive, along with a few tantalizing fragments. Based on the incredible works that have made it down the centuries intact, this is our loss. Sophocles was a singular talent who enthralled the audiences of his day.*

\* \* \* \*

EVEN TO A Greek public that was accustomed to seeing the works of contemporary playwrights Aeschylus and Euripides performed, Sophocles was considered a unique, towering, creative talent. His plays regularly won awards (of the 30 competitions he entered, he reputedly won 24) and he also seems to have been an important civic figure.

## What We Know

The ancient works of history and literature that have come down to us have passed a gauntlet of obstacles. Over the centuries, works may perish in fires, be censored out of existence, turn to dust on library shelves, be written over by works considered more important at the time, or even be torn up and used for other purposes. In Sophocles' case, only seven plays have survived. His total output was around 123 plays.

Sophocles' seven surviving tragedies are *Ajax, Antigone, Trachinian Women, Oedipus the King, Electra, Philoctetes,* and *Oedipus at Colonus.* If nothing else had survived, *Oedipus the King* alone would have assured Sophocles' place in dramatic history. The plot, dialogue, and devices used in this marvel of classical Greek drama have reverberated down the centuries. It portrays King Oedipus slowly and ominously discovering the facts of his own upbringing and fulfilling the terrible fate prophesied by the Delphic Oracle.

## What We Lost

Of the remaining plays that Sophocles wrote, little is known beyond their titles, and these give little indication of their subject: *Andromache, Chryseis, Creusa, Dolopes, Momus, Niobe, Oeneus, Palamedes, Priam, Procris, Sinon, Theseus, Troilus,* and *Tyndareos* are all typical play titles, which merely indicate the names of main characters. We do not know the order they were written in, when or where they were performed, or how they were grouped. We do know that Sophocles continued to evolve and hone his creative abilities throughout his life, and that he may have seen his work as having three stages. One rather convoluted translation of Sophocles' own assessment of his work, and his debt to his predecessor Aeschylus, puts it this way: "After practicing to the bigness of Aeschylus, then the painful ingenuity of my own invention, now in the third stage I am changing the kind of diction which is most expressive of character and best."

Tantalizing fragments of his lost works have sometimes come to us either from authors who quoted those works or from papyri discovered in recent centuries. Among these are, for example, lines from *The Searchers,* a play involving the escapades of the young god Hermes. Another, *Inachus,* portrays Zeus coming to Argos to seduce the king's daughter. And in *Niobe,* Sophocles tells how Apollo and his sister Artemis punish Niobe by killing her twelve children for some slight she committed. These fragments reveal what we might have deduced—that Sophocles actively mined and reworked Greek myths and legends as did other contemporary playwrights. Given the seven existing plays, that material should have been enough to give us many more masterpieces.

# A Lost Classic? Melville's Missing Novel

*Did the author of* Moby Dick *write another masterpiece that was never published?*

\* \* \* \*

THOUGH HARDLY A beloved literary figure during his lifetime, Herman Melville is now recognized as one of the most singular and talented voices in American literature. But his career was a financially and emotionally difficult one, filled with setbacks and disappointments.

In June of 1853, Melville visited the offices of his former publisher, Harper & Brothers, to submit the manuscript of his new novel, which was probably titled *Isle of the Cross*. He had recently published *Pierre* in 1852, and this had been a financial disaster. Critics panned it. His previous novel, *Moby Dick* (published in 1851), though now understood as a masterpiece, had also been something of a flop, eviscerated by critics who considered it irreverent and blasphemous. Melville took these critical failures very seriously—according to letters written at the time by friends and family, these setbacks led to Melville coming close to a mental breakdown.

## A Mysterious Rejection

Despite these disappointments, Melville apparently wrote *Isle of the Cross* fairly quickly, in a burst of feverish creativity. While we don't know how hopeful he might have been about securing a new deal with his publisher, he must have anticipated that they might be less than receptive to an author whose last two books had done so poorly. As it turns out, his manuscript was indeed received skeptically. Later in November of the same year, Melville mentioned a manuscript "which I was prevented from printing" in a letter to the publisher who turned him down. The reasons for Harper & Brothers' rejection are not given, nor is the title of the manuscript, but it seems likely that he must have been referring to *Isle of the Cross*.

## Touchy Subject Matter

Like so many other great artists, Melville had a habit of exploring subjects in alarming ways. *Pierre* dealt with themes of moral relativism and incest, infuriating almost every critic who read it. In the words of one reviewer, the novel was "perhaps, the craziest fiction extant." Another said the material "might be supposed to emanate from a lunatic hospital." Was his new work similarly provocative?

Why Harper & Brothers rejected the manuscript is unclear. The staff may have factored recent harsh reviews Melville's novels had received. They may also have considered the subject of the book; if the material was deemed too close to a real-life story, then they may have feared legal action. Melville apparently gave up on publishing the book after this one rejection. The manuscript then disappeared.

The critics who believe this work exists tend to agree that its subject was inspired by a story Melville had heard about: A young Nantucket woman named Agatha had nursed a shipwrecked sailor back to health and married him. The sailor then deserted her, only to reappear 17 years later, disappear again, and finally be exposed as a bigamist. Melville had suggested in a letter to his friend Nathaniel Hawthorne that he take up this subject himself, but Hawthorne declined. Painstaking reconstructions of Melville's life via anecdotes, letters, and his reading materials reveal support for this story being the initial inspiration. And while clues that such is the case abound, we lack proof. Unless an actual version of the novel resurfaces, we'll never know if it was a lost masterpiece.

# The Lost Works of the Cotton Library

*In the early hours of October 23, 1731, a fire broke out at Ashburnham House, home of Britain's Cotton library and one of the greatest collections of manuscripts in the country. The fire destroyed or otherwise damaged many priceless works from a collection that would become the basis of the British Library.*

✳   ✳   ✳   ✳

THE ENGLISH POLITICIAN Sir Robert Bruce Cotton began collecting valuable manuscripts in 1588. After his death in 1631, his heirs continued to add to the collection. The library was a well-known resource in the seventeenth century; it included official papers of state, books, manuscripts of antiquity, and medallions and coins. Sir Robert's grandson donated the library to the government in 1702. This transfer would become the basis of what is now the British Library.

By 1706, the collection had been moved from its original location to a new one, and after some logistical wrangling, was transferred to Ashburnham House. The reasoning was that this temporary location was safer than previous ones from chances of fire. Unfortunately, it was not. However the fire started (most agree it somehow escaped from a fireplace on the ground floor), once it reached the dry wood of the house's beams, walls, and molding, the blaze was unstoppable. The night ended with librarians and neighbors flinging books out windows and dousing flames. There is an anecdote that Westminster schoolboys spent the next day catching fragments of manuscripts that floated through the air like butterflies.

## The Aftermath

It is estimated that the collection held over 950 manuscripts. While only ten to twenty manuscripts were lost, many more were seriously damaged by fire, smoke, and water. Irreplaceable texts like a fifth-century Greek Genesis (containing over 300 illustrations), Asser's biography of King Alfred, and *The Battle of Maldon* were destroyed. Other noteworthy works damaged by the fire included four letters patent of King John that recorded the grant of the Magna Carta (including the Great Seal, which the heat turned into a shapeless blob), the 'G' manuscript of the Anglo-Saxon Chronicle, the only extant manuscript of Aethelweard's chronicle, the earliest copy of the Burghal Hidage, and the earliest manuscript of Gildas. Irreplaceable illuminated manuscripts from medieval Northumbria and the continent were also seriously damaged.

## Restoration and Preservation

In the immediate aftermath, an assembled rescue team attempted to dry, clean, and reassemble what remained. But contemporary methods of restoration were hardly up to the task. Leaves were hung on lines to dry, in some cases even dried before a fire. Vellum manuscripts were disbound, with their folios hung up to dry. A large number of charred pages and fragments were simply put into drawers when it was uncertain which books they had come from. All of this was done hastily and was completed within three months of the fire. The resulting chaos was then left for future generations to sort out.

In 1753, much of the remnants of the library became part of the British Museum as a "foundation collection." Over the ensuing decades, there were attempts to piece together charred remnants. Different curators and custodians attempted different methods of restoring the collection, with some work in fact being counterproductive. During the second half of the nineteenth century, editorial standards and curatorial methodologies improved. Cataloguing and access was further improved over the course of the twentieth century, but many charred fragments remain to be sorted and studied. That said, the digitized manuscripts of some sections of the Cotton collection can viewed online, making access to this rich slice of history available to virtually anyone.

# Chapter 5

# Imaginary Books, People, and Other Fictions

## Doyle and His Very Dynamic Asteroid

*Yes it was just a fictional treatise mentioned in passing in a Sherlock Holmes short story. But what readers might see as a trivial bit of backstory, writers see as an invitation...*

✳ ✳ ✳ ✳

S IR ARTHUR CONAN Doyle wrote four novels and 58 short stories about the iconic sleuth Sherlock Holmes. The mastermind detective first appeared in print in 1887, immediately becoming a popular fictional character and setting readers' expectations for the genre of detective fiction for decades to come. In the course of Holmes' adventures and investigations, we hear about a certain Professor James Moriarty, whom Holmes considers a kind of arch-criminal. Moriarty's first appearance was in the 1893 short story "The Adventure of the Final Problem." In this story we learn that Holmes has suspected Moriarty of having been involved in certain recent criminal activities.

This is typical of how Moriarty appears: a malignant force dwelling somewhere in background, directing criminal traffic. Fans of Holmes stories know that the brilliant professor cast a menacing shadow over the life of Holmes. His evil scheming even included a few attempts to murder the detective.

In the short story "The Valley of Fear" (published in 1914 but set in 1888), we learn that Moriarty is also a first-rate mathematician who had once published an astronomical treatise. In that story, Holmes says, "Is he not the celebrated author of *The Dynamics of an Asteroid*, a book which ascends to such rarefied heights of pure mathematics that it is said that there was no man in the scientific press capable of criticizing it?" It was a single off-the-cuff reference to an entirely fictional book. Doyle would probably be surprised by what that single mention started.

## Moriarty's Dastardly Theorems

What might be contained in *The Dynamics of an Asteroid*? Why would a criminal mastermind devote himself to writing a treatise on such a subject? Doyle never delved any deeper into that part of Moriarty's backstory. But we do learn elsewhere that the professor had written "A Treatise on the Binomial Theorem" at the age of 21, and that on the strength of this paper he was awarded a Mathematics Chair at a small university. Holmes himself called Moriarty "a genius, a philosopher, an abstract thinker. He has a brain of the first order." The fact that Moriarty published acclaimed papers in two very different realms of mathematics supports Holmes's characterization.

## A Treatise That Grew in the Telling

While Doyle never elaborated on what the contents of *Dynamics* might be, later authors used the title as a starting point for conjecture. Examples of this include Isaac Asimov's "The Ultimate Crime" (in which a fictional character is asked to write a story about what the actual contents of *Dynamics* are), Robert Bloch's "The Dynamics of an Asteroid," and "The Adventure of the Russian Grave," by William Barton and Michael Capobianco. And believe it or not, a Spider-Man novel (*The Revenge of the Sinister Six*) references Moriarty's book, noting that it was said to still be the authority on "orbital bombardment." A Moriarty reference has even found its way into *Star Wars* literature, via Timothy Zahn's warlord *Nuso Esva*, a character based on the professor.

As if these embellishments of a single sentence weren't enough, a 1993 Bradley E. Schaefer paper published by the *Journal of the British Astronomical Association* dives even deeper. His paper considers what might have been in such a work and how it would have fit with the prevailing theories and concerns of astronomy of the time.

Schaefer's work ("Sherlock Holmes and some astronomical connections") theorizes that "Moriarty must have been one of the astronomer/mathematicians so common in the era of positional astronomy." Schaefer suggests that Moriarty may have been based on one of the well-known astronomers of the day, such as Simon Newcomb. He also considers the precise wording of Moriarty's book. The title was "a peculiar one. This work was published sometime in the 1860s or soon thereafter. In 1867, Daniel Kirkwood had discovered and explained the 'Kirkwood Gaps', or regions in the asteroid belts where few asteroids are to be found since the orbits in the gaps are unstable to perturbations by massive Jupiter. But if Moriarty had anticipated or extended these discoveries, then his book title would have been something like *The Dynamics of Asteroids*. By the 1860s, over 100 asteroids had been discovered, so perhaps the singular asteroid had some special orbital property? But the first Earth-crossing asteroid (Eros) was discovered in 1898." And, referencing Asimov's short story, Schaefer notes, "Asimov concluded that the title could only refer to the single asteroidal planet with an orbit between Mars and Jupiter whose breakup created the many asteroid fragments seen today."

Schaefer essentially works out substantial historical support for an evil genius fascinated by the mechanics of planetary cataclysms. We'll never know how much Doyle considered the actual contents of *The Dynamics of an Asteroid*, but the case Schaefer lays out is certainly plausible.

Other writers and scientists have suggested that Moriarty's work could have presciently implied chaos theory 25 years before Poincare's work in that direction. And the mathematicians Alain Goriely and Simon Norton both suggested that, given the timing, the treatise could have been a submission to King Oscar II of Sweden's celestial mechanics contest. Of course, we'll never know if Doyle had ever developed additional backstory behind the treatise, but we do know somewhere there's probably a mathematician doing just that.

# Don't Believe Everything You Read!

*Howard Hughes's autobiography,* The Amityville Horror, *the astounding story of a young Holocaust survivor who lived with a pack of wolves—great stories, but none of them are true.*

✳   ✳   ✳   ✳

IN 2006, THE literary world reeled when it learned that writer James Frey's heart-wrenching memoir, *A Million Little Pieces*, was more fiction than fact. But literary hoaxes are nothing new. Over the years, dozens of books published as nonfiction have turned out to be nothing more than literary lies. Here are some of the most famous.

**The "Autobiography" of Howard Hughes:** Con artists Clifford Irving and Richard Suskind almost hit the big time in 1971 when they penned the "memoirs" of the world's most famous recluse. The book was allegedly based on interviews between Howard Hughes and Irving. Just months before the book's scheduled release, Hughes came out of hiding to denounce the work as a fraud.

***Misha: A Memoire of the Holocaust Years***: Belgian writer Misha Defonseca (real name: Monique de Wael) alleged in her 1997 best-selling autobiography that as a child she had escaped the horrors of the Holocaust by trekking across Europe, protected by a pack of wolves. In 2008, she admitted that neither that story, nor her claim of being Jewish, was true.

***The Amityville Horror: A True Story***: In 1977, George and Kathy Lutz fast-talked writer Jay Anson into penning this book about their terrifying experiences while living in a supposedly haunted house in the Long Island town of Amityville. Brimming with all manner of evil goings-on, the Lutz's story continues to be debated: Was it a clever hoax or a terrifying truth? Nevertheless, the experience was the subject of nine Amityville movies.

***Angel at the Fence: The True Story of a Love That Survived***: Herman and Roma Rosenblat convinced the world that they met and fell in love while Herman was a prisoner in a German concentration camp during World War II. Oprah Winfrey twice had the couple on her talk show and called their tale "the single greatest love story" that was ever told on her show. But, in 2008, Berkley Books cancelled *Angel at the Fence* at the last minute when it was revealed that their love story was pure fiction. In reality, the Rosenblats met each other on a blind date in New York after the war.

***The Heart Is Deceitful Above All Things***: This 2001 book spun the troubled life of author JT LeRoy, an HIV-positive former drug addict and two-bit hustler. Its popularity even led to a 2004 movie based on the book. In reality, "LeRoy" was New York writer Laura Albert. After the ruse was discovered, in 2007, Albert was convicted of fraud and ordered to pay reparations.

***I, Libertine***: Some literary hoaxes are done not so much to scam as to make a point. In this case, humorist Jean Shepherd wanted to prove that bestseller lists were compiled based not only on actual sales figures but also on requests at bookstores. In 1956, Shepherd encouraged his radio show listeners to visit their local bookshops and request the nonexistent book *I, Libertine* by Frederick R. Ewing. When shops actually became interested in carrying copies of *I, Libertine*, publisher Ian Ballantine hired science fiction author Theodore Sturgeon to write the book based on Shepherd's outline. Sturgeon churned out the manuscript in one exhausting session, with Ballantine's wife, Betty, penning the final chapter after Sturgeon fell asleep. Proceeds from the book were donated to charity.

# The (Mostly) Fictional Book of the Dead

*H.P. Lovecraft's infamous book is one of the most well-known and referenced texts in literature, TV shows, and movies in the twentieth century. But does this eerie tome merely serve as a multipurpose literary tool, or is it a grimoire filled with terrible and forbidden things?*

✳ ✳ ✳ ✳

NECRONOMICON IS A title that exudes the very essence of H.P. Lovecraft's intention: to instill terrified curiosity in all readers who learn of it. Lovecraft, though often contradicted by actual translators, noted that the book's title means "an image of the law of the dead" when translated from Greek. Other translations of the text's title include variations on "book of dead names," an apt alternate translation of the tome's title considering the connection between the fictional text and the real-life Egyptian *Book of the Dead*. Lovecraft's *Necronomicon* is a fictional amalgamation of real-life texts, and it has held a powerful allure for cultists and magic practitioners practically since the first mention of it in 1924. Lovecraft claimed throughout his lifetime that the book was entirely fictional and that readers would be disappointed in the book if it did actually exist, even leaving errors in the book's backstory to keep it from seeming too infallible. Despite all of this, exactly how close is the *Necronomicon* to reality?

# Pseudo-History

The legend of the *Necronomicon* survived its creator, via his own pseudo-history entitled *The History of the Necronomicon* published after Lovecraft's death. Within this short manuscript, Lovecraft provides a detailed account of the long, storied history of the tome, beginning with its author.

Lovecraft refers to Abdul Alhazred, a "half-crazed Arab" who lived in the eighth century. Alhazred worshiped the entities Yog-Sothoth and Cthulu and acquired the knowledge that would ultimately be recorded in the *Necronomicon*. Alhazred allegedly visited the ruins of Babylon, Memphis, and the Empty Quarter of Arabia before moving to Damascus, where he composed the tome, which he dubbed *Al Azif*. The title, as Lovecraft described and in an apparent reference to Beelzebub (Lord of the Flies), referred back to the sound of nocturnal insect calls often compared to and suggested to be the howling of demons. Alhazred reportedly died mysteriously in 738, an incident his contemporary Ibn Khallikan described as occurring when he was seized and devoured by an invisible monster in broad daylight.

Theodorus Philetas of Constantinople translated *Al Azif* into Greek in 950. Copies were subsequently seized and burned by Patriarch Michael in 1050. Almost two centuries later, the book was translated from Greek into Latin by Olaus Wormius in 1228, a suggestion entirely inconsistent with the fact that Wormius actually lived from 1588 to 1654. Lovecraft posits that Pope Gregory IX banned both the Latin and Greek versions in 1232, though Latin editions were produced in fifteenth century Germany and seventeenth century Spain. A Greek edition was printed in Italy during the sixteenth century. During the Elizabethan era in England, John Dee undertook the final reported translation of the text. Though he completed a translation of the *Necronomicon*, this version was never printed and only fragments of this translation survived.

Lovecraft's pseudo-history of the *Necronomicon* includes a stark warning: Beware the contents of this book. According to Lovecraft, and entirely in line with most descriptions of arcane magic within the horror genre, the pursuit of ancient and dark knowledge almost inevitably leads to a gruesome end.

### Liber Fictionis

The *Necronomicon* first appeared in Lovecraft's 1924 short story, "The Hound." When the narrator and his friend, St. John, uncover a centuries-old grave, they find within it a jade amulet that they recognize from the *Necronomicon*. The theft of this object brings about a series of odd and unfortunate events that eventually drive the pair into madness. This story sets the tone of the Cthulhu Mythos in general.

Additionally, the book appeared within two of Lovecraft's novellas, *At the Mountains of Madness* and *The Case of Charles Dexter Ward*. Despite making cameos in several different written works and being a major item within the Cthulhu Mythos, not many specifics were ever divulged about the book's contents. This was not done out of negligence—Lovecraft once wrote, "If anyone here were to try to write the *Necronomicon*, it would disappoint all those who have shuddered at cryptic references to it." With that said, it's likely that Lovecraft intentionally kept details about the content sparse so as to maintain the potential horror suggested by its unknown contents. If every reader knew exactly what was in it or what it looked like, it would no longer be an enigmatic object filled with secret horrors. Additionally, Lovecraft placed a lot of importance on the accessibility of the *Necronomicon* and the Cthulhu Mythos—he wanted other horror writers to use it and add to it, creating a large shared world—a precursor to the Marvel cinematic universe, it might be argued. If no one knows exactly what's inside of the book, then it can be used however the author requires. It can contain any sort of information, curses, or history that proves useful, or detrimental, to the story's characters.

## What We Do Know

The *Necronomicon* is a fairly large and substantial text. In *The Dunwich Horror*, one of the characters visits a library to consult an "abridged" copy of the *Necronomicon* for a spell that appears on the 751st page. This is one of the few instances where a passage from the actual book is written down, and it shows how dense and detailed the book is. Here is but a snippet of the long paragraph: "The Old Ones were, the Old Ones are, and the Old Ones shall be. Not in the spaces we know, but between them, they walk serene and primal, undimensioned and to us unseen. Yog-Sothoth knows the gate. Yog-Sothoth is the gate. Yog-Sothoth is the key and guardian of the gate."

The *Necronomicon*'s physical appearance has never been plainly described in any of Lovecraft's works, but it is typically portrayed as bound in leather of various types and having metal clasps. According to Lovecraft's *History of the Necronomicon*, copies of the original *Necronomicon* are only held in five different institutions in the world: the British Museum, the Bibliothèque Nationale de France, the Widener Library of Harvard University, the University of Buenos Aires, and the library of the fictional Miskatonic University in Massachusetts. However, there are a few characters in various Lovecraft stories who have private copies of the *Necronomicon*.

## Reality Is Often Stranger Than Fiction

Despite the fact that Lovecraft himself stated on several occasions that the book was fictional, this has not stopped rumors to the contrary. Pranksters have listed it as "for sale" in bookstore newsletters and have made fake entries for the book in library card catalogs. There is also a belief that the Vatican Library holds a copy of the book, resulting in it receiving requests for information about the book from enthusiasts.

An indecipherable version written in a fake language was issued by Owlswick Press in 1973, and a book claiming to be the "real" *Necronomicon* was published by a person known only as

"Simon." It had little connection to Lovecraft's *Necronomicon*, instead being based on Sumerian mythology, and has been dubbed the *Simon Necronomicon*. It has been in print since 1980 and has sold over 800,000 copies, making it the most popular "real-life" version of the book.

In 1978, another fake version of the *Necronomicon* was released. Written by occultist Robert Turner and edited by George Hay, this hoax version claims that it was written from a computer analysis of a cipher text written by Renaissance mathematician, astronomer, alchemist, and occultist John Dee. Despite being a fanciful façade, this version is apparently far truer to the Lovecraftian version than the Simon text, even incorporating quotations from Lovecraft's stories in its passages.

## Everybody's a Critic!

Many books have claimed to be the true *Necronomicon*. Some have claimed to have determined whether the tome actually exists or ever existed. One of the latter is *The Necronomicon Files* published in 1998. It covered the aforementioned well-known versions of the *Necronomicon*, along with a few more obscure ones. In 2004, Canadian occultist Donald Tyson published *Necronomicon: The Wanderings of Alhazred*, which is also thought to be fairly close to Lovecraft's version, but Tyson did clearly state that the *Necronomicon* is fictional. Despite this statement, critics have claimed that Tyson must be working on behalf of "The Old Ones" due to his statements lulling readers into a false sense of security. It seems as though you can't win no matter what you say!

In his 1972 book, *The Magical Revival*, Kenneth Grant suggests that there was an unconscious connection between Aleister Crowley and H.P. Lovecraft. As a British occultist and a disciple of Crowley, Grant believed that they both drew on the same occult forces, albeit through magic in Crowley's case and through dreams for Lovecraft. His ideas were featured heavily in the *Simon Necronomicon* and supported by Tyson.

# The War of the Worlds: Misinformation and Misdirection

*Would you believe it if the radio told you that aliens were invading New Jersey?*

✳ ✳ ✳ ✳

I
T WAS 1938 AND tensions were rising around the world. Radio had become the American public's main source of news and entertainment and few questioned the validity of what they heard on the air, considering even the president used the format for his famous fireside chats. The day before Halloween, the Mercury Theater presented their holiday special, an adaptation of an H.G. Wells novel.

As the hour went on, people tuning in after the initial introduction were more and more convinced that the program was a real news account rather than a fictional drama. The sound effects and production convinced millions of Americans that Martians were invading New Jersey. Calls to emergency services clogged up phone lines and people ran through the streets, desperate to reach loved ones.

There is no question that *The War of the Worlds* broadcast, similar to today's mocumentaries, happened—it's recorded and well documented. It is also responsible for catapulting its director, Orson Welles, to stardom. The question today is how much panic it actually caused.

After all was said and done, the FCC declined to reprimand anyone involved in the production and there's actually little surviving evidence of mass hysteria. Instead, it's more likely that newspapers of the time deliberately inflated the reports, attacking radio with a zeal. At that time, many major and local newspapers believed that radio would ultimately make them obsolete, giving reporters and newsrooms every reason to pick up the first opportunity to attack the utility of the service.

Orson Welles' response to the program's controversy oscillated between regret and glee for the rest of his career. It undoubtedly served as the singular event that propelled him to a status in Hollywood that few other directors have achieved. To this day, there's no clear answer as to whether or not he intended to create panic with the program, but later references to it in entertainment and associated discussions of media literacy continue to view it as a major moment in broadcast history.

## The Baker Street Detective

*He's the most famous detective in the world, with over 25,000 adaptations on film and stage by the 1990s—and all of his feats are fictional.*

✳    ✳    ✳    ✳

THE RECLUSIVE DETECTIVE that has defined detective fiction more than any of his predecessors first appeared in Arthur Conan Doyle's 1887 book *A Study in Scarlet*. Sherlock Holmes' popularity exploded, prompting a loyal fan base so dedicated that Conan Doyle's attempt to kill off the character failed and he was forced to bring the detective back from the grave. The character is undeniably ubiquitous within the genre, to the point that some fans believe him to have been a real person. A character that feels as real as Holmes has to have some basis in reality, right?

Over the century since Holmes's first appearance in print, a number of figures have emerged as the inspiration for the Bohemian detective. On the literary side, Conan Doyle acknowledged Edgar Allan Poe's C. Auguste Dupin (the first fictional detective) as the first archetype for his most famous character. Holmes savants have also found similarities between the detective and Monsieur Lecoq, another famous fictional detective invented around the same time as Holmes. In real life, Conan Doyle acknowledged two inspirations for the character. These real-world inspirations were Joseph Bell, a surgeon at the Royal Infirmary of Edinburgh whose attitude and ability to draw quick conclusions from small details heavily influenced the development of Holmes. Sir Henry Littlejohn also served as an inspiration, providing a direct connection between medical investigation and detective work that allowed Conan Doyle to expand Holmes's scientific know-how through his cases.

# The Legendary Lumberjack and Fakelore

*From Minnesota's 10,000 lakes to the Grand Canyon, America's legendary lumberjack has been ever present in American culture for over a century.*

✳   ✳   ✳   ✳

FROM ANIMATED CHILDREN'S shows to forty-foot statues, the giant lumberjack known as Paul Bunyan is one of the most recognizable American folk heroes. In 1916, William B. Laughead produced the first known written record of the Paul Bunyan legend in the form of advertisement pamphlets. The campaign, produced for the Red River Lumber Company, took off after the second round of pamphlets was produced and the oral legend of Bunyan originally shared in logging camps and among workers grew and transformed into a something of a cultural zeitgeist.

Bunyan's life story includes fantastical tales of an enormous blue ox, creating the Grand Canyon with an ax, and the making of Minnesota's 10,000 lakes by way of giant footprints. Obviously, Paul Bunyan didn't exist in a literal sense, but the origin of his story is also contentious. Many modern scholars believe the nine-foot lumberjack is an example of fakelore, referring to a legend that's inflated by its creators to convince the public it's a much older tale than it is.

The legitimacy of earlier oral traditions surrounding Paul Bunyan is also up for debate. It's hard to say if Bunyan was ever a real person or whether his biography was entirely fabricated by Laughead for an advertising campaign.

Advertising lore notwithstanding, there is at least one possible real-life inspiration for the legendary lumberjack. Fabian Fournier, also known as Saginaw Joe, was born in Canada in the mid-nineteenth century, where he lived until shortly after the American Civil War, when he moved to Michigan to take advantage of the state's high-paying logging jobs. He was reputedly over six feet tall, far above the average for an American male at the time, and he spent much of his free time drinking, carousing, and brawling. He ultimately died in either 1875 or 1876 during—what else?— a bar fight. His bones ended up at the University of Michigan due to his unusual jawbone and alleged two rows of teeth, ultimately leaving the school with one of the best claims to being the resting place for the inspiration for Paul Bunyan.

# The Tornado-Wrangling Texas Cowboy

*Pecos Bill was an iconic symbol of westward expansion with a wild cast of characters to match.*

✳ ✳ ✳ ✳

AMONG THE VAST cast of American folk heroes, who could better fill the role of Southwestern cowboy than Pecos Bill? The chaotic cowboy's story was riddled with wild tales. In childhood he supposedly was lost near the Pecos River. Then he was raised by coyotes. He only returned to civilization years later. The cast of his story included his horse Widow-Maker, who was the most prolific folklore-based killer in Texas history, a snake named Shake that Pecos Bill used as a lasso, and Slue-Foot Sue, his one-time wife who was bounced off Widow-Maker so hard that she ended up either on the moon or in Russia for a match-up with Baba Yaga.

Like Paul Bunyan, Pecos Bill is credited with creating some rather preposterous landmarks, including the Gulf of Mexico and the Rio Grande. In Pecos Bill's lore, a severe drought prompted the cowboy to head to California and lasso a storm cloud to bring back to Texas. The storm raged for too long, though, and ultimately formed the Gulf of Mexico. In another instance Pecos Bill and Widow-Maker were stuck in the middle of the desert without any water, prompting Pecos Bill to pick up a stick and dig the famous Rio Grande.

Obviously, Pecos Bill as he's known in folklore and literature never existed in real life. He, like so many other figures, represents the American spirit of expansion during the nineteenth century and put a face to the movement that the American public could identify with. Pecos Bill might not have existed as a physical person, but he definitely exists within American culture.

# John Henry: The Legendary Steel Driver Who Took on the Railroads

*The tragic John Henry folk tale has unsurprisingly resonated with blue-collar workers, and the character has become a mythical figurehead within the American labor movement. Did the tale have a real-life origin?*

✳   ✳   ✳   ✳

ONE OF THE most urgent causes of the nineteenth century was obvious, considering the vast westward expansion that defined so much of early American history: connecting the country via railroads. After the Civil War, rail companies contracted heavily with prisons, using prisoners as cheap labor to lay rail at breakneck speed. The legend of John Henry arose from around this time: the story of an African American freedman working on the rail resonated with many people during the time period.

Historians believe the story spread primarily through a classic blues folk song. This song claimed to document John Henry's competition against a steel drill—a competition that ultimately led to his death. The legend says that John Henry competed against the railroad company's new steam-powered drill to prove that humans could beat the new technology.

He won the competition at the expense of his own life. The intense nature of the competition caused something in his body to fail, either his heart or a blood vessel in his brain, and he dropped dead shortly after the competition.

Given some of the very realistic elements underlining the story, scholars have sought a real-life origin for the legendary steel-driving hero. It is generally agreed that there are two primary options for such a historical person.

The first is less likely and involves West Virginia's Big Bend Tunnel. This theory relies on the fact that some versions of the song reference this specific tunnel. However, there is little other evidence to support the theory. In fact, the company that constructed the tunnel denied that steam powered drills were ever used in the tunnel.

The other (more convincing) theory involves the Lewis Tunnel. Modern researchers have traced the story of a prisoner from the Virginia Penitentiary at the time who was sent to work on the railroad. He participated in a competition that took place 40 miles away from the prison at the Lewis Tunnel, where steam drills were by then regularly employed alongside prison laborers—a situation that likely drew the ire of some. Scott Nelson, the main proponent of this theory, further points out that the earliest versions of the song suggest that Henry was buried in a pauper's grave near a "white house." Though tangential, it is suggested that this was in fact a mass grave located behind a real-life white building at the Virginia State Penitentiary. Quite possibly the tale has its origins here.

# William Tell's Tale

*The European country now known best for its seeming perpetual neutrality has a long history of being not so neutral.*

✳  ✳  ✳  ✳

OVER FIVE HUNDRED years before the unification of Germany, Central Europe was known as the Holy Roman Empire, with small states ruled by dukes and princes that ultimately reported to the Holy Roman Emperor, a title at the time vested in the House of Habsburg. In the early fourteenth century, a figure emerged within the Swiss resistance to a duke's rule. His legendary story endures to this day.

Albrecht Gessler was the tyrannical ruler of a part of modern-day Switzerland, going so far as putting his hat on a pole and requiring locals to pay deference to the inanimate object. One day, a certain William Tell, on a walk with his son, refused to bow to the hat while walking past. He was promptly arrested and jailed with his son. But he was offered a deal: If he could shoot an apple off his son's head, they would both go free. He complied, shooting an apple off the top of his son's head right before escaping and later assassinating Gessler for his tyrannical behavior.

The truth of the story has never been entirely proven or disproven and the historical veracity of Tell's existence and rebellion continues to be a mystery. However, his impact on modern Switzerland can't be overstated. The folk story of Tell has inspired a number of resistance acts over the years, with retellings and adaptations of the story keeping it firmly within the public eye. Tell acted as a symbol of resistance over the centuries, serving as a figure of inspiration for positive and negative figures, including John Wilkes Booth. Tell's story and figure is preserved around the world, with statues and plays commemorating the story of rebellion with little regard for whether or not it's accurate.

# Dracula, King of Darkness

*Possibly the most famous vampire in the world, Dracula has inspired countless artistic works in the century since he was penned into his existence. Bram Stoker's brilliant inspiration was to flesh out the monster lurking beneath the cape.*

✳   ✳   ✳   ✳

COUNT DRACULA WAS the archetypical vampire of the twentieth century. A Transylvanian nobleman, he was a highly intelligent military man in life, having successfully led troops against the Turkish empire. After rising from the dead as a vampire, he maintained a castle estate with three female vampire companions.

Upon becoming a vampire, Dracula gained several new strengths and weaknesses. Some of his most well-known powers were his supernatural strength and the ability to shape-shift into the form of different animals. Additionally, he could command animals to do his bidding and manipulate the weather in a few different ways, such as by creating fog and rain storms. He had hypnotic, telepathic, and illusion-making abilities that allowed him to affect humans in his domain and, particularly, humans he fed from. This enabled him to keep an iron-clad hold on his castle and territories, even aiding him in traveling to and from England.

But consider: The life of a centuries-old vampire wasn't all moonlight and daisies. Dracula had a number of lesser-known weaknesses, such as a blood thirst he had difficulty controlling, a weakness against garlic, crucifixes, and other holy symbols, and the inability to enter hallowed ground. He also could not supernaturally cross running water, and required assistance boarding and disembarking from boats. Contrary to common belief, Dracula would not burn to true death in the sun—he could actually travel quite freely during the day. However, he wasn't able to use most of his powers then. He was also compelled to enter a sleep-like state in which he couldn't awaken or move, and in this state he was unaware of people in his presence. This had the effect of putting him in an extremely vulnerable state daily. He could also be killed via sacred bullet while he was in his coffin.

One of Dracula's quintessential traits was his uncontrollable lust for blood. He required regular feedings—preferably on women—to survive, with all of his powers deriving from the stolen blood. Blood also had the effect of stalling his physical aging, even causing him to grow younger. He did not need to eat or drink anything else to survive and remain immortal.

## Making a Monster

Count Dracula first appeared in Bram Stoker's novel, *Dracula*, in 1897. It is said that on the night of March 8, 1890, Stoker had a nightmare involving blood-sucking creatures after having eaten too much "dressed crab." He began writing *Dracula* shortly thereafter.

In his process of developing the iconic character, Stoker took inspiration from a variety of sources. One of those came from stories his mother, Charlotte Blake, told him of life during famine. She told Stoker tales of starving people wandering the countryside, appearing gaunt and pale—as though they were the living dead. She also described to him accounts of cannibalism due to sheer desperation, including the practice of sucking blood from dead or nearly dead bodies. Horrifically enough, some people were buried alive during a cholera epidemic in the 1830s, so that they wouldn't spread the disease to other people. Additionally, bloodletting as a treatment for various illnesses was still commonplace at the time. All of these nightmarish, real-life horrors could have lent ample inspiration to Stoker for Dracula.

In addition to these real-life events lending some initial inspiration, Stoker would have certainly heard of the 1872 Gothic novel, *Carmilla*, written by fellow Irish author Sheridan Le

Fanu. *Carmilla* displays a lot of the tropes of Gothic horror fiction that *Dracula* employs, including the dangerous vampire antagonist, the setting of a dark castle, a mysterious atmosphere, controversial romance, and various elements of superstition and folklore.

While not being the earliest "modern" vampire, Dracula has transcended generations, inspiring countless horror authors, artists, and filmmakers. He has become the archetype of the modern vampire and has a legacy that continues to this day.

# The Detective Who Wrote His Own Story

*Who do you remember most? The author or the protagonist?*

✳   ✳   ✳   ✳

ELLERY QUEEN HAS the somewhat unique distinction of being both a fictional detective and a pen name. Created in 1928 by Frederic Dannay and Manfred Bennington Lee for a contest, the famous pen name was created due to the authors' belief that readers would always remember the detective's name and almost never remember the authors. Little did Dannay and Lee know at the time what their creation would lead to.

Ellery Queen has served as the protagonist of dozens of novels, forming one of the most famous collections of detective fiction from the golden age of the genre, as well as serving as the *nom de plume* for dozens of novels, some of which were written by authors other than Dannay and Lee. Originally, many readers believed the detective was created by SS Van Dine, the creator of Philo Vance, the obvious fictional inspiration for the character. Like SS Van Dine, Queen has a broad and elaborate backstory that rapidly changes after the first few books, with no true consensus on his background history—thanks to the authors' own inconsistencies regarding their character.

Ellery Queen's fair play mysteries have been adapted into radio and film several times over the years, a facet of the series' central role within the golden age of detective fiction. The detective also went on to serve as the namesake for the classic *Ellery Queen's Mystery Magazine*, which was founded in 1941 and continues to print new editions to this day. Dannay and Lee created one of the most iconic figures within American detective fiction, with a stature comparable to even Sherlock Holmes. It's safe to say that Ellery Queen lived on after Dannay and Lee's deaths in 1982 and 1971.

# Insult or Imitation: The Origin of Kilgore Trout

*Fictional characters usually have some element of reality ingrained in their personality or situation. When does that become a bad thing?*

✳   ✳   ✳   ✳

KURT VONNEGUT IS without a doubt one of the most notable authors of the twentieth century, with his novel *Slaughterhouse-Five* firmly seated within the canon of great American literature. But one of his most prolific characters has a fascinating though somewhat concerning origin story.

In 1957, Theodore Sturgeon, already a prolific science fiction author, moved to Truro, Massachusetts, the home of the up-and-coming Vonnegut. The two became friends, spending time together while in Truro. The pair subsequently moved to entirely different cities, at which point Vonnegut published *God Bless You, Mr. Rosewater*, marking Kilgore Trout's entrance to Vonnegut's literary universe.

Even Trout's name was a clear reference to Vonnegut's one-time friend, with the unpleasant characterization of Trout seemingly reflecting the author's view of his former friend. Trout had a struggling career as a novelist, paralleling the downward spiral of Sturgeon's real-life career, and Vonnegut ultimately acknowledged the connection between his character and Sturgeon after the latter's death.

Trout became a constant in Vonnegut's work, acting not only as a focal point but as a side or background character who connects seemingly entirely different stories. Throughout these stories, Trout's characterization and even appearance changes, apparently on the author's whim, giving him an inadvertent mythical quality where he changes into whatever is needed at a given moment.

One novel has even been attributed to Kilgore Trout in the real world. Philip José Farmer wrote *Venus on the Half-Shell* and published it under the pen name of Kilgore Trout. Due to the strong ties between the character and Kurt Vonnegut, many people believed the novel was written by Vonnegut, including critics. Vonnegut refuted this idea many times over the years, often via obscenity-riddled phone calls expressing his displeasure. Trout has also been referenced across a whole body of literature, placing him firmly within a class of fictional characters that transcend their original role.

# The King of Horror's Alter Ego

*Author Richard Bachman seemingly came out of nowhere. An unverifiable author bio, complete with a supposed stint in the Coast Guard and a vaguely-sketched life in rural New Hampshire, raised eyebrows. Did he even exist?*

✳   ✳   ✳   ✳

STEPHEN KING, ONE of the most iconic horror and thriller writers of all time, had a problem at the beginning of his career. At the time, most publishing houses believed that authors could only publish one book a year without oversaturating the market, leaving King, who is notorious for writing an almost absurd number of books every year, at a crossroads. He ultimately convinced Signet Books, his publisher at the time, to allow him to write under a pseudonym—Richard Bachman.

The pen name lacked longevity, however, as King wasn't particularly subtle in disguising his writing style. This led to a bookstore clerk discovering the connection and ultimately outing the alter ego with King's permission.

All told, King published seven books under the pseudonym, not including the four-book collection published in 1985 that incorporated the first four. Bachman's first novel, *Rage*, was published in 1977. It was allowed to go out of print in the 1990s after the text served as an inspiration for the Heath High School shooting.

In a later release, King supplies a sort of eulogy for his pen name, saying that Bachman had died in 1985 of "cancer of the pseudonym." King has continued to honor his former pen name, insisting that the writing credit for *The Running Man* movie be given to Bachman rather than himself and even playing Bachman in a TV adaptation of one of his books.

King has noted over the years that Bachman was also a way for him to explore his own career, though he considers the experiment a failure because of how quickly he was outed.

# America's Advice Columnists: Abigail Van Buren and Pauline Phillips

*Dear Abby is one of the most culturally ubiquitous newspaper columns in American culture, synonymous with the advice genre.*

✳ ✳ ✳ ✳

ABIGAIL VAN BUREN, a pen name based on an Old Testament prophetess and President Martin Van Buren, skyrocketed in popularity almost immediately after her debut, quickly becoming one of the most widely read columnists in the world. Her signature wit and commonsensical advice defined her long-time place within the American press and endeared her to readers. "Dear Abby" remains one of the quintessential advice columns to this day.

Pauline Phillips created the column and the pen name in 1956, a few months after her twin sister took over the Ann Landers column in Chicago, one of the most popular advice columns at the time. Phillips earned a place at the *San Francisco Chronicle* first. From there her column became syndicated, with a countrywide reach. By 1987, it was featured in over 1,200 newspapers.

For decades, Phillips and her twin sister, Esther Lederer, ran competing advice columns, leading to a great deal of animosity between the two. Phillips heavily contributed to the feud, including offering her column at a discounted rate to newspapers on the condition that the newspaper agree not to carry Lederer's column. The sisters later reconciled, though they maintained a cool distance.

Phillips continued to write the "Dear Abby" column by herself until her daughter Jeanne joined her in 1987. Jeanne Phillips became the primary author of the column in 2000 and the only author in 2002, when Pauline Phillips's battle with Alzheimer's disease prevented her from further contribution to the column. Pauline Phillips died in 2013 and her daughter continued to write the column.

Today, "Dear Abby" remains one of the most prominent advice columns in the country, with a national readership of the column reportedly reaching 110 million in 2016. The column has faced criticism, especially in recent years, but it doesn't appear to be going away. Abigail Van Buren has guided the country for over seventy years, and Pauline Phillips's legacy will survive in the media for years to come.

# Carolyn Keene: Mother(s) of an Icon

*What's in a name? Apparently not much when it comes to the much-loved "author" of one of America's most successful creations in young adult and children's literature.*

✳    ✳    ✳    ✳

SINCE THE FIRST Nancy Drew book was published in 1930, the character has appeared in hundreds of books, all purportedly written by Carolyn Keene—a feat that should be impossible for a single author to complete. And that's because it is. At least 29 writers contributed to the original Nancy Drew canon, because Carolyn Keene was a pseudonym invented by the Stratemeyer Syndicate as a part of their pioneering book packaging process, allowing multiple authors to contribute to the iconic character's canon over the decades, with new books still produced and published on a fairly regular basis to this day.

In the first three decades of the twentieth century, the Stratemeyer Syndicate came to define the industry of book packaging. The company would propose potential series to a publishing house, outline plots, and contract outside writers to produce the manuscript. This process was remarkably effective: a 1922 survey suggesting that over half of the books read by children in the United States were produced by the syndicate.

By the late 1920s, Edward Stratemeyer—the founder of the syndicate—decided to produce more children's mystery books. With the immense success of the Hardy Boys series, Stratemeyer decided that it would be a smart business decision to produce a female companion series. After a successful proposal to the syndicate's publisher at the time (Grosset and Dunlap), Stratemeyer moved forward with the first set of Nancy Drew books, contracting a writer who had worked with the syndicate previously to draft the first Nancy Drew book.

## Mildred Wirt Benson

Mildred Wirt Benson was a trailblazer from a young age, earning a degree in English from the University of Iowa in only three years and then returning to the same university to become the first student to receive a master's degree in Journalism from the university. After completing her education, she began a long, storied career of writing that would span multiple publishers, four pen names, and more than 130 books. Benson should also appear at the top of the list as contender for the title of the "real" Carolyn Keene.

Benson began working for the syndicate in the late 1920s, when she was hired to write entries to the Ruth Fielding series. Like other ghost writers for the syndicate, Benson was provided with a plot outline, which she converted into a manuscript in exchange for payment of anywhere between $125 to $250 (equivalent to multiple months of a journalist's wages at the time). She also had to sign away all rights to future royalties and agree not to admit to writing any specific series.

Her work impressed Stratemeyer enough that she was his first choice when the Nancy Drew proposal came down the pipeline. Provided with an outline and Stratemeyer's suggestion that the character not fall out of line with societal expectations for the time, Benson created an unexpected titular character. She infused pieces of herself into the character and developed a fiery, independent teenage detective—one that flew in the face of Edward Stratemeyer's original vision. Nonetheless, Nancy Drew became a near-instant cultural icon. Benson would go on to write 23 of the original 30 Nancy Drew books, having arguably one of the greatest impacts on the character's development over the long course of her history.

## Harriet Adams

Harriet Stratemeyer Adams, the daughter of the founder of the Stratemeyer syndicate, would take over operations after his death in 1930. She became heavily involved in the Nancy Drew series, at first writing outlines for each book as her father had and asserting, like her father, that the titular character should take on a softer demeanor, with notable changes to the character's actions and dialogue in later books marking the beginning of Adams' changes to the series.

Most glaringly, after management changes in the 1950s forced Mildred Benson out, Adams began rewriting the original books, making major deviations in the characterization of Nancy Drew and softening the assertive girl detective to a more pliable version of the character.

While Benson created the character, Adams redefined her, creating a more familiar version of the iconic series heroine—still in print to this day—giving Harriet Adams the second claim to being the "real" Carolyn Keene.

## The (Legal) Battle of the Publishers

By 1979, Harriet Adams was becoming increasingly frustrated with Grosset & Dunlap, and made the decision to switch publishers to Simon & Schuster. At this point, Grosset & Dunlap sued the syndicate for breach of contract. The lawsuit brought the syndicate into the public eye, a place the company had long avoided, and Mildred Wirt Benson was called to the stand, where she acknowledged her role in writing the original series, despite Adams's assertion that she had written all the books by herself within her tenure at the syndicate.

The court ultimately decided in the syndicate's favor, allowing them to switch publishers, but the secret was out. There was no Carolyn Keene, just a series of ghost writers and a company that controlled it all. In the end, the Stratemeyer Syndicate was sold to Simon & Schuster, who contracted out to another book packaging company to produce even more books focused around Nancy Drew. The character's contribution to popular culture is undeniable, as is the impact of both Mildred Wirt Benson and Harriet Stratemeyer Adams.

# The Burger-Slinging Clown and Charity

*The very first version of the McDonald's clown wore a cup as a nose and featured a burger-producing belt buckle. Today, the iconic red-headed clown raises millions of dollars for chronically ill children.*

✳ ✳ ✳ ✳

FROM A BURGER-SLINGING clown to the mascot of an international charity providing lodging for sick children and their families, the clown that debuted in 1963 has remained in the American eye for over half a century. Ronald was born out of the absence of another clown–Bozo–who served a similar role in advertising for the company before he was taken off air. The figure of a friendly burger-slinging clown had been so popular that McDonald's executives decided to create a more permanent, trademarked character to serve the same role.

Ronald McDonald served as the mascot of the iconic golden-arched restaurant for decades, facing down controversy surrounding his role in promoting childhood obesity with a stiff lip and a refusal to change, in whatever outfit and with whatever sidekicks he had at any given time. This continued until the clown sightings of 2016. After a series of reputedly "creepy" clown sightings across the country brought about a general feeling of unease about clowns in public areas, McDonald's decided to pull Ronald from public appearances and gave him a greatly reduced profile.

Despite his removal from McDonald's restaurants, Ronald has remained a fixture in another area: Ronald McDonald's House Charities. As the namesake and mascot, Ronald plays a large role in raising money and awareness for the charity, providing funding for over 380 Ronald McDonald Houses in 64 countries, providing lodgings to chronically ill children and their families near hospitals and medical facilities. The houses' proximity to specialized care facilities eases the burden on families who otherwise would not be able to access the care their children need. The houses are not the only thing the RMHC provides. They also maintain family rooms within hospitals and care mobiles for communities who otherwise would not have access to basic care at all. Ronald McDonald's role has shifted over the years, from beloved restaurateur clown to the emblem of a charity that has helped hundreds of thousands of children access healthcare.

# The Smoking Cowboy

*A tobacco advertising campaign's casual invention, the Marlboro Man has become synonymous with the tobacco industry—and just as controversial.*

※　※　※　※

ONE OF THE most iconic character archetypes to arise from the American cultural mythos is the cowboy. Master of the west, free to make his own path, the American cowboy has earned a place in this country's cultural pantheon. And one of the most famous, or even infamous, examples of this character is the Marlboro Man.

In the early twentieth century, Marlboro's specialized filtered cigarettes had become a staple across the country, having been specifically tailored for women. At that time, they were considered to be cleaner, healthier, and taste less harsh—characteristics favored by women of the age who saw smoking as a step towards freedom. For much of American history, women smoking in public wasn't just a cultural taboo—in many places it was even illegal. By the 1920s, women were looking for ways to express their newfound freedom and Marlboro was more than happy to step in and provide a product that, at first, was marketed for and bought almost exclusively by women.

A few decades later, Marlboro was facing a new problem: Their early advertisements had been successful but had had the effect of narrowing their market, limiting their ability to expand the brand. They hired Philip Morris & Co. to develop an advertising campaign that would lure men to buy their product. Leo Burnett was the driving force behind that campaign. Burnett focused on searching for the most masculine figures possible to photograph smoking a filtered cigarette. From sea captains to construction workers, Burnett tried everything. But his first photograph, inspired by a 1949 *Life* magazine photo shoot, proved to be the winner. The quintessential cowboy, the Marlboro Man was portrayed by dozens of men, from actors and models to actual cowboys. And the brand had a hit on their hands.

The Marlboro Man was a constant in the advertising sphere for decades. He was the face of a generation of new smokers and attracted new customers for Marlboro. Those customers included five of the models for the Marlboro Man—Wayne McLaren, David McLean, Dick Hammer, Eric Lawson, and Jerome Edward Jackson—who later died as a result of disease caused by smoking. The success that the Marlboro Man brought to the tobacco industry was also a contributor to the epidemic of lung diseases that followed.

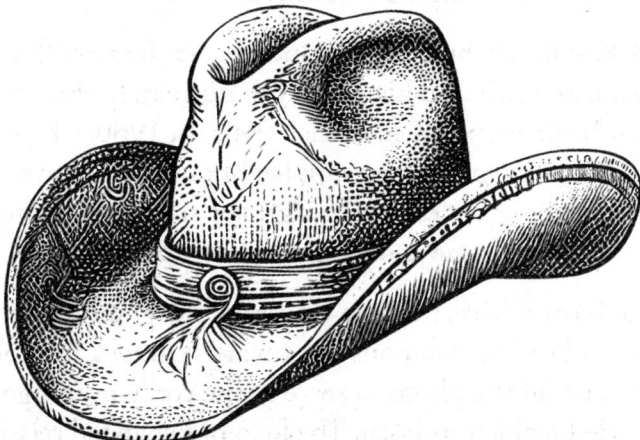

# From the Great Depression to the Digital Age: Snack Cakes and a Family Bakery

*The iconic figurehead of the first company to mass-produce and sell individually packaged snack cakes has been a part of the company since she was four, and still plays an integral role in the company's function.*

\* \* \* \*

TODAY, MOST PEOPLE can't imagine a world without pre-packaged food. From individual bags of chips to packs of cookies, today's market is full of snack packs perfected over decades of consumer selection. But the first company to market family packs of pre-wrapped snack cakes is the one that's had the same logo since 1960—Little Debbie.

The origin story of Little Debbie starts almost thirty years before the iconic logo appeared. O.D. McKee began selling snack cakes out of the back of the family car as a way to make money during the Great Depression, a business that proved successful enough for the family to buy a small bakery relatively quickly. The family lived on a tight budget for years, often living in the back of the bakery to make ends meet.

The McKee family business expanded over the next few decades, with O.D. and his wife Ruth ultimately able to buy out their business partners in the 1950s. In 1960, when O.D. was talking to his packaging supplier about their new run of family packs of snack cakes, the supplier suggested using a family member's name and likeness on the packaging.

O.D. took the advice, taking a picture of his granddaughter, Debbie, and having a famous pin-up artist draw a full color image based off the photo to serve as the company's logo. And thus Little Debbie was born. The logo has changed relatively little over the years and the original subject of the inspiration, Debbie McKee-Fowler, has even taken on a leadership role in the company, continuing the family business that has made millions with her face on grocery store shelves in every state.

# America's Baker: Betty Crocker

*Who was the kitchen maestro behind the iconic red spoon?*

✳ ✳ ✳ ✳

SPORTING AN ICONIC red logo on the side of a box, and present on the shelves of almost every grocery store in this country and many others, Betty Crocker is one of the most well-known brands in the world. Betty Crocker is an anonymous, yet seemingly real woman. She was created in the 1920s within the company that would become General Mills by an advertising executive named Bruce Barton.

Her ostensible purpose was to answer consumer questions. That role evolved over time, and she began to appear in radio and television programs, as well as on coupons for flatware, and even once being named the second most influential woman in the country, behind Eleanor Roosevelt. For almost two decades, most of the American public believed that Betty Crocker was a real person. The fact that she only answered letters and hosted radio shows meant that the public never really realized that she was more an amalgamation of many people than a real woman.

Despite many actresses portraying Betty, only one woman has a solid claim to being the iconic baker. Marjorie Husted was the original woman used as the public-facing persona for Betty Crocker. She answered to the name when visitors to General Mills inquired about her, and she played the character on the radio. Her believable presence was a driving force behind the rise of the Betty Crocker empire. Husted maintained an exceptional level of realism, including even being present for testing stages that involved home bakers interpreting General

Mills recipes before they went to market. Husted's legacy within the brand included reportedly contributing more to the company's sales than any other person who worked there at the same time she did.

# World Exploration and a Legendary Christian King

*From the Crusades to European exploration across two continents, the surprising impact of this mythical Christian king can't be overstated.*

✳ ✳ ✳ ✳

IN THE MIDDLE ages, Christianity dominated every aspect of life in Europe. When the Crusades engulfed the continent, kings and princes who would otherwise be at war with each other united in the pursuit of reclaiming the Holy Land. Out of these centuries-long holy wars came legends that endure to this day, including the story of Prester John.

Prester John arose as an emblem of Christianity outside of Europe. He provided a kind of fantasy hope for exhausted European leaders who wanted aid and allies outside of the continent in their ongoing fight against Islam. The general failure of the second crusade decreased the legendary Christian king's popularity, but curiosity surrounding his mythos and whether or not he actually existed persevered for centuries.

The legendary church leader was the target of a number of searches over the centuries. He was, at different times, believed to be from India, Mongolia, or Ethiopia. Throughout the late Middle Ages and the early Renaissance, Prester John represented a fantasized view of Christianity, whose scope extended beyond the European continent. For a time, the prevalence of Christianity in Ethiopia kindled hope, suggesting that the religion had somehow made its way to far corners of the world.

He was never found by his supposed contemporaries of course, and there is no evidence that Prester John ever actually existed. However, his impact was incredibly tangible. Without the legend of Prester John, Europe could have remained more isolated throughout most of the premodern period. Instead, European kings and the Catholic church practically threw money at explorers, resulting in numerous expeditions that ultimately mapped out sea routes between continents and informed European understanding of Africa, Asia, and distant ocean islands. Prester John may not have been a real person, but his legend was the catalyst for centuries of exploration and development that otherwise would never have had the resources needed for success.

## The King Everyone Knows and No One Can Find

*King Arthur is one of the most well-known figures in European literature. But was he a real person?*

✳   ✳   ✳   ✳

ONE OF THE most prolific subjects of folklore in Western history, the fantastical world of Arthur and the knights of his famed Round Table has endured for millennia, passing from generation to generation in chronicles, primitive novels, and oral storytelling, rivalling the stories of any other dark age civilization.

One of the first significant mentions of Arthur in the historical record comes from the chronicle *Historia Brittonnum* by Nennius. His work was based heavily upon previous Latin works and gave mention to a Celtic warlord named Arthur. This warlord was supposed to have fought and won many battles against the invading Saxons. Nennius's work, along with the Welsh Annals, loosely linked Arthur to the Battle of Badon, which delayed the Saxon invasion by almost a full generation.

The first person to call Arthur a king was Geoffrey of Monmouth in his chronicle of English royalty, the *Historia Regum Britanniae*. This manuscript is the foundational document of what would become Arthurian lore, laying out Arthur's legendary origin as the son of Uther Pendragon and describing his friendship with Merlin. The legend grew from there, developing in French medieval literature specifically and becoming an important foundation of medieval romantic literature. Arthur and his Round Table were here to stay.

## The Legend of Arthur

The tale of King Arthur was spun by a multitude of authors, but the central components of his story have remained relatively consistent over the centuries. His father, King Uther Pendragon, convinced the sorcerer Merlin to transform him into the likeness of a local duke in order to seduce his wife, Ygraine. Ygraine became pregnant with Arthur. Arthur succeeded Uther at the age of only fifteen after his father's death, becoming the king of Britain. He acquired Excalibur either by pulling it from a legendary stone or by receiving it as a gift from the Lady of the Lake, depending on the story version.

His rule was good for Britain. He successfully defeated a series of invaders, securing the island for his people before extending his reach across the sea to Ireland. His conquests continued until he discovered Mordred (possibly his nephew in some accounts or his son in others) had betrayed him and was making a play for the throne. Arthur returned to Britain to fight in one last battle, killing the treacherous Mordred but also sustaining a fatal wound himself.

After the battle, his knights brought Arthur to the vale of Avalon, his sword's magical place of origin, in the hopes that he would heal in this powerful location, but he ultimately died in the vale. Some legends create a messianic version of Arthur, suggesting that one day he will return to free his people from another dark age.

# The Knights of the Round Table

There is even more variety in the stories of the legendary knights of the Round Table. Depending on the source, the number of knights—and chairs at the table—ranges from as few as a dozen to as many as 1,600. When King Edward III attempted to create his own Order of the Round Table, the number settled at about 300.

Notable occupants of King Arthur's Round Table typically include Galahad, Lancelot, Gawain, and the aforementioned Mordred. The knights were introduced to Arthurian legend primarily through French authors, who picked up medieval romantic traditions and concocted the story of the wondrous Round Table as a way to expand the storytelling potential. The knights are most prevalent in the stories connecting Arthur to the Holy Grail.

Galahad was a late addition to the Arthurian world, appearing in a thirteenth-century French epic as the illegitimate son of Sir Lancelot. He was associated with the medieval quest to find the Holy Grail. Galahad was knighted after beating his own father in a duel at the age of 15, ultimately traveling to Camelot and assuming the vacant seat reserved for the knight who would succeed in the Grail quest.

Gawain was a particularly important member of the Round Table, acting as King Arthur's closest confidante and companion while also notably being Mordred's maternal half-brother. This knight's legend and character draw heavily from a legendary hero of Welsh mythology, Gwalchmei, who was a major figure in one thread of the Welsh oral tradition.

Lancelot is easily the most well-known of the knights, infamous for his affair with Arthur's wife, Queen Guinevere. Lancelot was raised by the Lady of the Lake and became an icon of the medieval code of chivalry, though he failed in his quest for the Holy Grail due to his sins. This was the quest that his son would ultimately complete. Lancelot is most likely based on two earlier figures: Llenlleawc, an Irishman, and the Welsh hero Llwch Llawwynnauc, though there have been some suggestions that he could even be based on characters from Greek mythology.

## Merlin

The legendary magician's role in Arthurian lore is extensive, from playing an integral role in the conception of the future king to his relationship with the Lady of the Lake to his role as an advisor to both Uther Pendragon and Arthur. Merlin's origin story often casts him as a half-mad *cambion*, the son of a mortal mother and an incubus, a lineage which granted him supernatural abilities. In most tales, he is known as a prolific shape-shifter and prophet as well as possessing a wealth of knowledge concerning all types of magic.

Merlin's end is less consistent and more open-ended throughout Arthurian legend. Some authors suggest that he can't die until the end of the world. Instead, he must transform into a bird and wander this world and the otherworld until then as a form of temporary limbo or retirement. Other versions of the story have him dying at the hands of the Lady of the Lake. Regardless, Merlin is an extremely odd character who almost always disappears from the story with little forewarning and little future recognition regarding his contributions to Camelot's safety. Merlin is likely based on two legendary prophets: Myrddin and Ambrosius, whose origins have absolutely nothing to do with Arthur.

## The Villain

Mordred acts as the quintessential villain, the traitorous family member who attempts to usurp the throne and steal the queen for his own purposes. In some versions he is cast as the legitimate son of Arthur's half-sister Morgause and her husband King Lot. In others he is the son of Morgause and Arthur. Regardless, all versions agree that Mordred was knighted by Arthur at some point, joined the Round Table, and eventually attempted to take the throne while Arthur pursued Lancelot through France after the king discovered his wife's affair with the knight, a discovery set into motion by Mordred himself. Ultimately, Arthur discovered the plot, rushing back to Britain in time to fight in the Battle of Camlann, where according to most versions of the story he killed Mordred while also sustaining the wound that would later kill him on Avalon.

## The Women

Within Arthurian lore, two women are linked to Arthur strongly enough to maintain important roles over centuries of retelling. Guinevere and Morgause both play major roles in the legend, Guinevere as the fallible queen and Morgause as Arthur's sister and the mother of Mordred.

Guinevere is one of the most recognizable female figures in Western literary tradition, acting as the center of a love triangle between herself, King Arthur, and Sir Lancelot, and unknowingly playing a part in her husband's downfall and ultimate death. Guinevere's marriage to King Arthur is largely considered to be a political deal with some versions of the legend even suggesting that the Round Table was a part of her dowry. Her conflict with Morgan Le Fay (a sister of Morgause's and also Arthur's half-sister) over her infidelity acts as a secondary source of conflict within many stories.

Morgause has had many names and many stories over the centuries, but she's always portrayed as related to Arthur, either as his full or half-sister. She marries the King of Orkney for love and gives birth to anywhere from two to ten children, including Gawain and Mordred. Her role in the stories is not as robust, confined mostly to an indirect presence in relation to her sons and their roles in the downfall of her brother. Morgause's character is often combined with her sister, Morgan Le Fay, in more modern versions of the legend. The original version of her character (named Anna) in Geoffrey of Monmouth's chronicles has been lost.

## The Witches

Morgan Le Fay, a prototype of the morally murky witch in western literature, found her start as the ambiguous and vengeful half-sister of King Arthur. Modern researchers believe her character could trace back to the Celtic goddess Morrigan, to Circe or Madea from Greek myth, or even to the real-life empress Matilda. Morgan's role in the legend is vast, with no concrete explanation for her morals or motivations. In the Lancelot-Grail tradition, she acts as a kind of foil to Sir Lancelot himself—a debauched and treacherous witch who would go to any lengths to seduce the chivalrous knight. In other versions, she goes to great lengths to expose Guinevere's infidelity to her brother, believing it to be the right thing to do. Regardless of her actions in any version of the legend, she's always one of the cloaked women who brings King Arthur to Avalon in a last-ditch effort to heal him after his fatal battle with Mordred.

The Lady of the Lake is an equally ambiguous presence throughout the legend, acting simultaneously as Merlin's protege, his potential captor, Arthur's advisor, and even the source of Excalibur. One of the Lady's many given names, Nimue, suggests a link between her and a figure in Irish mythology known as Niamh, a figure from the otherworld most often linked to Merlin. The Lady is always the ultimate keeper of the legendary sword Excalibur. Arthur's dying wish is frequently that the sword be returned to his old advisor, and this is carried out by his loyal knights.

## The Hunt for King Arthur

There has been no shortage of effort by historians to discover a legitimate source for the real Arthur. One of the most popular theories relates that there was a Roman military leader named Arturus, a Latin predecessor of the name Arthur, who led the Celtic resistance to the Anglo-Saxon invasion of the fifth century. However, there is little evidence from this period to definitively prove the theory. There are traces and hints of a military leader from the period who could fit the bill. This leader's father was a duke (a very high title of the time), and there are other biographical tidbits that tease out a potential connection. Yet nailing down a truly concrete personage a millennium and a half after the supposed events occurred continues to elude us.

Regardless of who King Arthur might have been historically, the sites attributed to him and his court still survive as ruins, visited by thousands of people every year. Lauded by kings from Edward I to Henry VIII, the mere mention of his name continues to inform our ideas of kingship.

# The Sherwood Forest Bandit

*From the Sherwood Forest to a purported grave near the Kirklees Priory, Robin Hood's life is shrouded in mystery.*

✳   ✳   ✳   ✳

ONE OF THE most enduring characters from early ballads and folk tales, Robin Hood has captured the imaginations of people the world over with stories of his exploits as an outlaw in medieval England, taking from the rich and giving to the poor, while upholding the rule of his king. As a character, he's so noteworthy that his name has become shorthand for anyone acting as an anti-hero or a rebel against tyranny. To this day, he represents a sort of gray morality that suggests that the ends are often much more important than the means.

Historians and folklore scholars have proposed at least eight possible real-life origins for Robin Hood, some of which are more plausible than others. One of the broadest suggestions is that the moniker never referred to an individual person, but rather served as an alias used by or in reference to bandits at the time that the myth was originally composed.

Another possible historical figure is Robert Hod of York, who was mentioned in legal records from 1226 detailing how his goods were confiscated after he was deemed an outlaw for owing money to St. Peter's in York. He is the only person of this name (Robin being a diminutive of Robert) known to be an outlaw in England during the relevant time. However, there's no evidence that Robert Hood ever became a bandit.

Robert and John Deyville may also have been inspiration for the legend. They were present at the Battle of Evesham, and their exploits seem to parallel parts of the legend. Finally, Roger Godberg makes the list for a string of events that could serve as a template for the legendary bandit.

Whether or not Robin Hood was a real person remains a mystery. Regardless, his story is a staple of English folklore and has shaped our perception of this time period for generations. The outlaw bandit has something of an archetypal status thanks to his alliance with the poor and provides a historical moral compass for those who question the intentions of power-hungry leaders.

# Pope Joan: Scandal or Satire?

*Some of the most basic qualifications for becoming Pope include being male, baptized, and Catholic. "Joan" was two of those things, but apparently not the third.*

✳ ✳ ✳ ✳

PICTURE THIS: IT'S the mid-ninth century, and the Pope is parading through the streets in a typical papal procession. There's nothing particularly out of the ordinary going on during this parade. But then something very peculiar happens. The Pope, who by definition of the role is supposed to be male, goes into labor and gives birth in the middle of the procession. Pope John is revealed to be Joan, a fact that horrifies the crowd to the point that some versions of the story end with onlookers ripping her from the procession and dragging her behind a horse until her ultimate death.

The story of Pope Joan first emerged in an early thirteenth-century chronicle and remained an accepted story in church history until the sixteenth century. In fact, a bust of Pope Joan was placed among other pontiffs at the Siena Cathedral until protests prompted its removal in 1600.

## The Life of Pope Joan

Pope Joan was born John Anglicus of Mainz and her reign as Pope was first included in Jean de Mailly's early thirteenth-century chronicle, *Chronica Universalis Mettensis*, where she is said to have disguised herself as a man, become a curial secretary, then a Cardinal, then Pope, thanks to her own character and talents.

Martin of Opava's thirteenth-century *Chronicon Pontificum et Imperatorum* was the most important source of the legend, providing a birth name to the secretive female pope (John Anglicus) and claiming that she was Pope for two years, seven months, and four days. In this account, John Anglicus was led to Athens as a young girl and dressed in men's clothes by one of her lovers.

She subsequently received a broad education and departed for Rome, where she taught liberal arts. She gained so much respect through this vocation, that she was ultimately elected Pope. However, while serving as Pope, she became pregnant by one of her companions. She ultimately gave birth on a street then known as Via Sacra. In Martin of Opava's telling, Joan died on that street and was buried there. Joan was furthermore removed from all lists of pontiffs and every existing historical record at the time.

These two extensive chronicles are the only undisputed references to Pope Joan, with some earlier writings dismissed due to questions of validity. Regardless, the example of Joan was used as a successful defense in a number of court cases against church reformers who opposed elements of the Catholic church.

## Poking Holes in the Story

After centuries of the Pope Joan story providing sundry forms of ammunition for various religious reformers, Pope Clement VIII unilaterally declared the legend of a female pope untrue in 1601. But then the legend became the subject of contention between Catholic and Protestant writers during the reformation, with each side choosing elements of the legend to count or discount depending on what benefitted their side.

Later historians have examined the story in detail and the general consensus is that there is little to no chance that a female Pope existed during the ninth century, as the reigns of Leo IV and Benedict III are heavily documented and occurred sequentially with no substantial gap in between. However, modern historians have suggested that a period of unrest in the church (including a series of antipopes between 1086 and 1108) would be a more likely time for such an event to occur. This theory would support Jean de Mailly's original account of the legend, considering he placed the story in 1099. The supposed existence of the *sedes stercoraria*, a mythical rite that would have confirmed the incoming pope's gender, is also mentioned. Later chronicles suggest that this practice was still occurring as late as the fifteenth century.

The truth of Pope Joan's existence still draws intense scrutiny and speculation, with most researchers firmly believing she never existed and a few fervently looking for any clues that support her actual existence. Regardless, her legend has had immense impact on the world and the church and remains a fascinating conundrum.

# Saint Nicholas to Santa Claus

*Saint Nicholas was revered as the patron and protector of everyone from sailors to orphans. From the Protestant reformation to the American Revolution, Santa Claus has played a surprising role in a lot of historical events.*

✳ ✳ ✳ ✳

TODAY, SANTA CLAUS is synonymous with Christmas. The holly jolly gift bringer provides joy to kids around the world on Christmas day with toys made by an army of elves in a secret North Pole workshop. But our image of Santa has only been around for a few centuries. His character is a curious amalgamation built upon previous figures associated with winter holidays, starting with the most well-known example: Saint Nicholas.

The original St. Nick lived during the third and fourth centuries in an area that is now part of Greece and Turkey. His faith was a large part of his life from an early age. After his parents' deaths, he took his sizable inheritance into the priesthood with him, giving freely to the less fortunate and living a humble, pious life. He spent his life traveling the countryside and aiding the poor and sick, even saving a trio of sisters from being sold into slavery by providing a dowry for them. After his death, he was revered by locals, who built and named a church after him in Myra, the city where he died. Most of his bones were stolen from the church, following a schism between the Catholic and the Greek Orthodox churches, and his skeleton was taken to two churches in Italy during the First Crusade.

Nicholas was canonized in 1446, quickly becoming one of the most popular saints in Europe. His feast day, December 6, became associated with giving small presents and contributed to the traditions surrounding Christmas within the church. Things quickly changed during the Protestant reformation, however, when Martin Luther discouraged the worship of saints and tried to steer Christians towards gift giving on Christmas, citing the *Christkindl* or Christ child as the giver.

Nicholas remained a central figure in the Dutch tradition, acquiring a shortened version of his name, *Sinter Klaas*. This tradition was brought to North America by Dutch settlers, where colonists adopted the story and anglicized the name. Santa Claus became a key figure differentiating American Christmas tradition from British. Santa Claus was here to stay, though he only took on his modern role at the end of the nineteenth century. Today, Santa Claus has little in common with his historical counterpart, though he does maintain the giving spirit that Saint Nicholas was so well known for.

# The History of the Easter Bunny

*From Germany to the United States, the Easter Bunny has brought joy to children across the world for centuries.*

✳  ✳  ✳  ✳

THAT WHITE BUNNY who delivers colorful eggs, candy, and toys to children on Easter morning seems a rather random sort of figure. Easter, one of the holiest Christian holidays, has little to do with rabbits or eggs, much less the mythical bunny known in many parts of the world. The Easter bunny has been around since the seventeenth century, even longer than our modern Santa Claus. So where did the Easter Bunny originally come from?

Hares, and later rabbits, once held a role within European pagan religions. During the Neolithic era, hares were given ritual burials with humans all across Europe, suggesting they had a symbolic role of rebirth within those early religious rituals. However, hares later became negatively associated with witches. Their previous stature was diminished, and in fact, a tradition of eating rabbit on Easter became a symbolic act of opposition to witchcraft and support for Christianity. This tradition was especially popular in Germany, where it was named *Oster Haws*. Somehow, the tradition grew to include the practice of children searching for colorful eggs in hidden nests on Easter day.

German immigrants brought the tradition to the United States, where it evolved further. Nests were replaced by decorated baskets and eggs replaced by candy and gifts. The Easter Bunny was here to stay, fully entrenched in American Easter tradition. Other animals have taken on similar roles in other countries. Today, questions seem to pop up annually about whether or not the Easter Bunny has pagan origins, specifically regarding its possible link to the Anglo-Saxon goddess of Spring, *Eostre*, who has been cited as an early inspiration for a festival celebrated close to the Spring equinox. The truth is a bit more complicated. Rabbits have a variety of pagan associations, but the Easter Bunny in and of itself isn't pagan.

# Tooth Be Told

*In the United States, the Tooth Fairy usually trades cash for baby teeth. But how do other cultures handle this rite of passage?*

✳  ✳  ✳  ✳

### Molar Mice

AS IT TURNS out, the Tooth Fairy isn't universal. In fact, she only visits kids in the United States, Canada, Australia, England, and Denmark (where she's called Tandfeen). But before you start feeling bad that the Tooth Fairy doesn't get around more often, know that in most parts of the world, it's a tooth *mouse* who reigns supreme.

Known as El Ratón in Mexico, El Ratoncito in Argentina, El Ratón Perez in Spain, and Le Petite Souris in France, this magical mouse has much the same purpose as the Tooth Fairy, taking baby teeth from under a pillow, or sometimes from a glass of water, in exchange for money or candy. But that's not the only place children put their baby teeth. In South Africa, mice swipe the tooth from a slipper, but in Uganda, the tooth is hidden behind a pot.

And not every culture trades teeth for trinkets. In Russia and Afghanistan, children drop their teeth down mouse holes in hopes that their teeth will grow in like mice's teeth: strong, sharp, and white. In Kazakhstan, teeth are dropped under bathtubs with similar wishes.

## Tooth Tossers

Strange as it sounds, tossing a tooth on the roof is common in many cultures, although it's not always a mouse who makes the trade but another sharp-toothed rodent. In Sri Lanka, it's a squirrel; among the Cherokee, a beaver.

In the Dominican Republic and Haiti, the tooth is simply tossed on the roof. In China, Japan, and other Asian countries, only a lower tooth is tossed on the roof; an upper one is thrown straight to the ground, buried, or placed at the foot of the bed. The belief is that the new tooth will grow in the direction of the old one.

## Dental Diners

Some cultures prefer to feed a child's tooth to a specific animal in hopes that the animal will replace the tooth with one like its own. The native Yupik of Alaska feed lost teeth to dogs. However, in the nineteenth century, children from Cornwall, England, had their first teeth burnt so as to avoid having "dog's teeth" grow in (that is, crooked teeth).

## Fangs of Fire

The ancient Egyptians believed the sun strengthened teeth, which may explain why in many North African and Middle Eastern countries, such as Egypt and Libya, teeth are tossed toward the sun.

## Bicuspid Burial

But why toss teeth when you can bury them? In Turkey, a tooth is buried at a site that symbolizes the parents' hope for their child's success. For instance, if they wish their child to become a doctor, the tooth is buried on the grounds of a hospital; a scholar, on the grounds of a university. Malaysian tradition believes that, as part of the body, teeth must be returned to the earth, and in Tajikistan, teeth are planted in a field so boys can grow into warriors.

The Navajo traditionally take a lost tooth to the southeast, away from the family home, and bury it on the east side of a young bush or tree. Other native cultures, such as the aboriginal Australians and the Yellowknife Dene of Canada's Northwest Territories, plant a tooth inside a tree in hopes that as the tree grows straight, so will the child's new tooth.

## Ivory Accessories

Still, there are cultures that are loath to part with their children's pearly whites. Lithuanians hang on to them as keepsakes, and in certain Central American countries, such as Chile and Costa Rica, a baby tooth is dipped in gold or silver and made into jewelry for the child to wear—a custom that resembles the Viking tradition of wearing baby teeth as good luck charms.

# The Mystery of the 700-Year-Old Piper

*It's an intriguing story about a mysterious piper and more than 100 missing children. Made famous by the Brothers Grimm, this popular fairy tale has captivated generations of boys and girls. But is it actually more fact than fiction?*

✳   ✳   ✳   ✳

THE LEGEND OF The Pied Piper of Hamelin documents the story of a mysterious musician who rid a town of rats by enchanting the rodents with music from his flute. The musician led the mesmerized rats to a nearby river, where they drowned. When the townsfolk refused to settle their debt, the rat catcher returned several weeks later, charmed a group of 130 children with the same flute, and led them out of town. They disappeared—never to be seen again.

It's a story that dates back to approximately the year 1300 and has its roots in a small German town called Hamelin. Several accounts written between the fourteenth and seventeenth centuries tell of a stained-glass window in the town's main church. The window pictured the Pied Piper with hands clasped, standing over a group of youngsters. Encircling the window was the following verse (this is a rough translation): "In the year 1284, on John's and Paul's day was the 26th of June. By a piper, dressed in all kinds of colors, 130 children born in Hamelin were seduced and lost at the calvarie near the koppen."

The verse is quite specific: precise month and year, exact number of children involved in the incident, and detailed place names. Because of this, some scholars believe this window, which was removed in 1660 and either accidentally destroyed or lost, was created in memory of an actual event. Yet, the verse makes no mention of the circumstances regarding the departure of the children or their specific fate. What exactly happened in Hamelin, Germany, in 1284? The truth is, no one actually knows—at least not for certain.

## Theories Abound

Gernot Hüsam, the current chairman of the Coppenbrügge Castle Museum, believes the word "koppen" in the inscription may reference a rocky outcrop on a hill in nearby Coppenbrügge, a small town previously known as Koppanberg. Hüsam also believes the use of the word "calvarie" is in reference to either the medieval connotation of the gates of hell—or, since the Crusades—a place of execution.

One theory put forward is that Coppenbrügge resident Nikolaus von Spiegelberg recruited Hamelin youth to emigrate to newly-settled areas in Pomerania near the Baltic Sea. This theory suggests the youngsters were drowned in a tragic accident while in transit to the new colonies. It was also suggested that they were murdered because they took part in summertime pagan rituals. But these are not the only theories. In fact, theories concerning the fate of the children abound. Here are more ideas put forth about what really happened:

* The children suffered from the Black Plague or some similar disease and were led from the town to spare the rest of the town's population.

* They were part of a crusade to the Holy Land.

* They were lost in the 1260 Battle of Sedemünder.

* They died in a bridge collapse over the Weser River or a landslide on Ith Mountain.

* They emigrated to settle in other parts of Europe, including Maehren, Oelmutz, Transylvania, or Uckermark.

* They were actually young adults who were led away and murdered for performing pagan rituals on a local mountain.

Most historians have since concluded that emigration, bridge collapse/natural disaster, disease, or murder are the most plausible explanations.

## Tracing the Piper's Path

Regardless of what actually happened in Hamelin hundreds of years ago, the legend of the Pied Piper has endured—and grown. First accounts of the Pied Piper may have had roots in an actual incident, but as time has passed, the story has taken on a life of its own, with embellishments accruing along the way.

One early account of the legend dates back to 1384, at which time a Hamelin church leader, Deacon von Lude, was said to be in possession of a chorus book with a Latin verse related to the legend written on the front cover by his grandmother. The book was misplaced in the late seventeenth century and has never been found.

The oldest surviving account—according to amateur Pied Piper historian Jonas Kuhn—appears as an addition to a fourteenth-century manuscript from Luneburg. Written in Latin, the note is almost identical to the verse on the stained-glass window and translates roughly to:

"In the year of 1284, on the day of Saints John and Paul on the 26th of June 130 children born in Hamelin were seduced By a piper, dressed in all kinds of colors, and lost at the place of execution near the koppen."

The sixteenth-century physician and philosopher Jobus Fincelius believed the Pied Piper was simply the devil. In his 1556 book, *Concerning the Wonders of His Times*, Fincelius wrote: "It came about in Hamelin in Saxony on the River Weser...the Devil visibly in human form walked the lanes of Hamelin and by playing a pipe lured after him many children...to a mountain. Once there, he with the children... could no longer be found."

In 1557, Count Froben Christoph von Zimmern wrote a chronicle detailing his family's lineage. Sprinkled throughout the book were several folklore tales, including one that referenced the Pied Piper. For some unknown reason, the count introduced rats into his version of the story: "He passed through the streets of the town with his small pipe... immediately all the rats... collected outside the houses and followed his footsteps." This first insertion of rodents into the legend led a string of other writers to follow suit. It remains to be seen whether this was an embellishment or a reference to an earlier story, now lost.

In 1802, Johan Wolfgang Goethe wrote "Der Rattenfanger," a poem based on the legend. The monologue was told in the first person through the eyes of the rat catcher. Goethe's poem made no direct reference to the town of Hamelin, and in Goethe's version the Piper played a stringed instrument instead of a pipe. The Piper also made an appearance in Goethe's literary work Faust.

Jacob and Wilhelm Grimm began collecting European folktales in the early 1800s. Best known for a series of books that documented 211 fairy tales, the brothers also published two volumes between 1816 and 1818 detailing almost 600 German folklore legends. One of the volumes contained the story "Der Rattenfanger von Hameln."

The Grimm brothers' research for "Der Rattenfanger von Hameln" drew from 11 different sources, from which they deduced that two children were left behind (a blind child and a mute child); the piper led the other children through a cave to Transylvania. Subsequently, a street in Hamelin was named after the event.

## No End in Sight

While the details of the historical event surrounding the legend of the Piped Piper have been lost to time, the mystique of the story endures. Different versions of the legend have even appeared in literature outside of Germany: A rat catcher from Vienna helped rid the nearby town of Korneuburg of rats. When he wasn't paid, he stole off with the town's children and sold them as slaves in Constantinople. A vagabond rid the English town of Newton on the Isle of Wight of their rats, and when he wasn't paid, led the town's children into an ancient oak forest where they were never seen again. A Chinese version had a Hangchow district official use magic to convince the rats to leave his city.

The legend's plot has been adapted over time to fit whichever media format is currently popular and has been used as a story line in children's books, ballet, theatre, and even a radio drama. The intriguing story of the mysterious piper will continue to interest people as long as there is mystery surrounding the original event.

## ✳ Chapter 6

# The Translator's Dilemma

## Stumping a Nation: The Beale Ciphers

*The Beale ciphers have stumped treasure enthusiasts, the greatest minds in cryptanalysis, and specialty computers since 1862. Do the ciphers actually lead to massive riches, or has this been one of the longest-lasting hoaxes in history?*

✳  ✳  ✳  ✳

THOMAS J. BEALE lived on-and-off in Lynchburg, Virginia, in the 1820s. Before he left for the last time, never to return, he left an "important" locked box with an acquaintance, Robert Morriss. After holding onto it for twenty years, Morriss finally looked inside, where he found a note written by Beale, detailing how he and 29 others had been traveling across the United States when they unearthed a large quantity of gold and other precious metals. His travels then led him to Lynchburg, where he found a suitable location to bury his treasure.

The three encrypted sheets accompanying the note were purported to state the location of Beale's treasure, the exact contents of the treasure, and the names of the treasure's owners and their next of kin.

After working on the ciphers for two decades to no avail, Morriss confided in a friend about Beale and the treasure. The friend, identity unknown, managed to crack the second cipher, which detailed the contents of the treasure. He was able to figure out that each of the 800 numbers corresponded to a word in the Declaration of Independence. Beale's treasure was purported to be worth around $43 million in U.S. dollars as of 2018. Unfortunately, the mysterious friend was unable to crack the remaining two ciphers, which led to him giving them to his friend, James B. Ward, who published a pamphlet of Morriss's account and Beale's ciphers in 1885.

## Cracking the Code

Over the decades, several notable people have attempted to crack Beale's ciphers: Treasure hunters George and Clayton Hart tried for decades before Clayton gave up in 1912 and George in 1952. And Beale aficionado, Hiram Herbert Jr., made attempts from 1923 all the way until the 1970s. Professionals in the field of cryptanalysis also gave it a try, such as Herbert O. Yardley, the founder of the U.S. Cipher Bureau, and Colonel William Friedman, an impressive figure in American code breaking; both of them made no progress. Retired director of computer science at Sperry Univac and one of the pioneers of computer code breaking, Carl Hammer, has this to say regarding the difficulty of the Beale ciphers: "At least 10% of the best cryptanalytic minds in the country [have attempted it]. And not a dime of this effort should be begrudged. The work—even the lines that have led into blind alleys—has more than paid for itself in advancing and refining computer research."

The Beale ciphers are not without their critics; many people have debated whether or not the ciphers are just an elaborate hoax. The key evidence that its detractors—particularly professional skeptic and paranormal investigator Joe Nickell—bring to bear is that the paper that was enclosed in the box, and supposedly written in 1822, uses language that would not have been seen in print at the time, such as "stampede." However, arguments to the contrary claim it could have been used colloquially in the Old West much earlier, and Beale could have picked it up in his travels. Additionally, Nickell has studied the writing style of the papers and believes that James B. Ward is actually Thomas J. Beale himself. Another argument against the ciphers considers whether the numbers are merely random. But the aforementioned Carl Hammer has plugged the cipher numbers into various cryptanalysis computers, and they have confirmed that the numbers do have a pattern to them.

Whether the treasure is there or not doesn't appear to be the end-goal of modern cryptanalysts like Hammer. "There is a message in those codes, and if it turns out to be something like, 'April Fool, Sucker,' so what? If Tommy Beale has played a trick on me, I've come out ahead, because this whole affair has been fascinating and just plain fun."

# One Heck of a Hoax? The Mysterious Voynich Manuscript

*Dubbed the "World's Most Mysterious Book," the Voynich manuscript contains more than 200 vellum pages of vivid, colorful illustrations and handwritten prose. There's only one small problem: No one knows what any of it means—or whether it means anything at all.*

✳   ✳   ✳   ✳

IT WAS "DISCOVERED" in 1912 after being hidden from the world for almost 250 years. An American antique book dealer named Wilfried Voynich came across the medieval manuscript at an Italian Jesuit College. Approximately nine inches by six inches in size, the manuscript bore a soft, light-brown vellum cover, which was unmarked, untitled, and gave no indication as to when it had been written or by whom.

Bound inside were about 230 yellow parchment pages, most of which contained richly colored drawings of strange plants, celestial bodies, and other scientific matter. Many of these pages were adorned by naked nymphs bathing in odd-looking plumbing and personal-size washtubs. Handwritten text written in flowing script accompanied the illustrations.

Although Voynich was an expert antiquarian, he was baffled by the book's contents. And today—nearly a century later—the manuscript that came to bear his name remains an undeciphered mystery.

## Weird Science

The mystery surrounding the Voynich manuscript begins with its contents, which read (so to speak) like a work of weird science presented in six identifiable "sections":

* a botanical section, containing drawings of plants that no botanist has ever been able to identify.

* an astronomical section, with illustrations of the sun, moon, stars, and zodiac symbols surrounded by naked nymphs bathing in individual washtubs.

* a "biological" section, showing perplexing anatomical drawings of chambers or organs connected by tubes—and which also features more nymphs swimming in their inner liquids.

* a cosmological section, consisting mostly of unexplained circular drawings.

* a pharmaceutical section, depicting drawings of plant parts (leaves, roots) placed next to containers.

* a recipe section, featuring short paragraphs "bulleted" by stars in the margin.

Weirder still are the ubiquitous nymphs—a nice touch perhaps, but how they relate to the book's subject matter is anyone's guess.

## Many Mysteries, Still No Answers

And then there's the manuscript's enigmatic text. The world's greatest cryptologists have failed to unravel its meaning. Even the best American and British code breakers who cracked the Japanese and German codes in World War II came away stumped. To this day, not a single word of the Voynich manuscript has been deciphered.

This, of course, has led to key unsolved questions, namely:

* Who wrote it? A letter found with the manuscript, dated 1666, credits Roger Bacon, a Franciscan friar who lived from 1214 to 1294. This has since been discredited because the manuscript's date of origin is generally considered to be between 1450 and 1500. There are as many theories about who wrote it as there are nymphs among its pages. In fact, some believe Voynich forged the whole thing.

* What is it? It was first thought to be a coded description of Bacon's early scientific discoveries. Since then, other theories ranging from an ancient prayer book written in a pidgin Germanic language to one big, elaborate hoax (aside from that supposedly perpetrated by Voynich) have been posited.

* Is it real writing? Is the script composed in a variation of a known language, a lost language, an encrypted language, an artificial language? Or is it just plain gibberish?

## What Do We Know?

Despite the aura of mystery surrounding the manuscript, it has been possible to trace its travels over the past 400 years. The earliest known owner was Holy Roman Emperor Rudolph II, who purchased it in 1586. By 1666, the manuscript had passed through a series of owners to Athanasius Kircher, a Jesuit scholar who hid it in the college where Voynich found it 250 years later.

After being passed down to various members of Voynich's estate, the manuscript was sold in 1961 to a rare-book collector who sought to resell it for a fortune. After failing to find a buyer, he donated it to Yale University, where it currently resides—still shrouded in mystery—in the Beinecke Rare Book and Manuscript Library.

## The Search for Meaning Continues...

To this day, efforts to translate the Voynich manuscript continue. And still, the manuscript refuses to yield its secrets, leading experts to conclude that it's either an ingenious hoax or the ultimate unbreakable code. The hoax theory gained some ground in 2004 when Dr. Gordon Rugg, a computer-science lecturer at Keele University, announced that he had replicated the Voynich manuscript using a simple, low-tech device called a Cardan grille. According to Rugg, this proved that the manuscript was likely a fraud—a volume of jibberish created, perhaps, in an attempt to con money out of Emperor Rudolph II. So, mystery solved? Well, it's not quite as simple as that. Many researchers still remain unconvinced. Sure, Rugg *may* have proven that the manuscript might be a hoax. But the possibility that it is not a hoax remains. And thus, the search for meaning continues...

# Can You Crack the Code?

*Located in Langley, Virginia, the Central Intelligence Agency is a service of the United States federal government that is focused on overseas intelligence gathering. The agency has a reputation for being secretive and covert, and most Americans know little about it aside from its portrayal in numerous books and films. Which makes the bizarre sculpture that sits on the CIA's grounds even more mysterious.*

❋ ❋ ❋ ❋

## A Unique Commission

IN 1990, WORK began on a new building in which to house the headquarters of the CIA. Fittingly dubbed the New Headquarters Building (NHB), the agency decided that the courtyard of the building should be spruced up with a bit of artwork. Using a federal program called "Art in Architecture," which oversees the creation of artwork for federal buildings around the country, the agency evaluated potential artists in order to choose one for the project. They eventually gave the $250,000 commission for the NHB artwork to Washington, D.C., artist Jim Sanborn.

The CIA laid out several principles for the artwork to be displayed at the agency, including requirements that it to be "positive," and reflect "well-being" and "hope." But Sanborn's final piece was more than just an aesthetically pleasing statue in the middle of a courtyard. In fact, it went well beyond mere artwork, inspiring the imaginations of not just the employees at the CIA and visitors to the building, but curiosity seekers worldwide. So exactly what is it that is so unusual about Sanborn's art piece?

## "Hidden" in Plain Sight

The sculpture, entitled "Kryptos" (the Greek word for "hidden"), is made up of several parts. Two red granite and copper plated constructions begin the piece, which are engraved with International Morse code and ancient ciphers. There is also a stone slab with an engraving of a navigational compass, which points to a lodestone, or a naturally magnetized rock.

While these pieces are certainly unique, it is the centerpiece of the installation that has been causing a stir for three decades. It consists of a large sheet of copper, shaped like a giant S, with exactly 1,735 alphabetic letters cut into it. At first glance, it seems to be random and nonsensical, the jumbled letters haphazardly carved into the metal like a giant sheet of gibberish. But nothing about Kryptos is random; Sanborn actually designed his sculpture to be a cryptographic message.

## An Enigma Wrapped in a Puzzle

Kryptos contains four encoded messages, which, according to Sanborn, will reveal one final puzzle once they're decoded. But decoding the strange cypher has proven to be quite the challenge, even for the code experts at the CIA. It took nine years for anyone to come forward with a solution to part of the code, although computer experts at the NSA later proved to have solved the same sections in 1993 (presumably they kept quiet so as not to ruin the fun for anyone else!).

While the first three sections of Kryptos have now been solved and can be found on many websites, the fourth, while relatively short at only 97 characters, has confounded even the smartest people in the world and remains unsolved. Sanborn has offered help by releasing several clues: the words "NORTHEAST," "BERLIN," and "CLOCK," along with their positions within the code. But even with the clues, the message remains elusive.

It is fitting that an art piece at the CIA should honor the history of cryptography, which is the art of writing and solving codes. Sanborn's puzzle within a puzzle has provided cryptographers—both amateur and professional—a challenge worthy of the most gripping spy novel.

# A Composer's Cipher

*A cryptogram enthusiast penned a cipher to his dear friend and the mystery of its contents has endured for over a century. What attempts have been made to crack it, and will anyone ever reveal his cryptic message?*

✳ ✳ ✳ ✳

THE DORABELLA CIPHER is a letter written by Edward Elgar to Dora Penny. It entirely consists of an 87-character cipher spread over three lines. It appears to be made up of 24 symbols with each symbol consisting of one, two, or three semicircles oriented in one of eight directions. It's unknown as to why Elgar sent this cipher to Penny—not only did she never crack it in her lifetime, but it remains unsolved to this day. Penny and Elgar were friends for many years, having met in 1897 when her family invited him and his wife to stay at the Wolverhampton Rectory for a few days. Elgar's wife, Alice, was good friends with Dora's stepmother, and the two families would meet on several occasions.

Edward Elgar was a music teacher who would become a successful composer. Additionally, he was apparently fascinated by secret writing, and was supposed to have cracked an "uncrackable" cipher published in *Pall Mall* magazine. The same cipher alphabet used in the Dorabella Cipher appears elsewhere in notes of his, most notably in the left margin of a concert program for Hungarian composer Franz Liszt that Elgar annotated in 1886. He also wrote the symbols in one of his notebooks, penned sometime in the 1920s, along with the supposed solution to the aforementioned *Pall Mall* cryptographic challenge, and diagrams resembling clock faces. The original note with the cipher is lost, but it was made public when Penny published it in her memoir, *Edward Elgar: Memories of a Variation*, in 1937. The name "Dorabella" was a nickname Elgar gave to Penny, even naming one of his 1899 compositions *Dorabella* in dedication to Dora Penny.

## Notable Attempts

Several enthusiasts have made attempts at solving the Dorabella Cipher. Eric Sams, a British musicologist and Shakespeare scholar, produced an interpretation in 1970. However, his crack adds around 22 extra letters, which he claims to be necessary to expand the phonetic shorthand into full words.

A few people, such as Javier Atance, have suggested that the solution is actually a *melody*. He claims that the eight different positions of the semicircles, when turned clockwise, correspond to the notes of the musical scale. He adds that each semicircle has three different levels corresponding to natural, flat, or sharp notes. While intriguing, this theory hasn't led anyone to a solution either.

In 2007, the Elgar Society proposed a Dorabella Cipher Competition in an effort to finally crack the elusive code. While a high number of entries were received, none of them were deemed satisfactory.

The Elgar Society noted, "One or two entries did contain some impressively ambitious and thoughtful analysis. These entries, though, having matched Elgar's symbols to the alphabet, invariably ended up with a fairly arbitrary sequence of letters. Another solution suggested that the code was a form of musical notation. Whilst an interesting idea, when transcribed, the resulting somewhat messy arrangement of notes can hardly be called music."

Two more notable claims occurred in 2011 and 2020. Richard Henderson, a Canadian cryptography enthusiast, claimed to solve it as a substitution cipher, while Wayne Packwood claimed to have produced a complete decryption in the journal *Musical Opinion*. Both solutions do produce legible writing, although Henderson's solution is rather nonsensical: "whY AM I VERY SAD, BELLE. I SAG AS WE SEE ROSES DO. E.E. IS EVER FOND OF U, DORA. I kNOw I PeN ONE I LOVe. All Of My Affection." The solution Packwood came to is significantly more legible, but he is unable to explain the logic he used to come to the solution. "A WOMAN IS LIKE CHESS ONE HAS TO MAKE MANY SACRIFICES FOR ITS QUEEN IT IS VICTORY SHE COMMANDS NOT DO BETTER."

In 2018, Thomas Ernst, a Dorabella Cipher enthusiast, put forth the theory that Dora Penny may have faked Elgar's ciphers. Ernst calls into question the fact that the original cipher no longer exists—thus, making it possible that she forged it. He also brings up how the cipher seems to be a simple letter substitution, yet all attempts to solve it have failed, and how patterns within the cipher can't be explained linguistically, but do follow Penny's writing patterns.

Cryptanalysts have found Ernst's claims to be intriguing, but have ruled that they are ultimately circumstantial. As of 2023, there have still been no satisfactory solutions to the enigmatic Dorabella Cipher.

# Cretan Hieroglyphs

*A writing system more than 4,000 years old still baffles scholars with its mystery. Details surrounding an ancient culture could be hidden within the surviving clay tablets and seals.*

✳ ✳ ✳ ✳

**F**OUND LARGELY ON the island of Samothrace in the northeastern Aegean Sea, Cretan hieroglyphs are a hieroglyphic writing system dating back to Bronze Age Crete during the Minoan era. Predating Linear A (another unknown language) by about a century, they were both used at roughly the same time. Cretan hieroglyphs remain undeciphered, although recent excavations of artifacts displaying the dead language bring new hope that they may one day be cracked.

So far, archeologists have discovered 832 signs on seals and sealings, and 723 signs on other documents. The first collection of signs was published by Arthur J. Evans in 1909, and a more updated collection known as *Corpus Hieroglyphicarum Inscriptionum Cretae* (CHIC) was published in 1996. The items included in CHIC are clay documents with incised inscriptions, sealstones and sealstone impressions, the Malia altar stone, the Arkalochori Axe, and seal fragment HM 992.

In the years since the publication of the CHIC, several changes and refinements have been made. The primary adjustments were the inclusion of images that were originally left out due to scholars mistakenly believing that they were decorative. Additionally, more Cretan hieroglyphic inscriptions were found on the island of Samothrace in the northeastern Aegean Sea. The three main symbol inventories of Cretan hieroglyphs were compiled by Evans in 1909, Louk C. Meijer in 1982, and Jean-Pierre Olivier and Louis Godart in 1996.

The collection in CHIC has 96 syllabograms, which represent sounds, words, or portions of words. Ten of those also double as logograms (written characters that represent words). It has been determined that many of these symbols seem to have Linear A counterparts.

Even to this day, new artifacts are being found. One example is a sealstone found on a foundation deposit at the Neopalatial area of the Cult Centre of the City of Knossos that was dated to the Final Palatial Period. With each new discovery, scholars may be closer to deciphering this ancient writing system.

# Proto-Elamite Script

*An undeciphered script more than 3,200 years old could reveal untold secrets about the ancient civilizations of Iran. Scholars and amateurs alike are making new discoveries that may aid in finally cracking this age-old mystery.*

\* \* \* \*

THE PROTO-ELAMITE SCRIPT is an Early Bronze Age writing system that was in use over a very large geographical area. Most tablets and fragments were found in Susa, with over 1600 having been discovered, but others have been found in Anshan, Tepe Yahya, Tape Sofalin, Tepe Sialk, Ozbaki, Shahr-e Sukhteh, and Tal-e Ghazir. These ancient Elamite cultures existed in an area that eventually became Persia and later Iran. The development of Proto-Elamite started with clay *bullae*—marked tokens and envelopes—in the ninth millennium BC. The tokens remained in use around Susa and Uruk even after a more advanced Proto-cuneiform system was firmly in use. The earliest tablets are largely numerical, but the system would later evolve into symbols read left-to-right.

Proto-Elamite is still largely undecipherable. Scholars have been able to surmise that a lot of the tablets are economical in nature, perhaps for the accounting of goods; they've been able to figure this much out due to similarities between Proto-cuneiform and Proto-Elamite. All of the Proto-Elamite texts that have been discovered thus far have been published, but the proposed sign list is still a work-in-progress. While there are still disagreements over the meaning of some signs, there has been enough of a consensus to allow decipherment to progress. In 2012, Dr. Jacob Dahl of the University of Oxford made the nearly 1600 images of Proto-Elamite tablets available as high-resolution images online on a wiki of the Cuneiform Digital Library Initiative. What he hopes is that crowdsourcing by academics and amateurs will lead to greater progress in understanding the script.

Archeologist François Desset of the University of Tehran in Iran announced a proposed decipherment and translation in 2020, further publishing a paper in 2022. Essentially, he used an ancient set of silver beakers to propose a method for reading Linear Elamite. Additionally, Desset seems to believe that Proto-Elamite and Sumerian cuneiform were used in the same time period, despite radiocarbon dating showing that Proto-Elamite tablets date slightly later than Sumerian cuneiform. His proposal has been met with skepticism from his colleagues.

# The Somerton Man's Cryptic Code

*When the corpse of a mysterious man was found on the beach with no explanation, the world's curiosity was piqued. Even stranger still, a torn page was discovered in his pocket, leading authorities to a notebook that contained a coded message. What could the cryptic message mean, and does it have anything to do with his mysterious death?*

❋ ❋ ❋ ❋

THE SOMERTON MAN is an unidentified man whose body was found on the beach at Somerton Park, Adelaide, Australia, on December 1, 1948. The case is also known as "tamám shud," ("is over" or "is finished" in Persian) named after the text on the scrap of paper found on his person at the time of discovery. It was later discovered that it had been torn from the last page of the book, *Rubaiyat of Omar Khayyám* by twelfth-century poet Omar Khayyám. The theme of *Rubaiyat* is that "one should live life to the fullest and have no regrets when it ends." That, along with no obvious health issues and no signs of foul play, caused authorities to theorize that he may have taken his own life with poison. Once authorities managed to locate the exact copy the scrap was torn from, they discovered the indentations of prior handwriting: a local telephone number, an unidentified number, and a coded message.

## The Mystery Deepens

The coded message consists of five lines of text in capital letters. The second line has been struck out; experts are unsure if it was intentional or an error. Additionally, it is unclear whether the first line begins with an M or W, but when compared to other Ms in the code, it is suspected to be a W. Experts are also unsure whether the L in the crossed-out line of text reading MLIAOI is actually an L and not an I with a deletion line or underline. Lastly, there is an X above the last O in the code; it is unknown whether this is part of the code or not.

Experts in cryptography and amateur code breakers alike have attempted to crack it for decades, to no avail. In 1978, Department of Defence cryptographers analyzed the handwritten text, but reported that it would be impossible to provide "a satisfactory answer." They explained that the short length of the code made it impossible to glean anything from it.

In 2004, Gerry Feltus, retired detective, wrote that the last line, "ITTMTSAMSTGAB" might stand for "It's Time To Move To South Australia Moseley Street," but that proved an unsatisfactory interpretation. So too with the analysis by John Rehling, a computational linguist. In 2014, he suspected that the letters might be the initials of some English text; however, he's never found a match in any of the large surveys he's conducted. Thus, he sadly concluded that the code may be shorthand, and the meaning will probably never be determined.

# The D'Agapeyeff Cipher

*Can you solve an 80-year-old cipher that even its creator couldn't crack? Ponder the challenge that is the D'Agapeyeff cipher.*

✳   ✳   ✳   ✳

T HE D'AGAPEYEFF CIPHER is an unsolved cipher that appears at the end of the first edition of *Codes and Ciphers*, a 1939 beginner's book on cryptography written by cryptographer and cartographer Alexander D'Agapeyeff. The cipher text is as follows:

75628 28591 62916 48164 91748 58464 74748 28483 81638 18174

74826 26475 83828 49175 74658 37575 75936 36565 81638 17585

75756 46282 92857 46382 75748 38165 81848 56485 64858 56382

72628 36281 81728 16463 75828 16483 63828 58163 63630 47481

91918 46385 84656 48565 62946 26285 91859 17491 72756 46575

71658 36264 74818 28462 82649 18193 65626 48484 91838 57491

81657 27483 83858 28364 62726 26562 83759 27263 82827 27283

82858 47582 81837 28462 82837 58164 75748 58162 92000

It was originally described as a "challenge cipher," presumably there to test the new knowledge of those who had finished studying his book. However, the cipher has remained unsolved for over eighty years. When asked for clues on its solution, D'Agapeyeff confessed that he has forgotten how the cipher is solved!

It is possible that not all the numbers used in the cipher text are related to the puzzle, and are actually "nulls." D'Agapeyeff mentions this himself on page 111 of his book: "The cipher is of course easily made out, but if every third, fourth, or fifth letter, as may be previously arranged, is a dummy inserted after a message has been put into cipher, it is then extremely difficult to decipher unless you are in the secret." However, cryptographers have noted that the letter frequency (the number of times letters of the alphabet appear on average in written language) distribution is too flat for a 196-character message written in English.

Another theory of cryptographers is the Polybius Square method, which is also detailed within *Codes and Ciphers*. The Polybius Square is an encryption device where you place the alphabet into a 5×5 grid with the numbers 1–5 listed across and down the sides of the square, and use the numbers to encrypt the letters. The main evidence for this theory's relevance is that the structure of the D'Agapeyeff cipher has similarities to the Polybius Square. However, the plaintext of the exercise for the Polybius square within his book has a mistake in it, which may mean that the D'Agapeyeff cipher has mistakes within it too! For this reason, it may be impossible to solve.

# The Zodiac Ciphers

*The serial murderer known as "Zodiac" made international headlines and frightened and enthralled Americans in the late 1960s and early 1970s. Operating in Northern California, he murdered at least five victims between December 1968 and October 1969. He remains unidentified to this day, inspiring professional and amateur detectives who think they can solve this long-lasting mystery.*

✳  ✳  ✳  ✳

PERHAPS ONE OF the most unique and eccentric things the killer did while active was to mail taunting letters and cards to regional newspapers. Zodiac's messages included the threat of more violence if they weren't printed. Some of these letters contained cryptograms, of which there are four. The first cryptogram was solved fairly quickly, but the second wasn't solved until 2020, and the other two remain unsolved to this day.

## The Solved Ciphers

The first cipher, sent in three pieces to three newspaper organizations in the Bay Area, was solved in a week's time by Donald Gene and Bettye June Harden. They managed to solve it without any technological help, which was quite a feat even in the 1960s. To summarize, the message rambled on about how the Zodiac Killer enjoys hunting people instead of wild animals, how it gives him a thrill that's better than any other experience one could have, how he will be reborn in paradise after death, and how his victims will be his slaves in the afterlife. It concludes by proclaiming that he will not give up his name because he needs to collect more slaves for his afterlife.

The cipher didn't give authorities any clues as to the killer's identity, but it did clue them in to delusions he may have been experiencing. It also gave them a probable motive for the killings, but didn't shed any light on when he could strike again or at whom.

While this first cipher would prove relatively quick to solve, authorities and cryptanalysts wouldn't be as lucky with the remaining few. One of the most famous ones—the one containing 340 characters—eluded code breakers and cryptanalysts until 2020 when David Oranchak, Sam Blake, and Jarl van Eycke used state-of-the-art software to help them crack the cipher. About the 50-year struggle to solve it, Oranchak says, "It took a lot of computational effort, and it's been a real source of frustration for a lot of people. So many people conjure coincidences out of thin air, and the more coincidences they generate, the stronger their evidence." Each code breaker had been working on it independently for years, but they joined forces in 2018 after Blake saw Oranchak's talk about the cipher at the annual meeting of the American Cryptogram Association in Asheville, North Carolina. After Blake responded to his talk, the pair began corresponding and discussed hundreds of thousands of possible ways to read and crack the code.

To aid in sifting through their hypotheses, Orenchak brought in van Eycke, a code breaker who wrote AZdecrypt, a piece of software used for decoding homophonic substitutions (a method wherein you replace each letter with a variety of substitutes, the number of potential substitutes being proportional to the frequency of the letter). In late 2020, an updated version of his software churned through all of the trio's theories and possibilities, finally returning two phrases: "trying to catch me" and "gas chamber." They put those phrases in the software, ran it again, and more words, such as "paradice [sic]" and "slaves," appeared. After working at it a bit more, they had their completed message in December of 2020. Oranchak sent in their results to the FBI, who verified the results:

I HOPE YOU ARE HAVING LOTS OF FUN IN TRYING TO CATCH ME

THAT WASNT ME ON THE TV SHOW

WHICH BRINGS UP A POINT ABOUT ME

I AM NOT AFRAID OF THE GAS CHAMBER

BECAUSE IT WILL SEND ME TO PARADICE [sic] ALL THE SOONER

BECAUSE I NOW HAVE ENOUGH SLAVES TO WORK FOR ME

WHERE EVERYONE ELSE HAS NOTHING WHEN THEY REACH PARADICE [sic]

SO THEY ARE AFRAID OF DEATH

I AM NOT AFRAID BECAUSE I KNOW THAT MY NEW LIFE IS

LIFE WILL BE AN EASY ONE IN PARADICE [sic] DEATH

When asked about how the cipher remained a mystery for so long, Oranchak theorizes that it's due to the code being so computationally-heavy. "No one in 1969 could likely have decoded the Zodiac's message." But because the Zodiac Killer sent these messages as ways of taunting investigators and the media, it is unlikely he intended them to be unsolved for this long. Could it be that he, himself, had no idea how difficult he had made them? Regardless of his intentions, the two remaining ciphers—13 and 32 characters long respectively—have yet to be solved.

# Linear A, the Lost Language of Crete

*Early forms of the Greek language have been heavily studied for centuries. But have you ever wondered what previous language Greek developed from? How much do we know about it? Let's take a look at Linear A, a probable precursor to Greek. Remnants of this language exist in written form, but Linear A continues to be shrouded in mystery.*

✳   ✳   ✳   ✳

LINEAR A IS a writing system that predates the first written examples of the Greek language. Used by the Minoans of Crete from 1800 to 1450 BC, Linear A was primarily used in palace and religious writings. It would later develop into Linear B, which is a syllabic script used for writing in Mycenaean Greek, an early version of the Greek language.

Linear B is fairly similar to Linear A, sharing many symbols and a similar syllabic structure. It may have partially derived from Cretan hieroglyphs. However, while Linear B has yielded some secrets, Linear A remains undeciphered. The only parts of the script that can be read with any degree of certainty are the numbers—and even then, the words for those numbers remain unknown.

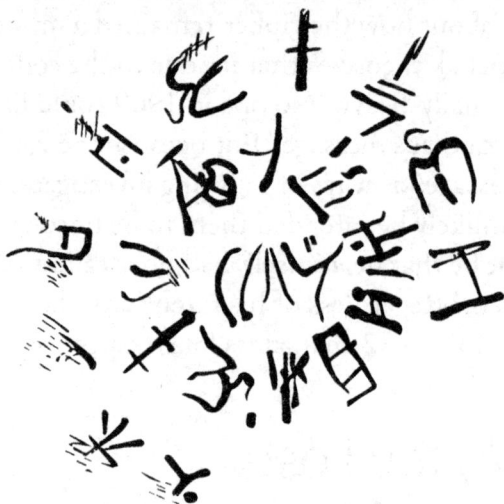

Attempts to decipher Linear A and the Minoan language typically begin with Linear B due to their similarities. The written language consists of numerals, phonetic signs (sounds), ligatures, and composite signs (characters composed of two or more letters joined together, i.e. æ), and ideograms (pictures or symbols that represent things or ideas, but not particular words); this results in hundreds of different signs.

Compared to the complexity of the script, numbers are slightly more straightforward. They follow a decimal system, where units are represented by vertical dashes, tens by horizontal dashes, hundreds by circles, and thousands by circles with rays. They even have special symbols to indicate fractions and weights.

While Linear A is considered a deceased Cretan language, script relics have also been seen at sites in Greece, Turkey, and Israel. Paleographers have seen it written on stone offering tablets, gold and silver hairpins, roundels (a round figure or object), and ceramics. The earliest object that has Linear A on it was dated around 1800 BC. It became more common around 1625 BC before falling out of use around 1450 BC. Linear A is an interesting bridge between the Cretan hieroglyphs of a previous age and the true syllabic script of Linear B.

# Chapter 7

# Without a Trace: Ships and Airplanes

## This Tiger Left No Tracks

*Multiple mysteries—from the very nature of its mission during the Vietnam War to its eerie disappearance in 1962—surround Flying Tiger Line Flight 739. Details of the worst accident involving a Lockheed L-1049 Super Constellation airplane will likely never be known.*

✳    ✳    ✳    ✳

F AMILIES OF SOME of the 93 American soldiers aboard Flying Tiger Line Flight 739 claim the passengers seemed especially hopeless before the 1962 Vietnam War mission. While "company line" said the soldiers were specialists heading to South Vietnam to train others, some maintain that this flight had a top-secret mission that has never been revealed. Some allegedly referred to their flight as a "death warrant," leading historians to believe that there was more to the mission than training.

Along with 11 crew members and three South Vietnamese soldiers, the soldiers on the L-1049 Super Constellation took off from Travis Air Force Base on March 14, 1962, due for four fuel stops on the way to Saigon. The aircraft had logged more than 17,000 hours over five years in service. Fuel stops were routine for the Lockheed staple, and the first stops were just that—a few minor maintenance issues were quickly resolved. The leg of the trip from Guam to the Philippines, however, produced a mystery for the ages.

The plane had nine hours' worth of fuel for an eight-hour flight. The captain requested clearance to reach 18,000 feet from an altitude of 10,000 feet. The request was granted. A few hours later, however, Guam reported that it was the last time they had received radio contact from Flying Tiger Line Flight 739. Multiple attempts to contact the flight were made—none successful. Ten hours after departure time, officials concluded it had crashed.

## Searching for Answers

One of the largest searches for an aircraft in the Pacific Ocean ensued, with 48 planes scouring hundreds of thousands of square miles. Sadly, no remnants of the plane or its passengers have been found to this day. We know it's impossible for a plane and its passengers to completely vanish in midair, but no other explanation exists due to the lack of evidence. Why did some soldiers express such dismay before leaving their families to board the plane?

One theory suggests there may have been foul play, perhaps relating to another Flying Tiger Line flight carrying military cargo that crashed on the same day. Some speculated that the passengers of Flying Tiger Line Flight 379 might have been kidnapped, or that the plane had been hijacked. Though the two planes departed from the Travis Air Force base the same day, there is no concrete evidence showing any connection between the two Flying Tiger Line flights.

Another theory speculates that Flying Tiger Line Flight 379 exploded midair before falling into the ocean. This idea comes from witnesses on a ship, the SS *T L Linzen*, who described seeing a bright flash of light followed by two red lights plummeting toward the sea at differing speeds. The sighting occurred where the flight's expected position would be, so search crews went to the area to see what they could find. But after eight hours of searching, officials discovered no evidence of the plane or its passengers.

# Doomed Round-the-World Flight Leaves Ongoing Mystery

*Pan Am Flight 7 from San Francisco to Honolulu was supposed to be just the first leg in a luxurious, round-the-world trip. Instead, it turned into a fatal crash that took 44 lives and spawned a search for answers that continues more than 65 years later.*

\* \* \* \*

IT WAS THE conclusion no one could bear to hear. "Insufficient tangible evidence at this time to determine the cause of the accident." It came from the U.S. Civil Aeronautics Board after a long investigation into the November 8, 1957, crash of Pan American Airways Flight 7 from San Francisco to Honolulu that killed 36 passengers and eight crew members. It was not a conclusion Gregg Herken and Ken Fortenberry were going to settle for.

Herken and Fortenberry had close connections to two people who died on the PAA-944, Clipper *Romance of the Skies*, a double-decker plane that had been called the "ocean liner of the skies." It was a Boeing 377 Stratocruiser, a sprawling aircraft that had experienced significant mechanical issues over the years but offered a luxurious voyage for its passengers, including champagne and caviar, a large cocktail area, and seven-course dining.

Herken was in elementary school in California's Bay Area at the time. His favorite substitute teacher, Marie McGrath, was a flight attendant on Pan Am Flight 7, the first leg of what was to be an around-the-world, once-in-a-lifetime trip. Fortenberry was also a child at the time, the son of the doomed flight's second officer, Bill. As the years passed, the two started separate searches for evidence as to what caused Pan Am 7 to crash into the Pacific Ocean some 900 nautical miles northeast of Honolulu, and later they joined forces to find answers for the families who also lost loved ones in the tragedy.

## Nothing Routine About Routine

The weather could hardly have been better when Flight 7 took off from San Francisco. Clear skies over smooth seas. The pilots announced that the 10-hour expected flight time would be smooth. The 36 passengers could turn their attention to food, drink, conversation, or sleep.

Flight 7 contacted ground control on the hour with routine position reports. There was nothing unusual about them, up to and including the 5:04 p.m. report. The plane was cruising at 10,000 feet at that time, east of Hawaii. One hour later, however, there was no report at all. No check-in, but no distress call either. Concern began to well up. No contact could be made with the plane. At 6:35 p.m., a half hour after the hourly report should have been made, air traffic control issued an alert that Flight 7 was missing. The Coast Guard sent search planes.

An intense air and sea search began at daylight, but to no avail. It was not until November 14, six days after the crash, that a search plane reported wreckage based on its radar. It led to the discovery of floating debris and 19 bodies 955 miles northeast of Honolulu, indicating the plane had gone off course after its last position check. Watches found on some of the victims had stopped at 5:25 p.m., presumably on impact, 21 minutes after the plane's last report.

What happened in those 21 minutes has never been conclusively determined. The lengthy official investigation led to an announcement in January 1959, more than a year after the crash, that "no probable cause" could be identified. The Stratocruiser line had experienced mechanical failures in the past, including propeller failure that had led to engine loss. The maintenance log for this particular plane had noted a "constant fluctuation" in oil pressure, leaks from the turbochargers, and persistent cooling problems. No one, however, could be certain.

## Sabotage? Insurance Fraud? Negligence?

Herken and Fortenberry looked into the long list of mechanical issue these planes had experienced in the past. They devoured the accident reports, noting that several victims were found to have had elevated levels of carbon monoxide in their systems. They wondered if a fire or gas in the cabin had incapacitated those on board in the moments after the final position report.

They also noted similar patterns in previous mechanical failures, where propeller issues caused engine separation from an airplane. In the Flight 7 crash, the top section of an engine cowl ring was found embedded in a scorched pillow. Four years earlier, the pilot of a sister Stratocruiser had saved his aircraft from a similar circumstance by dumping fuel from a wing tank. The two wondered if perhaps the Flight 7 pilot might have decided not to do so because an existing fire/smoke situation could have turned a fuel dump into an inferno.

Herken and Fortenberry also considered a couple of possible foul-play suspects on the passenger list. One of the passengers, William Payne, was an ex-Navy underwater demolitions expert who had bought three insurance policies—one that paid double for accidental death—and a one-way ticket to Hawaii. He had told his family he was going there to collect a debt, but his family said the money would have been less than the price of the ticket. Though no one could be certain he even boarded the plane, his wife ended up collecting on the insurance.

Then there was Eugene Crosthwaite, a Pan Am employee who had changed his will days before the flight, leaving an updated copy in the glove compartment of the car he'd parked at the airport. He was known to have been upset with the airline. Fortenberry said he heard from Crosthwaite's stepdaughter during his investigation, and she told him Eugene was "suicidal and out of his mind." Could he have terrorized the plane?

While Fortenberry focused on Crosthwaite, Herken favored the mechanical failure theory. Both men acknowledge that, at a time when Pan Am Airways was struggling financially and trying to stay in the black, corners were being cut around inspection protocols. One thing the duo was in complete agreement on was their quest to keep the memories of Flight 7 victims alive. A memorial to the victims was unveiled at California's Millbrae History Museum in 2023.

## Art Heist? Soviet Plot? Accident? Varig 967 Remains a Mystery

*Of the 240-plus crashes, accidents, and mishaps suffered by Boeing 707 aircraft over the years, only one disappeared under circumstances that remain unknown. There are many theories as to why Varig Flight 967 is the only plane in that category, but a definitive answer remains elusive.*

\* \* \* \*

CAPTAIN GILBERTO ARÚJO was an experienced pilot with more than 23,000 flying hours on his resume. He had survived a crash in 1973. On paper, his flight from Japan to Brazil on January 30, 1979, should have been routine. The plane was a Boeing 707-323C cargo aircraft and was carrying 53 paintings by Manabu Mabe, then valued at more than $1 million. Five crew members were on board with him. Varig Flight 967 was about 40 minutes from Narita International Airport toward a layover at Los Angeles International Airport when it went radio silent.

The flight took off at 8:23 p.m., and the crew was able to check in with the Narita tower 20 minutes later, when they were about 300 miles from the coast of Japan. It would be their final check-in. Less than half an hour later, no one could reach them. Workers in the tower continuously tried to communicate with the flight for the next hour, to no avail. More drastic measures

were taken once the situation was deemed an emergency. The Navy and Air Force were dispatched to search for the plane, but after eight days of combing the area where it was suspected to have crashed, they came up with nothing. No remains of the plane, its paintings, or passengers were ever found. What actually happened to the plane is still unknown to this day.

Several theories swirl around the mystery. One is that the flight was hijacked by art thieves. Another theory posits that the plane accidentally flew into Soviet territory and was shot down. Lastly, some have speculated that the flight was carrying valuable aircraft components that Russia wanted to acquire. Some believe it's possible the Soviets tracked down the flight and forced it to land in their territory in order to obtain whatever these components might have been.

Each of these theories is purely speculative—they are not backed by hard evidence and, in some cases, admittedly far-fetched. What is more likely to have happened is that the plane simply became depressurized, resulting in everyone on board passing out and the plane crashing into the Pacific Ocean—a territory so vast that it is unlikely any remains of the wreckage will ever be recovered.

# Controversy Surrounds Mount Erebus Disaster

*A computer system update the morning of a sightseeing flight contributed to the deadliest accident in Air New Zealand history, and a controversial investigation, when a DC-10 slammed into a mountain on Antarctica in 1979. All 257 people aboard the plane perished, through many of their photos and videos live as a reminder of the deadly day.*

✳  ✳  ✳  ✳

S OME OF THE photos and video salvaged from the wreckage of Flight TE 901 show spectacular views of Antarctica. After all, that was the purpose of the trip. Most flights are designed to get people from Point A to B. This one, an Air New Zealand DC-10 carrying 257 passengers and crew, was for the express purpose of witnessing the spectacular, snowy terrain of Antarctica—a sightseeing tour covering 5,300 miles and 12 hours from New Zealand and back.

Those who boarded the plane on November 28, 1979, were excited, to say the least. Their seats weren't cheap, it was the last such tour flight of the season, and rising fuel prices had some wondering whether this might be the last for some time. Sir Edmund Hillary had served as a tour guide on previous flights. But this time, prior commitments caused the famed New Zealand explorer to give those duties to his climbing companion, Peter Mulgrew.

Captain Jim Collins and first officer Greg Cassin were experienced flyers, though neither had made the Antarctica trip before. Their engineer, Gordon Brooks, had, and the preflight briefings had everyone prepared for what should have been a routine and enjoyable trip. As it happened, there was a massive snag that no one saw coming. The route taken by the previous sightseeing tours had, unknowingly, veered by about

20–30 miles from the officially approved flight path near Mount Erebus. The "erroneous" route was actually safer, allowing the plane to fly at a lower altitude in decent weather, which was better for sightseeing.

The error was apparently reported to the airline sometime before the November 28 flight. And in the early morning hours—several hours before departure—someone at Air New Zealand fixed the error in the computer system. No one told the crew.

### Too Close. Too Low. Too Little Visibility.

As passengers loaded their cameras—even some high-end, high-tech video cameras for the time—with images from their already spectacular tour of the Antarctic coast, those manning the cockpit thought they were in the clear as they approached 12,448-foot Mount Erebus. Thinking they were a safe distance away, as previous tours were, they received clearance to descend to a lower altitude. However, the snow-covered ground below, white clouds, and an icy mountain caused a "whiteout," keeping the pilots from identifying their danger until it was too late.

A little before 1 p.m., the automated warning system detected the plane was too close to the ground, or, in this case, the mountain. "Whoop, whoop, pull up," repeated several times, were its last warnings before the sound of impact with Mount Erebus. There were no survivors.

Air New Zealand was accused of hiding and shredding paperwork, blaming pilot error, and refusing to comply with the investigation after the crash. As it turned out, the late updating of the system and the lack of communication with the plane's crew were among administrative blunders that certainly contributed to the disaster.

Then-New Zealand Prime Minister Jacinda Arden used the fortieth anniversary of the crash, in 2019, to finally issue a government apology to the families of the victims. "After

40 years, on behalf of today's government," Arden said, "the time has come to apologize for the actions of an airline then in full state ownership, which ultimately caused the loss of the aircraft and the loss of those you loved."

# TWA Flight 800 Forever Changed Airline Safety

*Airborne just 12 minutes before an explosion took it down off the eastern coast of the United States, killing all 230 aboard, TWA Flight 800 unveiled a mechanical issue that should never again arise. A long, pricey investigation put to rest any conspiracy theories—at least for most.*

✳   ✳   ✳   ✳

THE FLIGHT ITSELF, regrettably, lasted just 12 minutes. The investigation into what caused the explosion of Trans World Airlines Flight 800, on July 17, 1996, took four long years. There were valid reasons it was—at the time—the longest and costliest ($40 million) investigation in the history of the National Transportation Safety Board. In the final analysis, the explosion that killed all 230 people on board was found to have resulted from a mechanical failure.

Some still question that finding, based largely on eyewitness accounts from more than 30 people who described seeing at least one streak of light that appeared to be ascending near the Boeing 747 bound from New York's JFK International Airport to Paris. Such descriptions, which some scientists attributed to optical illusions that occur with certain types of explosions, caused some to question whether a terrorist missile strike might have been responsible for blowing up the 170-ton jet.

The FBI got involved early in the investigation, advancing the speculation that something nefarious might have been involved. The long investigation ruled out foul play, however, focusing on a fuel tank in the center wing area of the plane.

"The explosion that occurred on TWA 800 was in the center wing fuel tank and was not from anything external," said John Purvis, head of Boeing's accident investigation department at the time. "The NTSB was never able to pinpoint the precise cause, but it was clear that it [the explosion] was from within the tank."

## From Out of the Blue

There were no indications of any danger when 230 people—including 18 crew members and 20 off-duty airline employees—boarded the flight at JFK. More than half of those on the flight were Americans, including a group of 16 students and five chaperones from a high school French club in Pennsylvania. Forty passengers were French, with eight other countries represented. The 25-year-old jet had completed more than 16,000 successful flights.

The weather had been muggy but the skies were mostly clear when the plane took off at 8:19 p.m. There were no distress calls from the cockpit during the mere 12 minutes the flight was in the air, though the captain did mention a "crazy" reading about two minutes before the explosion took place—a sudden, fiery event seen by more than 250 witnesses that sent the aircraft in pieces into the Atlantic.

Search teams sprang into action the following morning, eventually recovering most of the wreckage from the flight. The plane was pieced back together in a Long Island hangar during the investigation, and family members of the victims were later allowed to visit the reconstruction. No sign of a strike by a missile or anything external was detected during the long investigation. If such a strike had occurred, there would be the additional unusual circumstance of no group claiming responsibility, which would normally be the case in a terrorist attack.

Though no conclusive reason was ever determined for the igniting of a fuel tank in the center wing area, the NTSB report did call it an "overpressure event"—a rapid increase in pressure that resulted in a structural failure. In the wake of the tragedy, the airline industry adopted several recommendations in inspection activities and in the structure of center wing tanks in 747s.

# Nosedive Leads to Deadly Halloween, Dueling Theories

*Egypt and the United States maintained far different conclusions over what caused EgyptAir Flight 990 to crash on Halloween Day 1999. It was not for a lack of evidence indicating it was the deliberate act of a pilot that caused one of the deadliest crashes in the history of Boeing 767 aircrafts.*

✳    ✳    ✳    ✳

HALLOWEEN MORNING, 1999, brought no tricks or treats to those in the airline industry, those with loved ones aboard EgyptAir Flight 990, or those who were on a Merchant Marine ship that came across airplane wreckage and human remains floating in the Atlantic Ocean about 60 miles south of Nantucket. Some of the sailors gagged at the sight, combined with the smell of kerosene—unburned jet fuel—rising from the water.

They had stumbled across the wreckage of a morning flight bound from New York's JFK Airport to Cairo, and it became quickly apparent that no one lived. On board had been 203 passengers and 14 crew members, including veteran captain Ahmed El-Habashi, first officer Adel Anwar, relief captain Raouf Noureldin, relief first officer Gameel Al-Batouti, and the chief pilot for EgyptAir, Hatem Rushdy. A relief crew was required due to the 10-hour flight time, and customarily would take over 4–5 hours into such a trip.

About 20 minutes after their 1:20 a.m. takeoff, however, Al-Batouti insisted he take over for Anwar as first officer. Anwar was hesitant at first, but eventually agreed. This left only El-Habashi and Al-Batouti in the cockpit. After the plane reached an altitude of 33,000 feet, El-Habashi put the Boeing 767 on autopilot and left the cockpit to use the restroom. Just 10 seconds later, the plane began descending rapidly, causing the aircraft to experience zero gravity.

The captain hurried back to the cockpit, repeatedly asking, "What's happening?" Al-Batouti's only response was, "I rely on God." It is said that Al-Batouti had taken control of the plane, turning off autopilot, and started the sudden descent. El-Habashi tried to increase power by pushing the throttles, but then realized the fuel had been cut off from both engines. Against those odds, he managed to temporarily stop the nose-dive and reached a steady altitude of 25,000 feet.

Because the engines no longer had fuel, however, the plane lost electrical power. A few minutes later, the plane started descending again at a rate of 20,000 feet per minute. The left engine and other parts of the plane broke loose, falling into the ocean. What remained of EgyptAir Flight 990 hit the water around 1:52 a.m., killing all 217 people on board. It became the deadliest crash in the history of EgyptAir and one of the deadliest ever for a Boeing 767.

## Egypt Calls It 'Mechanical Failure'

As soon as the plane dropped off radar, a search and rescue mission began. The Egyptian government, lacking the resources to support the mission some 5,000 miles away in 250 feet of water, signed over the investigation to the U.S. government. Sunrise brought the discovery of the oil sheen, wreckage, and human remains. DNA helped identify the victims. The National Transportation Safety Board (NTSB) found the cockpit voice recorder, which held the frantic conversation between El-Habashi and Al-Batouti, and they determined the latter to be responsible.

Their official report pinned the cause on "the relief first officer's flight control inputs," and went on to say that "the reason for the relief first officer's actions was not determined." The Egyptian

Civil Aviation Authority did not agree with the NTSB's conclusion and decided to launch their own investigation. They later released a statement saying "the Relief First Officer did not deliberately dive the airplane into the ocean," blaming mechanical failure.

Whether it was a political agenda coloring the ECAA's conclusion is the stuff of conjecture, but the Egyptian government held to its notion that those in the cockpit were working together to try to regain control of a plane in a deadly dive. The U.S. government was unable to determine whether Al-Batouti's motives were suicide, terrorism, a combination of the two, or something altogether different. The last words captured by the flight recorder were those of a frantic El-Habashi yelling, "Pull! Pull with me! Pull with me! Pull with me!"

# "Miracle of the Andes" a Testament to Human Will

*One of the most inspiring and talked-about survival stories in history followed a plane crash in the Andes Mountains in 1972. Just 16 of the 45 people on board Uruguayan Air Force Flight 571 survived after a 72-day struggle in some of the harshest conditions imaginable.*

✳ ✳ ✳ ✳

**M**ILAGRO DE LOS Andes. Miracle of the Andes. Their story was a big-screen or made-for-TV movie waiting to happen. And happen it did. The crash of Uruguayan Air Force Flight 571 and the ensuing struggle for survival of those who lived through it has been the subject of numerous documentaries, a Netflix movie, and the popular 1993 feature film *Alive*, among others. It was referenced in a Stephen King novel (*The Shining*) and written about extensively. It's one of those instances where the facts, including cannibalism, seem crazier than anything a fiction writer might dream up.

The story began, innocently enough, with a rugby match. The Old Christians Club, from Uruguay, was due to face an English team, the Old Boys Club, in Santiago, Chile, and decided to charter a plane for the trip. It was a Uruguayan Air Force twin turboprop Fairchild FH-227D, on which five crew members and 40 passengers—19 team members—boarded on October 12, 1972. They were supposed to fly direct from Montevideo to Santiago, but a large storm over the Andes forced an overnight stay in Argentina. The next day, weather again became an issue.

The captain, veteran Air Force pilot Colonel Julio César Ferradas, waited until afternoon to take off to give the storm time to clear. There was still considerable cloud cover, forcing Ferradas and his crew to rely on their instruments rather than visual clues.

Thinking they had already cleared the Andes, the cockpit requested and was granted permission to descend—before they should have, as it happened. The plane struck a mountain, shearing off both wings and splitting the fuselage in half. Three crew members and nine passengers were killed by the impact. The harrowing experience, however, was just beginning.

## 72 Unimaginable Days

The plane came to rest on a remote mountain glacier in Argentina, almost 12,000 feet above sea level. The aircraft was white, which gave air crews on the search mission almost no chance to spot it among the snowy and icy conditions. Unknown to the survivors, the wreckage sat just 13 miles from an abandoned hotel that might have been able to provide limited shelter from the harsh conditions. As it was, they turned the fuselage into a makeshift shelter, removing seats to "wall off" the small cabin from the elements.

The first night saw the copilot and four others die from injuries suffered in the crash. One of the players, Nando Parrado, had a fractured skull and remained in a coma for three days. Upon awakening, he learned that his mother was among the dead and his 19-year-old sister was severely injured. He tried to keep her alive, but she perished on the eighth day. Temperatures were dropping well below zero, and some of the survivors had never seen snow in their lives. It became clear in the first week that sustenance was going to be a life-or-death ordeal. Eight chocolate bars, a tin of mussels, three jars of jam, a tin of almonds, a few dates, dried plums, candy, and several bottles of wine amounted to the survivors' rations after the crash.

Parrado wrote in his autobiography that, over one three-day span, he ate a single chocolate-covered peanut. The 28 survivors after the first few weeks adhered to strict rationing as they waited, hoped, and prayed someone would find them. At a certain point, they agreed in an unthinkable conversation that, when conditions would take some of their lives, it would be advisable—even imperative—for the survivors to eat the flesh of those who expired.

"I thought if I would die, I would be proud that my body would be used for someone else," recalled Roberto Canessa, a 19-year-old medical student who survived the ordeal. "We laid thin strips of frozen flesh aside on a piece of sheet metal. Each of us finally consumed our piece when we could bear to."

## The Long Trek to Survival

Seventeen days after the crash, an avalanche overcame the fuselage and killed eight more. Those who survived were trapped with the dead bodies in a further confined space for three days. They dug out, only to be greeted by a blizzard, and eventually the group decided Canessa and Parrado would make an attempt to go out and find help. Without climbing gear and seriously underdressed and underprepared for the elements, the duo climbed 4,000 feet to a higher peak. They slept in makeshift sleeping bags, crafted from remnants of the plane.

They found, after 10 days of perilous hiking, a group of Chilean shepherds. The group went for help, and Parrado was able to lead three Chilean Air Force choppers to the crash site for a rescue. In all, 16 people survived. The bodies of the others were left at the peak for some time before finally being buried in a mass grave near the site. Mountain climbers still visit the spot today.

All 16 survivors were Roman Catholic, and many feared damnation for the lengths they took to stay alive on the mountain. Their confessions were heard by reassuring priests in the aftermath, and Pope John Paul II and the Uruguayan Catholic Church absolved them.

# Worst Terrorist Attack in Canadian History Still Conjures Pain

*The fact no one truly paid a price for orchestrating the worst terrorist attack in the history of Canada stings globally, but nowhere more so than in Canada and India. The bombing of Air India Flight 182 in 1985 took the lives of all 329 people on board.*

✳   ✳   ✳   ✳

UNTIL THE SEPTEMBER 11 attacks on the United States in 2001, the "Kanishka Bombing" of Air India Flight 182 was the deadliest act of aviation terrorism in world history. All 329 people flying on a Boeing 747 from Montreal to London, England—a stop on the way to India—were killed when the plane blew up off the coast of Ireland. The victims included 268 Canadian citizens, most of Indian origin, and 24 citizens of India. Those responsible were thought to be Sikh separatists seeking revenge for a 1984 attack by the Indian Army.

Many people in Canada and India remain angered, hurt, and any number of other emotions knowing that only one person involved in the terrorism that brought down the plane was ever punished for a crime, and even that was minimal. Electrician Inderjit Singh Reyat, a dual British-Canadian citizen, was jailed in the UK for 10 years for his role in a related explosion in Japan and pleaded guilty to manslaughter for constructing the bomb that was placed in a suitcase and detonated on Flight 182. For that, he received an additional five years but was released in 2016.

Reyat's purported partner in the bombing, Talwinder Singh Parmar, was the leader of an extremist group called Babbar Khalsa that's now banned in Canada and India. Thought to be the mastermind of the attack, he was arrested by the Royal Canadian Mounted Police, but the flimsy case against him was later dropped. Parmar wound up being killed by Indian police in 1992. It was only after the fact that word came that a Canadian secret service member had followed Parmar and Reyat into a wooded area weeks before the bombing and disregarded a "loud, explosive sound." There were other indications Canadian police had been warned months before the flight that a plot was underway to take down a plane.

Canada launched a public inquiry looking into the attack in 2006. Four years later, then Canadian Prime Minister Stephen Harper made an apology to the families of the victims after the report determined that a "cascading series of errors" had led to the "largest mass murder in Canadian history." The plane had been named after Indian Emperor Kanishka. In 2011, Canada launched the Kanishka Project, a $10 million initiative aimed at countering extremism.

# Firestorm of Controversy Follows Fiery Crash

*The cause of a fire that sent South African Airways Flight 295 crashing into the Indian Ocean on November 28, 1987, remains unknown. Because of that, and without any survivors to tell their story, the tragedy remains heavy with speculation, theories, and unanswered questions.*

✳   ✳   ✳   ✳

THE AIRCRAFT HAD a name, the *Helderberg*, and a very unique feature. It was a version of the 747 and was sometimes called a "combi" (short for combination), as it had a moveable partition that acted as a separator between its passengers and cargo. When South African Airways Flight 295 departed from Chiang Kai-shek International Airport on November 27, 1987, it was carrying six pallets of cargo, 140 passengers, and 19 crew members.

One stopover was scheduled in Mauritius before the flight was to land at its final destination in Johannesburg, South Africa. The flight took off at 2:23 p.m. local time, and everything seemed to be going smoothly. About nine hours later, however, air traffic control was notified that Flight 295 had declared an emergency. A smoke alarm had signified that a fire had broken out where the cargo was being held. The last communication from the flight occurred four minutes past midnight on November 28—some 15 minutes after the first mention of an emergency. By daybreak, the first remnants of the plane were spotted on the Indian Ocean's surface.

United States and French Navy crews conducted an immediate search and rescue about 130 nautical miles northeast of the island nation of Mauritius. They found debris, oil slicks, and eight bodies floating on the ocean. Two months later, in January 1988, the rest of the wreckage was found 4,000 meters below the ocean's surface. As much of the plane as possible was reassembled as part of the investigation led by the Republic of South Africa, which issued a report stating that "some of the recovered items such as cabin paneling, furnishings, and cargo showed traces of fire damage, such as heat discoloration and soot." There was heat damage on a section of the rear bulkhead as well on pieces of the main deck cargo floor. These findings helped to confirm the suspicion that a fire had broken out in the cargo area.

## Politics Fuels Speculation and Theories

Determining the cause of the fire proved far more difficult. South Africa's apartheid-based political tensions had planes bearing the South African flag restricted from flying over certain other African countries at the time. It caused flights like 295 to have to travel longer routes, making the "combi" option a more economical one at the time. However, the cargo area became the focus of some speculation about the cause of this flight's demise.

One theory held that the South African government had secretly placed a rocket system in the cargo area, due to the arms embargo South Africa was under at the time. It is thought that the vibration of the aircraft might have caused it to ignite and start a fire. Officially, the cargo on the plane consisted of electronic components including computer hardware, paper, textiles, sports equipment, and medicines.

Other theories suggest that perhaps a short circuit started a flash fire in the area, perhaps related to the computer or electronic equipment. Though we might never truly know what caused the Flight 295 fire, one silver lining came in the form of changes to the design and safety protocols of "combi" aircraft in subsequent years.

# First Western Hemisphere Bombing Goes Largely Unpunished

*The first midair bombing of a civilian airliner in the Western Hemisphere, the attack on Cubana de Aviación Flight 455 came in the form of two bomb explosions. All 73 on board, including the entire Cuban national fencing team, were killed in the crash.*

❋　❋　❋　❋

AMONG THE 73 CASUALTIES in the bombing of Cubana de Aviación Flight 455 on October 6, 1976, were every member of the Cuban national fencing team. The Douglas DC-8 had reached 18,000 feet and was still climbing on a scheduled three-hour flight from Barbados to Kingston, Jamaica, when two bombs exploded. It was the first known midair bombing of a civilian plane in the Western Hemisphere, and it killed all on board.

One blast took place in a bathroom at the back of the airplane, ruining the plane's control cables. The other bomb was located in the midsection of the cabin; its explosion created a hole and started a fire. The plane then began descending rapidly. The last contact Flight 455 had with the radio control tower was the captain frantically explaining, "We have an explosion aboard— we are descending immediately! Fire on board! —we have a total emergency!"

The pilots tried to return to the airport. Once they realized they wouldn't make it, the captain turned the plane so it would crash into the Caribbean Sea, five miles away, potentially saving the lives of travelers and airport workers.

Two Venezuelan men were arrested a few hours after the crash. They had gotten off the flight after an earlier leg from Trinidad to Barbados, despite having booked tickets to Cuba—the final destination. The men, Freddy Lugo and Jose Vasquez Garcia, confessed to planting the bombs and claimed they were working for Luis Posada Carriles, a CIA operative. He and fellow CIA operative Orlando Bosch were thought to be involved.

The offices of one of Posada's companies were raided; explosives, weapons, and a radio transmitter were found. Lugo, Garcia, Posada, and Bosch were all taken to a military trial, where the judge ordered them to be tried by a civilian court. In the end, Lugo and Garcia were given the lowest sentencing possible due to not having a prior criminal record. Bosch was acquitted because the evidence against him had not been translated into Spanish, and Posada escaped from the San Juan de los Morros penitentiary, never facing any legal consequences.

# Swissair 111: What Could Go Wrong Did

*There were likely no conspiracies or malicious intentions behind the failure of Swissair Flight 111, which claimed the lives of all 229 crew members and passengers on the plane. What there were, however, were malfunctions, questionable decisions, and a fire that led to the deadliest crash ever involving a McDonnell Douglas MD-11.*

✳ ✳ ✳ ✳

THE MYSTERIES SURROUNDING Swissair Flight 111, which crashed into the Atlantic Ocean near Halifax, Nova Scotia, on September 2, 1998, are tantalizing and numerous. In the end, however, the ones that have been solved have brought little comfort to the friends and families of the 229 passengers and crew who died when the plane, its cabin engulfed in flames, struck the water's surface around 10:30 that evening.

Some curious things about the flight came to light after the fact, though their relation to the crash must still remain speculative. For example, once-imprisoned British intelligence agent Richard Tomlinson was thought—at least for a time—to have been on the flight. It prompted one author to speculate that the British might have had an interest in taking the plane down with an explosive device. But Tomlinson was actually not on the flight between New York's JFK Airport and Geneva, a popular route for government and United Nations officials. In another twist, a former Royal Canadian Mounted Police sergeant who had been involved in the investigation claimed that the Transportation Safety Board suppressed evidence that an incendiary device had contributed to the fire that broke out on the plane.

The facts showed otherwise. Though the McDonnell Douglas MD-11 was relatively new—built in 1991 and equipped with an in-flight entertainment system that was considered state-of-the-art at the time—an extensive (and expensive) search and the largest air crash investigation in Canadian history turned up the faulty wire that caught fire in the cabin. The flight crew smelled what they thought was smoke coming from the air conditioning system at first. Minutes later, the smoke became visible and a radio call was made, requesting an emergency landing in Boston.

Air traffic control instead routed the flight to Halifax International Airport, which was closer, but the crew requested time to dump fuel before attempting to land. They were 30 nautical miles from Halifax, but needed to fly out to 40 miles away in order to safely dump the fuel. It might have been a costly mistake. The same can be said for the decision to cut power to the cabin, which was done according to the Swissair checklist when "smoke of unknown origin" is detected. It shut off the air circulation fans, and just 10 seconds later the flight's final transmission was made: "...we are declaring emergency now, Swissair one eleven."

Two more "mysteries" of note: the plane's flight recorder (black box) contained no data from the fateful final six minutes of the flight. And for 13 minutes early in the journey, there was no communication between the crew and air traffic control. The latter anomaly was chalked up to the pilots having turned their radios to the wrong frequency, a mistake that was cleared of any impact on the crash.

# All Roads Led to Pilot Error Aboard Indian Airlines 491

*A 1993 Indian Airlines flight that barely got airborne when it collided with a truck, struck power lines, and broke into flames was the subject of much scrutiny and speculation in a post-crash investigation. The root causes turned out to be more man-made than mysterious.*

✳   ✳   ✳   ✳

IN 1953, EIGHT regional carriers merged to form Indian Airlines, a state-run airline that was launched to serve as the domestic equivalent to the more established Air India. Until the 1990s, when other companies were allowed to compete for business, it was actually the only domestic airline flying in the country. As such, Indian Airlines developed a poor track record for safety. In addition to relatively frequent fatal crashes, it was susceptible to security breaches. Indian Airlines was the target of no fewer than 16 hijackings in the 1970s, '80s, and '90s.

One of those hijackings took place on April 24 and 25, 1993. The very next day, on April 26, a jammed plane of 112 passengers and six crew members boarded Indian Airlines Flight 491 at Aurangabad Airport with the intent of reaching Bombay. Unfortunately, the Boeing 737-2A8 made it only a few kilometers, and 56 of those passengers wound up dead after an unusual crash.

The flight was cleared for takeoff at 1 p.m. It had just started to climb toward the end of the 6,000-foot runway. The airport's perimeter wall was a few hundred feet beyond the end of the runway, and the plane was able to clear it without issue. But just beyond that, of all things, was a truck carrying 36 bales of cotton moving north on Beed Road. Combining the height of the road with an approximately 11-foot-tall stack of cotton bales, this presented an obstacle far greater than the perimeter wall the plane had just cleared some 70 feet earlier.

The left landing gear and left engine made contact with the vehicle. Despite considerable damage to much of the left side of the plane, Flight 491 managed to stay airborne for about three kilometers. At that point, a loss of thrust on the left side caused it to veer left into some power lines. That sent it crashing to the ground, where an inferno erupted and consumed the main cabin. Slightly more than half of those on board managed to escape with injuries; 56 perished.

## Inexperience and Error

Because of the hijacking just one day earlier, there was speculation that perhaps terrorism was involved in the crash of Flight 491. The plane was also heavy—just 54 kilograms (120 pounds) below its maximum takeoff weight. The Indian Ministry of Civil Aviation interviewed dozens of witnesses, pored over 146 documents, and retrieved burned flight recorders to try piecing together the clues. In the end, all roads led not to terrorists, but to the airplane's pilots.

The captain, 38-year-old S.N. Singh, had logged just 140 flying hours since his promotion to captain. His co-pilot, 30-year-old first officer Manisha Mohan, had fewer than 1,200 hours total under her belt and had her license granted on the condition that she be subject to every-other-week checks. Both pilots shrugged off the weight concerns, which experts said threatened the plane's ability to achieve the proper climbing gradient to ascend safely to cruising altitude.

After ruling out terrorism, investigators focused on the weight problem. They conducted three flight simulations under the same circumstances. Only one resulted in a crash, and it turned out weight was not the issue. The simulated crash occurred due to a late rotation by the pilot. With that being the most probable cause of the crash, Singh had to plead his case in court. A judge ruled that Singh knowingly kept the plane on the ground for too long, resulting in "improper rotation technique, directly leading to the failure of the aircraft to clear the obstacle."

Singh had his license revoked, while Mohan's was temporarily suspended. The judge also placed fault on Indian Airlines for promoting Singh to captain, considering his poor reports throughout pilot training. The airline was held liable for not adhering to weight restrictions, and for its lack of proper emergency training on behalf of its flight attendants.

While it turned out there was not much mystery in what happened to Indian Airlines Flight 491, there certainly was an element of disappearance. What disappeared, in this case, were shoddy protocols, a lack of rigor around safety, and a road so close to a runway. It was moved some 1,700 feet away, ensuring a plane-vehicle collision will not happen there any time soon.

# The Ghostly Trials of the *Mary Celeste*

*What would cause a perfectly intact ship to be found adrift off the coast of Portugal, with no one on board and all possessions and cargo in place? The answer might never be known, as the Mary Celeste—filled with a history some might call cursed—tells no tales.*

✻ ✻ ✻ ✻

IMAGINE THE SURPRISE on the face of David Morehouse, captain of the Canadian ship the *Dei Gratia*, upon learning that the abandoned 282-ton brigantine he'd just discovered 600 miles off the coast of Portugal, the *Mary Celeste*, belonged to a good friend of his. He and *Mary Celeste* captain Benjamin S. Briggs had recently shared dinner together, and now he was finding his buddy's boat adrift in the ocean—a ghost ship, with no one at all on board, in 1872.

When he spotted the ship, Morehouse sent first mate Oliver Deveau to investigate. His first thought was that Briggs and his crew might have come down ill and incapacitated. After what turned out to be a difficult time boarding the ship while strong winds against the sails caused it to continue speeding along, it was discovered that Briggs, his wife, their daughter, and all eight crew members were nowhere to be found. What's more, their belongings and cargo seemed perfectly intact, including the 1,700 barrels of crude alcohol the ship was carrying. A single lifeboat was missing.

Had pirates been responsible, surely the *Mary Celeste* would have been ransacked. There was no logical explanation for a perfectly seaworthy vessel to have been left adrift. Theories would start to surface, not the least of which pointed to the ship being cursed.

## Trouble by a Different Name

The *Mary Celeste* was built in Canada and originally christened as the *Amazon* in 1861. She carried timber across the Atlantic, running a series of successful voyages, but there were also some mishaps. Three of her captains died in its first several years at sea. She also hit and sank a brig in the English Channel, collided with fishing equipment off the coast of Maine, and was abandoned by her owners in October 1867 after running ashore in a storm in Nova Scotia. Could the ship have been cursed from the start?

Sold as a wreck, seized by creditors, and rebuilt to bigger dimensions in the early 1870s, she resurfaced as the *Mary Celeste*. Briggs, his family, and their small, carefully-chosen crew sailed from New York's Pier 50 in November 1872. Briggs wrote to his mother, "Our vessel is in beautiful trim and I hope we shall have a fine passage."

Morehouse spotted the ship between the Azores and the coast of Portugal about a month later, on December 4, 1872. Her sails were set oddly and the ship was moving erratically, leading the *Dei Gratia* crew to believe something was amiss. They were not prepared to find no one at all aboard the ship once they finally made their way aboard.

The last entry on the ship's log noted strong winds and rough seas. Malfunctioning pumps, mutiny, UFOs, and the Bermuda Triangle have all been invoked as possible explanations. The salvagers from the *Dei Gratia* netted a sixth of the $46,000 dollars for which *Mary Celeste* was insured, leading some to suspect foul play was involved. The *Mary Celeste* was run aground in Haiti in January 1885 on her final voyage, presumably for an insurance claim.

# Many Questions Rest at the Bottom of the Sea

*Instrumental in developing nuclear submarine combat tactics, the USS* Scorpion *was a fixture of the United States navy fleet in the 1960s. Questions abound as to what happened when she went missing on May 22, 1969, and was subsequently found in pieces at the bottom of the North Atlantic.*

✳    ✳    ✳    ✳

RUNS BETWEEN NORFOLK, Virginia, and the Mediterranean Sea were routine for the USS *Scorpion*, a nuclear-powered, Skipjack-class attack submarine. The U.S. Navy had made huge strides in the development of nuclear submarine warfare tactics during the 1960s. The *Scorpion* first hit the water in 1959, and between 1961 and '68 she took part in both U.S. and NATO operations of the highest magnitude.

After operating with the Sixth Fleet in the Mediterranean during May 1968, *Scorpion* headed west for Norfolk. On May 21, she reported her location: 50 miles south of the Azores.

Evidence later showed that the sub was having trouble sending signals to naval stations at that same time. Six days later, she was overdue—no one knew what could have happened. Search crews hit the water, to no avail, and she was listed as "presumed lost" on June 5. All 99 on board were presumed dead.

Dr. John Craven, chief scientist of the navy's Special Projects division, employed a statistical theory to the search parameters and was instrumental in locating portions of the sub about 400 nautical miles southwest of the Azores in October—five months after its disappearance. Gordon Hamilton, using underwater acoustics, also contributed significantly to the discovery of the sub. It is one of two nuclear subs the U.S. Navy has lost, along with the USS *Thresher*.

What happened to *Scorpion* remains a hotly-debated topic to this day. The navy released tapes that contained underwater sounds of the destruction of the sub. The Structural Analysis Group (SAG) concluded that an explosive event was unlikely, though some speculated the detonation of a torpedo was the most likely cause of the vessel's demise. In 1984, *The Norfolk Virginian-Pilot* obtained records related to the inquiry and reported that the most likely cause was a torpedo that detonated while the *Scorpion* crew was trying to disarm it.

Because *Scorpion* had been patrolling for and monitoring Soviet activity, one theory holds that the Soviet Union destroyed it. That theory was espoused in a 2008 book by Kenneth Sewell and Jerome Preisler. A hydrogen explosion during a battery charge, the accidental (or intentional) detonation of a torpedo, and the malfunction of a trash disposal unit are among the many additional theories as to what might have happened.

There were also structural concerns about the sub. Once a fit vessel, it was no longer up to the standards of the Thresher-class subs of the time. Its heavy workload over the years had also taken a toll. Some of its crew members had started referring to her—perhaps hauntingly in retrospect—as "Scrapiron."

# "*Titanic* of the Southern Seas" Remains Lost

*The SS* Waratah *disappeared mysteriously somewhere between Australia and South Africa more than a century ago. All 211 passengers and crew aboard were presumed dead, but no one has ever found the place where it all went wrong—or a remnant of the "unsinkable" ship.*

✳  ✳  ✳  ✳

IT REMAINS ONE of the greatest mysteries of the sea—the fate of the SS *Waratah*, which disappeared on her second voyage in 1909, three years before the *Titanic* went down. The *Waratah*, sometimes known as the "*Titanic* of the Southern Seas," was a cargo steamship built to travel between Europe and Australia. She left Durban, South Africa toward a stop in Cape Town, South Africa, on July 26, 1909, with 211 people aboard.

Other ships in the Indian Ocean off South Africa's rugged coast either spotted the *Waratah* or presumed they did, as stormy weather turned the seas dangerous. *Clan MacIntyre*, a slower steamer, traded customary info via signal lamps about eight hours into *Waratah*'s journey. As the weather grew worse and the seas more turbulent, there were a few other, unconfirmed sightings. Some aboard the *Harlow*, 180 miles from Durban, described vanishing lights that concerned some, while others chalked them up to fires onshore. A few aboard the *Guelph* reported signals coming from a ship that bore the last three letters "T-A-H."

It was not unusual, particularly in poor weather in those days, for ships to arrive at their destinations a few days late. But as more and more days passed, concern began to grow around the whereabouts of the *Waratah*. Search parties went out, but none found the ship that many thought "unsinkable."

Over the years, efforts continued. How could a larger, sturdy liner with eight staterooms, a music lounge, and 211 people just disappear without a trace? A rogue wave, common in that area of the sea, is the likely answer, but others have speculated about whirlpools, explosions, or a sudden cargo shift that might have caused the ship to capsize. The National Underwater and Marine Agency thought they had a breakthrough with findings off the South Africa coast in 1999, but it turned out to be a false alarm.

## Pacific Ghost Ship: The MV *Joyita*

*Lost ships typically get found on the ocean floor, or in pieces after a wreck. Yet five weeks after going missing, the MV Joyita was discovered still afloat in 1955. It had been abandoned, with none of the 25 people aboard to be found.*

✳   ✳   ✳   ✳

ONCE A LUXURY yacht for American dark film director Roland West, the MV *Joyita* ("little jewel," named for West's wife Jewel Carmen) was built in 1931 and had certainly made the rounds by the time she left Samoa for the Tokelau Islands on October 3, 1955. *Joyita* had made 1939 and '40 trips to the Golden Gate International Exposition in San Francisco, had been used to patrol Pearl Harbor for the U.S. Navy during World War II, and had come to be used as a trading and charter fishing boat in the 1950s by Captain Thomas Miller, a British sailor living in Samoa.

Miller and first mate Chuck Simpson were setting out on a seemingly mundane trip that October day. They led a total crew of 16 along with nine passengers and a cargo of medical supplies, timber, flour, sugar, rice, and empty oil drums bound for the Tokelau Islands, a trip that was expected to take about 48 hours.

They got off to a rocky start when departure was delayed due to a failed port engine clutch. Despite this setback, Miller decided to set sail with one engine. On October 6, the day after the ship was expected to arrive, a New Zealand Air Force search and rescue mission was launched. There was no sign of the ship. That is, until about five weeks later, when the *Tuvalu* of Captain Gerald Douglas found the *Joyita* listing at a 45-degree angle some 600 miles off her original course, near Fiji. The ship was abandoned.

Investigators were able to make some notable discoveries to try to explain what might have happened. The dinghy and three lifeboats were gone, indicating they were used for an escape. The radio was set to the international distress channel, despite no signal having been received. Enough fuel remained for 50 or so more miles, but cargo, navigational equipment, log books, and guns were missing. Finally, a leak was spotted in the engine room. Could that leak have prompted all to abandon ship? Given the ship's sturdy design—a design that had it floating intact five weeks later—some wondered why such a decision might have been made.

One hypothesis suggests Miller might have died mid-journey. If so, the remaining crew and passengers might have seen the leak as reason to panic. Along the same lines was an idea that Miller and Simpson, who were known to have feuded, got into a fight that sent both overboard, leaving everyone else on board to fend for themselves. Pirates seemed another possibility.

Perhaps the most credible hypothesis comes from Robin Maugham, a British author who once owned *Joyita* and published his theory in *The Joyita Mystery*. In the book, he claims Miller knew the ship would not sink and wanted to press on, while the rest onboard, including Simpson, wanted to turn back. Amid heavy swells and strong winds, an altercation occurred that injured Miller, leaving Simpson in charge. Even though the leak might have caused the engine to fail and killed power, Simpson would have known the ship wouldn't sink. He would not have suggested leaving it, Maugham claims, unless he thought he'd seen a reef or island that could be reached by lifeboat. Strong winds might have prevented such an escape, carrying everyone out to sea.

# The SS *Cotopaxi*

*From one of several mysteries of the Bermuda Triangle to a bit part in a famous Steven Spielberg movie to a "fake news" boom on the internet that led to a revealing documentary, the SS* Cotopaxi *has been almost as well-traveled after its 1925 wreck than before it.*

✳   ✳   ✳   ✳

THOUGH FOR YEARS she was chalked up to being one of those mysterious victims of the Bermuda Triangle, the SS *Cotopaxi* carried a rather run-of-the-mill shipwreck story in real life. The steam-powered "Laker," commissioned in 1918 under the United States Shipping Board's emergency shipbuilding program during World War I, was one of 17 bulk carrier ships of its kind.

The ship's wartime runs were mainly between the east coasts of the U.S. and South America. After the war, she was purchased for $375,000 by the Clinchfield Navigation Company and was used, among other things, for coal runs. On one trip from Charleston, S.C., to Havana, Cuba, in 1920, she sunk a tugboat in a collision. The *Cotopaxi* was unharmed in the accident.

Another trip from Charleston to Havana in 1925, however, did not bring such fortune. The *Cotopaxi*, filled with 3,800 tons of coal and a crew of 32 under captain W.J. Meyer, encountered a tropical storm in the Atlantic. The crew sent a radio distress call on December 1, saying they were taking on water and listing—leaning one way. They were not heard from again.

## Let the Drama Live On

A lawsuit filed by crew relatives argued the ship was not seaworthy when making her final voyage. It gave coordinates off the east coast of Florida where the ship was said to have last been, and claimed hatch covers in terrible condition were likely to blame. Others invoked the Bermuda Triangle theory, as the area of the Atlantic connecting Bermuda to the U.S. east coast and Puerto Rico has been a popular area for mysterious disappearances. This one, in reality, lacked great mystery.

But the story had legs that have led it to unexpected places. Steven Spielberg's 1977 blockbuster, *Close Encounters of the Third Kind*, connected the SS *Cotopaxi* to the mysteries of the Bermuda Triangle and had her being discovered in—of all places—the Gobi Desert, put there by extraterrestrials.

Meanwhile, off the big screen, a shipwreck off the Florida coast near St. Augustine was discovered in 1980 and, because it was not identified, was for decades called the "Bear Wreck." Around 2010, however, marine biologist Michael Barnette determined on scuba diving excursions it was actually the SS *Cotopaxi*. Barnette wrote about it in a 2013 book, *Encyclopedia of Florida Shipwrecks*. He decided to try spreading the word more widely two years later when a story started on social media claiming that Cuban authorities had intercepted a ghost ship that had been floating around undetected for 90 years. When he saw that the tale was claiming the ship was the *Cotopaxi*, Barnette began setting the record straight.

His interviews with major media outlets and publications let the world know that the "Bear Wreck" was indeed the long-lost *Cotopaxi* and that its disappearance was not an unsolved Bermuda Triangle tale. There was even enough interest to prompt a Science Channel television documentary, *Shipwreck Secrets*, in which he documented his discovery. "It's very satisfying," Barnette told *Esquire*, "to be able to put a real explanation to what happened."

# Chapter 8

# Mysterious Cataclysms and Disasters

## Incendiary Impact

*On October 7, 2008, an asteroid four meters across came barreling into Earth's atmosphere, exploding and disintegrating about 37 kilometers above northern Sudan. It was the first asteroid to be observed and tracked in space.*

✳　✳　✳　✳

### Aiming for Earth

AT APPROXIMATELY 6:39 UTC (Universal Time Coordinated—the time standard used by NASA) on the morning of October 6, 2008, astronomer Richard Kowalski discovered a small object that appeared to be on a collision course with our planet. The object, provisionally called 8TA9D69, was picked up in images taken by the Catalina Sky Survey, a NASA-funded project conducted near Tucson, Arizona. Every day, the survey sweeps the sky searching for dangerous asteroids.

Within hours, three other observatories reported similar sightings. Discovery observations were promptly sent to the Minor Planet Center (MPC) in Cambridge, Massachusetts. There, a preliminary orbit computation indicated that the object was indeed going to make contact with the planet within 24 hours. This news was groundbreaking: This would be the first time an asteroid was discovered and tracked *before* impact. 8TA9D69 was given a more formal name: 2008 TC3.

## A Downward Trajectory

As more and more observations poured in from professional and amateur astronomers alike, the asteroid's trajectory began to take shape. The sheer number of different observers, along with their distribution around the globe, allowed for much greater precision than what could normally be expected from an unexpected collision, especially given such a small window of observation opportunity. JPL scientist Paul Chodas confirmed the initial impact prediction: TC3 would enter Earth's atmosphere around 2:45:28 UTC and reach maximum deceleration around 2:45:54 at an altitude of about 14 kilometers.

On October 7, 1:49 UTC, the asteroid entered Earth's shadow, rendering further observations impossible. But it didn't matter by then. With the immense amount of data collected—586 astrometric and almost as many photometric observations—astronomers could confidently predict that TC3's atmospheric entry would occur over northern Sudan.

## Raining Rocks

As predicted, the meteor entered Earth's atmosphere above the Nubian Desert at 2:46 UTC—5:46 a.m. local time—on the morning of October 7, 2008. Because of TC3's immense speed—approximately 46,000 kilometers per hour—as it approached Earth's surface, the air in front of it compressed and heated. This caused the meteor to begin glowing. Then, only tens of kilometers above the ground, TC3 exploded with the energy of about one *kiloton* of TNT explosives. Multiple reports claimed that its light was so intense that it lit up the sky like a full moon. A KLM airline pilot flying over Chad, approximately 1,400 kilometers away, also reported seeing the bright flash.

The meteor completely disintegrated. Dust from the explosion expanded into the air as a vast cloud. The rest of TC3 rained down as more than 600 fragments of rock across the desert. These rocks, or meteorites, ranged from tiny grains and specks to visible stones. A dedicated search was conducted to recover the fragments.

## Brace for Impact

Although small impact events like TC3 occur every year, never before had an asteroid's trajectory been mapped in real time. Being able to predict ground zero helps astronomers discover more about the history and composition of our natural world. The remnants were composed of fragile, carbon-bearing ureilite—a rare type of stony meteorite with a unique mineralogical composition. But scientific progress isn't the only benefit of such forecasting. Safety, too, remains a big concern. The Nubian Desert is a remote location for an impact, but TC3 still could have been disastrous for the few people that call it home. Larger collisions, though commensurately rarer, are even more dangerous. TC3's unprecedented impact, not only on Earth's surface, but also in the fields of humanitarian issues and scientific discoveries, remains strong to this day.

# The Case of the Carancas Chondrite

*A chondritic meteor barreled across the sky, landing and carving a large crater in a remote Peruvian field. Those who approached the site were immediately stricken with nausea, digestive problems, and vomiting.*

✳ ✳ ✳ ✳

## Going Down in Flames

AT 11:40 A.M. local time on September 15, 2007, a large fireball with a smoky tail streaked across the Peruvian sky. As it fell, it shattered the windows of a nearby health center. Locals observed its strong light, mistaking the bright orange streak for a crashing plane. Then came a loud bang.

The meteorite landed in a field near the village of Carancas, a sparsely-populated highland village near Lake Titicaca and the Bolivian border. The impact created a huge crater over 40 feet wide and 15 feet deep. Visibly scorched earth smoldered around the site, forming a column of smoke that lasted several minutes. When farmers came over to investigate, they found boiling water bubbling out of the crater. Particles of rock and cinders were strewn about. More than this, however, was a "strange odor." Local health department official, Jorge López, reported this finding to Peru's RPP radio. Fetid, noxious gasses were making people ill.

## Inexplicable Illness

Over 600 villagers visited the site, many of whom began to complain of headaches and dizziness. Some residents even experienced vomiting and diarrhea. When the police arrived to investigate the crater, they too fell ill. A medical team was dispatched to help alleviate symptoms using oxygen masks and rehydration, but still the sickness persisted. "The odor is strong and it's affecting nearby communities," said López.

Five days later, all Peruvian scientists could confirm was that there had indeed been a meteorite strike. No further information about the impact could explain the subsequent maladies. Engineers, like Renan Ramirez of the Peruvian Nuclear Energy Institute, did not detect any radiation with their instruments. Astronomers were stumped: No other meteorite caused this much harm to this many people, especially if it did not strike a residence. Within Peru, another meteorite had fallen months prior in the Arequipa province and did not cause nearly as much trouble. Something wasn't adding up.

## In Hot Water

Although only a conventional, chondritic meteorite, Peru's 2007 impact event was highly unusual in that it occurred at such a high altitude. Normally, meteorites strike the earth at lower temperatures, but because of the high elevation of the region, this particular meteorite's surface did not have ample time to cool. When it hit the ground, it reacted with the numerous deposits of arsenic inside Carancas' groundwater. According to nuclear physicist Modesto Montoya, natural arsenic deposits in groundwater are not uncommon for this region.

It was concluded that the arsenic in the water triggered the illnesses: Arsenic poisoning occurred when Carancas residents inhaled the fumes of the boiling contaminated water. Fortunately, the Puno region's health ministry confirmed that none of the villagers were in serious condition. As for the crater, it was largely left alone.

# A Meteorite of Magnitude

*On February 12, 1947, an iron meteor fell on the Sikhote-Alin Mountains in southeastern Russia. It was one of the largest, most spectacular falls of its kind in recorded history.*

✳ ✳ ✳ ✳

### A Picture-Perfect Landing

IT WAS 10:48 a.m. local time in Primorsky Krai, a remote province of Russia, when the Sikhote-Alin meteor was first seen. It came from the north, descending at an angle of about 41 degrees. Witnesses reported a massive bolide (the fireball-like appearance of a meteor exploding in the atmosphere) that seemed brighter than the sun. Behind the bright flash was a long trail—nearly 20 miles—of smoke and dust. It lingered in the air for several hours.

Soviet artist P. I. Medvedev had just sat at his window to start a sketch when the fireball came into view. Quickly, he began to draw what he saw. The resulting painting was seen as such an iconic image of the event that on November 20, 1957, the Soviet Union issued a postage stamp reproducing the artwork for the Sikhote-Alin's tenth anniversary. The original painting was placed in the Fersman Mineralogical Museum in Moscow.

## Shower in Siberia

The bright lights and deafening noise of the fall were observed for hundreds of miles around the point of impact. The meteor—more accurately the group of meteors—sped into the atmosphere at incredible speed. When the cluster reached an altitude of about 3.5 miles above the surface, the largest of the pieces exploded violently, shattering into a shower of rocks. This was a very low altitude for such an event, half as low as the cruising altitude for passenger jets. In total, 25 tons of meteor fragments rained down on Siberian taiga forest.

The group of fragments largely fell together, scattering over an elliptical area of about half a square mile. Many fragments—especially the larger pieces—violently shattered upon reaching the frozen Siberian ground and bedrock. As such, the Sikhote-Alin did not leave much of a footprint upon the earth: Most of the 120 impact craters and pits were rather small.

That is not to say that there were no large craters whatsoever. One crater, the largest of the bunch, measured 85 feet across and 20 feet deep. This was likely the result of eight individual fragments all falling in close proximity. The biggest craters were all located at the far end of the field.

## How Iron-ic

Inside the craters were fragments of the Sikhote-Alin. According to E. L. Krinov, a Russian astronomer and geologist, the largest recovered individual piece weighed around 1,700 kilograms, while the smallest measured a mere 6 milligrams. Some meteorite fragments were not found in craters at all, but instead were embedded in the bark of surrounding trees. There are two distinct types collected from the impact: angular shrapnel which exploded as a result of atmospheric pressure, and fragments that flew through the atmosphere on their own. The latter melted into unusual shapes, leaving behind a unique, thumbprint-like texture. These coveted cavities are called *regmaglypts*.

Iron meteorites such as Sikhote-Alin only constitute about two percent of all the space rocks that make it to Earth's surface. Of these impact events, only a very small fraction have fallen recently. The Sikhote-Alin was one of the first of its kind to be witnessed, and was certainly the first of its kind to be witnessed in such magnitude. Avid meteorite collectors hold specimens of Sikhote-Alin meteorites in high regard, selling them for hundreds, even thousands of dollars.

# A Flood of Biblical Proportions

*Noah's ark is one of the best-known stories from the book of Genesis. But could such a catastrophic worldwide event actually occur? And if it did, wouldn't it leave behind some evidence?*

✳  ✳  ✳  ✳

## The Great Flood

INDEED, PRACTICALLY EVERYONE is familiar with the story of Noah's ark, perhaps the most famous floating menagerie in history: Seeing only wickedness and violence, God decided to wipe the land clean with a global flood. Not everyone would perish, however. God found one righteous man—Noah—and instructed him to build a massive ship out of wood, which he was then to fill with a mated pair of every kind of animal. Noah was also instructed to stock food for all the animals as well as for himself and his family, which included his wife, three sons, and their wives. The ark itself, as designed by God, was to be 300 cubits long, 50 cubits wide, and 30 cubits high.

What followed was a horrifying event. God produced torrential rains for 40 days and 40 nights, enough to flood the planet past the mountaintops and kill everyone and everything on it. As the waters receded, the ark came to rest in the mountains of Ararat. It took several months for the world to dry completely. When finally invited by God to exit the ark, Noah built an altar and worshiped God with burnt offerings. God was pleased, and he promised never to destroy the earth by flood again.

It's a remarkable story, sure, but it's also one that begs a lot of questions. How did Noah fit thousands of animals—plus their food—into the ark? How did the ark survive such tumultuous waters? How much devastation did the flood cause across the world? The simplest answer, of course, is that God was responsible for all of it. After all, the entire event was supernatural in origin, from God instructing Noah on what to do and how to do it to God creating the flood itself. But there are also those who believe that these supernatural incidents are more than just a cautionary tale and carry real, concrete evidence. Surely, if such a catastrophe occurred exactly as it was described in the Bible, we'd see proof of it somewhere, right?

## Reviewing Records

The geologic column and fossil record are used as major sources of evidence regarding the development and evolution of Earth and its inhabitants. Not everyone agrees on how to read the evidence, however. Those who give credence to flood geology believe that all strata were laid down by the Great Flood approximately six thousand years ago. Geologists, however, have determined that the same strata were deposited gradually over many millions of years.

Erosion, too, is a topic of contention. Flood geology claims that the Great Flood occurred worldwide, but such a phenomenon would have produced evenly-distributed levels of erosion. Geologists argue that different regions of the world, like the Appalachians and the Rocky Mountains, for example, differ significantly in this regard.

Just as flood geology believes the Great Flood is responsible for laying down layers of strata, it also holds the flood responsible for fossilization: God's violent rains scoured and dumped sediments onto all sorts of creatures, burying them and turning them into fossils. The order of the fossil record can be explained by the regions its victims occupied: First, fish were affected. Then, as the water levels rose, lowland-living animals like amphibians and reptiles were buried, too. Finally, as the flood surged upward and into the hills, so were mammals. But geologists claim that this simplified way of thinking does not accurately represent the fossil record. If the flood was solely responsible, then that would mean that all the animals now fossilized lived together on Earth at the same time.

## Searching Stories

Many different cultures from around the world have flood stories of their own. Proponents of flood geology highlight how these stories, whether documented as history or legend, frequently parallel the Bible. According to the Northwest Creation Network, similarities include warning of an incoming flood, construction of a boat, storage of animals, and the release of birds to see if the water level had subsided. The consistency across these stories are thought to indicate that they were derived from the same origin: the Great Flood.

Anthropologists, however, reject this view. Over the course of history, much of the human population has lived near rivers, coasts, and other sources of water. It stands to reason that unusually severe floods occurred on occasion and were incorporated into local mythologies. Just because multiple civilizations have a flood story does not mean they each experienced the same flood.

## Fact or Fiction?

Whether the story of Noah's ark is true or not has been the subject of debate for centuries. Even amongst theologians there is contention: Some believe it literally, while others posit that the flood did occur, but that it was regional rather than global. And some believe the story is more allegory than fact—a fable designed to illustrate God's intolerance toward wickedness. Interestingly, some explorers believe that Noah's Ark still rests atop Mount Ararat in eastern Turkey. Over the years, several expeditions have searched the mountain looking for concrete proof of the vessel, though nothing conclusive has been found.

Although it cannot be fully proven true, the story of Noah's ark and the Great Flood is a remarkable tale, full of compelling characters and wild adventure, with a simple yet important moral: Righteousness always prevails over wickedness.

# The Johnstown Flood

*On May 31, 1889, a catastrophic breach of Western Pennsylvania's South Fork Dam delivered unimaginable destruction to gritty Johnstown, a steel company town in a valley 14 miles below. With 2,209 deaths attributable to the dam break, the tragedy ranks among the worst in American history.*

✳   ✳   ✳   ✳

A S IF SUCH loss of life weren't unsettling enough, subsequent reports of improper dam maintenance and outright neglect led to a startling conclusion: The Johnstown Flood could have been avoided.

During the Gilded Era (1845–1916), the South Fork Fishing and Hunting Club membership roster read like a veritable "Who's Who" of wealthy industrialists. Such magnates as Andrew Carnegie and Henry Clay Frick would summer at the fishing and boating oasis at Lake Conemaugh, conveniently located just a short train ride from Pittsburgh.

But there was a major problem brewing beneath the lake's surface. Since the club had acquired the property, dam maintenance had gone by the wayside. Worse still, members had lowered the dam's height and installed fish traps in the spillway to prevent stocked fish from escaping. These screens would at times collect debris to the point of rendering the spillway almost useless. In addition, critical discharge pipes had been removed and never replaced. Despite warnings and recommendations from dam inspector Daniel Morrell, the members maintained this dangerous status quo. The stage was set—and disaster ensued.

# Grote Mandrenke: The Great Drowning of Men

*Few storm tides in European history were as large or as devastating as the Grote Mandrenke in 1362. With an estimated 25,000 casualties, the huge surge of water drastically changed the shape of the North Sea coast.*

✳ ✳ ✳ ✳

## The Calm Before the Storm

IT WAS THE start of the Little Ice Age, a period of regional cooling in the North Atlantic. Waning solar radiation levels, combined with changes in ocean circulation and increased volcanic activity, left the northern parts of Europe prone to unsettled and fluctuating weather conditions.

It wasn't just the weather that changed. Along the coastline from Denmark to Holland, people migrated to and settled in the marshy swamp regions closer to shore. The unclaimed land, newly exposed by falling sea levels, was exploited for cooking salt, peat fuel, and agriculture. The new resource came with great risk, however. As it was used, parts of the region's ground level fell below sea level, and the already-fragile environment grew even weaker.

## A Whirlwind of Destruction

The first signs of the storm were seen in Ireland, where a huge southwesterly gale reportedly devastated Dublin homes and buildings. Southern England experienced the brunt of the storm next. Howling winds blew down thousands of trees. Local reports in the *Chronicle of Anonymous of Canterbury* described how "houses and buildings for the most part [came] crashing to the ground."

The wind famously caused massive damage to taller buildings, including the spires and towers of multiple churches. Norwich Cathedral lost its wooden spire. St. Pancras Church in London suffered horrible damage, as did St. Albans Abbey. Salisbury Cathedral was so badly destroyed that the bishop had to appeal to the Pope in order to fund the building's repair.

The following day, on the feast day of St. Marcellus, conditions worsened. As the storm reached the North Sea, it combined with the high tide. The resulting storm surge swept across the east coast of England and then across the sea into the Netherlands, Germany, and Denmark.

Because of the recent migration into the marshes, the storm easily overtook the landscape. Floodwaters spread more than 15 miles inland. The water tore up the coastline, breaking up existing islands, then dividing up the mainland into new islands. It wiped out numerous villages and districts. Rungholt, a wealthy trading town of about 3,000 people, completely sank beneath the waves.

## Silver Linings

The Grote Mandrenke spread its unprecedented devastation far and wide across northern Europe. An estimated 25,000 people perished in the extratropical cyclone, and many more lost their homes, loved ones, health—everything—to its powerful winds and floodwaters.

Still, the storm left another, more positive, legacy. Like other storm tides of its size during the thirteenth and fourteenth centuries, the Grote Mandrenke played a role in the formation of the Zuiderzee, a vast inland sea in the Netherlands. This body of water became a hub for extensive trade connections for the Dutch, trading with ports in England, on the Baltic Sea, and beyond.

# Disaster in Pakistan: The Indus River Flood

*In January 1841, an earthquake triggered a huge landslide off of Nanga Parbat Mountain in Pakistan, forming a natural dam. When the dam finally burst several months later, it unleashed a gargantuan flood wave nearly 100 feet high.*

✻  ✻  ✻  ✻

## Troublesome Topography

ALTHOUGH THE 1841 FLOOD was the largest of its kind, historic records of other Indus River floods in the 1800s indicate that it was not an isolated, chance event. The Peshawar Basin, where the Indus River is located, has physiographic characteristics that make it prone to catastrophic flooding. According to Douglas Burbank of the University of California, Santa Barbara, it's a "broad, low-lying depression" that exhibits only minor topographic relief. Along the basin's border, however, the landscape couldn't be more different.

The Attock-Cherat Range forms the southern boundary of the Peshawar basin. This mountain range is underlain and transected by active thrust faults (a type of convergent fault where two tectonic plates are pushed together). Because the Attock-Cherat Range has a much higher elevation than the Peshawar Basin, it forms a physical barrier perfect for impounding, or collecting, the high flows of the Indus River.

## Dangerous Dam

An earthquake shook the region in January of 1841, triggering a massive landslide on the slopes of Nanga Parbat, the ninth-tallest mountain on Earth. So much bedrock tumbled off the mountain that it blocked the flow of the Indus River for six months, creating what's called a landslide dam. Landslide dams, as their name suggests, collect water. The subsequent lake that formed was 500 feet deep and several dozen miles long.

Landslide dams occur under a variety of circumstances, including rainstorms, rapid snowmelt, and, as in the case of January 1841, earthquakes. Because landslide dams have no controlled outlet, they can be unstable and subject to failure. The dams with high levels of blockage in confined valleys have the greatest potential for danger. Once the water inside is able to escape, a massive flood is bound to follow.

## Fatal Flood

The natural dam finally burst that June, emptying the lake at a rate of 540,000 cubic meters per second. The Indus River rose nearly a hundred feet in four hours, washing over several hundred miles of the Indus Valley. Even the Indo-Gangetic Plain, where the river drains, experienced great destruction. Entire villages were wiped completely off the map, and 500 soldiers in Raja Singh's army were reportedly swept away.

Although breaches of landslide dams represent only a small percentage of the world's largest floods, they are still a significant hazard. The number of casualties of the Indus River flood is not known, but current dam-breach modeling suggests that it was probably the largest flood in recorded history. When the waters finally receded, all that remained was a fine layer of silt.

# Mississippi 1927: The Most Destructive Flood in U.S. History

*Known as the most devastating flood the country has ever seen, the Great Mississippi River Flood of 1927 inundated over 16 million acres of land along the Mississippi Delta. In addition to destroying towns, agricultural fields, and hundreds of thousands of homes, the flood also brought about long-term social and political change.*

❋  ❋  ❋  ❋

## Open the Floodgates

THE GREAT MISSISSIPPI Flood of 1927 actually began in the summer of 1926. Exceptionally heavy rains pummeled the Mississippi basin for several months, and people all along the river began to fear the prospects of a great, catastrophic flood. Numerous publications, like the *Memphis Commercial Appeal*, warned its readers about the encroaching disaster: "The roaring Mississippi River, bank and levee full from St. Louis to New Orleans, is believed to be on its mightiest rampage." Still, floods along the Mississippi River were not uncommon. The US Army Corps of Engineers assured the public that the river's levees would hold.

The rain continued pouring, and unprecedented amounts of runoff flowed into the river's many tributaries. The Mississippi swelled with the extra load. As spring approached, melting snow added to the mix. Wind, too, churned its waters. The flood defenses protecting the Mississippi Valley floodplains stood no chance. On April 16, the first levee broke along the Illinois shore.

Five days later, just upriver from Greenville, Mississippi, the levee at Mounds Landing Mississippi gave way. The levee lay just below the junction with the Arkansas River and, when broken, opened a huge crevasse one hundred feet deep and half a mile wide. Greenville flooded completely. Over the next few weeks, the entire levee system along the river collapsed.

## Troubled Waters

Over 27,000 square miles were submerged under water. Mississippi, Louisiana, and Arkansas suffered the greatest amount of damage. Financially, property losses totaled $350 million dollars, equivalent to approximately $5 billion dollars today. Economic losses were estimated at $1 billion. At the time, this was worth almost a third of the federal budget.

The flood displaced nearly 640,000 people, approximately 555,000 of whom were racial or ethnic minorities. Somewhere between 250 and 1,000 people died. African Americans were disproportionately impacted, tens of thousands of whom lived and worked in the lowlands as cotton tenants, sharecroppers, and plantation wage hands. African American families made up 75% of the lowland population, supplying nearly 100% of the entire agricultural labor force. Plantation owners, along with the railroad industry, feared that the flood and its devastation would cause their laborers to leave the Mississippi Delta entirely. To remedy this, they partnered with the American Red Cross and set up a system of flood refugee camps.

These "relief" camps became a home to more than 200,000 African Americans. The camps varied in both size and quality of living conditions. Some were acceptable, others disgraceful. At the camps, thousands of plantation workers were impressed into service and forced to endure dangerous and deplorable work conditions to help fix the levees near Greenville. Men and women worked tirelessly to stack sandbags atop the structures that remained.

## Change on the Horizon

Prior to 1927, flood control was largely the responsibility of town, country, and district levee boards. The great Mississippi flood changed all that. The Flood Control Act of 1928 gave the federal government authority over containment of the

Mississippi River. The Army Corps of Engineers transformed the entire Mississippi River Valley, constructing a system of new levees that incorporated strategic floodways, locks, dams, and runoff channels.

Eventually, the waters began to empty into the Gulf of Mexico. By July 1, the Mississippi still measured 70 miles wide in some areas, and 1.5 million acres continued to be submerged. The flood waters did not completely subside until August. But the flood hasn't completely disappeared. Instead, it has found a new home inside folklore, music, literature, and films. In 1929, Kansas Joe McCoy and Memphis Minnie wrote "When the Levee Breaks," a phrase which continues to reverberate in American history and culture.

# Nightmare in the Netherlands

*St. Felix's Flood destroyed the ancient city of Reimerswaal in the Netherlands, killing over 100,000 people in the process. It is considered the fifth-deadliest flood in human history.*

✳ ✳ ✳ ✳

## Evil Saturday

IT WAS NOVEMBER 5, 1530, the day of St. Felix's feast. Holy Roman Emperor Charles V reigned over the land, having inherited the Burgundian Netherlands from his father, Philip the Handsome. The area was largely below sea level and, as a result, flooding was always a potential risk. The Netherlands continuously tweaked their flood defenses, creating an extensive system to help maintain low water levels. Even so, floods were known to cascade through the land, transforming the Dutch landscape each and every time. This flood, however, would be different. Generated by a combination of a high spring tide, severe windstorm, and surrounding low pressure, St. Felix's Flood would raise the North Sea over 18 feet above average sea level. This day—later known as Evil Saturday—would dramatically change the Netherlands and its people.

## Drowned Land of Reimerswaal

Two regions along the North Sea shore, Flanders and Zeeland, were largely washed away by the flood. According to Audrey M. Lambert, author of *The Making of the Dutch Landscape: An Historical Geography of the Netherlands*, "all the Oost Wetering of Zuid-Beveland was lost, save only the town of Reimerswaal."

But the town of Reimerswaal was not unaffected by the catastrophic flood. Reimerswaal was once the third largest town in its province, having had a population of around six thousand residents. It was granted city rights in 1374 during the reign of Holy Roman Emperor Charles IV, although the Netherlands would not become an independent country until a few centuries later. After St. Felix's Flood ravaged Reimerswaal, all that remained of the city was a single, small island.

Over the next hundred years, more floods and fires continued to plague the few people left until, by 1632, the city of Reimerswaal was completely abandoned. Nothing remained. Today, the sunken city (known as *Verdronken Land van Reimerswaal*, or, "Drowned Land of Reimerswaal") serves as a shellfish fishery, providing rich breeding grounds for the mussels that are harvested there.

## The Aftermath

All in all, more than 100,000 people were killed by St. Felix's Flood. The island of Zuid-Beveland could not be reclaimed from the sea. Reimerswaal never recovered, also becoming lost to the waves. In Zeeland just two years later, on November 2, 1532, another major flood destroyed much of the repair work that had taken place after St. Felix.

The aftermath of St. Felix's Flood, considered one of the deadliest in history, forever changed the landscape of the Netherlands. Although the country now boasts beautiful beaches and seaside towns, its past of deadly destruction is still apparent to those that search for it.

# Flood and Famine: A Year of Unrest in Bangladesh

*Just three years after the Bangladesh Liberation War in 1971, heavy rainfall generated a series of troubling floods along the Brahmaputra River. What followed was one of the most devastating famines of the twentieth century.*

✳ ✳ ✳ ✳

## Moments Before Disaster

During the first few years of its independence, the newly-formed country of Bangladesh was listed as one of the poorest nations in the world. Nearly 90 percent of its total population lived in rural areas, although a majority of these people did not own land themselves. Life expectancy for both men and women was very low, and approximately 15 percent of all children died before reaching the age of five.

The country's economy was based around agriculture: The agriculture sector provided over half of the national gross domestic product and supplied employment to 80 percent of the population. Despite this, over 50 percent of households struggled with food insecurity.

Warnings of a famine began to emerge in March of 1974 as the price of rice grew more and more expensive. Newly-appointed government officials—corrupt and incompetent in the years after a major civil war—reiterated to the nation of 75 million people that the crisis would only be temporary. Still, prices continued to rise. Reports of starvation grew more frequent by April. In such a fragile state, even the slightest complication could lead to widespread starvation.

## A Wealth of Water

Heavy rainfall came to Bangladesh from April to July. A series of devastating floods along the Brahmaputra river caused massive destruction, bursting the river banks a total of six times. More than half of the country was inundated by floods—affecting approximately 35 million people. At least 2,000 Bangladeshis were killed in August alone. A number of those displaced attempted to move to the nation's capital, Dhaka, but broken road and rail communications made their journey exceedingly difficult.

But the worst was yet to come. The flood washed away a major part of Bangladesh's principal rice crop, *aus*, which was typically harvested in July and August. Two weeks later, the water level rose again, drowning *aman* seedlings—a type of rice crop transplanted between July and September. Another major rice crop, *boro*, was also damaged. With food production strained, the Bangladesh government officially declared a famine.

## Feast or Famine

Because the flood wiped out a large portion of rice, seasonal labor was not needed as harvest time approached. Those who could have earned money gathering the crop were left empty handed—a fate worsened by the still-rising rice prices.

The Bangladesh government could not procure enough rice to bring these prices down, especially while the food was being stockpiled and hoarded by wealthy speculators. Although the government managed a *langar khana*, or food distribution program, the relief effort was so poorly run that it did not offer much assistance.

A ration system was put in place to help provide subsidized food, but this kept supplies only in Bangladesh's urban centers. While the politically-important urban population was kept fed, rural Bangladeshis suffered even further starvation.

Famine occurred in all districts, but those affected by concurrent flooding—Mymensingh, Rangpur and Sylhet—had it worse. If the rice shortage had instead been shared equally across the country, there would have been much less hardship.

Equally as culpable was the lowered import of food grains from abroad—down 28 percent from the previous year. Bangladesh, like other developing countries at the time, received regular food aid from the United States. After three million dollars' worth of jute gunny sacks were shipped from Bangladesh to Cuba earlier that spring, however, the U.S. purposely withheld millions of tons of food aid. American wheat was not loaded for export until mid-November, when the worst of the famine was already over.

### A Famine Soon Forgotten

The famine officially ended in July of 1975, officially incurring a mortality rate of 26,000. Other estimates indicate a much higher figure, though, raising the number to one and a half million. Although the famine remains one of the best-documented and most-analyzed of its kind in world history, it remains a sensitive and painful topic for Bangladesh. The shame and guilt felt across the nation leave it in danger of being forgotten.

# An Unholy Upheaval: The All Saints' Flood of 1570

*The All Saints' Flood of 1570 was one of the greatest flood disasters in Dutch history. Its effects were felt from Belgium to the Netherlands, Germany, Denmark, and even Norway.*

✳    ✳    ✳    ✳

### Keeping a Weather Eye Open

EUROPEANS IN THE sixteenth century were accustomed to wild and tempestuous weather. According to the *Weather Eye*, October 1570 saw a storm devastate the North Sea coast of England, nearly obliterating the town of Mumby Chapel in Lincolnshire. One month later, another catastrophic storm swept across the coast of the North Sea. Water rose from the northwest, swelling with the spring tide. The storm only pushed the water to rise to unprecedented heights.

Because much of the North Sea coast lies below or very near sea level, the threat of flood is always present. Therefore creating and maintaining safety measures in the form of dikes, dams, sluices, and polders is extremely important. Even so, each century witnessed these defenses fail. Stronger and higher floods would regularly take over the land, breaching levees and inundating the countryside.

## Throwing Precaution to the Wind

The morning before the disastrous storm surge, on November 1, 1570, the Domain Council in the city of Bergen op Zoom issued a flood warning—the very first of its kind. They recorded their deed, describing how "a warning [had been] given about the very excessive high flood" to the dike works of both the south and north quarters. Unfortunately, their warning did not have its intended effect. Most victims, having not been alerted in time, were caught unprepared.

The All Saints' Flood, named for the holiday on which it occurred, rose more than thirteen feet above the mean high water—well exceeding the height of the protective dikes that existed at the time. The flood broke innumerable dikes on the Dutch coasts, many of which were already severely neglected. Coastal sections of the Netherlands, Belgium, Germany, and Denmark were overrun by the water masses, causing immense damage and devastation.

In Belgium, four villages near the city of Antwerp completely disappeared under a thick layer of mud and silt (they are now referred to as the *Verdronken Land van Saeftinghe*, or "Drowned land of Saeftinghe"). The westernmost province permanently lost the small islands of Wulpen, Koezand, Cadzand, and Stuivezand to the North Sea. Nearly all of the province of Holland was inundated. East Frisia, alongside its offshore islands, was also hit hard. In some places, entire stretches of land were under water for up to four weeks.

## Blowing It Out of the Water

Salt water rendered fields and meadows unsuitable for growing crops. Livestock was lost in huge numbers. Barns full of winter stocks of food and fodder were destroyed. An estimated 20,000 people perished in the flood, and many tens of thousands more became homeless. Of all the floods in the North Sea, only St. Felix's Flood of 1530 claimed more lives.

At the time, many saw the storm surge and resulting flood as God's punishment for their evildoing. In the Protestant provinces of the Netherlands, however, the death toll was seen as a call to rebel against Spanish oppression. In 1572, the Geuzen, a confederacy of Calvinist Dutch nobles, succeeded in conquering the provinces of Zeeland and Holland.

Several floods have plagued the region for centuries, and flood protection systems have always been built to combat them. After the North Sea Flood of 1953, the Delta Works project, a series of water defenses, was constructed. Since its completion, the Netherlands has remained dry.

# Caribbean Catastrophe: The Violent Hurricane of 1666

*In 1666, a violent hurricane swept across the Caribbean islands of Guadeloupe, Martinique, and Saint Christopher. It destroyed all the boats along their coasts, including a fleet of 17 British ships and 2,000 troops.*

❋　❋　❋　❋

## Winds and Waves

HURRICANES HAVE DEVASTATED the Caribbean region for millennia. Although cycles of storm activity have fluctuated in both time and intensity, with some years and decades being worse than others, hurricanes remain one of the most frequent and deadly natural disasters to impact the region. The strongest Caribbean hurricanes typically originate off the western coast of Africa, gaining strength as they pass westward over the Atlantic Ocean.

Hurricanes are tropical cyclones with strong, sustained winds. They are created when humid air rises from the ocean to meet the troposphere. Then, high pressure pushes the air down towards the storm's center, clearing out an eye. In the Caribbean, high amounts of humidity and warm air create near-perfect hurricane conditions. As such, these storms have always presented a threat for those living there.

In August of 1666, midway through the Atlantic hurricane season, a major storm struck the islands of Guadeloupe, Martinique, and Saint Christopher (now Saint Kitts). The strong winds and waves completely demolished homes. Island batteries—barrier walls six feet thick—were destroyed. Large, 16-pounder cannons washed away. With no such thing as weather forecasting, people had little time to hide from the path of the storm.

## The Fall of Francis Willoughby

The hurricane also posed a substantial threat to any boats along its trajectory. After learning of the recent French seizure of Saint Christopher, English Admiral Francis Willoughby formed a relief force of 17 ships: two Royal Navy frigates, 12 large vessels, a fire ship, and a ketch. The admiral and his fleet departed from Barbados on July 28, planning to first anchor in Nevis, Montserrat, and Antiqua to the north to gather supplies and reinforcements before engaging the French. As his crew passed Martinique and Guadeloupe, Willoughby ordered the capture of two merchant vessels.

This small victory would never be exploited, however. That very night, a majority of his force was destroyed by the hurricane. Of the 17 ships bearing over a thousand men, only two ships survived. Admiral Willoughby, at sea on board his flagship *Hope*, was lost.

## Somewhere Beyond the Sea

Although frequent in occurrence, each Caribbean hurricane never fails to shake up the islands and their inhabitants. In just one tempest, hundreds—even thousands—of lives could be lost. The 1666 hurricane itself killed thousands of people. In the aftermath of every large-scale disturbance, it seems unlikely that people will remain and rebuild. Yet, every time, they have. It wasn't until the early 1870s that a first hurricane warning service was implemented in Cuba. Since then, the Caribbean islands have developed myriad ways to monitor the movement of catastrophic, natural disasters.

# Buried Secrets of the Treasure Coast

*On July 24, 1715, a fleet of 11 ships departed from Havana, Cuba, on a journey to Spain, carrying with it millions of pesos' worth of gold and silver coins. One week later, a savage hurricane swept across the Bahamas Channel from the northeast. The fleet never reached its destination.*

\* \* \* \*

## A Fleeting Moment

SINCE THE BEGINNING of the eighteenth century, Spain regularly sent fleets of ships from the New World to the Old. The ships were loaded with various treasures and natural resources, including tobacco, exotic spices, indigo and other dyestuffs, gemstones, and gold and silver bullions. The July fleet was heavily laden when it departed for Spain. The Spanish king, Philip V, was dependent on its arrival. His fortune rose and fell with the arrival or loss of every fleet, and he often faced bankruptcy. This particular fleet was the first to leave the New World in over three years.

The 1715 Spanish Plate Fleet—named for the Spanish word for silver, *plata*—was actually a combination of two Spanish treasure fleets: The Nueva España Fleet (five ships) under the command of Captain General Don Juan Esteban de Ubilla, and the Tierra Firme Fleet (six ships) commanded by Captain General Don Antonio de Echeverz y Subiza. Another ship, the French frigate *Le Grifon*, sailed with the fleet, too. While the Spanish ships stayed close to the Florida coast, the French captain elected to stay further out from the shore. As the heavy, treasure-laden ships turned into the Bahamas Channel, they encountered northeasterly winds. Once the ships were between Cape Canaveral and Fort Pierce, these winds picked up dramatically.

## Sink or Swim

Although the ships were heavily fortified against pirates, hurricanes were another threat entirely. At two in the morning on July 31, just seven days after their initial departure, a hurricane struck the east coast of Florida and overtook the fleet. Three of the ships sank in deep water. The remainder were wrecked on the jagged rocks and coral reefs just north of present-day Vero Beach. The sinking of the *Nuestra Senora de la Regla* sent 200 people and 120 tons of coins to a watery grave. The *Santa Cristo de San Ramon* went down with another 120 sailors aboard. All in all, over a thousand sailors lost their lives, including fleet commander General Ubilla. It was a disaster to both the fleet and to the finances of Philip V of Spain.

Survivors assembled on the desolate Florida coast, managing to access food and clothes at the nearby Spanish colony of St. Augustine. Tools were used to try and salvage what was left of the ships and their cargo. When Havana learned of what had happened, a relief expedition was immediately dispatched. *Le Grifon*, the French frigate, was able to ride out the storm and returned to Europe safely.

## Another Man's Treasure

Over the next decade, the Spanish government attempted to recover the treasure, establishing several coastal salvage camps.

Spanish salvors braved Florida weather, mosquitos, and pirates as they sought to retrieve every bit of their lost fortune but, ultimately, a great quantity of treasure remained. After these initial salvage attempts were abandoned, the 1715 tragedy was surrendered to Davy Jones's Locker.

Then, in the late 1950's, another treasure hunter, Kip Wagner, discovered several silver coins on the beach following a storm. Wagner searched further, recovering more artifacts. He and his team exhibited their collection at the National Geographic Society Museum in Washington D.C. for visitors around the world. Since Wagner's discoveries, other treasure seekers have made their own discoveries. Thousands of precious pieces of gold, silver, and jewels have been recovered, inspiring the region's new alias: Treasure Coast.

# The Great Hurricane of 1780: The Deadliest Atlantic Hurricane Known

*In October of 1780, a powerful storm swept across the Caribbean. Although exact details of its strength are unknown, it caused significant damage, destroying buildings, sinking ships, and leaving behind thousands of casualties. It became known as the Great Hurricane of 1780.*

✳   ✳   ✳   ✳

A N OFFSHORE BOAT first spotted the storm on the horizon of the eastern Caribbean Sea. At the time—the night of October 9, 1780—it was only over the Atlantic. The following morning, however, the Eastern Caribbean islands began to feel its effects. First, only a light rain and wind. Then, full destruction. The hurricane made landfall in Barbados on October 10 before it charged across its neighboring islands, decimating the region over the course of one week.

Barbados suffered horrifically. The wind, which reached speeds as high as 200 miles per hour, was obtrusively loud—so deafening that people could not hear their own voices. Trees were stripped of their bark. Even the strongest buildings and fortifications were affected. Some were torn up off their foundations. In the capital of Barbados, churches, public buildings, and homes were completely leveled. The death toll on the island totaled over 4,500 persons.

Then, on October 11, the hurricane hit the neighboring islands of Saint Lucia and Martinique. Once again, sturdy stone forts and buildings were ripped away from their foundations. Heavy cannons were effortlessly carried hundreds of feet. In Saint Lucia, nearly every home on the island was destroyed. In Martinique, a 25-foot storm surge took an estimated 9,000 lives. As the storm moved northwest across the Antilles, it wiped entire towns off the map. The attorney general of Guadeloupe described the onslaught, claiming that "Grenades, St. Vincent, St. Lucia, Martinique, suffered more than any person can conceive."

## A Revolutionary Tale

Of course, it wasn't just the islands that were affected. The naval forces of Great Britain and France, both of whom were fighting in the American Revolutionary War, had a number of warships concentrated in the Caribbean. Both sides sustained heavy losses. The worst losses in the British fleet were those under the command of Vice Admiral Peter Parker and Rear-Admiral Joshua Rowley. Although the two men were fighting elsewhere (in Jamaica and New York, respectively), many of their ships remained directly in the hurricane's path. HMS *Thunderer*, HMS *Stirling Castle*, HMS *Scarborough*, HMS *Barbados*, HMS *Deal Castle*, HMS *Victor*, and HMS *Endeavor* were all lost. Several other ships were dismasted. A fleet of French ships was struck near the coast of Martinique, killing roughly 4,000 soldiers. The French military's only ship loss, however, was the frigate *Junon*.

## Deadly Destruction

Specifics about the Great Hurricane of 1780, such as its strength or point of origin, are unknown. The official Atlantic hurricane database only began keeping records in 1851, so the storm predates the advent of modern storm-tracking records and technology. Even so, there is no doubt that the Great Hurricane is among the deadliest Atlantic hurricanes ever recorded. More than 22,000 people perished as the storm swept through the eastern Caribbean Sea. Barbados, Martinique, and Saint Lucia were among the islands hit hardest, but thousands more casualties were found across the Caribbean. Only Hurricane Mitch, which occurred 200 years later in 1998, has dared approach the Great Hurricane in terms of fatalities and destruction.

# Dominican Disaster: The Hurricane That Gave a Country a 31-Year Dictatorship

*The 1930 Atlantic hurricane season was exceptionally quiet, all things considered. Only three tropical storms were known to have occurred. One of the three, however—Hurricane San Zenón— managed to devastate Santo Domingo in the Dominican Republic. It is known as the fifth deadliest Atlantic hurricane in recorded history.*

✳ ✳ ✳ ✳

## From Tropical Storm to Hurricane

ALTHOUGH THERE WERE no ships close enough to the storm at the time of its development to be sure, the system is estimated to have formed on August 29 about halfway between the Lesser Antilles and Cape Verde islands. It was only a tropical storm when its activity was first recorded. As it moved westward, however, it gradually intensified.

The storm was estimated to have become a hurricane on August 31, approximately 385 miles east of Guadeloupe. Operationally, however, it was first observed on the first day of September, while the storm passed through the Lesser Antilles. The hurricane was named San Zenón. At the time, there was no World Meteorological Organization, so hurricanes were given names of the saints of the day from the Roman Catholic liturgical calendar.

Wind reports from Dominica and Barbados showed evidence of San Zenón approaching, and a warning was immediately sent out to the surrounding island nations. After it passed Dominica and entered the Caribbean Sea, the hurricane reached Category 2. Before passing south of Puerto Rico, it strengthened into a Category 3. It continued intensifying until making landfall on the third of September near the city of Santo Domingo in the Dominican Republic. At the time, peak winds were estimated at 155 miles per hour.

## Grave and Terrible Devastation

The worst damage occurred in a two-mile diameter around its landfall location. Nearly half of the entire city of Santo Domingo was destroyed, and three of its districts were wiped away entirely. Stronger buildings, such as those located in the historic Colonial City, managed to survive the storm, but most houses lost their roofs. The strong winds disabled the city's communication infrastructure, making it difficult to assess the level of destruction even when the storm had passed.

Residents of Santo Domingo went outside to take in the devastation after the storm had calmed—only to be surprised by the other side of the eye of the storm. Many were killed by flying objects picked up by the fierce winds. Others died as a result of flooding. The people of the Dominican Republic suffered a great loss. The Red Cross estimated that 2,000 perished in Santo Domingo alone, with an additional 8,000 people injured.

## Dictator Rafael Trujillo

General Rafael Leónidas Trujillo Molina had come into office just two and a half weeks prior to Hurricane San Zenón's landfall. The newly-elected president personally organized relief efforts after the storm, deploying the country's entire military to assist with clean-up and reconstruction. In only a short amount of time, the capital flourished once more—now renamed Ciudad Trujillo, or "Trujillo City." Streets, monuments, and landmarks across the country were also named to honor the leader. This would be the beginning of one of the longest dictatorships in the Americas.

## A Lasting Impact

Although Hurricane San Zenón impacted many islands around the Atlantic basin, the Dominican Republic reported the most damage—an amount equalling nearly $50 million at the time. The island of Dominica suffered, too, recording failing crops, damaged buildings, and the deaths of at least 20 people. No significant reports came from Cuba, Florida, or Haiti—and, in Puerto Rico, the hurricane actually provided six inches of much-needed rainfall.

Small as it was, San Zenón has had a lasting impact on Santo Domingo—renamed once more following Trujillo's assassination—and its people. The storm itself, however, gradually weakened in the cold waters of the North Atlantic Ocean, and finally dissipated on September 17, just west of the Azores.

# Hurricane Flora: Cross-Caribbean Catastrophe

*Hurricane Flora, among the deadliest Atlantic hurricanes in recorded history, ravaged the Caribbean and Florida between September and October of 1963. It caused more than 7,000 deaths and cost over $525 million in damages—that's 5.02 billion dollars today.*

✳ ✳ ✳ ✳

## Flora's Formation

FLORA DEVELOPED ON September 26, 1963, as a tropical depression in the Intertropical Convergence Zone, a region along the equator where trade winds converge. It was first noted on TIROS satellite imagery about 750 miles southwest of one of the southernmost islands in Cape Verde. Though initially poorly organized, the depression managed to grow in size over the next day before disappearing from satellite view. Then, two days later on September 29, Flora reappeared about 350 miles north of Cayenne, French Guiana: In that time it had secured improved convection levels and rapidly developed into a tropical storm.

Flora continued to intensify. On September 30, ship reports noted that the system had developed a small but well-defined eye. With winds of 120 miles per hour, it was official: Hurricane Flora had reached Category 3.

## Picking Up Speed

Flora moved west toward the Windward Islands and made landfall on the island of Tobago. Heavy rainfall poured over the island, followed by strong winds. A mudslide off Mount Dillon completely buried a road leading to the seaside village of Castara. Meanwhile, tides swelled to five to seven feet beyond what was considered normal, sinking several heavy ships in Scarborough harbor.

Banana, cocoa, and coconut plantations were especially vulnerable. Half of all coconut trees were utterly destroyed, and many more were considered significantly damaged. Nearly 75 percent of all forest trees fell, and those that remained standing were also negatively affected. Though not estimated, heavy damage to other crops was reported too. Around 6,250 of the total 7,500 houses on the island were destroyed, claiming the lives of 18 people. On Tobago alone, Hurricane Flora caused $30 million (1963 USD) in crop and property damage.

Tobago's neighbor, Trinidad, was largely unaffected by the storm: The island's mountain range along the north coast protected its residents from the degree of harm that devastated Tobago. Grenada, another island, was hit with winds of 125 miles per hour for nearly 90 minutes. Though it did not receive the same degree of devastation as Tobago, it also reported damage to its airport and bridges. In some areas, roads were blocked by fallen trees.

## On the Warpath

As it entered the Caribbean Sea, Hurricane Flora strengthened to Category 4 status. It reached a peak wind speed of 150 miles per hour on October 3, just 105 miles south of Haiti and the Dominican Republic. Excessive rainfall set records for the nearby islands. At Polo Barahona, the highest amount reported was 40 inches. In Miragoâne, 57 inches fell over the course of three days.

At Côtes-de-Fer on the south coast of Haiti, Flora made its second landfall. Flash flooding washed out large sections of several towns. Other towns were buried by mudslides triggered in the country's more mountainous regions. Still others were left roofless by Flora's strong winds. The hurricane killed 5,000 people in Haiti alone. In southwestern Haiti, many of those who died were found to have first suffered from intense wind burns.

The Grise River crested at 14 feet above its normal level, seeping into surrounding banana plantations. As with Tobago, Haiti's crops were almost entirely destroyed. Although the coffee crop was harvested prior to Flora's arrival, the intense rainfall and flooding ruined existing plants for years to come. Monetary losses in Haiti amounted to $180 million (1963 USD).

## Slowing Down

Flora made another landfall on October 4, in Cuba. Although the hurricane—now a Category 3—had weakened significantly, its vast amounts of rain still caused significant devastation. A quarter of coffee, ten percent of corn, and 15 percent of sugar crops were ruined. Significant beach erosion occurred along the northern coast of Camagüey Province. Transportation infrastructures were damaged across the island, as were tens of thousands of Cuban homes. Approximately 1,750 people were killed. Of those who remained, many were left stranded on top of their homes.

As Flora turned to the northeast, heavy rainfall fell across the island of Jamaica, leading to numerous landslides. Rough seas affected the Bahamas and the southeastern Florida coast. Finally, at the end of its 17-day lifespan, Flora was downgraded to an extratropical cyclone.

With a death total of at least 7,193 people, Hurricane Flora was so detrimental to the people of the Caribbean nations that its name was officially retired by the World Meteorological Organization, never to be used again.

# Independence Hurricane:
# A One-Two Punch

*The 1775 Newfoundland Hurricane, also known as the Independence Hurricane, was a tropical cyclone that struck both the British colony of Newfoundland as well as the Thirteen Colonies. It is believed to have killed 4,000 people, making it one of the deadliest Atlantic hurricanes to hit the northern coasts of North America in history.*

✳   ✳   ✳   ✳

## A Hurricane of a War

ON AUGUST 27, during the opening months of America's War of Independence, a hurricane hit the Outer Banks of North Carolina. Dubbed "Independence Hurricane" by author David Ludlum, the storm traveled northeastward out of the state. "We had a violent hurricane," recounts one letter from New Bern, "which has done a vast deal of damage here, at the Bar, and at Mattamuskeet, near 150 lives being lost at the Bar, and 15 in one neighborhood at Mattamuskeet."

September 2 brought heavy wind and rain to southeastern Virginia. Even rebels holding the Bunker Hill heights in Boston noticed the storm swirling overhead. "Every day last week it rained more or less, and sometimes continued the chief part of the night; but on Saturday it never ceased pouring down," the September 8, 1775 edition of the *Virginia Gazette* reported. "Infinite damage has been done to the crops of corn and tobacco." Norfolk bridges were swept away by the raging waters, and numerous wharves and storehouses were devastated.

Along the coast—ravaged from Currituck to Chincoteague— approximately 25 vessels were thrown ashore and damaged. The HMS *Otter's* tender, named *Liberty*, was driven aground in Back River, near Hampton. The next day, local inhabitants boarded the vessel, captured the crew, removed the guns and stores, and burned it. Between the two states, at least 163 people were killed.

## Canada's Deadliest Natural Disaster

One week later, on September 9, the hurricane struck the eastern coast of Newfoundland. A localized storm surge reportedly raised ocean levels to heights "scarcely ever known before"—nearly 30 feet. Two armed schooners, one stationed on the Grand Banks of Newfoundland and the other on the northeast coast of the province, were wrecked, but only two crew members were lost to the storm.

Conception Bay was filled with a number of fishing boats. The squid catch was late that summer, and the working men were oblivious to the growing storm. They "received a very severe stroke from the violence of a storm of wind, which almost swept everything before it," wrote Commodore Governor Robert Duff. "A considerable number of boats, with their crews, have been totally lost, several vessels wrecked on the shores." The Newfoundland storm was responsible for over 4,000 deaths, most of which were sailors from England and Ireland. For some days after, bodies—sometimes up to 30 at a time—were drawn up from the depths in fishing nets. The 1775 storm was the first Canadian hurricane to ever be recorded. It is also the eighth-deadliest hurricane in the history of the Atlantic Ocean.

## Hurricane? Or Hurricanes?

There is no doubt that the Independence Hurricane brought about immense damage and destruction. But what historians and meteorologists struggle to understand, however, is if the extreme weather conditions were part of one singular storm or two storms hitting in close succession. It is possible that the 1775 Newfoundland Hurricane was its own storm, and it is also possible that it was a remnant of the hurricane that crossed the Outer Banks one week prior.

Experts in science and communication have chosen to focus on what comes next. People 250 years ago did not have any warning about the impending storm. Nowadays, we can better recognize the many risks associated with the unforgiving Atlantic waters.

# The Long Hurricane: A Month of Terror

*The 1899 San Ciríaco Hurricane devastated Puerto Rico and the barrier islands of North Carolina's Outer Banks for four grueling weeks. It was the longest-lived Atlantic hurricane on record.*

✳ ✳ ✳ ✳

## An Advancing Storm

THE TROPICAL STORM system was first observed on August 3 by a ship southwest of Cape Verde. Typical of other Cape Verdean hurricanes, San Ciríaco originated at low latitudes in the deep tropics. It moved across the Atlantic into the Caribbean and, on August 7, appeared east of the island of Martinique. Moving at a slow speed of 17 miles per hour, the storm crossed directly over the island of Guadeloupe, then moved 50 miles north toward St. Kitts. There, San Ciríaco finally crossed the Leeward Islands—but not before its 150 mile-per-hour winds earned it a shiny new rating of Category 4 on the Saffir-Simpson hurricane wind scale.

The hurricane continued on its northwestern track. Along its journey, its wind speeds lessened—but only slightly. On the morning of August 8, Hurricane San Ciríaco made landfall on southeastern Puerto Rico with winds of 140 miles per hour.

## Puerto Rico

At the time, warnings of an approaching hurricane came strictly through observations: increasing winds, rising tides, and falling atmospheric pressure. Although it was August, the height of Atlantic hurricane season, the island of Puerto Rico had not suffered a major storm in over two decades. As residents made arrangements for the Feast of San Ciríaco, they were unprepared for the fury of the most destructive hurricane in Puerto Rican history.

It rained for 28 days straight. At Humacao, a city located on the eastern coast, 23 inches of rain reportedly fell in the span of a single day. Other localities reported similar findings. Rivers like the Abacoa and the Portugués rose rapidly, resulting in massive flooding that washed away important coffee plantations. Along the coast, the sea furiously beat against the shore.

The storm and its accompanying floods caused the deaths of approximately 3,400 people—more than three times the amount of lives lost in all other Puerto Rican hurricanes. Thousands more were left without food, shelter, or work. Total damages were estimated to be over 30 million pesos—a cost the municipal governments were virtually powerless to alleviate. Taking place only a year after the U.S. invasion of the island, Hurricane San Ciríaco seemed only to add to Puerto Rico's existing pain.

## North Carolina

The hurricane continued onward—now a Category 3—skimming the northeast coast of the Dominican Republic on August 9. It crossed the Bahamas next, striking several islands. Then, on August 13, it moved north to Jupiter, Florida. It traveled nearly parallel to the U.S. coast over the next couple of days and initially appeared to be moving out to sea. By August 17, however, that was no longer the case. San Ciríaco turned back to the northwest and made landfall near Hatteras, North Carolina. Never again would a hurricane of this magnitude terrorize the Outer Banks.

The U.S. Weather Bureau station measured wind gusts reaching speeds up to 140 miles per hour—that is, before its measuring equipment was blown away in the storm. Nearly all the buildings in Diamond City and Shackleford were lost to storm surge—as high as ten feet in certain places. Fishing equipment was destroyed, as were boats. Several people reported seeing dead livestock float atop the incoming tide. After two days of terror, Hurricane San Ciríaco turned eastward, leaving the U.S. coast for the Atlantic as a mere Category 1.

## Atlantic Aftermath

After abandoning the waters of the United States coast, Hurricane San Ciríaco traveled over the Atlantic until it became an extratropical cyclone on August 22. Later, its stormy remnants reorganized enough to develop into a tropical storm once more. Moreover, once San Ciríaco turned farther east, the storm strengthened enough to regain its hurricane status. This new stage of its life wouldn't last long, however. The following day, San Ciríaco would be no more.

Hurricane San Ciríaco is on record as the longest-lasting Atlantic cyclone, existing for a total of 27.75 days. With an estimated 3,800 fatalities, it is also considered to be one of the worst storms to hit the U.S. Atlantic coast. The storm was so terrifying and devastating that approximately 500 North Carolina residents decided to move inland. What's more, some 5,000 Puerto Ricans chose to migrate halfway across the world to another island: Hawaii. For those who remained, the only choice left was to rebuild.

# The First Hurricane Warning Broadcast Via Radio

*Also known as the San Felipe Segundo hurricane, the Lake Okeechobee hurricane caused heavy casualties and extensive destruction all along its path, from the Leeward Islands to Florida. It ranks among the deadliest disasters in the history of the North Atlantic basin.*

✳ ✳ ✳ ✳

## Crisis in the Caribbean

ON SEPTEMBER 6, 1928, a tropical depression began to form off the west coast of Africa. Hours later as it passed south of the Cape Verde islands, it strengthened and became a tropical storm. It was only a Category 1 when it was first detected on September 10, approximately 900 miles east of Guadeloupe. But by the time it struck the island, the storm system had reached a dreaded Category 4.

The island of Dominica faced only mild winds while Martinique suffered three fatalities. Guadeloupe, however, received a direct hit with little warning. Damage reports relayed through Paris—Guadeloupe is an overseas region of France—proclaimed "great destruction." Nearly every building on the island was destroyed, save for a single police station built with reinforced concrete. Approximately three-fourths of the island's residents were left homeless. Over 1,200 people died.

Montserrat, another nearby island, lost a great deal of crops during the event, amounting to conditions of near-starvation before relief could arrive. St. Kitts suffered nine deaths, six of which occurred in the collapse of a wooden schoolhouse. On the island of Nevis, 13 people were killed.

The hurricane struck Puerto Rico on September 13. Although the storm had grown to reach a deadly Category 5 with wind speeds of up to 160 miles per hour, residents of the island were well-prepared: The U.S. Weather Bureau sent a hurricane advisory via telegraph to police districts across the island. The warning was broadcast from the naval radio station every two hours—the first time a hurricane warning was broadcast by radio. Even though heavy rain and wind caused disastrous property damage and several thousand people were rendered homeless, Puerto Rico had a fairly low death toll of around 300. By comparison, the San Ciríaco hurricane of 1899 killed approximately ten times as many Puerto Ricans.

## Fiasco in Florida

On September 16, the storm made landfall in West Palm Beach, Florida, with sustained winds of 145 miles per hour. Although it had weakened to a Category 4, the hurricane caused a ten-foot storm surge that greatly impacted the towns of Jupiter, Delray, Lake Worth, Pompano, Palm Beach, and West Palm Beach. In West Palm Beach alone, 1,711 homes were destroyed. 6,363 more were damaged.

The greatest devastation, however, occurred along the south shore of Lake Okeechobee in central Florida. Just like in Puerto Rico, residents had been warned to evacuate the area, particularly its low ground. But the hurricane did not arrive on schedule. After noting clear skies, many residents returned home, thinking that the storm had moved elsewhere. Little did they know, the hurricane might have been behind schedule, but it was right on track.

In the weeks prior to the storm, heavy rainfall had caused the lake's water level to rise three feet. The hurricane's downpour only raised it further. When the worst of the storm crossed the lake, it created a three-foot surge that washed over Lake Okeechobee's small, five-foot dike. Floodwaters covered hundreds of square miles and reached the rooftops of houses. Bodies and survivors alike were washed out into the Everglades. Most of the estimated 2,500 people dead were farm workers— African Americans and Bahamians who lived near the lake.

Because the ground was flooded for weeks, the burial of Lake Okeechobee's victims was virtually impossible. Segregation laws at the time forced Black families to cremate their loved ones for later burial in a West Palm Beach mass grave. They did not receive a formal memorial service.

## Calm in Canada

After decimating Lake Okeechobee, the weakened hurricane moved up the coasts of eastern Georgia and the Carolinas. It swung inland over Pennsylvania, then deteriorated into a tropical depression as it entered Canada on September 20. All in all, total damages from the storm amounted to approximately $100 million (1928 USD).

Hurricane warning and flood prevention systems are being improved all the time. Even in 1928, radio broadcasting proved to significantly decrease the amount of hurricane casualties. Today, recent technological advancements further help save lives and reduce the extent and severity of structural damage. Improved building codes, floodway channels, levees, medical equipment—all of these advances help prevent another Lake Okeechobee disaster.

# A Cascadia Conundrum: What Do Ghost Forests, Orphan Tsunamis, and Native American Legends Have in Common?

*At 9:00 p.m. on January 26, 1700, a massive megathrust earthquake—one of the world's largest—occurred along the coast of the Pacific Northwest. Neskowin Ghost Forest on the Oregon coast is one piece of evidence for this story. What's stranger, however, is another piece of evidence: eighteenth-century written records. They aren't found on the North American continent, but rather an ocean away in Japan.*

❊   ❊   ❊   ❊

## The Earthquake Event

JUST NORTH OF the San Andreas fault lies another, lesser-known fault line. Known as the Cascadia subduction zone, it runs for 620 miles from northern Vancouver Island, Canada, passing through Oregon and Washington before finally terminating around Cape Mendocino in northern California. Cascadia gets its name from the Cascade Range, a chain of volcanoes that parallel the fault about a hundred miles inland.

Subduction zones are regions of Earth where one tectonic plate slides underneath, or subducts, another. In the Cascadia subduction zone, the smaller Juan de Fuca plate is thrust under the larger North American plate. Most of the time, the movement of tectonic plates is slow and harmless—tectonic plates move at around the same speed as your fingernails grow. Occasionally, however, they shift rapidly. The overriding plate will lurch upwards, producing tremendous shaking and generating dangerous tsunamis. Subduction zones like Cascadia are capable of generating the largest earthquakes on the planet.

The 1700 Cascadia earthquake had an estimated magnitude between 8.7 and 9.2 on the Richter scale, a logarithmic scale that measures seismic waves. For reference, that's about the same magnitude that struck the northeast of Japan in 2011 (9.0). An earthquake of such magnitude can last five whole minutes—or longer. It would leave few, if any, structures standing in its wake.

## Seeing the Forest for the Trees

Neskowin Ghost Forest is a grove of Sitka spruces on the Oregon coast. Like many other ghost forests in Oregon and Washington, it bears leafless, branchless, and barkless tree stumps, worn down over time into a smooth, silvery gray. Scientists suspected that the trees had died as a result of rising sea levels. But how?

Specialists in dendrochronology were called to study the trees' growth ring patterns. Most trees grow a new ring every year, and the thickness of these rings directly corresponds to the quality of that growing season. By matching up the stump rings to those of living trees farther inland, scientists were able to determine that the ghost forests had died simultaneously sometime between the 1699 and 1700 growing season. This discovery matched up with previous evidence of sudden land subsidence along the Washington coast: When the ground beneath the trees plummeted 36 feet, a rush of incoming ocean water killed the entire forest instantly. This was the work of a powerful earthquake and tsunami.

## An Orphan Tsunami

The people of Japan have kept careful records of tsunamis dating back to at least the fourth century, and it's no secret why: Japan's coast is extremely vulnerable to these dangerous walls of water. Over the years, one incident has stood out for its peculiarity: On the eighth day of the twelfth month of the twelfth year of the Genroku era, a wave of water approximately six hundred miles long struck the coast. No earthquake was felt before it. Japan understood that tsunamis were the result of earthquakes, but this tsunami had no such origin. The mysterious event was referred to as an "orphan" tsunami.

It was only later, after the origin of the ghost forests along the Washington and Oregon coasts had been discovered, that seismologist Kenji Satake was finally able to match the orphan tsunami to its parent. Using a computer model, it was determined that a magnitude 9.0 earthquake would have taken ten hours to cross the Pacific Ocean. The earthquake occurred at approximately nine o'clock at night on January 26, 1700.

## Here All Along

Scientists did not have to go all the way to Japan for reports of earthquakes and saltwater floods. As it turned out, the quake was present in the oral traditions of numerous First Nations and Native American legends.

Oral accounts from tribes living on the coast of the Pacific Northwest have been passed down from generation to generation, detailing a violent shaking of land on a cold, winter night. In present-day Washington, the Makah tribe's land was inundated by the waters of Neah Bay. Farther north, on Vancouver Island, the shaking was so violent that it was difficult to stand. The Cowichan people suffered landslides and numerous collapsed houses. The Pachena Bay people were eradicated entirely.

In 2005, seismologist Ruth Ludwin collected and analyzed these reports in a study. In every account, low-lying native settlements were completely destroyed. Only those living 75 feet above sea level survived. The 1700 tsunami must have been enormous.

## What the Future Holds

The geological record tells us that the January 26, 1700 event was not unique: A major quake occurs in the Cascadia subduction zone about once every 500 years. At least 13 of these earthquakes have occurred in the past 6,000 years. A similar event is bound to occur in the future, and it may be sooner than we think. According to recent research, because multiple magnitude 8 earthquakes have disrupted the area in the tectonic plates' intervening years, the average time between megathrust earthquakes has decreased to a mere 270 years.

Because there hasn't been a major earthquake in the Cascadia subduction zone in over 300 years, the people who call the region home are unaware of its dangers. Without earthquake survival in mind, cities like Seattle, Tacoma, Portland, Salem, and Olympia might one day suffer the consequences.

# 78 Hours of Category 5

*The 1932 Cuba Hurricane, known alternately as the Hurricane of Santa Cruz del Sur, was by far the deadliest and one of the most intense tropical cyclones to have ever made landfall on the island of Cuba. It was also the only Category 5 Atlantic hurricane recorded in November.*

✳   ✳   ✳   ✳

## A Storm Is Brewing

THE 1932 CUBA HURRICANE was first identified as a tropical depression roughly 200 miles east of Guadeloupe. It strengthened into a tropical storm after passing over the islands of Dominica, Martinique, and St. Lucia, and then, strangely, continued its course towards the southwest. On November 2, while north of the Netherlands Antilles, the storm intensified and gained hurricane status. By November 5, the hurricane reached Category 5.

As it gathered strength near the coast of northern South America, the hurricane interrupted rail telecommunications and severely damaged swaths of banana plantations in Colombia. In the city of Santa Marta, several docks, railways, and multiple homes were inundated. Even inland farms suffered extensive flooding. Jamaica took a barrage of intense winds as strong as 70 miles per hour, causing some areas of the island to lose as many as half of their banana trees. The Cayman Islands, lying 700 miles south of Cuba, reported a storm surge as high as 33 feet. Homes and government buildings were washed out to sea.

## Cuban Calamity

On November 9, the 1932 hurricane came ashore in Cuba's Camagüey province. The resulting storm surge was reported to reach over 20 feet, effortlessly sweeping away the coastal town of Santa Cruz del Sur in a huge wall of water. Hundreds of homes were either destroyed or damaged. Electricity was only available in a few places, and a food shortage was imminent. Approximately 2,870 people lost their lives.

The *Madera Tribune* reported on the survivors distributed across several emergency hospitals, "Many were limping and others were bandaged. One died en route. All were underclad and some had no clothes at all." A Camagüey attorney, Dario Castillo, remarked on Santa Cruz del Sur's stricken state. "It is a city of the past," he said. "Nobody remains except a few distracted, obdurate refugees searching among the dead for relatives, and small squads of volunteer workers. The latter buried 472 bodies today. They will burn the other bodies, which are still strewn for several miles around."

## The Calm After the Storm

After hitting Cuba, the Hurricane of Santa Cruz del Sur weakened and began to wander northward toward the Bahamas and Bermuda. The hurricane finally dissipated on November 14, but not before setting a notable record for the longest duration of an Atlantic hurricane at Category 5 intensity. Over the course of 78 grueling hours, the Category 5 monster hurricane ravaged the Caribbean, sweeping away entire cities without any trouble. In total, over 3,100 people were killed.

# The Case of the Missing Earthquake Epicenter

*You might expect the origin of a powerful earthquake—strong enough to rattle seven states and provinces—to be pretty clear. It wasn't until recently, however, that geologists finally cracked one of the biggest seismological mysteries in the Pacific Northwest: the source of the 1872 North Cascades earthquake.*

✳ ✳ ✳ ✳

## The Inciting Earthquake

O N THE EVENING of December 14, 1872, long before the transcontinental railroad reached Washington state, and even longer before the first seismometer was installed in the Pacific Northwest, an earthquake struck the Pacific Northwest. In the sparsely-populated hills near Wenatchee, both settlers and Native Americans reported a massive landslide that temporarily dammed the mighty Columbia River. Trees toppled in Puyallup. Reports of cracked chimneys surfaced in distant Olympia. Fissures even split open the ground just south of Seattle. And at Snoqualmie Pass, people were knocked off their feet.

The effects weren't just limited to Washington, either. Compelling eyewitness testimonies noted windows shattering as far away as Victoria, British Columbia. Based on these historical accounts, experts estimate the quake's size to have ranged between magnitude 6.5 to 7.5. U.S. Geological Survey researcher Brian Sherrod, who led the modern-day hunt for the quake's source, remarked: "No matter how you define it, that's a big earthquake."

## Gathering Clues

Because of the region's low population, information trickled in slowly. Early newspaper reports put the epicenter not far from Vancouver, British Columbia. Other observers assumed the quake was centered under Puget Sound, an inlet of the Pacific Ocean in northwestern Washington. Still others centered the most intense damage near Wenatchee.

One hundred years later, in the 1970s, legions of consultants were tasked to pinpoint the location of the 1872 earthquake. Interested in building expensive nuclear reactors in Washington, each of the two companies involved—one planning to build in Hanford, the other on the Skagit River near Sedro-Woolley—did not want to risk their operations with another large earthquake. The series of reports that followed lobbed the epicenter back and forth across the Cascades. According to *The Columbian*, one Seattle politico dubbed the 1872 tremor "the earthquake that wouldn't stay put."

In the decades that followed, people continued to guess where the big 1872 earthquake occurred. "To be able to finally pinpoint this thing on a map would be really important in helping us get the seismic hazard assessment correct in that part of the state," said Craig Weaver of the USGS.

## Hot on the Trail

Brian Sherrod and his colleagues started their hunt for the epicenter near Entiat. The Chelan County city experiences recurring swarms of small earthquakes and is located near many faults. It is also close to 1872's infamous river-clogging landslide. Using lidar, an airborne laser-mapping tool commonly used to make detailed, high-resolution maps, Sherrod and his team identified a fault scarp in Spencer Canyon. These are left where a fault moves the ground surface during an earthquake.

But there was only one way to be sure: digging, and lots of it. Because the only road to the area was too narrow for an excavator, Sherrod and his colleagues were forced to dig two trenches by hand. Across the fault scarp, they exposed layers of rock and sediment needed to determine the region's geology through time. Colored pins delineated strata. Charcoal and ash were used to pinpoint the date of several ancient events. At the end of their backbreaking labor, the geologists had uncovered evidence of at least two past earthquakes. The new fault was named the Spencer Canyon fault after the valley in which it was found.

### Mystery Solved

Every new scientific discovery brings us closer to the truth about our planet and its many processes. With the new data collected at Spencer Canyon, it appears that Central and Eastern Washington are more prone to earthquakes than previously thought. There is, of course, always room for further research. Future studies planned by Sherrod will reveal how often the Spencer Canyon fault had ruptured in the past, as well as illuminate what risks it presents to the infrastructure—and homes of 1.5 million people—nearby.

# Effulgent Earthquake Enigma: What's Causing These Mysterious Lights?

*Videos shared on social media purportedly show mysterious, aerial phenomena lighting up the sky moments before a powerful earthquake. Experts aren't sure what causes them. Some doubt they're associated with earthquakes at all.*

✳   ✳   ✳   ✳

### Bringing It to Light

ACCOUNTS OF THESE strange earthquake lights actually go back centuries. The Nihon Sandai Jitsuroku, an officially-commissioned Japanese history text, described the lights as having occurred around the time of the 869 Sanriku earthquake. At least 65 instances of these aerial luminous phenomena were documented throughout the eighteenth, nineteenth, and twentieth centuries, and modern technology has made it possible to witness the phenomenon even after the fact.

In 2007, a security camera caught bright flashes that lit up the sky right before Pisco, Peru's 8.0 magnitude earthquake. Two years later, more flickering lights were spotted right before an earthquake in L'Aquila, Italy. Then, eerie images of blue and green lights appeared across social media when an 8.1 magnitude earthquake struck Mexico in 2017. More videos of these unexplained lights keep finding their way onto every front page and news feed—some as recently as September 8, 2023. This time, the lights were seen illuminating the night sky during a magnitude 6.8 earthquake in the High Atlas Mountains of eastern Morocco.

They may be short-lasting, but these lights have captivated people's imaginations around the world. What's stranger, however, is that they don't all appear to be the same: Some lights are described as flashing, others as softly-glowing clouds. Still others are compared to hovering orbs, or even flames emanating from the ground. They range in color, too. The lights seem to occur above sites of seismic stress, but they differ in their timing. Some occur before an earthquake, while others occur during. Though rarer, some are said to occur after an earthquake is over.

## Seeing the Light

With all these variations in place, it's difficult for scientists to distinguish between which lights have actually occurred, and which are likely a product of the imagination. In fact, the U.S. Geological Survey is circumspect about whether any of these reported lights exist at all. Even in cases where photographic evidence exists, the supposed earthquake lights cannot be confirmed. One analysis, in Mexico City, suggested that the light was actually the result of electric sparks being reflected by a cloud. Earthquake lights seen during the Turkey-Syria earthquake in 2023 were a combination of lightning, electric discharges, and fires. In Morocco, scientists speculate the lights were caused by exploding transformers in the city's streets.

But other scientists believe the explanation is hidden beneath the surface. Perhaps electric charges are activated in certain types of rocks during seismic activity. According to Friedemann Freund, senior researcher at NASA's Ames Research Center, basalt and gabbro rocks "have tiny defects in their crystals that could release electrical charges into the air." These could account for the lights seen in less than 0.5 percent of earthquakes worldwide.

## Lights Out

One of the biggest complications in studying earthquake lights is that earthquakes are impossible to predict. Without knowing when or where an earthquake will strike, scientists cannot begin to unravel the many mysteries surrounding the short-lived earthquake lights that accompany them.

For now, the debate remains. Whether the result of lightning strikes, crystalline defects, or UFOs, earthquake lights have captured the attention of people everywhere.

# The Largest Earthquake in History

*Scientists have found evidence of the largest known earthquake in history—a terrifying northern Chilean quake coming in at a magnitude of 9.5 on the Richter scale. The earthquake reportedly propelled car-sized boulders hundreds of yards, created massive waves 66 feet high, and prompted human populations to abandon their homes for over a thousand years.*

✳   ✳   ✳   ✳

## Ancient Megathrust Earthquake

BEFORE THE ANCIENT megaquake was discovered, another Chilean earthquake topped the list. The 1960 Valdivia earthquake, also known as the Great Chilean Earthquake, hit southern Chile with a magnitude between 9.4 and 9.6 and killed approximately 6,000 people. The rupture that caused the earthquake was enormous—about 500 miles long. According to new research, however, the ancient quake was even larger: Its originating rupture measured roughly 620 miles in length.

Like the Valdivia earthquake, the ancient quake 3,800 years ago was a megathrust earthquake, a type of earthquake that occurs at convergent plate boundaries. As the two tectonic plates collide, one plate is forced, or subducted, under the other. Most of the time, the movement of tectonic plates is slow and harmless. Occasionally, however, the plates will have gathered so much strain that the overriding plate will suddenly lurch upwards to release it. This sudden movement creates a gigantic rupture, generating some of the largest earthquakes on the planet.

## Clues Left Behind

Such a massive earthquake is bound to leave behind evidence—even if that evidence is thousands of years old. Evidence of the earthquake's resulting tsunami—with waves as high as 66 feet—was found all over the world. Australia, Vanuatu, Japan, and Russia were all affected, and in New Zealand the tsunami was so strong that massive boulders were effortlessly carried about one kilometer inland.

In every country affected, marine sediment (boulders, pebbles, and sand) and animal bodies were found a significant distance away from the coast, pushed across the land by the enormous wave. The evidence was discovered at high elevations, so it could not have been a regular storm that sent objects there. Further evidence came in the form of ancient stone structures: Large stone walls, built by ancient humans, were found beneath the tsunami's deposits. According to archeologists, some of the structures pointed toward the sea, toppled over by the strong currents of the tsunami's backwash. Other walls looked to have been pushed over by a retreating tsunami.

## Learning from Catastrophe

Even though most of the region is an inhospitable desert, ancient northern Chile hosted a thriving maritime community. Before the earthquake, people had been living off the nearby ocean for over 12,000 years. After the quake, the local population was left with nothing. Those who survived completely abandoned their villages and moved inland beyond the reach of tsunamis. It took over 1,000 years for people to venture out toward the coasts once more, suggesting that there was a long-lasting memory of this tragic event.

Understanding how communities adapt to devastating disasters helps better inform us of how we can cope when another catastrophe strikes. Chile and its surrounding South Pacific islands are more populated now than ever before, and many of these places are popular tourist destinations. When another earthquake comes along, we need to be prepared.

# Not-so-Good Friday: The Great Alaskan Earthquake

*The Great Alaskan Earthquake, the most powerful earthquake ever recorded in North America, shook the earth for a total of four minutes and 38 seconds. During that time, it caused ground fissures, collapsed structures, and generated a tsunami that claimed the lives of 122 people.*

✳ ✳ ✳ ✳

### An Earthquake of Great Magnitude

ON MARCH 27, 1964, just as many Alaskans were sitting down to dinner, the earth began to tremble. It was Good Friday that day, though "good" was hardly the proper term. In the four and a half minutes of intense shaking, eyewitnesses described hearing a crunching, grinding noise. Asphalt roads rose and fell like ocean waves, and the ground split open before them. Water shot up to fill the ensuing cracks. Unsurprisingly, water, sewer, and gas lines across the area broke. Above ground wasn't safe either: Telephone poles, buildings, docks, and cars were all destroyed.

The earthquake rupture started approximately 15 miles beneath the surface in Prince William Sound, about 75 miles southeast of Anchorage. But, being a magnitude 9.2, the earthquake was easily felt across the state—and beyond. 1,200 miles away, Seattle's Space Needle was seen wobbling back and forth. Farther south in Freeport, Texas, gauges used for measuring tides instead recorded the earthquake's seismic surface waves. The earthquake was so powerful it registered in every U.S. state except Connecticut, Delaware, and Rhode Island. Even beyond North America, seiches, or standing waves, were detected in multiple wells.

## A Wave of Tsunamis

For as bad as the tremors got, the worst was yet to come. In the early 1960s, the paradigm of plate tectonics was still in its infancy. Scientists did not understand it at the time, but Prince William Sound sat on top of a fault between the Pacific and North American plates—two convergent tectonic plates, one subducting under the other. As convergent plates move toward one another, they accumulate strain between them. Eventually, during particularly large earthquakes, the strain is released with drastic consequence. In the case of the Great Alaskan earthquake, parts of the Alaskan coast sank eight feet down, while other parts rose nearly 40 feet. There was such a severe shift in the coast's topography that, as soon as the tremors ended, local tsunamis sprang up to take their place.

Residents had little to no time to flee for higher ground before a massive tidal wave inundated the small, coastal village of Chenega. The town lost about a third of its population. Valdez, another Alaskan city, was left with 32 dead. Port Alberni, a Vancouver Island city, was hit twice, washing away 55 homes and damaging 375 more. Tsunami waves were noted in over 20 countries worldwide, including Mexico, Peru, Japan, and New Zealand. Nine people are believed to have died as a result of the earthquake itself, but an additional 122 died from the subsequent tsunamis.

## The Aftershocks and Aftermath

For weeks after the initial earthquake, thousands of strong aftershocks were recorded—some reaching magnitudes greater than 6.0! It became abundantly clear that scientists had a lot to learn about the mechanics of subduction zones. Data gathered after the 1964 earthquake was put to good use: A new broad earthquake-monitoring system was created to gather data and help seismologists predict future earthquakes—as well as minimize their potential damage.

# The Year of No Summer

*"The Year Without a Summer" may sound like the beginning of Armageddon, but these words describe an actual year in human history—the year 1816, which Americans nicknamed "eighteen-hundred-and-froze-to-death." It was a year of floods, droughts, and incredible, unparalleled summertime frosts that destroyed crops, spread diseases, incited riots, and otherwise wrought havoc upon the world. The culprit of this global meteorological mayhem was the eruption of Tambora, a volcano on the Indonesian island of Sumbawa—the largest explosive eruption in recorded history.*

✳   ✳   ✳   ✳

## Monster Eruption

TAMBORA WAS CONSIDERED inactive until 1812, when a dense cloud of smoke was seen rising above its summit. But neither the smoke, which grew denser and denser over the next three years, nor the occasional rumbles heard from the mountain, could prepare the islanders for what was to come.

When Tambora exploded in April 1815, the blast was heard 1,700 miles away and so much ash was ejected into the atmosphere that islands 250 miles away experienced complete darkness. Only a couple thousand of the island's 12,000 inhabitants survived the fiery three-day cataclysm.

Altogether, the eruption and its aftereffects killed more than 90,000 people throughout Indonesia, mostly through subsequent disease, pollution of drinking water, and famine. Ash rains destroyed crops on every island within hundreds of miles.

## Global Cooling

Along with about 140 gigatons of magma, Tambora expelled hundreds of millions of tons of fine ash, which was spread worldwide through winds and weather systems. It is this ash that scientists now blame for the subsequent "Year Without a Summer."

The sulfate aerosol particles contained in it remained in the atmosphere for years and reflected back solar radiation, cooling the globe. The effect was aggravated by the activity of other volcanoes: Soufrière St. Vincent in the West Indies (1812), Mount Mayon in the Philippines (1814), and Suwanose–Jima in Japan, which erupted continuously from 1813 to 1814. To make matters worse, all of this took place during an extended period of low solar energy output called the Dalton Minimum, which lasted from about 1795 to the 1820s.

## Spring of 1816 in the New World

Although the last three months of 1815 through February 1816 were all warmer than usual, the mild winter seemed to hesitate to turn into spring. Under the influence of the hot ash winds from the equator, the low pressure system usually sitting over faraway Iceland at this time of year shifted south toward the British Isles, and North America was penetrated by a series of polar air masses. By March, the weather was becoming decidedly erratic.

On Sunday, March 17, Richmond, Virginia, was treated to summerlike temperatures. However, the next day, there was hail and sleet, and on Tuesday morning, the flowers of apricot and peach trees were covered with icicles. At the end of May, there were still frosts and snowfall from Ohio to Connecticut.

## June 1816

The first days of June were deceptively warm, with typical temperatures of 70s, 80s, and even low 90s in the northeastern United States. But on June 6, temperatures suddenly dropped into the 40s and it began to rain. Within hours, rain turned into snow. Birds dropped dead in the streets and some trees began shedding their still unexpanded leaves. This distemper of nature continued through June 11, when the wind shifted and the cold spell was over—or so people thought.

But strange weather continued to vex the country. Gales and violent hailstorms pummeled crops. On June 27, West Chester, Pennsylvania, reportedly experienced a torrential storm where hailstones the size of walnuts fell from the sky.

## July 1816

Just as the farmers were beginning to think that the damage to their crops might be minimal, another cold spell checked their optimism. On July 6, a strong northwestern wind set in, and for the next four days, winter descended upon New England and the Mid-Atlantic states once more as temperatures again dropped to the 30s and 40s. The outlook for a successful harvest was looking bleaker day by freezing day; what vegetation remained intact in New England was flavorless and languid.

## August 1816

The folk wisdom that bad things come in threes proved itself that summer. On August 20, another wave of frost and snow finished off the fruit, vegetables, vines, and meager remains of corn and bean crops. The fields were said to be "as empty and white as October." For many farmers, that spelled ruin. Even though wheat and rye yielded enough to carry the country through without mass starvation, panic and speculation drove the price of flour from $3 to nearly $20 per barrel. Animal feed became so expensive that cattle were instead slaughtered. Many New England farmers, unable to cope with the disaster, loaded up their belongings and headed west.

## Summer Overseas

Meanwhile, Europe was faring no better. Snow fell in several countries in June. Alpine glaciers advanced, threatening to engulf villages and dam rivers. In France, grapes were not ripe enough to be harvested until November, and the wine made from them was undrinkable. Wheat yields in Europe reportedly fell by 20 to 40 percent, both because of cold and water damage and because rains delayed and hampered harvesting.

Famine hit Switzerland especially hard. People began eating moss, sorrel, and cats, and official assistance had to be given to the populace to help them distinguish poisonous and nonpoisonous plants. In Rhineland, people reportedly dug through the fields for rotten remains of the previous year's potato harvest. Wheat, oats, and potatoes failed in Britain and Ireland, and a typhus epidemic swept the British Isles, killing tens of thousands. Grain prices doubled on average; in west-central Europe, they rose between three and seven times their normal price. This was a disaster for the masses of poor people, whose average expenditures for bread totaled between one quarter and one half of their total income.

Food scarcity led to hunger, and high prices led to increased poverty, which led to mass vagrancy and begging. People looted grain storages and pillaged large farms. There was a wave of emigrations to America. The European economy was still unsteady from the aftermath of the Napoleonic wars, and the crisis of 1816 led to a massive retreat from liberal ideas. By 1820, Europe was in the grip of political and economic conservatism—thanks in no small part to a single volcanic eruption in Indonesia!

## Who's to Blame?

Theories for why summer failed to come in 1816 abound. Many lay the blame directly on the sun. Due to volcanic particles in the air, the solar disk had been dimmed all year, which made large sunspots visible to the naked eye. Others believed that the ice persisting in the Atlantic and the Great Lakes was absorbing great quantities of heat from the atmosphere.

## Silver Lining

In 1816, Geneva, Switzerland, had experienced the coldest summer it would face between 1753 and 1960. It was this bad weather that kept Mary Wollstonecraft Godwin, Percy Shelley, and Lord Byron indoors at the Villa Diodati on the shores of Lake Geneva in June 1816. As they listened to the wind howl and watched the awesome thunderstorms rage over the lake, they recited poetry and told each other ghost stories, which they vowed to record on paper.

His mood very much under the weather, Lord Byron penned his lengthy poem "Darkness," a vivid imagining of the Apocalypse, which the weather no doubt contributed to. ("Morn came and went, and came, and brought no day....") Mary Wollstonecraft Godwin, who would later become Mary Shelley, began work on a masterpiece that would eventually bear the title *Frankenstein, or, the Modern Prometheus*.

# The Strange Seismicity at New Madrid

*When people think of earthquakes in the United States, they tend to think of the great subduction zones of the west coast. But earthquakes can happen anywhere, including right in the middle of the country. In the winter of 1811 and 1812, three powerful tremors shook the New Madrid seismic zone near Missouri. Their effects were felt throughout much of the central and eastern United States.*

✳  ✳  ✳  ✳

## Seismic Sequence

THE FIRST OF the three large New Madrid earthquakes hit on December 16, 1811. At around 2:15 in the morning, local time, a magnitude 7.2–8.2 quake rattled what is now northeast Arkansas. And only six hours later came a magnitude 7.4 aftershock. Two additional earthquakes of similar magnitudes walloped the area in January and February of 1812.

Although these earthquakes occurred in the central Mississippi Valley, they were felt strongly throughout the central and eastern United States. Minor structural damage was reported as far away as Cincinnati, Ohio, and St. Louis, Missouri. Cattle bellowed in fear in Illinois. Church bells rang in Charleston, South Carolina. Even President James Madison and his wife Dolly reported feeling the earthquakes from the White House.

Closer to the epicenter, the earthquakes dramatically affected the surrounding landscape. They destroyed several settlements along the Mississippi River: The Great Prairie settlement, which flourished prior to the tremors, was broken up and reduced to nothing. Landslides were reported along the Chickasaw Bluffs in Kentucky and Tennessee. Throughout the Mississippi River floodplain, large tracts of land were shifted, uplifted, and subsided. Lakes were either formed or expanded, and several islands disappeared under the water.

## Sand Boils, Fissures, and Backward-Running Rivers

Some consequences of the earthquakes were stranger in nature. The world's largest sand boil—a phenomenon where pressurized groundwater wells up through and ejects beds of sand— was created by the New Madrid earthquakes. Located in the boot heel of Missouri, it measures 1.4 miles long and expands across 136 acres. Locals refer to the area as "The Beach."

Chasms regularly opened up, ripping apart fields. Some were as long as five miles. While working on the land, people discovered that most of these crevices ran from north to south. To prevent trees from falling in and being lost to the earth, lumberjacks began to routinely chop down trees in an east-west direction. This also provided them with bridges.

The most glaring example of these peculiarities occurred after the third large earthquake on February 7. The great upheaval of the Mississippi River floodplain turned the river against itself and caused the Mississippi to actually run backwards for several hours. Two temporary waterfalls were created, and thousands of acres of virgin forest were devastated. Yet surprisingly, the boatmen aboard flatboats were able to survive the experience unharmed.

### Intraplate Imminence

Most earthquakes occur at the boundaries of the earth's massive, powerful tectonic plates, but New Madrid sits right in the middle of a tectonic plate. Even so, in the known history of the world, no other sequences of earthquakes have lasted as long or produced as much evidence of damage as the New Madrid earthquakes. In fact, these three remain the most powerful known earthquakes to hit the contiguous United States east of the Rocky Mountains. They remain on the list of America's top earthquakes.

# The Eruption Heard Around the World

*Located in the Sundra Strait between the larger land masses of Java and Sumatra, the small, uninhabited island of Krakatoa doesn't make much of a statement when viewed on a map. But in August of 1883, Krakatoa erupted explosively. The combination of ash, falling tephra, pyroclastic flows, and tsunamis claimed the lives of 36,000 people.*

✳   ✳   ✳   ✳

### Under the Radar

KRAKATOA WAS JUST one of many islands in the Dutch East Indies, present-day Indonesia, and it certainly wasn't one of the bigger ones. The island measured only about five miles long and three miles wide. It rose 2,667 feet above sea level.

Below the surface, however, Krakatoa was much more active: Situated along the convergences of the Indian-Australian and Eurasian tectonic plates, the island was a hub of both volcanic and seismic activity. Within the past million years or so, it built up a cone-shaped mountain made of alternating layers of volcanic rock, lava, and ash.

In the early morning of May 20, 1883, the captain of the German warship *Elisabeth* spotted ash-laden clouds rising six miles above Krakatoa. The captain didn't know it at the time, but his documentation would be one of the first recorded Krakatoan eruptions in over two centuries. Over the next two months, other vessels would document similar sightings: swirling black clouds, sprinklings of ash, and explosive noises.

The inhabitants of Batavia, the capital of the Dutch East Indies in what is now Jakarta, noticed a dull booming noise followed by a violent rattling of their doors and windows. The tremors continued through to the next day. Then, the vibrations ceased. Over the next several weeks, Krakatoa would continue to eject volumes of molten stone, pumice, and volcanic ash.

## Loud and Clear

Around 1:00 p.m. on August 26, the first of a series of increasingly violent explosions occurred. By 2:00, a black cloud of ash had risen 17 miles above the volcano. The following morning on August 27, an even bigger explosion shook the island.

Clouds of ash were propelled miles into the air, blanketing about 300,000 square miles. The area was plunged into darkness for two and a half days and, because the ash filtered incoming solar radiation, global temperatures were lowered by as much as one degree Fahrenheit over the course of the following year. In fact, temperatures would not return to normal until 1888—five years later.

What was even more impressive, however, was the noise: Krakatoa had just produced the loudest sound in recorded history. It was heard across more than ten percent of the Earth's surface—in the Andaman Islands, in India, and nearly 2,000 miles away in Perth, Australia. Nearly 3,000 miles away, the island of Rodrigues near Mauritius heard it too. Within a few hours, pressure waves in the atmosphere were recorded all around the world.

A devastating explosion of this size is not without some consequence to the volcano itself: The northern two thirds of the island collapsed beneath the sea, generating a violent pyroclastic flow of blistering hot ash and rock. But relatively few of Krakatoa's 36,000 victims were killed by the volcano itself. Instead, tens of thousands more drowned in the subsequent series of massive tsunamis. When Krakatoa collapsed into a caldera, it displaced an incredible volume of ocean and generated a 120-foot-high wall of water. Approximately 165 coastal villages on Java and Sumatra were completely wiped out. The tsunami waves reportedly traveled as far as the shores of Hawaii and South America.

## The Child of Krakatoa

Krakatoa remained relatively quiet until December 1927, when volcanic activity began again. The smaller eruptions have created a new cone in the center of the caldera. Referred to as Anak Krakatau, or "child of Krakatoa," this fourth island produced lava flows more quickly than the surrounding ocean could erode them. In 2017, Anak Krakatau was reported to have an elevation of 1,300 feet above sea level. After a collapse in December 2018, that height was reduced down to just 361 feet.

Krakatoa's 1883 eruption was one of the first volcanic eruptions to be scientifically recorded and extensively studied. Between the sighting of its first ash plume on May 20 to its eardrum-shattering explosion on August 27, the observations made at Krakatoa have proven invaluable to the continued studies of volcanic eruptions across the globe.

# Laki's Worldwide Impact: Famine, Pestilence, and Decreased Global Temperatures

*Beginning in the summer of 1783, Laki, a volcanic fissure in Iceland, violently erupted 3.7 quadrillion gallons of lava, sulfuric acid, and hydrofluoric acid for a period of eight months. It decimated the Icelandic population, destroyed crops and livestock, contaminated European soils, and caused a temperature decrease across much of the world.*

✳  ✳  ✳  ✳

## A Flood of Fire

THE DATE WAS June 8, 1783. On the Laki volcanic mountain ridge in southeastern Iceland, a 15-mile-long fissure of 135 volcanic vents suddenly erupted with violent, phreato-magmatic explosions. Large pieces of *tephra*, or solid rock, were ejected alongside brilliant lava fountains, some of which were estimated to have reached heights of 2,600 to 4,600 feet. Over the next few days, however, the eruptions became less explosive. Rather than launching thousands of feet up into the air, Laki's lava emerged from its crater like a great river of fire.

An estimated 3.7 quadrillion gallons of basaltic lava poured out near the town of Klaustur, covering up an estimated 965 square miles of land. Jón Steingrímsson, a Lutheran clergyman who led a church in the Síða district not far from the Laki eruption, described the unfolding disaster in his diary. "The flood of fire flowed with the speed of a great river swollen with meltwater on a spring day," he wrote. "In the middle of the flood of fire great cliffs and slabs of rock were swept along, tumbling about like large whales swimming, red-hot and glowing."

Volcanic gasses were carried out by Laki's convective eruption column to altitudes of about 50,000 feet. Over the course of eight long months, the volcano sent 80 metric tons of sulfuric acid across much of the northern hemisphere—that's about 80 times more sulfuric acid than Mount St. Helens in 1980. It resulted in one of the most widespread climatic and socially-significant disasters of the last millennium.

## Close to Home

Iceland bore the brunt of Laki: Over one fifth of the country's total population perished as a result of the eruption. Nowhere was safe, either. Volcanic ash was carried far and wide by the forces of the wind and sea. By eating the fluorine-contaminated grass, animals began to develop strange ridges and growths on their legs. The pestilence killed half of the Icelandic cattle population. About 80 percent of the island's sheep and 75 percent of its horses died, too.

People did not fare any better. Clergyman Jón Steingrímsson recounted how "ridges, growths, and bristle appeared on their rib joints, ribs, the backs of their hands, their feet, legs and joints." "Their bodies became bloated," he wrote. "The insides of their mouths and their gums swelled and cracked, causing excruciating pains and toothaches."

Thousands of these "eruption-people," as they came to be called, attempted to escape their poisoned homes. But with air pollution and acid rain having decimated the land, the resulting famine killed more Icelanders than the initial lava and tephra ever did.

## Far and Wide

It wasn't only Icelanders that had to deal with the Laki's consequences. In the months following the eruption, a strange haze covered the larger European sky. The "dry fog" made breathing difficult, leading to respiratory problems, headaches, and other health issues affecting millions of Europeans. Just like in Iceland, soil, crops, and animals were decimated. The resulting famine may have been responsible for the French Revolution of 1789–1794, one of the most famous insurrections in history.

When the ash and gas from Laki's 1783 eruption entered the uppermost layers of the atmosphere, it absorbed incoming solar radiation and cooled the planet for years to come. Throughout the northern hemisphere, surface temperatures plummeted.

The years 1784, 1785, and 1786 were the coldest of the second half of the eighteenth century. In the United States, scientists including Ben Franklin kept logs of one of the coldest winters on record—ice blocks even appeared in the Mississippi River at New Orleans! To the east, Japan suffered exceptionally low summer temperatures, leading to one of the country's worst famines ever recorded.

The 1783 eruption of Laki may have been a low energy basaltic eruption—earning a 4 on the Volcanic Explosivity Index—but its effects had long-lasting and far-reaching impacts.

# Peléan Explosion— The First of Its Kind

*On the morning of May 8, 1902, Mount Pelée sent a massive pyroclastic surge rocketing toward the port of Saint-Pierre. The event was so deadly and dramatic that the name of the mountain was adopted (Peléan) to describe a particular kind of eruption with viscous magma, hot volcanic ash, and lava domes.*

✳   ✳   ✳   ✳

### Martinique

AT THE TURN of the twentieth century, the city of Saint-Pierre, Martinique, was known as the "Paris of the Caribbean." Cafes and shops lined the streets, and residents strolled in its beautiful parks and botanical gardens. A bustling harbor of ships carried away precious loads of sugar and rum—outpacing powerhouses like Jamaica and Guyana. With all it had to offer, Saint-Pierre easily usurped Martinique's official capital—Fort-de-France—as the island's cultural center.

Looming over it all, about five miles away, was Mount Pelée. As far as the residents of Saint-Pierre were concerned, it had always been a harmless, gentle giant: The volcano had not erupted in several generations, and even the most adventurous hikers who climbed its summit only occasionally reported smelling small bursts of putrid gases. As nineteenth-century writer Lafcadio Hearn described it, the dead volcano was rather picturesque: a "verdant violet-shaded mass" whose smooth slopes ambled down toward the placid blue waters of the Caribbean Sea.

## Reawakening

What residents did not understand, however, was that Mount Pelée was a lot more active than it seemed. Like most of the Lesser Antilles, Martinique was formed at the boundary between two tectonic plates: the Caribbean plate and the South American plate. As one plate subducted under another, it forged islands, mountains, and volcanoes.

The first signs of Mount Pelée's reawakening emerged in April 1902: Clouds of sulfurous vapor appeared from volcanic vents, or fumaroles, near the mountaintop. A string of light tremors rattled the ground, and a small dusting of cinders covered Pelée's southern and western sides. Étang Sec, a dry crater near the summit, was now filled with water, forming a lake approximately 600 feet across.

On the night of May 2, a small eruption captured the town's attention. A massive pillar of dense, black smoke carried ash and fine-grained pumice across the northern half of the island. "The whole population of the city is on the alert, and every eye is directed toward Mount Pelée," wrote Clara Prentiss, the wife of the American consul in St. Pierre. "Everybody is afraid that the volcano has taken into its head to burst forth and destroy the whole island."

A few days later, on May 5, part of the Étang Sec crater collapsed, propelling a *lahar*—a mass of boiling water and mud—down the Blanche River. The Guérin sugar works and 150 victims became buried under layers of hot mud, and survivors from other areas rushed into Saint-Pierre for safety.

On May 7, the Soufrière volcano on the neighboring island of Saint Vincent erupted and killed 1,500 people. This actually reassured the people of Martinique: Although their neighbor had suffered a devastating loss, the explosion was surely a sign that Mount Pelée's internal pressure had been relieved. There was nothing to fear. In fact, people assumed that everything could go back to normal.

## Raining Down Destruction

At last, on the morning of May 8, it was Mount Pelée's turn. A dense, black cloud hung in the air, darkening the sky. The upper mountainside ripped open as a blast of superheated steam, gases, ash, and rocks—a pyroclastic surge—raced down the volcano's slopes towards the city of Saint-Pierre at one hundred miles per hour.

The surge obliterated the town in one fatal moment, covering every surface and igniting everything combustible. Ships in the harbor caught fire and sank. All but a handful of its 28,000 residents died. Of those who survived the initial explosion, many succumbed to burns that scorched their skin and lungs.

The violent explosion of the Mount Pelée volcano is what most people picture when imagining an erupting volcano. May 8 still stands out for the magnitude of tragedy it produced. The 1902 eruption of Mount Pelée was one of the deadliest eruptions in recorded history and, unlike the 1815 eruption of Tambora or the 1883 eruption of Krakatoa, which also killed through subsequent disease, famine, and tsunamis, Pelée's devastation was direct and instantaneous. The extensive study of this disaster led to the first documentations of pyroclastic flows, surges, and other deadly hazards, marking the beginning of modern volcanology.

# Ilopango, El Salvador: Was One Volcano to Blame for Global Cooling?

*With widespread ash clouds and pyroclastic flows that devastated Mayan cities, the Ilopango volcano no doubt produced one of the largest volcanic events on Earth in the past 7,000 years. But was it also responsible for subsequent cold weather events during the sixth century?*

❋　❋　❋　❋

## Crater Lake Ilopango

THE LARGEST LAKE of El Salvador, Lake Ilopango, is actually an immense caldera of the Ilopango volcanic complex. It's a part of the Volcanic Arc of El Salvador, a geologic feature that includes a total of 21 active volcanoes. Formed by numerous eruptions in the past two million years, the caldera now sports a scalloped rim between 500 and 1600 feet tall.

The lake was present when Ilopango experienced its incredible fifth- or sixth-century eruption. As lava boiled lake water into steam, Ilopango's eruption became even more explosive than before. It is estimated that about 20 cubic miles of *tephra* was expelled from the volcano—several times more than was ejected during the 1980 eruption of Mount St. Helens.

## Young White Earth

Ilopango's eruption plume rose nearly 30 miles into the air, covering about 4,000 square miles of Central America in waist-deep volcanic ash and pumice. Today, these deposits are known collectively as *Tierra Blanca Joven* (or Young White Earth). They buried forests, waterways, and Mayan settlements, rendering a 50-mile area uninhabitable for years to come. According to Victoria Smith, associate professor from the University of Oxford, the ashfall would have plunged the region into darkness "for at least a week." What's more, every living thing within 25 miles of Ilopango would have immediately succumbed to the volcano. Even those Maya living farther away were affected: Attempts at agriculture suffered for decades, and the subsequent famines directly led to the abandonment of many towns by their original inhabitants.

## Global Cooling

Although evidence of its eruption can be seen throughout El Salvador's geography, precisely when Ilopango erupted—as well as its more far-reaching effects—remained a mystery for quite some time. Originally, Ilopango was thought to have been responsible for the anomalously cold decade in Europe around AD 530. Recently, a team of researchers determined that, based on volcanic shards taken from ice cores in Greenland and radiocarbon dating of a charred tree found in volcanic ash deposits, the eruption likely occurred around AD 431—one whole century earlier than previously thought.

Ilopango's *Tierra Blanca Joven* eruption took place during the start of the Early Classic period—just as the Maya began to expand across Central America. Although the eruption dealt the local Maya a blow that altered their trajectory, they were able to overcome it: The Maya went on to construct the La Campana pyramid in San Andrés—using blocks of the same volcanic tephra that buried their previous home.

# The Great Unzen Disaster: Earthquakes, Eruptions, and Tsunamis

*Mount Unzen, a large volcano group of overlapping volcanoes in western Kyushu, Japan, is synonymous with disaster. In 1792, it spawned the deadliest eruption catastrophe in Japanese history when the eastern flank of its Mayuyama dome collapsed, generating a massive landslide and tsunami.*

✳ ✳ ✳ ✳

## Steam, Lava, Earthquakes

EAST OF NAGASAKI, in Japan's Shimabara Peninsula, lies a complex of composite volcanoes. Although composite volcanoes can be the most picturesque of all volcanoes, they are also much more prone to explosions.

Near the end of 1791, a series of earthquakes struck the western flank of Mount Unzen and gradually moved toward Fugen-dake, the highest volcano in the complex. In February of the following year, Fugen-dake experienced a phreatic eruption, a type of steam-driven explosion. For two months, lava flowed in a continuous stream from this volcano's summit. But the earthquakes did not abate.

## Earthquake-Induced Landslide

On the night of May 21, 1792, two large earthquakes collapsed a large portion of the Mayuyama peak, a 4,000-year-old lava dome in front of Mount Unzen and above the city of Shimabara. This caused a mass of earth equivalent to nearly a sixth of the mountain's body to rush down the mountain slopes, sweeping through the city of Shimabara. Thousands of people are thought to have been killed by the landslide alone. The mountain scar created from the Mayuyama landslide remains visible today.

## Landslide-Induced Tsunami

After burying the city and its inhabitants, the surge of debris and rocks dropped down into Ariake Bay, displacing the water from above and generating a massive mega-tsunami: Its initial wave reportedly reached a height of 330 feet. In Futsu, a former town in Nagasaki, the seafloor's topography caused waves of 187 feet.

The tsunami caused further damage far and wide. About 12 miles across the Ariake Sea, it killed 5,000 people in the Higo Province. The tsunami here gained a new name that translates to *Shimabara erupted, Higo affected*. After hitting Higo, the tsunami returned to devastate Shimabara. Altogether, it is estimated that 15,000 people were killed.

# Nevado del Ruiz and the Armero Tragedy

*After nearly 70 years of dormancy, the Nevado del Ruiz volcano surprised Colombia with a massive explosive eruption in 1985. A violent mix of hot ash and lava was ejected into the atmosphere. Pyroclastic flows melted the ice and snow of the volcano summit, generating dangerous lahars that engulfed the town of Armero. Approximately 23,000 people were killed.*

✳  ✳  ✳  ✳

## Precursor Activity

LOCATED ABOUT 80 MILES west of Colombia's capital, Bogotá, Nevado del Ruiz is a cone-shaped stratovolcano made up of successive layers of lava, ash, and pyroclastic flow deposits. The volcano is located at the boundary between the Nazca and South American tectonic plates: As the Nazca plate subducts under the South American plate, it melts into magma that then rises towards the surface to form volcanoes. Although historical records of Mount Ruiz's activity go back to 1570, the most devastating eruption in recent history took place in 1985.

Geologists began to notice seismic activity in the area around Nevado del Ruiz as early as late 1984: increased fumarole activity, sulfur deposits, and multiple phreatic—or steam-based—eruptions. September 11, 1985, saw a major phreatic event, and smaller ash ejection episodes followed through the end of the month. Activity declined in October, but by November 7, seismicity had steadily increased. All the while, local officers began planning for an evacuation, but the hazard map they produced was poorly distributed to residents across the region.

## Eruption Day

A little after 9 p.m. on November 13, 1985, Nevado del Ruiz erupted. Dacitic tephra was ejected more than 20 miles into the atmosphere. Pumice and ash rained down in Mariquita and Armero. Manuel Cervera, a cargo pilot for Caribbean Airlines, attempted to land at Bogotá through the eruption cloud. Smoke and sulfur filled his cabin, which made it nearly impossible to see. After Cervera's first two attempts failed, he stuck his head out of a side window and managed to land safely in Cali.

The eruption also produced pyroclastic flows: hot, mobile mixtures of rock, gas, and ash that quickly flow along the ground away from a volcano. Because of their high temperatures, the pyroclastic flows melted away several of Nevado del Ruiz's glaciers. As a result, several thick lahars were generated. Unlike other debris flows, lahars originate on the slopes of a volcano and are made up of pyroclastic material, rocky debris, and water. When the lahars cascaded down the volcano's flanks at 40 miles per hour, they picked up everything in their path: sediment, water, trees—even vehicles.

## Armero Aftermath

The town of Armero, which had only experienced falling volcanic ash, was suddenly pulverized and entombed by three huge flows of volcanic mud, one after another. The largest of the lahars was approximately 100 feet deep, moving at a rate of 39 feet per second. Massive torrents of mud almost entirely buried the town, killing an estimated 23,000 people, or 70 percent of all residents.

Armero wasn't alone, however: The nearby Gualí River spilled over into several surrounding villages, and more lahars inundated the town of Chinchiná on the Claro River. All in all, the 1985 eruption of the Nevado del Ruiz volcano constituted history's fourth-largest single-eruption death toll, behind only Tambora in 1815 (92,000), Krakatau in 1883 (36,000) and Mt. Pelée in 1902 (28,000).

# Mount Pinatubo, 1991: One Disaster After Another

*On the afternoon of June 15, 1991, the Philippines' Mount Pinatubo exploded in a spectacular display of ash, tephra, and gas-charged magma. It was the second-largest volcanic eruption of the century, made up of high-speed pyroclastic flows, lahars, and a giant column of smoke and ash. But it wasn't just the volcano that devastated Luzon island: On that same day, the Philippines was also struck by Typhoon Yunya.*

✳   ✳   ✳   ✳

## A Waking Mountain

LOCATED IN WESTERN Luzon, the northernmost island of the Philippines, Mount Pinatubo had a reputation of keeping quiet. Despite its size—prior to 1991, it rose to a height of about 4,800 feet—Pinatubo's eruption history was something of a mystery to those living under its shadow. In July of 1990, however, that began to change.

On July 16, a magnitude 7.7 earthquake struck about 60 miles northeast of Mount Pinatubo. It was a large earthquake, comparable in size to the great 1906 earthquake in San Francisco. Steam emissions increased for a time, and a landslide cascaded down the volcano's flanks, but otherwise Pinatubo seemed to continue slumbering. Below the surface, however, things were not as they seemed.

In March and April of the following year, magma was detected rising toward the surface, triggering thousands more earthquakes—smaller this time—and a series of powerful steam explosions. Three craters were formed on the volcano's north flank, and these emitted thousands of tons of noxious sulfur dioxide gas.

Still, the activity did not diminish. By early June, tiltmeter measurements reported that the volcano had swelled in size—an indication of magma filling the reservoir beneath its summit. Seismic activity increased. June 7 saw the first magmatic eruption—not an explosion, but an oozing of molten rock from a new lava dome.

## Explosive Eruptions

It was Philippine Independence Day (June 12), when Mount Pinatubo began its new, more violent state. Large pyroclastic surges came barreling down the mountain, and eruption columns—plumes of suspended gasses and ash—soared to heights of 62,000 feet. June 13 saw more seismic activity, more eruption columns, and more pyroclastic flows.

The eruptions reached a peak on June 15, when Mount Pinatubo experienced a cataclysmic explosion that ejected over a cubic mile of material. Its summit completely collapsed. The subsequent column of smoke rose 22 miles high, blanketing the countryside in pumice and ash. U.S. Clark Air Force Base, located ten miles east of the volcano, was first forced to evacuate, then close entirely.

But it was about to get even worse. The volcanic ash was blown in every direction by the intense winds of Typhoon Yunya, which had just made landfall in the Philippines on that same day. Heavy rainfall, combined with Pinatubo's superheated pyroclastic flows, generated flooding and fast-moving lahars. The damage was catastrophic: Two million people were impacted directly. Reports estimated $700 million in damages—$100 million to aircraft alone. Nearly 850 people were killed. Approximately 20,000 people were compelled to evacuate, and of the people that stayed behind, at least 10,000 were left homeless.

## Evacuation and Lasting Effects

As devastating as the 1991 eruption was, it could have been even more deadly. Fortunately, scientists from the Philippine Institute of Volcanology and Seismology, as well as the U.S. Geological Survey, had forecast Pinatubo's 1991 eruption far enough in advance for civil and military leaders to be able to undertake several precautions. Ships had previously been made available and were able to evacuate thousands of U.S. Department of Defense civilian personnel and their dependents, resulting in the saving of at least 5,000 lives and $250 million in property.

Still, evacuation can only do so much. The indigenous Aeta people, who called the slopes of Mount Pinatubo home, were completely displaced. Even after the areas surrounding the volcano were declared safe, many Aetas chose to remain in government-organized resettlement sites.

The hazardous effects of Pinatubo's 1991 eruption lingered for years. The significant quantity of aerosols and dust expelled into the atmosphere resulted in a volcanic winter, a ten percent reduction in the normal amount of sunlight reaching the Earth's surface.

Global temperatures dropped by about one degree from 1991 to 1993, and ozone layers at middle latitudes reached new lows. And it's no wonder: Mount Pinatubo was by far the largest eruption to affect such a densely populated area. The impacts of its eruption continue to this day.

# The Ignored Warning
# Signs of Santa María

*The 1902 Plinian eruption of the Santa María volcano was one of the three largest eruptions of the twentieth century. For 19 days, Santa María generated 1.9 cubic miles of pyroclastic debris, devastating much of southwest Guatemala. All in all, the eruption earned a rating of six on the volcanic explosivity index.*

✳ ✳ ✳ ✳

## A Naked Volcano

LOCATED IN THE western highlands of Guatemala near the city of Quetzaltenango, Santa María is the most prominent in a chain of large stratovolcanoes which rise dramatically over the Pacific coastal plain. Before the arrival of the Spanish in the sixteenth century, the volcano was known in the local Kiche language as *Gagxanul*, or "Naked Volcano," for its stark lack of vegetation. Even back then, Santa María had a reputation for being quiet: The volcano had been inactive for half a millennium, at least.

Starting in January 1902, however, a series of earthquakes began to shake up the region. On April 18, a major earthquake—a magnitude 7.5—destroyed a number of Guatemalan roads, water pipes, huts, and cathedrals. Nowadays, seismic activity is considered a clear indication of an imminent volcanic eruption. But because there were no historical records of previous volcanic activity at the time, these warning signs were largely ignored.

Santa María erupted violently beginning October 24, although it wasn't until the next day that its largest explosion occurred. The sound of that eruption could be heard from Costa Rica over 500 miles away.

Shock waves rattled windows in the city of Cobán, and sulfurous odors filled the air. Off the Pacific coast, a Captain from the mailboat SS *Newport* estimated the volcano's eruption column to be approximately 16 miles high, reaching well into the stratosphere. The ash darkened Guatemalan skies for days on end. Thousands of people were killed.

## A Smoking Crater

The Santa María stratovolcano produced one of the three largest eruptions of the twentieth century, following only the 1912 Novarupta eruption and the 1991 explosion at Mount Pinatubo. Although its worldwide impact was significant—ashfall was detected as far away as San Francisco—no significant temperature deviations were reported.

The eruption also left a large, oval-shaped crater in the volcano's southwest flank, about 0.6 miles in diameter and 980 feet deep. Although the 1902 eruption was followed by nearly 20 years of dormancy, a dacite lava dome began growing in the crater in 1922. The dome, called Santiaguito, remains active today.

# Chapter 9

# Plagues and Epidemics

## Dance of the Black Death

*The Black Death, the epidemic best known for devastating Europe between 1347 and 1350, was as deadly in the east as it was in the west. By the time the plague reached the outskirts of Europe, it had already killed an estimated 25 million people. Within three years, approximately 25 million more Europeans would follow in the first wave of a cycle of plagues that continued to hound Europe for three centuries.*

※   ※   ※   ※

THE PLAGUE ISN'T pretty. Whether primarily in the lymph nodes (bubonic), blood (septicemic), or lungs (pneumonic), the plague is caused by the bacterium *yersinia pestis*, which lives in the digestive tract of fleas. It primarily transmits from animals to humans through flea bites, though humans in close contact can transmit pneumonic plague to each other. The bacteria was discovered by Japanese and European researchers in the late nineteenth century. Patients manifest symptoms such as swollen and tender lymph nodes (buboes) in the area of the bite, fever, bloody sputum and blotching, rapidly worsening pneumonia, and—as the bacteria overwhelms the nervous system—neurological and psychological disorders. Untreated, plague has a morbidity rate of 50–60 percent; the rate is even higher for pneumonic plague. Between 1,000 and 3,000 cases are reported each year worldwide.

## Origins of a Disease

The Black Death originated in China in the 1340s. Making its way along the Silk Road, the epidemic ravaged India, Egypt, the Middle East, and Constantinople before spreading rapidly through trading ports to Europe. Even Greenland and Iceland were struck. From 1347 to 1350, a third of Europe's population died an agonizing, dramatic, mysterious—and sudden—death. In cities such as Florence, the death toll reached 75 percent, and many rural villages were wiped out completely. Nearly annual outbreaks of the plague continued, culminating in the great 1665 plague of London, in which perhaps 100,000 Londoners died. Overall, some estimates of the combined death toll reached 200 million people.

It would be hard to underestimate the pervasive effects of the plagues on Europe. All aspects of society and culture suffered intense disruption and experienced profound change as the plagues brought on economic stress, social dissolution, religious extremism, and skepticism. The trauma on the European psyche as a result of living in circumstances where, as the fourteenth-century Italian writer Boccaccio put it, people could "eat lunch with their friends and dinner with their ancestors in paradise," can be seen in the pervasive use of skeletons in art and drama. They act as grim and often ironic reminders of *memento mori* ("remember, you die"), illustrations of *quod es fui, quod sum eris* ("what you are I was; what I am you will be"), and participants in the "Dance of Death" (Danse Macabre, Totentanz) throughout this period.

## Was That the Last Dance?

Although the Black Death and its subsequent outbreaks ended in the seventeenth century, its rapid spread and descriptions, as well as the patterns of known outbreaks do not in some cases correspond well to this plague's pathology, nor to the complex conditions required for the bacteria to find its way into fleas that can then infect humans. This has recently led some researchers in Britain and the United States to advance the theory that the plague was actually caused by a human-borne virus that can lie dormant in the earth until it is introduced into the population. If so, another round of "Black Death"— especially in an age of continuous global travel and trade— remains a frightening possibility.

# Why Was Smallpox Deadly for Natives of the New World, but Not Europeans?

*The Europeans were not good guests in the New World. Whether it was conquistadors in South America or Pilgrims in New England, they left a calling card no one wanted: diseases that killed thousands of people. Some experts think that smallpox and other diseases, such as measles and influenza, killed up to 95 percent of the native populations in some areas.*

❊   ❊   ❊   ❊

YET THE EUROPEANS remained ridiculously healthy while nearby villages of Indians might be wiped out. And when they sailed back home, they brought no new illnesses with them. Why did diseases seemingly only flow in one direction?

First of all, the Europeans had already been exposed to epidemic diseases—or at least their ancestors had. Smallpox was known in ancient Egypt, and a smallpox epidemic killed millions of Romans in the second century AD. The disease hit Europe so frequently that the folks who had no natural immunities died off. Those who lived passed their immunities on to their children. Over the centuries, with so many nasty plagues hitting big population centers, the surviving Europeans became more resistant to the killer microbes.

Where did all these diseases originate? Was there a Patient Zero? No. Most of the epidemic bugs—smallpox, measles, influenza, and even tuberculosis—came from livestock. When

Asians and Europeans began herding cattle and penning up ducks and pigs thousands of years ago, they breathed in the strange germs that hung around the animals. Sometimes these pathogens were able to infect humans. Once humans started living in cities in large numbers, these germs were able to spread like wildfires. Europe suffered through the same plagues that killed so many of the native populations they came into contact with, but Europe's experience took place hundreds of years earlier, and its populations eventually recovered, each time with better immunity.

The conquistadors, Pilgrims, sailors, and settlers who crossed the Atlantic during the Age of Exploration came from families that had survived waves and waves of disease. Without realizing it, they brought smallpox, measles, and influenza germs with them to infect people who had never seen cattle, might never have herded animals, and never, ever been exposed to any of these diseases.

You know the result: Millions died. Exactly how many millions is unknown because experts aren't sure about the sizes of pre-encounter populations. The first wave of smallpox to hit Mexico's Aztec Empire in 1520 killed half the kingdom. Up to ten million perished, including the emperor. More disease followed, and a century later, the area's native population numbered only 1.6 million.

Here's another infamous example: In 1837, smallpox hit the Mandan, an Indian tribe in North Dakota. The disease, brought by someone who was on a steamboat traveling up the Missouri River, nearly wiped out the entire tribe. Within weeks, the Mandan population of one village lost over a thousand inhabitants.

And since no one back then knew about germs, microbes, or how sicknesses spread, the Europeans weren't even aware of what they'd done.

# The Great Influenza Epidemic of 1918

*The 1918–1920 flu pandemic was the deadliest known global influenza pandemic in the world's history. The path of the virus began in Kansas and quickly spread to war-weary Europe and the rest of the world.*

✳ ✳ ✳ ✳

D UE TO ITS misnomer, "The Spanish Flu," most believe that the 1918 flu pandemic emerged from Spain. However, the earliest documented case was actually in Kansas in March of 1918. It is believed that it received its connection to Spain due to wartime censors. During World War I, the countries involved suppressed news they deemed "bad for morale." However, Spain—which was neutral—freely reported on its outbreaks. This gave a false impression to the world that the virus originated there, which resulted in its popular moniker. What made this outbreak different and more concerning from previous flu outbreaks was that it disproportionately killed young adults. Typically, the flu is most concerning for the very young and the very old. However, this one's targeting of young adults right at the end of a world war caused it to absolutely decimate populations worldwide during four waves over the course of two years.

## Transmission and Symptoms

The Great Flu Epidemic was caused by the H1N1 influenza A virus. The first recorded case of someone contracting H1N1 was Albert Gitchell, an army cook at Camp Funston in Kansas. However, there were cases before him, and the virus had been observed 200 miles away in Haskell County a few months prior. Due to no precautions being taken, the virus spread through the camp incredibly quickly. Within days of Gitchell's case being recorded, 552 men at the camp had reported sick. With the US having recently entered into WWI, the virus spread to other U.S. Army camps and into Europe, quickly becoming an epidemic in the Midwest, the American east coast, and several French ports by April, 1918, reaching the front lines a week later. It reached North Africa, India, and Japan in May, China in June, and Australia in July. In this first, early wave, 75,000 people died from the flu. Additionally, it heavily disrupted military operations, with significant portions of the French, British, and German forces falling ill.

Thankfully, the majority of the infected only experienced typical flu symptoms—sore throat, headache, and fever. However, during the second wave, the virus was often accompanied by bacterial pneumonia. This more serious type would cause *heliotrope cyanosis* to develop, which turned the victim's skin blue and caused their lungs to fill with fluids. The majority of deaths were due to bacterial pneumonia, but the virus also killed people directly by causing massive hemorrhages and edema in the lungs. Additionally, malnourishment and poor living conditions in the trenches caused the virus to not only spread incredibly quickly, but it caused the stronger strains to spread due to the far sicker soldiers being sent on crowded trains to crowded field hospitals. Climate conditions are cited as having had a significant role in victims' immune systems, due to it being unseasonably cold and wet for extended periods of time. This especially affected soldiers who were exposed to these harsh conditions for the duration of the war without much of a reprieve. This climate anomaly is said to have influenced the migration of birds infected with H1N1, spreading it even faster and contaminating water sources.

## The Great Flu's Legacy

At the time, there were no vaccines or effective treatments for the flu. Schools, theaters, churches, and businesses were forced to close, and there were ordinances in place to compel people to wear masks in public in an attempt to slow the spread. Undertakers, gravediggers, and casket manufacturers couldn't keep up with the rate of the deceased, resulting in caskets being stacked haphazardly outside of mortuaries. With public gatherings being prohibited, families were unable to hold funerals for their loved ones. This was compounded by the stream of dead soldiers arriving daily from the front lines, which only added to the struggles in laying the dead to rest.

The Great Flu is considered one of history's deadliest pandemics, having infected over 500 million people worldwide and claiming the lives of approximately 50 million. Despite how gravely it affected so many, the 1918 epidemic has largely been "forgotten" over time. Historians theorize that the rapid pace of the pandemic, which claimed most of its victims in the U.S. in around nine months, resulted in limited media coverage. Additionally, people of the nineteenth and twentieth centuries contended with several different outbreaks—typhoid, yellow fever, diphtheria, and cholera—around similar spans of time. This may have caused most people of the time to "shrug off" H1N1 as just another illness making the rounds.

Another theory is that, because the outbreak coincided with the deaths and media focus of WWI, the pandemic deaths may have become overshadowed by it. Particularly in Europe, many may have thought that the flu was merely an extension of the war's tragedies.

# The Plague of Justinian

*The Black Death is one of the most well-known pandemics in the world, but that event was not the first time the world would feel its murderous rage. The Plague of Justinian was an epidemic that claimed the lives of millions of people from AD 541–549.*

✳    ✳    ✳    ✳

THE PLAGUE OF Justinian was the first known outbreak of the Bubonic Plague—aka the Black Death—which would ravage Europe again centuries later. The plague affected the entire Mediterranean Basin, Europe, and the Near East, and it decimated the Sassanian Empire and the Byzantine Empire, particularly Constantinople, which lost about a fifth of its population. It is for that reason that the outbreak was named after the Byzantine Emperor Justinian I who, according to his court historian Procopius, contracted the illness and survived at the height of the epidemic. Having been the first part of the first plague pandemic, and having ravaged the continent for seven long years, it had profound effects across societies in Europe and the Near East.

## Timeline of the First Plague Pandemic

The information we have about the plague is thanks to two sources: a Syriac church historian, John of Ephesus, and a child named Evagrius Scholasticus who would grow up to become a church historian too. Evagrius caught the disease, even contracting the buboes that it's known for, and survived. However, he would go on to lose his wife, a daughter and her child, other children, most of his servants, and people from his country estates, as the disease returned a total of four times over the course of his lifetime.

Contemporary sources believe that the plague in Constantinople was brought in and spread by flea-bitten, infected rats on grain ships. The city imported an enormous amount of grain, mostly from Egypt, to feed its large urban population. This allowed the infected rats to spread the disease rapidly to large groups of mobile people.

The true number of daily deaths due to the plague will likely remain unknown, although unverifiable sources assert that it was as high as thousands per *day*. Historians concur that this plague was ultimately one of the deadliest pandemics in world history, having killed an estimated 15 to 100 million people over the course of 200 years; that number would have accounted for approximately 25 to 60 percent of Europe's population over that time.

The plague was particularly devastating to the countryside, wiping out countless farmers and crippling those who survived. They received no aid from Emperor Justinian due to his heavy spending on wars and churches, while the decrease in tax revenue brought many of the empire's plans to a screeching halt. The plague also weakened the empire by slowing down and even halting its conquests across Italy and the western Mediterranean coast.

# The Antonine Plague

*One of the most destructive epidemics of the ancient world nearly wiped out the Roman Empire during the height of its power. This plague would spend 15 years killing a tenth of its people, with no regard for age, wealth, or class.*

✳   ✳   ✳   ✳

THE ANTONINE PLAGUE—ALSO known as the Plague of Galen, after the physician who diagnosed it as a fever plague—took place between AD 165 and 180. It spread throughout the Roman Empire and into nearby areas, bringing death and destruction in its wake. Millions of people were infected, with as many as 2,000 people dying per day in the city of Rome at the plague's height. With a fatality rate of 25 percent, it's estimated that 5–10 million people died over the course of the plague, which was an astounding amount of the global population at the time.

While pandemics were commonplace in the ancient world, the Antonine Plague had exceptionally cruel timing, taking place during the "golden age" of the Roman Empire, during the reigns of emperors Lucius Verus and Marcus Aurelius. Unfortunately for them, the plague would take the life of Emperor Verus and nearly decimate the Roman army.

There are a number of theories regarding why the Antonine Plague was so devastating. One major reason is that 20 percent of the Roman population was living in cities at the time, which was a huge amount for the ancient world. The high-density urban populations coupled with poor sanitation resulted in ideal conditions for a plague to spread quickly through the major cities. And of the city dwellers, the majority would have been quite poor and unhealthy, which we can surmise through the average height of Romans. Prior to and after the Roman Empire, Italians' average height was taller than during. This might seem odd for a civilization that was so advanced for the time, but historian Kyle Harper explains that, "not for the last time in history, a precocious leap forward in social development brought biological reverses."

## The Spread and Effects

The first documented case of the Antonine Plague came from Smyrna (a Greek city located on the Aegean coast of Anatolia) in AD 165. We know this thanks to the orator Aelius Aristides, who almost died from the plague himself. From there, the plague spread westward until it reached Rome in 166. It had covered the entire empire by 172, lingering in pockets until 180. Another pandemic struck in 189, but historians are unsure if the two epidemics were related. However, the Roman people of the time believed that the disease was carried to the Empire by the Roman army from a temple in the city of Seleucia.

While the Roman army didn't spread the initial cases into Rome, they were responsible for spreading it throughout the Empire. They were far from safe from it as the plague decimated their numbers. Germanic tribes took advantage of this by invading the Empire's lands in what is now the Czech Republic and Slovakia. It got so bad that Marcus Aurelius had to spend two years training gladiators and slaves in order to replenish the army's numbers so that they could retake the land from the invaders. Unsurprisingly, many historians mark the plague as the beginning of the decline of the Roman Empire.

# London's Seventeenth-Century Plagues

*Most people are familiar with the Black Death, the Spanish Flu, and, now, the Covid pandemic of 2020. But there have been plenty of other pandemics in history that have ravaged populations. Unfortunately for Europeans of the Middle Ages and subsequent centuries, there would be multiple plagues that ripped apart families and destroyed entire villages. London was no exception.*

\* \* \* \*

WHILE THE WORST plagues of history have received a great deal of attention from historians, there were plenty of other horrific plagues that, while not as history-altering, still decimated populations and wreaked havoc on society. London had the unfortunate distinction of enduring two at the same time: the pneumonic plague and septicaemic plague. The former attacked the lungs and was spread to others through coughing and sneezing. The latter was caused by bacteria entering the bloodstream, and was almost always fatal. In all cases, a combination of ineffective treatments were used in an attempt to slow the spread of infection. A few of the most common were bloodletting by leeches—which was believed to remove the diseased blood—and ridding a room of "impure air" through flowers, oils, smoke, and vinegar-soaked sponges.

## Frogs, Mice, and Flies, Oh My!

The primary way the plagues were able to spread so quickly was due to the extremely poor living conditions in London. The poorer parts of seventeenth-century London had nearly no proper sanitation infrastructure and overcrowded tenements were the norm. Open sewage drains flowed alongside the streets, and nearly everyone had to trudge through muck and waste while dodging buckets of used water and other liquids that were tossed from the windows of nearby shops and homes.

The city tried to do something about the state of things by hiring "rakers" to clean up the piled-up waste and transport it to mounds outside the city walls, but it just moved the problem to one central location. Outside of the city was no better, with shantytowns housing an estimated 250,000 people springing up all over the area. These conditions and circumstances created the perfect storm to quickly spread the plagues throughout the county.

In addition to the wretched living conditions of most people, no one knew how to contain diseases. The most practical method was to force households with diseases to quarantine. While that did sometimes protect the neighbors, it might also result in entire households dying. In fear and panic, people blamed everything from unusual weather and livestock sickness, to the number of frogs, mice, and flies, and even to any unusual celestial phenomena, like a strange comet streaking across the sky.

# The 1889–1890 Flu Pandemic

*What happens when you combine industrial travel, a virus, and medieval medicine? You get over one million deaths during one of the worst global pandemics ever known.*

✳   ✳   ✳   ✳

THE 1889–1890 FLU PANDEMIC was the last great pandemic of the nineteenth century. Also known as the "Asiatic flu" or the "Russian flu," it is believed to have originated in Western Siberia. Considered one of the deadliest pandemics in history, it killed an estimated one million people, which was approximately 0.067 percent of the world's population at the time. It was first believed to have begun in Bukhara—modern-day Uzbekistan—in May of 1889. However, a commission of four doctors in 1889 (supported by a 2023 study) subsequently determined that that particular outbreak was of malaria instead of influenza.

It actually originated from the Tomsk province of Western Siberia. It was believed to have then spread to major cities such as Moscow and St. Petersburg thanks to the Russian military. From there, it spread to Stockholm and all of Sweden, then Norway, and finally Denmark—all in November 1889. By December, it had spread to the German empire, Paris, Vienna, Rome, Spain, and the United Kingdom.

It didn't take long for it to travel across the Atlantic, reaching the U.S. that same month; it landed on the East Coast before spreading to Chicago and into Kansas. The first American death is widely reported to have been Thomas Smith of Canton, Massachusetts, on December 25, 1889. The five-week-long wave would finish spreading across the country by January before making its way down into Mexico City and Buenos Aires by the end of the month. On the other side of the world, it had spread to India, Singapore, and the Dutch East Indies by February, and then Japan, Australia, and New Zealand by April. It had done a complete lap as it reached its origin at around the same time. Over the course of four months, it spread across most of the northern hemisphere and much of the south as well.

## A Viral World Tour

How did this nineteenth-century flu outbreak become a global pandemic? Primarily, it was due to the modern transportation of the era. Railroads were the travel method of choice for those who remained on land, and transatlantic sea travel took as little as six days. That allowed the virus to remain safely within hosts until they were able to pass it on to others on different continents. This made it the first pandemic that didn't remain confined to one particular region, as with the pandemics and epidemics of the past.

Despite the improvements of modern travel, this was an era before the time of effective influenza treatments. Quinine and phenazone were used to help treat fever, ear pain, and malaria symptoms, and strychnine was used in incredibly small doses. Some of the sick would use traditional treatments like whisky and bourbon to help alleviate symptoms, while others would use cheap treatments such as linseed, salt and warm water, and glycerin. Some believed that one could reduce a fever by starving the sick. Of course, we now have a much better idea of how to handle the flu and bring fevers down, but this was at a time when some doctors still believed in miasma theory (the belief that epidemics were caused by "bad air" emanating from rotting matter). This flu pandemic was unfortunately perfectly positioned at the intersection of newly modernized travel and antiquated medicine.

# The Sixth Cholera Outbreak

*In the late 1800s, a cholera outbreak would rip across Asia, decimating towns and cities in India before spreading west, destroying towns and nearly annihilating an army in Romania.*

✳   ✳   ✳   ✳

THIS PARTICULAR OUTBREAK of cholera began in India in 1899, where it killed more than 800,000 people. From there, it spread to the Middle East, North Africa, and Eastern Europe and Russia. After this, it slowed, taking quite a good while to travel further west—not reaching the United States until 1910. That portion of the outbreak began on a boat carrying passengers from Naples, Italy, to New York City.

Thankfully, the proper authorities had been alerted before the passengers were able to disembark, and it was possible to quarantine them within a facility on Swinburne Island. Eleven people died—including children and one health care worker—at the facility, but the outbreak did not spread onto the mainland. And so, the epidemic largely didn't affect Western Europe and North America thanks to improvements in public health and sanitation.

Eastern Europe was not as lucky, however, particularly Romania. The outbreak killed 1,600 members of the Romanian Army in 1913, when it was invading Bulgaria during the Second Balkan War. By 1919, India had lost more than half a million people to the disease. By the time the epidemic officially ended, most countries were free of widespread cholera cases.

# The Japanese Smallpox Epidemic

*An ancient smallpox outbreak decimated the population of Japan and left many starving and displaced.*

✳   ✳   ✳   ✳

KNOWN AS THE "Epidemic of the Tenpyō era," the Japanese smallpox epidemic took place in AD 735–737. It affected most of Japan, and killed a third of the entire Japanese population. It began in Dazaifu, Fukuoka, in August 735 from a shipwrecked Japanese fisherman who had been stranded on the Korean peninsula. It quickly spread throughout the northern countryside, resulting in a poor agricultural season and crop yields—creating a countrywide famine. The adult mortality rate was somewhere between 25 and 35 percent of Japan's entire population, with some areas being hit harder than others.

When a group of Japanese government officials traveled through northern Kyushu in 736—during the height of the epidemic—some grew sick and died, while others brought it back to the capital. This spread the disease to eastern Japan and Nara, the capital city of the Nara prefecture. The disease's toll was so great that a tax exemption had been granted to all of Japan by August 737.

All levels of society were affected. Many court nobles died, including all four brothers of the Fujiwara clan. This allowed the ascension of their rival, Tachibana no Moroe (Japanese imperial prince), to a high official position within the court of Emperor Shomu. For the common people, the epidemic particularly affected construction and farming. Due to this, it triggered a significant movement in labor and population. The reason we know so much about this ancient epidemic is because the government had begun to report disease outbreaks among the general population a few decades prior to this small-pox epidemic.

# Major Plagues of the Eighteenth Century

*Three major bubonic plagues occurred in Europe in the 1700s, affecting much of Europe, Russia, and Ukraine.*

✳ ✳ ✳ ✳

THE FIRST OF these major plagues was the Great Plague of Marseille—also known as the Plague of Provence. It was first reported in Marseille, France, in 1720, where it killed over 100,000 people over the course of two years. Trade remained largely unaffected, but the French population wouldn't return to pre-plague numbers until 1765.

Marseille actually did have a sanitation board, established after the plague of 1580. It had established a three-tiered control and quarantine system to attempt to prevent future plagues. This system included inspecting all incoming ships. Not only would the ship be inspected, but it, along with its crew, would be required to quarantine on one of the nearby islands for eighteen days before the crew would be permitted to disembark.

This particular plague is believed to have originated from the merchant ship *Grand-Saint-Antoine*, which had passed through a plague-ridden Cyprus. Upon reaching Marseille, it was placed under quarantine by the port authorities. Due to its cargo of silk and cotton, which was wanted for the great fair at Beaucaire, powerful city merchants pressured the city to lift the ship's quarantine.

The first cases of the plague were reported mere days later. After the plague had run its course and began to subside, the government increased port defenses to try to ensure this would never happen again.

## The Great Plague of 1738

The Great Plague of 1738 was an outbreak of the bubonic plague that affected areas of the Habsburg Empire—the modern-day countries of Romania, Hungary, Ukraine, Serbia, Croatia, Slovakia, Czechia (the Czech Republic), and Austria. It is believed that the plague began in the Banat region, probably brought there by the Imperial Army.

The 1740 Diet of Hungary (the most important political assembly of Hungary until the modern period) reported that the Great Plague claimed 36,000 lives. The hardest hit area was southeastern Transylvania, with the plague killing about a sixth of the population of Timișoara, the capital city of the Timiș County, Banat (the main economic, social, and cultural center in Western Romania). More than 10 percent of the population of Cluj-Napoca, the second most populated city in Romania, was reported to have been killed by the plague.

## The 1770–1772 Russian Plague

The Russian plague epidemic of 1770–1772, also known as the Plague of 1771, took place in central Russia and was particularly rough on the city of Moscow. It originated in the Moldovan theater of the 1768–1774 Russian-Turkish war before moving northward through Ukraine and into central Russia. It peaked in Moscow in September 1771 and caused the Plague Riot, which was a mass protest against protective measures that culminated in rioters breaking into the Kremlin, destroying the Chudov Monastery, killing Archbishop Ambrosius, and destroying the two quarantine zones.

Originally, the plague was concealed by Commanding General Christopher von Stoffeln. Thankfully, Field Marshal Pyotr Rumyantsev forced the troops to quarantine.

When medical quarantine checkpoints would have protected the major cities during peacetime, they were largely ignored or not enforced during this time of war. While this resulted in the plague reaching Poland and Ukraine by August 1770, Empress Catherine II would not even acknowledge the plague in public. The epidemic in Moscow alone was estimated to have caused 52,000–100,000 deaths out of a total of 300,000 infections.

# Awake: Decades-Long Comas and No Known Cause

*A disease that starts out with symptoms consistent with the flu and ends with a decades-long coma or death:* Encephalitis lethargica *is both a medical mystery and the stuff of nightmares.*

✳   ✳   ✳   ✳

ONE OF THE greatest human fears came true for the million-plus people who contracted the sleeping disease. It turned well over half a million people into living statues between 1917 and 1928. At the time, the disease terrified the public, partially due to the fact that its origins were mysterious and unknown. Considering contemporary events, scientists at the time postulated that it could have been related to the Spanish Flu epidemic or even be a side effect of the mustard gas used during World War I.

Autopsies performed by Constantin Von Economo at the time suggested that the disease caused an enlarged hypothalamus, the part of the brain responsible for sleep. Likely due to that inflammation, hundreds of thousands of people fell into catatonic and comatose states, leaving families devastated and doctors scrambling to find a cause.

Forty years later in the 1960s, doctors employed a new drug aimed at treating Parkinson's disease to wake up a number of patients who had remained unresponsive for decades at that point. Upon waking, these people reported a spectrum of experiences, from no awareness whatsoever over the course of that time to awareness but limited memories of the experience. However, most of the patients who woke up thanks to this drug ultimately fell back into their comatose state, and were lost to the world forever.

Doctors named this disease *Encephalitis lethargica* and continued to search for its origin. It has mostly fallen out of public awareness, but the search for a cure is ongoing. To this day, there's no definitive conclusion as to what the cause could be, with most theories revolving around a virus or a subtype of *streptococcus* bacteria that evolved to specifically target the brain. Scientists' fear of the disease has not been unfounded, as cases continue to appear sporadically every few years with seemingly no explanation.

# Chapter 10

# Mass Hallucinations and Bizarre Afflictions

## Hammersmith Ghost Hysteria

*In the early nineteenth century, a mysterious ghost terrorized the people of Hammersmith, England. Was it a vengeful spirit or something else entirely?*

✳   ✳   ✳   ✳

IN 1803, PEOPLE claimed to have seen or been attacked by a ghost in the Hammersmith area of London. Some locals described the ghost as being "clothed in a winding sheet," wearing a blanket or some sort of shroud, or wearing a "calf skin with horns."

The legend circulated that the Hammersmith ghost was a man who had taken his own life by cutting his throat. At the time, there was a common superstition that suicide victims would become restless if they were buried on consecrated ground, which explained why the Hammersmith ghost was terrorizing the cemetery.

The locals reacted in various ways to the ghost. In the beginning, most were too afraid to go out at night. After a few weeks, some became a little braver, but would still refuse to travel alone. Some young men took it as a sort of masculine challenge to bravely go after the ghost.

## Tragedy Strikes

The most tragic event surrounding the Hammersmith ghost wouldn't involve the ghost at all. Francis Smith, a 29-year-old excise officer (someone who makes sure that taxes and duties are paid) was infuriated about the ghost terrorizing his fellow citizens. Armed with a fowling gun, he patrolled the area where the ghost sightings had occurred, particularly in the field attached to Black Lion-Lane. During one of these nights, while hidden and watching the area, Smith saw a figure donned in all white. Steeling himself, he jumped out and shot the figure, causing it to fall to the ground. Unfortunately, he soon discovered that the figure wasn't a ghost at all—rather, it was a 22-year-old bricklayer named Thomas Millwood. At the time, bricklayers dressed in all-white garb. He had been traveling to meet his wife when Smith mistook him for the ghost.

Smith had fatally shot Millwood through his neck and jaw; he was indicted for murder and ultimately found guilty of manslaughter by a jury of his peers. However, due to Smith's "good" intentions, the hysteria surrounding the Hammersmith ghost, and it genuinely being an accident, he was only sentenced to one year in prison.

While the accidental killing was an absolute tragedy, it did cause the "real" Hammersmith ghost to come forward—a man by the name of John Graham, a boot and shoemaker. Graham had been in the habit of dressing in all white and jumping out at people at night. On one occasion he had jumped out at a wagoner, who promptly abandoned his wagon out of fright; this put his horses and passengers in danger. Additionally, Graham's "pranks" caused a pregnant woman to become so frightened that she fainted when he rushed at her and took her in his arms. As to why he would put his neighbors in danger, Graham was reportedly trying to get revenge on his apprentices who had terrified his children with ghost stories. He "expected to check them of this disagreeable bent . . . by presenting to them, as they passed homewards, a figure of a ghost."

# Seattle Windshield Pitting Epidemic

*Could aliens or nuclear testing have terrorized the people of the greater Seattle area? The strange rash of windshield damage would captivate and confuse the country for years.*

✳   ✳   ✳   ✳

THE SEATTLE AREA's windshield pitting epidemic occurred in April 1954 in Bellingham, Seattle, and other communities in Washington. Many people suddenly noticed holes, pits, and dings in windshields. Some residents believed that vandals were responsible, while others attributed the phenomenon to greater powers involving government conspiracies and nuclear bomb testing. At first, when it was only happening in Bellingham, police seemed to think that teens using BB guns might have been causing destruction. However, this theory seemed less and less likely as cases began popping up in nearby Sedro Woolley, Mount Vernon, and Anacortes on Fidalgo Island, off the coast of Washington. Soon, the news of this pitting epidemic reached Seattle and newspapers began writing sensational articles about the odd events. With the news spreading far and wide, the reports of windshield pitting only increased, with parking lots and garages seeing the majority of the damage reports.

The most common hypotheses for this strange phenomenon were: a new million-watt radio transmitter at the nearby Jim Creek Naval Radio Station producing waves that caused physical damage in glass; cosmic rays; some atmospheric weather phenomenon; and sand fleas laying eggs in the glass, causing bubbles to form. However, Sergeant Max Allison of the Seattle police crime laboratory explained that the pitting reports consisted of "5 per cent hoodlum-ism, and 95 percent public hysteria." Likewise, Dr. D. M. Ritter, a University of Washington chemist who had been assigned to work with authorities on the pitting case, proclaimed, "Tommyrot! There isn't anything I know of that could be causing any unusual breaks in windshields. These people must be dreaming."

Despite these explanations, over 3,000 reports had been collected by local law enforcement by the middle of April, which prompted Seattle Mayor Allan Pomeroy to seek help from Washington Governor Arthur B. Langlie and President Dwight D. Eisenhower. It's unknown if the president did anything to help the frantic citizens of Washington, but Langlie did request that a committee of scientists from the University of Washington help try to explain the phenomenon. They found the damage to be "overly emphasized," and most likely "the result of normal driving conditions in which small objects strike the windshields of cars." And they were correct: The Seattle windshield pitting epidemic is a textbook example of collective delusion, wherein a spontaneous, temporary spread of false beliefs occurs within a given population.

# The Blackburn Faintings of 1965

*For three weeks in 1965, girls in Blackburn, England, experienced dizzy and fainting spells out-of-the-blue. It would stop as quickly as it started, leaving no concrete explanation.*

✳ ✳ ✳ ✳

I N OCTOBER OF 1965, several girls at a school in Blackburn, England, mysteriously fainted. First complaining of dizziness, 85 girls ended up fainting over the course of a few hours. The ones in the worst condition were rushed to the hospital where they came-to and experienced side effects of swooning, moaning, clattering of teeth, hyperpnea (increased volume of air taken during breathing), and tetany (a type of seizure). All of the girls were of different ages and didn't seem to have any sort of preexisting conditions that would make them more susceptible to fainting spells. All the remaining girls at the school were released to their homes until the following Monday. When they returned, a similar epidemic occurred yet again—this time, 54 girls were taken to the hospital. A week later, another 40 girls had similar symptoms, although none had to be taken to the hospital.

An explanation was never found, but doctors noticed a few trends: The faintings began with the 14-year-olds, but the majority of girls affected were younger. Despite this, the younger girls did recover quicker than the older girls, who also had more severe symptoms. They also noticed that those affected had higher scores for extraversion and neuroticism according to the Eysenck Personality Inventory.

Other than those odd trends, no direct cause for the faintings could be found. There was no evidence of food poisoning, viruses, or gas leaks. There had been a recent polio outbreak in town, which led some to believe that the faintings were a result of a "mass hysteria." Another theory was that seeing their peers becoming dizzy and fainting created a sort of mass hypochondria in yet others (a condition also known as illness anxiety disorder) wherein the girls, becoming worried that they would faint next, ended up manifesting the symptoms and effects in themselves. Each time they returned after the weekend, concerned girls would be worried that it would begin again, creating a sort of self-fulfilling prophecy.

# The Hollinwell Incident of 1980

*An unexplained event occurred at England's Hollinwell Showground in 1980 wherein over 300 people experienced mysterious dizzy spells that resulted in widespread fainting.*

✳ ✳ ✳ ✳

ON JULY 13, 1980, at 9:00 a.m., around 500 children from several different marching bands were lining up to participate in the Junior Brass and Marching Band competition. This was a charity show that was part of the annual Hollinwell

Show at Kirkby-in-Ashfield, Nottinghamshire. At around 10:30 a.m., random children in the marching bands started collapsing with fainting spells, seemingly out of the blue. The fainting also seemed to be contagious as adults, kids, and even infants were also affected. By the end of the event, around 300 victims were reported, and 259 of those had to be taken to nearby hospitals.

Over 50 years later, the exact cause of the illness—if it truly was an illness—is still unknown. There are a number of theories that range from plausible to fringe, such as contaminated water supplies, food poisoning, radio waves, and crop spraying in nearby fields.

Pesticides seemed to be the favored explanation of the day, particularly the use of the pesticide tridemorph, which the World Health Organization described as "moderately hazardous." However, the official investigation seemed to settle on mass hysteria being the cause.

People who were there were adamant that their symptoms were real and not made up, but the crowd could have easily manifested "real" symptoms if they saw the people around them drop like flies. Unfortunately, the marching bands and visitors to the Hollinwell Showground would never receive a satisfactory explanation.

That wasn't for lack of trying. While the council that investigated the incident announced in 2003 that they had no plans to reopen the case, a number of television and radio broadcasts were made over the years to attempt to explain or solve the incident. Radio researchers had reached out through the newspaper, urging locals to come forward with their experiences. Additionally, in August 2013, an episode of *Punt PI* on BBC Radio 4 investigated the incident; this was followed up by a further examination during an episode of *Mystery Map* on ITV just three months later.

The latest exploration into the incident occurred on its 42-year anniversary. A local BBC reporter created a podcast about the events and interviewed a forensic science lecturer from Nottingham Trent University. The lecturer hypothesized that different cleaning products used in a block of temporary restrooms for the event could have caused a buildup of chlorine gas, which could create similar symptoms if allowed to spread across a crowd.

# The Kosovo Student Poisoning of 1990

*Over the course of a year, thousands of young Kosovars would fall ill due to an alleged mass-poisoning. Although this would trigger an international investigation, the incident remains a mystery to this day.*

\* \* \* \*

ON MARCH 22, 1990, thousands of young Albanian Kosovars were allegedly poisoned by toxic gasses. The first to fall victim were students, who saw a "white powder" on their desks. If they touched it, they quickly experienced frothing around the mouth, widespread cramping, inflamed eyes, and facial flushing. These would typically evolve into fainting, vomiting, and violent convulsions. The first school to report the symptoms was Duro Dakovic high school in Podujevo, but many more would fall ill in the ensuing days. Soon, around 200 of Podujevo's students fell ill, with most being driven to Pristina for first aid. By the end of the year, 7,421 Albanian Kosovars had been stricken with the illness. Thankfully, there were no reported deaths.

Most victims received aid from Catholic nuns. One of the nuns provided information through an interview for *Glas Koncila*, a Croatian Roman Catholic, weekly newspaper. Her interview helped give advice to fellow nuns throughout the region who were treating children with the "mysterious disease." The Faculty of Medicine of the University of Pristina subsequently organized a group of Albanian and Serbian doctors to intervene. They announced that the epidemic was a disease, but would need the results of toxicology reports of the blood and urine of the victims.

Three days after the initial outbreak, the first results of the samples, processed at the Military Academy in Belgrade, were released. The verdict was that the samples did not contain any poison. However, these results were controversial because these tests typically took at least six weeks to process.

## Targeted Attack?

It has been pointed out that the poisoning occurred just a few months after the Serbian government decided to segregate Albanian and Serbian students in schools throughout Kosovo. Thus, a wide variety of accusations and conspiracy theories have been lobbed by both sides. One doctor spoke on Serbian television and claimed that the episode was all "pure acting" for the Cannes Film Festival. Serbian doctors came to the defense of their Albanian colleagues, claiming that no such thing was happening.

Slovenian doctor, Anton Dolenc, declared that there was no actual poisoning, explaining the phenomenon as a "psychogen reaction." Two British doctors, Alastair Hay and John Fran, also found no hints of poisoning, acknowledging that the only explanation for the widespread symptoms was "mass hysteria." However, the chief of epidemiology of Kosovo, Jusuf Dedushaj, fiercely denied that the disease was mass hysteria. He claimed that if it were something psychological, this event would have more likely happened the year prior when "young Albanians were afraid to be vaccinated by Serbian doctors." His opinions were quite controversial, and they landed him in prison for five days. To this day, a common conclusion has not been reached, despite experts from all over the world examining the event.

# The Ganesha Milk Drinking Miracle of 1995

*One morning in 1995, a strange phenomenon occurred all over India: Statues of Ganesha, the popular, elephant-headed Hindu god, absorbed offerings of milk in temples. Could this be a modern-day miracle, or something more sinister?*

❋ ❋ ❋ ❋

THE PHENOMENON BEGAN early in the morning on September 21, 1995 in New Delhi, India. A worshiper at a temple made an offering of milk to the trunk of a statue of the Hindu deity, Ganesha. When the milk touched the trunk, it appeared to be drunk up by the statue, with no liquid remaining after. In a state of absolute shock, the worshiper spread the word around only to find that other statues throughout India had also taken up milk. By the afternoon, word had spread to Hindu temples outside of India, and they also began to claim to reproduce the phenomenon.

Word of the purported miracle spread far and wide, resulting in major vehicle and pedestrian traffic jams at temples in New Delhi. The gridlock lasted until late in the night. Sales of milk jumped over 30 percent as people desired to witness the miracle for themselves. Unfortunately for those who had traveled to bear witness, many statues were less cooperative.

The statues would not drink milk at a variety of important locations, such as the South Mumbai Ganapati temple, the bulls and bears at the Delhi Stock Exchange, and the Siddhivinayak temple. Oddly enough, however, were reports of statues from other religions taking in milk, such as a statue of the Virgin Mary in Singapore, and statues of Ambedkar and Buddha. Locals in Mumbai reportedly offered alcohol to a Gandhi statue, and it apparently took that in too.

## Are the Statues Just Thirsty?

In an attempt to explain this phenomenon in a scientific way, Ross McDowall led a team of scientists from India's Ministry of Science and Technology to a temple in New Delhi to see what exactly was occurring. The team offered spoonfuls of milk containing food coloring to a statue. The statue did take the milk, and the scientists hypothesized that after the milk was taken, it coated the statue beneath where the spoon was placed. They believed that capillary action might explain the phenomenon: The surface tension of the milk pulled the liquid up and out of the spoon, but then gravity caused it to run down the front of the statues. Due to normal milk being so light in color, observers had not noticed the milk doing this. The colored milk made the process more apparent.

The labor minister in the Narasimha Rao government, Sitaram Kesri, had a more sinister explanation for the milk-drinking reports. Quoting internal reports, he stated that a temple in Jhandewalan Park near the RSS headquarters (a far-right Hindu nationalist paramilitary organization) in Delhi was where the "miracle" originated. Thus, he claims that this whole event was a ploy by Hindu nationalists to gain votes in the upcoming Lok Sabha elections. He further claimed that they made late-night phone calls to various temples all over India and the world so that they would all experience the phenomenon on the same day.

# The Great Clown Panic of 2016

*Odd and frightening clown sightings occurred all over the world in the late summer and fall of 2016. Was it merely a viral media event, or evidence of something more sinister?*

✳ ✳ ✳ ✳

THE 2016 CLOWN SIGHTINGS are considered a case of mass hysteria that occurred mainly in the United States, Canada, England, and Australia. The common element of these reports was that people dressed as "evil" or otherwise frightening clowns were being spotted in strange places, such as near forests, schools, and cemeteries. The sightings began in August of 2016; by October, clown sightings and attacks had been reported in nearly all U.S. states, nine of the provinces and territories of Canada, and 18 other countries.

Reports of clowns in odd locations isn't something completely new: Since 2013, odd sightings of clowns have occurred all over the world, but nearly all of them could be explained as being related to social media stunts to drum up publicity for horror films. However, 2016 seemed to usher in a whole new wave of clown terrors.

The phenomenon apparently began in Green Bay, Wisconsin, when five pictures of a creepy clown roaming a vacant parking lot in downtown Green Bay went viral on the internet. A Facebook page was soon created, claiming that the clown was named "Gags," but it was soon revealed that this was a marketing campaign for an upcoming horror short film called *Gags*. There were also sightings of creepy clowns in Greenville County, South Carolina, later that month. Rumors spread that the clowns intended to lure children into the woods with money and treats. Fuel was only added to this fire when a clown was sighted in Winston-Salem, North Carolina, offering treats to children.

## And Then They Multiplied

After the virality of the Wisconsin incident, numerous other sightings popped up around the United States. Reports of evil clown sightings extended into Canada, and then the United Kingdom and Australia. Pressure was placed on police to keep the frightened communities safe from this "menace." In the coming weeks, there were at least 12 clown-related arrests and, unfortunately, one death—a 16-year-old boy in Reading, Pennsylvania, was wearing a *Purge*-style clown mask when he was fatally stabbed by 29-year-old Avery Valentin-Bair.

While communities were terrified of these clown sightings, it seemed to have a more detrimental effect on those who were harmless professional clowns or people who enjoyed dressing up as scary clowns during the Halloween season. In fact, students at Pennsylvania State University and Michigan State University formed mobs that searched for clowns on campus after reported sightings. The World Clown Association president, Randy Christensen, took a hard stance against people dressing up as clowns in order to scare or intimidate others.

Many U.S. schools decided to ban clown costumes and masks outright during the run-up to Halloween, and Target and similar stores even removed clown costumes and masks from their stores and websites. Employees of theme parks that were doing Halloween events—such as Universal's Halloween Horror Nights—were instructed to remove their clown makeup and costume before leaving work so as to avoid trouble from hostile or paranoid people.

# The Meowing Nuns

*A long-told tale of French nuns being overtaken by a bout of feline-like "meowing" has long puzzled those who study mass hysteria events.*

\* \* \* \*

A PARTICULARLY ODD EVENT of mass hysteria occurred in a convent in France possibly during the Middle Ages (dates have vaguely been given between AD 500 and 1500). According to the book *Epidemics of the Middle Ages* by J. F. C. Hecker, one nun randomly started meowing like a cat. Soon, others in the convent began to meow as well. Due to cats being closely associated with the devil in Catholicism, this drew a lot of fear and attention. Soldiers were brought in to try to contain the situation. Unfortunately for the nuns, their "solution" was to whip and beat the nuns until they stopped.

Our primary source for information about this event comes from Hecker's book, published in 1844. This book is actually a compilation of Hecker's three previous books *The Dancing Mania*, *The Black Death*, and *The Sweating Sickness*, all published in German. However, what's interesting is that the story about the meowing nuns isn't in the original compilation—it wasn't there at all until it was added in a note by English translator Benjamin Guy Babington. Babington studied medicine and received his doctorate in 1831, and he had a keen interest in epidemics and was a huge fan of Hecker's work. Unfortunately for us, however, he failed to include any sort of citations for the origin of the meowing nun story.

Despite there being no solid proof that the meowing nuns ever existed, there's also no proof that anyone was lying about them. Many young women were forced into convents due to the lack of options for them at various times in the Middle Ages. Nuns were required to practice celibacy, lived in poverty, and often did hard manual labor. Thus, it would be the perfect storm of circumstances to result in episodes of hysteria.

## The Dancing Plague of 1518

*On a summer's day in 1518, a woman in Strasbourg started feverishly dancing and could not stop.*

✳    ✳    ✳    ✳

THE DANCE EPIDEMIC of 1518 occurred in Strasbourg, Alsace (modern-day France) from July to September. The outbreak started when a woman named Frau Troffea began to dance fervently in the street and kept it up for a week. Soon after, a dozen others joined in. Dancers did collapse, and some died of strokes and heart attacks. While there is controversy around the number of deaths that occurred, rumors of the time stated that around 15 people died each day. Estimating from these numbers, the total death toll would be in the hundreds.

No one knows exactly what triggered this epidemic, but a popular theory, originally suggested by Historian John Waller, is that it was stress-induced mass hysteria. Other theories include ergot poisoning (fungi that grows on rye and related plants) and religious explanations.

Historical documents from the time confirm that there was an outbreak of dancing, and it did begin after a single woman started dancing. It lasted for so long that the authorities began to get involved. Physicians of the time could merely scratch their heads and recommend that the victims be left to dance it all out of their systems. Some claims mention areas being cleared out and turned into dance halls, and that musicians were called to accompany the dancers. Others were brought to help the dancers stay upright. However, when people joined in on the dancing, believing that it was punishment from Saint Vitus, the Strasbourg city council decided to ban public dancing and music—a dramatic move in a culture where dancing was so important.

The most frantic dancers were then ordered to go to the shrine of Saint Vitus, where the first dancer, Frau Troffea, had apparently been cured of her mania. The dancers, still thrashing about, were placed underneath a wooden carving of Vitus. Then, small crosses were placed in their hands and red shoes were placed on their feet. Holy water was sprinkled on the tops and soles of these shoes while Latin incantations were chanted and incense was burned. This apparently worked, with the victims being cured of their dancing plague.

# The Writing Tremor Epidemic of 1892

*An odd epidemic of girls experiencing hand tremors and body seizures occurred in Poland and Switzerland in the late 1800s. Doctors were unable to find anything wrong with the girls, nor an exact cause of the events.*

✳ ✳ ✳ ✳

IN 1892, SCHOOLGIRLS in Groß Tinz, Poland, suddenly started experiencing tremors in their hands when they attempted to write. Some developed full-body seizures. At first, only one ten-year-old was affected, but the tremors soon spread to 19 other girls. In the following year, a similar epidemic occurred in Basel, Switzerland, where more girls were affected with the same symptoms. The event wouldn't happen again until 12 years later where the Basel school would have another outbreak of the hand tremors in 27 students.

To this day, doctors have no idea what caused the tremors. Some speculate that the folklore surrounding the very first instance is what caused the subsequent epidemics, while some believe that the girls wanted to get out of class. Dr. Robert E. Bartholomew theorizes in his article, "Protean nature of mass sociogenic illness" in *The British Journal of Psychiatry*, that "the writing tremor of the latter nineteenth century Europe was a direct result of a new teaching method which viewed the mind as a muscle that needed exercise. This [tremors] was a subconscious way to get out of the dreaded writing classes." There is a problem with Dr. Bartholomew's theory: The tremors only affected girls. One would think that if students wanted to get out of writing classes, boys in various schools would experience similar phenomena. Additionally, writing classes were not unique to European students at the time. Thus, it's odd that there weren't reports of similar epidemics in other parts of the world, or similar instances of these tremors since.

# The Mad Gasser of Mattoon

*Over the course of two weeks in the 1940s, a small Illinois town was terrorized by a mysterious figure who reportedly broke into homes and gassed the occupants. Was this a simple case of mass hysteria, or the actions of one sick individual?*

❋  ❋  ❋  ❋

THE MAD GASSER of Mattoon—also known as the "Anesthetic Prowler," the "Phantom Anesthetist," or just the "Mad Gasser"—was the name given to a person who allegedly broke into houses and gassed residents of Mattoon, Illinois, in 1944. In the span of two weeks, over two dozen cases of gas attacks were reported to police. The most common symptoms of these attacks were leg paralysis, coughing, nausea, and vomiting. More people were said to have spotted the unknown assailant, but no one was ever charged with a crime. The most popular description of the gasser was given by Mr. and Mrs. Kearney of 1408 Marshall Avenue: a tall, thin man dressed in dark clothing and wearing a tight-fitting cap. However, another notable sighting describes the assailant as being a woman dressed as a man. The Gasser was also described as carrying a flit gun, an agricultural tool used to spray pesticide.

Police remained skeptical throughout the event due to most reported gassings being easily explained by odors caused by spilled nail polish, animals, or nearby factories. No one died from the gassings, and all victims recovered from their symptoms quickly with no long-term side effects. In recent times, the Mad Gasser is considered to have been a mass hysteria event. However, some experts suspect that industrial pollution was responsible for the gassing events. Some have concluded that there may have been someone roaming around and gassing homes, but that was the less likely explanation. Rather, it was probable that the vast majority of accounts were from paranoia caused by the few sightings of the true Mad Gasser.

# The Mysterious June Bug Epidemic of 1962

*A classic example of hysterical contagion, the June Bug Epidemic of 1962 was a baffling occurrence involving a group of textile workers who believed they were the victims of some mysterious affliction, possibly caused by insects. Despite very few of the afflicted having any bite marks, dozens of workers fell ill over the course of the month.*

✳ ✳ ✳ ✳

IN JUNE 1962, 62 workers in an American textile mill became the victims of a mysterious illness. The source was thought to be the result of some strange insect infesting the mill. Victims experienced numbness, dizziness, nausea, and vomiting. Entomologists (people who study insects) and other scientists were called in to find the cause of the illness, but no evidence of bugs or pests was ever found. Nor did they find any other potential cause.

This mysterious event is now dubbed the June Bug Epidemic, and it's an example of a mass sociogenic illness: a form of mass hysteria characterized by the rapid spread of illness symptoms through a population where there is no agent responsible for the contagion. Despite there not being any concrete cause, mass sociogenic illness events can still result in severe physical symptoms and even require hospitalization.

In the case of the June Bug epidemic, it's likely that anxiety coupled with unhappiness was the cause for the "spread" of the symptoms. Additionally, workers stated that the environment was extremely stressful, with the work pace being excessively busy and organization being poor.

Some of the affected workers took time off to recuperate after the hectic event, but ultimately all workers recovered with no long-term effects.

# Months of Uncontrollable Laughter: The Case of the Tanganyika Laughing Epidemic

*Laughing till it hurts doesn't sound like fun, especially when you can't seem to stop. But the strange epidemic of uncontrollable laughter that afflicted students in Tanganyika revealed how societal pressures can manifest in bizarre ways.*

✳   ✳   ✳   ✳

SPANNING A 100-MILE radius, an 18-month crisis overtook the new country of Tanganyika in 1962. After decades of British colonial rule, Tanganyika had just gained its independence, plunging the still-fragile country into a period of instability and political transition.

A mission-run boarding school in Kashasha saw the possible effect of that instability in January of 1962, when three female students began laughing uncontrollably—and couldn't stop. Over the next couple of months, the bizarre phenomenon spread to almost 100 students, with most episodes lasting an average of one week.

The event was significant enough that the school had to be temporarily closed in March of that year, sending the girls home to their families and subsequently spreading the laughing epidemic to their home communities. Over the course of the 18 months that followed the initial occurrence, a total of 14 schools had to shut down and at least one thousand people were affected.

Most experts concluded that the Tanganyika Laughing Epidemic was a clear and simple example of mass hysteria. In terms of those affected, young people and women with little power in their communities were the most likely to be affected, as is expected in most cases of mass psychogenic illness.

The strict culture of the mission-run boarding school and the differences between the traditional values of the country and those taught at the school could have provoked the initial onset of the epidemic.

Sociologists who have studied the Laughing Epidemic have termed the incident as a "conversion reaction." From there, the generalized instability and change in the country most likely heavily contributed to the illness and allowed it to spread between villages. Laughter quickly became a simple exhibition of unease and distress, emotions that many people in the country at the time had no viable outlet for expressing. Like other cases in Africa under similar circumstances, the period of unrest immediately following independence from a colonial power could very easily produce an incident of mass hysteria.

# Chapter 11

# It Came from the Archeological Record

## The Curious Case of the Tucson Artifacts

*In the 1920s, dozens of unusual lead objects were discovered in the Sonoran Desert. While some believe that these relics are proof of European colonization of North America prior to Columbus, others are convinced that they are nothing more than an elaborate hoax.*

✳　✳　✳　✳

THE PLAINS OF the Sonoran Desert just outside Tucson, Arizona, may seem like the last place anyone would expect to uncover Roman artifacts from the eighth century. So when Charles Manier and his father were exploring the area near Picture Rocks on September 13, 1924, they were probably rather surprised when they found a 64-pound lead cross engraved with Latin lettering.

Manier discovered the mysterious cross buried near an abandoned lime kiln, where all but two inches of the object was concealed by gravel, rock, and soil. Unable to translate the Latin inscription on the object, Manier enlisted the help of Dr. Frank H. Fowler, a Latin professor at the University of Arizona. Along with Fowler, Manier's friend Thomas Bent and several members of the university's faculty soon joined in excavating the site where the anomalous cross was found.

Altogether, 31 objects were uncovered in the area, including crosses, swords, spear points, and religious symbols. In addition to Latin, many of the items were engraved with Hebrew lettering, and featured images of temples, angels, menorahs, portraits of humans, and even what looked to be a dinosaur. When Fowler translated the engravings on the items, he discovered that the people who created them referred to their colony as "Calalus," and they supposedly had lived in the area between AD 790 and 900. The inscriptions also listed leaders of Calalus and the length of their reign, as well as stories of civil wars and the defeat of a city called "Rhoda," thought to perhaps be a part of the Mesoamerican Toltec civilization.

## Lead and Latin

Manier and Bent were quick to believe that the artifacts they'd uncovered near Tucson were genuine archeological finds, which proved that a settlement of Roman Jews existed in North America 700 years before Columbus set foot on the continent. Others, however, including Fowler and experts from Harvard University, the Metropolitan Museum of Art, and the Smithsonian Institution, were just as quick to dismiss the relics as forgeries. Many of these experts cited the poorly refined lead and crude casting techniques used to make the objects, as well as inscribed Latin phrases which either seemed to be directly copied from basic Latin primers or plagiarized from works of classical authors like Virgil, Horace, and Cicero. The strange "dinosaur" image found on one of the items also raised red flags when researchers were determining the artifacts' authenticity.

But not all experts agree that the Tucson finds are forgeries. Donald Yates Ph.D., author of *Merchant Adventurer Kings of Rhoda: The Lost World of the Tucson Artifacts*, contends that the "poorly refined" lead used in the artifacts perfectly matches the lead available in the area at the time, and it's unlikely that a small colony of settlers would have had an expert metalworker to create items. Thus the "crude casting techniques." Yates also argues that the "dinosaur" found on one of the objects isn't a dinosaur at all, but rather a stylized depiction of a sea monster—a symbol of ancient seafaring and trade. What's more, while some of the Latin phrases may be familiar from Latin primers and classical texts, many of the details in the inscriptions are not found anywhere else, and the use of Hebrew is quite curious and still unexplained.

Manier and Bent remained believers in the artifacts' authenticity for the rest of their lives, although most experts agree that the items are fake. Ironically, even if experts could prove that the items were fake, that answer would create even more questions: Who made the items, and why? Why were they buried in a remote location? Why would someone go to the trouble of creating such an elaborate hoax if they knew they would never profit from it? Today, more than 100 years after the Tucson Artifacts were first discovered, the only one to know the answers to these questions is the lonely Arizona desert.

# P. T. Barnum's Giant Sucker

*P. T. Barnum, the consummate huckster, supposedly laughed at the audiences he tricked, saying, "There's a sucker born every minute." But have we misjudged America's Greatest Showman?*

✳   ✳   ✳   ✳

THE PHRASE—WHICH SUGGESTS that every scam, no matter how obvious, will find a gullible mark—has been attributed to several late-nineteenth-century sources, including con man Joseph "Paper Collar Joe" Bessimer and humorist Mark Twain. Most often, it is attributed to P. T. Barnum.

### What a Circus!

Phineas Taylor Barnum (1810–91) both amused and appalled his audiences with his collections of freaks, oddities, and wonders. Writer Herman Melville boldly declared him "sole heir to all…lean men, fat women, dwarfs, two-headed cows, amphibious sea-maidens, large-eyed owls, small-eyed mice, rabbit-eating anacondas, bugs, monkies and mummies." In the name of entertainment, he promoted "humbugs"—obvious hoaxes designed to delight and entertain, such as the "Feejee Mermaid" and a woman he claimed was George Washington's 161-year-old nanny.

Barnum insisted that people enjoyed being fooled so long as they got "several times their money's worth." Though it seems likely that such a showman would utter this dismissive phrase, Barnum's acquaintances denied it upon inquiry from his biographer, saying that Barnum actually treasured and respected his patrons.

## Start of the Punch Line

The true story behind the phrase can be traced to George Hull, a businessman from Binghamton, New York. In 1868, Hull (a fervent atheist) argued with a fundamentalist preacher who insisted the Bible be taken literally, including Genesis 6:4 ("There were giants in the earth in those days"). Hull purchased an enormous slab of gypsum and hired a stonecutter to carve it into a ten-foot-tall statue of a giant with lifelike details such as toenails, fingernails, and pores. The statue was stained with sulfuric acid and ink and shipped to a farm near Cardiff, New York, where it was then buried.

A year later, Hull hired workers to dig a well near the spot where the statue was buried. As intended, the workers found the statue and were excited by their find. (Months earlier, fossils had been dug up, with much publicity, at a nearby farm.) Hull had the workers excavate the statue, and then he charged people to see the Cardiff Giant, as it had become known.

Hull sold his statue for nearly $40,000 to a group of exhibitors headed by David Hannum. Barnum became interested in the find and offered to rent it for $50,000, but Hannum refused.

Rather than make a higher offer, Barnum decided to build his own Cardiff Giant, which he put on display, declaring that Hannum had sold him the giant after all and that Hannum's was the actual forgery. Newspapers widely publicized Barnum's story, causing audiences to flock to Barnum while Hannum bitterly declared, "There's a sucker born every minute," in reference to the duped crowds.

### Careful What You Sue For

Hannum sued Barnum for calling his giant a sham. At trial, Hull admitted that the original giant was a hoax. The judge ruled in Barnum's favor, saying that it is not a crime to call a fake a fake!

Afterward, one of Barnum's competitors, Adam Forepaugh, mistakenly attributed (or intentionally misattributed) Hannum's purported phrase to Barnum. The consummate showman didn't deny saying it; in fact, he thanked Forepaugh for the publicity.

# By Land or Sea?

*Scientists long believed that humans first arrived in North America about 14,800 years ago by way of land, traversing across the Bering Strait and through Canada after melting glaciers created an ice-free path. But an archeological discovery in Idaho suggests that humans may have first arrived by sea. And it also points to an arrival on the continent much earlier than has long been assumed.*

✳   ✳   ✳   ✳

TENS OF THOUSANDS of years ago, ice sheets covered vast portions of North America. When this ice began to melt, around 14,000 years ago, it resulted in gaps throughout central Canada. Humans could migrate through these pathways and were eventually able to settle in the interior of the continent. For many years, scientists believed that the first humans

to make their way into North America and call it home were
the Clovis people, best known for their creation of "Clovis
points"—arrow-shaped tools first discovered in Clovis, New
Mexico, in 1929. Evidence of Clovis culture has been found
throughout North America, with the oldest artifacts dating
back 13,500 years. In the second half of the twentieth century,
the "Clovis First" theory became popular amongst scientists,
who had concluded that no evidence existed to suggest any
other culture had settled in North America before the arrival of
the Clovis culture.

But in recent years, a series of archeological discoveries have
begun to challenge the "Clovis First" hypothesis, including
remains of a Paleolithic settlement at the Buttermilk Creek
Complex near Salado, Texas, and knives and mammoth
bones found in a Florida sinkhole that all date back to before
the Clovis era. But perhaps the strongest evidence against
the "Clovis First" theory has come from discoveries made at
Cooper's Ferry in western Idaho. Here, along the banks of the
Salmon River, a tributary of the Columbia River basin, excavations have uncovered tools, animal bones, and charcoal once
used in cooking hearths. When an archeological team sent
some of the items to researchers at Oxford University for dating, they were astounded to learn that the oldest artifacts were
between 16,300 and 16,500 years old.

## A Connection to Asia?

Since this time predates the existence of the unglaciated cor-
ridors that would have provided humans with a land route
into the North American interior, scientists concluded that the
humans who settled at Cooper's Ferry must have had ancestors
who came by sea. With so much ice covering the northern part
of the continent at the time, it seemed likely that early peoples
sailed down the Pacific coast until discovering the Columbia
River, where they were able to easily access the interior of
North America.

While not all scientists are convinced that the items at Cooper's Ferry are definitive proof of a pre-Clovis human settlement, many, including Oregon State University anthropologist Loren Davis, consider the "Clovis First" theory debunked. Davis has also raised intriguing questions about the identity of the Cooper's Ferry peoples, stating that some of the artifacts found at the site are similar to items uncovered in northwestern Asia and Japan. This raises the possibility that the first humans in North America may have migrated across the Pacific from this area. Whether scientists prove such a theory or not, the artifacts at Cooper's Ferry remind us that we still have much to learn about our past.

# Step into the Past

*Scientific research has often caused us to question the things we thought we knew. This was certainly the case when a discovery made in New Mexico's most popular national park revealed a surprising possibility about North America's first humans.*

＊　＊　＊　＊

STRETCHING ACROSS 275 SQUARE miles in the Tularosa Basin of New Mexico is the world's largest gypsum dune field. This soft sulfate mineral makes up the unique white sands of White Sands National Park, which encompasses about 41 percent of the dunes. The word "gypsum" is derived from the Greek word *gypsos*, meaning "plaster"—a fitting description for the mineral, which is often used in plaster, drywall, chalk, and as a medium for casts and sculptures. But its plaster-like properties have proved to be valuable to scientists, as well, and may give us a rare glimpse into our ancient past.

Tens of thousands of years ago, the dry, sandy Tularosa Basin was decidedly different than it is today. Lush green vegetation provided food and shelter to a variety of animals, and a large body of water, now known as Lake Otero, was nestled within the basin. Docile plant eaters, including ancient camels, mammoths, and giant ground sloths, were common in the area, as were predators like dire wolves and American lions. In the 1930s, long after these animals were extinct, researchers noted an interesting phenomenon: Any time it rained, animal tracks would be visible on the wet ground, but when the earth dried up again, the tracks would be much less visible. These elusive tracks in the dry ground became known as "ghost tracks."

The "ghost tracks," scientists theorized, were created thousands of years ago as Lake Otero began to dry up and shrink in size, exposing soft layers of silt, clay, and gypsum. And the more scientists searched for these prints, the more they discovered. What started as only a small collection of prints eventually turned into hundreds, and then thousands, of tracks in the Tularosa Basin.

## Tracking History

Then, in 2009, National Park Service biologist David Bustos found an intriguing set of tracks that no one else had noticed yet. They appeared to be human footprints, situated right next to those of a mammoth.

At first, Bustos's fellow scientists were unconvinced that the tracks belonged to a human, assuming instead that the prints were made when a camel slipped in the mud. In fact, it would take more than a decade before researchers not only admitted that Bustos was correct, but also began to study the tracks more closely. By 2021, teams of researchers were able to uncover more than 60 sets of human footprints, located within different levels of sediment.

Using radiocarbon dating to analyze grass seeds that were found within the sediment, scientists were able to estimate that the human footprints were made between 21,000 and 23,000 years ago. This was an amazing discovery for the researchers. At the time, most estimates of human arrival in North America did not go farther back than 16,000 years ago.

Knowing that their timeline was off by thousands of years, scientists were forced to rethink everything they thought they knew about the first humans on the continent.

The human tracks found in White Sands vary from a hunter following in the tracks of a giant sloth, to a mother walking next to a child. Many of the tracks appear to belong to teenagers and children, possibly suggesting that younger people may have been sent out from settlements to gather food or water. Perhaps the most interesting detail of the footprints is how many of them are found right next to tracks of ice age animals, showing that humans and these extinct animals coexisted for many years.

Sadly, erosion in the Tularosa Basin has begun to eradicate some of these rare traces of ancient history. Scientists are racing against the clock to continue their work, and are planning to carbon date pollen found near the prints to help corroborate the dates offered by these traces. Until then, the footprints found in White Sands will serve as reminders of the prehistoric humans who once lived their lives in the Tularosa Basin.

# Who Built America's Stonehenge?

*Mystery Hill in Salem, New Hampshire—sometimes dubbed "America's Stonehenge"—truly lives up to its name. The question of who created the site has been widely debated; but William Goodwin, the owner of the property in the early twentieth century, may have come up with the most fanciful story of all.*

✳ ✳ ✳ ✳

AMERICA'S STONEHENGE HAS very little in common with the famous Stonehenge in England, aside from the fact that both locations feature structures made of rock. The American site was originally called "Mystery Hill" by William Goodwin, who purchased the 30-acre property in 1937. The wooded area features several large stone structures, stone walls, and underground chambers of unknown origin. Some of the stones seem to be situated as an astronomical calendar, with some monoliths that align with the sun on the summer and winter solstice, and others pointing toward stars. The strangest structure at the site may be the so-called "sacrificial table," a large, flat slab of stone with grooves carved into it, presumably to channel liquid.

Before Goodwin purchased the land, the area had been owned by the Pattee family, colonial settlers who paid little mind to the unusual stone structures dotting the landscape. In fact, aside from a brief mention in the 1907 book *History of Salem, N.H.*, the configurations of stone were largely ignored by everyone. The book called the area "weird and fantastic," descriptors that Goodwin would later take to heart when forming his own theory of the land's history.

## Theories Spanning the Ages

Goodwin was interested in the stories of "Vinland," the name given to a purported pre-Columbian North American Viking settlement. Evidence of such a settlement has since been found in the Canadian province of Newfoundland, but Goodwin's hope was that his "Mystery Hill" might feature proof of early European visitors closer to home. He began to believe that the site had been created by the Culdees, a group of Irish monks who first appeared in the Middle Ages. According to legend, a member of this sect, an Irish priest named St. Brendan, was said to have sailed to North America in the sixth or seventh century. And while no evidence of such a journey has ever been found, Goodwin was convinced that Mystery Hill was the site where St. Brendan, or his fellow monks, settled down.

Goodwin was so certain of his theory that he began to rearrange some of the rocks in the area to more accurately fit his narrative. Some archeologists who have visited the site have even suggested that much of what is seen today at Mystery Hill was "created" by Goodwin. But Goodwin's story, fanciful or not, sparked an interest in the long-neglected area, resulting in other origin theories. The most widely accepted theory is that the stone structures were created by eighteenth- and nineteenth-century farmers who used to live in the area. But radiocarbon dating of artifacts on the land have shown evidence of human occupation as long as 4,000 years ago, convincing some that the site was created by Native Americans.

Still others believe the truth is a combination of all these theories. Native Americans occupied the site thousands of years ago, colonial farmers constructed stone structures, and Goodwin's wishful thinking led to the site as it exists today. And what of the "sacrificial table" with its sinister-looking grooves? Most archeologists believe it was used for the innocent purpose of extracting lye from ashes for the manufacture of soap.

Mystery Hill was officially renamed America's Stonehenge in 1982, in an effort to give the site more archeological credibility. While we may never know who actually built it, America's Stonehenge will no doubt continue to fuel the imaginations of visitors for generations to come.

# A Lofty Point of View

*Geoglyphs—large designs that are created in the landscape on the ground—are found throughout the world. In modern times, these interesting works of art can be seen from planes, helicopters, and hot air balloons. So why were so many of these geoglyphs created before flight was possible?*

✳ ✳ ✳ ✳

IN 1932, a pilot flying between Las Vegas, Nevada, and the small city of Blythe, California, noticed a curious sight as he peered through his window. Large figures, including three humans, two four-legged animals, and a spiral, were carved into the landscape below. The giant geoglyphs, also known as *intaglios*, were discovered in the middle of the Colorado Desert, about 15 miles north of downtown Blythe, close to the Colorado River.

When scientists studied the figures, they noticed that the huge drawings were created by scraping away the darker top layer of rock to reveal a lighter layer underneath. The lower layer was then packed down so vegetation wouldn't grow. Estimations of their age have been varied, with some researchers believing they could be around 450 years old and others suggesting they could be up to 2,000 years old. But regardless of how many centuries they have rested on the desert mesa, their large size, ranging from 95 feet long to 171 feet long, would have made it impossible for their makers to see them in their entirety from ground level. This has prompted scientists to wonder why the huge works of art were created in the first place. If their own creators were unable to appreciate them, why did they make them?

## Eyes in the Sky

One theory is that the drawings were meant for the eyes of sky deities. While no Native American groups have claimed the intaglios as their own, members of the Mohave and Quechan tribes believe the figures may represent Mastamho, considered the creator of life, and Hatakulya, the creator's helper. In more modern times, the area was sometimes used for religious dances and gatherings in celebration of creation. A more outlandish theory suggests that the huge figures were, indeed, meant to be observed from the sky, but by ancient extraterrestrials.

The discovery of the Blythe Intaglios sparked an interest in searching the area for more of the mysterious figures. Altogether, hundreds of similar rock drawings have been found throughout the American Southwest, but the Blythe Intaglios remain the largest and most well-known. Whether they were created for gods in the sky or aliens from a far-off planet, they have stood the test of time. But who made them, and why, may always remain a mystery.

# Set in Stone

*Jackson County, North Carolina, boasts a large Cherokee population, with around ten percent of the residents identifying as Native American. The county is also home to an unusual and mysterious collection of historic petroglyphs that are still significant to the Cherokee peoples today.*

✳   ✳   ✳   ✳

ACCORDING TO CHEROKEE legend, a giant by the name of Tsul'kalu once lived in the mountains of western North Carolina. The giant was said to be a master hunter who had seven fingers on each hand. When the giant leaped from his mountain home to the ground below, his huge, many-fingered hands scratched a large rock. Over time, the giant's name, Tsul'kalu, morphed into "Judaculla," and became the namesake of the boulder with the largest collection of petroglyphs on any single rock east of the Mississippi River.

With more than 1,500 individual markings, Judaculla Rock is literally covered in petroglyphs. The soapstone outcropping has a surface area measuring approximately 240 square feet and features circles, lines, crosses, cupules, stick figures, and even what appears to be a seven-fingered handprint, presumably left by Tsul'kalu. Nearby, evidence of soapstone quarrying is found, where rock was carved out to create stone bowls. Using this information, some archeologists have deduced that the petroglyphs may date back to when the stone quarry was active, sometime between 2000 and 1000 BC. But other researchers believe the patterns carved into the boulder more closely resemble the style of the pottery and ceramics of the Middle Woodland and late Mississippian cultures, which stretched from AD 200 to 1400.

## Protecting the Past for the Future

Although no one is certain of when the petroglyphs were created, the Cherokee peoples consider Judaculla Rock spiritually significant to their tribe. The rock is located on what is believed to have been a path between two Cherokee settlements, leading some to believe it may have been considered a "map" of sorts, and many researchers note that the markings appear to contain stylized depictions of the surrounding landscape.

On March 27, 2013, Judaculla Rock was added to the National Register of Historic Places. While this action will help preserve and protect the site, Cherokee peoples will also continue to preserve and protect their heritage by passing down the stories of their history and traditions, including the importance of Judaculla Rock, to future generations.

# Mysterious Dighton Rock

*In southern Massachusetts, a 40-ton boulder covered in strange markings has long stirred the imaginations of those who have studied it. While some believe the rock was carved by Native Americans, others have attributed its creation to ancient visitors from far-off lands.*

✳   ✳   ✳   ✳

IN 1680, AN English colonist and recent Harvard graduate named John Danforth happened upon a strange rock in what was then the town of Dighton, Massachusetts. The boulder was covered in carvings of geometric shapes, lines, outlines of people, and some kind of unusual writing. Danforth, wanting to show other people what he'd discovered, copied the carvings onto paper, resulting in a drawing that now resides in the British Museum.

Because it was situated along the riverbed of the Taunton River, the boulder face was partially concealed by water when Danforth created his drawing. In subsequent years, many more drawings and descriptions of the rock would be made, including of those lower layers that had been submerged when it was originally discovered.

Danforth's immediate theory about the markings on the rock was that they had been created by Native Americans, who had carved a depiction of a battle onto the stone. But as more people studied the boulder, more theories began to emerge.

## From Portugal to China

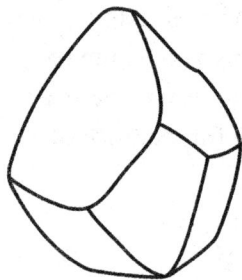

One suggestion came from Ezra Stiles, an eighteenth-century American educator and theologian, who believed that the writing was proof of a visit from ancient Phoenicians. In the nineteenth century, a Danish historian named Carl Christian Rafn proposed that the rock may have been carved by Vikings. Edmund Delabarre, a professor at Brown University in the early twentieth century, theorized that the writing was created by Portuguese explorers. And more recently, author Gavin Menzies posited in his 2002 book, *1421: The Year China Discovered America*, that the rock was carved by Chinese explorers who, he believes, visited the North American continent before Columbus.

In 1963, the five-foot-tall rock was removed from its home in the river and now resides in a museum in Dighton Rock State Park. After centuries spent near the water, the sandstone has undergone erosion, meaning the unusual markings on the boulder have faded considerably. Most historians agree with Danforth's original assessment and believe the rock was carved by Native Americans, although its meaning and intention has been lost to time.

Delabarre suggested that the markings may not have had a single meaning, but rather were meant to be significant in different ways to different people. If his theory is correct, perhaps the mystery of Dighton Rock's meaning is for the observer to decide.

# Hitting a Wall

*Throughout history, humans have built walls for various purposes. From the Great Wall of China to the Berlin Wall, many of these structures have been used for protection from enemies, to delineate borders, or merely as simple dwellings. But the East Bay Walls in California have surrounded researchers with questions and mystery.*

✳  ✳  ✳  ✳

IN THE HILLS surrounding the San Francisco Bay Area, hikers often run across an interesting sight: Miles of stacked stones and lines of rocks, forming crude walls that cut across the landscape. The walls range from around one to three feet high and are built with a wide variety of stones. Some are small enough that a single person would have been able to lift them into place, while others weigh more than a ton. No mortar was used to build the walls, which were created in broken sections ranging from a few feet to more than half a mile long. Some of the walls are straight and some are angled; some form rectangles while others form circles. And for more than a hundred years, people in Northern California have pondered the origin of this strange mishmash of walls scattered throughout the area.

Some of the first scholars to examine the walls, including Dr. John Fryer, a professor of Oriental languages at Berkeley University in the early 1900s, believed that the walls were thousands of years old. Fryer, perhaps falling back on his own field of study, theorized that the walls were built by Mongolians— though how they would have arrived in California is unclear. Other theories embraced this idea of an ancient origin, including an 1896 article in the *San Francisco Chronicle* that suggested the stone walls were the work of the Aztecs, or perhaps a "long forgotten race" of people. The newspaper revisited the subject in 1904, this time wondering if residents of the lost city of Atlantis created the structures.

## Ancients and Aliens

In addition to serious researchers and semi-serious journalists, the enigmatic East Bay Walls have fueled the imaginations of amateur historians and conspiracy theorists for decades. Some believe the walls are the work of the Lemurians, a mythical race of beings who once inhabited the lost continent of Mu. Others wonder if the walls were created to appease Native American gods, who expressed anger through the earthquakes that frequently plague the region. And of course, some insist the walls were created either by extraterrestrials or by humans to guide extraterrestrials to Earth.

Beyond the "who" is also the "why." Why were these strangely arranged, randomly shaped walls built in the first place? Because the walls appear to have been constructed in broken sections, most researchers believe they could not have been used as fences. They are also not tall enough to have been useful for defensive purposes. These puzzling details have confounded most observers, although some think the various walls could have been used to mark property lines or been used as hunting blinds.

## Unsolved Mysteries

More recent research has suggested that the walls are not as "ancient" as originally thought, but rather date only to the mid-1800s. And at least one researcher, San Francisco State University archeology professor Jeff Fentress, thinks there is a much simpler explanation for who built the walls: European and Mexican immigrants, who began settling the area around this time. But even Fentress admits that this theory is only a guess, and the true nature of the walls is still unknown.

Perhaps the best explanation for the East Bay Walls was written in a 1972 issue of *Pursuit*, a journal published by "The Society for the Investigation of the Unexplained." In it, an amateur researcher named Seth Simpson summarized his conclusions about the walls by stating, "All I can suggest is that they were built by unknown persons, in an unknown year, for an unknown purpose—and very possibly they will remain a puzzle for the indefinite future."

# Circle Back to the Past

*The city of Miami draws in more than 25 million visitors every year, who flock to the oceanside locale for its weather, beaches, and nightlife. But few of these tourists know that a 2,000-year-old archeological puzzle sits in plain sight amidst the glass towers and glittering lights of downtown.*

✳   ✳   ✳   ✳

IN 1998, A developer was preparing to build a luxury condominium in the Brickell neighborhood of downtown Miami, but before construction could begin, a routine archeological survey needed to be conducted on the property. So, the developer enlisted the expertise of Dr. Robert S. Carr, the director of Miami-Dade's Historic Preservation Division. Carr may not have been expecting to find much of interest during his inspection of the area, where an old apartment building from the 1950s had recently been demolished. But surprisingly, Carr and a team of employees and volunteers uncovered a number of clearly man-made holes cut into the limestone bedrock.

Upon further excavation, the team discovered 24 holes that formed a perfect, 38-foot diameter circle, as well as artifacts made of shell, stone, and bone. Charcoal found at the site was radiocarbon tested, with results showing that the burned wood was between 1,800 and 2,000 years old. The discovery quickly attracted the attention of local scientists, who conducted independent research of the find and corroborated the conclusion that the circle was not a modern creation.

Researchers who have studied the site believe the circle may have been the footprint of an important structure, perhaps a religious or ceremonial building, that once existed on the land.

Some have even suggested it may have been created by Olmec or Mayan civilizations, but many archeologists think it is more likely the work of the Tequesta, a local Native American tribe that lived in southern Florida from the third century BC until the 1800s.

### Saving the Circle

Although its origin and purpose is largely still a mystery, Carr believes the site, dubbed the "Miami Circle," is a hugely important find. After its discovery was announced in 1999, Carr stated that the Miami Circle "may be of national significance as it is believed to be the only cut-in-rock prehistoric structural footprint ever found in eastern North America."

Fortunately, appeals from archeologists and the public to halt the proposed condo project reached the ears of Florida legislators, who recognized the importance of preserving the site. After some legal wrangling, the plans to build a condominium on the historically significant property were scrapped and the State of Florida purchased the land from the developer. Today, the Miami Circle National Historic Landmark sits in a park at the mouth of the Miami River, serving as a small reminder of the past in the middle of the modern bustling city.

# Secrets of the River

*The Ohio River flows for almost a thousand miles, wending its way through seven states, from Pennsylvania to Missouri. The waterway is considered the sixth-oldest river on the North American continent, and the prehistoric artifacts found along its banks reflect its historic story.*

✳    ✳    ✳    ✳

IN 1838, AN antiques dealer named James McBride was exploring the Ohio River about four miles north of Steubenville, Ohio. The date was the Fourth of July; but instead of celebrating the country's independence, McBride was marveling over an unusual rock he had stumbled upon. Located on the West Virginia side of the river, which provides a natural boundary between the states of West Virginia and Ohio, the rock was made of sandstone, and covered an area of about nine feet wide and seven feet long.

But it wasn't the rock itself that amazed McBride; rather, it was what was carved into the rock's surface. McBride immediately took out a notebook and began drawing an image of the strange rock, which was covered with carvings of human figures, footprints, animal tracks, snakes, turtles, and other drawings.

The details of McBride's find were later recounted in *Ancient Monuments of the Mississippi Valley*, the first book published by the Smithsonian Institution. The scientific work was written by American archeologists Ephraim George Squire and Edwin Hamilton Davis in 1848 and it includes McBride's drawing and a description of the petroglyph-covered rock.

## Artifacts of the Valley

While McBride's account of the unusual Ohio River rock may be the most well-known, it was not the first time the rock had been viewed with curiosity. In fact, when the first pioneers began to settle in what is today West Virginia, they encountered the same rock, standing steadfast in the river. They also discovered burial mounds, stone walls, shards of pottery, and other artifacts in the area.

But while the settlers were able to learn some of the region's past thanks to the Native Americans who lived in the valley, even the natives were unsure of the significance of the carvings on the stone in the river. McBride indicated that the stone was inclined toward the water, almost like a monument or a sign, but what it was meant to communicate, and who was trying to communicate, remain a mystery.

Today, the rock, located in an area known as the Half-Moon Site, is submerged under the water of the Ohio River. But it is just one of many such rocks that have been located in the Ohio Valley. Some, like the so-called Ceredo Petroglyph—a three-foot-wide, six-foot-long rock weighing a ton and covered in carvings of unknown meaning—have been removed from the river and are now on display in museums. But others still stand in the river valley, just as they have for hundreds, or perhaps thousands, of years. These artifacts are so important that archeologists have, at times, sworn their locations to secrecy, to protect them from vandals.

Aside from McBride's notes, no written records of the Half-Moon site petroglyphs exist. Without such information, we may never understand why they were created or know their true meaning. But we can rest assured that if their messages were important enough to be set in stone, they are important enough to protect for future generations.

# Cactus Hill Controversy

*The Cactus Hill archeological site in southeastern Virginia is one of an increasing number of sites in North America that have challenged and toppled the once-dominant "Clovis First" theory regarding who the earliest inhabitants on the North American continent were. But some researchers also believe it suggests that the first humans to visit North America originated from a surprising location.*

\* \* \* \*

THE SAND DUNES surrounding Cactus Hill were once river banks, but today the site sits above the Nottoway River about 45 miles south of Richmond. The sandy soil provides the perfect environment for prickly pear cacti, which grow abundantly in the area and lend the site its name. But it wasn't a cactus that caught the attention of archeologists when the site was discovered in 1988. Rather, it was the evidence of human occupation in the area which dated back tens of thousands of years.

At the time the Cactus Hill site was discovered, most archeologists still adhered to the "Clovis First" hypothesis, which theorized that the first humans to occupy North America, known as the Clovis culture, arrived to the continent via land bridge over the Bering Strait. But thanks to its location along an ancient riverbank, the Cactus Hill site was uniquely preserved in a way that challenged this theory. Over millennia, wind and the shifting river deposited sand and silt in layers, one on top of another. Each layer marks a different time period, many of which retain evidence of human occupation.

## A European Migration?

To the surprise of archeologists who excavated the site, a layer which included stone tools, carbonized wood, and various animal bones was located several inches underneath the layer that corresponded to the Clovis time period. The lower layer is believed to date to between 18,000 and 20,000 years old, predating the Clovis culture and making Cactus Hill one of the oldest archeological sites in the United States. But with its location along the eastern coast of the country, the discovery of this pre-Clovis culture prompted a question: How did these prehistoric peoples end up so far from the Pacific Ocean and the Bering Strait land bridge?

Some archeologists believe they found an answer when they examined the ancient tools found at Cactus Hill. Instead of appearing as if they were created using Clovis techniques, the tools looked as if they had been made using the techniques found at Solutrean sites. Solutrean tool-making originated in the Solutré region of France around 22,000 years ago, and evidence of that culture is found throughout Western Europe. In what has become a controversial theory, some scientists, including the late Smithsonian Institution archeologist Dennis Stanford, have hypothesized that Solutrean people may have migrated over pack ice in the Atlantic Ocean and found their way to North America, becoming some of the first humans on the continent.

While most researchers reject this theory, the discoveries at Cactus Hill have forced scientists to rethink their original ideas about the earliest humans in North America. As more archeological finds are discovered, it is possible that one day we'll have an entirely new understanding of who the first humans to occupy North America were, where they came from, and how they managed to migrate such incredible distances.

# Refuge in the Rock

*When a researcher began excavating the grounds of a Pennsylvania farm in the early 1970s, he assumed his work would be mundane and inconsequential, making little impact on the world of archeology. Instead, it made history.*

✳    ✳    ✳    ✳

IN 1955, FARM owner Albert Miller was exploring his property, which had been owned by generations of his family since 1795. Along his hike, he discovered a groundhog burrow, which is not an unusual find in the western Pennsylvania township of Jefferson. But inside the burrow, Miller discovered flint flakes, burnt bone, and a flint knife. Considering himself a bit of an amateur archeologist, Miller was convinced that he had found something important, and he kept his discovery a secret for years to protect the area from looters.

Finally, in 1973, he was able to procure the expertise of a professional archeologist, James Adovasio, a professor at the University of Pittsburgh. Adovasio had recently founded the Cultural Resource Management Program at the university, which oversaw the first excavations of Miller's property.

The professor had low expectations about what he might find at the site, but he was eager to give the students in his newly created archeological program some work to keep them busy and give them experience. So when the excavation began revealing artifacts that dated back more than 16,000 years,

Adovasio was astounded. The team uncovered projectile points, pottery fragments, wooden instruments, and tools, some of which were still completely intact. One particular artifact, a piece of cut bark believed to have been used as a basket, was dated to be up to 19,000 years old.

## An Ideal Sanctuary

The surprisingly ancient artifacts were discovered in a rock shelter—a shallow, cave-like opening—in a bluff overlooking the Cross Creek tributary of the Ohio River. But an examination of the site produced more than one surprise finding. Not only did the discoveries in the rock shelter suggest that humans occupied the area thousands of years earlier than originally theorized, but they also revealed evidence that the site had been continuously inhabited up until 700 years ago. This would make it one of the oldest sites to boast continual human occupation in North America.

The site's location may provide an explanation for why it was occupied so regularly. In its position, the shelter was high enough to be protected from flooding, but close enough to Cross Creek that fresh water was readily available. Deer were common in the woods nearby, but if a hunt was unsuccessful, fish and mollusks were also available. And the shelter itself, naturally carved into the sandstone, would have provided pro-tection from the elements and a convenient refuge for rest.

## Preserving Meadowcroft

Adovasio's discoveries were announced to the world just nine days before President Nixon resigned in the summer of 1974. But even competing with the politics of Washington D.C., the archeologist's findings caused quite a stir. Archeologists still believed that Clovis culture artifacts were the oldest in North America, and they refused to accept the dates suggested by Adovasio's dig. Over the years, however, as the discoveries of many other sites obviously predating the Clovis era have been discovered, Adovasio's theories have become accepted.

After several decades of meticulous research, more than 20,000 artifacts have been uncovered at the site, and excavations have also revealed the largest collection of flora and fauna in one location in eastern North America. Approximately 1.4 million plant remains and 956,000 animal remains have been found, including the remains of elk, a species no longer found in western Pennsylvania. Today, Miller's once-anonymous property is a National Historic Landmark known as Meadowcroft. The property, which is open to the public, includes replicas of a nineteenth-century rural village and a prehistoric Native American village for visitors to explore. But the true draw is the rock shelter itself, where members of the public can see the prehistoric refuge and imagine what life might have been like in the distant past.

# Clues in the Caves

*Archeological sites in North America are often found to contain the scant remnants of a civilization. Pottery shards, tools, and the remains of cooking fires are all common. But scientists may have discovered something much rarer in a cave system in Oregon: prehistoric human DNA.*

✳   ✳   ✳   ✳

IN 1938, AN archeologist from the University of Oregon, Luther Cressman, assembled a research team to excavate a cave system in south-central Oregon. Known today as the Paisley Five Mile Point Caves, the site is located in a basalt ridge in the Summer Lake basin. Tens of thousands of years ago, the basin was covered by a huge freshwater lake called Lake Chewaucan, and waves from the ancient lake gradually carved the caves into the volcanic rock.

Cressman, known as the "father of Oregon archeology," was one of the few scientists exploring the state's ancient past, a subject which had been mostly ignored up until the 1930s. But the discoveries made by Cressman's team quickly caught the interest of archeologists across the country. In the caves, the researchers uncovered evidence of many extinct Pleistocene-era animals, including species of camels, horses, and bison. There was also evidence that humans occupied the area along with these pre-historic animals.

## Unlikely Evidence

As amazing as these finds were, many scientists at the time were cautious about estimating the dates of the artifacts. Just a year earlier, an extensive excavation of a site near Clovis, New Mexico, was completed, and believed to have proven the Clovis culture was the oldest in North America. Although Cressman had a hunch that his discoveries in the Paisley Caves could be older than those found at Clovis, the widely popular "Clovis First" theory, coupled with the limited technology of the 1930s, was gaining traction, and this emerging consensus hampered efforts to definitively date the Oregon site. Sadly, Cressman died in 1994, never knowing that the most intriguing discovery at the location was still to come.

In the early 2000s, archeology students from the University of Oregon returned to the work that Cressman began, this time with the help of state-of-the-art technology. In addition to finding more Pleistocene-era animal bones, the researchers uncovered tool fragments made of obsidian and bone, evidence of fire hearths, sage cords, and wooden pegs. But perhaps the most unusual, and revealing, find was the discovery of fossilized human waste—known as *coprolite*—which was collected and sent to Danish evolutionary geneticist Eske Willerslev at the University of Copenhagen.

## You Are What You Eat

Willerslev's analysis concluded that the coprolites contained mitochondrial DNA that matched that of the first peoples known to have journeyed to the Americas from Asia. The scientist was also able to determine that these humans ate an omnivorous diet, subsisting on grasses, seeds, fish, insects, and small mammals. The most exciting revelation came from radio-carbon dating the coprolites, which determined their age to be at least 14,000 years old, making them contemporary with the earliest known Clovis artifacts.

Even with this evidence, some archeologists are still skeptical, raising doubts about whether the coprolites are definitively human. Some have expressed concern that human DNA may have leached into the coprolites from layers of soil and sand above, or been transferred during the excavation process. And indeed, some samples have been found to contain both human and animal DNA, while others contain no human DNA what-soever. Even so, other finds from the caves, including a serrated tool made of bone and a human-made bulrush spear, have been dated to the pre-Clovis era, and do not bear any resemblance to the tools found at the Clovis site, bolstering claims that humans lived in the caves prior to the Clovis culture.

The work started by Cressman in the 1930s became the foun-dation for one of the most significant archeological excavations on the continent. Despite some controversy about the site, most scientists agree that the caves contain the oldest DNA evidence of humans that has ever been found in North America.

# Caribbean Curiosity

*Christopher Columbus is famous for being the first known European to set foot on a Caribbean island, making landfall on what is now the Bahamas in October of 1492. But he was not the first human to discover the islands of the Caribbean, as people had inhabited the islands for thousands of years. So, who discovered the Caribbean?*

✳   ✳   ✳   ✳

ON CHRISTMAS EVE 1492, Christopher Columbus sailed two of his ships, the *Niña* and the *Santa María*, around the island of Hispaniola. The *Santa María* ran aground, and, instead of attempting to repair the ship, the explorer ordered it to be used to create a small fort, which he dubbed *La Navidad*—The Nativity. Although it was destroyed by the Taino people less than a year later, the fort, and the small group of men who unsuccessfully tried to govern it, was considered the first European colony established in the New World.

Today, the island of Hispaniola is divided into two countries: On the west side is the French/Haitian Creole-speaking Haiti, and to the east is the Spanish-speaking Dominican Republic. While *La Navidad*, which was believed to have been located on the Haiti side of the island, was the first European attempt to set down roots in the area, other peoples had been living on the island for many generations. Because of the presence of the Taino people when Columbus arrived to the area, many assume they must have been the original inhabitants of Hispaniola. But the Taino are now believed to have emigrated to the island from the Orinoco Delta in what is currently Venezuela, thousands of years *after* Hispaniola had already been settled. That would mean that even this "native" tribe cannot claim to be the original inhabitants.

For years, scientists have called the mysterious true first inhabitants of the Caribbean the "Archaic" peoples, and archeologists have occasionally found artifacts that point to this shadowy group, such as stone hammers and distinctive butterfly axes that are a hallmark of the culture. But searching for ancient artifacts in the Caribbean is often a lost cause: The humid climate and changing sea levels can destroy anything organic, and modern construction, agriculture, vandals, and looters frequently disturb sites of interest.

## Little Well, Big Questions

But in 2021, scientists got lucky when they discovered an untouched patch of land at the end of the Samaná Peninsula, in the northeastern part of the Dominican Republic. Italian archeologist Alfredo Coppa found a natural spring bubbling in the area, and instinct told him to start digging nearby. Along with a team of Italian and Dominican researchers, Coppa uncovered a treasure trove of Archaic artifacts, including the ubiquitous butterfly axes and a small ceremonial well filled with 12 polished stone pestles.

Coppa dubbed the location "El Pozito," meaning "little well," and estimated its age to be at least 2,000 years old. The well-crafted pestles, and their suggestion of ritual ceremonies, were particularly intriguing to researchers, who had assumed that the Archaic peoples were much less sophisticated. Excavation at the site is ongoing, and Coppa is optimistic that his team may one day uncover a necropolis in the area. Such a find would be immensely valuable, perhaps even providing DNA to give scientists a better idea of who the Archaic people were.

Although their true identity is still unknown, the first peoples to discover the Caribbean would have had to be adventurous, seafaring explorers, who set off from the known comforts of their homes into an ocean full of unknowns. Such curiosity and courage is admirable; and thanks to El Pozito and sites like it, we may one day finally be able to answer the question, "Who discovered the Caribbean?"

# Bones and Stones

*Mastodons—large, elephant-like mammals that sported tusks up to 16 feet in length—roamed prehistoric North America in herds, until their extinction about 10,000 years ago. Fossils of the animals have been found throughout the continent, but one particularly interesting specimen in San Diego, California, was discovered with some surprising artifacts.*

✳    ✳    ✳    ✳

IN 1992, A construction crew was preparing to create a drainage system for a new freeway on California's State Route 54. As they dug about nine feet down through the soil with a backhoe, they suddenly uncovered what appeared to be bones. The digging was immediately stopped, and the crew contacted researchers from the San Diego Natural History Museum, who carefully began the excavation. One of the researchers, paleontologist Richard Cerutti, identified mastodon bones in the dirt of the construction area, and the site was quickly dubbed the Cerutti Mastodon site.

Along with the mastodon bones, which included tusks, molars, ribs, and more than 300 other bone fragments, scientists also uncovered the bones of a dire wolf, ground sloth, camel, and a mammoth. These finds alone would be remarkable, but the most amazing discovery at the site wasn't even a fossil—it was a collection of stones.

The stones, which exhibited impact marks and signs of wear, were found next to some of the mastodon bones. The bones appeared to be sharply broken, suggesting the stones had been used as tools to cut them. Spiral fracturing of the bones indicated they were fresh when the stones were used to hammer them apart. Studying the site, researchers theorized that humans living alongside the mastodons may have broken the bones of newly dead animals to extract the marrow or to fashion the bones into tools.

## An Unexpected Result

But the truly stunning implication of the stones discovered at the Cerutti Mastodon site came when uranium-thorium dating was used to date the bones. Results showed that the bones were more than 130,000 years old, meaning, if the interpretation is correct, that humans were present in North America long before even the oldest estimates of most archeologists.

In fact, the age of the bones appeared to be so ancient that many researchers were immediately skeptical of the results. Is it possible that humans were present on the continent more than 100,000 years earlier than almost every estimate? Some scientists have observed that no human bones or human-made tools were found at the site, and others theorize that the construction that had been taking place may have affected the appearance of the stones. Perhaps the backhoe scraped the stones and caused marks that appeared to be man-made?

More recent examinations of the Cerutti Mastodon artifacts have seemed to support the original conclusion. Microscopic bone residue was found on the stones, reinforcing the idea that they had been used by humans to hammer the mastodon bones. While skeptics are still critical of the findings, some scientists have been shocked and amazed by the implications of this archeological site. If nothing else, the discoveries made at the Cerutti Mastodon site have forced researchers to once again rethink their ideas about the earliest humans in North America, and to understand that when it comes to archeology, nothing is set in stone.

# Who Built Teotihuacán?

*The word "pyramid" immediately conjures up images of Egyptian sands and pharaohs. But Egypt isn't the only region known for these giant structures. In Mexico, two pyramids hold clues that speak of the lost ancient civilization that once inhabited this area of Mesoamerica.*

✳   ✳   ✳   ✳

TEOTIHUACÁN, ONCE A thriving metropolis in the middle of Mesoamerica, lies about 30 miles north of Mexico City. Its name can be translated to mean "the place where men become gods" in the Nahuatl language of the Aztecs. However, the Aztecs were not the founders of the impressive city. It is believed that they stumbled upon the ruins of the eight-square-mile complex sometime in the 1300s, after it had been abandoned for centuries. Scientists are still unsure of who created the many structures and roads that make up the city, but excavations at the site have revealed glimpses of an influential and sophisticated culture.

Archeologists believe Teotihuacán began as a small religious center around 100 BC, but continuous population growth over the next three centuries prompted construction of extraordinary buildings, some of which still stand today. The city was notable for its multi-floor apartment complexes which housed its many inhabitants. But the focal point of Teotihuacán was a long street known as the Avenue of the Dead. And located along this street were two of the most impressive structures in the entire city: The Pyramid of the Sun and the Pyramid of the Moon.

## Perplexing Pyramids

Although not as tall as the famous Pyramids of Giza, the buildings are the two largest pyramids in Mesoamerica, with the Pyramid of the Sun standing around 246 feet high and its counterpart reaching 141 feet. Like the city itself, the names of the pyramids come from the Aztecs, and their original names are unknown. But researchers have been able to glean some understanding about the mysterious builders of the structures.

It is theorized that the Pyramid of the Sun was constructed to honor a Teotihuacán god, but it is unclear which deity it may have been venerating. Lime plaster was used to cover the structure when it was completed, and then painted with colorful murals, which faded and disappeared over the centuries. But inside the pyramid, archeologists have discovered many tunnels and cave systems, including a large cave located deep underground, directly beneath the center of the pyramid. In Mesoamerican religions, caves were often thought to be sacred, and the place from which life sprang. So building a pyramid above this holy place would have had great ceremonial significance for the people in the city. Only a few artifacts, like arrowheads and human figurines, have been recovered from the pyramid, which has been well picked over by looters and vandals. But one artifact, an alabaster sculpture discovered in 1889 known as the Teotihuacán Ocelot, now sits on display in the British Museum.

## A Macabre Past

The Pyramid of the Moon, although the smaller of the two buildings, has yielded much more tantalizing information about the peoples of Teotihuacán. The structure, which was built in seven layers, each layer built over an older layer, seems to have been used for ceremonies and ritual sacrifices. These sacrifices involved both animal and human victims. When archeologists began exploring the pyramid's layered areas, they discovered several intact tombs containing human skeletons, animal remains, jewelry, obsidian tools and figurines, and ceremonial knives.

The humans found in these tombs are believed to have been sacrificial victims, offered up during the dedication of each new layer. Many more such ritualistic sacrifices have been found in the pyramid's foundation, where the remains of humans, felines, birds, and snakes have been uncovered. Scientists who studied the tooth enamel and bone of the humans concluded that they were not originally from Teotihuacán, suggesting that the victims may have been captured during a war or conflict of some sort.

## Lost Civilization

But the Pyramid of the Moon was not exclusively used for such disturbing reasons. Both the Pyramid of the Moon and the Pyramid of the Sun were built to line up with astronomically significant events, such as the changing of the seasons. And the entire plaza surrounding the Avenue of the Dead was a social gathering place for the people of Teotihuacán, who visited the pyramids for political, ceremonial, and socioeconomic reasons.

The city of Teotihuacán began to collapse sometime around AD 550 and was completely abandoned by the eighth century. The amazing structures left behind by this culture continue to amaze both scientists and visitors alike. But how this civilization went from being one of the largest cities in the Americas to a ghost town may always remain a mystery.

# The Undiscovered Continent

*Ahmed Muhiddin Piri was an Ottoman explorer, geographer, and cartographer who was born sometime between 1465 and 1470. His more well-known name, Piri Reis, means "Captain Piri," as he served in many naval wars for the Ottoman Empire, eventually rising to the rank of admiral. But he is most well-known for compiling a very unusual world map.*

✳ ✳ ✳ ✳

## A Forgotten Map

IN 1929, A German theologian named Gustav Adolf Deissmann was commissioned by the Turkish Ministry of Education to catalogue items in the Topkapi Palace library in Istanbul. As he sorted through some discarded bundles of material, he discovered a strange map drawn on gazelle skin parchment. Deissmann showed the parchment to German Paul Kahle, who identified it as a map drawn by the Turkish cartographer Piri Reis in the year 1513.

Inscriptions on the map claimed that Piri used at least 20 different maps and charts as source material to compile his own map, including Portuguese maps, Arabic maps, a map from Christopher Columbus, and Ptolemaic maps, which were maps based on Ptolemy's book *Geography*, written in the second century. The inclusion of the Christopher Columbus map caused a particular stir amongst geographers, as the Piri Reis map was the only known copy of a map drawn by Columbus. The map was also notable for its accurate renderings of the Iberian Peninsula, the northern part of South America, and Africa.

## Before the Ice Age

But one detail puzzled the geographers who pored over the map. Below the portion of the map that depicted the South American coast, the map appeared to show a representation of Antarctica. While this would seem totally normal on a modern map, the Piri Reis map, created in 1513, was drawn at least 200 years before Antarctica was known to exist. And that wasn't even the strangest part: The land mass on the map seemed to be a relatively accurate depiction of Antarctica *before* it was covered in ice. This would mean that the map displayed the continent as it appeared thousands of years ago.

How could anyone have created a map of Antarctica— especially before it was covered in ice—in the sixteenth century? Researchers considered the dozens of source maps Piri Reis claimed to have used to compile his map; could one of them have had knowledge of this sort? In 1965, a college professor named Charles Hapgood published a book entitled *Maps of the Ancient Sea Kings*, in which he argued for the affirmative. Hapgood believed that it was possible that an ancient, but advanced, civilization knew of Antarctica long before modern humans discovered it, and they had mapped its location when it was free of ice.

## Ancient Aliens, Ancient Peoples

Others have suggested that this ancient civilization may have been alien in origin, and Hapgood himself believed that who-ever mapped the continent would have to be not only able to navigate the sea, but also the air. Were ancient aliens flying across the globe millennia before the Wright Brothers? Or did a technologically advanced human civilization exist thousands of years ago, only to be inexplicably wiped out?

Skeptics point out that even in the sixteenth century, most sailors and geographers did believe that a continent existed somewhere in the south, so it's possible Piri Reis simply added one to his map. But others believe the map is too accurate for the land mass to have been added as a placeholder for a yet-to-be-discovered southern continent. We may never know the truth of how Piri Reis compiled his mysterious map, but it does make us question our ideas about "ancient" peoples. Did they possess more knowledge than we are aware of?

# An Ancient Computer at the Bottom of the Sea

*After millennia—possibly as long ago as the second century BC—at the bottom of the Aegean Sea, an artifact that NASA would later cite as the first computer was pulled off a previously undiscovered shipwreck.*

✳ ✳ ✳ ✳

IN 1900, A group of Greek divers looking for sponges near Antikythera, off the coast of Greece, discovered something incredible. Diver Elias Stadiatis had reached a depth of almost 150 feet when he requested a return to the surface. He claimed to have come across a pile of human and horse corpses on the seafloor—a statement the rest of the crew didn't immediately believe. Still, Captain Dimitrios Kondos put on his diving gear and descended to the site, eventually returning with his own discovery: the arm of a bronze statue.

After this initial discovery, the crew marked the area and continued on their mission, only returning at the end of the season to again dive to the wreck to investigate and bring several more artifacts to the surface. After this second visit, Captain Kondos brought the wreck to the attention of the Greek authorities, at which time the navy was able to send ships to examine the wreck. Salvage efforts began in earnest in November of 1900.

## The Shipwreck

The Hellenic Navy's recovery efforts were immensely successful. They extracted bronze and marble statues from the bottom of the Aegean Sea, along with artwork, ship equipment, and a variety of everyday objects, all of which made their way to displays at the National Archaeological Museum in Athens. Unfortunately, the salvage expedition came to a halt in the summer of 1901 after one diver died and another two were paralyzed from decompression sickness.

In 1902, archeologist Valerios Stais visited the museum. He realized that a corroded piece of bronze within the exhibit wasn't just a piece of metal—it had a gear embedded in it and legible Greek inscriptions.

## An Astrolabe, a Clock, or a Calendar

Stais originally suggested that the mysterious object pulled off the wreck could be an astronomical clock, though even his contemporaries believed such a device would be too advanced to have been constructed during the period in question. Albert Rehm, a German philosopher, was the first to suggest that it could be an astronomical calculator. Further studies have examined the mechanism from a variety of angles, with X-ray and gamma-ray images of the fragments taken in 1971. Further analysis has continued, including reexamination of the Antikythera wreck site along with examination of another wreck site considered to have been connected to the artifacts found at Antikythera. To this day, the Antikythera mechanism's full purpose is not understood.

## The First Computer

That said, the mechanism is now widely considered to be the first known analogue computer. The complexity of the mechanism's features has led many researchers to suggest that there are probably undiscovered prototypes of the same kind from even earlier times. The mechanism's construction relied heavily on theories of math and astronomy consistent with the knowledge of contemporaneous Greek astronomers.

A 2008 report by the research project associated with the Antikythera mechanism suggested that the device originated in Corinth or one of its colonies, citing a connection between the mechanism and the Metonic Spiral of Corinth. The report also suggested that the presence of the school of Archimedes in Corinth during the time period of the wreck could account for the production of the mechanism. Further research in 2014 suggested the mechanism may be even older, possibly dating back to 200 BC. Research is ongoing, with a 2017 study suggesting that prototypes of the mechanism originated in Rhodes, and that the version discovered at Antikythera was modified for a northern client.

# The Venus of Hohle Fels: 40,000-Year-Old Art

*A statue carved from mammoth ivory lay undiscovered in a cave in southern Germany for thousands of years. Its discovery has shaken up long-held views of early human history.*

✳  ✳  ✳  ✳

THE OLDEST KNOWN—AND undisputed—artistic depiction of a human being was discovered by an archeological team in 2008 in the Swabian Alb. This region is known for its high concentration of surviving artifacts from the Paleolithic period.

The Venus of Hohle Fels was found in six pieces ten feet below the ground. The left arm and shoulder were missing. There was no head to the figure, but a carved ring in its place suggested that the statue's original purpose was as some sort of pendant or amulet. The general shape of the figure was consistent with other Venus sculptures from the same period across Europe, though every other surviving example dates from later than the Venus of Hohle Fels. In fact, the find at Hohle Fels pushed back the estimates of the earliest carvings depicting humans by thousands of years—it was created nearly 41,000 years ago!

Like other Venus figurines, the Venus of Hohle Fels is considered a fertility symbol by researchers. Its emphasis on certain physical characteristics and not others (for example, indistinctive legs and a complete absence of a head) supports this conception. The physical attributes of the carving may reveal the values of prehistoric human society, but more than anything, it provides a vivid snapshot of human artistic development during this era of prehistory.

## Venus Statues and Early Figurative Art

The prevalence of Venus statuettes across Eurasia, all dating from tens of thousands of years ago, presents the picture of a relatively culturally united prehistoric Europe. All of these figures resemble the Venus of Hohle Fels, exaggerating reproductive characteristics while neglecting to detail other features. The first of these figures to be discovered was the *Venus impudique*, which was found in 1864 by Paur Hurault in France. The most famous example, the Venus of Willendorf, was discovered in 1908 in the Austrian Danube valley. In the century and a half since that first discovery, hundreds of such figurines have been unearthed in Europe and parts of Asia.

There has been some debate regarding the intent of the figurines. Some researchers suggest that the current theory simply reflects a century of confirmation bias. But regardless of their original purpose, Venus figurines—and the Venus of Hohle Fels in particular—tell us that the impulse to create artistic representations of the human form have been present in the human species for at least 41,000 years, and probably much longer.

# A Construction Site Find: The Discovery of the Pesse Canoe

*How can a wooden canoe survive unprotected in the ground for 10,000 years?*

✳  ✳  ✳  ✳

IT'S NOT UNUSUAL to find evidence of ancient and not-so-ancient life and culture during construction projects. In fact, it's such a common occurrence that construction companies often will contract with a consultant or the local government in order to handle whatever relics are discovered during a project. In 1955, those measures weren't in place yet and an incredible gem of a find was almost lost.

During the construction of the A28 motorway in the Netherlands, a crane operator found what he initially believed to be an old log. It was so inconspicuous that he almost disposed of it along with other debris from the area. Luckily, he mentioned it to a local farmer, Hendrik Wanders, who realized that the carving marks on the wood weren't incidental. Wanders took the find home to inspect it further, but quickly realized that he was out of his depth and took it to the nearby University of Groningen.

The University examined the log and realized that it was no mere log. Rather, it was an ancient and somewhat primitive boat. Scientists took samples of the wood. Carbon dating placed it somewhere between 8040 and 7510 BC, making it the oldest known boat in the world.

## Early Seafaring Vessels

The Pesse canoe is an example of a dugout canoe, a common style of boat that was still being created by hunter-gatherers into the modern era. Created from a single piece of wood, dugout canoes will never come apart. Dugout canoes were vital to the growth of fishing as a method of survival for many early peoples. The Pesse canoe's date of origin pushed back the time that people were known to travel via watercraft.

That being said, there was some early controversy surrounding whether or not the Pesse canoe was actually seaworthy or if it was another object simply mistaken for a boat by modern researchers. Skepticism was put to rest in 2001, however, when a replica was created and tested on the water. The test was successful and proved that the original likely served as a boat when it was created.

How the artifact managed to survive into modern times is another story. Thanks to its being trapped in a peat bog, the boat managed to last for thousands of years. The low oxygen environment prevented the wood from decomposing, preserving the canoe long enough to give modern researchers vital information about the development of human civilization. After initial testing, the canoe was freeze-dried, thus removing the moisture from the wood and arresting any subsequent deterioration. The log boat is now preserved and on display in the Drents Museum.

# Roman Dodecahedrons

*From Switzerland to the United Kingdom, mysterious metal objects crafted by the Romans have been found across Europe—with no apparent function.*

✳   ✳   ✳   ✳

THE ROMAN EMPIRE liked to document many things. From the minutiae of its political history to the aqueducts that still span parts of Europe today, very few things that originated with Rome remain unexplained. Roman dodecahedrons are one of the exceptions. These mysterious objects have been found across northwestern sections of the former Roman Empire. These objects, characterized by twelve equal sides and in most cases small knobs on the vertices and holes in each face, have baffled historians since the first one was unearthed in 1739. With over 100 similar objects found since that first discovery, it is reasonable to assume that they served enough of a purpose to justify such large-scale production.

A number of factors surrounding the objects' discoveries have led to speculation about their possible purposes. Some dodecahedrons have been discovered within caches of coins and other valuables, suggesting that they could have served as a symbol of wealth and status or have been worth a great deal of money. The discovery of one dodecahedron with zodiac symbols engraved on its faces has led to speculation that these objects could have been used in fortune telling or other ritual practices when they were produced. Discoveries in areas the Romans heavily developed have led to speculation that the objects could have been used as survey tools for construction and conquest.

And one hypothesis even suggests that the small objects were used as spool knitting devices to produce gloves, which could explain why the dodecahedrons are only found in the colder regions of the Roman empire. However, this theory is often discounted because the dodecahedrons seem to predate the invention of spool knitting.

Researchers are no closer to definitively proving a use for these objects than when the first one was discovered almost three hundred years ago. The mystery of these objects has proven to be as resilient as the metal they're made of, lasting far longer than tales of their origin and original purpose.

# The Tartaria Tablets

*Either the oldest known form of writing in the world or an elaborate hoax, the Tartaria tablets are one of the most fascinating archeological finds of the twentieth century.*

✳ ✳ ✳ ✳

THE ORIGIN OF written language has long been associated with the beginning of advanced civilization. The transition from primitive hunter gatherer societies to the boom of Ancient Sumerian cities was recorded on clay tablets, the oldest form of written language available to modern scholars.

Or is it? The Tartaria tablets, discovered in a grave in 1961, date back to an ancient culture in the Balkans. The tablets were radiocarbon dated to circa 5300 BC, predating known Mesopotamian proto-writing and pushing the origin of human writing back further, entirely disrupting our modern understanding of this slice of the distant past.

The tablets are primitive, consisting of three unfired clay tablets found amongst a hoard of goods located in an ancient burial site. Two are rectangular and one is round. All have symbols on one side. The symbols are a mix of abstract and clear representation, with primitive animal figures on one of the rectangular tablets. The symbols are controversial, with diverging opinions on whether or not they actually constitute writing and whether they merit the status of predating both Sumerian cuneiform and Egyptian hieroglyphs.

While there is no consensus about many aspects of the burial site, most researchers believe that the woman in the grave was likely a local shaman or religious figure. There is also debate surrounding the authenticity of the site as a whole due to the circumstances of the find and certain scientific elements of the dig. Like most archeological finds, the Tartaria tablets have their share of controversy. Their existence and validity call into question many assumptions we hold about ancient history and the origins of writing, but there isn't enough evidence to entirely prove that they were produced in that region during the time period they were dated to. It's very likely that the symbols on the tablets were not useful in communicating between people or communities and the grave is likely to be a mystery for decades to come.

## The Shigir Sculpture: Oldest Wooden Statue in the World?

*How does a wooden sculpture twice as old as the Great Pyramid still exist surprisingly intact?*

✳ ✳ ✳ ✳

AFTER OVER TEN thousand years in a peat bog, the oldest known wooden sculpture was unearthed on January 24, 1890, about 60 miles from Yekaterinburg, Russia. Though it was recovered in pieces, it was later reconstructed into a sculpture standing almost ten feet tall, though it likely stood more than 17 feet tall when it was originally created.

The first round of carbon dating on the sculpture took place in the 1990s. Scientists estimated that the statue was created 9,500 years ago. That date initially shocked researchers, who at the time believed that the hunter-gatherers of the period would not have been capable of carving and decorating the idol. A second analysis took place at the hands of German scientists who returned the shocking conclusion that the statue was even older than initially believed. They dated it to at least 11,500 years ago. The most recent analysis in 2021 pushed that estimate back even further, dating the statue to at least 12,000 years ago.

The statue's body is indefinite, with no limbs beyond vague hands, and entirely covered in detailed motifs. Its head, however, depicts eyes, a nose, and a mouth carved in a fashion that some viewers find vaguely disturbing. But more than anything, the enormous statue evokes questions about its origins and ultimately its purpose.

## What Does It Mean?

Initial reactions to the idol by researchers were heavily influenced by the widespread belief that hunter-gatherers were incapable of the workmanship necessary to produce such an object. Later discoveries and the use of carbon dating technology has proven those assumptions wrong, however, and the Shigir Idol has cast doubt about what we have assumed hunter-gatherer cultures were capable of in the distant past. The idol's meanings and original purpose are lost, considering the lack of written records from that time in history, but there are a number of theories on the idol's origins and purpose.

The idol was likely erected or propped up near a body of water. There is no evidence to show how it was held up. It may have been an emblem of protection, representing some entity that the people of the time found significant enough to preserve in effigy. Some researchers believe the motifs on the idol's body represent a local creation story.

Regardless of the original purpose and meaning, the idol represents a new understanding of people in the distant past, drastically changing our perception of hunter-gatherer groups.

# Two Thousand Years at the Bottom of a River: The Battersea Shield

*Dredged from the bottom of the River Thames in the nineteenth century along with artifacts from the Roman invasion of Britain, the Battersea Shield significantly predates the Roman occupation of the island.*

✳ ✳ ✳ ✳

THE BATTERSEA SHIELD consists of a metal facing, long detached from the wooden shield it likely covered at the time of its creation. It is covered in ornate decoration and has no damage that would indicate it was used in battle. It was discovered in the river Thames in 1857, during the construction of a bridge near the modern-day location of the Chelsea Bridge. Workers discovered a trove of Roman and Celtic artifacts in the area, along with skeletons, suggesting that the site could have been the location where Caesar crossed the river during the invasion of Britain. The Battersea Shield, however, was not a casualty of the battle.

Modern researchers believe the shield was a votive offering, created specifically to be thrown into the river as a ritual offering to the gods. The shield is ornate, typical of a style of metalwork popular among the Celts during the Iron Age. Its construction is dated to around 350–50 BC. The bronze shield is too thin to have provided substantial or even effective protection during combat and that fact, combined with a complete lack of battle damage on the metal, paints a very specific picture of the shield's purpose.

Votive offerings were common at the time. These offerings were a way of appeasing the gods at the center of the Celtic religious tradition. The shield was most likely originally created as a status symbol or a piece to be used in parades prior to battle, honoring the gods in a way that functional military equipment wouldn't have achieved.

The bronze shield, still attached to either a wooden or a leather shield, would have then been thrown into the river, sacrificed to the gods in hopes their favor would allow a victory in battle. Today the shield remains on display at the British Museum in London, the same city where it was discovered.

# Treasure Hunters and a Bronze Age Jackpot

*How could the discovery of a couple of illegal treasure hunters in Germany entirely upend our understanding of ancient history?*

✳   ✳   ✳   ✳

BARELY A FOOT wide and weighing just under five pounds, the Nebra sky disc is considered to be the oldest known depiction of astronomical phenomena in the world and is considered one of the most important archeological discoveries of the twentieth century. The disc is made of bronze with a characteristic teal patina. Gold symbols are carefully inlaid on the surface. Represented on the disc is the moon, the sun, several golden arcs, and a series of stars widely considered to represent the Pleiades constellations. The configuration correctly indicates the angle between the positions of sunset at both the summer and winter solstices—precisely at the latitude where the disc was found.

The figures on the disc most likely gave its creators a way of tracking time via astronomical phenomena, showing them how to synchronize solar and lunar years by using a leap month. The level of astronomical savvy this revealed was stunning, implying that its creators had spent decades carefully tracking the movements of celestial objects.

The disc was discovered on a hill near Nebra, Germany, and was ultimately dated to the early Bronze Age. In 1999, Henry Westphal and Mario Renner were treasure hunting on the hill, an activity that the pair engaged in without a license and with full understanding of the illegality of their hobby. The pair actually damaged the site, and nicked the disc with their spade, before selling the entire hoard to a dealer. The collection changed hands a number of times until 2002, when a police sting operation ultimately led to the disc finding its way into safer hands. Testing led to the conclusion that the metal within the object came from a number of sources, with some of the copper originating in Austria, the gold from the Carpathian mountains, and some of the tin and gold even tracing to Cornwall, England. Thus, the discovery of the Nebra sky disc draws a picture of a deeply interconnected European continent during the Bronze Age and even suggests that its people had acquired a more sophisticated understanding of astronomical phenomena than anyone previously suspected.

# Iron Age Silverwork and Sacrifice: The Gundestrup Cauldron

*How did the largest example of Iron Age silverwork end up in a peat bog? Are scholars any closer to understanding the civilization that created it than they were when the cauldron was found in 1891?*

✳   ✳   ✳   ✳

MODERN FASCINATION WITH the Gundestrup Cauldron, found in a Danish peat bog in 1891, arises from the many tantalizing mysteries surrounding it. Researchers believe that its creation dates to some time between 200 and 300 BC, and there is nearly unanimous agreement that it is one of the most brilliant examples of European silverwork during the Iron Age. Beyond that, the cauldron's origins and purpose are largely a mystery.

The cauldron is fragmentary, with the National Museum of Denmark possessing the only known surviving pieces, made up of the cup-shaped bottom, five interior plates, seven exterior plates, and two sections of a rounded rim that would have topped the cauldron. Researchers believe that there was at least one more exterior plate and pieces of rim that have been lost.

One of the most hotly debated mysteries surrounding the Gundestrup Cauldron involves its ultimate origin. It was found in a peat bog in Denmark near the town it was named for. The images depicted on the metalwork link the artifact to Celtic culture and religious practices. The methods required to produce the cauldron, however, were, as far as we know, entirely foreign to the Celtic people during the time period when it was created. Instead, it bears a striking similarity to both Gaulish and Thracian metalworking techniques known to be used during the Iron Age.

Modern researchers believe that the cauldron's origin lies with one of those two cultures and that it found its way to modern day Denmark through one of three methods: trade, as a gift, or as a spoil of war. Even the silver itself provides confusing clues: Its pieces were clearly taken from multiple sources and worked by different artisans.

The purpose of the cauldron also remains a mystery. There is very little information regarding cultural practices in the region during this time period. But we do know that the cauldron underwent extensive repair work, probably over the course of several centuries.

Scholars today tentatively suggest the cauldron may have been used ritualistically and it may have also been used in hospitality-related practices as well. The iconography on the cauldron's face features religious motifs, including what seems to be a reference to bull sacrificing, which was a known practice of Celtic societies at the time. The mysteries of the Gundestrup Cauldron may never be explained.

# One Night or Three Decades: The *Codex Gigas*

*Measuring three feet long and almost two feet wide, the largest medieval illuminated manuscript in the world boasts both a storied history and a bizarre creation legend.*

✳  ✳  ✳  ✳

OVER 700 YEARS AGO, a monk named Herman the Recluse lived in a Benedictine monastery in what would become modern day Czechia. In some unknown way, he broke his monastic vows. As a result, he faced punishment by his brethren. They harshly decided that he would be subjected to live entombment and left to die. Herman the Recluse begged for his life, offering to complete a tome of "all knowledge" in a night's time. His brethren, believing the task to be impossible, agreed. They then went and picked out his pauper's grave outside the monastery.

Of course Herman realized the task would be impossible and so he summoned the devil, offering his soul and a brilliant depiction of the prince of darkness within the book if the devil would only help him finish the task. And thus, the book that would become known as the Devil's Bible was created, featuring a full-page image of the devil. At least that's how the legend goes.

The book is the largest illuminated medieval manuscript in the world, weighing in at 165 pounds. It was likely completed by one scribe over the course of several decades. The impressive calligraphy and art appear on over 300 sheets of vellum made from the skin of at least 160 donkeys. It reveals no style variations that might be expected from a work that took so long to create. The treasured book stayed at its monastery of origin for hundreds of years before being borrowed, never to be returned, by the Holy Roman Emperor at the time, Rudolf II. Only

50 years later, the book was stolen by the Swedish Army during the Thirty Years' War. Thus it was carried off to Sweden, where it remains. The *Codex Gigas* is on display at the National Library of Sweden in Stockholm. It contains the full text of the Bible, a number of historical texts, and, of course, a colorful drawing of the legendary co-creator of the manuscript.

# Tenea

*For over two millennia, the city of Tenea was suspected to be no more than a myth of ancient Greek history. It took almost 40 years to discover the truth.*

✳  ✳  ✳  ✳

THE ANCIENT CITY of Tenea was a part of the legends surrounding the Trojan War. There was no archeological record of the city. But in 2018, after decades of research by a dedicated archeologist, the legend became a reality. Eleni Korka, who would later become the Director General of Antiquities and Cultural Heritage in Greece, was dedicated to the search for Tenea from the beginning of her career.

In 1984, after only five years on the job, Korka was contacted by a group of villagers who had discovered an ancient sarcophagus while digging a water channel in the area. Korka realized almost immediately it was something unique. The relic came from a period that had little documentation in the archeological record. Despite her intuition, she was considered too inexperienced to demand the resources that would be necessary for a full excavation at the site. Eventually, however, the excavation was begun in 2013. The dig yielded irrefutable evidence of the lost city in 2018.

Since then, digs in the area have produced an impressive trove of artifacts, filling in gaps in the archeological record and revealing things about ancient Greece never known before. Tenea, however, still holds many mysteries.

## Legend

Tenea's existence was a constant in myth and legend, showing up in stories about Oedipus and Agamemnon, and even getting a mention in Virgil's *Aeneid*. The city's origins are even the subject of myth, with some stories suggesting that the city was founded by Trojan prisoners of war who were brought to the area by the King of Mycenae.

Greece would later fall under Roman rule but, unlike many other conquered cities, Greek Tenea would continue to exist and even prosper, at least for a while. This may have been due to its legendary link to the Trojans as well as its status as a trading market.

Thanks to the stream of unearthed artifacts and structures, including coins and Roman-style bath houses, it is clear that the city continued to be occupied well into Roman rule. The artifacts that have already been unearthed provide a glimpse of daily life in the city. However, the cause of the city's subsequent demise is unclear.

## The Mystery

There is no confirmed story of what happened to Tenea, nor is there a clear record of when the city was deserted or why. Some speculation has been made regarding the role of Visigothic or Slavic invaders, who were present in the region at the end of Tenea's known history, and certainly caused mayhem elsewhere in the Roman Empire. However, there's no clear explanation of what happened to the ancient city. Whether a plague, natural disaster, or economic decline was responsible, archeologists have more questions than answers at this point. The archeological site itself is incredibly large—ongoing excavation efforts must grapple with the massive scale of the endeavor.

That said, the lost city of Tenea has now left the shadows of legend and become a part of the real history of Greece. It should continue to provide researchers with new and fascinating information as the digs continue.

# The Tamil Tools

*It was once believed that humans arrived in India from Africa around 125,000 years ago. But a discovery of stone tools in the Tamil Nadu region of India may point to a much earlier arrival than archeologists ever expected.*

❋ ❋ ❋ ❋

I N 1863, ROBERT Bruce Foote and William King, geologists with the East India Company's Geological Survey, uncovered some stone tools in the village of Attirampakkam, located about 37 miles west of Chennai, India. At the time, Foote and King probably thought the simple-looking, primitive tools were relatively unimportant to the field of archeology. That turned out to be far from the truth.

More than a century later, in 1999, archeologists from the Sharma Centre for Heritage Education in Chennai returned to the creekside village where Foote and King had once excavated and began an excavation of their own. Over the next two decades, researchers uncovered more than 7,200 stone tools created with a technique called *Levellois*. This technique is named after the Levellois-Perret suburb of Paris, France, where tools fashioned in this manner were first discovered in the nineteenth century. The technique consisted of chipping flakes off of stone cores to create blades, which could then be attached to sticks to make spears.

## Unexpected Age

Levellois was first developed around 300,000 to 400,000 years ago in Africa and Europe, and was thought to have been brought to India 125,000 years ago from Africa. But when scientists began to date the tools found at Attirampakkam using a process called luminescence dating, they discovered that the artifacts were an astounding 385,000 years old. This means that India may also be part of the cultural leap forward observed at the same time in Africa and Europe.

Researchers are unsure of whether this means a migration from Africa to India occurred much earlier than they believed, or if humans were already living in India and developed their own Levellois technique independently, along with Africans and Europeans. Unfortunately, no fossils or human bones have been found in the area, so any conclusions made have to be speculative. But the discoveries made at Attirampakkam are a reminder to scientists, archeologists, and curious truth-seekers to keep digging for answers.

# Army of the Dead

*Qin Shi Huang was the founder of the Qin Dynasty and the first emperor of a unified China, which he ruled until his death in 210 BC. But he is remembered less for his accomplishments as emperor and more for his imposing, elaborate mausoleum.*

✳   ✳   ✳   ✳

ON MARCH 29, 1974, a group of farmers was digging a well almost a mile east of where the tomb of Qin Shi Huang was believed to be located, in the Mount Li region of the Shaanxi Province of China. For many centuries, occasional discoveries of roofing tiles, bricks, and pieces of terra-cotta were reported in the area, but the farmers found something much more interesting this time. As they removed buckets of dirt from the hole they were digging for the well, they were surprised to see a head made of terra-cotta along with a bronze arrowhead in the ground.

The farmers, thinking they'd simply found a head-shaped jar, notified authorities, who sent out a team of archeologists to the site. Under the leadership of Zhao Kangmin, the team scoured the area, collecting fragments of terra-cotta. Zhao had a theory about what the terra-cotta head might actually represent, and no shard of terra-cotta was too big or too small—he wanted to collect as much material as possible.

When he had a large number of pieces, he took them back to the Lintong Museum, where he painstakingly assembled them until his hunch was confirmed and a remarkable artifact emerged: a life-sized figure of an armored warrior.

## Silent Sentinels

It is rumored that when Qin Shi Huang became king at the young age of 13, long before unifying China and beginning his reign as emperor, he made a strange request. He ordered the construction of his own tomb. But this was not to be just any tomb; this tomb would be guarded by thousands of silent warriors, who would protect the emperor from evil spirits in the afterlife. And more than two millennia later, Zhao was certain that he'd found one of these warriors.

When the Chinese government learned of Zhao's discovery, they ordered a large-scale excavation of the area where the terra-cotta pieces had been unearthed. What they slowly uncovered became one of the most awe-inspiring archeological sites in the world.

More than 6,000 life-sized warriors were buried beneath the dirt, along with terra-cotta horses, chariots, and weapons. These figures, which were originally painted in colorful pigments and carefully constructed to feature different heights, clothing, and hairstyles—lending them even more of a "lifelike" effect—guard the eastern side of the emperor's mausoleum.

## Underground Afterlife

Using ground-penetrating radar, researchers have estimated that the size of the entire necropolis is an impressive 38 square miles. Qin Shi Huang envisioned his final resting place to be a reflection of his earthly life, and the subterranean complex mirrors his imperial palace with underground gateways, offices, stables, and even a park, where bronze statues of cranes and ducks have been found. The actual tomb, which is about the size of a football field and remains unopened, is said to have been lined with precious gems and other treasures.

According to the Han Dynasty historian Sima Qian (c. 145–86 BC), the tomb also contained an unusual, and rather dangerous, feature: rivers made of silvery, flowing mercury. It is said that the emperor believed the element had life-giving powers, and by surrounding himself with it in death, he could live forever. Interestingly, scientists who have tested the earth around the tomb have found very high levels of mercury in the dirt, lending credence to the claim that the element was purposely included in the mausoleum.

The huge number of figures, the expansive mausoleum complex, and the intricate craftsmanship of the warriors has led some researchers to conclude that an incredible number of workers must have been required to build the necropolis. And indeed, Sima Qian claimed in his writings that 700,000 men were used to construct the complex.

However, some historians have questioned this number, as no city in the world is believed to have had a population that large at the time, so recruiting that many workers may have been a challenge. But even the lowest estimates assume that tens of thousands of men were needed to create the expansive complex. And seeing the underground city filled with thousands of ghost-like figures, it's not hard to imagine that an unprecedented number of craftsmen had a hand in its making.

Many of the terra-cotta figures at the mausoleum site still remain buried today. We may never know exactly how many warriors, horses, or weapons Qin Shi Huang required to guard him in the afterlife. But his tomb, and the surrounding complex, has no doubt made him one of the most famous emperors in world history. Perhaps in that way, he achieved his goal of immortality.

# First in the Philippines

*Luzon is the largest and most populous island in the Philippines, and the location of the country's capital, Manila. Recently, its name has also been lent to an intriguing fossil discovery made on the island, which may add another branch to our human family tree.*

✳ ✳ ✳ ✳

CALLAO CAVE IS a limestone cavern located in the Cagayan Province in the northeastern tip of Luzon. The cave is notable for being within the Callao Cave National Park, now known as the Peñablanca Protected Landscape and Seascape, which was one of the first national parks to be established in the Philippines in 1935. But decades later, the cave became known for an ancient discovery that surprised archeologists.

Between 2007 and 2019, more than a dozen bones, consisting of teeth, hand and foot bones, and part of a femur, were uncovered in the cave. When the first bone was discovered, researchers were quick to dismiss its importance because most believed it was just a modern human bone. But as more human fossils were excavated from the cave, scientists began to realize they were dealing with something much older.

Although the fossils closely resembled features of modern humans, the bones were significantly smaller, and the finger and toe bones were curved—as if the hands and feet had often been used for climbing.

But the biggest differences were observed in the teeth, which were unlike any human species previously discovered. They were simpler and smaller than modern human teeth or those of *Australopithecus*, one of humanity's earliest ancestors. And they were even smaller than those of *Homo floresiensis*, an ancient hominin species discovered in Indonesia that had been dubbed the "hobbit" due to its diminutive size.

## A New Species?

The bones were dated to between 50,000 and 67,000 years ago, putting them in the same time period as Neanderthals, Denisovans, and *H. floresiensis*. But the unusual teeth suggested to scientists that this might be a different species altogether. They named it *Homo luzonensis*, in honor of the island of Luzon on which it was discovered.

Researchers are unsure of where *H. luzonensis* fits in the evolutionary tree, but one theory is that when *H. erectus* migrated out of Africa, some hominins, including *H. luzonensis* and *H. floresiensis*, made their way to the islands, where their isolation and limited resources resulted in smaller statures. But this raises another puzzling question: How were such primitive humans able to cross large bodies of water to reach islands?

Although we may never know just how they arrived to the island, the unusual hominins are now considered the oldest known inhabitants of the Philippines. Scientists attempted to extract DNA from the remains but were unsuccessful, closing off another avenue to answers. For now, with a limited number of bones and no DNA, the origin of *H. luzonensis* must remain a mystery.

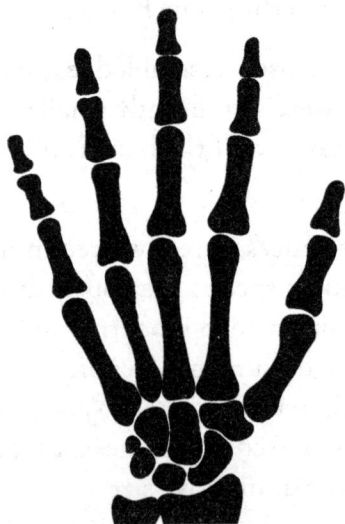

# The Mysterious Seima-Turbino Phenomenon

*The Bronze Age was a time period that lasted from about 3300 to 1200 BC. This era saw some of humanity's greatest innovations, including writing and the establishment of unique new urban civilizations. But some of the period's most impressive metalwork was created by a culture that remains shrouded in mystery.*

✳   ✳   ✳   ✳

IN 1912, A discovery was made in the village of Borodino in what is now the Odessa region of Ukraine. Workers excavating rock discovered two silver spear tips, a silver dagger, a gold pin, four stone axes, and several bronze artifacts. At about the same time, 930 miles away in the village of Seima, now known as Volodarsk, Russia, a similar set of relics was uncovered. Just over a decade later, in 1924, yet more artifacts, bearing a striking resemblance to the Borodino and Seima discoveries, were found in Turbino, in the Perm Krai region of Russia, more than 600 miles to the east of Seima.

The artifacts found in these locations displayed many similarities and seemed to have been constructed using the same methods. Many of the weapons found were made with a tin-bronze alloy. They were created using lost wax and hollow mold casting techniques. Artistic touches were added to blade hilts, with horses and geometric designs being the most popular.

Over time, additional artifacts bearing the same hallmarks were discovered everywhere from Greece to China to Sweden. Most of them were dated to between 2100 and 1900 BC, placing them in the middle of the Bronze Age. But other than their shared qualities, these artifacts didn't seem to belong to any specific culture. Nothing that would normally be found in a cohesive culture, such as settlements, pottery, or grave sites, was found in any of the locations where the relics were found.

## Cultural Expansion

Researchers realized that they were looking at a very unusual phenomenon. These artifacts were not part of a single culture, but rather, the techniques and artistry used for their creation were shared between different cultures spanning a vast area of more than 4,000 miles. This surprising interaction between the different cultures was dubbed the "Seima-Turbino phenomenon," in honor of two of the first locations where the artifacts were discovered.

Studies of the metal used in many of the relics determined that the tin-bronze ore used to create them originated from the Altai Mountains in western Mongolia and northern China. Scientists assume this is where the artifacts were first created, but how they spread from this location to areas far and wide is a mystery.

Some theorize that climate change forced the people in the Altai Mountains region to rapidly migrate east and west, where their metallurgy techniques were adopted by various cultures. Others think that the peoples living in the Southern Urals, including the Sintashta culture and the Andronovo culture, may have been a threat to the mysterious Seima-Turbino toolmakers and other cultures in the Siberian steppes, who stocked up on their well-made tin-bronze weapons in anticipation of any future conflict that might come their way. The steppe cultures then took their new-found knowledge of metallurgy and shared it with other cultures as they journeyed to other parts of the world.

The artifacts of the Seima-Turbino phenomenon are considered some of the most advanced and well-crafted pieces of the Bronze Age. While the creators of these relics remain mysterious, their far-reaching influence is a reminder that humans can always find a way to share knowledge, connect with others, and leave a mark on history.

# The Buddhas of the Desert

*Many religions feature art that reflects and honors deities, such as the intricate Christian-themed paintings of the Sistine Chapel, the symbolic jewelry of Hinduism, and the colorful mosaics of Islam. In China, a series of caves once offered a glimpse into the artistic works of Buddhism.*

✳ ✳ ✳ ✳

SITTING ON THE cliffs of the Mutou Valley in the Xinjiang region of western China are a collection of rocky, ancient caves. From the outside, the unassuming caves look as if they may have been used as modest dwellings by the Uyghurs of the Qocho Kingdom who called the area home until the fourteenth century. But inside the 77 caves, colorful murals once adorned every wall and ceiling, depicting religious scenes of Buddha and various other figures. So many Buddhas covered the walls and ceilings, sometimes hundreds in a single cave, that the area was named the Bezeklik Thousand Buddha Caves.

*Bezeklik* is a Uyghur word meaning "where the paintings are," and during their prime, that was certainly the case for these rock-cut grottoes. Construction of the caves is believed to have begun around the sixth century AD, with the majority dating back to between the tenth and thirteenth centuries. Inside, the caves consist of rectangular spaces with arched ceilings, sometimes divided into sections. Many of the spaces were painted with murals of Buddha surrounded by Turks, Indians, and Europeans, while other paintings depicted musicians, Uyghur princes and princesses, and scenes of daily life.

## Lost and Found

Archeologists believe that the caves were once the main religious center of Gaochang, the capital of the Qocho Kingdom. But near the end of the thirteenth century, Islam began to increase in popularity in the region, and by the end of the fourteenth century, the Buddhists in the Qocho Kingdom had been converted. Over time, the religious significance of the cave murals was forgotten, and the paintings were damaged and neglected. Since Islamic art prohibits the depiction of living beings, locals chipped away the faces of many of the figures in the murals, while other paintings were broken apart to be used for fertilizer.

But thanks to the dry desert conditions of the Mutou Valley, some of the murals were preserved for centuries under layers of sand and discovered by European and Japanese explorers in the late nineteenth and early twentieth centuries. Large sections of the cave paintings were removed and shipped to museums around the world, including the British Museum in London and the Tokyo National Museum in Japan, where they are still on display today.

While the caves in the Mutou Valley have lost much of their original colorful glory, the area has been carefully preserved to protect this historic site from the many visitors who come to see it every year. The Bezeklik Thousand Buddha Caves serve as a reminder that human accomplishments and achievements can be fragile, but they deserve our remembrance.

# Ancient Urban Planners

*Most archeologists agree that Mohenjo Daro, located in Sindh, Pakistan, was the largest settlement of the ancient Indus Valley Civilization, boasting a population of 40,000 people at its height. But recent findings in India may call that record into question.*

✳   ✳   ✳   ✳

THE NORTHERN INDIAN state of Haryana surrounds the country's capital state of Delhi (containing the capital, New Delhi) on the north, west, and south. Haryana is one of the smallest states in India, containing only about 1.4 percent of the country's land area, but the region is rich in culture, natural beauty, and ancient history.

A peek into this ancient history can be found in the village of Rakhigarhi, about 100 miles to the northwest of New Delhi. This site was once the location of an Indus Valley Civilization settlement, dating to between 2600 and 1900 BC. Along with ancient Egypt and Mesopotamia, the Indus Valley Civilization was one of the most important Bronze Age cultures, notable for its thoughtful urban planning that allowed the populations of its settlements to grow into the tens of thousands.

The ruins of some of these settlements, including Harappa in Punjab, Pakistan, and Mohenjo Daro in Sindh, Pakistan, were discovered in the late nineteenth and early twentieth centuries. Archeologists believe that each of these settlements was home to between 30,000 and 60,000 people, and Mohenjo Daro, covering around 600 acres, is one of the largest cities of the Indus Valley Civilization.

## Statues, Skeletons, and Seals

In the late 1960s, researchers discovered the Rakhigarhi site, and began excavations, which continue into the present. The site has proven to hold a treasure trove of Indus Valley artifacts, some more than 5,000 years old, including pottery, bricks, statues, copper fishhooks, jewelry, gold, and semiprecious stones. Also uncovered were several burial sites with complete skeletal remains dating to at least 4,600 years old. Rakhigarhi shows evidence of the Indus Valley Civilization's impressive urban planning, with paved roads, drainage systems, houses, and storage structures discovered. Some of the excavated houses feature brick-lined drains for removing sewage.

Amongst the pottery and jewelry and other artifacts found at Rakhigarhi are a large number of seals bearing what researchers have called the Indus script. Measuring between one to two inches long, the seals feature pictographic representations of animals and humans, similar to Egyptian hieroglyphics. But unlike Egyptian script, scholars have been unable to decipher the symbols on the seals found at Rakhigarhi, making them question whether the script is a language at all. Since most of the scripts are very short, some researchers theorize the writing was used by merchants as a form of accounting, or perhaps the marks denoted the property of specific people or families. For now, the Indus script remains a mystery, but scholars are hopeful that one day it will be deciphered and provide us with new insights into the Indus Valley Civilization.

According to many archeologists, the Rakhigarhi site covers an area of about 100 to 250 acres. But some researchers disagree with this assessment, estimating the actual area to be around 1,360 acres, or about 2.1 square miles. If this measurement is correct, it would make Rakhigarhi the largest Indus Valley Civilization settlement ever discovered. With only about five percent of the site currently excavated, there is still plenty to be discovered underneath the dusty soil of Rakhigarhi.

# Jars of the Giants

*According to a Laotian legend, there was once a giant named Khun Cheung, who ruled as king over his people. After winning a hard-fought battle, he created large stone jars to hold celebratory wine, which now sit in the foothills of the Xiangkhoang Plateau. But who really created these giant jars, and why?*

✻ ✻ ✻ ✻

XIANGKHOANG PROVINCE IN northeast Laos has the unfortunate distinction of being the most heavily bombed place on Earth. This is mostly due to the Laotian Civil War, fought between the Royal Lao Government and the Communist Pathet Lao between 1959 and 1975, in which U.S. forces, also fighting in Vietnam, dropped hundreds of millions of cluster bombs in the region.

One of the areas most affected was the Plain of Jars, an ancient site consisting of thousands of huge stone containers. The jars are spread out over at least 90 different sites on the plain, each site containing from one to 400 jars clustered together. The carved rock vessels range from three to almost ten feet tall and are mostly carved out of sandstone. The remainder are made up of granite, limestone, conglomerate, and breccia.

## Fire, Ash, and a Theory

The unusual jars were largely ignored by Westerners until the 1930s, when a French geologist named Madeleine Colani began exploring the location. Colani was intrigued by the giant jars, inside which she discovered colored glass beads, burnt teeth, and charred bone fragments. In the area just outside the containers, there were more human bones and glass beads, as well as pottery fragments, bronze and iron artifacts, ceramics, and charcoal. Nearby, Colani discovered a natural limestone cave, in which two openings had been dug out through the top. The presence of burned bone and ash in the cave led her to theorize that the cave had been used as a crematorium, with the holes in the top acting as a chimney for burning fires.

Piecing all of this information together, Colani concluded that the huge jars were probably used as funeral urns, perhaps for chieftains and other highly revered members of whatever community once lived there. She published her findings and theories about the Plain of Jars in the two-volume, 600-page work, *The Megaliths of Upper Laos*.

## Risky Research

Decades later, after the bombing raids had damaged or destroyed some of the stone vessels, archeological interest in the site began anew. In the 1990s, new excavations began in the area, some of it coinciding with bomb removal operations. While many researchers agreed with Colani's original theory about the jars, other suggestions have been proposed over the years. Some believe that the jars, which have been dated to between 1240 and 660 BC, were used to collect rainwater during the monsoon season, which would then be used by travelers passing through the region. The discovery of similar jar clusters stretching in a path all the way to India suggests they were part of a trade route, which may lend some credence to this idea. Other archeologists think the containers may have been nothing more than symbolic monuments that marked the site of nearby burials.

While many of the theories about the purpose of the giant jars seem plausible, the question of who created them still remains a mystery. Millions of unexploded bombs are still scattered in the region, making research of the vicinity difficult and dangerous. But work slowly continues to clear the ancient site of these hazards, increasing the likelihood that one day, the enigmatic people who created the Plain of Jars will get the recognition they deserve.

# A Circular Mystery

*The country of Jordan is probably best known for the archeological marvels found in Petra, including the famous Al-Khazneh rock-cut tomb. But the country's desert is also home to little-known wonders that have stumped scientists for decades.*

✳   ✳   ✳   ✳

THE INVENTION OF flying machines has been one of humanity's greatest accomplishments. With the ability to fly, we can travel to far-flung locations and see the world in a way that would have been impossible for our ancient ancestors. But this raises the question: Why would ancient peoples create large structures and designs, such as the Nazca Lines in Peru, that were only visible from such heights? Lionel Rees, a British pilot, may have been asking himself this very question when he flew over the Jordanian desert in the 1920s. From his plane window, Rees could make out the shape of several giant stone circles standing out from the dusty landscape. He took some pictures to document his discovery, but at the time, few archeologists showed interest in the strange circles and they were soon forgotten.

It took another 70 years before David Kennedy, a researcher from the University of Western Australia, caught wind of Rees' sighting in the desert and began working on documenting the archeological sites. By flying over the country and using satellite images, Kennedy and his team have found a total of 12 giant circles in Jordan, ranging from 720 to 1,490 feet in diameter. The structures consist mostly of field stones and boulders, stacked only a foot or two high, and while some are irregular in shape, others are nearly perfect circles.

## Unanswered Questions

Kennedy has theorized that in order to create the giant structures, at least a dozen workers would have been needed. The "architect" of the circles would have anchored a post of some sort into the ground, and tied a long rope to it. They then could have walked around the post holding the end of the rope, plotting the area to be used for the circular structure. The age of the circles is unknown, but they are thought to have been created between the Bronze Age and the seventh century, AD. One of the structures was later bisected by an ancient Roman road, suggesting that at least some of the circles existed before the Roman Empire.

With such limited information gleaned from the archeological sites, scientists are still unsure of who built the circles, exactly when they were built, or what purpose they could have served. Their stone walls would have been too low to use as corrals for animals, and no structures have ever been found within the walls. Kennedy and other scientists are scrambling to learn as much as they can as soon as possible, since land development and city expansions have begun threatening some of the structures. Some walls have already been partially destroyed, with modern roads wending across the circles and farmland encroaching around the edges.

With little data to go on and ever-dwindling sites, it is possible that the mystery of the Jordanian circles will never be solved.

# The Burnt City of Iran

*Archeologists often uncover interesting finds, such as pottery, weapons, and jewelry, that help them piece together the past lives of our ancestors. But the excavation of a 5000-year-old site in Iran has offered up some surprising artifacts that reveal a truly unique civilization that once flourished in the region.*

✳ ✳ ✳ ✳

THE LUT DESERT in southeastern Iran is one of the hottest places in the world, with temperatures as high as almost 160 degrees Fahrenheit recorded near the surface of its sands. But thousands of years ago, the climate in this region was much more hospitable, with marshland, rivers, and lakes providing water sources and cooler temperatures inviting human settlers.

It was near the eastern edge of this desert that Hungarian-British archeologist Aurel Stein discovered the ruins of a great civilization in the early 1900s. Although he brought attention to the region, it would take decades before other scientists began researching the site. Stein, who died in 1943, never got to see just how significant his find was.

The Bronze Age, mud-brick settlement spans around 494 acres, and is believed to have first been founded around 3200 BC, which would have made it one of the largest cities in the world at the time. Strangely, the city burned down and was rebuilt three times over the course of its existence, before finally being abandoned sometime between 2300 and 1800 BC. This led to its current name, *Shahr-i Sokhta*, meaning Burnt City.

## Pottery, Games, and Brain Surgery

The city was developed with several distinct zones, each with a different main purpose, displaying a complexity in urban planning never before seen in the area. These zones included a residential area, an industrial craftsman zone, a monumental area, and a cemetery, which is believed to hold between 25,000 and

40,000 graves. Archeologists theorize that the city was at the junction of a trade route with other Bronze Age cultures, a hypothesis supported by the different types of pottery found at the site, ranging from styles associated with Turkmenistan in the north, to Pakistan in the south, to Afghanistan in the east.

But the different pottery styles may be the least interesting artifacts discovered at Shahr-i Sokhta. Other finds include a ruler made of ebony wood that can precisely measure units of 1.5 millimeters, and what may be the world's first board game, complete with ancient dice and 60 playing pieces. Archeologists also uncovered a skull showing signs of having undergone brain surgery, another sign that this city was marked by significant civilizational achievement.

One of the most interesting finds is that of an earthen goblet which features sequential drawings of a goat leaping off the ground, eating leaves, and landing back on the ground. If viewed quickly in sequence, the pictures form an animated scene—possibly the first animation to ever be produced!

## The One-Eyed Woman

Perhaps the most intriguing discovery is the skeleton of a young woman, believed to be at least 4,800 years old. The woman is estimated to have been between the ages of 25 and 30 when she died, and she measures six feet tall—much taller than most women of her time. That in itself may have made the woman extraordinary, but her skull was found sporting a remarkable feature: the earliest known artificial eyeball. Scientists believe the eye was made of natural tar and animal fat, and it was covered in a thin layer of gold. A circle was carved in the center to represent the iris, and small holes were drilled in the sides of the eye through which a thin golden wire was threaded, which held the eye in place. It is unknown how the woman lost her eye, but due to her height and her golden prosthetic some have hypothesized that she was an important priestess. Most researchers, however, theorize that the woman was wealthy or a member of the city's nobility. But, like the story of how she lost her eye, the truth is unknown.

Why the creative, curious inhabitants of this carefully planned urban city chose to abandon it is still debated by scholars. Many believe that climate change caused nearby water sources to dry up, forcing the population to move. The dry desert air and dusty soil then preserved the many unique artifacts of the settlement for thousands of years. The details behind the rise and fall of Shahr-i Sokhta may remain a mystery, but this unusual city and its people were clearly ahead of their time.

# The Hidden Humanoids

*Humans have created and sculpted statues for thousands of years. From the Moai of Easter Island to Michelangelo's David, these representations of the human form are a testament to the creativity and determination of the people who carefully constructed them, even when their intended purpose is a mystery.*

✳   ✳   ✳   ✳

IN 1982, EXCAVATIONS began on the archeological site of Ain Ghazal, which had been discovered several years earlier as developers built a road to connect the Jordanian cities of Amman and Zarqa. Although the road construction had damaged some of the site, researchers were still able to learn much about the society that once lived there. The Neolithic settlement was first occupied around 7250 BC, and over the next 300 years the population grew from a few hundred to a few thousand. People lived in houses made of field stones covered with mud and lime plaster, which were then painted with red pigments. Crops like barley, chickpeas, lentils, and wheat were grown nearby, and domesticated goats were raised. Although at first, the settlers also foraged for additional plants and hunted various animals, over time they transitioned into a fully agrarian society, eating only the plants and animals they raised.

A year into the excavation of the settlement, archeologists were examining a path in the earth that had been carved out by a bulldozer when they discovered a pit dug eight feet down into the dirt. Inside the pit, they found a collection of humanoid statues. Two years later, they uncovered another pit filled with similar statues. In total, 15 full statues and 15 busts were found in the two pits, which had been created 200 years apart.

## Unknown Purpose

The statues were made by placing layers of lime plaster over bundles of reeds and grasses, which had been assembled into human-like shapes. The resulting figures are small, the largest being only about three feet tall, and their bodies lack detail. However, extra care was taken when sculpting the faces, which feature large, well-defined eyes lined in bitumen. It is believed that when they were first created, the figures were fitted with clothing, as imprints of woven articles are seen in some of the hardened plaster.

Because of the way the statues were made, researchers have theorized that they were not intended to last long. In fact, these figures seem to have been buried quite soon after being created, suggesting that they were only made for the sole purpose of being buried. But why would the people of Ain Ghazal go to the trouble of creating these statues only to then hide them underground?

One theory is that the statues were meant to represent the lives of the people who lived in the settlement. After the statues were created, they were perhaps used in some sort of religious ritual, and then buried, as if dead. This hypothesis is lent some credence by the discovery of human remains buried under the floors of houses. Some of the human skulls were even given masks made of the same lime plaster used to create the statues.

Regardless of what their true purpose was, the 9,000-year-old statues found in Ain Ghazal are notable for being one of the earliest examples of human figures created by Neolithic peoples. Today, these ancient examples of human creativity are on display in the Jordan Museum, the British Museum, the Louvre, and the Louvre Abu Dhabi.

# The Enigmatic Ostracon

*There are very few known written documents from tenth- and eleventh-century BC Jerusalem. So, when writing was found on a fragment of pottery—known as an ostracon—discovered in the area in 2008, researchers were excited to examine it. But the writing has proved to be much more difficult to decipher than anyone expected.*

✳   ✳   ✳   ✳

KHIRBET QEIYAFA, ALSO known as Elah Fortress, overlooks the Elah Valley about 20 miles southwest of Jerusalem. The six-acre site was largely ignored by scholars until 2007, when excavations of the area began in earnest. They revealed the remains of an Iron Age city, dated to between 1050 and 915 BC, encircled by a 2,300-foot-long stone wall.

Archeologists have offered several theories about the site's origins, with many believing it to be a biblical city, possibly either Sha'arayim, Neta'im, or Azekah. The dates of the city's occupation would coincide with the reign of King David, who may have at one time lived in an apartment in the center of the highest point of the city. But not all scholars agree with this assessment, and some suggest the site was not a walled city, but rather a walled-off cultic compound.

Within the city—whether it was the home of King David or a gathering place for cultists—archeologists found an artifact that has prompted much discussion. In one of the many rooms of the city, they found a fragment of pottery, measuring about 6 inches by 6.5 inches, on which an inscription was written. The exciting find is considered the longest Proto-Canaanite text ever discovered, and yet no one is quite sure what it says.

## A Mystery Message

Some scholars have suggested that the inscription is a list of names, or perhaps a list of random words. These words could have been part of a writing exercise which novice scribes were required to learn to practice their craft. Others have offered much more detailed translations, believing the text encourages its reader to care for slaves, widows, and orphans. This theory has been supported by the University of Haifa, which pointed to the inclusion of what appear to be Hebrew words in the text. But because the ostracon is not complete and some of the text is faded, it is difficult to know whose interpretation is the correct one.

While scholars may not agree on a translation, they do agree that the ostracon proves that humans were learning, writing, and reading in the Holy Land more than 3,000 years ago. Perhaps one day, we'll understand exactly what they were trying to say.

# The Ruins of Sirwah

*In late 2014, a civil war broke out between two rival political factions in Yemen. Both claimed to be the official government of the country. A tense ceasefire in 2022 briefly lessened the fighting, but some areas of the country—including many containing ancient archeological treasures—remain dangerous destinations. Sirwah is unfortunately one of those destinations.*

✻    ✻    ✻    ✻

THE ANCIENT YEMENI city of Sirwah was located between the high mountains in the western part of the country and the vast deserts in the east. The site was considered the second most important city in the kingdom of Saba, believed by some to be the biblical land of Sheba, which was founded sometime around 1200 BC. The Sabaeans were engaged in the spice trade of the time, selling frankincense and myrrh, and were believed to practice a religion with customs similar to Islam. King

Yada'il Dharih I, a seventh-century BC Sabaean ruler, chose Sirwah as the location for a temple in honor of Almaqah, the Sabaean moon god.

But for all that is known about Sirwah and the Sabaeans, far more is unknown. Any artifact or ruin that is uncovered in the area is considered a huge find to archeologists, but one discovery has the literal distinction of being "huge."

## Protecting What's Important

In the middle of the ruins of the temple of Almaqah, whose six-pillared portico and smooth stone floors still stand, an almost 23-foot-long inscription was found. Austrian archeologist Eduard Glaser first made the discovery in 1888, and he and an assistant spent days meticulously copying the text and taking pages of notes. More than a hundred years later, in 2005, researchers unearthed another inscription within the ruins. Together, these two inscriptions are considered the longest and most important Sabaean writings found in Yemen to date.

The inscriptions, carved into huge blocks of stone that once stood as a central feature of the temple, date back to between 685 and 715 BC, and they talk in detail about wars fought by the Sabaean army, including numbers of people killed and prisoners taken, and mention place names that still exist today. The inscriptions also describe construction work on an irrigation system, a sophisticated project for the time.

The city of Sirwah was abandoned around AD 290 after it was defeated by the southern Himyarite tribe, its temples, towers, and city walls forgotten for thousands of years. Today, archeologists mourn the irreparable damage to the structures wrought by the rockets and shrapnel of the civil war, and are often unable to reach excavation sites due to ongoing conflict. Sirwah was added to the UNESCO World Heritage List in 2023, in an effort to protect the endangered ancient city. Hopefully peace will prevail soon, and Sirwah will continue to reveal the story of its ancient past.

# The Jericho Skulls

*Almost 10,000 years ago, the biblical city of Jericho, today located in the West Bank, was one of the biggest settlements in the Middle East. Excavations in the area have been ongoing since the 1800s, giving researchers insights into the lives of the people who once lived there. But one discovery has been particularly eye-opening.*

✳ ✳ ✳ ✳

IN 1953, BRITISH archeologist Kathleen Kenyon was leading excavations of Tell es-Sultan, also known as ancient Jericho. Kenyon and her team made some remarkable discoveries, including 17 walls dating to the Bronze Age and the Tower of Jericho, a 28-foot-tall Neolithic stone structure considered to be one of the earliest stone monuments built by humans.

But one of Kenyon's most significant findings was a collection of human skulls, which had been covered in plaster to mimic faces, with small shells used for the eyes. Some of the skulls showed evidence of paint that once recreated hair, facial features, and mustaches.

The skulls are believed to have been created around 9,000 years ago, making them, as one researcher put it, "the first evidence of facial reconstruction in the world." They are also one of the earliest examples of sculpted portraits in the art world.

## New Technology, New Life

The skulls are thought to have been part of a burial ritual that was commonplace within the settlement, wherein the deceased were often buried under the floors of homes. Researchers aren't sure why certain skulls were removed and used to create plaster sculptures, as all ages and genders seem to be represented. But one hypothesis is that the skulls were a form of ancestor worship, and were a way for the people of Jericho to show their veneration for the dead. Signs of wear on the skulls suggest that they were often handled, and it is believed that they may have been passed down through generations, until they were eventually respectfully reburied as symbols of long-dead ancestors.

Recent technology has been able to give new life to some of these ancient citizens of Jericho, as scientists have used X-rays, CT scans, digital imaging, and 3D printers to recreate faces from the skulls. One such recreation, that of a man who lived and died at least 9,000 years ago, was recently on display at the British Museum. These methods have also revealed a peculiar characteristic in many of the skulls—an artificially elongated shape. Scientists believe that this was caused by binding the head in childhood, but why this practice was performed is a complete mystery.

More than 50 Jericho skulls have been unearthed in the area, their shell eyes gazing into a past that's still unclear. But with new technologies and curious researchers determined to learn more, there's no doubt these ancient faces have many more stories to tell.

# The Eyes Have It

*In the late 1930s, archeologists unearthed some unusual artifacts in northeastern Syria. Known as "eye idols," hundreds of the figures were found in a single location. But why so many of these idols were created, and why no other examples have been found elsewhere, are questions that remain unanswered.*

\* \* \* \*

EYES HAVE BEEN a recurring theme throughout much of artistic history. Ancient Egyptian art often featured the "eye of Horus" to represent protection, fertility, royalty, and good health. Byzantine portraits paid particular attention to the eyes, as they were said to symbolize a portal to the afterlife. In the eighteenth century, "lover's eyes," tiny portraits of eyes that could be worn on rings, pendants, or brooches, were a popular fad. And the eyes of daVinci's famous *Mona Lisa* seem to have been painted with the viewer in mind, having an uncanny ability to follow the gaze of whoever looks upon her. Certainly, eyes held significance for the creators of these works.

So, when British archeologist Max Mallowan (also known for being novelist Agatha Christie's husband) began excavating Tell Brak in Syria in 1937, he was probably not surprised to uncover an idol featuring huge carved eyes. But then he found another, and another, and soon it was evident that these "eye idols" had been a particularly important part of the culture around Tell Brak, which was one of the largest settlements in early Mesopotamia around 3500 BC.

## View to a Mystery

Hundreds of the eye idols were uncovered in what is now called the "Eye Temple." The figures are very small, no more than 2.5 inches tall, and were created from various materials including limestone, soapstone, alabaster, and baked clay. Many of the figures feature a flat, trapezoidal body and a thin neck supporting huge, oversized eyes.

Some idols have more than one set of eyes, while others have smaller eyes and bodies carved into the larger trapezoidal body shape, presumably to represent children. Scholars theorize that the idols may have been personalized by individuals, as their appearance varies widely. Some appear to have carved lines and zigzags to represent jewelry and clothes.

Tell Brak, also known as Nagar or Nawar, was an international city during its time, having cultural and trade relationships with several different cultures in southern Mesopotamia. Archeologists believe the city became a religious pilgrimage site, where worshipers would come to honor the deity Belet Nagar and visit the Eye Temple, perhaps leaving an eye idol as an offering.

The temple itself resembles other temples discovered in ancient Mesopotamian cities like Uruk and Eridu; however, while eye symbolism was common in Mesopotamia at the time, no other artifacts like the eye idols of Tell Brak have ever been found in the region.

The origins and reasoning behind the eye idols are a mystery even Agatha Christie, who often accompanied her husband on digs, never solved. Most archeologists believe the figures were offerings to gods, but why all the figures feature oversized eyes is anyone's guess. Some even insist that the prominent features represent aliens who visited Earth in ancient times. Sadly, parts of Tell Brak and some of its unusual artifacts have been destroyed by the much more terrestrial threat of civil unrest in Syria. Still, many of the eye idols can be found in museums around the world, where visitors can see these unique artifacts that appear to see right back.

# The Written Records of Uruk

*The ancient city of Uruk, located in what is now Iraq, is considered by some historians to be the "first city in world history." A discovery made in this urban metropolis suggests that the people of Uruk were not only the first to create a city, but the first to create a writing system, as well.*

✳   ✳   ✳   ✳

AT THE HEIGHT of its power, around 3100 BC, the city of Uruk boasted a population of around 40,000 inhabitants, with another 80,000 to 90,000 living in the surrounding areas. Its location along the Euphrates River made it a prime location for cultivating grains and other crops, along with trade, which gave the city—the largest urban area in the world at the time— a distinct advantage over other Mesopotamian settlements. As the population grew and its agriculture flourished, the people of Uruk found themselves in need of a reliable way to keep track of their grain stores, the trade they engaged in, and other important details of everyday life in the busy city.

This, according to many archeologists, is how the very first writing system in the world was developed, created before cuneiform. Cuneiform, named for the Latin word *cuneus,* meaning "wedge," was written by using reeds to make wedge-shaped marks on a clay tablet. This system was used to write several ancient languages, including Sumerian, Aramaic, and Old Persian. But before cuneiform was adopted by these civilizations, the people of Uruk developed a "proto-cuneiform" system of writing.

## Early Accountants

Proto-cuneiform consisted of basic pictographic depictions of numbers, people, and places, and was often used as an administrative tool, such as to keep economic records of livestock and grain. Archeologists have unearthed approximately 6,000 proto-cuneiform tablets in and around Uruk, which give a glimpse into the daily life of the ancient city. The earliest known writings recorded amounts of grain, livestock, fish, and beer, or listed names of city officials and their occupations. As time went on, some of the pictographs evolved to not only represent their intended meaning, but also a sound or group of sounds. To use an example from English, this would be similar to a picture of an eye referring either to a literal "eye," or to the pronoun "I."

Researchers have identified around 2,000 proto-cuneiform symbols, including 1,100 that represent individual ideas or items—the earliest "words"—and 600 complex combinations of more than one symbol. The fact that the vast majority of the Uruk tablets concern administrative matters suggests that the city's rapid growth and a need for organization prompted the development of the civilization's writing. It would take another 700 years or so for writing to advance into a more literary form, when religious texts, historical documents, letters, and stories would begin to emerge. But the proto-cuneiform writing system of Uruk paved the way for more significant leaps in humanity's development of communication.

# Kenyan Cave Exploration

*According to scientists, all humans living today can trace their origins to Africa, making the continent an important source of artifacts and information from our past. The Panga ya Saidi cave in Kenya is one location that has proven to be especially enlightening, offering evidence of human activity for at least 78,000 years.*

✳    ✳    ✳    ✳

ABOUT NINE MILES from the Indian Ocean, along the southeastern coast of Kenya, sits the Panga ya Saidi Cave. Perched on a bluff close to lush tropical forests and grassy savannahs, the flora and fauna of the area has changed little over many tens of thousands of years. But it wasn't until 2010 that scientists took a serious interest in the ancient cave and wondered what it could tell us about the history of the area. That year, archeologists from both the German Max Planck Institute for the Science of Human History and the National Museums of Kenya partnered to explore and excavate the cave.

Working through 19 layers of stratified soil, the researchers found a wealth of evidence pointing to human activity. The earliest layers, which date back 78,000 years, were found to have bone fragments, mollusk shells, ash deposits, and charcoal flakes, hinting at sporadic human occupation of the area for thousands of years. Later layers featured remains of houses, including collapsed walls and roofs, as well as cooking hearths, stone tools, and evidence of crops like millet and sorghum.

## Mtoto's Burial

But perhaps the most remarkable find in the Panga ya Saidi cave is what is known as the oldest modern human burial in Africa. Ten feet below the current cave floor, archeologists discovered a small pit containing a cluster of bones. The bones were so old, decayed, and fragile that scientists weren't even sure they were human. They immediately worked to carefully preserve and protect the bones so they could be moved to a laboratory for analysis.

Once they began to study the remains, researchers confirmed that the bones, were, in fact, human. They belonged to a small child, around two to three years old. The scientists named this human *Mtoto*, meaning "child" in Swahili. As researchers painstakingly continued excavating the remains in the lab, they discovered that Mtoto had been deliberately buried shortly after his death, just as in modern burial. He had also been placed in the burial pit with a support under his head, possibly a pillow, and arranged on his right side with his knees drawn toward his chest, suggesting that Mtoto's burial had been carefully thought out and planned.

The burial of Mtoto, similar to burials of Neanderthals discovered in Eurasia, shows us that funeral rites for the dead seems to be a cultural practice shared by all early humans. There is little doubt that the Panga ya Saidi cave will continue to offer up insight into the past that we all share.

# The Birds of God

*The flag of Zimbabwe features green, red, yellow, and black stripes and a prominent golden bird sitting on a pedestal. This same symbol can be found on the country's money, stamps, passports, and in more than 100 corporate and sports logos. How did this bird come to be Zimbabwe's most recognized emblem?*

✳   ✳   ✳   ✳

THE RUINS OF the city of Great Zimbabwe, located near the southeastern city of Masvingo, were first explored by Europeans in the late nineteenth century. The area is believed to have originally been settled in the fourth century, but the stone enclosures and towers that caught the interest of archeologists were constructed between the eleventh and fourteenth centuries. The city was built by people of the Gokomere culture, the predecessors to the modern Shona people of Zimbabwe, and at its cultural height was home to at least 10,000 inhabitants.

The name Zimbabwe is believed to be derived from the Shona words *Dzimba-dza-mabwe*, meaning "houses of stone." The city covers an area of about 2.7 square miles and features impressive stacked-stone walls, some as high as 36 feet, that were built without the aid of mortar. Researchers believe Great Zimbabwe was home to a royal palace and was a center for political power and trade. This theory is supported by the many artifacts found at the site, including elaborately carved beads, bracelets, and pendants made of ivory and gold, as well as glass beads and porcelain from China and Persia. Ivory and gold were the main items traded with other cultures, and the amount of gold extracted from the ground in the city is estimated to be around 20 million ounces.

## Colonial Controversy

But the most notable artifacts found within these "houses of stone" were not made of gold or ivory. In 1889, a European hunter named Willi Posselt traveled to Great Zimbabwe to explore the city after hearing rumors of its treasures. After climbing through the ruins, he discovered a collection of eight soapstone birds set in the ground around an altar. Each bird measured about 16 inches tall and was perched atop a three-foot-tall column, all carved out of a single piece of stone.

While Posselt's discovery was significant, his subsequent actions, as well as the actions of other Europeans, have been a source of controversy for decades. As local tribesmen looked on, Posselt dug out one of the soapstone birds and then sold it to British mining magnate Cecil Rhodes, today best known for his creation of the Rhodes Scholarship.

Rhodes was so intrigued by the bird that he mounted it in the library of his house, Groote Schuur, in Cape Town, South

Africa, and commissioned an excavation of the ruins of Great Zimbabwe. Eventually, he came into possession of four more of the soapstone birds.

## Waiting for Home

While Rhodes believed the birds to be Phoenician in origin, most scholars today attribute the carvings to the ancestors of the Shona people. Their meaning, however, is still debated. Some think a bird was carved every time a new king came to power, but others think the birds merely represented an animal that was sacred to the Shona. Most think the bird probably represents a bateleur eagle, which, in the Shona religion, was believed to be a messenger from Mwari, the Supreme Creator god, and an omen of good luck.

Even before Zimbabwe gained its independence in 1981, the Great Zimbabwe bird had national significance. It was featured on the coat of arms of Rhodesia, the flag of Rhodesia, and Rhodesian money. Some call the bird *Shiri ya Mwari*, or the "bird of God," and consider it a symbol of Zimbabwean freedom. According to legend, the country will never experience true peace until every Great Zimbabwe bird has been returned to its homeland.

Four of the stone birds that had been sent to Rhodes in South Africa were returned to Zimbabwe in 1981. Fragments of other birds had made their way to Germany in the early 1900s, and the last of these was returned to Zimbabwe in 2003. This leaves only one bird that has yet to return to its country of origin: the bird that first intrigued Rhodes and prompted his exploration of Great Zimbabwe. This bird still sits in the library of Groote Schuur, waiting for the day it can fly back to its ancestral home.

# Stories in the Sahara

*The Sahara Desert is the largest hot-weather desert in the world, dwarfed only by the "deserts" of Antarctica and the Arctic. But the area hasn't always been an arid desert. Thousands of years ago, trees, grasses, and lakes were common features in the region, providing a more comfortable climate for humans, who left behind permanent evidence of their daily lives.*

✻   ✻   ✻   ✻

Tassili n'Ajjer is a national park in the Sahara Desert, spanning 28,000 square miles across southeastern Algeria. The highest point in the park sits at an elevation of 7,080 feet, at the peak of Jebel Azao, also known as Adrar Afao. The combination of the high elevation and the region's porous sandstone, which can retain large quantities of water, allows vegetation to grow more readily on the eastern side of the park than in other areas of the desert. Thanks to this characteristic, Tassili n'Ajjer is known for its cypress and myrtle trees, and is classified by UNESCO as a Biosphere Reserve.

But Tassili n'Ajjer is even better known for the drier areas of the park, which have been noted for their unusual lunar features. Deep gorges, sprawling forests of rock, and almost 300 natural rock arches dot the area. It was in this landscape, in the early 1900s, that Westerners first laid eyes on the abundance of engravings and paintings that adorn the rock throughout the park. In total, 15,000 pieces of rock art have been identified in the area, mostly dating between 10,000 and 1,000 years old, with some dating back as much as 12,000 years.

## Rock Records

Archeologists have categorized the rock art into five time periods, which are noted as Archaic, Round Head, Pastoral, Horse, and Camel. Each category corresponds with the main type of art produced during the time period. Archaic, which spans from 10,000 to 7500 BC, depicts mostly large wild animals, including antelopes, sheep, and crocodiles, in a simplistic etching style. The "Round Head" period, as its name suggests, features human figures with round heads and is the earliest painted art, created between 7500 and 5050 BC. Humans are depicted dancing, hunting, and participating in masked ceremonies, and while wild animals are often shown, there are also early examples of animal domestication.

The Pastoral period art, created between 4500 and 4000 BC, corresponds with the domestication of animals, and features cattle, sheep, goats, and dogs. The art of this time also suggests that humans were forming nomadic groups due to climate shifts in the Sahara. Differences in style in the Pastoral period rock art reflects the different cultural groups who moved through the area. The Horse and Camel periods overlapped, beginning in 2000 BC and continuing past 1000 BC, and corresponded with the desertification of the Sahara. As the climate became less hospitable, humans sought new ways to travel through the desert. Their rock art first depicted horses and horse-drawn chariots, and then camels, which came to be the preferred mode of transportation across the sands.

## Timely Art

One of the most interesting aspects of the Tassili n'Ajjer rock art is how the engravings and paintings clearly show the progression of climate change, animal migrations, and the evolution of human life in the Sahara. The oldest art depicts water-dependent animals such as hippopotamuses and crocodiles and shows humans engaging in hunting and gathering. Later art features the camels that became the main source of transport for trade caravans across the desert and depicts men outfitted with swords, shields, and spears.

Because of the huge range in time between the first pieces of rock art and the last, and the fact that the humans in the area made no permanent settlements but rather lived nomadic lifestyles, researchers are unsure of which cultural groups were responsible for the thousands of examples of rock art in the region. In 1982, Tassili n'Ajjer was added to UNESCO's World Heritage Site list, ensuring that these extraordinary pieces of art will be protected and preserved for as long as possible.

# The Benin Bronzes

*For thousands of years, cultures around the world have found ways to record important events and time lines. Whether oral storytelling passed down through generations or journals written on parchment, these records provide researchers with vital information. But one kingdom in Africa found a way to take historical archives and turn them into true works of art.*

✳ ✳ ✳ ✳

THE KINGDOM OF Benin was established in 1180 and lasted until 1897, when it was annexed by the United Kingdom. Not to be confused with the modern country of Benin, the Kingdom of Benin was located in what is now southern Nigeria. The kingdom was founded by the Edo people, who originally called it *Igodomigodo*. Their kings were referred to as *Ogisos* ("kings of the sky") and later *Oba*, meaning "ruler." One of these kings, Oba Ewuare, who ruled from 1440 to 1473, commissioned a great wall to circle the capital city of Edo, now known as Benin City. Discovered by archeologists in the 1960s, this earthen wall stretched for seven miles around the center of the capital, and was surrounded by a 20-foot-deep moat.

Smaller earthen walls were found throughout the region, the wending and winding ramparts adding up to an astounding 4,000 to 8,000 miles total. These walls would have taken hundreds of years to build, and researchers theorize that they marked the borders of towns and cities as the kingdom expanded. By the fifteenth century, the Kingdom of Benin was a center of political and military power, which grew wealth through trade with not only other African kingdoms, but with Europeans, as well.

## A Story Set in Bronze

The kingdom traded pepper, cloth, ivory, and iron with other cultures, but it was most famous for its artistic expression, especially plaques and other sculptures that today are known as the Benin Bronzes. These metal sculptures date to between the thirteenth and sixteenth centuries, and consist mostly of plaques depicting warriors, kings, animals, and scenes of the kingdom's history, but also include portrait heads and jewelry. "Bronzes" is a bit of a misnomer, since the majority of pieces consist of brass mixed with other materials, as bronze itself was often difficult to obtain. The pieces were expertly crafted by specialist metalworking guilds, who used the lost wax casting technique to create the art.

The Benin Bronzes were often commissioned by Obas to honor their predecessors, and new bronzes were also created to commemorate new Obas. But the most well-known pieces are the plaques that display historical records of the Kingdom of Benin. Once lining the hallways of the Oba's sprawling palace in Edo, the plaques record the history of the royal families who lived there, as well as the social history of the kingdom. Of particular interest to many researchers are the depictions of the kingdom's first diplomatic contacts and trade with Europeans, mainly the Portuguese. By studying the plaques, a story of relationships between different cultures can be pieced together, from first contacts to profitable trading arrangements.

## A Slow Journey Home

When the Kingdom of Benin was annexed by the United Kingdom in 1897, the British looted centuries of art from the royal palace and other residences. This controversial move resulted in most of the bronzes winding up in British, German, and American museums. After Nigeria gained its independence in 1960, the Benin Bronzes began to make their way back home, although in some cases the Nigerian government was forced to pay for the artwork. In more recent times, bronzes that had been on display at the University of Aberdeen, the

Metropolitan Museum of Art, and the Smithsonian Institution were repatriated to Nigeria. But the largest collections of the artifacts are still found at the British Museum in London and the Ethnological Museum of Berlin.

In the last weeks of his administration in early 2023, Nigeria's President Muhammadu Buhari declared that the fortieth Oba of Benin, Ewuare II, is the sole owner of the Benin Bronzes. The Oba, who admits that the display of the bronzes around the world has served to introduce Benin culture internationally, nonetheless hopes to one day have all of the bronzes back in Nigeria, where he intends to build a museum near the royal palace to showcase their splendor.

# Masks of Mali

*The traditions and rituals practiced by cultures around the globe teach us about the unique differences, as well as similarities, of humans. Although these traditions often change drastically over the centuries, one group in northern Africa still engages in a masked ceremony that began a thousand years ago.*

✳   ✳   ✳   ✳

MALI, THE EIGHTH-LARGEST country in Africa, is located on the western side of the continent and is surrounded by Algeria, Niger, and Mauritania in the north, east, and northwest, and Burkina Faso, Cote d'Ivoire, Guinea, and Senegal in the south and west. In the central, southeastern region of the country lies the Bandiagara Escarpment, a sandstone cliff that rises 1,600 feet above a sandy plain. Dozens of villages are located along the escarpment, which today are home to the Dogon people.

The Dogon villages were first established around a thousand years ago, as Muslims began conquering land in northern Africa and converting inhabitants. The escarpment, with its natural caves and underground tunnels, was a perfect retreat for the Dogon people, who were much more familiar with the location than outsiders. This allowed the people and their religious traditions to thrive, and over the centuries the Dogon became known for their architecture, their sculpture, and, especially, their masks.

The Dogon are said to have more than 70 types of masks that are used in ritual dances and religious rites, the most famous of which is called a *kanaga* mask. A kanaga mask features a double-barred cross with shorter, vertical bars projecting from each horizontal bar. The design has been interpreted by some to be an animal, such as a bird or lizard, but it is also considered a reflection of the god Amma, considered to be the creator god of the Dogon.

## Traditions and Secret Societies

For a millennium, the masks of the Dogon have been used for funeral rituals known as *dama*. The Dogon believe that performing these rituals increases the respect and honor for the deceased as well as for their descendants. The rituals are performed over six days, ending with traditional masked dancers escorting the souls of the dead out of the village so they can enter the spiritual realm. Dama rituals are performed years, or even decades, after a death, due to the cost and the elaborate preparations needed, and in modern times these rituals are sometimes performed for tourists to provide income to the tribe.

These ancient rituals, and the masks required to perform them, are so important to the Dogon that most of the men in the village are initiated into *Awa*, or the Society of Masks. The society has a strict code of ethics for its members and even a secret language, known as *sigi so*, from which the word awa—referring to both the masks and the dancers—is derived. While the Awa Society has a certain political influence over the Dogon, its most important role is in the dama rituals and the creation of its unique masks.

Dogon masks, including the distinctive *kanaga*, can be seen in museums around the world. These artifacts serve as a reminder of the remarkable and diverse history of the human race.

# Millions of Years in the Making

*In 1974, paleoanthropologist Donald Johanson was exploring northeastern Ethiopia when he noticed a bone sticking out of the dirt. The bone would turn out to belong to a hominin called Australopithecus afarensis, now known to be one of our earliest ancestors. Affectionately named Lucy, her story, and the story of others like her, is still unfolding today.*

＊　＊　＊　＊

IN ETHIOPIA, A landlocked country in eastern Africa, archeologists and anthropologists have long discovered evidence of humanity's past. Not only is the country one of the oldest in the world, but some scientists believe that this may be the area in which modern humans first emerged millions of years ago. Lucy, dated to about 3.2 million years ago, may be the most famous of the fossils discovered in the country, and her bones encompass the best-preserved and most complete fossils found, but she is not the oldest. That distinction goes to *Ardipithecus ramidus*, believed to be around 4.2 million years old. By studying the leg bones of these finds, scientists have determined that they most likely walked on two feet. But it was unknown whether these ancient ancestors shared some of our more complex traits, such as our ability to use tools. Once again, Ethiopia seemed to provide an answer when archeologists in the town of Bouri uncovered animal bones, dated to 2.6 million years ago, with distinctive cut marks.

The marks on the bones were easily distinguishable from marks that would have been created by natural sources, such as being trampled by animals, due to a distinctive "V" shape and sharply defined edges. The find seemed to confirm that early humans were using tools millions of years ago.

## From Bones to Phones

Then, in 2000, while working in the same region of Ethiopia—the Afar region in the northeastern portion of the country—archeologists discovered two 3.3-million-year-old bones in Dikika. These fossilized remains were named "Selam." This hominin was found to be about 120,000 years older than Lucy.

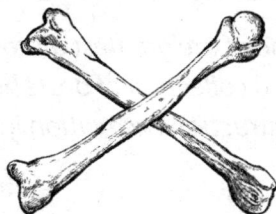

While this discovery was impressive enough, the discovery of more animal bones nearby was also revolutionary. The bones featured marks similar to the cuts found in the bones from Bouri, but scientists were cautious about assuming they were tool marks, due to the age of the fossils. But one researcher, University of Chicago paleoanthropologist Dr. Zeresenay Alemseged, believes the evidence is conclusive: The cut marks are proof that early humans used tools many thousands of years earlier than originally thought.

According to Alemseged, the fossil marks were made when our early ancestors used stone tools to remove meat from the bones and to break them to extract marrow. The researcher even believes that Selam, who was found a mere 218 yards away from the bones, may have been one of the humans who helped to butcher the animals with other members of her family.

While the use of simple stone tools may not seem impressive by contemporary standards, it was this first step that led to the creation of more complex tools and encouraged more sophisticated skills. These, in turn, eventually transformed into humanity's penchant for problem-solving and creativity, giving us inventions like cars, microwaves, and microchips. So, the next time you're scrolling through social media on your smart phone, remember that its creation was 3.4 million years in the making. Perhaps we should thank Lucy, Selam, and their families for paving the way to our modern world.

# Heads of the Gods

*Some of the greatest discoveries in history have been accidental.
And a collection of brass heads, found by accident during a
construction excavation in Ife, Nigeria, is no exception.*

✳ ✳ ✳ ✳

THE CITY OF Ife lies in the southwestern region of Nigeria,
and was founded by the Yoruba people sometime between
the tenth and sixth centuries BC. According to legend, the
city, and the world itself, was founded by a divine spirit named
Obatala, who was given the task of creation by the Supreme
God Olorun. But when Obatala was negligent in his task, his
brother, Oduduwa, took over, creating a new dynasty of sons
and daughters who then became the rulers, or *Ooni*, of the
Yoruba people.

During a construction project in Ife in 1938, a collection of
brass and copper heads were unearthed. The most famous
of these heads is now on display at the British Museum in
London, and features a head rendered in a naturalistic style,
topped with a crown decorated with beads, tassels, and a
rosette. The leaded zinc-brass head, like all of the heads uncovered at Ife, was created using the lost wax casting technique.
Archeologists theorize that the head depicts Oduduwa, or perhaps another Ooni, who, according to Yoruba religious tradition, are all said to be descended from the original creator god.

## A Head Above the Rest

The head was created sometime between the fourteenth and
fifteenth centuries, a time of prosperity for the Yoruba people,
who traded metals, ivory, and glass beads with other civilizations along the Niger River. The head, and the others like it,
may have been created at the request of the Third Ooni of Ife,
Obalufon Alayemore. As the Yoruba people still consider him
to be a descendant of the gods, Obalufon is today known as the
patron deity of brass casters. He is also associated with a brass

mask discovered in Ife, known as the Obalufon mask, which shares many similarities with the Ife heads.

When the heads were discovered, there was a pervasive belief amongst Western scholars that ancient African civilizations were not capable of such complex artistic processes. Some even insisted that the heads were created by the ancient Greeks. But today, archeologists agree that not only were the heads created by indigenous Africans, but they were most likely produced in a single workshop by one artist.

The Ife head has become a recognizable symbol in Nigeria, often used in branding for corporations and educational institutions, and is considered one of the best examples of artistic achievement in the country.

# The Question of Pedra Furada

*While the "Clovis First" theory still has some adherents and continues to be debated amongst some archeologists, discoveries like Pedra Furada in Brazil provide a tantalizing counter-history suggesting that humans arrived much, much earlier.*

✳   ✳   ✳   ✳

IN 1973, BRAZILIAN archeologist Niede Guidon began exploring the area around the state of Piaui in northeastern Brazil. A decade earlier, Guidon had seen photos of unusual rock art in Piaui, and she was curious to see the art with her own eyes. While excavating an area that is now the southeastern portion of Serra da Capivara National Park, Guidon and her team discovered a collection of more than 900 rock shelters, including one that stretched to 55 feet deep, covered in hundreds of prehistoric paintings.

Over the next 13 years, Guidon continued exploring the area, uncovering thousands of flaked tools, charcoal deposits, and a structure that seemed to be a man-made hearth, dating back to 48,700 years ago. Testing over time has confirmed the age of the ancient site, with some results even suggesting the artifacts may date back to as much as 60,000 years, far predating the Clovis culture. The rock paintings, created with red ochre and burned bone charcoal, number more than 1,150, and date back between 5,000 and 11,000 years ago. The paintings, which are scattered throughout the hundreds of rock shelters, feature animals such as deer, turtles, llamas, and iguanas, and human forms that appear to be hunting, dancing, and fighting.

## Questions and Theories

Guidon divided the site and its artifacts into three phases according to their dates. The pre-Clovis phase is known as *Pedra Furada*. The middle phase, dating between 12,000 and 7,000 years ago, is *Serra Talhada*, and the earliest phase is called *Agreste*. But not all scholars agree that Pedra Furada is proof of a pre-Clovis culture. One critic, American archeologist James Adovasio, claims that the flaked stone tools found at the site were more likely created by natural means.

Adovasio theorizes that the "tools" resulted from rocks falling from cliffs and shattering when they hit the ground. Another theory concerns the wild bearded capuchin monkeys that are often seen in the area. These monkeys have been observed smashing stones against larger rocks, creating flakes that might resemble the artifacts uncovered by Guidon. Adovasio has also theorized that the charcoal found in the area may have come from natural forest fires, as opposed to man-made fires.

But Guidon remains steadfast in her belief that Pedra Furada was once home to some of the earliest humans in the Americas. Contrary to the usual theories that propose an overland migration from Asia, Guidon suggests these humans may have come by boat from Africa as far back as 100,000 years ago. Regardless of who is correct about Pedra Furada, recent finds across the Americas continue to challenge the "Clovis First" theory, showing us that we still have much to learn about our ancient history.

# The Bay of Jars

*Many of us have heard the old children's rhyme, "In 1492, Columbus sailed the ocean blue." The story of Christopher Columbus' journey to the Americas is as familiar to us as tales about other explorers like Lewis and Clark, Neil Armstrong, and Amelia Earhart. But we have known for some time that Columbus wasn't the first European to set foot in the Americas. Who was?*

✳ ✳ ✳ ✳

RIO DE JANEIRO's Guanabara Bay has achieved notoriety in recent years for all the wrong reasons. Although the area features breathtaking views of the surrounding green mountains and city skyline—and is spectacularly visible from the top of the city's most recognizable tourist attraction, the Christ the Redeemer sculpture—it has also become a terribly polluted health hazard. Garbage and sewage that end up in the water from the surrounding area, populated by more than 11 million people, is a big part of the problem. But another issue concerns the dozens of abandoned ships and wrecks that have been left in the bay to disintegrate, leaking fuel and other toxic chemicals into the water.

But in the early 1980s, amidst these rusting, dilapidated ships, a mystery unfolded. In 1982, marine archeologist Robert Marx, who had gained notoriety 20 years earlier when he recreated Columbus' voyage across the Atlantic in an exact replica of the *Niña*, was scuba diving in Guanabara Bay when he discovered something unusual. Far from shore, located underneath 100 feet of water, Marx found a collection of what appeared to be Roman amphorae, large ceramic jars which were designed to nestle together to be safely transported across the sea. But Roman amphorae were used most often several thousand years ago in the Mediterranean region, long before the first European to visit Brazil, Portuguese navigator Pedro Alvares Cabral, arrived in 1500.

## A Cover-up or a Hoax?

Marx dug through three feet of mud to uncover pieces of the amphorae, and found other pieces attached to nearby coral and rock formations. He theorized that the jars came from an ancient Roman shipwreck, and believed they proved that Europeans visited the Americas thousands of years earlier than previously believed. But skeptics were quick to question Marx's claims, as no other archeologists were able to examine the artifacts in person. Some, including the Brazilian government, accused him of being more of a "treasure hunter" than an archeologist, believing he was more interested in fame and fortune than science. Marx countered by making the accusation that the Brazilian government (which had strong ties to Portugal and made it easier for Portuguese immigrants to obtain citizenship) wanted to cover up the unusual Roman find. The country had a high rate of immigration from Italy, and the argument was that Italian immigrants might use the discovery to demand an easier process of naturalization.

The story became even more complicated when a Brazilian businessman named Americo Santarelli claimed he was the person who placed the jars in the water. Santarelli said he had had the jars made in Portugal in the 1960s, and had submerged them underwater to produce an authentic, weathered, and ancient look. But after they had spent some time in the water, Santarelli was only able to retrieve four of them, and the rest were abandoned in the bay.

So, what is the real story? Were the amphorae once cargo on a Roman ship that sunk in Guanabara Bay? Or were the jars a twentieth-century creation, placed in the water deliberately? Was Santarelli part of a government cover-up to preserve Brazil's Portuguese heritage?

Unless another curious explorer like Marx, who died in 2019, comes forward to ask questions, the world may never know the truth about the strange jars in Guanabara Bay.

# Rock of the Andes

*El Fuerte de Samaipata lies in the eastern foothills of the Bolivian Andes Mountains, where it showcases a unique collection of three different cultures. But the focal point of this archeological site is a huge rock covered in carvings. It represents one of the largest pre-Columbian ceremonial works in the Andes.*

❋　❋　❋　❋

THE ORIGINS OF El Fuerte probably lie with the Chané people, who were members of the Arawak indigenous peoples of northeastern South America. The Chané began moving into the area around AD 200, and by 300, they had firmly established the region around what is now the town of Samaipata as a residential and ritual location. Archeologists believe it was the Chané who first began to shape and carve the huge rock that now sits in the center of the site, and that makes up most of what is known as the ceremonial sector.

Encompassing an area more than 720 feet long and almost 200 feet wide, the imposing red sandstone is covered in carvings of animals, geometric shapes, long channels, and niches. At the highest point of the rock, 18 niches set into a deeply carved circle, known as the *coro de los sacerdotes*, or "choir of the priests," is believed to have once been used for important ceremonies and rituals. The base of the rock contains 21 large rectangular niches, which may have been used for storage or perhaps for residences for the priests.

## Cultures Collide

Along with the ceremonial sector, El Fuerte is also made up of a residential and administrative sector. This area, set on artificial platforms south of the large rock, was established when the Incas began absorbing the Samaipata region into their empire in the late 1400s. Samaipata became a religious and political center for the Incas, and the ruins now found at El Fuerte reflect its importance to the culture. This sector contains the remains of the *Acllahuasi*, or "house of the chosen," where women dedicated to a religious life lived, made clothing, and were occasionally chosen to be sacrificed in rituals. It is also the location of the *Kallanka*, a large building that was used for public gatherings, feasts, and military housing.

The Incan influence at El Fuerte continued until the early sixteenth century, when the Spanish arrived and built a settlement in the area, constructing buildings in the Arab Andalusian, or Moorish, architectural style they adopted at the time. Today, this unique archeological wonder is a UNESCO World Heritage Site. As one of the most popular tourist destinations in Bolivia, visitors can see all three of the influences—Chané, Incan, and Spanish—that are still evident at El Fuerte.

# All That Glitters

*The Sican culture of Peru flourished between AD 750 and 1375 and was notable for its religious practices, social hierarchies, art, and metalworking, including its distinctive gold cups and ceremonial masks. One of these masks was found to have been created in an especially unusual way.*

✳ ✳ ✳ ✳

ANTHROPOLOGIST IZUMI SHIMADA first discovered evidence of a pre-Hispanic culture along the northern coast of Peru in the 1970s. He named this culture *Sican,* meaning "temple of the Moon," and divided its existence into three historical periods: early, middle, and late. The early period, beginning around 750 and lasting until 900, is marked by a signature ceramics style featuring a polished black finish that derived from the Moche civilization, the culture that preceded the Sican. But while the Sican may have initially borrowed this ceramics style from the Moche, their artistic expression, iconography, religion, and funerary practices began to transform into a style all their own.

## Metal and Masks

By the middle period, which lasted from 900 to 1100, the Sican had created a unique, distinguishable civilization. Society was divided into classes, and religious ideology was an important aspect of the culture. Both of these were evident in the precious metal objects crafted by metalsmiths, which were produced according to hierarchy. Elites possessed items made with high-karat gold alloys, lesser classes had ceramics layered with thin sheets of lower-karat gold, and the lowest classes were granted only copper metals. But all metalwork, regardless of hierarchy, featured the Sican deity, believed to be Naylamp, a god often depicted with birdlike features and upturned eyes.

Metal objects featuring Naylamp included cups, cooking vessels, bottles, jewelry, and architectural ornaments. But perhaps the most striking artifacts found within the ruins of the Sican civilization are the golden masks, used for funerary rites and other ceremonies.

One such mask was discovered in a Sican tomb in the 1990s, still covered in a layer of remarkably preserved bright red paint. The pigment was identified as cinnabar, a mineral often found near hot springs or areas of volcanic activity and used since antiquity as a cosmetic and coloring agent for pottery. But researchers were perplexed by how the pigment had been so securely bound to the gold surface of the mask.

## The Ties That Bind

In 2014, scientists were finally able to discover the secret of the binding agents used in the paint on the mask by using advanced analysis techniques. What the analysis revealed surprised everyone: The bright red paint contained proteins from both chicken egg and human blood. And interestingly, the blood may have been less intriguing than the chicken egg! Human sacrifice was a common practice in certain cultures at the time, and the presence of blood may also suggest that the Sican were aware of blood's importance for life. But the chicken egg was truly confounding, as chickens were believed to have first arrived on the continent with the Spanish in the 1500s. But the mask seems to suggest that chickens were present in Peru hundreds of years earlier, posing a conundrum for archeologists.

In the year 1020, a 30-year drought caused agriculture in the Sican civilization to weaken, and the population began to drop off. The late Sican period began around 1100, after many of the civilization's inhabitants lost faith in their deities, who had failed to protect them from the natural disaster, and burned and abandoned the religious temples. Although they established a new religious center and rebuilt their civilization over the next 250 years, they were eventually conquered by the Chimú in 1375. But their impressive metalwork has survived for centuries, much of it hidden in tombs and protected from the elements and looting. Today, many of the Sican's beautiful gold artifacts can be viewed, including some that still feature bright red cinnabar, in museums around the world.

# The Ancient Wise Men

*In many cultures, the dead are buried in the ground, often in holes dug "six feet under." But the interment of some members of the pre-Incan Chachapoya culture was just the opposite. Their unusual sarcophagi are located high on a cliff overlooking a Peruvian valley.*

✳ ✳ ✳ ✳

THE FIRST OUTSIDER to set eyes on the Chachapoya Sarcophagi must have wondered what in the world they were seeing. Seven human-like shapes, each standing around eight feet tall and perched on a seemingly inaccessible cliff, stare down into the surrounding countryside. Constructed of clay, sticks, and grasses, and featuring large heads with sharply defined jawlines, these strange sarcophagi were created to be the final resting place of the most revered members of the Chachapoya culture.

Also known as the "warriors of the clouds," the Chachapoya lived along the eastern slopes of the Andes Mountains in what are known as "cloud forests." These tropical or subtropical forests have a unique ecosystem characterized by frequent low-level cloud cover and abundance of moss and vegetation.

The Chachapoya first settled in the cloud forests around AD 800 and lived in the region until they were conquered by the Incas in the fifteenth century.

## Cliffside Capsules

The Chachapoya created distinctive circular stone architecture and red-painted textiles. But they are perhaps best known for their unusual funerary practices. Some of their deceased were buried in mausoleums that were carved into caves in the sides of cliffs. But the elite of society were given an even loftier resting place. They were wrapped in mortuary cloths, then seated on animal skins. Along with ceramics and other gifts, the deceased were then placed inside large, human-shaped capsules and sealed inside. These anthropomorphic sarcophagi were then situated on a high cliff, in a remote area that would be nearly inaccessible to looters.

Thanks to this impressive process, most of the sarcophagi still survive today and remain unmoved from their original positions. However, one was damaged during an earthquake in 1928, and this allowed researchers the opportunity to study its contents. Carbon dating determined the sarcophagus was placed on the cliff sometime between 1460 and 1520.

Today, the Chachapoya sarcophagi still keep a vigilant watch at Carajía in the Utcubamba Valley of Peru, where locals have dubbed them simply the "ancient wise men." Adventurous visitors can rent horses to take them down a steep descent through the valley, where they can view the silent sarcophagi on the side of the cliff.

# The Paracas of Peru

*The name of the Andean Paracas culture, which thrived between 700 and 200 BC, is said to mean "sand falling like rain." And it was the dry, sandy climate of the coastal desert that helped preserve evidence of this culture, including their distinctive carved gourds.*

✳  ✳  ✳  ✳

THE EARLIEST PARACAS settlement along southern Peru's Pacific coast is believed to have been around 1200 BC. The region is one of the driest in the world, with expanses of sandy deserts nestled against the Pacific Ocean. It would have presented a challenge to its ancient inhabitants, who, over the next several centuries, became experts at irrigation and water management. Thanks to freshwater rivers flowing down from the Andes and the abundance of available marine life, the Paracas were able to create a flourishing culture in what some may have considered an inhospitable region.

The first evidence of this culture was discovered in the 1920s by Peruvian archeologist Julio Tello. Tello had purchased some ancient textiles in the city of Pisco in 1915, and, curious about their origin, began investigating the pieces. His research led him to what is now the Paracas Peninsula, where the dry desert meets the blue ocean.

## Desert Discovery

It was here that Tello discovered an underground necropolis containing ritual burial chambers filled with more than 400 mummy bundles. Each mummy had been placed in a sitting position and wrapped with large textiles. Most of the mummies were simply and plainly wrapped, but some, believed to be the elites of the civilization, were covered with elaborately embroidered and brightly colored cloths. These textiles were made from cotton grown in the river valleys and wool from domesticated or wild alpacas and llamas.

Under many conditions, similar textiles would have broken down and decayed; but because of their arid underground locations, the Paracas burial cloths were remarkably well-preserved, even after almost 2,000 years. Bright reds, yellows, greens, and blues are still visible in the woven textiles, which feature animals like birds, snakes, and felines. They also feature supernatural figures known as "Oculate Beings," named for their large eyes. These figures feature prominently in the textiles, where they take on both humanoid and zoomorphic forms.

## Story Gourds

But colorful textiles weren't the only amazing find within the Paracas necropolis. The mummies were also found with jewelry, ceramics, and intricately carved gourds that had been shaped into bowls, rattles, and even musical instruments. These gourds were of particular interest, as gourd carving is an art that is known to have been practiced in Peru for more than 4,000 years.

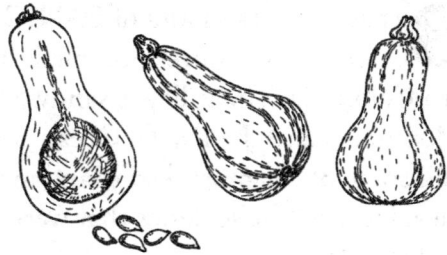

The ancient gourds were skinned, cleaned, and dried, then carved to create designs, which were often used as a way to pass along folklore or to tell stories of celebrations or tragedies. In fact, modern Peruvians carry on this tradition, using gourd-carving as a way to pass on their heritage and tell family stories.

All that we know about the Paracas culture comes from the burials uncovered by Tello. Much of their history and way of life remains unknown, but their artistic work, including their colorful textiles and carved gourds, imply that they had a great appreciation for the natural world and a strong belief in the afterlife. Today, Paracas artists are considered some of the most accomplished in Peru's history.

# Lost Treasure

*In the early twentieth century, settlers from the northern mountains of Colombia began migrating to the coffee-growing regions in the west. There, in an area rich with history and volcanic soil, the newcomers engaged in a pastime known as* guaqueria. *But we might simply call it treasure hunting. While many treasures and artifacts have found their way to museums, looting remains a serious concern.*

✳   ✳   ✳   ✳

**B**ETWEEN THE YEARS of 200 BC and AD 400, four pre-Columbian cultures occupied the Cauca Valley in western Colombia. The valley is sandwiched between the Andes Mountains and the Pacific Ocean, and features rivers, jungles, and some of the most fertile land in the country, making it an ideal location for societies that were dependent on agriculture and fishing.

The four civilizations that once called this area home—the Ilana, Yotoco, Sonso, and Malagana—are collectively known as the Calima culture. They first appeared in the area along the Calima River, where they developed efficient agricultural techniques to grow yuca, maize, beans, and achiote. They also created textiles and ceramics, and, of greatest interest to those practicing *guaqueria*, became experts at metallurgy.

Thousands of Calima-era tombs, many containing items made of gold, were discovered in the early twentieth century by these treasure hunters. They would take the gold to the National Bank of Colombia, where it was melted down and turned into bullion. No doubt this practice would have shocked professional archeologists, who take painstaking steps to preserve even the smallest artifact.

Luckily, in 1939, an especially beautiful golden artifact was taken to the National Bank, where it was deemed too impressive to melt down. From that point on, any gold brought into the bank was protected, and eventually Colombia established its famous gold museums to house all of the precious metal artifacts discovered in the country.

## Treasures Found, Treasures Lost

Among the gold items discovered in Calima burial tombs are life-sized hammered masks. Each mask was created from a single sheet of high-carat gold and often featured generic details of a human face. While all of the masks were found in tombs, researchers believe they may have also been worn for ceremonial purposes. This is because many of the masks have cutout eyes and mouths, as well as small holes on the side that could have been used to tie the mask to a face. While the gold masks are believed to have been buried with the elite members of society, the Calima, like many ancient indigenous groups, probably assigned little monetary value to gold, but rather prized it for some symbolic or religious reason.

The Calima left behind no written records of their lives, so archeologists must do their best to piece together a picture of how this culture lived based on the artifacts uncovered. And although the National Bank of Colombia no longer melts down golden artifacts, looters have proven to be an issue. In 1992, a site once occupied by the Malagana, one of the four Calima cultures, was discovered and immediately looted. An estimated four tons of artifacts disappeared from the location within several days. Sadly, because so much evidence of the Calima has been stolen or outright destroyed, we may never truly know all we should about these ancient peoples.

# Chapter 12

# Lost Cities and Mysterious Sites

## The Lost City of Thinis

*While archeologists continue to uncover new wonders in the land of the pharaohs to this day, Thinis remains elusive.*

※   ※   ※   ※

THOUSANDS OF YEARS ago, ancient Egypt was divided into two regions: Upper Egypt and Lower Egypt. Named for their locations in relation to the south-to-north flow of the Nile River, Upper Egypt (which was upriver) was the southern portion of the land, whereas Lower Egypt (downriver) was the northern portion. Perhaps even the ancient Egyptians found this up-and-down geography a bit confusing, because by 3100 BC, the two regions unified, ushering in the Archaic or Early Dynastic Era of Egypt.

This era was also known as the Thinite Period, named after the first capital city of the newly unified Egypt, Thinis. According to Manetho, an Egyptian priest who authored a chronology of the kings of ancient Egypt, the pharaoh who united the two regions was a member of a tribal group based in Thinis called the Thinite Confederacy. This pharaoh, named in various sources as either Menes or Narmer, declared the city to be the capital of the newly created Egypt, and it remained the capital into the First or Second Dynasty of Egypt.

## A Religious Center

It may be assumed that archeologists have uncovered a plethora of artifacts from this important city, but the truth is just the opposite: The city of Thinis has never been found. Along with the writings of Manetho, Thinis was mentioned in many ancient manuscripts, including the religious text *The Book of Going Forth by Day*, often known by its more common name, the *Book of the Dead*. Through the recordings of ancient peoples, we can be certain that Thinis existed; but its location remains a mystery to this day.

While its location may be unknown, most scholars believe it was probably situated close to Abydos, one of the oldest cities in Egypt. Records show that the city possessed great wealth, and provided food, weapons, and troops to the pharaoh's army. Thinis was also a religiously significant city, containing a temple to the god of war, Anhur. Anhur's consort, the goddess Mehit, was also worshipped in the city. But gods and goddesses were not the only recipients of the Egyptians' reverence. According to the Book of the Dead, Thinis itself was associated with the afterlife, existing as a celestial city in the heavenly realm.

## Farmers and Taxes

The significant wealth enjoyed by the city of Thinis continued even after the city of Memphis became the capital. This was clearly recorded in tax documents of the era, which showed that Thinis was taxed gold, silver, cattle, and honey on an annual basis. The city was also required to pay 65 sacks of grain yearly, compared to the three paltry sacks that were paid by nearby Abydos. This suggests that farming and agriculture were hugely important to Thinis, and probably made up the majority of its industry.

Could this large focus on agriculture explain why Thinis has never been found? Some archeologists believe so. Farmers often lived in structures made of easily perishable materials like wood and mud, whereas stronger materials like stone were reserved for temples and tombs. If Thinis, as the first city in the first era of a unified Egypt, was lacking many stone structures, it's possible that it simply disappeared under the sands of the desert. But its religious significance can't be forgotten, either; certainly the city had a stone temple or two, even if most of its residents were simple farmers. Either way, Thinis grew less and less vital as the eras of Egypt moved on, and by the Roman Period in 30 BC, it was all but forgotten.

With all of the written evidence we have, one thing is certain: The city of Thinis existed, somewhere. Perhaps one day someone will stumble upon its sand-shrouded remains in the Egyptian desert. But in the meantime, we can only guess where its location may be, and ponder how this modest farming city sparked the beginnings of the great kingdom of Ancient Egypt.

# Abydos: City of the Dead

*One of the great cities of ancient Egypt continues to reveal new details about the lives and rituals of its people.*

✳    ✳    ✳    ✳

IN 2021, ARCHEOLOGISTS made an unusual discovery in the Egyptian city of Abydos, which lies about 280 miles south of Cairo. The researchers uncovered a 5,000-year-old brewery, believed to have been capable of making more than 5,900 gallons of beer at a time. The brewery, possibly the oldest in the world, provided beer to the kings of Abydos and was used for many sacrificial rites and rituals.

Ritual practices were especially important to the people of Abydos. The city was established around 3100 BC as a necropolis for royalty. This "city of the dead" counted the jackal-headed god, Khenti-Amentiu, as its protector. But by the Fifth Dynasty, beginning around 2465 BC, reverence for Khenti-Amentiu gradually transformed into a worship of Osiris, the god of life, death, and the afterlife.

## Cult of Osiris

Abydos became a destination for pilgrims in the cult of Osiris. They believed that the god himself was buried within the city. Pious Egyptians would travel to the city, desiring to one day be buried as close to the tomb of Osiris as possible. Records of journeys to Abydos undertaken by wealthy families are found all throughout Egypt. But even those who could not afford the travel or the cost of burial in the city found a way to leave a piece of themselves in Abydos: Archeologists have found thousands of stelae, or stone slabs, engraved with the names and titles of Egyptians who could not make a final trip to the city. The stelae were also engraved with prayers to Osiris, an effort to make sure the deceased person would be close to the god in the afterlife.

Over the centuries, pharaohs built and expanded a temple to Osiris in the city, eventually calling it the Great Temple of Osiris. It was here that Egyptians would gather to worship Osiris and his counterpart, Isis. Every year, pilgrims would gather for a celebration of their god, carrying a likeness of Osiris from the temple to where his tomb was believed to be, in a great, elaborate procession. The jubilant participants would then carry the likeness back to the temple, passing many private and royal chapels that were located along the route.

## Seti I and the Mother of Pots

The Great Temple of Osiris was important to the people of Abydos, but it was not the only temple they built in the city. One of the best known, and surviving, temples is the Temple of Seti I, also known as the Great Temple of Abydos.

Built by the pharaoh Seti I around 1300 BC, the temple was built to not only memorialize Seti himself, but to honor the pharaohs of previous dynasties. This was accomplished with a gallery featuring a relief of Seti and his son, Ramesses, making offerings to the cartouches of 76 predecessors. Known as the Abydos King List, the gallery is especially valued by modern researchers because it is the only known record of many of the kings of the Seventh and Eighth Dynasties of Egypt.

Abydos is also known for Umm el Qa'ab, the royal cemetery where the kings of the First and Second Dynasties were buried. Umm el Qa'ab means "Mother of Pots," and it was so named because the site is littered with pottery shards and other items that were left by religious pilgrims. Archeological excavations that began in the 1970s discovered inscriptions on many of the objects that suggested Egyptian writing had become more advanced much earlier than originally assumed.

The temples and city of Abydos continued to be expanded, revamped, and used until the Thirtieth Dynasty of Egypt, which lasted until 343 BC. Today, while the Great Temple of Osiris has been reduced to ruins, many of the ancient structures from this civilization still stand, giving researchers a valuable look into the lives of ancient Egyptians. It is no wonder that Abydos is considered one of the most important archeological sites in the world.

# Akhenaten: The City of Light

*In 1912, a German archeological team discovered a 19-inch-tall, 44-pound, limestone and stucco bust in what had once been the workshop of a fourteenth-century BC sculptor named Thutmose. The bust became one of the most recognizable pieces of ancient art in the world, depicting one of the most famous women of the ancient world: Nefertiti.*

\* \* \* \*

THE BUST WAS found in the deserted city of Akhenaten, also known as Amarna, which had been founded around 1346 BC by Nefertiti's husband, Pharaoh Akhenaten.

The pharaoh—who, before the fifth year of his reign, was known as Amenhotep IV—had some unusual ideas that were previously unheard of in ancient Egypt. As king, he was entrusted with preserving *ma'at*, or harmony and balance, in Egypt. Traditionally, an important part of ma'at was maintaining the rites and rituals that served to honor the gods and goddesses. At first, the pharaoh continued these practices; but in the fifth year of his reign, he abolished the polytheistic ancient Egyptian religion and created his own monotheistic religion based on the sole worship of Aten, a minor deity who personified the light of the sun. The pharaoh's new name, Akhenaten, meaning "the horizon of the Aten," or "effective for the Aten," reflected his new devotion to the deity.

Aten represented the life-giving light of the sun, possessing no weaknesses or harmful traits. By merely existing, Aten caused all things to exist. The god may have been a "minor" deity in his polytheistic past, but to Akhenaten, Aten was supremely powerful on his own. The pharaoh did not believe that such a significant god should be worshiped in temples that were created for other gods; so, he decided to build a city devoted to his new monotheism.

## A New Capital

The city, Akhenaten, was situated along six miles of the east bank of the Nile River, between the cities of Memphis and Thebes. Completed around 1341 BC, the city immediately became the capital of the Eighteenth Dynasty. Akhenaten was laid out in four distinct areas, which today are known as the north city, central city, southern suburbs, and outskirts.

The north city was the location of the Northern Palace, where guests were received and the royal family resided. The palace was constructed without a roof, a common feature of the buildings in the city, which was seen as a gesture of welcome for Aten. The central city was the location of administration buildings and two important temples to Aten, the Great Temple and the Small Temple. Wealthy residents lived in large estates in the southern suburbs, whereas peasants and farmers occupied the outskirts of the city.

## A Singular Problem

While the city of Akhenaten flourished under the pharaoh's rule, the same cannot be said for the rest of Egypt. Akhenaten's singular focus on the worship of Aten distracted him from many affairs of state, and as his reign progressed, he seemed to care less and less for his kingly duties. And while he may have meant well by creating his monotheistic religion, Egypt's economy suffered greatly because of it. Temples were key sources of economic activity, employing thousands of people and engaging in local trade and industry. When the pharaoh imposed worship of only Aten, many temples were forced to close, while others lost much of their support. Even Egypt's military lost clout during Akhenaten's reign, and the country lost some of its standing with other kingdoms at its borders.

When Akhenaten died after 17 years of rule, his son, the famous Tutankhamun, reestablished the old polytheism in Egypt, reopened the temples that had been closed, and moved the capital to Thebes, the city of his birth. The city of Akhenaten struggled to survive for at least a decade but was eventually abandoned. Perhaps the empty city could have one day found life again, had it not been for one of Tutankhamun's successors, Horemheb.

## Downfall and Discovery

Horemheb had been a military general under Akhenaten, and while he served the king well, he greatly disagreed with his monotheistic religious policies. When Horemheb became pharaoh, he wanted no record of Akhenaten's kingdom. He ordered the city razed, and used the bricks and stones that were left over for his own projects.

It is no wonder that the ruins of Akhenaten sat undiscovered for thousands of years. It was not until the eighteenth century that archeologists began excavating the ancient capital, uncovering foundations of temples, monuments, and a collection of 300 cuneiform tablets known as the Amarna

Letters. These letters include official documents from Akhenaten's reign as well as correspondence with foreign nations. Archeologists also discovered the king's tomb, although Akhenaten himself was nowhere to be found, possibly a victim of grave robbers.

The famous bust of Nefertiti, which happily survived Horemheb's destruction of the city, is now known worldwide as a symbol of beauty. Ironically, very little is definitively known about Akhenaten's royal wife, yet she has become one of the most instantly recognizable faces of the ancient world. Hopefully, the city in which she once lived will continue to reveal secrets of its complicated and controversial past.

# The Treasures of Timbuktu

*It is quite common in our modern age to equate "Timbuktu"— today a city in the West African country of Mali—with a far-off location or a long trip. Throwing out an exasperated, "I had to drive from here to Timbuktu!" tells a listener just how arduous a journey was, even if only in the mind of the speaker. The fact that we still, in modern times, equate Timbuktu with faraway lands speaks to the enigmatic history of the city, and to our ongoing curiosity with ancient cultures.*

✳ ✳ ✳ ✳

TIMBUKTU HAS LONG been considered a mysterious place. In fact, a 2006 survey in the United Kingdom found that a third of young Britons wrongly believed the city to be fiction. It's hard to blame anyone for this misunderstanding, as stories of Timbuktu have often been awash in fantastical anecdotes that spark imaginations.

Of course, the truth of Timbuktu is not nearly as opulent as the rumors; but that doesn't mean that the city's history is any less impressive. Archeologists have found evidence of human occupation of the region around Timbuktu dating back to the

Iron Age, but the city was not actually formally established until medieval times. At first, the location was used as a seasonal camp by salt traders; but by the early twelfth century, the area became a permanent hub for caravan trade of all kinds. Many of these traders decided to put down roots in the area, and soon, Timbuktu was a thriving and prosperous city, where travelers from the west brought gold to exchange for salt from the east.

## The Midas Touch

According to many scholars, an event in the early 1300s first ignited the swirling rumors of Timbuktu's wealth and helped to spread its fame far and wide. By this time, the Mali Empire was the most powerful kingdom in West Africa. Mali was already well-known for the wealth of its ruler, Mansa Musa, who is still often called one of the wealthiest people in history. A devout Muslim, Musa decided to undertake a pilgrimage, or *hajj*, to Mecca in 1324, a journey of 2,700 miles. Musa wasn't alone, however: His entourage comprised an astounding 60,000 men. This included 12,000 slaves who carried four pounds of gold each, plus 80 camels carrying bags of gold dust. The entire procession was outfitted in Persian silks, and heralds carried gold staffs.

This display of wealth was obvious enough, but Musa didn't simply show off—he also shared what he had. All along the journey, the ruler made stops to share his gold with other pilgrims and those in need, and was said to have financed the building of mosques in many cities along the way. Some accounts claim that Musa handed out so much gold on his pilgrimage that by the time he reached Cairo, the price of the metal had dropped greatly.

Musa's pilgrimage to Mecca became fodder for myth and legend, spawning a persistent rumor that his nearly endless supply of gold came from the city of Timbuktu. In reality, the gold had come from mines west of the city, but that didn't stop the story of the gold-laden kingdom of Timbuktu from taking on a life of its own. Like the mythical El Dorado of the Americas, Timbuktu was thought of as a hidden, mysterious city, a place that explorers and adventure-seekers might stumble upon in the middle of the desert. Soon, people in other parts of the world were dreaming of a secret paradise brimming with gold in the far-off, exotic land. These rumors of opulent palaces and gold-lined streets reached the ears of Europeans around the time when plagues began to ravage the continent. Imagining a warm, desert paradise full of treasure surely would have been a preferable distraction to the realities of disease, and may explain why the stories of Timbuktu at the time were so fanciful and flamboyant.

## Africanus in Africa

Gold or no gold, Musa annexed the city of Timbuktu when he returned from his pilgrimage, making it part of the prosperous Mali Empire. But Musa wasn't the only character who helped place Timbuktu on the world stage. Another was Leo Africanus, a diplomat and author best known for his book *Description of Africa*. Africanus was born al-Hasan ibn Muhammad al-Wazzan in Andalusia, Spain, in 1485. The area was under Muslim rule until the reconquest of Spain by King Ferdinand and Queen Isabella in 1492, when the rulers exiled all Muslims in the country, including Africanus's family, who moved to Fez, Morocco.

Africanus was an intelligent man who not only traveled throughout North Africa extensively, but also spoke Latin and Italian, in addition to his native Arabic. After impressing Pope Leo X with his knowledge and intellect, Africanus converted to Christianity and took the Latin name Johannes Leo de Medicis, or, in Italian, Giovanni Leone. The pope commissioned him to write a book about the continent of Africa, which was published in Italian in 1550. *Description of Africa* became hugely popular and was eventually translated into French, Latin, and English.

Africanus's book, which was one of the few contemporary texts Europeans had relating to Africa, included several descriptions of Timbuktu. The author described the "rich king" of the city, detailing his many gold objects, "some whereof weigh 1300 pounds." Africanus also described the prosperous resources the city possessed, including food, livestock, and an abundance of "learned men." Europeans were once again fascinated and intrigued by this city which had already captured their imaginations centuries earlier. But this time, they had a first-hand account from someone who had visited the city in person, instead of simply rumors and gossip.

## Wealth of Information

While Africanus did write of the gold and prosperity within Timbuktu, he highlighted another aspect of the city that gave it what many scholars consider its true source of wealth: its love of books. In fact, the fifteenth and sixteenth centuries are considered Timbuktu's "Golden Age," but not because of literal gold; rather, these centuries were marked by a rise in education, literacy, and a trade in books that gave Timbuktu a reputation in the Islamic world as a center of learning and culture.

During this time, Timbuktu was home to several hundred maktabs, or Quranic schools, which attracted students from all over the region. Some historians estimate that at the height of its Golden Age, Timbuktu was crowded with 25,000 scholars. Many of them were also scribes, creating manuscripts of religious, philosophical, historical, and scientific works. Thousands of texts were written, and hundreds of thousands were gathered through a bustling book trade. Manuscripts ranged from those written by local astronomers, mathematicians, religious scholars, and other experts, to texts translated from famous historical figures like Plato and Hippocrates.

In addition to the maktabs, Timbuktu created madrasahs, which were informal but religious institutions modeled after European medieval universities, where scholars gave lectures on their subjects of expertise. The city so prized learning and knowledge that even visitors passing through were seen as possible sources of new information. Guests were warmly welcomed and treated like royalty, in the hopes that they could share new wisdom with the citizens of Timbuktu. Even more than gold, Timbuktu considered literacy and books to be symbols of its power and wealth.

## End of the Golden Age

Unfortunately, this power and wealth was not to last. In 1591, Morocco invaded Timbuktu. The scholars of Timbuktu were disbanded and scattered: Some were imprisoned or even executed for disloyalty to the new rulers, while others were exiled or escaped to nearby countries. The Golden Age of Timbuktu came to an abrupt end.

The city's once lively book trade was over, but those who remained in Timbuktu during Moroccan rule understood the importance of the variety of manuscripts the city had collected over the years. In an effort to preserve this knowledge and keep it safe from those who might attempt to destroy it, families began hiding copies of everything they could get their hands on. Texts were hidden in cellars, buried underground, lowered into wells, and concealed behind walls, where they were kept safe like precious treasure, sometimes for centuries.

It wasn't until the 1800s that the first Europeans began exploring the Sahara—enduring malaria, hunger, and other dangers—to reach the long-imagined city of Timbuktu. By then, the city's Golden Age was long past. When stories of the realities of the legendary city reached Europe, they were much less impressive than what centuries of rumors had led some to believe. No streets of gold, no opulent palaces, no silk-adorned kings. French explorer René Caillié, the first European to journey to and from Timbuktu, described it as desolate and quiet, a city which "exuded the greatest sadness." In modern times, the city has struggled with droughts, increasing desertification, and an influx of terrorists and extremists, which has often led governments to discourage travel to the region.

Despite its modern-day struggles, the Western world often still thinks of Timbuktu as a mysterious, hidden city of gold. But as the city itself once understood, its true sources of wealth were the books, education, and knowledge it possessed. Today, historians are searching for the real hidden treasure of Timbuktu and working to restore its greatest legacy: its collection of nearly 700,000 manuscripts. Three of the city's original madrasahs—Djinguereber, Sidi Yahya, and Sankore—are still standing today and are collectively known as the University of Timbuktu. These structures, and the manuscripts they contain, are reminders of this once-wealthy kingdom, and the knowledge that it yearned to gather and share with the world.

# Timgad: Lost and Found

*As with so many other ancient cities that once flourished around the Mediterranean within the protection of the Roman Empire, Timgad eventually succumbed to misfortune.*

✳ ✳ ✳ ✳

THE ANCIENT CITY of Pompeii is famous not only for its destruction after the eruption of the volcano Mount Vesuvius, but also for its remarkably well-preserved state. Contemporary visitors can wander the same streets Pompeii residents once walked, and see a glimpse of the past frozen in time. This famous city is visited by millions of people a year; but few have heard of another well-preserved ancient city that many liken to Pompeii: the city of Timgad.

Timgad was founded by the Roman Emperor Trajan around AD 100, in what is now northern Algeria. The emperor gave the city the rather unwieldy name Colonia Marciana Ulpia Traiana Thamugadi, in honor of his family—his mother, Marcia; sister, Ulpia Marciana; and father, Marcus Ulpius

Traianus. The last part of the name, Thamugadi, was a word used by the indigenous Berber tribes in the area, and is believed to mean "peak" or "summit." This reflects the city's location in the Aurès Mountains of Algeria, at just over 3,000 feet above sea level.

## Gridlock

Timgad was originally created to house Roman military veterans, and to act as a show of strength against the local Berbers. Since it was founded on an unsettled area of land, the Romans were able to construct the city exactly how they wanted. The result was an impressive feat of ancient urban planning, with streets laid out in a grid system around two main thoroughfares: the *decumanus maximus*, which ran from east to west, and the *cardo*, which ran north to south. A stately sandstone gate known as the Arch of Trajan was constructed at the west end of the decumanus maximus, featuring an 11-foot-wide central arch. The city also included a library, a basilica, several bathhouses, an amphitheater, and a temple dedicated to the god Jupiter which rivals the size of the Pantheon in Rome.

For several hundred years, Timgad's residents enjoyed peace and prosperity. The city became a center for commerce and trade, and expanded from its original population of Roman military veterans to more than 15,000 citizens from across the Roman Empire. The city grew so much that it could no longer be contained within the orderly grid of its original design, causing it to spill out into a much more haphazard pattern.

## Lost to the Desert

But the peace would not last forever: In the fifth century, Germanic Vandals sacked the city, looking to expand their own influence and power in North Africa. Weakened, Timgad was then nearly destroyed by marauding Berbers from the surrounding mountains. Although it was repopulated for a short time, the city was completely abandoned by the eighth century. It was left to the slow encroachment of desert winds and sands.

Timgad was slowly buried underneath more than three feet of dry ground. Then it was forgotten for a thousand years.

In 1765, a British explorer named James Bruce reached the neglected city and described it in a book about his African travels. Still, it took more than a hundred years for others to seriously take note of the once-remarkable city, and in 1881, French archeologists began excavating Timgad. They discovered that the dry air and sand of the desert had perfectly preserved much of the city. By the 1960s, most of Timgad had been uncovered, revealing an outline of the once vibrant city. Nearly every building in the area is still clearly outlined by the remains of walls and foundations. The precisely laid out streets are paved with large limestone slabs, some of which clearly display worn chariot tracks. Private houses and villas are adorned with intricate mosaics, hinting at the wealth of the city's residents. A visit to the upper seats of the amphitheater provides a view of the entire city, including the public forum, bathhouses, and the imposing Arch of Trajan.

## What's Old Is New

One thing that surprises archeologists about this ancient city is how familiar it feels in our modern age. Researchers were clearly able to see how the growing population of Timgad had caused it to branch out into nearby locations, with newer buildings constructed on the outskirts of the city in a less ordered fashion than the central area. This is not unlike most cities found in the world today: a downtown area contains the highest concentration of businesses and people, whereas growth leads to less-organized suburban areas. Timgad may have been one of the first cities to feature "suburban sprawl."

Today, Timgad is a UNESCO World Heritage Site. Visitors can come and explore this bit of ancient history themselves. Although Timgad's citizens are long-gone, they left behind some advice in the form of a Latin motto engraved on the steps to the large basilica: *Venare, lavari, ludere, ridere, occ est vivere.* "Hunt, bathe, play, laugh, that is life." It would seem that during its glory days, Timgad provided comfort, prosperity, and contentment to its lucky inhabitants. While Pompeii may have had a more dramatic ending, Timgad deserves some attention for being one of the best-preserved ancient cities in the world.

# Heracleion: Lost to the Sea

*Now lost to the waters of the Mediterranean, was Heracleion the Atlantis of its day?*

✳  ✳  ✳  ✳

THE FAMOUS "LOST city of Atlantis" was a fictional island first mentioned in the works of Plato. The philosopher wrote about the island in 360 BC in his works *Timaeus* and *Critias*. The imaginary civilization represented an arrogant naval power that attacks Athens. Athens is able to fight off the attack, and Atlantis, which loses favor with the gods, is submerged into the sea. It was a minor tale in Plato's vast collection of works, but it immediately took hold of the imaginations of those who read it.

In fact, not everyone who read about Atlantis was convinced that it was imaginary. Since Plato's first mention of the island more than two thousand years ago, scholars have scoured the planet, hoping to find this lost underwater city. Today, most historians agree that Atlantis is a place of fiction; however, many believe that Plato may have based the island on a real place. While the idea of such a sunken city may seem far-fetched, natural occurrences like earthquakes and tsunamis have, in reality, consumed once-thriving cities.

## A Once-Bustling Port

One such example is the underwater city of Heracleion, also known as Thonis or Thonis-Heracleion. Located near the mouth of the Nile River, Heracleion was an ancient Egyptian port founded around the eighth century BC. The city served as the main port of entry for Greek ships traveling to Egypt, and also became a city of religious significance due to its large temples devoted to the Egyptian god Amun and his son, Khonsou. Built on several neighboring islands, Heracleion featured many canals and harbors lined with houses and wharfs, all connected by a network of bridges and ferries.

While Heracleion was a thriving city for centuries, it grew weaker over time as it fell victim to earthquakes, tsunamis, and rising sea levels. By the second century BC, the main island of the city began eroding due to soil liquefaction. The once hardened ground was inundated with sea water, and gradually the buildings fell into the sea. While people did continue to live on adjacent islands for several more centuries, eventually the city of Heracleion completely disappeared into the Mediterranean Sea.

## From Forgotten to Found

But the city didn't only vanish from dry land; it also almost vanished from historical memory. Ancient historians and philosophers made note of the city, sometimes working it into mythological chronicles such as the story of Helen of Troy. Hard evidence of its existence, however, was rare and hard to come by. While archeologists discovered several stone slabs inscribed with mentions of Heracleion, they were mostly forgotten, perhaps set aside in favor of researching easier-to-locate Egyptian ruins.

It wasn't until airplanes became commonplace that the ruins of Heracleion were once again seen by human eyes. In 1933, a British Royal Air Force pilot was flying over Abu Qir Bay just east of Alexandria when he spotted what looked like the outline of a city underwater. Even so, it took until the year 2000 for French underwater archeologist Franck Goddio to reach the ruins, which are located 4.3 miles from the shore, and to begin excavating the city.

Goddio helped to set the record straight about the city's name, which, until his discovery, had been assumed to be a separate city from Thonis. But an engraved stele found underwater helped to explain the disparity: Heracleion was the city's Greek name, whereas Thonis was its Egyptian name. Today, most scholars refer to the city as Thonis-Heracleion.

## Underwater Treasure

Clarifying the city's name helped to solve a long-standing archeological puzzle, but Goddio's discovery revealed so much more. A large number of coins, gold jewelry, and pottery were found dating between the sixth and fourth centuries BC, leading researchers to conclude that this was the city's most prosperous time. The busy port city enjoyed immense wealth and grandeur during this era, evidenced by its grand temples, intricate architectural details, and bronze statues. Researchers also found more than 70 shipwrecks and 700 ancient ship anchors in the area, a testament to Heracleion's importance as a port city.

Some of the most impressive discoveries were several nearly colossal statues resting on the sea floor, some more than 16 feet in height and weighing more than five tons. Usually made of red or pink granite, these statues represented Ptolemaic kings and queens, as well as Hapi, god of the Nile flood. The flooding of the Nile was an annual occurrence that resulted in fertile soil and good crop conditions, making Hapi an important god of abundance and fertility. This statue was the largest representation of a god ever found in Egypt, pointing to Heracleion's dependence on, and appreciation for, the Nile River.

Researchers estimate that only around five percent of Heracleion has been excavated, and archeological research continues. The artifacts that have been recovered have been given to the Grand Egyptian Museum in Giza, so that these amazing finds can be shared with the world. But it is hard not to wonder what sorts of treasures remain underwater, patiently waiting to reveal more secrets about the city consumed by the sea.

# Naucratis: Greek Culture in Egypt

*Located approximately 45 miles southeast of Alexandria, on the western edge of the Nile River delta, the ancient city of Naucratis was the first permanent Greek settlement in Egypt, founded around 570 BC. It is a fascinating example of the early cosmopolitanism that thrived in the eastern Mediterranean in ancient times.*

✳   ✳   ✳   ✳

WHILE EVIDENCE OF Greek influence in Egypt dates back to at least 1600 BC, the two civilizations were at first merely engaged in trading and commerce. But in the seventh century BC, Greek mercenaries joined the fight of Egyptian pharaoh Apries, who attempted to defeat a former general named Amasis. Although Amasis prevailed and consequently became pharaoh, the new monarch took a liking to the Greeks and allowed them to settle in what would become Naucratis.

The area, once the site of an Egyptian town, soon turned into a major trading port between Greece and Egypt. It was also a trading destination for other Mediterranean civilizations wishing to trade with Egypt. Greek traders began to settle in significant numbers in the region, and soon Naucratis had a large, prosperous Greek population.

The town became a pivotal link between Egypt and the Mediterranean world, and its influence stretched from Phoenicia, Cyprus, and the Levant in the east to Italy in the west. By the time Alexander the Great conquered Egypt in 332 BC, Naucratis had established itself as a hub of Greek culture, which contentedly coexisted alongside Egyptian society.

Some of the goods exported by Naucratis included wool, textiles, flax, papyrus, perfumes, and natron, a sodium-based chemical used during the mummification process. The discovery of such things along trade routes and in the homes of ancient peoples living in the Mediterranean and Aegean regions, has proven to researchers just how influential Naucratis was during its span as a trading port. Evidence suggests that it remained an important city until well into the Byzantine Period of the Roman Empire, but the rise of Alexandria and the shifting Nile eventually led to the city's downfall. The once-vital port city began its fade into obscurity sometime after the first century AD.

## Two Cultures, One City

Fortunately, an English Egyptologist by the name of Flinders Petrie discovered the ruins of Naucratis while he was excavating in the area in 1884. Since then, archeologists have discovered the city's unique mix of Greek and Egyptian culture. The site covers the modern-day villages of Kom-Ge'if, el-Niveria, and el-Niqrash, and, although the city has been almost entirely covered by vegetation, researchers have uncovered a large quantity of artifacts. These include Greek-style pottery, stone statuettes, amulets, and large quantities of coins. Archeologists have also found evidence of Egyptian-style "tower houses," or tall homes fabricated from mud bricks, a construction commonly found along the Nile during the time period.

The remains of sanctuaries dedicated to Greek gods including Castor and Pollux, Hera, Apollo, and Aphrodite were discovered, as well as sanctuaries reserved for many Egyptian gods, such as Amun-Ra, Nut, and Khonsu. These findings served to illustrate the blend of Greek and Egyptian cultures that coexisted within the location. Scholars estimate that at its height of influence, Naucratis had an impressive population of approximately 15,000. This mix of Greek and Egyptian residents not only gave the city a distinctive and cosmopolitan perspective on the ancient world, but it also left an indelible mark on the many other civilizations throughout the region. There is no doubt that this Greek city on the coast of Egypt was enormously important during its existence.

# The Sunken City of Canopus

*Homeric legend tells the story of Menelaus, the king of Sparta, who led the Greek army during the Trojan War. At sea, the king had a ship that was piloted by a handsome young captain named Canopus, who, while visiting the Egyptian coast, was bitten by a poisonous serpent and died. Menelaus built a monument to his ship captain right there on the Egyptian shore, and eventually, a city grew up around it.*

\* \* \* \*

REFERENCED BY NUMEROUS classical scholars, including ancient Greek historian Herodotus and the philosopher Seneca, the city was said to be the ship captain's namesake, Canopus. The city, believed to date back to the sixth century BC, was said to be an extravagant and decadent city, known for its luxuries. The Roman poet Juvenal noted its "debauchery" in his writings, and the emperor Hadrian was said to have enjoyed a visit to Canopus so much that he built a replica of part of the city at his villa in Tivoli. But the town was also an important religious sanctuary to the gods Osiris and Serapis, and drew pilgrims from all around the region, who believed they could be miraculously healed in the temples there. But the gods were unable to save the city from its eventual demise. Earthquakes, tsunamis, and rising sea levels gradually weakened the land on which Canopus sat, and by the end of the second century BC, the city sank beneath the waves.

## Past, Present, and Future

After it succumbed to the sea, the city faded from memory and became, like so many lost settlements, merely a topic of stories and legends. But in 1933, a pilot was flying over Abu Qir Bay on the Mediterranean coast of Egypt when he spotted what looked like ruins beneath the water. The eagle-eyed pilot had discovered not one, but two ancient, submerged cities: the city of Thonis-Heracleion and the city of Canopus.

While excavations of the area around Canopus began in the 1930s, the most significant discoveries have come more recently, under the supervision of French underwater archeologist Franck Goddio. Goddio and his team have found many large architectural elements in the sea, including a 338-foot-long wall that was preserved beneath six feet of sand. The wall is thought to have surrounded a temple, which, if true, would make this Canopus temple the largest ancient Egyptian shrine found in the region.

Limestone blocks, red granite columns, and stones inscribed with hieroglyphs have also been discovered in the area. These stones are of particular interest to archeologists, as they were part of a shrine called the Naos of the Decades, which was dedicated to Shu, the god of the air. Many statue fragments have been found in the area, including a marble head of the god Serapis, and smaller items, like jewelry and coins, hint at the wealth that Canopus once enjoyed.

Researchers believe that only a small percentage of this city beneath the sea has been explored, so there are no doubt many treasures yet to be discovered. Meanwhile, Canopus patiently waits beneath the waves, just as it has for thousands of years.

# The Catalhoyuk Settlement of Anatolia

*The 9,000-year-old remains of a settlement in Turkey reveal a trove of artifacts and a society in transition.*

✳   ✳   ✳   ✳

IN 1962, A British archeologist named James Mellaart was accused of smuggling priceless antiquities, supposedly discovered in the Turkish city of Dorak, out of the country. Mellaart claimed to have met a woman who owned many artifacts that dated back to ancient Troy, but she would not allow them to be photographed. Instead, Mellaart drew sketches of the items and took notes, later publishing his findings in *The Illustrated London News*. The Turkish authorities, however, said there was no evidence of this mysterious woman who supposedly showed Mellaart the collection of artifacts, and they concluded that the archeologist had fabricated the entire story to cover up his own theft. The "Dorak Treasure," as it came to be known, was never found, and James Mellaart was subsequently barred from reentering Turkey.

This was a shame, as only a few years earlier, in 1958, Mellaart had uncovered the remains of a large settlement near the city of Konya. Mellaart's excavations revealed 18 layers of buildings, suggesting many eras of civilization in the region. The lowest layers dated back to at least 7100 BC, whereas the top layers dated to 5600 BC. After Mellaart's involvement in the "Dorak Affair" and his subsequent banishment, this impressive discovery remained unexplored for decades.

## Settling Down

It wasn't until 1993 that excavations of the site, now known as the Catalhoyuk settlement, began again in earnest. What Mellaart had discovered were the ruins of a town that flourished about 9,000 years ago and boasted a population of between 8,000 and 10,000 residents. Over time, as the civilization traversed multiple centuries, there is evidence that the society transitioned from more of a hunter and gatherer lifestyle to one of agriculture and animal husbandry. The city itself is considered an illustration of the progress humans in the Anatolian region achieved when they shifted from nomads to settlers.

Years of modern excavation at the site have revealed much about these ancient city dwellers. One of the most unique aspects of the Catalhoyuk settlement is the arrangement of the houses. There were no roads or paths in the town; rather, the mud brick houses were constructed in an interconnected style, as if they were a large, human-sized honeycomb. Doors to the houses were located in the rooftops and accessed by ladders, so the roofs themselves served as pathways through the settlement. Large communal ovens were located above the homes, suggesting that the rooftops also served as a gathering place for the residents. Over the centuries, houses were periodically demolished and new houses were built on top of the rubble, leading to a "tell," or a mound, made up of accumulated debris.

## Equality and Art

The Catalhoyuk society was believed to be egalitarian, with men and women holding equal social status. This is evident in the civilization's burial practices, which seem to be relatively similar for everyone within the culture. The dead were tightly wrapped in reed mats and buried right inside the village, often under floors, hearths, or even beds, inside homes. The only exceptions made in burial practices were for children, who were often decorated with beads and colorful ochre, suggesting that children were valued in the society, possibly because of a need for help with household labor and a desire for descendants.

Perhaps the most striking feature of the Catalhoyuk settlement is the artwork that the civilization left behind. Nearly every house excavated at the site was found to contain decoration of some sort, including geometric designs and figures of animals, painted directly on to plaster walls. The plaster seems to have been reapplied every season, or even as often as every month, and then drawn on again, suggesting that this art was a central part of the villagers' lives.

Many clay figurines of humans and animals have also been found, scattered in garbage pits or buried in floors or walls. Researchers theorize that these figures were used as tokens to ward off bad luck or evil spirits. Even more interesting was the use of animal remains to create artwork. Often the skulls of bulls, with horns prominently pointing into a room, would be mounted into a wall, along with teeth, beaks, and tusks of various other animals.

## A Nod to the Past

Some scholars think that the use of these animals in the art-work of the Catalhoyuk settlement was a way of honoring the past, when hunting was vital for survival. Toward the end of its existence, the Catalhoyuk society was much more reliant on domesticated animals and agriculture for sustenance. Archeologists have discovered storage bins that were used for wheat and barley, and the society also grew peas, almonds, pistachios, and fruit near the village. Although hunting continued to be a source of food, it was not as crucial once the civilization began to raise sheep and cattle.

For unknown reasons, the Catalhoyuk settlement was abandoned sometime before the Bronze Age. But the inhabitants left behind a wealth of clues to help us paint a picture of their society. Today, visitors can travel to this UNESCO World Heritage Site, which features a museum and a protected excavation area. Curious history buffs can also view a recreation of a Catalhoyuk house, constructed by archeologists to show what life may have been like in this village 9000 years ago.

# The Jewel of the Mongol Empire: Karakorum

*The Mongol Empire was the largest contiguous empire in the history of the world. At its height, it reigned from the Sea of Japan all the way to eastern border of Europe, covering a massive amount of land. The empire is probably best known for its original leader, Genghis Khan, who united the nomadic tribes of East Asia before setting out to expand his rule in all directions.*

✳   ✳   ✳   ✳

IN 1220, THE Khan chose a village called Karakorum, located in what is now northwestern Mongolia, as his base of operations for an invasion of China. Aside from being the Khan's base, the town remained relatively inconsequential until the

Mongol conquest of the Jin Dynasty in 1234. Genghis Khan himself died in 1227, but after the defeat of the Jin Dynasty, his son, Ögedei, began to construct walls around Karakorum and ordered a palace be built.

## A Quickly Growing City

Karakorum's location, on a well-traveled east to west trading route on what is now known as the Silk Road, was considered ideal to serve as the capital of the rapidly expanding Mongol Empire. The rectangular walls built by Ögedei measured approximately one mile by one and a half miles and enclosed brick buildings, a dozen shamanistic shrines, mosques, and the palace itself, which featured 64 wooden columns standing on granite bases.

Ögedei and his successors continued to enlarge and build upon Karakorum, until it became a central location for world politics. At times, especially when the Khan's court was present, the population of the town would grow to such an extent that temporary yurts would be raised just outside the city to accommodate everyone. Merchants and craftsmen sold their wares in the city center, while traders frequently passed through with merchandise from far-off locations.

The city was known for its metallurgy, and produced an abundance of iron cauldrons, metal ornaments, axle rings for horse-drawn carts, and arrowheads. Artisans created glass beads for jewelry and cloth from the wool they gathered from their flocks of sheep. Rich silks from China made their way to the city through trade, and were highly prized by the Mongol elites.

## The Stunning Silver Tree

To the Khan and his court, Karakorum was an extraordinary city that deserved an extraordinary centerpiece for its palace courtyard, and Parisian goldsmith Guillaume Bouchier was asked to carry out the task. Bouchier created a large tree sculpted of silver and other precious metals, with branches extending over and into the palace. Four golden serpents wound their way around the trunk, and a trumpet angel stood atop the tree. The serpents and angel were automatons—moving machines with control mechanisms—that must have stunned the thirteenth-century crowds who gathered in the palace courtyard to watch. At the Khan's word, the angel would raise the trumpet to its lips and the four serpents would pour beverages from their mouths into a large silver basin at the base of the tree. The Silver Tree of Karakorum, as it was called, delighted the palace's guests.

Sadly, the magnificent Silver Tree of Karakorum, and much of the city itself, were razed in the late 1300s as the Ming Dynasty rose to power. Much of what we know today about Karakorum comes from the detailed account of a Flemish Franciscan missionary named Friar William of Rubruck. The friar described a cosmopolitan, religiously tolerant, and multicultural city. But he also spoke of the "arrogance" of the Mongols, who assumed William had come to barter for peace and an alliance on behalf of King Louis IX. Many of the people he met in Karakorum had been captured by the Mongols during raids on their lands, including the talented goldsmith, Guillaume Bouchier.

## Discovery and Excavation

For centuries after the city was razed, its location was unclear; but the Erdene Zuu Monastery, the oldest monastery in Mongolia, provided clues. This Buddhist monastery was built using stones from the ruins of Karakorum, but this fact didn't quite click in the minds of archeologists until 1889. In that year, Serbian archeologist Nikolai Yadrintsev discovered that the monastery did, indeed, stand directly adjacent to the Mongol capital.

Excavations of Karakorum began in earnest in 1933, revealing paved roads, brick buildings, kilns, and evidence of metalwork. The kilns were of particular interest to researchers, who concluded that the Mongols used them to produce ceramic roof tiles, tableware, sculptures, and, most impressively, water pipes. There is even evidence that the Mongols created heated floor systems as well as "bed-stoves," traditional heated platforms used in cold weather for both sleeping and for general activities during the day.

Although the Mongol capital was eventually moved from Karakorum to Khanbaliq—today known as Beijing, the capital of the People's Republic of China—the city remained a symbol of Genghis Khan's power for centuries. Referring to his first impression of Karakorum and its people, William of Rubruck wrote, "When I found myself among them, it seemed to me of a truth that I had been transported into another world." It is a shame that this "world," at one time impressive, grand, and magnificent, has been lost to time.

# The Demise of Mohenjo Daro

*Located west of the Indus River in the Sindh province of Pakistan, the ancient city of Mohenjo Daro is notable for its advanced infrastructure, which was unusually complex for its time. While the people who lived here seemed to possess greater knowledge and resources than their ancient counterparts, they abandoned their great city for unknown reasons, leaving behind some chilling clues.*

✳  ✳  ✳  ✳

### An Amazing Find

AS EARLY AS the 1850s, British colonial officials discovered bricks belonging to the Mohenjo Daro site, but they were unaware of their importance. It was not until 1920, when an Indian archeologist by the name of R.D. Banerji visited the area, that the site was discovered. Banerji was excavating what he believed to be a Buddhist stupa—a mound-like structure used as a place of meditation—when he stumbled upon artifacts made of flint. Further excavation revealed an impressive Bronze Age city. The city, thought to have been established around 2500 BC, exhibited an impressive and advanced level of city planning, with a grid-like layout, a sewer system, and houses with bathrooms and toilets. Even the bricks used to build the city, once thought to be insignificant, were found to be more well-constructed than other bricks of the age.

Other finds included carved figures, copper and stone tools, metal bowls and pots, jewelry, and toys. Archeologists also discovered tablets written in Indus Script. The script has never been fully deciphered, thus leaving researchers to glean what information they could from the other discoveries at the site. Even so, it was clear that the inhabitants of this city were advanced for their time. Although its original name is unknown, archeologists dubbed the city Mohenjo Daro, which is often interpreted to mean "mound of the dead."

## The Mystery of the 44

Much of Mohenjo Daro had the appearance of a city abandoned. But in the uppermost levels of the city, researchers made a chilling discovery: 44 human skeletons, scattered throughout streets and houses, buried under layers of rubble, ash, and debris. The bodies were contorted into strange and unnatural positions. Some of the people appeared to have died while attempting to crawl to safety, which led archeologists to assume that these 44 people had died a violent death. Had the city been attacked by an enemy? Some believed that an armed band of Indo-Aryans, a nomadic tribe from the northwest, ambushed the city as the 44 attempted to defend it. However, no weapons were found near the bodies, and, significantly, none showed evidence of violent injuries.

Others believed that the bodies' contorted appearance was not due to violence, but rather illness. Cholera outbreaks were common at the time, and evidence seems to suggest that Mohenjo Daro was prone to flooding. Even with their advanced sewer systems, a flood could have resulted in an outbreak in the city. But even this theory is not well-accepted, as modern scientific dating techniques have shown that these 44 people did not die at the same time. Some died years—and perhaps even centuries—earlier than others. Most scientists now conclude that the 44 probably died of natural causes.

### The Mystery Deepens

Even if the 44 skeletons found at Mohenjo Daro are the result of natural deaths, questions remain. Why, in a city so obviously advanced and orderly, were these people so unceremoniously and haphazardly buried? To archeologists, it appears as if the 44 were simply "dumped" into hastily-dug graves. Why have no other cemeteries or burial sites ever been found within the city? Estimates put the population of Mohenjo Daro at around 40,000; surely these 44 were not the only people who died while the city existed.

But perhaps the most perplexing question is also the most basic: Why did the thousands of inhabitants of Mohenjo Daro abandon their sophisticated city? With only an indecipherable language and few clues to go on, we may never know.

# Magical Nan Madol

*Pohnpei is the largest of the Senyavin Islands, which belong to the Pohnpei State in the Federated States of Micronesia. But at only 129 square miles and with a population of just over 36,000, this "large" island is quite small, occupying less space than the Hawaiian island of Lanai. But one of the most significant features of this area is found on an even tinier island off the coast of Pohnpei known as Temwen. Here, sitting on a coral reef in a lagoon, are the incredible ruins of Nan Madol.*

✳  ✳  ✳  ✳

NAN MADOL WAS once the capital of the Saudeleur Dynasty, the first government to unite the people of Pohnpei, who had been disorganized and lawless after they first settled on the island. According to legend, the dynasty was established around AD 1100 by twin brothers, Olisihpa and Olosohpa, who were said to be sorcerers. They arrived at the island in a large canoe from a mythical place known as Western Katau and built an altar on Temwen Island to worship Nahnisohn Sahpw, the god of agriculture. After Olisihpa died, Olosohpa appointed himself king and married a local woman, siring at least 12 generations of Saudeleur rulers. This not-very-reliable legend also claims that when the brothers built their altar on Temwen, they magically levitated rocks with the aid of a flying dragon.

## City on the Reef

Unfortunately, the real story of how the Saudeleur Dynasty originated is unknown, but researchers do believe that part of the legend must be true. While they were certainly not sorcerers or magicians, the people who built the structures on Temwen were most likely a foreign tribe who migrated to Pohnpei. After they arrived, they chose a leader, known as the Saudeleur, who ruled from Nan Madol and successfully united the tumultuous peoples of Pohnpei.

Nan Madol is the only known ancient city built atop a coral reef, and is made up of more than 90 artificial islands. Tidal canals and waterways crisscross the city, giving it its nickname, "the Venice of the Pacific." In fact, "Nan Madol" can be roughly translated to "within the intervals," in reference to the winding watery pathways that provide a method of transportation through the city.

Buildings in the city were constructed of carved basalt stones of various sizes and weights. Some are light enough that a single person would have been able to carry them, while others weigh an incredible 50 tons. It is unknown how the builders of Nan Madol were able to not only construct durable structures without the aid of binding agents like mortar, but also were able to move the most massive stones, align them, and sink them into the lagoon.

## Kings and Priests

Nan Madol became the most important political and religious center in Pohnpei. While the population of Pohnpei numbered around 25,000, only about 1,000 people lived at Nan Madol. Archeologists believe that one of the reasons it was built was to isolate the nobility from the commoners. The largest homes were reserved for nobility and those with high social status, such as priests and religious leaders. The remainder were for commoners who served the nobility.

The religious leaders of Nan Madol were especially revered. The city was filled with altars, temples, oracles, and mortuaries, and some islands were occupied exclusively by priests. At first, the Saudeleur nobility continued to worship the agriculture god Nahnisohn Sahpw, just as the legendary Olisihpa and Olosohpa had, but the large concentration of religious leaders and symbols led to the development of many different cults. Over time, as new nobility came to power, the once benevolent and gracious Saudeleur aristocrats abandoned their old ideas of morality and embraced crueler ideals. Nan Madol was dependent upon the Pohnpei mainland for all of its food and water, as there is no fresh water or arable land in the lagoon. The increasingly cruel Saudeleur royalty would purposely starve the native population, and the oppression led to immense unrest.

## The End of the Saudeleur

By 1628, the unhappiness and discontent of the Pohnpei people paved the way for an invasion of the island, led by a warrior named Isokelekel. Pohnpeian legend calls Isokelekel a demigod, who was angry with the Saudeleur royalty and their abandonment of Nahnisohn Sahpw. But whether god or human, Isokelekel, with the help of the oppressed Pohnpei people, overthrew the Saudeleur and ran them out of Nan Madol. For a time, Isokelekel and his tribal chiefs lived at Nan Madol, but the effort of leaving the city for food and water, along with a population decline, led them to eventually abandon it altogether.

Today, Nan Madol is one of only two major archeological sites in the Oceania region. The other, Easter Island, attracts 50,000 visitors a year and is well-known even to those unfamiliar with the area. Yet Nan Madol usually hosts fewer than 1,000 guests, and many around the world have probably never even heard of this ancient wonder. Modern Pohnpeians like to say that magic was used to construct the city of Nan Madol, and with no evidence to the contrary, who's to say it wasn't? This "magical" place certainly deserves the interest and attention of the archeological world.

# The Submerged City of Pavlopetri

*In 1904, a Greek geologist named Fokion Negri thought he saw something that looked like the ruins of a city lurking in the blue waters of the Mediterranean Sea just off the coast of the Peloponnese peninsula in Greece. He noted the location of the curious underwater formations, somewhere between the island of Elafonisos and a small beach known as Punta, but it seemed that a simple report marked the end of his investigation.*

✳   ✳   ✳   ✳

DECADES AFTER NEGRI'S discovery, in 1967, British marine geo-archeologist Nicholas Flemming returned to this site and discovered a city submerged underwater. With the help of Greek professor Angelos Delivorias and a team of archeologists from the University of Cambridge, Flemming began mapping out the underwater city, now known as Pavlopetri. Buildings, streets, and public squares were all evident below the waves, in spite of the inevitable erosion that occurred after the city met its watery fate.

## Significant Discoveries

At first, the ruins were believed to be from the Mycenaean Period, the last phase of the Bronze Age in Greece that lasted from about 1750 to 1050 BC. But further research showed that while many of the buildings and streets do date back to this time, the area itself was first inhabited much earlier, around 2800 BC, making it one of the oldest known submerged cities in the world. In fact, some researchers believe that Pavlopetri is the oldest submerged city ever discovered.

Forty years after Flemming's discovery, interest in the sunken city returned, and researchers began studying the site in more detail. Using digital mapping techniques originally developed for the military, scientists were able to recreate a three-dimensional model of the submerged city. All told, 15 buildings, containing about 12 rooms each, have been discovered, as well as a sophisticated water management system, complete with canals and pipes.

The digital mapping also allowed archeologists to see tombs and religious buildings, as well as a clear layout of the city, still apparent after thousands of years. One of the most impressive finds was a possible "megaron," which, in ancient Greek buildings, was a large, rectangular room with an open porch at one end, sometimes supported by several columns. These types of buildings were occupied by the elites in society, suggesting that Pavlopetri was an important city during its time.

Divers, with the assistance of special robots from the Australian Center for Field Robotics, discovered a large number of loom weights throughout the site, indicating that Pavlopetri once had a thriving textile industry. They also recovered many pottery jars originating from Crete, which indicates that Pavlopetri had a significant trading relationship with the island, or perhaps that the city itself was considered a major trading port.

## Frozen in Time

Sometime around 1000 BC, Pavlopetri began to descend into the sea. Researchers are not certain why this occurred, but most believe it was probably due to a series of earthquakes, some of which may have been as strong as magnitude 8. Whatever the reason, the abandoned city sank into its watery grave, never to be inhabited again. This has given archeologists the unique opportunity to explore an ancient city frozen in time.

Because the ruins of Pavlopetri are so close to the surface of the water—some of the larger structures are less than two feet underwater—they face many environmental threats to their continued existence. Pollution from passing commercial ships, dragging anchors, shifting sediment, and looters looking for souvenirs are all dangers that must be addressed in order to maintain the integrity of Pavlopetri's ancient ruins. In 2016, the site was added to the World Monuments Watch list, which was created by the World Monuments Fund, an organization that strives to protect the world's most significant and vulnerable historic sites.

Flemming, who has revisited the site in recent years, envisions the city as an underwater museum and park, which would allow careful protection of the area while still welcoming visitors to explore the amazing ruins. He also believes that exploration has only just begun, and there is still much more Pavlopetri can reveal to the world. As research and excavation continues, archeologists are excited to see what else may be waiting just below the surface of the sea.

# Vijayanagara: An Architectural Marvel

*On the banks of the Tungabhadra River in the Karnataka region of India, the ruins of Vijayanagara still stand. Once the capital city of the empire of the same name, Vijayanagara now thrills archeologists and visitors with its architecture.*

✳ ✳ ✳ ✳

THE CITY WAS founded in 1336 by brothers Harihara I and Bukka Raya I. The region was already a site of pilgrimage for Hindu devotees of the god Shiva and the goddess Parvati, and it grew rapidly throughout the fourteenth and fifteenth centuries. At its height, it was believed to be one of the largest cities in the world, second only to Beijing, with a population that may have surpassed 500,000.

Within Vijayanagara is the UNESCO World Heritage site known as Hampi, which was built around an existing temple complex devoted to Parvati. In fact, the name Hampi is derived from Pampa, another name sometimes given to the goddess. Archeologists have uncovered pottery in the region dating back to the second and third centuries, so it is evident that humans were drawn to the location long before the creation of the Vijayanagara empire. Local folklore tells a tale of two hunters named Hakka and Bukka who saw a strange sight in the area before humans had settled there. The hunters were watching their dog chase a rabbit across the land, when suddenly, the rabbit turned and instead began chasing the dog. Hakka and Bukka took this as a sign that they had found a unique place within India, and moved their entire village to the new location.

## World-Renowned

Whether or not the story is true, Hampi certainly did become a unique place in India. The city attracted people from all over the world, who came to the crowded markets where merchants traded and sold their wares for spices, cotton, silver, and gold. Art and architecture were greatly prized, and magnificent temples, forts, palaces, shrines, water structures, and gateways were constructed. By the year 1500, Vijayanagara covered 250 square miles and was the richest city in India.

But all good things must come to an end and Vijayanagara was no exception. In the sixteenth century, the city was engaged in ongoing wars with Muslim sultanates. Five of these sultanates, who were normally rivals, formed an alliance, known as the Deccan sultanates. Together, they attacked the city in January 1565, capturing and beheading the leader of Vijayanagara, Aliya Rama Raya. The city was looted and burned over the next several months, and was finally abandoned.

Today, more than 1,600 structures spread over 16 square miles have been restored in Hampi. These include the Virupaksha temple, known for its 160-foot-high *gopuram*, or monumental tower, and the amazing Garuda shrine, a large stone chariot often referenced as a symbol of Hampi. Also restored are public plazas, water features, kitchens, dining halls, and elephant stables. The once magnificent Vijayanagara, which attracted visitors from far and wide, continues to welcome people from around the world, who marvel at its history and architecture.

# Xanadu: City of Dreams

*A city of fabulous myth to many, Xanadu was quite fabulous in reality as well.*

✳   ✳   ✳   ✳

FANS OF LITERATURE may recall Samuel Taylor Coleridge's poem "Kubla Khan," which begins with the lines:

In Xanadu did Kubla Khan

A stately pleasure-dome decree:

Where Alph, the sacred river, ran

Through caverns measureless to man

Down to a sunless sea.

The poem goes on to speak of "gardens," "towers," and "greenery," describing the area as "enchanted." According to Coleridge himself, he wrote the poem one night after reading about Shangdu, the summer capital which came to prominence under its leader, Kublai Khan. The poet also claimed to have partaken in opium, which fueled his imagination with vivid dreams.

Regardless of whether or not the poem was the result of a drug-addled dream, Shangdu, better known as Xanadu, was a real place. Shangdu came to be known for its gardens, waterways, and temples.

## Summering in the City

Located about 220 miles north of Beijing in what is now Shangdu Town in Inner Mongolia, the city was originally named Kaiping, meaning "open and flat," and was built between 1252 and 1256. In 1263, the capital of the Mongol Empire was moved from Karakorum to Kaiping, but just ten years later the capital was moved again to Khanbaliq. But Kublai Khan, who began his reign in 1260, enjoyed the cooler summer climate in Kaiping so much that he transferred his entire court to the city every year during the warmer months. He renamed it Shangdu, or Xanadu, meaning "upper capital," to reflect the importance of the city to the Mongol Empire.

Laid out in a square shape, the city was surrounded by earthen walls that were up to 18 feet high. Six towers were located on each side of the perimeter wall, just like the "towers" Coleridge spoke of in his poem. Xanadu was divided into an "Inner City," where the court resided in a palace built of wood, stone, marble, and glazed tiles, and the "Outer City," where most of the general population lived in houses built of mud and wood. The Inner City was surrounded by walls made of brick which were up to 16 feet high, and four more towers adorned the walls. Abundant natural springs provided water to the city, contributing to the "gardens" and "greenery" of the location. To the northwest of the city, the Mongols had created a preserve for one of their favorite pastimes, hunting. This area was surrounded by another earthen wall as well as a moat. The preserve was stocked with wild game such as deer, along with domesticated animals including falcons, horses, and cows.

## A Visit from Marco Polo

Xanadu became known for hosting great feasts and hunting parties, and was a gathering place for the Mongol tribal chiefs, who debated how best to run their empire. It was also a destination for travelers who had heard the tales of great Asian rulers and their kingdoms.

Perhaps the most famous of these travelers was the Venetian explorer Marco Polo, who visited Xanadu and served in Kublai Khan's court between 1275 and 1292. He wrote of his experiences in Xanadu in his book, *The Travels of Marco Polo*. In it, the explorer described two palaces used by Kublai Khan. One was a marble palace, complete with columns of gilt and lacquer. The other was built of cane or wicker and varnished to be watertight. The Cane Palace, as he described it, could be deconstructed and moved to a different location if the Khan so desired.

Xanadu embraced a combination of Mongol and Chinese traditions, which Kublai Khan believed symbolized the future. However, not everyone saw it the same way. Many Mongols thought the city was too Chinese, and they felt it was an abandonment of their own culture. The Chinese, on the other hand, believed the city encompassed a way of life that was too Mongol. They believed the city should adopt a more formal Chinese culture.

Over time, bitterness, struggle, and discontent among the populace began to weaken the city. This, coupled with droughts, floods, and famines that plagued the region in the mid-1300s, led to the fall of the ruling dynasty in 1368. Although Xanadu initially survived the fall of the empire, it suffered a period of neglect and was finally abandoned in 1430.

## Lasting Legacy

The city was effectively forgotten for centuries, reclaimed by the grasslands of Inner Mongolia and mostly hidden from view. In 1872, an English physician and amateur Orientalist named Stephen Wootton Bushell became the first known European to visit Xanadu since the time of Marco Polo. He described stone lions and dragons and a ruined palace strewn with marble tiles. By the time archeologists began to excavate the site in earnest more than a century later, much of what Bushell had described had been removed by inhabitants of a nearby town.

Even so, researchers have managed to uncover the ruins of more than 1,000 buildings, as well as the foundations of 700 other structures. Colorful roof tiles, marble columns, ceramics, jade sculptures, and coins have all been discovered in the area. In 2011, Xanadu, which is now recognized as a UNESCO World Heritage Site, was opened to visitors. The city has become synonymous with exotic splendor and mystery, and has been referenced in movies like *Citizen Kane* and the 1980 film *Xanadu*. Today, fans of Samuel Taylor Coleridge can visit the site of his poem's inspiration and imagine the grandeur that once enthralled travelers like Marco Polo.

# Aztalan: A Prehistoric Puzzle

*Few people know it, but a millennium ago, Wisconsin was the site of a thriving culture now known as the Middle Mississippians.*

✳ ✳ ✳ ✳

## A Mysterious Site

AZTALAN IS A fortified settlement of mysterious people who worshiped the sun. The Middle Mississippian culture erected stepped pyramids, may have practiced cannibalism, and enjoyed coast-to-coast trade. Some have linked the Mississippians to the Aztecs and even to the legendary city of Atlantis. All that is truly certain is that they lived at Aztalan for 150 years. Then they disappeared.

Aztalan, near present-day Lake Mills, is now a state park and a National Historic Landmark. Still, what happened at Aztalan is among the greatest archeological puzzles in the world. During the period when it was settled, sometime between AD 1050 and 1100, gunpowder was invented in China. Macbeth ruled Scotland. The Orthodox and Roman Catholic churches split. In America, across the Mississippi from St. Louis in what is now Illinois, there was a strange, 2,000-acre city of earthen pyramids later dubbed "Cahokia." Its population was roughly 20,000—more than London at that time.

Aztalan appears to be the northern outpost of the Cahokia peoples. Because of location, archeologists call their civilization Middle Mississippian. They are distinct from the Woodland peoples, who were there first and remained afterward. The Mississippians were quite enamored with the sun, and at Cahokia, residents erected wooden solar observatories, similar to Britain's Stonehenge.

Like Cahokia, Aztalan was something of an oddity: 22 acres surrounded by a stockade with 32 watch towers, all made from heavy timbers and then covered with hard clay. Inside, pyramidal mounds stood as high as 16 feet. Outside the fortifications, crops were planted. According to Cahokia experts, the Mississippians are responsible for introducing corn to this part of North America.

Today, Aztalan looks much different than it did at its peak. The mounds remain, and part of the stockade has been rebuilt. Also, the Friends of Aztalan group is trying to recreate antique agriculture with a small garden of gourds, squash, sunflowers, and an early type of corn, all planted just as the Mississippians would have.

In addition to vegetables, the Mississippian diet may have included some more interesting dishes—namely human flesh. At Cahokia there is evidence of human sacrifice. It was initially thought that Aztalan's residents practiced some sort of cannibalism as well. But science and interpretations change with time. There is speculation that the so-called "cannibalism" could have simply been a ceremonial or funerary practice that had nothing to do with eating human flesh.

## Gone Without a Trace

Another puzzle is why the Mississippians suddenly vanished from the Midwest sometime between AD 1200 and 1300. Author Frank Joseph has taken the folklore of three continents and made a case linking Atlantis, Aztalan, and the Aztecs in his books, *The Lost Pyramids of Rock Lake* and *Atlantis in Wisconsin.* Joseph's theory is that the people of Atlantis founded Cahokia and Aztalan, mined copper, cast it into ingots, and shipped it back east, fueling Europe's Bronze Age. After a cataclysm destroyed their Mediterranean island empire, leaderless survivors in the Wisconsin settlement migrated south. They created a new Aztalan in Mexico and eventually became the Aztecs.

The Aztecs themselves referred to their far-away, long-ago homeland—wherever it was—as "Aztlan." However, scholars deny that residents of Aztalan ever used that name. It was merely a fanciful label applied by European settlers.

Joseph's evidence is highly conjectural and sensationalist but contains some intriguing elements. For example, one of the great mysteries of Europe's Bronze Age is where all the necessary copper came from (bronze is made of copper and tin). Known low-grade deposits in Great Britain and Spain would have been quickly exhausted. Yet Lake Superior's shores have, and had, the only known workable virgin, native copper deposits in the world.

The Mississippians certainly knew of these copper deposits—they mined Michigan's Upper Peninsula. Farther back in time, according to legend, Atlantis was reigning supreme, enjoying great wealth derived from its trade throughout the known world of precious metals, especially copper. The Lake Superior mines closed precisely when Europe's Bronze Age ended. Coincidentally, or perhaps not, it was around this time that Atlantis supposedly sank and disappeared forever.

The answers to many more questions about the Mississippian culture are yet be found. According to the Cahokia Mounds Museum Society, archeologists have explored only a fraction of the site. Could the decisive link to Atlantis or the Aztecs still be buried beneath the grounds of Cahokia or Aztalan? While that is highly unlikely, only time will tell.

* As the name suggests, Mississippian culture spanned the length of the Mississippi River, including areas in what are now the states of Mississippi, Georgia, Alabama, Missouri, Arkansas, Illinois, Indiana, Kentucky, Ohio, Wisconsin, and Minnesota.

* It must have been desirable real estate! While Aztalan is usually considered to be a Mississippian settlement, there are many artifacts at the site from other groups of people that predate their arrival.

* For many years before it was studied and preserved, the area of Aztalan was plowed for farming; pottery and other artifacts were carted away by souvenir hunters.

* Aztalan became a National Historic Landmark in 1964 and it was added to the National Register of Historic Places in 1966.

* There is speculation that some of the mounds at Aztalan could have been used for astronomical purposes.

* It is believed that Aztalan was a planned community with spaces for the general public, ceremonial locations, residential areas, and sections designated for elite individuals.

* Based on the artifacts unearthed at Aztalan, it appears that the people living there were skilled at farming, hunting, and fishing.

# A Lost City in Kansas

*The state of Kansas, known for its agriculture and for being the home of Dorothy in* The Wizard of Oz, *is probably one of the last places that comes to mind when reflecting on lost civilizations. Yet Arkansas City, located in the southwestern part of the state along the confluence of the Arkansas River and Walnut River, was once the location of Etzanoa, home of the Wichita people.*

✳   ✳   ✳   ✳

THE FIRST RECORD of Etzanoa can be traced back to 1595, when an expedition of Spanish colonists, including an indigenous Mexican by the name of Jusepe Gutierrez, happened upon a "very large settlement" stretching for miles along a river. Six years later, Gutierrez guided Juan de Onate, the founder and governor of New Mexico, back to the same area the Spanish colonists had explored years earlier. The explorers, along with more than 70 Spanish and Indian soldiers, priests, and servants, ran into a group of Escanjaque Indians along the way, who led the Spanish explorers to an encampment of another Indian tribe. Onate called these other people *Rayados*, using the Spanish word for "striped," in reference to their tattooed faces.

## The Great Settlement

The Rayados were friendly and helpful to Onate and his contingent, but the Escanjaque had an ulterior motive for bringing the Spanish to the settlement. The two tribes were enemies, and the Escanjaque requested help from the Spanish in attacking the Rayados. Although Onate refused to attack the peaceful Rayados, he did take their chief, Catarax, hostage and used him as a guide. Catarax led the group to another large settlement on the banks of the Arkansas River, where they found more than 1,200 round houses, along with fields of corn, beans, squash, and pumpkins. The people from the village had fled, however, fearing an attack.

Catarax was soon rescued by his people, and Onate and his group decided to return to New Mexico lest they face the wrath of the Rayados for taking their chief hostage. But on their way home, it was the Escanjaque who attacked, resulting in casualties on both sides. Onate was able to capture one of the attackers, and, still fascinated with the large village on the river Catarax had shown him, asked the captive to draw a map of the area. The Escanjaque complied, calling the village the "Great Settlement" of "Etzanoa."

## New Translations of Old Stories

Over time, the story of Etzanoa faded into obscurity. The fabled "Great Settlement" was forgotten, even by the archeologists who had studied the area around the Arkansas River and the Walnut River many times since the 1930s. Although construction crews, road workers, and residents of Arkansas City had often found artifacts like flint arrowheads and pottery shards, these were assumed to be remnants of many different settlements and tribes. But Wichita State University archeologist Donald Blakeslee wasn't so sure. In 2015, he set out to prove that the huge settlement of Etzanoa was once located right in Arkansas City.

Blakeslee acquired newly updated, and more precise, translations of old Spanish documents and maps concerning the Rayados and Etzanoa. The documents, which had been compiled after Onate's 1601 expedition, described the geography of the area, the size and types of dwellings found, and the appearance of the native "Rayados," who, researchers now know, were the Wichita Indians.

The expedition members described seeing around 2,000 beehive-shaped, grass hut homes, spread out over a five-mile area on both sides of the Walnut River. The homes were approximately 70 to 80 feet in circumference, and about ten people lived in each home, making the population of the village around 20,000. Houses were arranged in clusters, and between each cluster of homes was land planted with crops. The women of the village tended to the gardens with tools made of stone, wood, bone, and deer antlers, and the men hunted for wild game with stone arrow points, knives, and spears.

## A Lost Settlement Found

Blakeslee was able to decipher two maps—which were drawn in an unfamiliar and unusual style compared to modern maps, making them difficult for previous researchers to understand—and believed that they both pointed to Arkansas City as the location of the settlement.

Over the next several years, Blakeslee, along with other archeologists and volunteers, began unearthing an overwhelming number of stone tools, weapons, and cooking utensils that would have been used by the Wichita. But even more compelling, volunteers found horseshoe nails, bullets, and a cannonball—items left behind by the 1601 Spanish expedition during their battle with the Escanjaque. Blakeslee was certain now: This was the site of the legendary Great Settlement of Etzanoa.

Researchers believe that the Wichita inhabited Etzanoa from about 1500 to 1720, eventually moving south into Oklahoma but leaving behind traces of their presence. And the Great Settlement is still giving up secrets today, thanks to new technologies and innovations.

A recent drone survey using LIDAR methods concluded that Etzanoa may have covered even more ground than originally believed, stretching into Winfield, Kansas, about 14 miles to the north. And a study led by archeologists from Dartmouth College recently found several circular earthworks in the area, which may be the remains of Etzanoa ceremonial sites. While the modern world may now surround it, it seems the Great Settlement of Etzanoa still quietly stands, waiting to reveal more of its mysteries.

# Ciudad Perdida: A City Found

*The discovery of Ciudad Perdida is reminiscent of an adventure movie! In 1972, a group of treasure hunters stumbled upon a very old stone staircase hidden deep within the greenery of the Colombian jungle. When they climbed the stairs, they found themselves in an abandoned city, covered with vines and vegetation, which they called the "green hell." What they discovered was far from being a hell, however, as it became clear that their quest for treasure was successful.*

✳   ✳   ✳   ✳

THE SITE CONTAINED many gold figurines and valuable pottery, and the looters loaded up with goods to sell. But when unusual gold and ceramic items began showing up on the black market, archeologists knew that something exciting had been found in the Columbian jungle. In 1976, researchers were finally able to find the elusive stone staircase in the jungle, and excavation of the abandoned city, now known as Ciudad Perdida, or "lost city," began.

## Not-Quite-Lost City?

But "lost" may be a misnomer in the case of Ciudad Perdida. Local indigenous groups, including the Wiwa, Arhuaco, and Kogi tribes were all aware of the location of the city, and even visited it on occasion. But they preferred to keep it a secret, possibly hoping to prevent treasure hunters, such as the ones who eventually found it, from looting it.

Built around AD 800, in the mountains of the Sierra Nevada de Santa Marta range, the city was one of many places inhabited by the Tairona people (forebears of the Kogis). Their villages were connected by stone pathways, not unlike the stone staircase that leads to the lost city. Within Ciudad Perdida, the largest of these villages, the Tairona people constructed more than 200 structures, including mountainside terraces, circular plazas, dwellings, storehouses, and ceremonial areas.

# A Life Upended

For centuries, life on the mountain was simple and peaceful. Communities grew tomatoes, corn, avocado, pineapple, and guava. With a location close to the Caribbean Sea, they were able to catch an abundance of seafood. The stone paths between villages allowed easy trade of food, textiles, pottery, and gold. Women and children wove fabric to create clothing and bags, and men took the status of warriors and protectors.

But everything changed after the arrival of the Spanish conquistadors in the 1500s. Years of conflict and struggle followed, and although the Tairona men fought to resist the hostility of the Spaniards, they were not a naturally violent people. After even offers of gold failed to appease the conquistadors, the Tairona people were eventually forced to flee Ciudad Perdida, leaving it to be consumed by the jungle.

Today, tourists can visit this ancient city, which can still be described as "lost" for good reason: In order to reach it, visitors must trek for 27 miles through the jungle, crossing several rivers and enduring steep climbs. The journey takes at least two or three days, and a local guide must accompany all hikers for safety. While the hike requires payment of a fee, much of the money is used to preserve the site and protect it from overgrowth and looting. It also ensures the indigenous peoples of the area have a say in how the site is run. For many visitors, the price is well worth it to have the chance to experience a bit of ancient history.

# The Atlantis of the Sands

*In the Quran, a story is told about a tribe of people known as the Ad. The Adites built a powerful city filled with "lofty pillars," which rivaled any other city in Arabia. But the people turned their backs on Allah, living wicked lives and engaging in pursuits that displeased their God. A prophet named Hud was appointed by Allah to caution the Ad people to turn from their sinful ways, but they did not heed the warning. To punish the Adites, Allah sent a huge sandstorm that engulfed their city for seven nights and eight days. When it was over, the city, known as Iram of the Pillars, had vanished beneath the desert sands as if it had never existed.*

✳ ✳ ✳ ✳

SOME PEOPLE BELIEVE that the story of Iram is simply a parable, a morality tale that illustrates the dangers of living a selfish, arrogant life. But others are convinced that there is truth within the narrative, and the city of Iram may have once existed. For centuries, explorers, archeologists, and travelers have been fascinated by the possibility of a hidden city in the desert. Even famed army officer, diplomat, and archeologist T.E. Lawrence, known best by his nickname, Lawrence of Arabia, was curious about Iram and its unknown location, dubbing it the "Atlantis of the Sands."

## Reimagined Embellishments

While there are a few mentions of a place called Iram in some pre-Islamic poetry, the main source for the story of the city is the Quran. Over the centuries, the relatively simple tale in the religious text received embellishment in retellings. The "lofty pillars" of Iram were now covered in silver and gold, and encrusted with jewels, pearls, and saffron. What's more, the desert city was an oasis of flower gardens and trees, with abundant flowing rivers providing fresh water. Perhaps the most detailed version of the story was found in *One Thousand and One Nights*, a collection of Middle Eastern folk tales.

Western audiences who were curious about the mystical, romantic land of Arabia were captivated by the stories when they were first translated into French in 1704. Translations into English, German, Italian, Russian, and other European languages quickly followed. *One Thousand and One Nights* describes Iram as a city full of hundreds of splendid palaces, each adorned with pillars, all of which took three hundred years to construct.

Some scholars argue that these elaborate, fanciful additions to the original story have prevented archeologists from taking the idea of a buried desert city more seriously. But others point out that the stories, especially the hugely popular *One Thousand and One Nights*, ignited an interest in explorers, travelers, writers, and researchers who otherwise would not have known about Iram. Whether it was jewel-encrusted or simply made of stone, many were determined to find this Atlantis of the Sands.

## Evidence in the Desert?

In the 1970s, a discovery was made which helped to bolster the claim that Iram was at one time a real city. Italian archeologist Paolo Matthiae led an excavation of the ancient city of Ebla in northern Syria, where he and his team carefully uncovered houses, temples, walls, and gates that dated back to between 2500 and 2250 BC. Also discovered were thousands of clay tablets and fragments of tablets containing Sumerian writing and cuneiform writing in a script now known as "Eblaite." And within these tablets, which seemed to describe nearby regions and cities that traded with Ebla, was the name Iram.

Decades later, in the 1990s, a team led by American filmmaker and amateur archeologist Nicholas Clapp excavated a location in Dhofar province of Oman. According to *The New York Times*, Clapp used "ancient maps and sharp-eyed surveys from space" to uncover what he believed to be Ubar, another name for Iram. He discovered a large octagonal fort with towers, which had partially collapsed when it fell into a sinkhole.

## Still Searching

While the site is located within the Rub' al Khali desert (the area most often suggested as the location of Iram), it should be noted that the ruins of the fort are also believed to be on what used to be a trade route for frankincense. This site was known for its large well, the only source of water within several days' journey, and, therefore, a logical choice to establish a town. Archeologists also believe that the city discovered by Clapp was not destroyed by a sandstorm, but rather by the sinkholes that once housed the area's well water. The Saudi Arabian press was also critical of the find, insisting that similar "lost" cities had been uncovered in the country's deserts and were better contenders for the title of Iram.

To date, no city has been discovered in the Arabian desert that truly fits the many descriptions of Iram of the Pillars, whether ordinary or fanciful. While many researchers believe that the city is entirely mythical, others are still convinced that the city of Iram and the Ad people who once occupied it were quite real. With around 250,000 square miles of desert to explore, it is possible that Iram of the Pillars is still out there, sleeping beneath the sands, waiting to be found.

# An Oasis in the Desert

*The Oxus civilization was part of a Bronze Age culture dating back to between 2300 and 1700 BC. Its remnant ruins and artifacts lie in a remote desert region of Central Asia, still waiting to yield all its secrets.*

✳  ✳  ✳  ✳

REMAINS OF THE Oxus civilization lie buried in an area known as the "Bactria-Margiana Archeological Complex." "Bactria" was the Greek name for northern Afghanistan and northeast Iran, and "Margiana" referred to what is today Turkmenistan and Uzbekistan. Flowing through this Central Asian region is the Amu Darya River, historically known as the

Oxus. Although the site was first discovered in the 1970s by Soviet archeologist Viktor Sarianidi, the 1979 Iran revolution and the Soviet invasion of Afghanistan prevented many of his findings from catching the attention of Western researchers. But Sarianidi's discoveries would eventually amaze the archeological world.

Sarianidi had first discovered many Bronze Age sites dating back to the second and third millennia BC, as well as graves full of large amounts of gold, in the region of ancient Bactria. These sites contained structures with thick fortification walls, buttresses, and gates, and were filled with art of a very distinctive style. Shortly after, Sarianidi was conducting another excavation in the hot, dusty, Kara-Kum desert in eastern Turkmenistan. The flat plain of the desert contained a large expanse of mounds, indicating the presence of man-made structures that had long been buried by the elements. The site was so expansive, in fact, that Sarianidi assumed it had been occupied as recently as medieval times. But while digging in the region, he was surprised to discover pottery that resembled the artistic style of ancient Bactria.

## New Research, Old Artifacts

The war in Afghanistan soon forced Sarianidi to abandon this site and explore other areas, but he made note of the sprawling, buried city, which the locals called Gonur. After the collapse of the Soviet Union, Western archeologists began to reexamine Sarianidi's findings, and this time, they not only traveled to the region to conduct their own research, but they also brought along more advanced technology than had been available to the Soviets.

Sarianidi, meanwhile, began excavating the ruins buried beneath the desert, discovering a walled citadel nested within a larger wall, and a vast oval wall surrounding the entire complex. The Western researchers were able to date the city back to 2000 BC, much earlier than Sarianidi had originally guessed.

The archeological teams also uncovered many pieces of intricate jewelry made of metal, including gold and silver, and semiprecious stones like lapis lazuli and carnelian. The sophisticated pieces, which often featured geometric designs, humanoid figures, animals, or mythical monsters, hinted at the skilled craftsmen who must have once lived and worked in the area.

The find also helped to solve an old archeological puzzle. For decades, researchers had found items displaying the same style as the artifacts found in Gonur in regions like Mesopotamia, the Persian Gulf, and the Mohenjo Daro site in Pakistan, but they were mystified by their origin. Finding a treasure trove of such items in Gonur seemed to confirm that their origin had been found.

## Oxus Origins

But Gonur was not the first settlement of the Oxus civilization. Researchers believe that the civilization's origins lie in the foothills of the Kopet-Dag mountain range near the city of Ashgabat in Turkmenistan. Here, in Anau, archeologists found more of the same ancient mounds found in Gonur, dating back to 2300 BC, a mere three centuries after the Egyptian pyramids were finished.

Researchers theorize that prior to Anau, small bands of people lived in the mountains of Kopet-Dag, where they established small towns and began creating rudimentary pottery that would eventually evolve into the more sophisticated pieces found at Gonur. This small civilization grew stronger, larger, and more structured. Eventually, it expanded throughout Turkmenistan, finally extending into Iran, Afghanistan, and Uzbekistan.

Although today the Kara-Kum desert is a very dry, dusty, and unforgivingly hot place, archeologists believe that when the Oxus civilization was thriving and expanding, the climate was significantly more temperate, with more rain and more extensive vegetation. Oases along the Murgab River, which flows from the mountains of the Hindu Kush, would have provided the irrigation needed for the civilization to grow the wheat, barley, lentils, and fruits that they cultivated. In addition to engaging in agriculture, the Oxus civilization also created their own impressive jewelry and pottery, and raised goats, sheep, oxen, and camels.

## Golden Bowls

Along with the excavations of Gonur and Anau, researchers have made many more discoveries concerning the Oxus civilization, some after organized digs, and some accidentally. The first evidence of the culture in northern Afghanistan was uncovered even before Sarianidi began his own investigations in the country. In 1966, farmers near the Afghan village of Fullol stumbled upon a grave that contained golden bowls depicting animal imagery as well as numerous silver cups and bowls. Not realizing what they'd found, the farmers began crudely removing these treasures with an ax.

Luckily, local authorities got word of these amateur excavations and managed to salvage several of the priceless artifacts before they were damaged or went missing. These artifacts turned out to date back to 2200 BC, and their distinctive style was eventually linked to the Oxus civilization.

The golden bowls were particularly fascinating, not just because they were crafted from precious metals thousands of years ago in the Oxus style, but also because some of the motifs they displayed suggested interaction with outside cultures.

One of the bowl designs featured the image of a bearded bull, a theme that was common in Mesopotamia far to the west. Other patterns were common in the area that is now Pakistan, far to the southeast. These clues suggested that the Oxus civilization was probably engaged in trade with these and other cultures, and it probably exchanged its own wares made of lapis lazuli, mined in the mountains of the Badakhshan province.

## The Capital and the Cannabis

Perhaps no place has served to reveal as much about the Oxus culture as the Gonur site itself, which many consider to be the "capital" of the civilization. Covering about 136 acres, Gonur is divided into three sections: Gonur North, Gonur South, and the Large Necropolis.

Gonur North features the huge walled citadel that Sarianidi first uncovered in the late 1980s, which spans 330 feet by 590 feet. It also contains temples, water reservoirs, and a royal palace, which features two courtyards and an inner chamber that may have been a throne room or audience hall. Also found in Gonur North is a royal necropolis, where eight underground burial pits were found. These pits contained numerous items of gold, silver, bronze, and ivory, reflecting the elite status of those who were buried there. Gonur South is a smaller complex surrounded by walls flanked with round towers. A shrine called the Temenos is located here, and within the shrine is a smaller fort in the shape of a cruciform.

The Large Necropolis covers about 24 acres and contains more than 3,000 graves of adults and older children. Young children were found to have been buried near houses or within buildings. The necropolis is notable for its mosaics, which decorate some of the walls as well as containers and boxes that were used to hold offerings of gold and silver.

Sarianidi made another interesting discovery in Gonur when he found what seemed to be a kind of boiler for making *soma*, a type of ritualistic drink. He also found bowls with the residue of cannabis, opium, and ephedra, which may have been the ingredients for this drink, as well as mortars and pestles for extracting these plants' juices.

If soma did, indeed, contain these various substances, it would explain why the drink often resulted in hallucinations. But a definitive recipe for soma has never been found, and a correlating identification of the residue Sarianidi found in the bowls has never been completed. However, most researchers agree that soma must have been made with some combination of plants with psychoactive properties, so it is plausible to imagine that the archeologist confirmed the use of these ingredients in the drink.

## Sharing Faith and Culture

The Oxus civilization not only engaged in the ritualistic consumption of soma, but it also adhered to a religion that Sarianidi believed eventually evolved into Zoroastrianism, sometimes considered the world's first monotheistic religion. Oxus artifacts have been found in the Indus Valley, the Iranian Plateau, and the Persian Gulf, giving evidence of their interaction and trade with peoples in those areas. It is possible that they also traded ideas about their religion, which, sometime before 500 BC, transformed into what is today known as Zoroastrianism. Some historians even believe that Zoroaster himself may have lived in Margiana.

The influence of the Oxus civilization in Bactria and Margiana is undeniable. The peoples lived in meticulously designed cities with homes, temples, streets, and sophisticated irrigation and drainage systems. They were experts at cultivating fruits and grains in the oases of the desert. They traded gold, silver, and semiprecious stones with cities far and wide, while also sharing their ideas about religion. But around 1900 BC, the cities of the Oxus civilization began to decrease in size, and within a few centuries, they simply vanished.

As is the case with so many ancient civilizations, the cause of their disappearance is unknown. But they left behind many echoes of their culture, to remind us that even when civilizations disappear, they do not have to be forgotten.

# Birthplace of Buddha

*Lumbini offers tantalizing historical clues about Buddhism's originator. Was it the true birthplace of Siddhartha Gautama?*

✳ ✳ ✳ ✳

ACCORDING TO LEGEND, sometime around 563 BC, a pregnant queen named Mayadevi, who lived in what is today Nepal, was traveling when she stopped in a beautiful flower garden. Under a sal tree, she gave birth to a son, who was named Siddhartha Gautama. Three and a half decades later, Prince Siddhartha would become Gautama Buddha, the founder of Buddhism.

Today, the supposed location of the garden where Buddha is believed to have been born is known as Lumbini, and it is one of the holiest sites for followers of Buddhism. Located in the Rupandehi District of the Lumbini Province in Nepal, the region is situated very close to the Indian border. While it was known to be a pilgrimage destination for Buddhist followers for several centuries after Prince Siddhartha was born, as Hinduism and Islam came to predominate in the area by the eighth century AD, Lumbini fell into neglect and eventually was forgotten.

### The Ashoka Pillar

A great benefactor of Buddhism, Ashoka the Great, emperor of the Maurya Empire, had formally declared in 249 BC that Lumbini was the birthplace of the Buddha. To commemorate the location, the emperor created an inscribed stone pillar so that future visitors would understand the significance of the place. Over time, the pillar was damaged, as documented by a Chinese Buddhist monk named Xuanzang, who made a pilgrimage to the site in the seventh century. Xuanzang noted a pillar, topped by a sculpture of a horse, that was split in two and lying on the ground.

After Lumbini's popularity waned, the pillar was forgotten. Over time, the fallen pillar became partially buried. Then, in 1869, German archeologist Alois Anton Führer, who specialized in the study of South Asian cultures, began excavating the Ashoka pillar, which had been discovered several years earlier. As Führer dug away the earth that had concealed the pillar for so long, he found something that the monk Xuanzang had not mentioned in the record of his travels: the inscription that Ashoka the Great had added to the stone pillar, marking the location of the Buddha's birth.

## Rediscovery

Although Führer was later found to have faked some of his archeological discoveries and was forced to end his career in disgrace, most scholars agree that the pillar of Ashoka is indeed authentic. The discovery served to reignite interest in the "lost" city of Lumbini, and placed the sacred location back on the map. Indian archeologist Purna Chandra Mukherjee took over the excavations of the area after Führer's misdeeds. Many modern researchers credit Mukherjee with truly "discovering" Lumbini, as he engaged in careful, methodical work in the area, uncovering ancient monasteries, temples, and sculptures.

Along with the ruins of ancient monasteries, researchers have found an ancient bathing pond and a bodhi tree, which, according to legend, is the same type of tree under which Buddha attained enlightenment in 500 BC. In the 1930s, the governor of the region ordered restoration projects at Lumbini, in order to make the destination more attractive to tourists. But the projects also resulted in the loss of some of the ancient artifacts, prompting the Nepalese Department of Archeology to take control of the site. It was later protected under the Ancient Monument Preservation Act of 1956.

## An Enlightened Destination

Modern Lumbini, which is three miles long and one mile wide, is divided into three sections: the Sacred Garden, the Monastic

Zone, and the Cultural Center and New Lumbini Village. The Monastic Zone contains monasteries and schools that represent the Theravada, Mahayana, and Vajrayana Buddhist traditions. The Cultural Center and New Lumbini Village is where visitors will find a museum, shops, research institute, administrative buildings, and the Lumbini Crane Sanctuary, which helps to protect sarus cranes and preserve the natural ecosystem of the area.

But the heart of Lumbini is the Sacred Garden, where the site of Buddha's birth has been marked with a stone. The area also features the Mayadevi Temple, the Ashoka Pillar, and a pond where Mayadevi was said to have ritually bathed before giving birth to the Buddha. The area is popular not only with followers of Buddhism, but with anyone seeking peaceful reflection or quiet meditation.

Interestingly, modern Lumbini has been designed to mirror the spiritual path of Buddhism. The first area that greets visitors is the Cultural Center and New Lumbini Village, a busy area of "worldly activities." From there, visitors leave the distractions of the world behind and journey through the Monastic Zone, which represents the process of learning more about Buddhism and its traditions.

Finally, the quiet enlightenment of the Sacred Garden awaits, where guests can reflect on their own spiritual paths. For tourists from around the world, Lumbini is not just an archeological site full of ancient artifacts, it is also a journey unto itself.

# Vanished: The Lost Colony of Roanoke Island

*Twenty years before England established its first successful colony in the New World, an entire village of English colonists disappeared in what would later become North Carolina. Did these pioneers all perish? Did Native Americans capture them? Did they join a friendly tribe? Could they have left descendants who live among us today?*

✳ ✳ ✳ ✳

## Timing Is Everything

TALK ABOUT BAD timing. As far as John White was concerned, England could not have picked a worse time to go to war. It was November 1587, and White had just arrived in England from the New World. He intended to gather relief supplies and immediately sail back to Roanoke Island, where he had left more than 100 colonists who were running short of food. Unfortunately, the English were gearing up to fight Spain. Every seaworthy ship, including White's, was pressed into naval service. Not a single one could be spared for his return voyage to America.

## Nobody Home

When John White finally returned to North America three years later, he was dismayed to discover that none of the colonists he had left behind were to be found. They seemed to have just vanished. He had stumbled upon a mystery—one that remains unsolved to this day.

The village that White and company had founded in 1587 on Roanoke Island lay completely deserted. Houses had been dismantled (as if someone planned to move them), but the pieces lay in the long grass along with iron tools and farming equipment. A stout stockade made of logs stood empty.

White found no sign of his daughter Eleanor, her husband Ananias, or their daughter Virginia Dare—the first English child known to be born in America. None of the 87 men, 17 women, and 11 children remained. There were no bodies or obvious grave sites offering clues about their fate. The only clues—if they were clues—that White could find were the letters CRO carved into a tree trunk and the word CROATOAN carved into a log of the abandoned fort. All White could do was hope that the colonists had been taken in by friendly natives.

## No Forwarding Address

Croatoan—also spelled "Croatan"—was the name of a barrier island to the south and also the name of a local tribe of Native Americans that once lived on that island. Unlike other area tribes, the Croatoans had been relatively friendly to the English newcomers, and one of them, Manteo, had even traveled to England with earlier explorers and returned to act as an interpreter for the Roanoke colony. Had the colonists, with Manteo's help, moved to the island? Were they safe among friendly natives?

White tried to find out, but his timing was rotten once again. He had arrived on the Carolina coast as a hurricane bore down on the region. The storm hit before he could mount a search. His ship was blown past Croatoan Island and out to sea.

Although the ship and crew survived the storm and made it back to England, White was stuck again. He tried repeatedly but failed to raise money for another search party.

No one has ever learned the fate of the Roanoke Island colonists, but there are no shortage of theories as to what happened. A small sailing vessel along with other boats that White had left with them were gone when he returned. It's possible that the colonists used the vessels to travel to another island or to the mainland. White had talked with others before he left about possibly moving the settlement to a more secure location inland.

It's even possible that the colonists tired of waiting for White's return and tried to sail back to England. If so, they would likely have perished at sea. Yet a few shreds of evidence suggest that the colonists might have survived in America.

## Rumors of Survivors

In 1607, Captain John Smith and company established the first successful English settlement in North America at Jamestown, Virginia. The colony's secretary, William Strachey, wrote four years later about hearing a report of four English men, two boys, and one young woman who had been sighted south of Jamestown at a settlement of the Eno tribe, where they were being used as slaves. If the report was true, who else could these English have been but Roanoke survivors?

For more than a century after the colonists' disappearance, stories continued to surface of gray-eyed Native Americans and English-speaking villages in what is now North Carolina and Virginia. In 1709, an English surveyor said members of the Hatteras tribe living on North Carolina's Outer Banks—some of them with light-colored eyes—claimed to be descendants of white people. It seems possible that the Hatteras were the same people that the 1587 colonists called Croatoan.

In the intervening centuries, many of the individual tribes of the region have disappeared. Some died out. Others were absorbed into larger groups such as the Tuscarora. One surviving group, the Lumbee, has also been called Croatoan. The Lumbee, who still live in North Carolina, often have Caucasian features. Could they be descendants of Roanoke colonists? Many among the Lumbee dismiss the notion as fanciful, but the tribe has long been thought to be of mixed heritage and has been speaking English so long that none among them know what language preceded it.

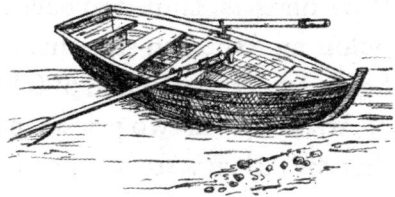

# Atlantis: The Philosopher's Fable

*Flight of fancy or glimmer of truth? The tale that traces back to Plato still holds a powerful allure.*

✳   ✳   ✳   ✳

THE FAMOUS PHILOSOPHER Plato is well-known for his dialogue-format literary prose in which two or more individuals discuss moral and philosophical issues, often applying the Socratic method. In two of these dialogues, *Timaeus* and *Critias*, composed around 360 BC, the philosopher wrote of a land called Atlantis, which he described as a huge island, "larger than Libya and Asia together," located somewhere beyond "the pillars of Heracles." Atlantis, said to be a major naval power, attacked Plato's concept of an ideal state, what he called "Ancient Athens." But this Athens successfully rebuffed the Atlantean attack, and the island subsequently fell out of favor with the gods. Eventually, the entire civilization was destroyed by an earthquake, causing the home island to sink into the Atlantic Ocean.

Even though the tale of Atlantis has been told countless times by numerous philosophers, writers, artists, and others, *Timaeus* and *Critias* are the only original sources of the story. Plato himself claimed to have heard about the island from Solon, an Athenian statesman and lawmaker, who visited Egypt sometime around 590 BC and heard about the history of Atlantis from two priests in a temple at Sais. It would seem that the Atlantis story is one of the earliest examples of "heard it from a friend of a friend."

## The Debate Begins

But as unreliable as these sorts of stories may be, its origins did not stop Atlantis from immediately capturing the imaginations and igniting the curiosity of subsequent writers and thinkers. Some, like Plato's student Aristotle, believed the story to be nothing more than a fictional illustration of a philosophical idea. Others, like Crantor, a Greek philosopher who became a leader in Plato's Academy, were convinced that Atlantis was historical fact. Some later historians and geographers, including Francis Bacon, Francisco Lopez de Gomara, and Alexander von Humboldt, believed that Plato was referring to the Americas when he described Atlantis. And the debate certainly didn't stop there. Today, the fact, or fiction, of Atlantis continues to be a topic of great interest for everyone from historians and archeologists to avid readers and travel buffs.

But with no other records of Atlantis beyond Plato's fictional account, how did this mythical, ancient island become so well-known in our modern world? A nineteenth-century Minnesota congressman named Ignatius Donnelly can take some of the credit. Donnelly was a bit of an amateur historian who dabbled in pseudoscience, and he had a theory about the achievements of the ancient world. He argued that knowledge of things like agriculture, language, and metallurgy must have originated with an earlier, but more evolved, society, since ancient civilizations were too primitive to have developed such skills on their own.

## Flooded or Frozen?

In 1882, Donnelly published a book called *Atlantis: The Antediluvian World*, in which he theorized that Atlantis may have been just such an evolved society, and that all of civilization's advancements in knowledge and technology could be traced back to it.

Donnelly suggested that the island, which he believed was once located in the Atlantic Ocean just outside the Strait of Gibraltar, was engulfed by shifting ocean waters during the Biblical Great Flood. In fact, *antediluvian* refers to the time period between the creation of the universe and the flood as described in Genesis. So, this antediluvian society, Donnelly argued, was the single origin of all great cultures in the world, where the Garden of Eden once flourished and humans rose from barbarism to civilized society.

While Donnelly's theory of Atlantis was eventually discredited by oceanographers, scientists, and even Charles Darwin, his book sold well and sparked renewed interest in the "lost" continent. Many believed that Donnelly's theory sounded plausible, especially since he placed Atlantis exactly where Plato said it should be. "The Pillars of Heracles" that Plato described was the name given to the rock formations in Gibraltar and Morocco that mark the entrance to the Strait of Gibraltar.

Of course, with the advent of modern oceanography, scientists have been able to determine that there is no giant island lurking beneath the waves of the Atlantic. But far from quelling interest in the story of Atlantis, its absence in the Atlantic only served to fuel more theories about the island. Some believe that Plato's story, while mostly fiction, may have been based on a kernel of truth, and the real Atlantis is simply in another location. One theory, popularized by author Charles Hapgood in his 1958 book *Earth's Shifting Crust*, is that Antarctica was once Atlantis. Hapgood posited that the continent used to be located much further north than its present location, in a more temperate climate. But 12,000 years ago, the Earth's crust suddenly shifted, and Atlantis's civilized inhabitants faced extinction under Antarctica's layers of ice.

In the 1970s, another author, Charles Berlitz, who wrote many books on paranormal phenomenon, suggested that Atlantis was, in fact, located in the Atlantic Ocean, but was a victim of the infamous Bermuda Triangle.

## The Wrong Pillars?

More recently, some scholars have noted that before the sixth century BC, the mountains on either side of the Laconian Gulf, in the southern Greek region of Peloponnese, were called the Pillars of Hercules. If Plato had been referring to these "pillars" in his writing, that would mean that Atlantis was more probably located in a nearby part of the Mediterranean Sea than in the Atlantic Ocean. Working off of this assumption, many researchers suggest that "Atlantis" may actually refer to the Minoan culture and the Thera eruption, which caused massive devastation to the civilization sometime between the seventeenth and sixteenth centuries BC. Such a catastrophic disaster would have no doubt led to embellished stories about the society's downfall, which were passed down from generation to generation.

But most historians and archeologists believe that Plato's story was simply that: a story. Many even think that his claim to have heard the story from Solon in Egypt was part of his fabrication, since no evidence of the Atlantis story has been found in Egypt. But fabrication or not, the story of Atlantis has inspired countless works of literature, musical compositions, paintings, sculptures, and even comics. Perhaps this "lost" island is right where it should be: alive and well in the imaginations of dreamers everywhere.

# House of the Round Table

*Where was Camelot located? Was it based on a real location? Or was it all a lovely story embellished during the Middle Ages?*

✳   ✳   ✳   ✳

IN THE TWELFTH century, British cleric Geoffrey of Monmouth helped to ignite interest in the famous King Arthur, mentioned in his book, *Historia regum Britanniae*, or *The History of the Kings of Britain*. But while Geoffrey may have brought the valiant king to the world's attention, he never mentioned a detail that is now synonymous with King Arthur: the castled city of Camelot, where Arthur held court.

In fact, the first mention of Camelot didn't come from Great Britain at all, but rather France, in a late twelfth-century poem written by Chrétien de Troyes. In the poem, entitled "Lancelot, the Knight of the Cart," the castle is merely mentioned in passing, giving no hint of the significance it would soon play in King Arthur's legend. Chrétien, like Geoffrey, placed King Arthur's main court in Caerleon in Wales, with many minor courts in various other cities and castles. But in the thirteenth century, French romances began embracing Camelot as King Arthur's seat of power.

These literary texts, known as the Vulgate and Post-Vulgate cycles, were written by an unknown author or authors and are composed of thousands of pages of texts. The stories contain hundreds of characters from King Arthur lore, engaging in various exploits that are woven together throughout the manuscripts. One story calls Camelot, "the city most full of adventures," and talks of a land filled with magicians, dragons, giants, and knights.

## The King and His Knights

According to a Vulgate story, Camelot was founded by Joseph of Arimathea, who was also said to have founded the Glastonbury Abbey, believed by some to be the final resting place of King Arthur. Joseph established the Church of St. Stephen the Martyr in the middle of the city, which would be Camelot's largest church. While the city was small, at times requiring visitors to shelter in tents and pavilions in the nearby forests and meadows, it still had plenty of space for knightly tournaments, which were a regular occurrence. It was also well fortified, surviving several wars against the Saxons.

In the fifth or sixth centuries, King Arthur held court in a castle in Camelot, which was said to be located near a body of water. The castle had a hall for feasts, many bedrooms, and a main courtyard, but the most famous feature of the castle was the Round Table.

The table was said to have been a wedding gift from King Leodagan of Carmelide, the father of Guinevere, King Arthur's wife. The table was so massive that 150 knights, who were entrusted with protecting the peace of Camelot, could be seated around it. These included such familiar names as

Lancelot, Galahad, Percival, and Gawain, among dozens of others. The Round Table, having no corners and therefore no head, was a symbol of the equal status of all participants in King Arthur's court.

By the end of the Vulgate stories, nearly every knight of the Round Table, despite their strength and bravery, was dead, as was King Arthur. While Camelot survived for a short time, eventually it was attacked by King Mark of Cornwall, who was once defeated in battle by Arthur and his knights. The people of Camelot, lost without their valiant protectors, were quickly defeated, and King Mark destroyed not only the city, but also the Round Table.

To the thirteenth-century readers of the Vulgate stories, it would have been evident that Camelot, if such a place had been real, no longer existed. But over the centuries, the legend of Camelot has been retold many times, with both King Arthur's story and the stories of his grand city reimagined and reinterpreted. Some even believe that Camelot was a real place, and perhaps King Arthur was a real person.

## Excavations and Evidence

Several places have been suggested as possible locations of what was once Camelot. One of the most popular candidates is Cadbury Castle, an Iron Age hill fort in Somerset County, England, which was proposed by poet and antiquary John Leland in 1542. Leland was convinced that King Arthur was a historical figure and not a fictional character, and his theory that Camelot was once located at Cadbury Castle prompted archeological digs in the area in the twentieth century. Excavations revealed evidence of human occupation of the area from the fourth millennium BC until the sixth century AD, and ruins of a large building, possibly a great hall, were found. Cadbury Castle is also located not far from Glastonbury Tor, which some believe is where King Arthur is entombed.

Another Camelot contender is Tintagel Castle, a historic site perched on the cliffs of Cornwall. According to Geoffrey of Monmouth, King Arthur was born in this location. In the 1980s, slate tablets with Latin inscriptions were discovered at Tintagel which mentioned "a descendant of Coll," which some researchers believe refers to King Coel, said to be one of Arthur's ancestors. Excavations at the site have uncovered pottery dating back to the fifth and sixth centuries, lending more credence to the site's possible history as Camelot; however, the castle ruins that now stand at the site date back only to the 1100s.

Many other locations have been associated with King Arthur and have been put forth as potential Camelot sites, but most scholars agree that the accounts of the city and its king are entirely fictional. But that hasn't stopped the theories and speculation from persisting into modern times. Camelot has inspired poems, songs, movies, television shows, a famous Broadway musical, and was even used to describe the presidency of John F. Kennedy. Kennedy was said to have been particularly fond of a line in the finale of the musical: "Don't let it be forgot/ That once there was a spot/ For one brief, shining moment/ That was known as Camelot." Whether it was real or imagined, the memory of this legendary city, the knights who protected it, and its famous king will not soon be forgotten.

# Out of the Mist

*In 1674, a man named W. Hamilton from Derry in Northern Ireland wrote his cousin a letter in which he described an incredible tale. Hamilton wrote of a ship captain named John Nisbet who sailed from Ireland with a small crew of men to transport butter, tallow, and animal hides to France. After dropping off their cargo, they filled the ship with French wines and headed back to Ireland. But a couple days into their return journey, a thick fog enveloped the ship, making navigation difficult. When the fog lifted after a few hours, the sailors found themselves just offshore of an unknown island, with a strong wind pushing the ship perilously close to rocks . . .*

✳ ✳ ✳ ✳

IN ORDER TO get their bearings and avoid running aground, they decided to drop anchor until the wind died down. Several sailors went ashore to explore the mysterious island, hoping to get an idea of where they were. Animals, including horses, cows, sheep, and rabbits, roamed the green hills, but not a single human, or even a house, was seen. But strangely, the group soon happened upon an old castle, which seemed to be the only structure on the island. The men knocked on the door of the castle incessantly, but no one answered and no sound came from within.

Assuming the castle, and perhaps even the entire island, was abandoned, the men made their way back to the shore, describing to Captain Nisbet what they'd found. Since it would soon be dark, the company of sailors gathered wood and built a huge bonfire on the beach, where they sat warming themselves as night fell.

## End of an Evil Curse

Suddenly, a terrifying sound erupted from the woods, seemingly emitted from somewhere near the old castle. The sailors immediately abandoned the fire and made their way back to the ship, where they hid in fear all night. When they ventured outside the next morning, they were startled to see a very old man leading a group of people toward the ship. When Captain Nisbet and his crew went ashore to greet them, the old man and his group began enthusiastically hugging the very confused sailors.

The old man told them that his ancestors had lived on the island for centuries, ruling as princes. But an evil necromancer had imprisoned dozens of important citizens inside the castle, and hidden the island from the eyes of mortals, for a period of one hundred years.

When the one hundred years had passed, the island again became visible to human eyes, as Captain Nisbet and his crew had discovered. But the people in the castle were doomed to be imprisoned until fire had been kindled upon the island. When the sailors made their bonfire, the curse was finally lifted, and the horrible sound of the necromancer's departing evil washed over the island.

The freed captives thanked the sailors profusely, offering them some of the gold and silver that were mined on the island. The island, the old man told Captain Nisbet, was known as O'Brazile, and it was not far from the sailors' home in Ireland.

## An Unapproachable Island

While Hamilton's story is quite fanciful—in fact, most historians agree that it was a work of fiction created by Irish playwright Richard Head—it is not the only story of this mysterious vanishing island.

Sometimes also known as Breasal, Brazil, Brasil, or most commonly Hy-Brasil, this island began appearing on maps in 1325, usually off the western coast of Ireland. Irish folklore claimed it was visible for only one day every seven years, otherwise it was perpetually shrouded in fog. But over the centuries, many sailors claimed to have seen the mysterious Hy-Brasil, some even claiming they were close enough to make out features of the island. One ship captain insisted he saw a harbor, but when he attempted to sail toward it, a mist rolled in and he was unable to reach the shore.

Despite these accounts, most historians agree that Hy-Brasil never actually existed. But that doesn't explain why so many centuries of maps featured the island. It was called Insula de Brasil on a chart created by Venetian cartographer Andrea Bianco in 1436. In 1562, Spanish cartographer Diego Gutierrez named it Isola de Brazil. French cartographer Guillaume de L'Isle named the island Rocher de Brasil, or Brasil Rock, on a map published in 1769. Hy-Brasil kept appearing on maps until at least 1872, when it was depicted on a British admiralty chart.

## Gone but Not Forgotten

Most scholars believe that the island was included on these maps simply due to hearsay. Rumors of Hy-Brasil's existence reached the ears of mapmakers, who included the mysterious island on their charts, even though there was no evidence that it was real. But not all cartographers believed the rumors: In 1753, British cartographer Thomas Jeffreys did include the island on a map, placed just southwest of Ireland. But his more scrupulous label read "Imaginary Island of O Brazil."

It's easy to assume that the appearance of "phantom islands" on maps is an issue from a bygone era. But a nonexistent island named Sandy Island, once said to be near the French territory of New Caledonia, was charted on maps from 1774 all the way up until 2012. In that year, an Australian marine research ship passed through the area and confirmed that the island did not exist, finally resulting in Sandy Island's removal from maps. While Hy-Brasil may have met the same fate, its exclusion from geographical charts has not quelled the interest in its legend. This mysterious island, shrouded in mist, will continue to be a fascinating part of Irish culture.

# Chapter 13

# Ancient Kingdoms and Peoples

## The Lost Kingdom of Benin

*Southern Nigeria's Edo Kingdom was the envy of its neighbors, with a fame that reached to Europe. As the world encroached, however, the kingdom would not prosper.*

※ ※ ※ ※

THE 2018 POPULAR FILM *Black Panther* gave audiences a depiction of the fictional African kingdom of "Wakanda." The fantastical country contained such stunning wealth and technology that its leaders hid its location from the rest of the world, lest their riches and technology be stolen or misused. Depicted as a kingdom ahead of its time, a place like Wakanda could only be found in the imaginations of filmmakers, right?

While Wakanda itself was entirely a place of fiction, the African continent did once contain a kingdom that was so far ahead of its time that it became the envy of the European world. Known as the Kingdom of Benin, or the Edo Kingdom, evidence of its founding by the Edo people of southern Nigeria dates to the eleventh century. The city was established within dense rainforest, providing its inhabitants with animals for food, plants for medicines, and wood for construction. And construct they did: Over the next several hundred years, Benin expanded to encompass around 500 separate villages.

## Walls All Around

More impressive than the expansion of the city, however, were the walls that surrounded it. According to archeologists, the main city of Benin and its outlying villages were surrounded by nearly 10,000 miles of earthwork banks and ditches, which would have taken the people of Benin as many as 150 million hours of digging to complete.

The walls and city itself may also have been planned and laid out according to fractal geometric design. Fractals are continuous patterns that demonstrate self-similarities across different sizes and scales. Examples in nature would include snowflakes, ferns, or seashells. In Benin, some researchers believe fractal designs were planned out in the walls, village plans, and even individual houses in the city, giving the entire kingdom a sense of mathematical symmetry.

The city contained some notable features that were, at the time, unheard of in many other parts of the world, including a sewer system beneath the streets that carried storm water away, wells for each house that provided fresh water, and "streetlights" fueled by palm oil that helped travelers find their way through the area at night.

Benin became a hub of creativity and culture, with artists working in bronze, iron, and ivory to create wall plaques, carvings, and sculptures, including life-sized bronze heads of their Obas, or kings.

## European Friends and Foes

In 1485, new waves of European explorers stumbled upon the kingdom of Benin when Portuguese explorers led by João Afonso de Aveiro found the city, sprawling and thriving, nestled in the rainforest. Soon, Benin was no longer an isolated city hidden by vegetation; it became a hugely popular destination for European traders, who raved about the city back home, noting its wealth, beautiful art, friendly citizens, and sophisticated government. In fact, it was said that Benin was so clean, prosperous, and well-managed, that crime was non-existent, and people lived in houses with no doors.

For several centuries, Benin and European traders enjoyed a civil and pleasant relationship, with the kingdom offering palm oil, ivory, and pepper in exchange for the guns brought from Europe. But by the late 1800s, British colonial influence began to crowd its way into Benin.

While the people of the kingdom were always happy to trade with the Europeans, it eventually became clear that British traders to the city were intent upon colonization. The Oba would not hear of it, and in 1896 he cut off trade with the British empire. When a British-led expedition, intent on reestablishing contact, tried to enter the city in January of 1897, they were ambushed and attacked, with only two British men managing to escape.

## Lost to the Jungle

Sadly, this was the beginning of the end for the kingdom of Benin. The British soon sent a "punitive expedition" of 1,200 men to the city, and over the course of nine days, Benin was sacked, looted, and burned. The Oba was captured and exiled. Many of the looted artifacts wound up in museums and universities, but recently there has been an effort to begin returning the items to Nigeria.

Today, a new Benin City stands where the ancient kingdom once thrived, but none of the old city's distinctive features remain. The fractal houses, the expansive walls, the clever streetlights—all have been lost to time and the surrounding jungle. Perhaps one day some enterprising explorer will discover a bit of earthen ditch or excavate the foundation of an unusual ancient house, and the world will be reminded of the remarkable lost city that was ahead of its time.

# D'mt and Keskese: Ancient and Enigmatic

*Two enigmatic sites in what are now the countries of Eritrea and Ethiopia continue to fascinate archeologists.*

✻ ✻ ✻ ✻

IN 2003, ARCHEOLOGISTS in Eritrea made an astounding discovery when they unearthed the skeleton of a young woman, which was dated to be more than a million years old. The remains were believed to show a link between early hominids and modern humans, giving scientists a small glimpse into our ancient history.

The discovery also served as a reminder that Eritrea and its surrounding areas are no strangers to antiquity. Much of the region's history has been well documented and studied, but there are still plenty of unknowns to explore, such as the mysterious kingdom of D'mt and its ritual site of Keskese.

## Cities of Mystery

Once located in what is now Eritrea and northern Ethiopia, little is known about the city of D'mt—sometimes known as Damot—but historians believe it existed between the tenth and fifth centuries BC. The ancient civilization may have called the city of Yeha, in northern Ethiopia, its capital. A temple to the moon god Almaqah still stands in Yeha, alluding to the formation of the city at a time before Islam or Christianity had made its way to the region. D'mt was an agricultural society, and the people constructed plows and developed irrigation systems to grow their crops, and also fashioned tools and weapons out of iron.

D'mt was believed to have been influenced by its South Arabian neighbors, including the area of present-day Yemen. Evidence of this fact is found in the nearby archeological site of Keskese, once the seat of ritual practices in D'mt. Stone inscriptions featuring the name of a South Arabian king have been discovered at the site, but the city is mostly known for its "stelae," a collection of stone pillars and obelisks which range in length from about 22 feet to almost 30 feet. Remains of walls and terraces have also been found, as well as remnants of tools and pottery.

Thanks to these bits of historic evidence, we can assume the people of D'mt spent their days tending to their millet fields, focusing on metalwork, or constructing the obelisks that marked their ritual site. But we may never know why, in the fifth century BC, D'mt and Keskese seemed to simply cease to exist. Their abrupt ending made way for the Kingdom of Aksum, which arose to great power in the early first century. But historians still have much to learn about these two enigmatic places, which left behind precious few clues to tell us about their once thriving societies.

# Songhai: Mighty African Empire

*What began as a small kingdom founded in the ninth century by fishermen along a bend of the Niger River eventually became the most important country in West Africa. This was the Songhai Empire, also called the Songhay, which dominated a vast geographical region during the fifteenth and sixteenth centuries.*

✳  ✳  ✳  ✳

BEFORE THE SONGHAI Empire could rise to ultimate power, it had to overtake the prevailing Mali Empire, a kingdom that had been prospering since the thirteenth century. The Mali Empire controlled both local and international trade in gold and spices, but the Songhai controlled the transport of goods along the river, making them troublesome neighbors for Mali. When civil wars in the mid-1400s began to weaken Mali's influence, the rulers of Songhai saw an opportunity to expand their territory.

## Merciless Expansion

In 1468, King Sunni Ali of Songhai ordered a military campaign of territorial expansion, making use of Songhai's river-borne naval fleet—the only naval fleet in this part of Africa. Sunni Ali conquered the Mali Empire, cementing Songhai's path to power in the region.

The king gained a reputation for ruthlessly striking down his opponents, earning him the nickname "Sunni the Merciless." He was able to quickly expand Songhai's territory, creating many new provinces. Each of these in turn were overseen by governors which he appointed. By 1473, the Songhai Empire controlled most of the centers of trade in the area, keeping a tight rein on the caravans of salt, cloth, horses, ivory, and spices that traversed the Sahara.

Sunni Ali was succeeded by his son, Sunni Baru, who, in turn, was overthrown by Mohammad I. Mohammad I, who was the first in the region to popularize the use of the title Askia, meaning "ruler," oversaw what would be the largest expansion of the Songhai Empire. By the early 1500s, the capital city of Gao was home to 100,000 people, and Songhai's territory spanned from the Senegal River in the west, to central Mali in the east, to the salt mines of Taghaza in the north.

## A Grain of Salt

In the late 1500s, the sultan of Morocco, Ahmad al-Mansur, took notice of Songhai's impressive salt mines, which were a vital part of the trade routes they controlled. The sultan demanded that Askia Daoud, the ruler of Songhai at that time, pay tax revenues for the salt mines. Askia Daoud attempted to satisfy al-Mansur's demands by offering large quantities of gold, but the sultan wasn't appeased. In late 1590, al-Mansur sent 4,000 men to attack Songhai.

In what became known as the Battle of Tondibi, al-Mansur's forces clashed with 40,000 men of the Songhai army. While there is no doubt that al-Mansur's men were outnumbered, the

Moroccans had a huge advantage: gunpowder. The Songhai Empire may have been expansive, but they had little more than spears and arrows for defense.

The Moroccans quickly won the battle, and the once formidable Songhai Empire was gradually absorbed and vanquished by the Moroccans. Its downfall was astonishingly fast and sadly absolute: Within two years, Songhai, the largest, most powerful kingdom in West Africa for more than 125 years, simply crumbled and vanished, demonstrating that the mighty can, most certainly, fall.

# The Dong Son Civilization

*The Dong Son, or Dongson culture, was a late Bronze Age civilization that arose between 1000 and 600 BC, in what is now the Red River Valley of northern Vietnam. They are best known for their large, ceremonial bronze drums, which could be more than three feet high and weigh up to 220 pounds.*

✳ ✳ ✳ ✳

THE DONG SON people lived in simple houses with thatched roofs set on stilts, and cultivated rice for food. They also fished and hunted, and raised water buffaloes and pigs. Because they were farmers, they fashioned many types of agricultural tools, including axes, spades, and hoes. They created arrowheads and spearheads for fishing and hunting.

Water and seafaring were an important part of Dong Son culture, and some scholars believe that the civilization was a state society that maintained control of the Red River region of Vietnam. Others think that the Dong Son peoples were merely a confederation of villages that shared cultural practices. But either way, evidence of their reverence and respect for the water is clear from their use of "boat burials," or the use of canoe segments in funeral customs. Archeologists have uncovered burial sites in which the deceased was wrapped in a shroud made of vegetable fibers and then placed in a segment of a canoe, with the head at the open end and the feet in the bow of the canoe. Coins, pottery, textiles, and weapons have also been found in Dong Son grave sites.

## The Beat of Their Own Drums

The most striking and well-known artifacts from the Dong Son culture are their drums, known as Dong Son drums. These were created using the lost wax casting technique, in which a metal object is created using a mold of an original object or sculpture. The Dong Son drums were intricately decorated with scenes of daily life, warfare, ritual ceremonies, and geometric patterns, or were created with more simple images of animals, plants, or boats.

The drums were used as musical instruments in weddings, festivals, funerals, and other ceremonies. They were also symbols of power and even objects of worship. They were sometimes used for trade as well, with some of their drums being found as far away as New Guinea. The Ngoc Lu drum, considered one of the best-preserved examples of a Dong Son drum, is considered one of the national treasures of Vietnam. This drum features three circular concentric panels, decorated with images of animals and people. The outer two panels show figures of deer, egrets, and hornbills, while the innermost panel appears to depict people taking part in a festival. The scene contains illustrations of rice growing and harvesting, but it also shows people playing the drums themselves, suggesting the importance the instrument must have played in the lives of the Dong Son peoples.

The Dong Son culture began to fade sometime around the first century AD, but many scholars believe the people of this civilization are the direct descendants of the modern Vietnamese people. The artifacts—and literal national treasures—they left behind continue to remind the people of Vietnam of their ancient past.

# The Achaemenid Empire

*Founded around 559 BC, the Achaemenid Empire, also known as the Persian Empire, became the largest empire the world had ever seen. Spanning the Balkan Peninsula in the west to the Indus Valley in the east, the empire covered around 2.1 million square miles and encompassed many parts of what is now Iran, Iraq, Egypt, Turkey, and parts of Afghanistan and Pakistan.*

\* \* \* \*

THE ACHAEMENID EMPIRE arose under the leadership of King Cyrus the Great. Before he was known as "great," however, Cyrus was the leader of one of many scattered tribes in Persia, the Pasargadae. The Pasargadae tribe was located near the sprawling but disjointed Median Empire. This kingdom was led by Astyages, Cyrus's grandfather. Despite the family relation, Cyrus laid siege to his grandfather's empire, resulting in many of the Medes revolting against Astyages and joining Cyrus. Cyrus conquered the Median Empire, becoming the Shah, or king, of Persia.

## Conquered with Kindness

Cyrus didn't stop with his grandfather's empire. He continued to expand his own empire, next capturing Lydia, a region of western Asia Minor. Lydia's capital, Sardis, was one of the richest cities in the Ionian region, giving Cyrus a quick advantage in his quest for expansion. He then set his sights on Babylon, considered the greatest city in the world at that time. Babylon's king, Nabonidus, was not popular with his people, and Cyrus used that fact to his advantage.

Nabonidus had attempted to quell the religious freedom of the Babylonians, introducing his own religious reform and confiscating religious icons from temples. Cyrus, instead of simply taking Babylon by force, went to the city and performed Babylonian religious rituals that had been suppressed by Nabonidus. He then returned the confiscated idols back to their temples, and told the people that under his rule, they could worship any gods they chose. The citizens of Babylon were enamored by this new leader, and gladly handed him control of the city.

Cyrus became well known for this religious tolerance and embrace of multiculturalism. He was also admired for his mercy, as he never mistreated the cities and kingdoms he conquered. Instead of killing a vanquished king, he would ask for the king's advice and guidance in ruling over a newly acquired city and its subjects. Cyrus the Great even earned praise in the Bible, which tells of his liberation of Hebrew captives in Babylon and his efforts to rebuild Jerusalem.

## Taxes at Work

When Cyrus died in 530 BC, he left behind the foundation of a strong kingdom, which saw its greatest height during the rule of Darius I. Darius, who began his reign in 522 BC, expanded the empire into the Indus Valley. Darius realized that his vast kingdom needed better organization if it were to run smoothly. He divided the empire into 20 provinces known as "satrapies," each of which was run by a "satrap," meaning "protector of the kingdom" or "keeper of the province." The satraps were required to pay a regular tribute to Persia, which was, in effect, a tax.

Darius used this tax to create a navy and to fund public works like irrigation projects, roads, and canals. Darius also designed a postal system, which was not unlike the "Pony Express" that would come to be used in America thousands of years later. The postal system interconnected the empire using a series of roads which couriers traveled by horseback. The horses would be switched out at predetermined locations to prevent the animals from suffering fatigue. This system was not simply an example of improved transportation efficiency, however; Darius used it as a way to keep tabs on each of his satraps, appointing spies to gather information and report back by way of the postal system.

## Great Riches, Little Humility

The riches of the Achaemenid Empire grew great, and Darius tasked craftsmen from all over the kingdom to construct an imperial capital at Persepolis. He established a common currency for the empire, and kept large amounts of gold and silver in a large vault in the new capital. Persepolis became a city that showcased the cultures and styles of peoples throughout the kingdom, a vision that the first king, Cyrus, had for the empire.

But Darius lacked much of the humility of Cyrus, seeing himself as exalted far above his subjects. He eventually dropped the title of Shah for the loftier Shahanshah (king of kings). His arrogance may have led to the unrest that began to plague the empire in 499 BC, when the Greeks staged a revolt. Darius, seeking to punish the Greeks for their rebellion, sailed a fleet to Athens only to be shockingly defeated. In order to appear strong and in control, Darius raised taxes to rebuild his fleet. But this only led to more unrest and instability, especially in the outlying region of Egypt.

Darius's son, Xerxes, who began his reign in 486 BC, attempted to quell the discontent in the kingdom, but he proved to be even more arrogant than his father. When the Babylonians began to riot in 482 BC, Xerxes, who, unlike Cyrus, had no interest in religious or cultural tolerance, sacked the city and tore down a golden statue of Marduk, the Babylonian's patron god. He melted down the gold and kept it for himself, using it to build an army to attack the mutinous Greeks. But the Greeks once again proved victorious, and Xerxes retreated to his wealthy palace to live out his days in luxury and decadence.

## The Next "Great" Ruler

The overconfidence and excesses of the last kings of the Achaemenid Empire no doubt contributed to its downfall. For the next 200 years, the rulers of the kingdom hid in opulent palaces, doing little more than raising taxes, as the once-united empire gradually grew disjointed. The satraps began to grow in power, taking more control of their individual regions. Meanwhile, the huge army of the kingdom, which had once been a multicultural success story, eventually descended into a confused mishmash of troops that spoke different languages and were all trained in different fighting styles. It was only a matter of time before the empire collapsed.

Cyrus the Great had created the world's first true empire, and had paved the way for its prosperity with his ideas of humble governance. Unfortunately, many of his successors saw only a path to power, and their pride led to the end of the kingdom. Someone else was paying attention to the downfall of the Achaemenid Empire: Alexander the Great. Alexander, who had been an enthusiastic admirer of Cyrus the Great, conquered what was left of the Persian Empire in 334 BC. But unlike the last kings of the Achaemenid Empire, Alexander the Great remembered Cyrus's example and used it as inspiration for his campaigns, swiftly accruing his own infamous empire.

# The Khmer Empire

*This Southeast Asian kingdom was both warlike and peaceful in turn. It left behind amazing works of art and iconography, like the Angkor Wat temple.*

✳   ✳   ✳   ✳

JUST NORTH OF the resort town of Siem Reap in Cambodia lies the sprawling Angkor Wat temple. Built in the early twelfth century, the massive work of art was constructed to honor the Hindu god Vishnu, but later became a Buddhist temple. It is still considered an important pilgrimage destination for Buddhists, and is believed to be the single largest religious monument in the world. The temple is even prominently featured on Cambodia's national flag, a testament to the continuing importance this structure holds in the hearts and minds of its people.

Angkor Wat is, no doubt, the most lasting symbol of the Khmer Empire of Southeast Asia, which lasted from the ninth to the fifteenth centuries. The empire was formed by the Khmer people, who, by the seventh century, inhabited much of the area along the Mekong River. Many kingdoms in the area often warred against each other, until a man named Jayavarman II set out to conquer these fighting factions. He successfully managed to overcome and unite a series of territories, and, once his victories were complete, declared himself Chakravartin, meaning "universal ruler."

## Peace, War, and Temples

Jayavarman II began his rule in AD 802, which is the date used to mark the beginning of the Khmer Empire, and reigned for 33 years. He and his successors expanded the empire without the use of violence and engaged in the trade of goods and services with nearby regions. The king Yasovarman I established the capital of the empire at Yasodharapura—also known as Angkor.

Over the next few centuries, the Khmer empire expanded, but their peaceful beginnings were soon marred by wars and conflicts. The kingdom annexed lands to the west and north, but the Vietnamese and the Cham peoples (located in what is today central Vietnam), proved to be fierce fighters who refused to allow their lands to be taken by the Khmer. As a result, although the Khmer empire eventually covered most of what is today Myanmar, Thailand, Laos, Cambodia, and part of southern China, it was never able to annex the bulk of Vietnam.

But the inability to conquer this area was ultimately of little consequence to the mighty Khmer empire. The people of the kingdom were prolific builders, creating not just temples and monuments, but a network of infrastructure including roads, bridges, canals, and reservoirs. The main highway constructed by the Khmers was almost 500 miles long. King Jayavarman VII, who ruled from 1181 to 1215, is credited with building more than 100 hospitals and establishing what could be considered the world's first known healthcare system.

## The Great City

Along with Angkor Wat, which was built between 1122 and 1150, the Khmers constructed Banteay Srei, a temple prized for its intricate carvings, and Ta Keo, the first temple to be built entirely of sandstone, in addition to many other impressive structures. In the late twelfth century, Jayavarman VII established Angkor Thom, meaning "great city," as the capital of the Khmer empire, with his own temple, Bayon, located at the center. This complex was built inside Angkor as a "city within a city," and at the height of the Khmer empire, Angkor was the largest pre-industrial urban center in the world. The city covered an area about the size of Los Angeles, and researchers estimate that its population may have topped one million.

During this time, the Khmer people enjoyed wealth and prosperity, engaging in festivals and celebrations year-round. Horse races, music, dancing, fireworks, and other entertainment were part of their culture. They relied heavily on rice farming, fishing, and other agriculture for their economy, selling their wares in open-air marketplaces.

Interestingly, most of the trade and commerce in the empire was run by women, who were respected for their abilities in these matters. Society was ordered according to the Hindu caste system, until Buddhism eclipsed Hinduism as the most popular religion in the region in the thirteenth century.

## Rise of the Sukhothai and Downfall of the Khmer

Scholars are unsure of why the Khmer empire began to steadily decline after the thirteenth century, although some propose the switch to Buddhism may have somehow contributed to the change in political and social systems. Others have suggested a breakdown in infrastructure or even a plague event may have pushed the kingdom to the point of collapse.

But the most likely reason for the downfall of the empire is a great migration of Thai peoples from the north of the kingdom. In 1238, many of these peoples, living in the Lavo kingdom, a state within the Khmer empire, revolted and gained independence. They chose the city of Sukhothai as their capital, and became known as the Sukothai kingdom, encompassing much of modern-day Thailand. Other Thai migrants began annexing regions for themselves, and in 1431, the kingdom of Ayutthaya took Angkor, driving out the last king of the Khmer empire, Ponhea Yat.

Today, visitors flock to Angkor to see the city's monuments and temples, which, until the nineteenth century, had been largely hidden by the thick surrounding forest. Dozens of archeological sites have been uncovered, restored, and preserved, and the tourism they attract is vital to Cambodia's economy. The intricate structures serve as a legacy left behind by the once great Khmer empire.

# The Lapita: Culture of the South Pacific

*Navigational savvy and feats of long-distance migration mark the Lapita as one of the greatest seafaring cultures known to us.*

❋   ❋   ❋   ❋

WHEN AMERICAN ARCHEOLOGISTS Edward W. Gifford and Richard Shulter Jr. began excavating a site in New Caledonia, an archipelago in the South Pacific, in 1952, they heard the locals using the word *xapeta'a*, which means "to dig a hole" or "the place where one digs" in the local Haveke language. But the researchers did not hear the word correctly, and from that confusion they coined the name "Lapita," using it to designate the remains of a civilization they had uncovered on Grande Terre, the largest of the islands in New Caledonia.

Gifford and Shulter discovered pottery fragments that were dated to around 800 BC, and which hinted at the ancient travels of a seafaring people. The Lapita are believed to have originated in the northern Philippines and nearby islands, and began migrating to the islands of the South Pacific Ocean around 1600 BC, becoming the first people to colonize the area. Evidence of their existence has been found at more than 200 sites, not only in New Caledonia, but also in New Guinea, Fiji, Tonga, Samoa, and the Solomon Islands. Many researchers believe the Lapita peoples made it to New Zealand, as well, and some even suggest they traveled as far as South America.

## Sailing and Settling

It is astounding to think that people who lived thousands of years before cruise liners and airplanes were able to traverse a vast ocean to find new lands. Yet that is exactly what the Lapita peoples accomplished. Sadly, there is little evidence to shine a light on how they traveled such long distances by sea, but the civilization must have possessed an impressive amount of navigational knowledge. They are believed to have been skilled sailors, who understood exactly how to use the wind to their advantage, and who used indications like the sun and stars, shadows, and the flight of birds as guides to keep them oriented and on course.

Regardless of how they accomplished their exploration of the Pacific, the Lapita left behind artifacts and evidence that give us a glimpse into their lives. The Lapita grew taro, coconuts, yams, bananas, and breadfruit, and supplemented their diet by fishing off the islands where they settled. This was an easy feat, since most of their villages were located right on the shoreline, rather than further inland. Researchers theorize this may have been to avoid disease-carrying insects, such as mosquitoes, or perhaps because areas inland were already occupied by other groups. This is not to say they avoided inland locations altogether, however. In the Bismarck Archipelago, a group of islands off the coast of New Guinea, most of the Lapita settlements were inland. These villages were located near sources of obsidian, which the Lapita used to create tools and as a commodity for trading with other cultures.

## A Face from the Past

The burial practices of the Lapita were particularly interesting, demonstrating that the culture went to great lengths to honor their dead. Most people were buried on their backs, but some were interred on their stomachs. Others were in what research-ers call "yoga positions," with legs bent in different ways. Special pottery, used only in burials, was often included in the grave sites. But the most unusual aspect of Lapita burials was the removal of the skulls after body decomposition. The skulls were then placed in ceramic pots and used for ceremonial purposes. The removal of skulls was a known practice to archeologists amongst the peoples of the Pacific, but many researchers believe the custom may have originated with the Lapita.

While this practice was common, it was not always carried out. In fact, in 2002, the discovery of a complete Lapita skeleton caused quite a stir in the archeological world. Discovered in central Fiji, the female skeleton was found in a settlement dating back to 1000 BC, buried in five feet of beach sand and surrounded by Lapita pottery.

The woman's skull was remarkably well preserved, and researchers were able to create a computer model of it, which they then used to create a representation of the woman's face. She was dubbed Mana, a word that means "truth" in the Lau dialect of Malaita, the most populous island of the Solomon Islands. Mana became the first depiction of a Lapita person the world had ever seen. She has since been laid to rest in the same area of Fiji where she was discovered.

While the Lapita culture may have faded away around 500 BC, the ancestors of this civilization are very much alive today in the people of Polynesia, Micronesia, and Melanesia. Some even believe that the modern tattoos favored by the people of

Oceania are based on motifs used in Lapita pottery. The people in these regions work to keep their traditions and spiritual values alive, ensuring that the customs that began with the Lapita will never truly disappear.

# A Kingdom Carved in Stone

*The Nabataeans left behind amazing architecture carved into the very rock of the desert. What was this culture like?*

✳ ✳ ✳ ✳

FANS OF THE classic film *Indiana Jones and the Last Crusade* will no doubt remember the last scenes of the movie, in which the titular character discovers the Holy Grail hidden in a booby-trap-ridden shrine called the Temple of the Sun. In the movie, the temple was said to be located within the Canyon of the Crescent Moon in the Republic of Hatay. Of course, well-traveled filmgoers recognized the façade of the temple as belonging to the famous Al-Khazneh, or The Treasury, one of the best-known structures in the historic Jordanian city of Petra. But even those who immediately recognized the remarkable carved sandstone Treasury may not have realized that the city of Petra was once known as Raqmu, and it was the capital city of the Nabataean Kingdom.

The Nabataean peoples were originally Arabian nomads who traversed the desert in search of sustenance for their herds. They continually traveled back and forth on what became known as the Incense Route, a trading route that stretched from Qataban, in what is now Yemen, to Gaza on the Mediterranean Sea. Aromatic resins, including frankincense and myrrh, were transported along the 1,200-mile route, which the Nabataean tribes became quite familiar with. Since they were so adept at finding water and preserving these locations, these peoples were able to become traders, carrying goods across the desert more quickly and efficiently than others.

## Masters of the Trade

By around the third century BC, the Nabataeans had control of many of the major cities along the trade route. Towns such as Haluza, Avdat, and Shivta became welcome stopover locations for those who were traveling the Incense Route. But these cities were not only places to rest and recharge before heading back out on the road; they were also important centers of trade in their own right. Travelers could purchase horses and trade goods, as well as find a comfortable place to sleep. But even more than comfort, the Nabataeans recognized the value of providing safety for the visitors passing through towns on the trade route. They began constructing forts along the route, to keep merchants and travelers safe, but they also began charging taxes to fund their hospitality.

Thanks to this tactic, the Nabataeans were able to grow their kingdom and accrue much wealth. By 312 BC, a thriving civilization had developed in the area that is now Petra. They constructed their capital city, which they knew as Raqmu, in the sandstone cliffs of what is now southern Jordan. Archeologists were at first perplexed as to why the wealthy peoples would build their capital in such a location, as the area lacks a natural source of water and is surrounded by inhospitable terrain. But the Nabataeans were experts at finding water, unlike any potential enemies from outside the area, and the harsh environment gave them a natural defense against enemies.

## Forgotten, Then Found

At its height, it is believed that Petra was home to about 20,000 inhabitants. For a while, the Nabataeans' strategy of living in such a hostile environment paid off. Even the Romans, who attempted to lay siege to the capital in 62 BC, gave up when they ran out of supplies and could no longer handle the difficult terrain. But by AD 106, Rome had succeeded in annexing the Nabataean kingdom, and the Nabataean people gradually lost control over their trade routes. The Syrian city of

Palmyra became the new center of trade in the region, and over time, the Nabataean people became scattered and powerless, until, by the seventh century, they were forgotten altogether.

In the nineteenth century, Swiss explorer Johann Ludwig Burckhardt rediscovered the city of Petra, and reignited interest in the lost Nabataean kingdom. In addition to Petra, many ancient Nabataean sites have been discovered by researchers, located along what used to be the Incense Route. The ruins of Haluza, Avdat, and Shivta lie in the Negev Desert of Israel, while other sites are located in Saudi Arabia, Syria, and Egypt.

But perhaps none of the sites are as well preserved or famous as Petra, which now attracts more than a million visitors every year. To reach the city, visitors must traverse a three-quarters-mile long gorge called the Siq. At the end of the dark, high-walled, narrow gorge, the magnificent Al-Khazneh, thought to be a mausoleum for a Nabataean king, comes into view. The site is also known for Ad-Deir, or The Monastery, the largest structure in Petra at 148 feet tall and 160 feet wide. Thanks to the Nabataean peoples' skills in architecture and stonemasonry, marks of their once-great existence have literally been carved in stone.

# The Badarian People

*Well before the pyramids were built, Egypt underwent a revolution in agriculture and contributed to one of humanity's greatest leaps forward.*

✳   ✳   ✳   ✳

U P UNTIL ABOUT 12,000 years ago, humans relied on hunting and gathering for food and shelter. This way of life required people to live as nomads, roaming to different locations in search of animals and plants for sustenance. While these early peoples harnessed the use of fire, created tools, learned to preserve their food, and had a wealth of knowledge about plant life, they were never able to settle down in a single location, as they were always forced to travel to new sources of food.

But then, in a drastic change of lifestyle that archeologists now dub the "Neolithic Revolution," humans developed agriculture. With the advent of farming, humans were able to settle in permanent locations for the first time in their history. Now that crops could be constantly cultivated and livestock continually raised, there was no reason to wander. Civilizations were founded, villages and cities were established, and the world's population increased.

## Discovery on the Nile

In Upper Egypt, the Badarian culture is the earliest example of an agricultural civilization in the region. Named for its discovery in El Badari, a town which is approximately 120 miles northwest of modern Luxor, the Badarian culture arose around 5000 BC and was at its pinnacle from 4400 to 4000 BC. It was discovered in 1922 by English archeologists Guy Brunton, who would go on to become the assistant director of the Egyptian Museum in Cairo, and Gertrude Caton-Thompson, one of the first women to significantly contribute to the field of archeology.

Brunton and Caton-Thompson uncovered around forty settlements, located on a 19-mile stretch along the eastern bank of the Nile River. Their excavations gave researchers insight into an ancient culture that flourished during what is called the Predynastic Era of Egypt.

Although none of the Badarian culture's structures remain, archeologists were able to uncover storage pits and holes for posts, some of which still had the remains of wooden stumps. The storage pits are believed to have been used to store the wheat, barley, lentils, and flax that the Badarian people culti-vated. Pottery, carved figurines, arrowheads, and jewelry were also found in the area. Along with agriculture, the Badarian people practiced fishing and also raised domesticated animals like sheep, goats, and cattle. The animals were an important part of the Badarian culture, and were often laid to rest in ceremonial burial sites.

At least 600 human burial sites were also found during the excavations, with bodies usually found interred in a westward-facing position. The Badarian people buried their dead wrapped in reed mats or animal hides, and placed items in the graves including ceramics, jewelry, fine cloth, amulets, and even cosmetic palettes. Some people were also buried along with figurines of female mortuary figures or fertility idols.

## Particular Pottery

Many of the tools used by the Badarian people were quite simple, but Brunton and Caton-Thompson were impressed and surprised by the quality and uniqueness of the culture's pottery. In fact, it is the pottery that sets the Badarian culture apart from other cultures of the time. The pottery was fashioned with red Nile clay, and often featured a black interior and rim. But the most distinctive detail was an unusual, spiraled rippling effect which covered either the entire surface of a piece, or part of it. Archeologists are still unsure of what sort of tool was used to create the decorative ripples, but the majority of the pottery found in the area displays the unique texture. Badarian pottery is also notable for its thin, sometimes almost sharp, edges, which were found nowhere else during this time.

Other items found in the region, such as turquoise, shells, and basalt vases, indicate that the Badarian people traveled to and traded with other cultures in the area. But for the most part, the Badarian people were settled and content to be at home in their civilization along the Nile. Thanks to their embrace of agriculture—and as the first people in Upper Egypt to do so—the Badarian culture was able to leave behind a wealth of information about their ancient lifestyle and practices.

# The Merchants of North Africa

*How did a small city-state on the southern Mediterranean coast rise to such historical prominence and remain Rome's nemesis for so long?*

∗  ∗  ∗  ∗

**H**ISTORY ENTHUSIASTS MAY recall the story of the military general Hannibal, who famously led his army and herd of North African war elephants through Spain and across the Alps into Italy. Although a risky and costly strategy, it was also a great surprise to his enemies, who probably never expected an army, and certainly not elephants, to make such a journey through formidable mountain passes. Hannibal's well-planned battles led him to many victories in Italy, and he controlled much of the southern half of the country for many years. But this was not the end of the wars that plagued the region, and eventually, Hannibal was forced to return to the city of his birth: Carthage.

Hundreds of years before Hannibal's famous trek through the mountains, Carthage was a small Phoenician settlement located on what is now the Tunisian coast. Founded around 814 BC, the site was chosen by the Phoenicians due to its access to the Mediterranean Sea and proximity to trade routes. While the Phoenicians had many settlements in the region, the vast majority of them were small, with populations rarely exceeding 1,000 people. Carthage, however, became the exception. The location of the settlement, with its ideal climate, arable land, and accessibility to the sea and trade routes, made it immensely popular. Within a century of the first settlers arriving, Carthage had grown to a population of 30,000.

## The Crème de la Crème

The founders of the city had been judicious in their choice of location. Carthage became an important center for trade between this part of Africa and the rest of the ancient world.

It was known for its luxurious goods, including jewelry, carved ivory, food, wine, spices, and rare purple dye extracted from the shells of marine snails. Beds, cushions, textiles, and mattresses produced in Carthage were considered premium indulgences, and those who were unable to afford them attempted to copy the furniture and linens that they so coveted.

Carthage also controlled much of the tin and silver that was mined in North Africa and southern Spain. Tin was an essential component in the creation of bronze, making it an especially lucrative metal and providing the settlement with further revenue.

The prosperous city was surrounded by walls that were said to be 32 feet thick and more than 40 feet high in some areas. These walls, which ran for 21 miles around the city, enclosed four separate residential areas as well as marketplaces, theaters, artisan workshops, religious districts, towers, and a necropolis. Outside the walls were the agricultural lands, where, according to the writings of a Carthaginian named Mago, landowners grew olive, pomegranate, almond, fig, and date palm trees. They raised cattle, sheep, and poultry, kept bees and bottled honey, and engaged in wine making.

## Independence and Expansion

For a time, the people of Carthage remained loyal to their Phoenician homeland, cultural background, and customs, and the city sent annual tributes to Tyre, which had originally been the powerful main city of the Phoenician civilization when Carthage was founded. But Tyre's strength and influence started to decline just as Carthage began to grow in wealth and power, and the settlement began wishing for independence. Sometime around 650 BC, Carthage gained its independence and set its sights on expanding its new empire. Perhaps emboldened by their growing prosperity, the Carthaginians sought out new sources to supplement their trade network and strengthen their economy.

Carthage set itself apart from other Phoenician settlements, not only by its success and population, but also by its military prowess. Unlike other Phoenician city-states, which rarely engaged in conflicts over territory, Carthage became a strong military power in the western Mediterranean.

The more docile Phoenician colonies, including Hadrumetum, Utica, and Kerkouane, were quickly absorbed into the rapidly growing Carthaginian empire. Carthage then gained control of a significant slice of coastal Africa, from Morocco to Libya, and the islands of Sardinia, Malta, Mallorca, Ibiza, and the western half of Sicily. The Iberian Peninsula was the next to bow under the budding empire's control, with some of the largest and most important Carthaginian settlements eventually being established there.

## A Growing Threat

But Carthage was not the only "superpower" emerging in the Mediterranean during this time. Rome, founded in 753 BC, had also begun as a small settlement like Carthage, but was growing in influence on the Italian peninsula to the north. In 509 BC, the two civilizations signed the first of several peace treaties in an attempt to lay out boundaries and protect interests. The two empires differed in their strategies for territorial expansion, with Carthage focusing on the sea and controlling trade routes, and Rome concentrating on acquiring more of mainland Italy.

Carthage soon controlled much more territory than Rome, and established a powerful navy to protect itself from the pirates and rivals who wished to get their hands on Carthaginian wealth. Mercenaries from Celtic tribes and African allies soon joined forces with Carthage as awareness of a new threat from the Greeks grew.

The Greeks had begun to establish their own Mediterranean trade routes, vying for dominance over the Carthaginians, especially on the island of Sicily. War soon broke out between these two well-matched groups. Both were expert in the art of maritime navigation, well familiar with the waters of the Mediterranean, and determined to gain control of Sicily. Eight wars, known as the Sicilian Wars, were fought over the span of more than 200 years.

## The Pyrrhic War

The last of the Sicilian Wars is known as the Pyrrhic War, named so after Pyrrhus of Epirus, a Greek king who fought both the Romans and the Carthaginians. In 278 BC, Pyrrhus was asked by several Greek cities in Sicily to come to the island and drive out the Carthaginians. The king obliged, and for a time, it seemed his campaign would be victorious.

Pyrrhus captured many of the strongest Carthaginian cities in Sicily, and was even planning to name his son heir to his future Sicilian kingdom. But the king did not fully anticipate how stubbornly the Carthaginians would hold on to their last major Sicilian city, Lilybaeum.

Carthage offered Pyrrhus money and ships if he would sign a peace treaty, but the king would only agree if Carthage turned over complete control of the island. Carthage refused, and the siege of the well-fortified and well-armed Lilybaeum continued. Try as he might, Pyrrhus could not wear down the Carthaginians, and he began to suffer heavy losses.

The king then made the mistake of forcing the Greeks, who had originally asked him to come to the island, to pay for his reinforcements, debts, and repairs. When they resisted, he treated them ruthlessly, even executing two Greek rulers on false charges of treason. The Greeks lost their faith in Pyrrhus, and after three years on the island, the king gave up and led his navy away to mainland Italy. According to some accounts, as he was leaving the island, he proclaimed prophetically, "What a wrestling ground we are leaving, my friends, for the Carthaginians and the Romans."

## The First and Second Punic Wars

Around 275 BC, the Romans became the protectors and leaders of a united Italy. But Sicily remained in Carthaginian possession. Due to the island's ideal location within their established trade routes, Sicily was extremely important strategically. Tensions mounted between the two civilizations, and Carthage placed its navy in the Strait of Messina, the narrow channel of water that separates the eastern tip of Sicily from mainland Italy. War finally broke out in 264 BC. Known as the First Punic War, this conflict lasted 23 years and resulted in Rome gaining control of Sicily—the first administrative territory outside of mainland Italy that would become a part of the Roman Empire.

But the conflicts between Carthage and Rome were far from over. In 219 BC, a Carthaginian army led by Hannibal captured the pro-Roman city of Saguntum in the Iberian Peninsula. This led to a declaration of war by the Romans, kicking off the Second Punic War. Hannibal took his large army, along with 37 war elephants, from the Iberian coast in the west to the Rhone River in the east, reaching the foot of the Alps in the autumn of 218 BC. Fighting frigid, snowy weather, difficult terrain, and hostile native tribes, the army crossed the mountains. After losing many men, and most of the elephants, to hunger, exhaustion, and falls from the slippery mountain heights, the army finally reached Italy.

Although Hannibal had early successes and even controlled parts of Italy for a time, Roman forces eventually found victory in 203 BC, and Hannibal sailed back to Carthage. Rome also gained control of Iberia, delivering a blow to the Carthaginians' main source of manpower for their armies. Finally, Rome took the fight directly to the heart of Carthage, attacking settlements in Tunisia. The Romans agreed to a peace treaty in 201 BC, but Carthage had lost everything it had worked so hard to acquire, save its North African city.

## Final War and Destruction

But soon, even the city of Carthage would be a thing of the past. In 149 BC, the Third Punic War was fought, after Roman senator Cato the Elder expressed the opinion that Carthage should be "destroyed." Despite the fact that the Carthaginians had been stripped of most of their resources and wealth, the city put up a fierce fight when the Romans invaded. Amazingly, they held off the Romans for three years, although they no doubt realized it was a lost cause. In 146 BC, Roman general Scipio Aemilianus ruthlessly sacked the city of Carthage, ordering it to be burned, razed to the ground, and plowed over. He killed or enslaved 50,000 Carthaginians.

Julius Caesar eventually rebuilt the city as a Roman seaport, and over the centuries, Carthage saw many different occupying forces, including the Vandals, Byzantines, Muslims, and Crusaders. But perhaps the empire is best known for the exploits of its military leader, Hannibal. Interestingly, Hannibal's surname, Barca, was derived from the Punic word *barqa*, meaning "lightning." It was a fitting name for a Carthaginian general who staged one of the most risky and surprising military campaigns in history, on behalf of an empire that once shone brilliantly and brightly.

# Dilmun

*Like many of the stories in the Bible, the tale of the Garden of Eden has fascinated readers for centuries. Described as a peaceful paradise full of lush greenery, flowing streams, and trees full of fruit, the garden was the home of Adam and Eve, the first humans created by God. The pair lived there happily until they ate fruit from the one tree God had commanded them to avoid, the tree of the knowledge of good and evil. They were then cast out, never allowed to return. Could the mysterious kingdom of Dilmun be the original basis of this story?*

✳ ✳ ✳ ✳

SOME BELIEVE THE Garden of Eden story is simply a myth, and the description of the plants and streams are the product of an active imagination. Others believe it is true, and, therefore, the garden must have existed at some point in history in some specific place. Still others settle on a mix of truth and fiction: Perhaps the tale isn't entirely true, but maybe it was inspired by an actual garden that once grew somewhere in the Middle East.

The Bible gives some clues about the location of the famed garden, describing it as the source of water for four rivers it names as the Gihon, Pishon, Tigris, and Euphrates. The Tigris and Euphrates are well known, running from the mountains of Turkey through Syria, and down through Iraq until they drain into the Persian Gulf near Kuwait.

## Myths and Stories

But the unknown locations of the Gihon and Pishon rivers have been debated by scholars for centuries. Some, including Austrian archeologist Eduard Glaser and Latvian-American archeologist Juris Zarins, posit that the Gihon corresponds to the Karun River in Iran, and the Pishon refers to the Wadi Al-Batin river system that runs through Saudi Arabia, Iraq, and Kuwait.

If these theories are correct, the Garden of Eden would have been situated at the head of the Persian Gulf, near present-day Kuwait, and right on the edge of an ancient civilization known as Dilmun.

Like the Garden of Eden, Dilmun was once thought to be nothing more than a myth. The mysterious civilization was a land mentioned in Sumerian mythology, where it was believed to be a paradise free of disease and death. Dilmun was filled with divine water sources, which transformed the dry desert into a garden of greenery, where the gods resided. These included Enki, the god of water, Ninlil, the goddess of wind, and Ninhursag, the mother goddess, who was said to be the caretaker of the plants in the sacred garden.

## Masters of the Sea

But more recently discovered evidence, including ancient Mesopotamian texts that mention Dilmun as an important trading partner and ruins excavated in Bahrain, have made it clear that this civilization was, indeed, real.

The first mentions of Dilmun date back to Sumerian cuneiform tablets from the third millennium, BC, but the society was most prosperous during the early centuries of the second millennium. By this time, Dilmun was controlling the trade routes in the Persian Gulf, which was frequently traversed by peoples from Mesopotamia, the Indus Valley, and China.

According to texts that have been found, Dilmun was considered a prosperous land which was filled with many great dwellings. It was said that all of the known countries in the world brought their wares to Dilmun for trade. Dilmun traded precious woods, ivory, gold, and pearls from the gulf in exchange for silver, tin, textiles, olive oil, and grains from their trading partners. They also may have had a monopoly on copper, which was mined in the area of modern Oman and found its way to Mesopotamian cities.

Sometime after 1720 BC, Dilmun began to decline in influence. By 1500 BC, foreign powers began to take over the civilization, including Mesopotamia, Babylonia, and Assyria. Dilmun also suffered from the effects of increasing piracy in the Persian Gulf, which interrupted their trading routes. After the collapse of Babylon in 538 BC, the name "Dilmun" was no longer found in texts. Dilmun fell into total obscurity.

## Uncovering Evidence

For centuries, a few ancient Sumerian writings were the only evidence known suggesting the existence of the Dilmun civilization. But in the 1950s, archeologists began to excavate a mound created from the rubble of different settlements on a single site, on the island country of Bahrain. The newest layer dates to the eighteenth century, when a Portuguese fort was built on the site. The Arabic word for "fort," *qal'at*, gives the location its name, Qal'at al-Bahrain. But it is the lowest layers, which date back to 2300 BC, that have given the location its reputation as Bahrain's "most important site in antiquity."

This site, which is situated on a Persian Gulf port, is believed to have been the capital of the Dilmun civilization. Three consecutive Dilmun cities are found one on top of the other. Evidence of ancient trade, such as ivory and copper artifacts, have been uncovered, as well as burial grounds, Dilmun stamp seals, the remains of houses and streets, and large warehouses, which hint at Dilmun's prosperity.

Nearby are carved stones marking the entrance of a chamber with an altar inside, and the presence of blackened animal bones and charred earth suggests that sacrifices to the gods were performed in the location.

And the ruins at Qal'at al-Bahrain aren't the only evidence of Dilmun that has been discovered in recent years. In the nearby town of Saar, even more ancient remains have been found. The ruins in this area include residential dwellings and a cemetery, which is laid out in a honeycomb pattern. Archeologists have even found what they believe are the remnants of restaurants and shops, suggesting that this region of Dilmun was quite a thriving city.

## The Two Seas

While Dilmun is believed to have encompassed eastern Saudi Arabia and Kuwait as well as Bahrain, it seems clear that the island was important to the entire civilization. At just under 300 square miles, the tiny country of Bahrain is the smallest Arab nation and the third smallest country in Asia. Its name is said to mean "two seas," but the "seas" it refers to are unclear. Some scholars believe it is in reference to the bay on the east and west of the island, or the seas to the north and south.

But perhaps the more likely meaning has to do with the two types of water naturally found on and around the island—saltwater and freshwater. Until modern times, when the population of Bahrain began to outgrow the resources, the island had an abundance of underground freshwater springs. For an island that receives barely more than three inches of rain a year, these springs were vital to the growth of the region. To ancient peoples, the sight of fresh, life-giving water bubbling up from the ground of an island surrounded by undrinkable saltwater must have seemed like a gift from the gods.

And that's exactly how the people of Dilmun described their land—as a fertile paradise fit for the gods. A Sumerian poem, featuring the gods Enki and Ninhursag, extols Dilmun as "pure," "pristine," and full of "fresh waters."

Whether or not this ancient land was the inspiration, or location, of the Garden of Eden may never be known for certain. But the myths and stories of the enigmatic Dilmun will no doubt continue to fascinate for generations to come.

# The Fiery Cucuteni-Trypillia Culture

*What do communism and the ancient Eastern European
civilization of Cucuteni-Trypillia have in common? Well, as it turns
out, much less than the former Soviet Union would have liked.*

✳   ✳   ✳   ✳

ORE THAN 6,500 YEARS ago, before the earliest known
cities arose in Mesopotamia, this civilization became one
of the first examples of urbanization in the world. Primarily
located in what is now Moldova, Romania, and Ukraine, the
culture was discovered in the late 1800s by both Romanian
scholar Teodor Burada and Czech-Ukrainian archeologist
Vikentiy Khvoyka. As a result, the culture was named for the
village of Cucuteni in Romania as well as the village of Trypillia
in Ukraine.

During the era it was in power, the Soviet Union took a
great interest in the Cucuteni-Trypillia culture, funding
excavations and research. At first, this civilization appeared to
be a classless society with no private ownership. The Soviets
called it "primitive communism" and praised the foresight
of these ancient peoples, living in their long-ago utopia. But
as excavation continued, the assumptions about the societal
makeup of the Cucuteni-Trypillia peoples began to unravel.
Archeologists were discovering huge buildings and technology
that called into question whether this society was, indeed,
classless. The discoveries were so unsettling to the Soviets that
any scholar who challenged the idea of the civilization being
"classless" was deemed an enemy of the state or accused of
being a terrorist spy.

## Early Urban Dwellers
Surprisingly, the fact that this ancient culture was able to cause
such strife within the Soviet Union thousands of years after
it existed isn't even its most interesting characteristic. Around
3,000 cultural sites have been discovered throughout Romania,

Moldova, and Ukraine, stretching from the Danube River in the southwest to the Dnieper River in the northeast. During the height of its existence, around 4000 to 3500 BC, the people of the Cucuteni-Trypillia civilization built settlements that consisted of thousands of structures. Researchers estimate that each settlement boasted between 20,000 and 46,000 inhabitants.

During the early era of its existence, the culture constructed mostly dug-out pit houses, then afterwards moved to above-ground clay houses with roofs of thatched straw or reeds. Later, they built homes by arranging vertical poles in the ground and attaching walls made of woven branches and clay. A clay oven was placed in the center of the house for heating and cooking. Using their building techniques, the Cucuteni-Trypillia peoples were able to erect large structures that could be up to 7,500 square feet in area.

## Female Influence

For sustenance and farm work, the civilization raised animals—including cattle, pigs, sheep, and, in later years, horses—and grew wheat, rye, and peas. They supplemented their diet with hunting, fishing, and gathering. Men and women of the Cucuteni-Trypillia culture had defined roles, with the men engaging in hunting, raising the livestock, and making tools out of flint, rock, clay, wood, and bone. The women made pottery, textiles, and clothing, and were also important leaders in the community. In fact, one of the most unique aspects of the culture is their apparent reverence for women. An abundance of statues and amulets depicting female forms have been discovered, with scholars theorizing that the civilization may have worshipped goddesses and been matriarchal in nature.

Cucuteni-Trypillia pottery and ceramic work is of particular interest to archeologists, who note the sophistication of the pieces. The Cucuteni-Trypillia peoples used temperature-controlled kilns to fire their pottery, with some kilns as big as

20 feet wide. Much of the pottery was intricately decorated with patterns, designs, or depictions of female figures, with minerals and other organic materials used to create different colors. The pottery was so well-made that even modern craftsmen have had a difficult time attempting to recreate it.

## Burn It Down

But perhaps the most unusual characteristic of the Cucuteni-Trypillia civilization was their perplexing habit of intentionally burning their villages to the ground every 60 to 80 years. Why, and even how, they did this is mostly unknown. Entire settlements were torched, requiring a huge amount of fuel and the cooperation of everyone in the community. Interestingly, the clay ovens located in the middle of each home were often removed before the conflagration ensued. Some theorize that the oven symbolized the "heart" of the home, and by removing it, the home "died" before it burned. The culture may have even believed that inanimate objects, such as houses, had souls, and burning them was a sort of ritual sacrifice.

Other theories for burning the settlements include a desire for urban renewal, a belief that a "fresh start" was needed every few generations, or simply a need to get rid of bugs or disease. One of the most striking examples of this practice is located in Poduri, Romania, where archeologists uncovered multiple distinctive layers of a single village, indicating it had been burned and rebuilt at least 13 times.

The Cucuteni-Trypillia culture's interest in fire may help to explain another strange discovery—or rather, lack of discovery—about the civilization. Very few human remains or cemeteries have ever been found in the settlement sites, and the culture created no funerary objects for their dead. It's possible that this culture was one of the first to make use of cremation, or they may have simply believed that their dead should be "returned" to nature, allowing animals and birds to consume the bodies.

## Ongoing Mystery

Sometime after 3000 BC, the Cucuteni-Trypillia culture began to decline and fade away. Like so many other aspects of this civilization, researchers are unclear about the cause. Many believe another, more war-like civilization may have crossed paths with the peaceful Cucuteni-Trypillia, driving them out or destroying them entirely. Others think climate change may have played a role, as the culture was largely dependent on agriculture and a drastic change in growing conditions would have been catastrophic.

Whatever their reasons for some of their unique behavior, the Cucuteni-Trypillia peoples have certainly made a name for themselves in the world of archeology. From angering communists to baffling scientists, this unique culture continues to fascinate today. With research work ongoing, archeologists are hopeful that the Cucuteni-Trypillia culture still has much to reveal.

# The Golden Tartessos Civilization

*The Colombian legend of El Dorado began with stories of Andean kings who were covered in gold dust as part of coronation rituals. The legend inspired other similar stories throughout the region. But such stories of treasure-filled cities are hardly limited to the Americas: A similar place full of gold, silver, and other riches, was once said to be found along the coast of what is today southwestern Spain.*

✳   ✳   ✳   ✳

THIS CULTURE WAS called the Tartessos, and it spanned the southern edge of the Iberian Peninsula, where it first emerged in the ninth century BC. Like El Dorado, the Tartessos civilization was something of a legendary, mythical place to the people of the Mediterranean, who often heard stories of the silver and gold said to be abundant in the area.

## Phoenician Influence

Tartessos was described by ancient historians and was even mentioned in the Bible. But 2,500 years ago it vanished, giving it even more of an air of myth. It wasn't until twentieth century archeologists began to find evidence of this lost civilization that it became clear that Tartessos was, indeed, once a real place with a plentiful supply of various metals.

The Phoenicians are believed to be the first outsiders who "discovered" the indigenous Paleo-Hispanic people of the Tartessos civilization sometime around the eighth century BC. The Phoenicians set up their own harbor, Gadir, which is present-day Cadiz, in order to load up their ships with the metal goods obtained in the area and carry them back across the Mediterranean.

The native peoples mined ore deposits in the mountain ranges of the Iberian Pyrite Belt, which contained copper, tin, lead, silver, and gold, and the Phoenician demand for the metals grew over time. Ancient historians recorded the great abundance of the metals extracted from the mines, describing silver anchors crafted to replace the stone and lead anchors of Phoenician ships, and claiming entire forests were cut down to fuel the constantly burning melting ovens.

Soon, the Phoenicians were settling colonies along the southern coast of Spain, with no resistance from the indigenous peoples. Paleo-Hispanic and Phoenician cultures melded together in Tartessos like the prized metals that were mined in the mountains. Populations increased rapidly, especially around Huelva and Cadiz, and word spread across the sea of a land filled with riches, fueling the legendary stories that would be told about Tartessos.

## A Golden Discovery

Tartessos remained a legend for centuries, with little to prove it ever existed, until a remarkable find in September of 1958. Just west of the city of Seville, in a hill called El Carambolo, archeologists discovered a Phoenician funeral urn filled with 21 pieces of gold jewelry and artifacts. Weighing just over five pounds, the golden items included bracelets, necklaces, and rectangular plaques. While the style of the items appeared to be Phoenician, the gold used to create them was mined merely miles away. The discovery was the first to hint at a larger trove of treasures from the Tartessos civilization, and sparked an interest in more research.

Soon after, hundreds of grave goods were found in a necropolis near Huelva. Cremated remains were found with items like bronze brooches, jugs, belt buckles, and incense burners, as well as iron knives with ivory handles. Thousands of fragments of Tartessos pottery were uncovered throughout the region, some of which was handcrafted, while other pieces were created on pottery wheels.

Many dwellings were found, but none large enough to be considered a workshop or manufacturing facility. This suggested to researchers that the people of the Tartessos civilization were self-sustaining and fashioned their wares in their homes, free from governmental or political control. But those who worked most closely with Phoenician traders were often the elites of Tartessos society.

The Tartessos civilization is also notable for its writing system, written in what is known as the Southwestern script. The writing is a mix of individual letters of an alphabet and symbols that represent syllables, known as a semi-syllabary. More than 95 inscriptions have been found, but so far, researchers have been unable to translate the script.

## Burned and Buried

For decades after these many discoveries, archeologists debated what had happened to the Tartessos civilization. Signs of a decline seemed to begin around the sixth century BC, when smaller villages appear to have been abandoned. The Phoenician homeland was conquered around this time by the Persians, and this may have prompted many Phoenicians to abandon Tartessos and seek more secure settlements. But in 2017, archeologists made a discovery that shed a new and disturbing light on the last days of the Tartessos civilization.

In the Extremadura region of Spain, just north of Seville, researchers uncovered the remains of more than 50 animals, including horses with hooves that had been deliberately and symmetrically crossed. These animals were found in a court-yard at the bottom of a large stone staircase. Also uncovered were bronze cauldrons and braziers, as well as intricately decorated bone and ceramic plates. To archeolo-gists, the finds suggested a large, elaborate banquet, during which dozens of animals were sacrificed. At the end of the banquet, the entire area was set on fire, and then buried beneath 14 feet of dirt and clay, an undertaking that would have taken many days of work.

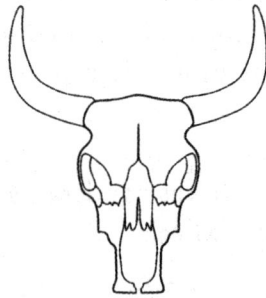

Were the people of Tartessos attempting to appease or bargain with their gods? One theory is that earthquakes and tsuna-mis near the coast destroyed many settlements, which would explain why the remains of the sacrificial feast were found inland. Perhaps the Tartessos peoples were simply asking their gods to protect them in their new location. However, this does not explain why they then burned and buried their new home, or why evidence of their existence vanished afterwards.

Archeologists believe that when ancient civilizations buried a site, it was to protect their relics from looters, and perhaps even to preserve them for future generations. Was this what they were doing? The Tartessos peoples may have deliberately left us a time capsule. Undoubtedly, the legends and stories of this civilization are far from over.

# Villanovans, Etruscans, and Romans

*In the hills and valleys of central Italy, the relics of a series of cultures continue to give archeologists tantalizing clues about cultural life from the dawn of the Iron Age to the rise of the Roman Empire.*

❋   ❋   ❋   ❋

AROUND 1000 BC, the Villanovan culture arose in central Italy, becoming one of the first Iron Age civilizations in the region. The name was taken from the site of a cemetery found near Villanova (now known as Castenaso), in northern Italy, where, between 1853 and 1855, archeologist Giovanni Gozzadini uncovered 193 tombs, most of which were filled with funerary urns.

The area's natural resources were ideal for an ancient society, providing a perfect area for crop production. Without a constant worry about food, the Villanovan peoples were able to explore other endeavors, such as the arts, manufacturing, and trade. As a result, their society flourished.

This civilization was the earliest phase of what would become known, by 750 BC, as the Etruscan culture. Researchers have looked for clues that might separate the two civilizations, like evidence of warfare or migration, but have found nothing to suggest that they are not one and the same. The small villages of the Villanovans appear to have gradually grown, until they became the first major Etruscan cities.

## Independently Wealthy

These cities were independent city-states, and they were scattered from the Tiber River in the south to the Po River valley in the north. Each Etruscan city developed its own industry, art, architecture, and government, so these achievements arrived at different times for every community.

The cities located near the coastline tended to develop more quickly, as they had more interaction with travelers and outsiders, and they would gradually pass along their knowledge to the cities located inland.

The Etruscans engaged in trade not only with each other, but also with tribes in northern Italy and the Alps, and with seafaring cultures that visited their shores, including the Phoenicians, Greeks, Carthaginians, and other Mediterranean societies. Etruscan land was rich in mineral resources, especially iron, which was offered for trade, along with wine, olive oil, grain, and pine nuts.

They also traded a form of pottery, known as *bucchero*, which was considered their "national" pottery. Bucchero was prized for its black color, which was achieved through a unique process called "reduction." After a piece was formed from red clay, it was placed in a kiln and the vent was closed. This helped reduce the oxygen available for the fire, forcing it to draw oxygen directly from the iron oxide in the pottery itself. The finished pottery displayed a striking black color, which was then polished to a glossy sheen.

## Eastern Influence

By the end of the eighth century BC, Etruscan contact with outside cultures led to what is known as an "Orientalizing period." Influences from the Eastern Mediterranean and Near East, including Syria, Assyria, and Egypt, first made their way into Greek art and pottery, and Etruscan interaction with the Greeks introduced them to the same ideas. Sculptures, ceramics, and metalwork all reflected this influence, but the Orientalizing period also affected food, clothing, and religion.

Perhaps most importantly, the Greek alphabet, derived from the Phoenician alphabet, was developed during this time period, resulting in a huge increase in literacy. Thousands of short Etruscan inscriptions have been found, most of which are epitaphs engraved on monuments. But several longer texts have been discovered, including the *Tabula Capuana*, a 390-word text that describes rituals to be performed at different times of the year.

## The Rise of Rome

In the fifth century BC, Etruscan cities began to feature large fortification walls with towers and gates. The reason for this is clear to archeologists: Rome, at one time the Etruscans' smaller neighbor to the south, was beginning to grow larger and gain power. By the late fourth century BC, Rome had begun annexing Etruscan cities, despite fierce opposition from the Etruscans, who occasionally allied with Celtic tribes from the north in their efforts to thwart the Romans.

For more than 200 years, battles raged between the ever-shrinking Etruscan cities and the growing empire of Rome. The independent organization of the Etruscan cities, once a unique aspect of their society, proved to hasten their downfall, as there was no centralized political unity amongst the peoples.

By 27 BC, the last of the Etruscan cities had been annexed by Rome. Their culture was overlain or replaced with the dominant Latin culture and language. The civilization of the Etruscans was then forgotten for nearly 2,000 years. Luckily, the amazing artifacts uncovered by archeologists—including bronze statues, gold jewelry, intricately carved sarcophagi, and colorful tomb wall paintings—have given researchers insight into this once-powerful culture.

Today, the small town of Civita di Bagnoregio, located 75 miles north of Rome, is one of the best-known Etruscan cities that still contains evidence of its founders in many locations. From the layout of the village, which is in an Etruscan style, to the Bucaione—an ancient tunnel carved through the lowest part of the city—signs of the Etruscans are everywhere. While Rome may have silenced this civilization for millennia, modern history buffs now have plenty of opportunities to learn about the ancient Etruscan culture.

# Myth and the Minoans

*Little is known about the culture birthed by the island people known as the Minoans. They left behind fragments of mysteriously advanced art and architecture. These remnants, as well as legends and stories, point to a civilization that accomplished much but ultimately succumbed to a string of unlucky catastrophes.*

✳   ✳   ✳   ✳

GREEK MYTHOLOGY TELLS the tale of the Minotaur, a fierce creature with the body of a man and the head and tail of a bull. To contain the beast, King Minos of Crete asked the architect Daedalus to build a convoluted labyrinth to imprison the Minotaur. The labyrinth was said to be so confusing and complicated that even Daedalus had difficulty escaping it after he designed and built it. Eventually, the Minotaur was killed by the Athenian hero Theseus, who found his way out of the labyrinth with the help of a thread he had tied to a doorpost at the entrance.

While the story may be myth, King Minos and the Minotaur inspired the name of the very real Minoan civilization, which arose on the island of Crete and other nearby islands in the Aegean Sea as early as 3200 BC. In recent history, the name was popularized by Sir Arthur Evans, a British archeologist who was a pioneer in the study of Aegean civilizations. Evans is most famous for excavating the ruins of Knossos, a winding palace complex that covers five acres and is composed of more than 1,000 rooms, which has itself been described as mazelike and labyrinthine.

## Early, Middle, and Late

Before the Minoan civilization began, the people of Crete mostly lived in small fishing villages along the shore or farmed in the fertile Messara Plain on the southern part of the island. When the Bronze Age began on Crete around 3200 BC, early

Minoans started to organize into centers of commerce and skilled work. Evans called this era the Early Minoan period, and much of what we know about it comes from the artifacts researchers have uncovered from burial plots. The evidence shows that great technological strides were made during this time in stone working, metalworking, and pottery, including the development of burnishing tools used to create decorations in these mediums.

Around 2100 BC, the Middle Minoan period began. Archeologists consider this the time during which the Minoans truly developed a civilization. Populations increased, cities were settled, and construction projects, like the massive Knossos palace, were undertaken. Crete and its resources were soon insufficient to support the burgeoning society, so the population began migrating to nearby islands.

Some researchers further divide the Middle Minoan period into the "Old Palace Period" and the "New Palace Period." This is because of a mysterious catastrophe that occurred around 1700 BC, believed to have been either an earthquake or a military invasion. The catastrophe destroyed many of the grand palaces that had been built. These "old" palaces were then rebuilt into "new" palaces which were even larger and more magnificent than the originals.

Unfortunately, this was not the end of the disasters to befall the Minoans. The beginning of the Late Minoan period, about 1600 BC, was marked by another catastrophe: the eruption of the nearby Thera volcano, in what was one of the largest volcanic eruptions in known human history.

Once again, the palaces were rebuilt and improved upon, but over the next several hundred years, earthquakes and subsequent eruptions of the Thera volcano—now known as the island of Santorini—caused a major decline in the Minoan population until eventually the civilization disappeared around 1100 BC.

## The Palaces of the Traders

At their pinnacle, the Minoans had significant influence in the Mediterranean region. The civilization relied on trading for much of its wealth and economy, exporting timber, textiles, foods, saffron, and olive oil in exchange for copper, gold, silver, tin, semiprecious stones, and ivory. The Minoan trading network stretched from the Old Kingdom of Egypt in the south, to the island of Cyprus and the Levant in the east, to the Anatolian region of modern-day Turkey in the north. There is even evidence that their trading influence may have reached as far west as the Iberian Peninsula.

Excavations by Evans and other archeologists have given us a glimpse into the lives of these prosperous traders. In addition to the palace at Knossos, similar structures have been discovered at Phaistos, Zakros, Malia, and Gournia. Although they're referred to as "palaces," researchers don't know if the elites of society actually lived in these buildings, or if they were only used for administrative, political, and economic purposes. The palaces were often multistory structures that were arranged around a paved center courtyard, and they featured indoor and outdoor staircases, light well openings, and sophisticated masonry. Huge storage areas found in some of the complexes suggest that they were, in part, used as distribution centers for agricultural commodities.

## Growing and Progressing

The Minoans had plenty of agricultural goods to share amongst the population. The civilization grew wheat, barley, legumes, grapes, figs, and olives, and raised cattle, sheep, pigs, and goats. On Crete, vegetables like lettuce, celery, and carrots grew wild, providing more variety for the Minoan diet. Minoans also domesticated bees and imported cats from Egypt to help control the rodent population. Their location in the Mediterranean Sea meant that seafood was plentiful, and fish and mollusks were regularly consumed. The diverse range of healthy food available helped the Minoan population thrive.

With the population growing, Minoan architects came up with clever systems for distributing water and for relocating sewage. Buildings were constructed with flat roofs and open courtyards that would collect rainwater and divert it to cisterns. Wells and aqueducts were located throughout cities to help manage water needs. The Minoans even created water treatment devices, such as pipes made of porous clay which would filter water until it was clean.

The thriving Minoan civilization also developed a system of writing, which may have been created as a way to keep track of inventory at the palaces. The writing consisted of both hieroglyphics, possibly inspired by Minoan interactions with Egypt, and a linear script known as Linear A, a precursor to the earliest known Greek writing. The language has proved difficult for scholars to translate, but much of what has been found seems to relate to accounting and recordkeeping. The scripts have mostly been found on sun-dried clay tablets, but writing is also found on ritual objects, pottery, and rings.

## Devoted to the Arts

Perhaps the most enduring aspect of the Minoan culture is the art they left behind. The Minoans were prolific artists, creating many paintings, frescos, sculptures, pottery, and jewelry. Some researchers are even convinced that Minoan artisans created art simply because they loved it, which would have been a major departure from the art that had been created before their time. Living in such a prosperous, flourishing civilization meant that citizens had plenty of free time to explore pursuits beyond those needed to meet basic needs, so many may have devoted their time to the arts.

Some Minoan art seems to have been influenced by Egyptian art, with human figures drawn in profile or with head and legs in profile, but the colors used are often more bright and vivid. Leaping bulls are found in many paintings, while the animal's head is used in pottery and sculpture, suggesting that bulls had some kind of religious significance in the culture. Marine animals are depicted in a large number of artistic pieces, so much so that "Marine Style" is a designation given to this art. Paintings of colorful dolphins and pottery featuring squids and octopuses with swaying tentacles are the hallmarks of this style. Small ceramic and stone figures were quite common, including two female figurines that Evans called a "Snake Goddess" and "Snake Priestess," but modern scholars are unsure of whether these sculptures represent deities.

Today, the largest collection of Minoan art can be found at the Heraklion Archeological Museum near the ruins of Knossos. Some scholars have called Knossos the oldest city in Europe, and there's no doubt that it was certainly one of the most influential. While the story of King Minos and the Minotaur may be mythical, the civilization whose name they inspired has left real, and remarkable, impressions of its once prominent culture.

# Sunken Civilizations

*Researchers have discovered the tantalizing remains of what appear to be advanced Mesolithic and Neolithic civilizations hidden for millennia under water or sand. Were these real, advanced cities or was the reality more mundane?*

\* \* \* \*

### La Marmotta: Stone Age Lakefront

WHAT IS NOW the bottom of Italy's six-mile-wide Lake Bracciano was once a lovely and fertile river floodplain. In 1989, scientists discovered a lost city, which they renamed La Marmotta. Dive teams have recovered artifacts ranging from ancient timbers to uneaten pots of stew, all preserved under ten feet of mud.

The site dates back to about 5700 BC, around the late Stone Age or Neolithic era. Though not much is known about the people who lived there, scientists do know that the city's residents migrated from the Near East or Greece in 35-foot-long, wooden dugout boats with their families. They had domesticated animals, pottery, religious statues, and even two species of dogs. They laid out their village with large wooden houses. Items such as obsidian knives and greenstone ax blades show that La Marmotta was also a Mediterranean trade center. But after 400 years of occupation, it seems the village was hastily abandoned. Why they fled still puzzles researchers.

## Atlantis Beneath the Black Sea

Ever since the Greek writer Plato described the lost island of Atlantis in the fourth century BC, scholars have searched for its location. One oft-suggested candidate is a grouping of underwater settlements in the northwest part of the Black Sea. Researchers claim this advanced Neolithic population center was once situated on shore along a freshwater lake that was engulfed by seawater by 5510 BC.

Ancient landforms in the area seem to have centered around an island that roughly fits the description of Atlantis. Similarities between the lore of Atlantis and this settlement include the use of a form of early writing, the existence of elephants (from eastern trade routes), obsidian used as money, and circular observatory structures.

## Japan, Gateway to Mu

According to Japanese geologist Masaaki Kimura, a legendary lost continent called Mu may have been discovered off the coast of Japan. Kimura says underwater formations that were found in 1985 at Yonaguni Island indicate that they were handmade and that they possibly once resembled a Roman city complete with a coliseum, a castle, statues, paved streets, and plazas. Although photos show sharp, step-like angles and flat surfaces, skeptics still argue these "roads" were actually created by forces such as tides or volcanoes. Nevertheless, Kimura maintains his belief that the ruins are the proof of a 5,000-year-old city.

## Ancient Alpine Lake Towns

Today, most people would associate the Alps, the mountain region that borders Germany, Switzerland, and Italy, with skiing, resorts, and beautiful views. But in the late Stone Age, or Neolithic period (6000–2000 BC), the region's lakes dominated the action. A dry spell in the mid-1800s lowered water levels and allowed evidence of ancient villages to surface within many lakes in the region. One site at the Swiss town of Obermeilen yielded exciting finds such as wooden posts, artifacts made from antlers, Neolithic clay objects, and wooden utensils. It is now believed that the posts supported large wooden platforms that sat over the water, serving as dock-like foundations for houses and other village structures.

## Hamoukar: City of Commerce

Until the mid-1970s, when the ancient settlement of Hamoukar was discovered in Syria, archeologists believed the world's oldest cities—dating back to 4000 BC—were in present-day Iraq. But the massive, 750-acre Hamoukar, surrounded by a 13-inch-thick wall and home to an estimated 25,000 people, was already a prosperous and advanced city by 4000 BC.

Situated in the land between the Tigris and Euphrates rivers, Hamoukar was sophisticated enough to support commercial bakeries and large-scale beer breweries. People used clay seals as "brands" for mass-produced goods, including delicate pottery, jewelry, and stone goods. The city was also a processing area for obsidian and later, copper. The settlement was destroyed in a fierce battle around 3500 BC, leaving more than 1,000 slingshot bullets in the city's ruins.

## The Great Danes

They sure ate a lot of shellfish—that much is known about the Mesolithic European culture that lived along the coast of what is now Denmark between 5600 and 4000 BC. Their now-underwater cities were investigated in the 1970s; the first is known as Tybrind Vig and its people are called the Ertebölle. The Ertebölle skeletons resemble those of modern Danes, but some also show Cro-Magnon facial features such as protruding jaws and prominent brow ridges. Archeologists have found implements made of antler, bone, and stone sticking out of the Danish sea floor. They also found large piles of shellfish at the oldest sites, indicating that the inhabitants relied on seafood. Preserved remains of acorns, hazelnuts, and various plants showed that their diet was well rounded.

The Ertebölle made clever use of local materials. They lived in wattle or brush huts; "knitted" clothing from plant fibers; made ceramic pots decorated with impressions of grains, cord, and bones; and created art from polished bone and amber. Eventually, it is assumed, the Ertebölle hunter-gatherers either evolved into or were replaced by people with farming skills.

## Mystery of the Bimini Blocks

The reason adventurers Robert Ferro and Michael Grumley traveled to the Bahamas was that they had read psychic Edgar Cayce's 1936 prediction that Atlantis would be found in the late 1960s off Bimini Island in the Bahamas. Needless to say, their discovery in the late '60s of what they described as giant rows of flat, rectangular blocks resembling a road off northern Bimini was a tad controversial.

The sunken, geometrically arranged rocks stretched for an estimated 700 to 1,000 feet. Several investigators estimated the "structure" dated back to 10,000 BC. Since then, other explorers have claimed to find additional stones that may have once formed part of an encircling wall around the entire island. Author Charles Berlitz observed that the stones resembled work by pre-Incan Peruvians.

However, geologists have countered that island shore rocks may split into regular planes due to a combination of solar exposure and shifting subsoil—formations resembling the Bimini Blocks also exist off the coast of Australia.

# The Anasazi

*Across the deserts and mesas of the region known as the Four Corners, where Arizona, New Mexico, Colorado, and Utah meet, backcountry hikers and motoring tourists can easily spot reminders of an ancient people. From the towering stone structures at Chaco Culture National Historical Park to cliff dwellings at Mesa Verde National Park to the ubiquitous scatters of broken pottery and stone tools, these remains tell a story of a culture existing across the arid Southwest during ancient times.*

✳ ✳ ✳ ✳

## Who Were the Anasazi?

THE ANASAZI ARE believed to have lived in the region from about AD 1 through 1300 (although the exact beginning of the culture is difficult to determine because there is no particular defining event). In their everyday lives, the Anasazi created black-on-white pottery styles that distinguish subregions within the culture, traded with neighboring cultures (including those to the south in Central America), and built ceremonial structures called *kivas*, which were used for religious or communal purposes.

## The Exodus Explained

Spanish conquistadors exploring the Southwest noted the abandoned cliff dwellings and ruined plazas, and archeologists today still try to understand what might have caused the Anasazi to move from their homes and villages throughout the region. Over time, researchers have posed a number of theories, including the idea that the Anasazi were driven from their villages by hostile nomads, such as those from the Apache or Ute tribes. Others believe that the Anasazi fought among themselves, causing a drastic reduction in their populations, and a few extraterrestrial-minded theorists have suggested that the Anasazi civilization was destroyed by aliens.

Today, the prevalent hypothesis among scientists is that a long-term drought affected the area, destroying agricultural fields and forcing people to abandon their largest villages. Scientists and archeologists have worked together to reconstruct the region's climate data and compare it with material that has been excavated. Based on their findings, many agree that some combination of environmental and cultural factors caused the dispersal of the Anasazi from the large-scale ruins seen throughout the landscape today.

## Their Journey

Although many writers—of fiction and nonfiction alike—romanticize the Anasazi as a people who mysteriously disappeared from the region, they did not actually disappear. Those living in large ancient villages and cultural centers did indeed disperse, but the people themselves did not simply vanish. Today, descendants of the Anasazi can be found living throughout New Mexico and Arizona.

The Hopi tribe in northern Arizona, as well as those living in approximately 20 pueblos in New Mexico, are the modern-day descendants of the Anasazi. The Pueblos in New Mexico whose modern inhabitants consider the Anasazi their ancestors include: Acoma, Cochiti, Isleta, Jemez, Laguna, Nambe, Picuris, Pojoaque, San Felipe, San Ildefonso, Ohkay Owingeh (formerly referred to as San Juan), Sandia, Santa Ana, Santa Clara, Santo Domingo, Taos, Tesuque, Zia, and Zuni.

# Culture and History
# of the Cherokee

*When sixteenth-century European explorers first began traveling
in what would later be called the United States, they found a
land already inhabited by a variety of groups. Among these
were a people living in the southeast corner of the continent
who referred to themselves as the Aniyunwiya, or "the principal
people." Their Creek Indian neighbors, however, called them the
Tsalagi, and English speakers gradually morphed that word into
Cherokee, the name generally used today.*

✳  ✳  ✳  ✳

THE ORIGIN OF the Cherokee is uncertain at best. Tribal
legend speaks of an ancient time of migration, which some
historians have projected as far back as the time of a land
bridge linking North America to Asia. Linguists report that
the Cherokee language is linked to the Iroquois, who lived far
to the north; others point out that traditional Cherokee crafts
bear a resemblance to those of the people of the Amazon basin
in South America. Regardless of their origin, the Cherokee
held sway over a great deal of land when Spaniard Hernando
de Soto made contact with this group in the 1540s.

De Soto did not find the gold he was looking for in Cherokee
territory. What he did find was a people who had heard of
his treatment of other tribes and did everything they could to
hasten his exit from their land. They quickly traded him some
food and other supplies—including two buffalo skins, the first
known European contact with the animal, which at the time
ranged as far east as the Atlantic coast—and suggested that he
might be better off heading to the west.

With that, de Soto left. The total number of people he
encountered living in their traditional lands is a matter of
speculation; the oldest reliable count dates from 130 years later,

long after the smallpox the Spaniard left behind had wreaked havoc on the tribe. The disease probably left somewhere between 25,000 to 50,000 people alive after killing an estimated 75 percent of the natives.

## Culture Shock

The Cherokee were quick to realize that white intruders were there to stay, and they did what they could to adapt to the changing world. On the arrival of the British, they became active trading partners, seeking to improve their situation through the acquisition of European goods and guns. They also became military allies—by many accounts, a trade at which they excelled—fighting with the British against the French and later against the Colonists in the American Revolution. The British, however, always viewed their Cherokee allies with suspicion, the effects of which ranged from the occasional massacre to the imposition of treaties demanding that the British be allowed to construct forts in Cherokee territory. This ceding of property was only the beginning of one of the biggest land grabs in history, culminating in the 1838 Trail of Tears, in which 17,000 Cherokee were forcibly sent west, resulting in thousands of deaths along the way.

Part of the difficulty with the early treaties was that the Europeans were in the habit of making them with anyone who claimed they represented the tribe; in reality, nobody could speak for all of the Cherokee. Their system was one of local autonomous government, with each village being responsible for its own affairs. The individual villages even had two chiefs: a White Chief in charge of domestic decisions and a Red Chief in charge of war and general relations with outsiders. The society itself was matrilineal and focused on a spiritual balance that the Cherokee believed existed between lower and higher worlds, with the earth caught in the middle. Europeans were ill-suited to understanding such a culture. In turn, the Cherokee realized that their society was ill-suited to dealing with Europeans.

## Changing Times

Cherokee society proved to be resilient, however. Part of the reason for this was due to people like Sequoyah. Sequoyah was a silversmith who devised the first syllabary for the Cherokee language in 1821. Although he was illiterate, he had studied the writing system used by the English. His Talking Leaves system, consisting of more than 80 symbols that each represented a syllable of Cherokee speech, was rapidly adopted and soon the Cherokee had a higher literacy rate than most of their white neighbors. One immediate result was the publication of a newspaper, *Cherokee Phoenix*, in 1828; it was soon renamed *Cherokee Phoenix and Indian Advocate* to indicate that its pages addressed issues faced by Native Americans of all tribes.

The 1820s proved a time of change for Cherokee society as a whole. Realizing that they must deal with the white man on his terms, the Cherokee had unified their autonomous tribes by the close of the decade, adopting a constitution that provided for a formal judiciary and elected legislature, electing John Ross as principal chief, and declaring themselves to be an independent nation. They took the nearly unheard of step of sending Indian representatives to Washington, D.C., to persuade both the Congress and the Supreme Court that the United States ought to be held to both the spirit as well as the letter of various treaties that were signed over the years. However, despite favorably impressing many with the quality of their arguments, their efforts proved fruitless, and the Cherokee joined their Native American brothers—being treated as second-class citizens for decades to come.

The repercussions from the almost unimaginable changes imposed on the Cherokee as European settlers came to dominate the continent echo to the current day. However, Cherokee society has proved itself equal to the task, and today its people are the most numerous of any Native American population, and the leadership of various parts of the tribe continues to actively work to remedy past inequities.

# The Mound Builders: Mythmaking in Early America

*The presence of mysterious mounds once led to the search for an improbable past. But what do we actually know about these ruins, and have we made mountains out of mole hills?*

✳  ✳  ✳  ✳

IN THE EARLY 1840s, the fledgling United States was gripped by a controversy that spilled from the educated parlors of Boston and Philadelphia—the core of the nation's intellectual elite—onto the pages of the nation's newspapers. In the tiny farming village of Grave Creek, Virginia (now West Virginia), on the banks of the Ohio River stood one of the largest earthen mounds discovered during the country's expansion westward. The existence of these mounds (frequently found throughout the Mississippi Valley, Ohio River Valley, and much of the southeast) was well known. The mounds had been the subject of speculation since Europeans had first arrived on the continent. Hernando de Soto, for one, had mentioned the mounds of the Southeast during his sojourns in that region.

## Money Well Spent

The colonists who settled the East Coast noticed that the mounds, which came in a variety of sizes and shapes, were typically placed near excellent sites for villages and farms. The Grave Creek mound was among the first of the major earthworks discovered by white men in their westward expansion. By 1838, the property was owned and farmed by the Tomlinson family. Abelard B. Tomlinson took an interest in the mound on his family's land and decided to open a shaft from its summit, 70 feet high, to the center. He discovered skeletal remains at various levels and a timbered vault at the base containing the remains of two individuals. More importantly, he discovered a sandstone tablet inscribed with three lines of characters of unknown origin.

## Who Were the Mound Builders?

Some Americans thought that the indigenous people were lazy and incapable of such large, earth-moving operations. The fact that none of the tribes who dwelt near the mounds had any knowledge of who had built them, led many to conclude that the mound builders could not have been the ancestors of current Native American in the area.

Wild and fantastic stories arose, and by the early nineteenth century, the average American may have assumed that the mound builders originated with a pre-Columbian expedition from the Old World—Vikings, Israelites, refugees from Atlantis—or entertained even more speculative assertions. There were theories that this part of the New World had once hosted a civilization as advanced as that of the Aztecs and Incas. It was asserted that this group had then succumbed to decline, possibly even being conquered by the tribes that now inhabited the land. Speculation on the history of the mound builders led many, including Thomas Jefferson, to visit mounds and conduct their own studies.

## Mormons and the Mounds

Meanwhile, the Grave Creek tablet inadvertently fanned the flames of a controversy that was roaring over the newly established, and widely despised, Church of Jesus Christ of Latter Day Saints, founded by Joseph Smith. The Mormon religion is based upon the belief that the American continent was once inhabited by the lost tribes of Israel who divided into warring factions and fought each other to near extinction. The last surviving prophet of these people, Mormon, inscribed his people's history upon gold tablets, which were interred in a mound near present-day Palmyra, New York, until they were unearthed and revealed to a teenaged Joseph Smith in 1823. Though many Americans were ready to believe that the mounds represented the remains of a non-indigenous culture, they were much less ready to believe in Smith's new religion.

Smith and his adherents were persecuted horribly, and Smith was killed by an angry mob while leading his followers west. Critics of the Saints (as the Mormons prefer to be called) point to the early nineteenth-century publication of several popular books purporting that the earthen mounds of North America were the remains of lost tribes of Israel. These texts claimed that evidence would eventually be discovered to support their author's assertions. That the young Smith should have his revelation so soon after these fanciful studies were published struck many observers as entirely too coincidental. Thus, Abelard Tomlinson's excavation of the sandstone tablet with its strange figures ignited the passions of both Smith's followers and his detractors.

## Enter the Scholar

Into this maelstrom strode Henry Rowe Schoolcraft, a mineralogist whose keen interest in Native American history had led to a government appointment as head of Indian affairs. While working in Sault Ste. Marie, Schoolcraft married a native woman and mastered the Ojibwa language. Schoolcraft traveled to Grave Creek to examine Tomlinson's tablet and concluded that the figures were indeed a language but deferred to more learned scholars to determine just which language they represented. The opinions were many and varied, and conjectures included Celtic runes and early Greek. Experts the world over weighed in with their opinions.

Schoolcraft was mostly concerned with physical evidence and focused on a close study of the mounds themselves. He remained convinced that the mounds and the artifacts they carried were the products of ancestors of the Native Americans. Schoolcraft's theory flew in the face of both those who sought to defend and those who sought to debunk the Mormon belief, and it would be more than three decades until serious scholarship and the emergence of true archeological techniques began to shift opinion on the subject.

## Answers Proposed, but Questions Still Abound

History has vindicated Schoolcraft's thoughtful study of the mounds. Today, we know that the mound builders were not descendants of Israel, nor were they the offspring of Vikings or any other Europeans. They were simply the ancient and more numerous predecessors of the Native Americans. They probably constructed the mounds for protection from floods and also possibly as burial sites, temples, and defense strongholds.

As for the Grave Creek tablet: Scholars today generally agree that the figures are not a written language but simply a fanciful design whose meaning, if ever there was one, has been lost to the ages. Though the Smithsonian Institute has several etchings of the tablet in its collection, the whereabouts of the actual tablet are no longer known.

# Caral-Supe: The First American Civilization?

*Did a technologically advanced civilization once flourish in the Peruvian mountains at the same time the ancient Egyptians were building their first pyramids?*

✳   ✳   ✳   ✳

THE FAMOUS PYRAMIDS of Giza are known not only as architectural wonders but as symbols of the ancient world. Their construction began around 2550 BC, and the painstakingly assembled, precisely designed structures have astounded archeologists and tourists for centuries. The Egyptian pyramids, and the ancient peoples who built them, may be the first things that come to mind when we think of ancient civilization; but surprisingly, at the same time Egyptian kings were creating pyramids, another civilization was thriving on the other side of the world.

The Caral-Supe civilization, named after its location in the Caral region of Peru near the Supe River, was first discovered in 1905. But the site, believed to be relatively recent, drew little attention from researchers. Some scholars, however, including Peruvian anthropologist and archeologist Ruth Shady, weren't so sure that the site was as recent as many assumed. In 1996, Shady began excavations of the area, with the help of a couple dozen Peruvian soldiers.

## An Exciting Excavation

Working on a tight budget—sometimes even using her own money—Shady and her team of soldiers searched the ruins for the remains of pottery, which are often found at archeological sites. But strangely, there was none to be found. The absence of any pottery shards suggested an exciting possibility to Shady: These ruins, at first believed to be recent, were not just older than originally thought; they were also older than the creation of pot-firing technology in the area. If Shady's hunch was correct, it would mean that she was uncovering one of the oldest civilizations in the Americas.

It took several more years before Shady had the chance to prove her hypothesis. In 1999, she and her team uncovered a number of preserved bags woven from reeds while excavating a pyramid at the site known as Pirámide Mayor. Since the reeds were, at one time, living organisms, they were the perfect candidates for radiocarbon dating. Shady sent samples to be dated to researcher Jonathan Haas at the Field Museum in Chicago, and the results were exactly what she was hoping for: the reeds were 4,600 years old.

## Impressive Architecture

Using samples found in the area, Haas was able to prove that the earliest city of the civilization, known as Huaricanga, dates back to 3500 BC. There is also evidence that humans may have been forming communities as early as 3700 BC, and human activity in the area can be dated all the way back to 9210 BC.

All of this evidence has added up to an amazing understanding for archeologists: this pre-ceramic society, sometimes known as Norte Chico or simply Caral, was the oldest-known civilization in the Americas. At the same time the Egyptians were building their pyramids more than 7,000 miles away, the Caral-Supe peoples were creating their own immense and impressive architecture, including huge, terraced pyramids, sunken circular plazas with 30-foot-wide staircases, amphitheaters, atriums, and residential buildings.

## Fish, Cotton, and a Trade Agreement

In addition to the Supe River, the society relied on the Fortaleza and Pativilca rivers to provide irrigation in the arid climate. This access to water allowed the Caral-Supe peoples to grow a variety of edible plants like squash, beans, sweet potato, and guava. But researchers pondered these inland locations of the settlements, which were about 14 miles from the coast of Peru. Why did this civilization choose to live so far from the coastland, where oceanic sources of protein were abundant? Shady and her team excavated several items that provided clues, including pieces of achiote, a fruit found in the rain forest, and necklaces made from coca seeds, a plant not found in the Caral region. Also discovered were remains of anchovies, sardines, and shellfish, which had to have come from the ocean miles away.

These items hinted that the Caral-Supe peoples enjoyed a thriving trade industry, one that allowed them to focus more on construction of their grand structures than on searching for food. Of course, this would mean that they must have possessed something of great worth with which to trade. More excavation at the site eventually uncovered the probable commodity: cotton. Shady discovered an abundance of cotton seeds and textiles in every area of the Caral-Supe site, leading the archeologist to conclude that the civilization must have traded cotton with other peoples in the region.

This would also serve to explain the presence of so many marine creatures at the site, even though it was so far inland. The Caral-Supe peoples probably traded their cotton to coastal fishermen, who needed the cotton to weave their fishing nets. In return, the fishermen provided Caral-Supe with plenty of seafood to supplement their mostly vegetarian diet, giving them vital access to protein. This relationship with the fishermen meant the Caral-Supe civilization was free to continue developing their infrastructure, without the need to be near the coast.

## A Mysterious Decline

Over time, the Caral-Supe civilization would encompass a 35-square-mile area, including within its territory 17 different pyramid complexes. The largest of these, the Pirámide Mayor, measures 520 by 490 feet at the base, and rises 59 feet high. Aside from its impressive architecture, the civilization is notable not only for its lack of pottery of any kind, but also its lack of sculpture, carvings, paintings, or drawings. But while Caral-Supe may not have had any visual art, there is evidence that the peoples enjoyed musical arts. Many flutes made of pelican and condor bone have been uncovered at the site. At its height, the civilization is believed to have been home to more than 3,000 people, making Caral-Supe one of the most densely populated regions of the world at the time.

Sometime around 1800 BC, the Caral-Supe civilization began to decline, for unknown reasons. Some of the structures appear to have been deliberately buried in an attempt to preserve them, suggesting the fall of the civilization didn't happen overnight. Researchers have noted that there is no evidence of warfare or violence in the location, so its disappearance is truly a mystery. But Caral-Supe's influence in the region is undeniable: The method of urban planning used by these ancient peoples was copied by other Andean civilizations for the next four thousand years. With ongoing research and excavation continuing at the site, the oldest civilization in the Americas may still one day provide us with answers to many questions.

# Ancient Artisans: Moche Culture

*Spanning 250 miles of desert coastline in what is now Peru, the Moche civilization flourished between the first and eighth centuries AD. While its culture was impressively advanced, the cause of its demise remains unknown.*

✳ ✳ ✳ ✳

THE CULTURE IS named after the Moche River valley, and the city of the same name is believed to have been the capital city of its peoples. Until the 1980s, most of what archeologists knew about the Moche culture came from the city of Moche itself, located just south of Trujillo, the second-oldest Spanish city in Peru. Here, two large adobe structures have stood since around AD 450, known now as the Huaca del Sol and Huaca de la Luna (Temple of the Sun and Temple of the Moon). At one time, Huaca del Sol stood 164 feet high, with a base spanning 1115 feet by 524 feet. Researchers estimate that more than 130 million adobe bricks were used to construct the temple, which was the largest pre-Columbian adobe structure ever built in the Americas. Sadly, almost two thirds of the original structure have been damaged or lost to erosion and looting. So, although Huaca de la Luna is the smaller of the two temples, it also has the good fortune of being better preserved, with faded murals that were once painted in bright colors still visible within the complex. Archeologists have also uncovered a large number of fine ceramic items, and they believe the two temples were once used for burials, as well as for administrative and religious purposes.

## Elaborate Tombs, Impressive Pottery

While these two temples are impressive, archeological excavation beginning in the late 1980s gave researchers even more insight into the Moche culture. Dozens of platform pyramids were discovered, divided between two distinct regions known as Southern Moche and Northern Moche. The Southern

Moche, which includes the Huaca del Sol and Huaca de la Luna, is believed to have been the center of Moche culture. The Northern Moche, centered around several valleys and rivers, was more independent and this area probably had its own individual governments.

The Southern and Northern Moche regions shared much of the same tradition and artwork, including an impressive variety of ceramics, textiles, and metalwork. The elites of society, such as royalty, warriors, and priests, were buried in elaborate tombs covered in artwork and filled with jewelry. Their burial chambers were quite unique, as each was adjacent to a smaller compartment that offered a representation of the tomb's contents, including a copper figure to symbolize the deceased.

Moche artwork and pottery was some of the most sophisticated in the pre-Columbian era. The peoples used mold technology to create their wares, which included high-quality water jars and pots. These were painted, mostly with red and white colors, with scenes depicting people, animals, plants, or fantastical beings. Some of the scenes illustrated the more disturbing aspects of Moche life, including human sacrifice and the ritual consumption of blood. These practices were also evident at the temples, where numerous skeletons have been unearthed that show signs of violence and head trauma.

## Masters of Metal

Moche culture is notable for its metalwork, which is considered very advanced. The civilization used sophisticated metalworking techniques, which have been difficult for even modern craftsmen to replicate. They perfected many techniques themselves, using gold, silver, and copper to create sculptures, jewelry, headdresses, and metal plating for vases and pots. Archeological sites excavated in the late 1980s found a wealth of these objects in their original locations, leading researchers to conclude that the Moche metal artwork was often associated with the elite of society and the power they wielded.

But this power was finite, and for reasons unknown, the Moche civilization began to wane around AD 700. Scholars theorize that climate change may have played a role, with a period of intense rain and flooding followed by years of drought taking a toll on the society. Others believe earthquakes or encroaching sand dunes may have disrupted daily life, while some think social unrest and warring factions may have been the culprits.

In all probability, a combination of these issues contributed to the downfall of the civilization. To this day, excavation continues and new discoveries await, ensuring the Moche will always hold an important place in the history of Peru and the ancient cultures of the world.

# The Goldsmiths: Quimbaya Culture

*Located between what are now the cities of Cali and Medellin, Colombia, the valley of the Cauca River was home to the pre-Columbian Quimbaya civilization. Scholars estimate that the culture arose around the first century AD, and flourished between the years 300 and 600. Much is unknown about the Quimbaya peoples, and few direct descendants of the civilization remain. Even the Quimbaya language is considered extinct, adding to the mystery surrounding the culture's ancient existence.*

✳    ✳    ✳    ✳

WITH THEIR TROPICAL location, the Quimbaya peoples were able to grow a variety of food, such as corn, avocado, and guava. Archeologists have found evidence that they also hunted for food, and remains of animals like deer, rabbits, opossums, foxes, and others have been found. Funerals were important occasions to the Quimbaya, and they carefully constructed distinctive tombs for each person who was buried. Inside, the deceased was provided with food, weapons, personal items, and ceremonial objects, which were believed to be necessary for the next life.

## Tumbaga and Poporos

One of the civilization's main industries involved the creation of textiles and cotton blankets. They also perfected a technique for extracting salt from the nearby river, and manufactured oil to be burned for lighting. Thanks to these resources, they enjoyed profitable trading relationships with neighboring regions. But the Quimbaya's primary claim to fame has nothing to do with blankets, salt, or oil. Rather, it is their skill in metalwork, particularly gold, that has impressed scholars and art lovers worldwide.

Gold was not terribly abundant in the Cauca River valley, so the Quimbaya developed a process to combine gold with copper into an alloy called *tumbaga*. Although the tumbaga was not pure gold, the alloy retained the brightness, beauty, and durability of the metal.

The most famous of the Quimbaya metal artifacts discovered by archeologists are called *poporos*. A poporo is a container with a long neck and a receptacle made to hold lime, which was made from powdered, roasted seashells. Indigenous cultures in Colombia, like the Quimbaya, used the lime during a sacred ritual called *mambeo*, in which coca leaves would be chewed along with the lime. To extract the lime from the container, a long metal pin was used. The poporos, and the mambeo ritual itself, were filled with symbolism and represented the idea of a dual god and the balance of opposites. The receptacle of the poporo symbolized femininity, while the long neck represented masculinity. The metallic pin joining with the lime was an illustration of the skies joining with the earth.

## Museum Quality

In addition to the poporos, Quimbaya artifacts include many human figures made from both metal and clay ceramics. These are often small figures, between 4 and 20 inches in height, which were buried in tombs as companions for the deceased. They also created an abundance of small animal and plant figures, including necklaces, earrings, and other decorative ornaments, as well as bowls, jars, and bottles. Some scholars believe that many of the anthropomorphic and zoomorphic figures found are meant to represent the gods worshiped by the Quimbaya, and the bond they shared with nature.

While the Quimbaya civilization eventually faded away sometime after the tenth century, the plethora of artifacts they left behind continues to mesmerize and educate history buffs. The Metropolitan Museum of Art in New York contains many Quimbaya items within its displays; but perhaps the most impressive collection is located at the Museo del Oro, or the Gold Museum, in Bogota, Colombia. Here, visitors can view the famous Poporo Quimbaya, which was purchased from grave robbers by the Banco de la Republica, the central bank of Colombia, in the 1930s. In an effort to preserve this priceless artifact as well as other pre-Columbian goldwork, the Gold Museum was established in 1939, and now houses hundreds of Quimbaya artifacts as well as thousands of other treasures. The Poporo Quimbaya has become a proud symbol of Colombia, and is a testament to the intricate skill of the Quimbaya peoples.

# The Kingdom of Quito

*Tombs and artifacts high in an Andean mountain valley beckon archeologists with hints of a thousand-year-old civilization.*

✳    ✳    ✳    ✳

THE ECUADORIAN CAPITAL of Quito lies in a valley on the eastern slopes of Pichincha, an active volcano in the Andes Mountains. Sitting at an elevation of 9,350 feet, just under two miles above sea level, the city is the second-highest capital in the world, after La Paz, Bolivia. Officially, the city was established in 1534, which is the date Spanish conquistador Sebastián de Belalcázar founded it after defeating the Inca warrior Rumiñawi.

But Quito's history goes back much further than its official founding date. In fact, researchers have found evidence of human habitation in the region that dates back to 8000 BC. American archeologist Robert E. Bell, while excavating a nearby extinct volcano in 1960, found tools made of obsidian glass left behind by hunter-gatherers. And in the Quito neighborhood of Cotocollao, researchers discovered the remains of a prehistoric village that once covered 64 acres. Burial sites, pottery, and stone figures were found near the ruins of ancient houses, which dated back to 1500 BC.

## The Cara Culture

Sometime in the late ninth or early tenth century AD, a civilization known as the Cara culture migrated from the coast of the Pacific Ocean up the Esmeraldas River to the area that is now Quito. After defeating the local Quitu tribe that inhabited the area, the Cara established a kingdom they called the Shyris, Scyris, or Caranqui civilization, but is now sometimes known as the Kingdom of Quito.

The kingdom was established in 980, and was ruled by a series of kings or tribal leaders, known as *shyris*, for almost 500 years. The Cara culture gradually spread into neighboring regions, building fortresses and leaving behind troops of fighters in each location. This was not without good cause: while the kingdom was the dominant culture in the region, it had not gained its place without making some enemies.

## Incan Empire

In 1462, the army of Quito was narrowly bested in a battle with an army led by Tupac Inca, the son of the emperor of the Incan Empire. Tupac Inca's son, Huayna Capac, built a capital city on what is today modern Quito, and the Cara culture, along with the Kingdom of Quito, was gradually absorbed into the Incan Empire.

When Sebastián de Belalcázar and the Spanish conquistadors arrived in 1534, the Incan general Rumiñawi decided he would rather see the city destroyed than fall into Spanish hands. He ordered the capital burned to the ground, destroying many artifacts of not only the Inca, but the Kingdom of Quito, as well. But recently, archeologists discovered 65-foot-deep Cara tombs found intact in the La Florida neighborhood of Quito. Efforts have been underway to preserve the artifacts found within and to learn more about the Cara culture. Perhaps one day we will have a much greater understanding of the civilization that once dominated Ecuador's mountainous capital city.

# The Tiwanaku of Bolivia

*Located near the Bolivian shore of Lake Titicaca, a freshwater lake in the Andes Mountains that straddles the border of Bolivia and Peru, the Tiwanaku archeological site was once the location of a culture that flourished more than a thousand years ago.*

✳ ✳ ✳ ✳

FOR DECADES, SCIENTISTS have debated the age of the Tiwanaku site, with some believing it dates back to 1500 BC or even thousands of years earlier. But most researchers agree that the Tiwanaku culture first emerged sometime between 200 BC and AD 200.

Unfortunately, much of the confusion may stem from the large amounts of looting and amateur excavations that began occurring at the site starting shortly after the fall of Tiwanaku and continuing unchecked into the early twentieth century. Some of the stones from the area were quarried for buildings and railroad projects, and structures were even used for target practice by the military. Needless to say, most of the buildings at Tiwanaku were destroyed or in poor condition by the time archeologists began studying and preserving the site. Luckily, the Bolivian government began restoring and protecting the area in the 1960s, and greater study of the site began in the late 1970s.

The archeological research at Tiwanaku has uncovered what was once an impressive civilization. The main structures at the site include the Akapana Pyramid, a rectangular enclosure known as the Kalasasaya, and a platform mound called the Pumapunku. These buildings, along with other reconstructed temples and courtyards, are open for public viewing.

## Pyramids, Courtyards, and Platforms

The Akapana is a platform mound or stepped pyramid, which is approximately 843 feet wide and 646 feet long, standing at about 54 feet tall. The entirely man-made mound, consisting of large and small stone blocks mixed with dirt, was excavated from the area. The pyramid was overlaid with a type of volcanic rock known as andesite, and stone blocks carved into puma and human heads were used to adorn the upper terrace. The largest of the andesite rocks is estimated to weigh more than 65 tons, suggesting the use of sophisticated construction practices which are still a mystery to archeologists.

The 300-foot-long Kalasasaya courtyard is notable for its monolithic "Gateway of the Sun," an arch which was discovered within the courtyard. The arch is carved with 48 squares, each representing what are thought to be angels or winged messengers. These messengers surround a central figure, a person holding staffs. The figure's head is surrounded by rays, possibly representing the sun. Researchers theorize that the figure is meant to be either the god Viracocha, who was said to be the creator of the universe, sun, moon, and stars, or the god Thunupa, who was known as a "Staff God" and controlled rain, lightning, and thunder.

The Pumapunku, similar to the Akapana, is a large man-made platform measuring approximately 549 feet long, 380 feet wide, and 16 feet tall. The structure is faced with megalithic blocks, and it also features a 22-foot-by-127-foot stone terrace that contains the largest stone block found within the Tiwanaku site, believed to weigh more than 144 tons.

## Skilled Architects and Farmers

Many of the stones, carved figures, and other artifacts found at Tiwanaku were so intricately and precisely cut that some researchers have suggested that extraterrestrials may have had a hand in their creation! Of course, it is far more likely that the Tiwanaku themselves were very skilled architects and artisans. The stonework and arches found at the site seem to suggest that the civilization had a good grasp of descriptive geometry and may have been familiar with mathematical concepts like the Pythagorean Theorem.

For decades, researchers believed that Tiwanaku had been largely a ceremonial site. But archeological excavations in the late twentieth century revealed a much different picture: that of a large and bustling metropolis that served as the capital city of a great civilization. The Tiwanaku civilization was especially knowledgeable about agriculture, which spurred a period of growth in the city between AD 300 and 700. They used a farming method known as the "raised-field system," consisting of raised planting areas separated by small irrigation canals. These canals helped to retain the heat of the sun even after it set, which was vital for keeping crops from freezing on cold nights. Farmers would also use the algae and plants that accumulated in the canals as fertilizer.

## Continued Influence

Tiwanaku grew to be very influential in the Andes, thanks in part to the civilization's agricultural economy. At its height, the city covered about one and a half square miles and had a population of between 10,000 and 20,000 people. Although the civilization disappeared around AD 1000, many believe that the Tiwanaku were the ancestors of the present-day Aymara indigenous peoples of the Andes and Altiplano regions of South America. The Tiwanaku also influenced many later cultures, including the Inca, and its impact was felt from what is now eastern and southern Bolivia to parts of Argentina, Chile, and Peru.

Today, researchers continue to make new discoveries in the area of Tiwanaku. Aerial photography, drones, and 3D laser scanning have revealed more buildings that have yet to be excavated, including about a hundred circular and rectangular structures that are thought to be residential homes. Archeologists have even discovered artifacts and the ruins of a temple and part of a village submerged in Lake Titicaca, which were once a part of the city of Tiwanaku. And the civilization continues to contribute more to the contemporary world than just archeological finds. Farmers in Bolivia have recently started to use the Tiwanaku's raised-field system for their own crops, which has had a significant effect on increasing agricultural production. The Tiwanaku civilization is proof that even in modern times, we can continue to learn from our past.

## Threads of an Ancient Culture

*Deep in the hills of Peru, an ancient society developed a unique culture that found expression in its textiles.*

* * * *

When it comes to ancient artifacts, textiles are often a rare find. This is because the fragile organic materials used to create textiles like blankets and clothing will break down over the centuries due to temperature changes and weather conditions. By the time archeologists have discovered the remains of an ancient civilization, any textiles that once existed have been lost to the ravages of time.

But this is not true for the Wari civilization, which grew along the coast and in the highland areas of Peru between AD 600 and 1000. This culture is known particularly for its vibrant, intricate textiles, which were well-preserved thanks to their use in desert burials. The dry desert air helped to protect the numerous tapestries, hats, and tunics that have been discovered, which have given archeologists a glimpse into the artistic expression of this culture.

## Capital and Quipus

But the Wari were far more than just prolific artists. Their civilization first began expanding from small villages in the Carahuarazo Valley of Peru and eventually established a capital at Huari, a city located 9,186 feet above sea level. Huari was spread out over almost six square miles, and at its height, had a population of about 70,000. The city was made up of densely packed rectangular buildings, usually two or three stories tall, which were divided into numerous rooms. Floors and walls were covered in plaster and painted white, and many buildings surrounded courtyards lined with stone benches. An underground network of conduits provided fresh water to the inhabitants of the city, which was said to be enclosed by stone and mortar walls up to 32 feet high and 13 feet thick.

Like many cultures before them, the Wari did not use any system of writing, so much of their social structure, political ideals, and other beliefs are unknown. However, the Wari did make use of *quipus*, the recording devices made of knotted strings. The knots were used to represent numeric and other values, and were often used as calendars or to keep track of taxes, census data, or military information. While many other civilizations, including the Incan Empire, have made use of quipus, many archeologists believe the Wari may have been its earliest innovators.

## Archeological Finds

While there may be a lack of written records, the Wari left behind quite a lot in the archeological record. Many structures have been identified at Huari, including a royal palace, a temple, and numerous residential buildings. Most were constructed with stone and mud brick, and were once painted either white or red. More Wari ruins lie approximately 380 miles to the southeast, in Pikillaqta, which is believed to have been an administrative and military center. Access was limited to a single, winding pathway, and the city was laid out in a geometric pattern of squares. Dozens of artifacts have been uncovered at Pikillaqta, including small figurines made of stone, copper, gold, and semiprecious stones. These tiny figures, which are no more than two inches high, depict elite members of society such as shamans and warriors.

The figures found at Pikillaqta are just a small sample of Wari art that has been discovered. Archeologists have also found pottery and ceramics such as bowls, vases, and urns, and sophisticated metalwork items made of copper, silver, and gold. These include a silver face mask, breastplate, gold bracelets, and jewelry found in a royal tomb.

## Abstract Art

It is the tombs which have provided the greatest examples of Wari art, preserved in their textiles. Vibrant threads of red, yellow, orange, green, indigo, and blue were woven together to create stylized and often abstract depictions of plants, flowers, pumas, condors, and llamas. Staff god iconography is also often featured in these textiles. As their civilization progressed, the Wari's artistic expression became even more abstract, until it was often difficult to know what they were attempting to represent within the fabric. Researchers theorize this may have been a purposeful act by the elite, who wanted to control the interpretation of the symbols on each piece. Or it may have been a representation of the drug-induced visions the Wari sought during religious ceremonies.

Up to nine miles of wool and cotton thread was used for a single tunic, resulting in what can only be called wearable artwork. The abstract designs, which many art historians have likened to cubism and abstract expressionism, would have come to life as the wearer moved, walked, or ran, giving each textile a life of its own.

## Modern Inspiration

While the Wari's skill with irrigation had allowed them to withstand a drought in the sixth century that brought an end to the nearby Nazca and Moche civilizations, they were not so fortunate when drought returned in the ninth century. This time, the dry conditions lasted for centuries, and archeologists theorize that this is the probable cause of the Wari's decline. Many of their buildings were purposely destroyed and ritually buried, while others were kept intact but had deliberately blocked doorways. It may have been their intention to one day return, but the long-lasting drought offered inhospitable conditions for far too long. By AD 1000, the Wari had faded into obscurity.

But thanks to their vibrant, creative artwork, the Wari have not been forgotten. Many of their textiles and other artifacts are on display in museums around the world. Some researchers even believe that artists such as Georges Braque and Pablo Picasso were influenced and inspired by the artistry of Wari textiles. Without the artwork of this ancient civilization, it is possible that our own modern art would be lacking. After all, we never know how our actions, inventions, and creations will one day affect societies that do not yet exist.

# Kingdom Beneath the Sea

*Standing at Land's End, near the town of Penzance in Cornwall, England, one might assume that the rocky cliff is, indeed, the end of the world. Sitting at the westernmost point on mainland England, the granite promontory is popular with tourists seeking the calm sounds of ocean waves as well as rock climbers looking for an adrenaline rush. But according to Arthurian legend and the tragic story of Tristan and Iseult, Land's End wasn't an end at all. Rather, it marked the beginning of a stretch of land known as the kingdom of Lyonesse.*

✳  ✳  ✳  ✳

ACCORDING TO LEGEND, Lyonesse spanned the area between Cornwall and the Isles of Scilly 30 miles away in the Celtic Sea, and was the home to Tristan, one of the Knights of the Round Table. Tristan's father, Meliodas, was the king of

Lyonesse, and his son was next in line for the throne. When the king died, Tristan was at his uncle's court in Cornwall, which turned out to be fortuitous; because on the night of November 11 in either the year 1089 or 1099, the kingdom of Lyonesse sank beneath the sea, never to be seen again.

## A Giant Wave and a Sole Survivor

But before its catastrophic destruction, Lyonesse was said to be home to a race of strong, hardy people who worked the fields and low-lying plains of fertile soil in the kingdom. They were particularly fond of churches, and built 140 in total, including a grand cathedral that sat on what is now the Seven Stones reef located halfway between Cornwall and the Isles of Scilly. But despite their apparent devotion to religion, Celtic lore tells of a grave crime or transgression committed by the people of Lyonesse that resulted in a swift and terrible punishment from God. In the dead of night, a ferocious storm rolled in, pummeling the kingdom with winds and rain. But the final blow was dealt by a massive tsunami wave, which engulfed Lyonesse and wiped it off the Earth.

The stories of Lyonesse never mention what terrible crime was committed by the people of the kingdom, but many liken the legend to the Biblical story of Sodom and Gomorrah. According to that story, Lot and his two daughters survived the destruction sent by God. And according to the story of Lyonesse, a single man, usually called Trevelyan, survived the wave that destroyed the city. The man had been out hunting and fallen asleep under a tree, only to be awoken by the sounds of the gigantic wave crashing into the kingdom. He jumped onto his white horse and galloped for higher ground. The horse ran so quickly that it lost a shoe, and the pair barely made it to what is now Land's End.

Today, several families in Cornwall claim to be descendants of Trevelyan and use family crests featuring either horseshoes or a white horse. But beyond the stories that have been passed down from previous generations, there is no evidence to suggest Lyonesse ever existed. Still, locals insist that on days when the sea is calm, the sound of church bells can be heard off the coast of Land's End, ringing from their resting place beneath the sea.

# The Amazons: Man-Eaters of the Ancient World

*They were the ultimate feminists—powerful, independent women who formed female-only societies that had no use for men beyond procreation. They were the epitome of girl power, fierce mounted warriors who often beat the best male fighters from other societies. They were the Amazons.*

✳   ✳   ✳   ✳

THE ANCIENT GREEKS were enthralled by a group of warriors known as the Amazons. Greek writers, like today's Hollywood gossip columnists, relished lurid tales of love affairs between Amazon queens and their Greek boy toys. Others wrote of epic battles between Amazon warriors and the greatest heroes of Greek mythology.

Given their prominent place in Greek lore, the story of the Amazons has generally been considered the stuff of legend. But recent archeological finds suggest that a race of these warrior über-women actually did exist.

## The Amazons According to the Greeks

History's first mention of the Amazons is found in Homer's *Iliad*, written in the seventh or eighth century BC. Homer mentioned a group of women he called the *Antianeira* ("those who fight like men"), who fought on the side of the Trojans against the Greeks. They were led by Penthesilea, who fought Achilles and was slain by him. According to some accounts, Achilles fell in love with her immediately afterward, though how exactly that worked is unclear.

From then on, the Amazons became forever linked with the ancient Greeks. Their very name is believed to derive from the Greek *a-mazos*, meaning "without a breast." This referred to the Amazon practice of removing the right breast of their young girls so that they would be unencumbered in the use of the bow and spear. Somewhat draconian, yes, but no one could accuse the Amazons of being anything less than hard-core. This may have made Greek, Roman, and European artists squeamish because their depictions of Amazons showed them with two breasts, though the right breast was often covered or hidden.

According to Greek mythology, the Amazons were the off-spring of Ares, god of war, who was the son of the mightiest of the Greek gods, Zeus. Though the Amazons may have had Greek roots, they didn't want anything to do with them. Like young adults eager to move from their parents' homes, the Amazons established their realm in a land called Pontus in modern-day northeastern Turkey, where they founded several important cities, including Smyrna.

The Greeks paint a picture of the Amazons as a female-dominated society of man-haters that banned men from living among them. In an odd dichotomy between chastity and promiscuity, sexual encounters with men were taboo except for once a year when the Amazons would choose male partners from the neighboring Gargareans strictly for the purposes of procreation. Female babies were kept; males were killed or sent back to their fathers. Females were raised to do everything a man could do—and to do it better.

## Soap Opera Encounters with Greek Heroes

The Greeks and the Amazons interacted in a turbulent love-hate relationship resembling something from a Hollywood soap opera. Hercules, as one of his labors, had to obtain the girdle of the Amazon queen Hippolyte. He was accompanied in his task by Theseus, who stole Hippolyte's sister Antiope. This led to ongoing warfare between the Greeks and Amazons as well as several trysts between members of the two societies. One account has Theseus and Antiope falling in love, with her dying by his side during a battle against the Amazons. Another account has Theseus and Hippolyte becoming lovers. Stories of Hercules have him alternately wooing and warring with various Amazonian women.

Jason and the Argonauts met the Amazons on the island of Lemnos. Completely unaware of the true nature of the island's inhabitants, Jason queried the Amazons as to the where-abouts of their men. They told him their men were all killed in an earlier invasion. What the Argonauts didn't realize was that the Amazons themselves were the killers. The Amazons, anticipating another opportunity for manslaughter, invited the Argonauts to stay and become their husbands. But Jason and the boys, perhaps intimidated by the appearance of the Amazons in full battle dress, graciously declined and hightailed it off the island.

## More Than Myth?

The Greek historian Herodotus perhaps provides the best connection of the Greeks to what may be the true race of Amazons. Writing in the fifth century BC, Herodotus chronicles a group of warrior women who were defeated in battle by the Greeks. These Androktones ("killers of men"), as he called them, were put on a prison ship, where they happily went about killing the all-male Greek crew. Hellcats on land but hopeless on water, the women drifted to the north shores of the Black Sea to the land of the Scythians, a nomadic people of Iranian descent.

Here, says Herodotus, they intermarried with local Scythian men on the condition that they be allowed to keep their traditional warrior customs. They added a heartwarming social tenet that no woman could wed until she had killed a man in battle. Together, they migrated northeast across the Russian steppes, eventually evolving into the Sarmatian culture, which featured a prominent role for women hunting and fighting by the sides of their husbands. The men may have even given their wives the loving pet name *ha-mazan*, the Iranian word for "warrior."

Though the Amazons are still mostly perceived as myth, recent archeological discoveries lend credence to Herodotus's account and help elevate the Amazons from the pages of Greek legend to historical fact. Excavations of Sarmatian burial grounds found the majority of those interred there were heavily armed women, all of whom got the very best spots in the site.

# The Colossal Olmecs

*The Olmec civilization was the earliest known civilization in Mesoamerica, originating sometime between 1600 and 1200 BC. The civilization may be best known for its monuments known as "colossal heads," which, as their name suggests, are giant human heads sculpted from basalt boulders. But the Olmecs weren't just good at sculpting; the peoples were also talented architects and engineers, had a rich religious mythology, and passed along traditions—such as the important tradition of drinking chocolate—to future civilizations.*

✳ ✳ ✳ ✳

IN FACT, THE Olmecs are considered one of a handful of "pristine" civilizations. These are cultures that arose on their own, without influences from outside sources. Later cultures, including the Veracruz, Maya, and Aztecs, borrowed from many of the traditions of the Olmecs, including the so-called "Mesoamerican ball game," which became a popular pastime for later civilizations.

The environment around the southeast portion of the Mexican state of Veracruz, where the Olmec civilization is believed to have arisen, may have been uniquely situated to support a growing population. Well-watered alluvial soil and easy access to the Coatzacoalcos River provided the foundation for agri-culture and trade, much like regions such as the Nile, Yellow River, and the Fertile Crescent of Mesopotamia. Today the area is known as San Lorenzo Tenochtitlán, and it consists of three archeological sites: San Lorenzo, Tenochtitlán, and Potrero Nuevo.

## The Mother Culture?

While today the contributions of the Olmec civilization to Mesoamerican history are well documented, the culture was unknown to archeologists and researchers until the middle of the nineteenth century. In the 1850s, a farmer in Veracruz was clearing away forested land one day when he stumbled upon a strange stone sculpture half buried in the ground.

The discovery caught the attention of an antiquarian traveler named Jose Melgar y Serrano, who excavated the sculpture and published a description of it. His description, of a "colos-sal head" now called Tres Zapotes Monument A, was the first recorded evidence of the Olmec civilization, and the first hint to archeologists that something exciting was lurking in the region of Veracruz.

Gradually, more Olmec artifacts were uncovered, but archeolo-gists debated where this newly discovered culture fit within the historical timeline. Some believed the civilization existed at the same time as the Maya, and some even assumed the artifacts were Mayan themselves.

But in the 1930s and 1940s, two researchers, a Smithsonian Institution archeologist named Matthew Stirling and a Mexican art historian named Miguel Covarrubias, began to contend that the items being uncovered in Veracruz actu-ally predated any other Mesoamerican civilization known at the time. By 1942, the arguments made by Stirling and Covarrubias had convinced Mexican archeologist Alfonso Caso to label the Olmecs as the *cultura madre* (mother culture) of Mesoamerica.

## Preserved Proof

While some archeologists accepted this declaration, others remained unconvinced for decades, even after radiocarbon dating provided more conclusive evidence. Then, in 1987, researchers made a remarkable discovery at an archeological site in the town of Hidalgotitlan. Known as El Manati, the site was once used by the Olmecs as a sacred sacrificial bog. The bog, with its anaerobic and temperature-stable environment, provided the perfect conditions to preserve the ritual offerings that were placed there by the Olmecs thousands of years ago.

Some of the objects discovered in the El Manati bog were dated back to at least 1700 BC, bolstering the argument that the Olmecs existed before any other Mesoamerican civilization. At the site, researchers discovered wooden sculptures, ceremonial axes, pottery, rubber balls, remains of infants, and even traces of cocoa drinks, all well-protected in the muck of bog. Of particular interest were the very well-preserved rubber balls, which were found to be made of a type of vulcanized latex. Vulcanization was a hardening process that would be unknown to the rest of the world until the nineteenth century, yet the Olmecs had already perfected their own method. In fact, the name "Olmec" was an Aztec name that translated to "rubber people."

## From Fun and Games to Somber Rituals

These rubber balls are believed to have been used for what is known as the "Mesoamerican ball game," a sport that was played for recreation and also for ritual purposes. While the rules of the game are unknown, it is thought that it may have been similar to modern day racquetball, with players using their hips to strike the ball. The game was played on a stone ball court between teams of between two and four players. The rubber balls used were around 10 to 12 inches across and weighed between three and six pounds, and researchers theorize that players may have finished games with some rather impressive bruises!

The Mesoamerican ball game became an important part of later Mesoamerican cultures, but some archeologists are convinced that the Olmec were the first to invent the pastime.

The infant bones found at El Manati were also an intriguing find for archeologists. Some have theorized that the Olmecs may have practiced human sacrifice, although the evidence supporting this is scarce. While it may be disturbing to uncover the bones of such young humans, there is no way for researchers to determine how they died. And unlike other civilizations that were known to practice human sacrifice, the Olmecs produced no art or artifacts that depicted the sacrifice of humans. However, archeologists believe they have found evidence that the civilization practiced bloodletting, a ritualized cutting or piercing of the body that was performed by many Mesoamerican cultures. Cutting instruments, including stingray tails, ceramic spikes, and cactus thorns have been found at Olmec archeological sites, leading researchers to conclude that these were used for the practice.

## Religion and Trade

Regardless of whether the Olmecs incorporated human sacrifice into their rituals, the civilization left behind indications that they did practice religious ceremonies. The archeological site of La Venta has provided clues to these practices, as researchers believe it was used as a ceremonial center. The site consists of stone monuments, altars, plazas, and one of the earliest known pyramids in Mesoamerica, but is lacking residential structures. American archeologist Peter Joralemon, who studies pre-Columbian iconography and art, identified eight different supernatural beings that he believes were important to the Olmecs. These include nature gods like the Water God and Maize God, as well as beings known as the Olmec Dragon and the Feathered Serpent. Some of these gods were later modified and adopted by the Maya and Aztec cultures, as well.

Sometime between 1200 and 900 BC, the Olmec had developed several major urban centers and began engaging in trade with other regions. This is evident from the presence of artifacts made of materials like jadeite and obsidian, which originated from the area that is now Guatemala. Likewise, Olmec objects, such as pottery, figurines, and rubber, have been found at the archeological sites of other cultures.

## Colossal Creations

While some of what researchers believe about the Olmec civilization is speculative and pieced together, most of what is known comes from the monuments and sculptures they left behind. Rock carvings, jade and stone masks, ceramic figurines, and carved wooden busts are just some of the works left behind by these skilled artisans.

But there's no doubt that the Olmec's best-known creations are the aptly named "colossal heads" that they somehow sculpted from massive boulders. All told, 17 of these heads have been found, ranging in height from around four feet to more than 11 feet tall, and some weigh up to 50 tons. Each of the heads represents a unique individual, and each head is topped with a different headdress.

The significance of the colossal heads is unknown, but archeologists believe they may have represented powerful Olmec rulers or other elites, dressed in ceremonial headgear or helmets worn for war. Many of the heavy stone slabs were transported almost 100 miles, from the Sierra de Los Tuxtlas mountains, which would have required an enormous amount of effort for the ancient Olmecs. Such a difficult task would probably only be undertaken for a person of vast importance.

Exactly how the colossal heads were transported and created is another mystery to archeologists. But we know it would have required countless laborers, boatmen, sculptors, and other artisans, as well as the support of Olmec society. A single head may have taken years to complete. The boulders were taken from an area in the mountains that had been affected by a volcanic mudslide, depositing the large basalt stones at the base of the mountain slope. The Olmec searched here for stones that were already relatively spherical in shape, to mimic a human head. After transporting the rock to a work area, the head was roughly shaped by chipping stone away, then rounded cobblestones were used to refine the shape further. Finally, abrasive material was used to create finer detail.

### A Lasting Impression

Today, it is possible to see many of the colossal heads at various museums throughout Mexico. Occasionally, heads are loaned to museums outside the country for temporary display. Miguel Aleman Velasco, the governor of Veracruz from 1998 to 2004, authorized the placement of many replica heads, which can be seen in locations including the Field Museum of Natural History in Chicago, Illinois, and the Smithsonian National Museum of Natural History in Washington, D.C.

Sometime around 400 BC, the Olmec civilization began to dwindle. Theories for the decline include possible environmental changes that made farming, hunting, and gathering more difficult, or nearby volcanic eruptions that forced settlements to relocate.

But the end of the Olmecs was just the beginning for other cultures that would be strongly influenced by their predecessors. The Feathered Serpent god, Olmec-style art, and the Mesoamerican ball game, for example, were all adopted by subsequent regional cultures. Some Olmec traditions, like the consumption of hot cocoa, have even survived into the present. The Olmec civilization is proof that the culture of ancient peoples is more than just ancient history; it continues to impact our world today.

# Idols of the Aztecs

*The Aztecs revered the master artisans who came before them—with good reason. The Toltecs left behind a culture worth emulating. Its myths and stories, as revealed in its architecture and chiselled stone motifs, revealed a culture that was both rich and strange.*

✳ ✳ ✳ ✳

FLOURISHING BETWEEN THE tenth and twelfth centuries AD, the Toltec civilization was often lauded and praised by the later Aztec culture which came after it. The Aztecs considered the Toltec capital city of Tollan an awe-inspiring achievement of human society. Of course, some researchers believe that the stories told by the Aztecs of the impressive and lavish Toltec culture were greatly exaggerated, and that the yarns they wove, detailing extravagant Tollan palaces filled with gold, jade, and turquoise, were more myth than truth. But regardless, the Toltec civilization made an incredibly deep impression on the Aztecs, who considered their predecessors master artisans.

In fact, in Nahuatl, the language of the Aztecs, one meaning for the name Toltec is "master artisan." Another meaning, however, is "inhabitant of Tula, Hidalgo," the region that was ruled by the Toltec when they were at the height of their prominence. The civilization is believed to have originated with the Tolteca-Chichimeca peoples, who, in the ninth century, migrated from the northwestern Mexican deserts to Culhuacan, which today includes the area around Mexico City. This was where the first Toltec settlement was established, before the capital was moved to Tollan.

## As Thick as Reeds

According to the Aztecs, the first ruler of the Toltecs was Ce Tecpatl Mixcoatl, followed by his son, Ce Acatl Topiltzin. But as with other accounts given by the Aztecs, these figures have been greatly mythologized, even at times conflated with deities such as the "Plumed Serpent" god Quetzalcoatl. But archeologists have uncovered more than stories and myths, giving them more quantifiable evidence of the civilization.

Tollan, and its alternate name, Tula, can both be translated as "place of reeds," which was used to describe a thriving city where "people are thick as reeds." True to its name, the city grew to span of around eight and a half square miles, and supported a population between 40,000 and 60,000 people.

While the Aztecs spoke of richly appointed palaces, intricate jewelry, and cotton textiles in red, blue, yellow, and green, very few artifacts have survived through the centuries. What have survived, however, are two large pyramids, the remains of a large palace, a colonnaded walkway, ball courts, and many residential structures. Also discovered are the ruins of a large workshop where the Toltecs shaped obsidian, mined from the nearby region of Pachuca, into arrowheads and cutting tools.

## Art, Offerings, and Admirers

Many carvings and friezes created by the Toltec master artisans are still intact today. The tops of the pyramids feature large columns, carved to look like warriors dressed for battle, which at one time held up roof-like structures. Interestingly, these columns are nearly identical, suggesting that the Toltecs had some type of workshop capable of mass producing these giant carvings. A 130-foot-long L-shaped wall, known as a *coatepantli* or "wall of serpents," stands near the pyramids.

Similar walls are found at other Mesoamerican archeological sites, but the coatepantli is a Toltec invention. The walls depict animals such as jaguars, coyotes, wolves, and eagles, some of which are devouring human hearts. There are also scenes of skeletons entwined with rattlesnakes, which are believed to be depictions of sacrifice.

Toltec artisans were also the first in Mesoamerica to create *chacmools*, sculptures of reclining figures holding bowls or vessels, which were used for offerings to the gods. Offerings could include food, alcoholic drinks, tobacco, incense, or feathers, but later civilizations, such as the Aztecs, used chacmools to offer the gods human hearts.

Researchers are unsure of why, in the twelfth century, the Toltec civilization began to decline, but they have found evidence of possible violence or war. Some of Tollan's architecture was purposely destroyed, burnt, and buried, and the Aztecs gradually looted the city. This was not done with malice, however, as the Aztecs held the Toltecs in the highest regard.

Many of the gods who were depicted in Tollan architecture were later adopted by the Aztecs, including Centeotl, the god of maize, Xochiquetzal, the goddess of beauty and love, and Quetzalcoatl, the god of life and wisdom. And whether true or not, the Aztecs claimed to be directly descended from the Toltecs. They even coined the expression Toltecayotl, which meant "to have a Toltec heart," when referring to members of their civilization who showed courage or excellence. Whether the stories told by the Aztecs are true or not, the Toltecs most definitely left an indelible mark on Mesoamerica.

# Move Over, Columbus

*Regardless of the high-profile explorers who came centuries later, the Vikings can claim the distinction of being the first known Europeans to visit the Americas.*

✳ ✳ ✳ ✳

CHRISTOPHER COLUMBUS'S TRANSATLANTIC voyages were undeniably world-changing events. Between 1492 and 1504, he traversed the vast Atlantic Ocean in what would today be considered quite small (and no doubt hazardously uncomfortable) ships, and visited many islands in the Caribbean, as well as parts of Central America and South America. While modern commentators often criticize Columbus and his actions, there is no doubt that his expeditions ushered in a period of European exploration that eventually helped create the world we know today.

It is now an established fact, however, that Columbus was not the first European to "discover" the Americas. That distinction could possibly be credited to Leif Erikson, a Norse explorer who, by some interpretations, reached the continent of North America hundreds of years before Columbus ever set sail.

Exploration was in Erikson's family lineage: He was the son of Erik the Red, who was believed to have founded the first settlement in Greenland, an impressive feat in itself. He was a distant relative of the Viking Naddodd, a ninth-century explorer who accidentally discovered the island country of Iceland. But according to oral traditions that were passed down through the centuries, as well as written sagas about the events that were recorded somewhat later, Erikson also made a discovery of a previously unknown land—farther even than Greenland. He called this land "Vinland," and researchers now believe that it was the northeastern coastal region of North America.

## Land of Grapes and Timber

Two Icelandic stories, known as *Grænlendinga saga,* or the *Saga of the Greenlanders* and *Eiríks saga rauda,* or *Erik the Red's Saga,* make note of Erikson's travels, although the two tales differ in a number of their details. In the *Saga of the Greenlanders,* a Norse explorer named Bjarni Herjólfsson was blown off course while sailing towards Greenland and spotted an unfamiliar land covered with hills and forests. He decided not to go ashore, however, so when Leif Erikson retraced Herjólfsson's steps years later, he may have become the first European to step ashore the unknown land.

Erikson and his crew explored an icy, rocky area he called Helluland ("land of flat rocks"), a wooded area he called Markland ("land of forests"), and a warmer, lush area that Erikson chose for his base, which he called Leifsbúdir ("Leif's camp"). The group later found forested areas of fine timber and vines full of grapes, inspiring the name they bestowed upon the place, Vinland ("land of wine").

But in *Erik the Red's Saga,* Erikson himself is the one who is blown off course during a voyage, becoming the first European to see and set foot on an unfamiliar land. In this tale, Erikson and his crew discovered an inlet in an area of strong currents, which they dubbed Straumfjordr ("fjord of currents"), and made their base there. In a warmer area further south, the group established a camp where they discovered timber and the wild grapes that inspired Vinland's name.

In both tales, subsequent expeditions to the new land are launched from Greenland. Norse colonists began to establish settlements, met groups of indigenous people, and engaged in peaceful trade for a short period of time before falling into conflict and violence. Outnumbered by the large number of indigenous peoples in the area, the colonists returned to Greenland, with ships full of timber and grapes, and abandoned their quest to create a new home in the "land of wine."

## Unknown Location

For hundreds of years these stories were little more than anecdotal, but most researchers agreed that they were quite plausible. Piloting a ship through the open waters between Scandinavian Viking territories and Greenland would have been no small feat in the era before precise navigation. Vikings relied on knowledge of tides, wind direction, landmarks, and even the movement of whales to help steer their ships, so it isn't hard to imagine that a bout of bad weather or fog could significantly alter a course. But finding actual evidence of these Viking voyages proved to be a challenge for researchers.

For years, archeologists debated the location of the legendary "Vinland" visited by Erikson. Historical records, including a narrative written by German chronicler Adam of Bremen between 1073 and 1076, tell of "islands" discovered by the Norse, which early cartographers believed could be anywhere from St. Lawrence Bay to Cape Cod Bay to Chesapeake Bay. Others placed Vinland much closer to Europe, assuming it was perhaps simply a previously unknown part of Iceland.

But in 1960, a husband-and-wife team, Norwegian explorer Helge Ingstad and archeologist Anne Stine Ingstad, discovered the remains of Norse buildings at L'Anse aux Meadows in the Canadian province of Newfoundland. Between 1960 and 1968, the Ingstads discovered the ruins of eight separate buildings that had been covered in sod and more than 800 Norse artifacts. Each building had a large hall alongside multiple rooms, with fireplaces, storage spaces, and workshops, and the entire settlement may have housed up to 90 people. Carbon dating proved that the site was about 1,000 years old, aligning with the time that Erikson would have explored Vinland.

## Abandoned but Not Forgotten

Researchers speculate that L'Anse aux Meadows may be the site where Erikson's group established their main base camp—the Leifsbúdir of the *Saga of the Greenlanders* and the Straumfjordr of *Erik the Red's Saga*—and from there, they explored other areas along the Canadian coast and further south. Since L'Anse aux Meadows is not known for its grapes or timber, the Vikings probably traveled south to at least eastern New Brunswick, a region with both grapes and impressive hardwood forests.

But is New Brunswick the famed "Vinland" the Vikings spoke of? So far, L'Anse aux Meadows is the only known Norse settlement in North America, although additional possible sites have been identified in Baffin Island, Labrador, and Prince Edward Island. New Brunswick, Nova Scotia, and Maine have been most often suggested as the "land of wine," but some researchers believe the "grapes" Erikson and his crew mentioned may have instead been wild berries, which could have been found in abundance at L'Anse aux Meadows.

The Norse settlement was apparently only occupied for between 10 and 20 years. Many have wondered why the Vikings simply abandoned L'Anse aux Meadows and never returned to establish another colony, and the answer is probably a simple matter of numbers.

The Norse population in Greenland was only around 400 to 500 at the time of Erikson's travels, and, considering the resources and risk required to journey to North America, it wasn't feasible or practical for the Vikings to attempt settling down in a new location. It made much more sense to merely continue exploring and settling in Europe, where resources were plentiful and political connections could be made.

Today, most archeologists use "Vinland" to refer to any area the Vikings visited in North America. Regardless of whether it was a specific location or not, Leif Erikson's discovery of the "land of wine" nearly 500 years before Christopher Columbus reached the Americas was an impressive accomplishment that reflected the curious nature of so many explorers who would follow his footsteps.

# The Old Kingdom: The Age of the Pyramids

*Although ancient pyramids have been found in many parts of the world, including China, Mexico, India, and Greece, the Great Pyramid at Giza is perhaps the most famous example of this type of architecture. For more than 3,000 years, this pyramid held the record for the tallest man-made structure in the world, rising 481 feet over the dusty Egyptian desert.*

✳ ✳ ✳ ✳

I**T'S NO WONDER** that the Old Kingdom of Egypt, a period spanning from approximately 2700 BC to 2200 BC, and encompassing the Fourth Dynasty during which the pyramids were built, is also commonly known as the Age of the Pyramids or the Age of the Pyramid Builders. It was during this time that pharaoh Sneferu devised innovative ways to construct the monolithic structures, helping to perfect the art and science of pyramid-building.

Along with the Fourth Dynasty, the Old Kingdom includes the Third, Fifth, and Sixth Dynasties, as well. Records of this period are scarce. However, scholars have been able to piece together a history of the time thanks to architectural monuments and the many inscriptions left behind by their builders. Because of this, historians like to say that the history of the Old Kingdom is literally "written in stone."

## Imhotep's Architecture

The Old Kingdom traditionally begins with the Third Dynasty of Egypt, a period of growth and change for the civilization. It was during this time that the once independent states of Egypt came to be ruled under a centralized government located in the capital of Memphis. The Third Dynasty also saw changes in architecture, politics, and religion, which would all serve to transition Egypt into the height of the Old Kingdom.

The Third Dynasty is also when King Djoser, who reigned for more than 20 years, began many building projects in the village of Saqqara, including the first pyramid constructed in Egypt. The pyramid was designed by Djoser's architect, Imhotep, who built the stepped pyramid to be used as a tomb for the king. Imhotep is often credited with being the first builder in Egypt to construct tombs out of stone. Prior to his designs, the structures were often created using mud bricks; but Imhotep was determined to create a lasting tribute to his king, building a stone pyramid and surrounding temples, and creating a model that would be followed by many dynasties after.

## Sneferu and the Three Pyramids

This era of change led to the Fourth Dynasty of Egypt. The first king of the Fourth Dynasty, Sneferu, commissioned several pyramids, but his structures relied on trial and error. Sneferu changed some of Imhotep's designs on his first try, aiming to construct a true pyramid and not a "stepped" pyramid, but these changes resulted in a collapsed pyramid. Today, what remains of this structure, which is located in Meidum and is known as the "false pyramid," looks more like a tower sitting atop a pile of gravel.

Sneferu's next pyramid, known as the Bent Pyramid, also hit a bit of a snag. As workers were assembling the structure, they realized that the angle of the walls was too steep. So halfway through the project, the angle was changed from 55 degrees to 43 degrees. This gave the pyramid its distinctive "bent" appearance. Undeterred, Sneferu started on his last pyramid, now called the Red Pyramid due to the reddish limestone which was used for its construction. After so many false starts, the Red Pyramid, built on a solid base with walls rising at a 43-degree angle, finally became the first true pyramid in Egypt. Sneferu was a much respected king, who established a stable, strong government and was careful with resources. His rule was the beginning of a golden age in the Old Kingdom, which continued once his son, Khufu, began to reign.

In contrast to his father, Khufu was described as a "tyrant" by the ancient Greeks, who claimed that the king oppressed and enslaved the people. However, a number of Egyptian texts, such as the Westcar Papyrus, a document discovered in 1824 by a British traveler named Henry Westcar, seem to refute this claim, praising Khufu and his treatment of his subjects. The Greek impression of Khufu as an oppressive tyrant seems to stem from a specific highlight of the king's reign: the construction of the Great Pyramid.

According to Herodotus (a historian who was not always reliable), Khufu forced hundreds of thousands to work on his pyramid for months at a time. This story gave the ancient Greeks, and even some modern historians, the idea that slaves were used to build the Great Pyramid. But Egyptian texts and physical evidence uncovered over hundreds of years tell a different story. Today, most scholars agree that Khufu was not only an admired ruler, but that the people who built his pyramid were treated well. More than likely, they were either paid for their labor or volunteered as a community service. Some people also helped with the construction during the Nile's annual flood, when their farming work was impossible.

## A Colossal Monument and a Small Pyramid

Khufu's sons Djedefre and Khafre were the next kings to rule during the Fourth Dynasty of the Old Kingdom, with Djedefre making an important pronouncement about Egyptian royalty. Djedefre, who ruled between 2566 and 2558 BC, was the first king of Egypt to associate the kingship with the sun god Ra, adding "Son of Ra" to the royal title. His brother Khafre took over in 2558 BC, and is often credited with the construction of the Great Sphinx of Giza. The Sphinx depicts the face and head of a king, with the body of a reclining lion. Because the statue is aligned perfectly with Khafre's pyramid complex, most scholars agree that his is the face depicted by the Sphinx.

Khafre's son, Menkaure, became king in 2532, BC. During his reign, Menkaure began building his own pyramid and temple complex, just as his father and grandfather had done, but the resources necessary for a project as colossal as the Great Pyramid had dwindled by this time. Foreshadowing the Old Kingdom's eventual decline, Menkaure's pyramid was much less grand than previous structures. Even with its smaller size, the pyramid was unfinished by the time of Menkaure's death, even after 30 years of reigning as king. His successor, Shepseskaf, completed the project; but, as there were not enough resources left to create another grand pyramid, after his death Shepsekaf himself was interred in a more modest burial chamber.

## The Sons of Ra

The death of Shepsekaf signaled the end of the Fourth Dynasty and ushered in the Fifth. The Fifth Dynasty saw a slight shift in the power dynamic between Egyptian citizens and kings, who, prior to the Old Kingdom, were believed to be human manifestations of gods. But Djedefre's declaration that the king was a "son of Ra," effectively reduced the power of the king from that of a god to that of a son of a god. Priests began to wield more influence, and the Egyptian people worshiped the god Ra directly, instead of venerating the king as a representative of their god.

So much significance was given to Ra during the Fifth Dynasty that it is often called the "Dynasty of the Sun Kings." No longer was the focus on grand pyramids; rather, temples were made for citizens to worship the sun god. The first king of this time period, Userkaf, is known for overseeing the construction of the Temple of the Sun at Abusir, the first real sign that the influence of the Egyptian kings was waning.

The worship of Ra and diminishing power of the king continued throughout the Fifth Dynasty, until 2414, BC, when Djedkare Isesi took the throne. For the first time during the dynasty, a king decided not to honor the sun god with a temple.

Djedkare Isesi reduced the number of priests in his kingdom and strengthened Egypt by renewing ties with Punt and revitalizing the economy. Some scholars believe that the king's decision to depart from worship of the sun god was because he was an early follower of the cult of Osiris, which would eventually replace the cult of Ra as the most popular deity worship in Egypt.

## The Collapse of the Kingdom

Whatever the reason, this departure from previous traditions served to reduce the king's influence even further. By the time the Sixth Dynasty began with the reign of Teti in 2345, BC, the idea that only kings should build elaborate monuments and tombs was falling by the wayside. Teti was the first king to be assassinated, possibly by his successor, Userkare, in a plot that would have been shockingly unthinkable in previous dynasties.

The assassination of Teti was a portent of the collapse of the Old Kingdom. Instead of a king with huge influence over the entire country, local administrators, called nomarchs, wielded most of the power. Instead of kingly, royal dynasties, local dynasties of nomarchs were created, as local officials passed their titles on to their descendants.

Struggles within the country, and even civil wars, sporadically broke out, but the symbolic end of the Old Kingdom was signaled by a drought. Without a strong ruler to lead the people of Egypt through this hardship, the country was beset with famine. The nomarchs could only attempt to help their own communities, as they lacked the resources to do more.

As the once grand Old Kingdom came to an end, Egypt descended into a period of political struggle, disorganization, and conflict. But while the Age of the Pyramid Builders was over, the impressive monuments, art, inscriptions, and temples they left behind have assured us that the Old Kingdom of Egypt will never be forgotten.

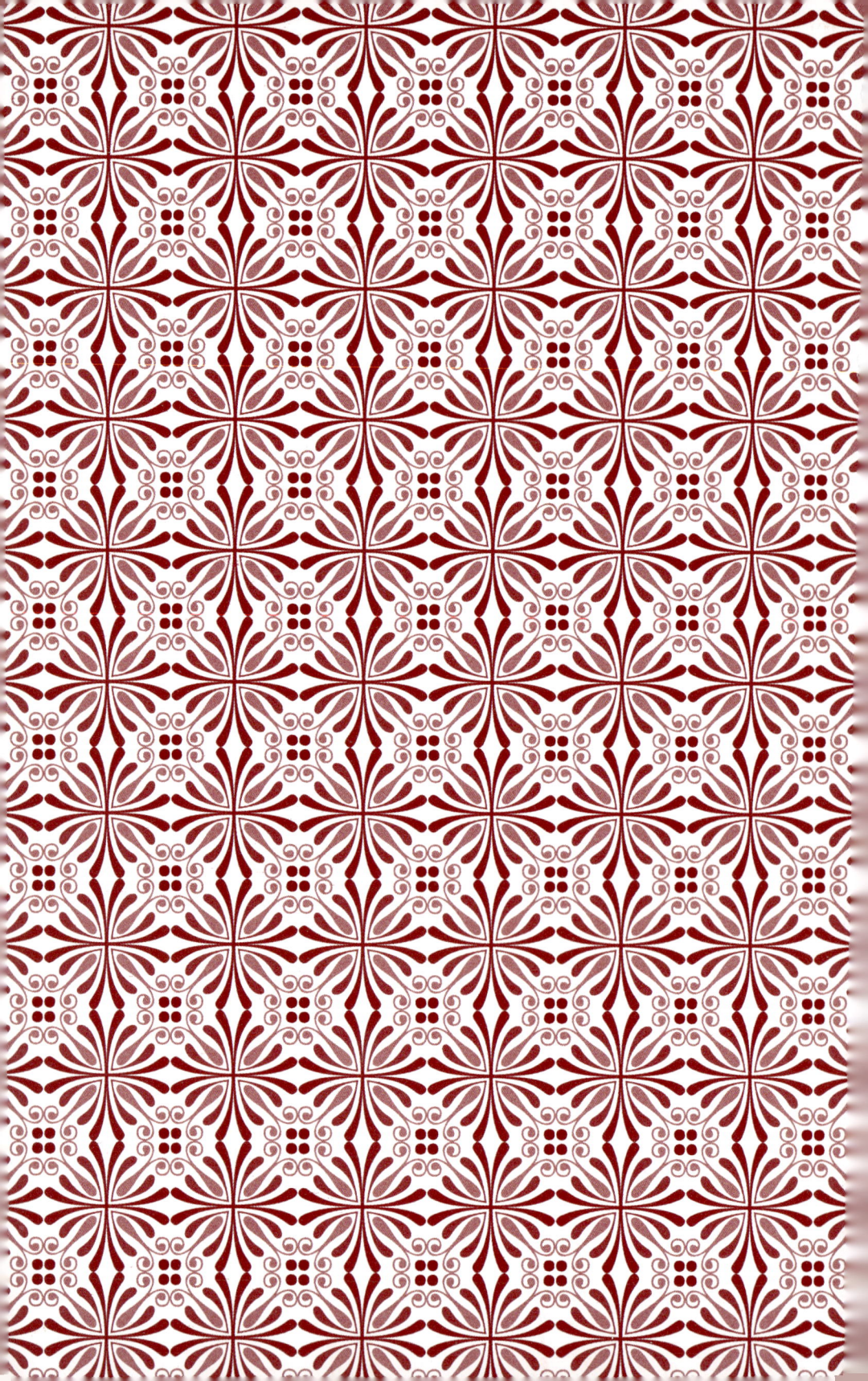